Handbook of Health Services Evaluation

Axel Kaehne • Julie Feather
Editors

Handbook of Health Services Evaluation

Theories, Methods and Innovative Practices

Springer

Editors
Axel Kaehne
Evaluation and Policy Analysis (EPA) Unit
and Medical School
Edge Hill University
Ormskirk, UK

Julie Feather
Evaluation and Policy Analysis (EPA) Unit
Edge Hill University
Ormskirk, UK

ISBN 978-3-031-87868-8 ISBN 978-3-031-87869-5 (eBook)
https://doi.org/10.1007/978-3-031-87869-5

This Springer imprint is published by the registered company Springer Nature Switzerland AG
The registered company address is: Gewerbestrasse 11, 6330 Cham, Switzerland

Preface

Evaluations have become a key mechanism to improve health services over the last decade or so. However, there has been no handbook to date which brings together the accumulated knowledge and expertise which evaluators across the world have developed in this field. This handbook is the first of its kind in the field of health service evaluations and, at the same time, unique in its scope and inclusivity of approaches, topics, and issues. We believe that the book you are holding in your hands is a collection of the most up-to-date and current evaluation practice in health services and will serve as an important reference tool as well as foster debates about the most suitable evaluation techniques, approaches, and theories whenever and wherever health services are assessed in their quality, their effectiveness, or their wider societal impact.

As we started to sketch the various topics and themes to be included in the book, we made two critical assumptions: that there is a (theoretical and empirical) difference between health services and health systems, and that the distinct nature of health services necessitates discrete evaluation approaches, tools, and techniques for health service evaluations to be done successfully. This may be uncontroversial at first glance but, when inviting contributors, we repeatedly ran up against issues of how evaluation practices or the terminology used in them often failed to distinguish between health system and health services. Pragmatically, in this handbook we decided to use an operational definition of health services as organizations, publicly or privately owned or of charitable nature, which directly deliver services to patients on a day-to-day basis.

Planning and commissioning organizations, for example, would fall outside this scope if they do not also *deliver* care, clinical or non-clinical, to members of the public. We recognize that health service evaluations and health systems analysis can and should learn from each other, yet we believe that health services possess a unique character and are of a special nature which compels evaluators (and researchers for that matter) to utilize distinct approaches sensitive to the fact that the objective of health service organizations, programs, or interventions designed are delivered to improve health among a target population or group of patients.

We do think, however, that the field is ready for a more detailed discussion about how innovative health system research and analysis can feed into health service evaluation practice to create a fertile link between the *system* aspects of services and the *delivery* aspects of systems and policy steering. A concrete example of this interplay between system and services is the chapter in this handbook on learning health systems which we believe we have rightly included here by virtue of the fact that learning has a system-wide dimension yet occurs and manifests itself through service-level benefits. It is this interdependency of system and service level which, arguably, warrants more attention from evaluators in the future.

The need for this book emerged from a dilemma which has plagued the evaluation of health services for a long time. Research of health services has gained increasing prominence in public debates as questions have been asked whether the services we have created maintain the health of our populations adequately over time. Yet evaluations have traditionally played a subservient and often neglected role to research. This has changed in the last decade or so as evaluation practice has adopted more theory-led approaches, morphing from a narrow, less scientific approach into an exercise complying with standards of scientific work: replicability and falsifiability, transparency, and the need to produce generalizable insights where possible.

In essence, evaluation has matured from producing specific individual and localized insights to knowledge with wider validity and utility. This development, however, has not necessarily been mirrored by the emergence of academic degree programs in health service evaluation. At the time of writing, there is no degree program in the United Kingdom dedicated to the development of skills and competencies in health service evaluation. In theory, anybody with some knowledge of health service research can conduct evaluations, yet no standardized canon exists of what constitutes good or acceptable standards of evaluation practice in health services.

Our handbook is trying to change this by bringing together a body of knowledge and expertise that covers the main established, as well as the most innovative, practices in the field of health service evaluation. For the first time, this handbook articulates a corpus of learning which can act as a key reference point for future evaluations in this area. It answers questions about how to conduct principle focused evaluations, how to use simulated patient techniques, and much more. We also strove to include aspects of professional development that should underpin good evaluation practice in health services such as which leadership qualities should evaluators have when investigating the impact of health services, and which competencies and skills are required for evaluators in this area. Our handbook therefore is large in ambition: we deliberately designed it not just as a repository of the existing knowledge of evaluations in health services but also as a vehicle to support the emergence of the embryonic scientific praxis of health service evaluation.

When we started to talk about this handbook with colleagues, we only had a rudimentary idea of how many exciting and innovative health service evaluations have mushroomed over the last years. We have tried to put order to rapidly developing fields by separating our book into sections representing evaluation's foundations, methods, theories, and models as well as innovative techniques, tools, and specific topics.

Each chapter in this book is self-contained and presents the currently best available evidence on the tool, technique, or approach it describes. Yet, we would argue, the sum of the book is larger than its part. Together, the chapters provide a currently unique source of information on how health services ought to be evaluated to answer the questions stakeholders of health services usually have: is my service effective; and does it make a positive impact on the community it serves and others. We believe that the expertise this handbook offers on the methods and the approaches of health service evaluations will also serve it well when used as a handbook for health service evaluation courses and academic degree programs as and when they will be developed.

The handbook thus has a twofold purpose, it looks to support evaluators in their daily practice but also seeks to enable standardized teaching and training of health services evaluators over time. It therefore speaks to the need to improve health service delivery as much as it speaks to the need to support how the community of practice in health service evaluation benchmarks excellence and scientific rigor.

However, we are conscious that evaluations in principle have a wider role to play in society beyond the confines of a narrow quality improvement tool. In the wake of various recent scandals in the United Kingdom's National Health Services (NHS), health care organizations have rightly come under increasing scrutiny by the public. In a free society this is to be expected and very much welcome. In this context, evaluations are providing the evidence not just on how services are performing but also generating pointers for the direction on how to improve them.

Evaluators thus have a role to play in providing legitimacy to the health services for the communities they serve. For many evaluators this may not be the most immediate and apparent aspect of their work. This wider societal role of evaluations has hence received little attention. But we, the community of practice, would ignore this crucial role at our peril. There is nothing natural or predetermined about health organizations providing effective services to their patients and communities. The history of health systems is littered with examples of poor or outright dangerous and harmful medical or clinical practices as well as organizational neglect and refusal to accept responsibility.

Holding health organizations to account requires daily efforts and pays its respect to the fundamental principle of a free society: that services using public resources should also respond to public health care needs, not being beholden or captured by narrow interests of professional groups. Evaluators play a crucial role in this effort. Their work provides the evidence which allows patients and community groups to challenge health services and hold those working in them to account. If anyone thought this is an easy feat, think about the way in which organizations habitually protect themselves from external criticism and how often hospital professionals have closed rank when responding to concerns from patients and the public.

Evaluators play a critical role in the process of accountability and they are contributing a key building block for public scrutiny. It is our work which permits transparency to emerge and allows processes of accountability to work in the long run. Arguably, this may lead us to stipulate a dual role of evaluators, one internal to the immediate task and duty at hand, another one external in nature and direction. While the work of evaluators is often commissioned, paid, and framed by health service organizations, they have a wider duty when conducting health service evaluations. Their work can often be a critical barometer of how far services address the needs of patients and public in a given area. Their reports often reveal strengths as well as shortcomings of health services and produce evidence of quality or the lack thereof.

This external role of evaluators has received surprisingly little attention in the literature. And this absence of regard hints at a prevalence of a narrow definition of evaluation work, framed by the parameters of the evaluation aims and objectives at hand. However, solely focusing on what commissioners want from evaluations, significantly underplays the responsibility evaluators have within the wider agenda of health service improvement. Surveying the contributions of our handbook, it becomes immediately obvious that health services are undergoing an important shift from organization-centered perspectives to patient and person centered approaches. If we interpret this shift in a limited, service orientation, way however we overlook how this move to more responsive service constellations are originating in demands for organizations to be rooted in robust doctrines of public duty.

The NHS Constitution grandly pronounces that the "NHS belongs to the people" of the United Kingdom. Yet, as anybody with only a modicum of awareness of recent or historical care scandals in the NHS knows, there is a disconnect between grandiose statements such as this and care reality on the ground. It is up to theorists and philosophers to interpret what it means for an institution to belong or be "owned by" the people. Fundamentally, however, all public institutions in a democratic society require legitimacy, and health services that do not command the confidence of the populations they serve are unlikely to justify their existence in the long run.

We would argue that there is a direct line between producing reliable evidence of how health services affect the health and wellbeing of their populations and the longer-term legitimacy of health services in the local as well as national context. Evaluators therefore have a wider role and duty to play in ensuring that their work effectively addresses the questions of impact and efficacy of service in reducing health inequalities and health disparities among other current concerns. It is here that the issues of leadership for evaluators can usefully be located which our handbook articulates. Evaluators without awareness of the wider implications of their work for maintaining and supporting legitimate health services serving communities are bound to overlook the critical legitimating role of their work in society. This means that evaluators have obligations beyond their immediate evaluation tasks predefined in tender documents. They have a function in the processes sustaining the legitimacy of publicly funded services.

Our handbook should be seen as a first attempt to shape this agenda of a critical evaluation practice conscious of its wider societal obligations for people, patients, and populations.

Who Is This Handbook For

We already mentioned that there is currently no academic qualification for health service evaluations. Our handbook hopefully provides a foundation for such future courses. The community of practice of health service evaluators have arguably long benefitted from the ability and license of professionals from many diverse backgrounds to conduct evaluations. We would be opposed to change this fecundity of practice stemming from its openness and cross-disciplinary fertilization.

Consequently, our book is for everyone who wants to conduct an evaluation of a health service in their community, regardless of position, professional status, or experience. We deliberately included the term "experience" here since we are aware how we, like many others, started as amateurs of evaluation practice many years ago and only gradually built up the experience and knowledge. Regardless of the ongoing standardization of evaluation practices and its increasing theoretical sophistication, it remains an indisputable fact that evaluators come from all walks of (professional) life and it is one key goal of our handbook to help them conduct better evaluations without being prescriptive of who can engage in evaluative work.

We do not only acknowledge the diversity of evaluators in the field but would argue that this is something we should celebrate as it gives our field the freshness, momentum, and vitality we cherish. In our mind, it is just as important to stress that evaluators may work inside the organizations they assess or, alternatively, may be external to them. Although there are well-versed strengths and benefits to external evaluations which revolve around notions of impartiality and objectivity associated to critical distance of evaluators, there still remains a case for internal evaluations as a tool for quality improvement of health services, not least since external evaluations have a cost attached which may be challenging for some organizations. Our aim with this book is therefore to speak to everyone who wants to conduct an evaluation of health services, be they part of the health care organization they evaluate or not.

How to Read This Handbook

The handbook is divided into five sections, each with a unique focus designed to address distinct aspects of health services evaluation. The first section, **Foundations and Purpose of Evaluation in Health Services**, lays the groundwork by establishing a robust theoretical and ethical basis for evaluation. It explores the fundamental questions of why we evaluate health services and how these evaluations can inform decision-making and improve outcomes. This section serves as an anchor, grounding the reader in the philosophical and ethical considerations that underpin the field.

The second section, **Evaluation Theory and Methods**, details key methodological frameworks and theoretical approaches that evaluators can employ to critically assess health services. We recommend this section to those who seek a deeper understanding of the tools and models that drive robust and insightful evaluations.

In the third section, **Instruments and Techniques of Evaluation**, readers will find a practical toolkit of methods for data collection, analysis, and evaluation. The section emphasizes the "how" of evaluation, offering tangible techniques that practitioners can apply directly to their work.

The fourth section, **Evaluation Themes**, takes a forward-looking approach, addressing contemporary challenges, innovations, and trends shaping the field. This section invites readers to engage with evolving practices and to consider the broader implications of health services evaluation in a rapidly changing healthcare landscape.

Finally, the fifth section, **Person and Community-Centered Evaluation Approaches**, highlights the growing shift toward participatory and human-centered evaluation. It underscores the importance of involving patients and communities as central stakeholders in the evaluation process, reflecting a move toward more inclusive and equitable practices.

We designed this handbook to be a resource that meets the needs of both newcomers and experienced evaluators. For those new to the field, it offers foundational knowledge and practical guidance, while seasoned professionals will find advanced tools and fresh perspectives to enhance their practice. We would encourage readers to navigate the handbook flexibly, selecting chapters or sections that align with their specific interests or needs.

Finally, we would invite everyone to approach the handbook with an open mind, considering both the more well-established and the more recent still emerging approaches to evaluation. The field of health services evaluation is dynamic and continuously evolving, shaped by new challenges, innovations, and societal needs. Our handbook aspires to be a living resource, not only reflecting the current state of the field but also inspiring its future development. If it motivates readers to reflect on how the practices outlined in the handbook can be adapted and expanded within the context of their own work, then the book has achieved a lot.

Ormskirk, UK

Axel Kaehne
Julie Feather

Contents

Editors and Contributors

About the Editors

Axel Kaehne is Director of the Evaluation and Policy Analysis Unit at Edge Hill University and Professor of Health Service Research at the university's Medical School. Axel was born in Berlin/Germany and educated at Free University and Humboldt University. He subsequently studied at Aberdeen University and the University of Wales. He settled in South Wales in 1996 and currently lives in Liverpool. Axel is Editor-in-Chief of the *Journal of Integrated Care* and the *Journal of Health Organization and Management* (Emerald Publishing). He is also Visiting Professor at the Department of Health and Social Management at the University of Eastern Finland, Kuopio, and appointed Governor of the Wrightingon, Wigan and Leigh NHS Hospital Foundation Trust. He is teaching postgraduate modules on leadership and research methods as well as delivering workshops for various organizations on AI in data analysis and evidence synthesis. He has published extensively on integrated care, health services, and complexity in research.

Julie Feather is a Senior Research Fellow in the Evaluation and Policy Analysis Unit at Edge Hill University, based in the UK, and an Associate Editor for the *Journal of Health Organization and Management*. With a particular expertise in realist evaluation, Julie designs and leads service evaluations across the health and social care sectors working collaboratively across disciplines to inform policy and practice improvements.As a qualified social worker with substantial experience in adult social work practice, Julie's research is rooted in her dedication to enhancing health and social care systems for individuals accessing services. Her PhD research focused on improving transitional processes for young people moving between children's and adult healthcare services, applying realist approaches to evaluate the implementation of person-centered transition programs.At Edge Hill University, Julie is actively involved in projects dedicated to improving services for children and young people, with a key emphasis on mental health, palliative care, and cancer care. Her research interests also extend to the integration of health and social care services and the delivery of interprofessional education. Julie is committed to co-produced, collaborative research that brings together academics, practitioners, and people with lived experience to drive impactful advancements in health and social care evaluation.

Contributors

Kathryn Ashton Policy and International Health, WHO Collaborating Centre on Investment for Health and Well-being, Public Health Wales, Wales, UK

Solange L. Baptiste The International Treatment Preparedness Coalition (ITPC Global), Johannesburg, South Africa

Naïma Bentayeb McGill University, SHERPA University Institute, Montreal, QC, Canada

Mai Berger First Nations Health Authority, Vancouver, BC, Canada

Antoinette Bewley Edge Hill University, Ormskirk, Lancashire, UK

Lucy Bray Edge Hill University, Ormskirk, Lancashire, UK

Jeremy Brown Edge Hill University, Ormskirk, Lancashire, UK

Judith Brown The National Autistic Society, London, UK

Jackie Chandler Health Innovation Wessex, Southampton, UK

Melanie Channon University of Bath, Bath, UK

Wei Wen Chong Faculty of Pharmacy, National University of Malaysia, Kuala Lumpur, Malaysia

Anja Christoffersen Centre for Health Services Research, The University of Queensland, Brisbane, QLD, Australia

Champion Health Agency, Fortitude Valley, QLD, Australia

Kate Churruca Australian Institute of Health Innovation, Macquarie University, Sydney, Australia

Jack C. Collins The University of Sydney School of Pharmacy, The University of Sydney, Sydney, Australia

James Copestake University of Bath, Bath, UK

Philippa Darnton Health Innovation Wessex, Southampton, UK

Emmanuel Defever Health Innovation Wessex, Southampton, UK

Helen Dickinson UNSW, Canberra, Australia

Mariana Dyakova Policy and International Health, WHO Collaborating Centre on Investment for Health and Well-being, Public Health Wales, Wales, UK

Douglas Easterling Department of Social Sciences and Health Policy, School of Medicine, Wake Forest University, Winston-Salem, NC, USA

Louise A. Ellis Australian Institute of Health Innovation, Macquarie University, Sydney, Australia

Stefanie Ettelt Department of Health Services Research and Policy, London School of Hygiene & Tropical Medicine, London, UK

Julie Feather Evaluation and Policy Analysis (EPA) Unit, Edge Hill University, Ormskirk, UK

David Fetterman Fetterman and Associates and Claremont Graduate University, Claremont, CA, USA

David Fetterman II Northwestern University, Evanston, IL, USA

Lara Gautier SHERPA University Institute, Montreal, QC, Canada

Emilie Gélinas School of Public Health, University of Montréal, Montreal, QC, Canada

Liz Green Policy and International Health, WHO Collaborating Centre on Investment for Health and Well-being, Public Health Wales, Wales, UK

Oliver Groene OptiMedis and University of Witten/Herdecke, Witten, Germany

Raphaëlle Ashley Guerbaai Rehabilitation, Ageing and Independent Living (RAIL) Research Centre, School of Primary and Allied Health Care, Monash University, Frankston, Australia

Daniela Holle Department of Nursing, Midwifery and Therapeutic Sciences, Hochschule für Gesundheit, Bochum, Germany

Ihoghosa Iyamu Centre for Advancing Health Outcomes, University of British Columbia, Vancouver, BC, Canada

School of Population and Public Health, University of British Columbia, Vancouver, Canada

Amanda L. Joseph School of Health Information Science, University of Victoria, Victoria, British Columbia, Canada

Majestic Global Consulting Inc., Vancouver, British Columbia, Canada

Axel Kaehne Evaluation and Policy Analysis (EPA) Unit and Medical School, Edge Hill University, Ormskirk, UK

Katherine Knighting Edge Hill University, Ormskirk, Lancashire, UK

Nicolas Larrain OptiMedis and Hamburg Center for Health Economics, University of Hamburg, Hamburg, Germany

Krista Lauer The International Treatment Preparedness Coalition (ITPC Global), Johannesburg, South Africa

Amanda Lees Health Innovation Wessex, Southampton, UK

Janet C. Long Australian Institute of Health Innovation, Macquarie University, Sydney, Australia

Kristiana Ludlow Centre for Health Services Research, The University of Queensland, Brisbane, Australia

Centre for Healthcare Resilience and Implementation Science, Australian Institute of Health Innovation, Macquarie University, Sydney, Australia

Nicholas Mays Department of Health Services Research and Policy, London School of Hygiene & Tropical Medicine, London, UK

Elizabeth McGee LEAP Consulting, New Haven, CT, USA

Kaileah McKellar Institute of Health Policy, Management and Evaluation, University of Toronto, Toronto, ON, Canada

Rebekah J. Moles The University of Sydney School of Pharmacy, The University of Sydney, Sydney, Australia

Per Nilsen Linköping University, Linköping, Sweden

Halmstad University, Halmstad, Sweden

Kelsey Pateman Centre for Allied Health Research, Royal Brisbane and Women's Hospital, Brisbane, QLD, Australia

Kristiina Patja Faculty of Medicine, University of Helsinki, Helsinki, Finland

Anna Perry Milken Institute School of Public Health, George Washington University, Washington, DC, USA

Quynh Pham Centre for Digital Therapeutics, University Health Network, Toronto, ON, Canada

Institute of Health Policy Management and Evaluation, University of Toronto, Toronto, Ontario, Canada

Laura J. Pitkänen Faculty of Medicine, University of Helsinki, Helsinki, Finland

Ministry of Finance, Helsinki, Finland

Steve Powell Causal Map Ltd, Bath, UK

Tina Quasdorf Institute of Nursing, School of Health Sciences, ZHAW Zurich University of Applied Sciences, Winterthur, Switzerland

Shibaab Rahman UNSW, Canberra, Australia

Fiona Remnant Bath Social & Development Research Ltd, Bath, UK

Amy Salmon Centre for Advancing Health Outcomes, University of British Columbia, Vancouver, BC, Canada

School of Population and Public Health, University of British Columbia, Vancouver, Canada

Monika Sanchez Centre for Community Health and Evaluation, Seattle, USA

Lea Saringer-Hamiti Institute of Nursing, School of Health Sciences, ZHAW Zurich University of Applied Sciences, Winterthu, Switzerland

Lisa Schafer Centre for Community Health and Evaluation, Seattle, USA

Carl R. Schneider The University of Sydney School of Pharmacy, The University of Sydney, Sydney, Australia

Walter Sermeus Healthcare Management, Department of Public Health and Primary Care, Leuven Institute for Healthcare Policy, KU Leuven, Leuven, Belgium

Sara Shearkhani Institute of Health Policy, Management and Evaluation, University of Toronto, Toronto, ON, Canada

Michael Garron Hospital, Toronto, ON, Canada

Nelson Shen Digital Mental Health Lab, Krembil Center for NeuroInformatics, Centre for Addiction and Mental Health, Toronto, ON, Canada

Institute of Health Policy Management and Evaluation, University of Toronto, Toronto, Ontario, Canada

Andrew Sibley Health Innovation Wessex, Southampton, UK

M. Elizabeth Snow Centre for Advancing Health Outcomes, University of British Columbia, Vancouver, BC, Canada

School of Population and Public Health, University of British Columbia, Vancouver, Canada

Carolyn Steele Gray Science of Care Institute and Lunenfeld-Tanenbaum Research Institute, Sinai Health, Toronto, ON, Canada

Institute of Health Policy Management and Evaluation, University of Toronto, Toronto, Ontario, Canada

Paulus Torkki Faculty of Medicine, University of Helsinki, Helsinki, Finland

Jyväskylä University, Jyväskylä, Finland

Elvire Toure-Pegnougo School of Public Health, University of Montréal, Montreal, QC, Canada

Michael S. Trevisan Washington State University, Pullman, WA, USA

Dale Trevor Champion Health Agency, Fortitude Valley, QLD, Australia

Consumer Representative, Metro North Health and University Partners, Herston, QLD, Australia

Tamara M. Walser University of North Carolina Wilmington, Wilmington, NC, USA

David Wiljer Institute of Health Policy Management and Evaluation, University of Toronto, Toronto, Ontario, Canada

Education, Technology & Innovation, University Health Network, Toronto, Ontario, Canada

Walter P. Wodchis Institute of Health Policy, Management and Evaluation, University of Toronto, Toronto, ON, Canada

Institute for Better Health, Trillium Health Partners, Mississauga, ON, Canada

Adrienne M. Young Centre for Health Services Research, The University of Queensland, Brisbane, QLD, Australia

Dietetics and Food Services, Royal Brisbane and Women's Hospital, Brisbane, QLD, Australia

List of Figures

List of Tables

The Foundations and Purpose of Evaluation in Health Services

Ontological and Epistemological Foundations of Health Service Evaluation

Axel Kaehne

Abstract

This chapter establishes the foundational ontological and epistemological principles guiding health service evaluations. It highlights the critical distinction between health service evaluation and broader public policy assessments, focusing on the interplay between objectivist and constructivist paradigms. The chapter emphasizes a pragmatic approach, recognizing the complementarity of reductionist and holistic methodologies in capturing the complexity of health services. Ontology and epistemology are explored in relation to their implications for evaluating healthcare performance, patient experiences and organizational practices. Emerging perspectives, including critical realism and pragmatism, are examined for their potential to bridge philosophical divides and inform actionable, context-sensitive evaluation frameworks. The chapter advocates for pluralistic, theory-led approaches that accommodate both quantitative and qualitative insights, aligning evaluation practices with the dynamic realities of healthcare delivery.

Keywords

Health service evaluation · Ontology · Epistemology · Pragmatism · Critical realism · Methodological pluralism

A. Kaehne (✉)
Evaluation and Policy Analysis (EPA) Unit and Medical School, Edge Hill University, Ormskirk, UK
e-mail: Axel.kaehne@edgehill.ac.uk

A. Kaehne, J. Feather (eds.), *Handbook of Health Services Evaluation*,
https://doi.org/10.1007/978-3-031-87869-5_1

1 Introduction

This first chapter will provide a foundation on the ontology and epistemological principles guiding health service evaluation. It acts as an anchor for the following sections of the handbook which champion a variety of methodological and theoretical perspectives. While I welcome the pluralism of approaches in the field, I think it is important to set out some methodological tenets of health service evaluation as a theory-led inquiry which can inform future discussions about the applicability and suitability of different approaches in different contexts. In what follows, I make no claim about contributing anything novel to the debate around either epistemology or ontology in applied social sciences. The purpose is simply to guide evaluators through the thicket of methodological perspectives.

The chapter will start by setting out the specific conditions pertaining to the health sector, which define the practice of evaluation work in distinction to other public policy program assessments. The aim is to demarcate the boundaries of suitable ontological and epistemological approaches for the type of evaluations likely to be undertaken in health services. Understanding the ontological and epistemological foundations of health service evaluations is essential, as these philosophical perspectives shape how evaluations are designed, conducted and interpreted. Ontology and epistemology will then be discussed in turn, and conclusions for evaluation work will be drawn at the end of the chapter. This will set the methodological foundation for the subsequent chapters.

2 Ontology in Health Service Evaluations

Ontology is generally perceived to encapsulate our understanding of the nature of phenomena in the world. The long-standing divide between those espousing the view that what can be observed exists and those who hold the view that human perception influences what and how something exists is characterizing health service research and evaluation as much as any other scientific inquiry. For health service evaluation, this rift between the two positions takes on the form of two main perspectives which promote either the view that reality is objective, measurable (wherever and whenever it can be observed) and independent of individual perceptions (Fraser and Robinson 2004; Stanley 2012) or the stance that reality as we perceive it is influenced by social, cultural, and personal viewpoints, indicating that reality is partially constructed through us as agents in the world (Peck and Mummery 2017).

In the past, much has been made of the alleged antithetical thrust of these two perspectives, but by now most researchers, while having preferences for certain methodological approaches, are likely to pragmatically acknowledge the complementary nature of both notions of reality (Sanderson 2009; Lynch et al. 2018; Kelly and Cordeiro 2020). It is not the aim of this chapter to arbitrate between those two perspectives. Instead, I want to draw conclusions from considering the implications of either position for health service evaluation as a scientific practice.

The divergence between both visions of reality results in different understandings of what can be measured and included in the daily analysis of health service performance (Strandberg-Larsen and Krasnik 2009; Siegel et al. 2011). While those who profess a more materialist disposition are more inclined to emphasize the robust nature of analysis based on observable indicators of health services, clinical or otherwise, those who adhere to a more constructivist position would generally champion types of analysis which include intangible aspects of health services such as patient satisfaction, trust, and confidence, and the like (Lee 2012; Peck and Mummery, 2017).

It is probably fair to say that, while health policy and policymakers are still highly dependent on data based on observable phenomena, politicians and commissioners have increasingly acknowledged the benefits of a more holistic view of health service performance which is grounded in the more constructivist ontological paradigm (Greenhalgh 2003; Wilson et al. 2021). In fact, arguably, the fundamental question at the heart of ontological disagreement, whether or not non-observable phenomena actually exist independently of human perception, is now rarely raised in methodological debates around health service evaluations, even though some faint echoes of this debate are still heard when discussing the issue of data validity generated by inductive research approaches.

In other words, evaluators tend to adopt a pragmatic stance when it comes to foundational debates about the nature of reality in health services, while their personal ontological preferences may resurface as and when they recognize or discount a type of evidence produced through methods whose claim to validity they may question. This pragmatism at the foundational level however does not necessarily extend to the next level up, so to speak, which is the argument on how to conceive of health service performance and how to investigate it practically.

The two broad positions adopted by most researchers fall into either a type of reductionism or holism (Nelson et al. 2007; La Placa et al. 2013). Effectiveness, so those who champion a reductionist approach, can be measured by assessing the impact of individual components of health services; the totality of their specific levels of effectiveness gives us an indication of their performance as a whole. This is challenged by those who champion a more holistic ontology maintaining that service components are interdependent and interconnected as well as influenced by perceptions, a view which has come to be echoed in more recent organizational studies as well (Geyer 2012; Kaehne 2016; Caffrey et al. 2016). Again, while the two positions sketched here may look mutually exclusive, evaluators often advocate a pragmatic use of both holistic and reductionist approaches which may sit side by side in practice.

Before we embark on considering the epistemological foundations of health service evaluations, it may be useful to look in more detail at the interplay between ontological perspectives and evaluative practice. In particular, it may be important to explore how researching health services intersects with newly emerging organizational theories and perspectives. This may provide us with insights into any particular blind spots of one or the other vision of reality in evaluation practice. I recognize that linking ontological positions to organizational theories is likely to narrow our focus in this chapter. Health service evaluations cover a much wider range of theoretical approaches than those borrowed from organizational studies (Shortell 2016; Bartlett and Ray 2021; Birken et al. 2023). However, I will show that probing how specific ontological perspectives interact with particular organizational theories creates additional insights or, alternatively, may perhaps prevent us from gaining insights into health service performance. Asking the question which ontological perspectives are most appropriate for health service evaluations, particularly in the context of organizational logics, we may glimpse opportunities to widen the methodological apparatus available to us and ensure genuinely patient-centered service perspectives (Kaehne 2017, 2022).

It is indisputable that ontology informs how we think about health services, patient experiences and organizational structures. The concept of agency is one specific lens through which researchers often conceptualize health service evaluation. Ontology thus predefines what we believe warrants investigation and how. Over the last decade or so, researchers have stressed the importance of accord parity of relevance to patient perspectives when assessing the performance of health services (Abma and Broerse 2010; Shimmin et al. 2017). The reductionist objectivist perspective, so they argue, may neglect important aspects of health service delivery as it de-emphasizes non-observable phenomena such as patient beliefs, patient or professional perceptions and the like. Championing a narrow, largely positivist approach may therefore overlook how health service delivery is not simply a matter of how many clinical procedures have been conducted, but arguably about judging the effectiveness of services including views and opinions on how these procedures are perceived, felt and experienced by patients and professional staff (Durand and Fleury 2021).

A casual look at the public debate about the health system performance in England reveals the predominance of positivist approaches, articulating consistently the number of clinical outcomes as the primary benchmark of performance (Coulter 1991; Kaehne et al. 2017; Calnan 2020; Maniatopoulos et al. 2020; Lewis et al. 2021). This is mirrored by research on health services, a more granular level for evaluation work. Here, equally, health services are most likely to be assessed through the sum of clinical procedures completed, as these are measured and reimbursed through various payment models for health providers (Fulop et al. 2013; Warner et al. 2022). However, shifting the emphasis from the sheer quantity of health service activity to the quality of delivering healthcare for patients requires a reappraisal of the importance of patient perspectives and patient experiences which, in turn, can only be generated through research favoring more constructivist ontological approaches. In particular, researchers have argued that the prevalent reductionist understanding of health stands in the way of a much-needed recognition that health and illness are not simply states combining the sum total of biological or clinical markers but are deeply influenced by social and cultural factors as well (Russell et al. 2008; Kaehne et al. 2018).

In addition, as I have previously argued, organizational logics do not necessarily align with patient experiences (Buntinz 2008; Kaehne 2022). There has now been ample evidence that the way in which services are organized around clinical tasks is often in contrast to perceived patient needs (Galbraith 1973, 1977; McCarthy et al. 2016; Gualandi et al. 2021; Ly et al. 2021). The long history of research on continuity of care and integration provides abundant insights into how patient experiences of care provision differ significantly from the way in which services are arranged (Kaehne and Catherall 2012; Temple 2012; Kaehne 2016; Kaehne 2017). Continuity of care as perceived by patients is rarely informing the way in which services are organized in hospitals or across local services which leaves patients with the challenging task to navigate their way through the care provider landscape.

Translating this into the field of health service evaluation, the question arises how we can ensure that narrow and reductionist attitudes to evaluating services can be reorientated from stressing efficiencies, cost-effectiveness and assessing observable standards of care or regulatory compliance to include emotional, social, and cultural dimensions which differentially influence healthcare outcomes for different individuals and communities. Healthcare researchers favoring a constructivist or interpretivist ontology are not the only ones who identify a significant risk when evaluation approaches side with mainly reductionist perspectives. Historians of public policy have long raised alarm at the effects of standardization in various policy areas (Scott 1998). They argue that wherever organizational structures are given precedence in shaping public policy, one-size-fits-all approaches eliminate any chances to provide services to the public which take account of individual differences and the diversity of needs in populations.

This also applies to healthcare services which are, by definition, charged with delivering standardized care. In addition, so the argument goes, assigning priority to reductionist or positivist perspectives may disregard individual patient outcomes at the expense of organizational goals. Anyone who has ever seen a hospital performance report will know that, notwithstanding some patient satisfaction survey results, organizational performance pegged to activity data, patient safety incidences and the like take center stage. In turn, performance reports mainly contain aggregated figures which fail to reflect the individual nature of health services for patients and their complex needs. A result may be a tendency to depersonalize care and to overlook unique patient circumstances.

Yet, how do constructivist approaches avoid this pitfall? What do research approaches based on a different ontology offer in order to produce more holistic appraisals of health service performance? The primary candidates from the constructivist or interpretivist camp are critical realism and pragmatism. I will consider both in turn.

Critical realism asserts that reality exists independently of our perceptions but is understood by us through social constructs (de Souza 2013; Williams et al. 2017). Please note how this differs from a strong, and nowadays rarely held, subjectivist belief which may posit reality as something which can only exist through human perception. Arguing that reality exists outside of human perception allows researchers to anchor their work and prevent radical subjectivism or relativism (Hollis 1994; Raz and Wallace 2011).

When they apply this ontological vision to their work, evaluators may be able to acknowledge both the impact of observable factors, such as resources and policies, while at the same time focusing on the impact of underlying structures which influence these policies and organizational delivery. In essence, their ontological conviction leads them to recognize that organizational structures enable and constrain human agency, be that for professionals working in the health services or patients (Gunn 2000; De Waele et al. 2005; Morgan 2006). Specifically, critical realism is adept at attending to how power dynamics between healthcare professionals and patients or between healthcare professionals may influence health service delivery. Research around the impact of status differentials between nurses and doctors attests to this issue (Laurant et al. 2018; MacLeod et al. 2023).

Pragmatism adopts a different defensive position in the trenches of ontological debates. It has long tried to steer a middle passage between the ontological foes of positivism and constructivism (Lynch et al. 2018; Martínez-García et al. 2019; Kelly 2020). It advocates a mix-and-match model of selecting the most suitable methods (not ontologies) when investigating complex health issues. However, pragmatism is not unprincipled. It maintains the primacy of practical solutions case by case regardless of theoretical alignment. This pragmatic approach may reflect the complex environment in which evaluators find themselves when having to find answers to challenging questions in difficult circumstances. Regardless of set preferences for specific types of evidence amongst those who commission evaluations, evaluators are acutely aware of the fact that evidence may not be forthcoming if it is too narrowly defined through the lens of standardized organizational metrics. In those cases, they may suggest alternatives based on more constructivist approaches if it reduces the risk of a successful completion of the evaluation. Offering a range of methodologies may avert evaluation failure and provide often welcome flexibility to produce more comprehensive evaluation findings. It also speaks to the now widely acknowledged context dependence of healthcare outcomes generating real-world insights into the effectiveness of services (Mukumbang et al. 2018; De Brún and McAuliffe 2020; Paparini et al. 2021).

Does pragmatism have an ontological leg to stand on? Its philosophical roots lie in the work of Charles Peirce and William James, American philosophers, who stipulated that truth is judged by how useful a specific piece of information is when it is acted upon. It is immediately obvious how radically different this position is from any other philosophical standing. It relocates questions of reality and what counts as real in the realm of human conduct and makes our efforts to orientate ourselves in our environment through our actions the primary measure of what does and does not exist. The argument between different philosophical camps does not need to detain us here; what is important, however, is the radical change in perspective this entails for evaluations grounded in pragmatic ontology.

It is human behavior, according to pragmatists, which reveals reality. Actions, in turn, are based on decisions and thoughts about their utility in specific circumstances; they are based on calculations about what is necessary for us to succeed in achieving our goals. It is this practical focus on the person as primary source for our understanding of reality which makes pragmatism so radically different from other approaches. By putting human conduct at the center and seeing it as a product of human calculations of utility of actions in specific settings, it transcends perennial questions about the primacy of thought or physical reality (Sanderson 2009).

The ontology pragmatists adopt is therefore marked by a substantial degree of flexibility. By positioning human action and experience at the core of what constitutes reality, pragmatism emphasizes that reality is constructed and continuously rebuilt through our interactions with the world. Note how this differs from the radical subjectivist position which stresses the sharp demarcation between thought and reality, assigning primacy and constructive power to human thought. In contrast, pragmatism develops a balanced vision of reality, in which we can understand human views of reality through human conduct. The key observation for pragmatists is that action is a product of human calculations about the behavior's utility when aiming to be effective in the world.

This lends pragmatism the ability to see reality as something fluid and dynamic and shaped by the practical consequences of human conduct. It eschews notions of immutable truths but posits understanding of reality as a result of lived experiences (Bonifanti-Romanelli 2018; Collins and Halliday 2020). This is the ontological bridge needed for an appreciation of patient experiences and their lived practical knowledge which informs so many of the most recent evaluation approaches.

In particular, utility, which is the central concept of pragmatic philosophy, serves a facilitating purpose to access reality or truth. The utility and effectiveness of actions or behavioral strategies may be seen as validation of truths or create the status of truth of individual and personal perspectives. This outcome-focused notion of utility binds human conduct to reality and allows evaluators to analyze behavior as signs of what is perceived as real in the world. By acting upon our environment, pragmatists maintain, we test and validate our ideas and reveal what exists in a practical sense. To put it succinctly, for pragmatists, human conduct is the measure of our existence in the world. Decision-making itself is at the heart of our ability (or failure) to make sense of the world. While this permits pragmatism to sidestep the perennial debates between idealism and realism, it concentrates our attention on the interplay between our perceptions of actions within concrete settings and their chances to be successful.

In the context of evaluation, this ontological position holds promise for evaluators in several ways. The first domain where pragmatism has a significant impact is evaluation itself as an example of human conduct. Evaluation strategies may or may not work in specific circumstances, and pragmatism recasts these as justifiable attempts to make evaluations effective in practice. It widens the horizon of evaluation approaches away from a narrow one size fits all to a more flexible and dynamic approach characterized by its utility influenced by local conditions. Pragmatism makes the case for adaptability and articulates an emphasis on problem-solving, rather than methodological purity. This extends to the usefulness of theory and theoretical underpinnings. Theories are valued as and when they contribute to the practical success of capturing the essence of health services in evaluation.

But pragmatic ontology casts its net wider than this. It also allows evaluators to embrace novel and innovative perspectives based on the recognition that human conduct should be placed at the center of evaluation work, acknowledging the experiences of agents in healthcare services as evidence of reality. At the same time, pragmatism's notion of conduct as product of utility calculations of human beings in specific environments supplies us with justifiable reasons to be contextually sensitive in our work. Human conduct varies as the use and effectiveness of behavioral strategies vary in different circumstances, requiring evaluators to be alive to the possibility that our methodological approaches should be tailored to the issues we investigate (De Brún and McAuliffe 2020; Paparini et al. 2021).

The significance of the shift to pragmatism in evaluation work only becomes apparent when we situate this in the context of previously prevalent approaches. It is probably fair to say that evaluations have long favored organizational perspectives which aligned with the policy and commissioning frameworks in which many health services operate. The dominance of organizational performance measures and metrics in health service assessment has however been challenged by more recent attempts to refocus evaluation work on patient experience, providing a more holistic perception of the utility of services. Please note how pragmatism redefines the notion of utility of impact as well by highlighting the patient's role in making services effective. Pragmatism shifts our gaze away from what makes organizations effective on their own terms to what makes them beneficial for patients. Success of services is hence measured by how they support and improve patient health and well-being. This does not preclude the possibility to gauge the performance of health services through analysis of quantifiable activity and their direct outcomes. But it does widen our range of vision across what contributes to the effectiveness of health services. In effect, it reshapes our conversation about health services by drawing new boundaries in relation to what counts as reality to include rich contextual data. Adherence to clinical protocols is certainly one aspect of health service performance, yet how patients experience, say, their hospital stay is also part of health outcomes.

This is not cost-neutral for evaluators. They need to recognize the diversity of patients and their specific needs and accommodate this within the evaluation framework they apply. Integrating cultural aspects into evaluation work is fraught with challenges since cultural positions and their impact on service outcomes are often contested (Karimi Madjid 2015; Slattery et al. 2020). Cultural sensitivity may help address this issue to some extent but, as often noted by observers and practitioners alike, barriers to mutual understanding remain. Health service evaluation as a scientific methodological practice is thus a mirror of our wider societal struggles to make sense of our differences and commonalities. But the alternative is less appealing. Traditional perspectives advancing organizational performance at the expense of wider holistic approaches to effectiveness of health services arguably produce fewer actionable insights and stifle innovation and learning. Volumes written on the shortcomings of health outcome frameworks and their implementation attest to this fact (Richards 2015).

Interestingly, this shift to a more holistic appreciation of health service reality within the pragmatist paradigm also draws attention to the issue of continuous service improvement through learning and adaptation which has taken root in most health service quality improvement policies and protocols around the world

(Hammermeister et al. 1994; Sheikh et al. 2004; Melder et al. 2022; Willmington et al. 2022). Ratings from patients are continuously collated to promote service practices enhancing their effectiveness on the basis of feedback. Methodologically, evaluators have championed "what works" approaches to health service assessments which span the bridge to critical realism and realist evaluation techniques (Feather 2018; Pawson 2018, 2019, 2020). By emphasizing "what works," evaluators assist commissioners to redirect resources to those services which are effective, with effectiveness defined in a broader holistic sense including patient experiences.

Yet, like all ontological perspectives, pragmatism has its challenges when deployed in evaluations. Highlighting utility as a benchmark for human action may gloss over the important conceptual difference between what is effective and what is ethically sound. Timely hospital discharge may be useful for patients and beneficial to hospitals reducing bed blocking, but it may be a deeply ethically flawed action where, in specific circumstances such as the most recent pandemic, risks to patient health are greater outside than inside hospitals (Pawson 2020). Utility is also a double-edged sword when applied from one perspective only. Evaluators are often aware that their work is framed narrowly through single measures or performance indicators which may underplay how health outcomes are combinations of contributions from many groups whose interest may be included or excluded from analysis. The role of informal carers for the health of patients is an illustration of how health services depend on other, often neglected groups with low public visibility (Chou et al. 2014; Gillibrand et al. 2024). This issue is linked to the question of what constitutes "useful evidence" and how it can be or should be defined.

Pragmatists recognize the subjective (in common parlance) nature of utility which requires evaluators to define usefulness and effectiveness as ultimate goals of health services collaboratively capturing a multitude of voices in the process. Stakeholders may put differing emphasis on the long- or short-term effectiveness of services and perceive service impact in different time horizons. This requires evaluators to engage different voices involving patients, providers, and policymakers when demarcating the boundaries of their evaluation and when interpreting the results. While conventionally applied in clinical interactions, shared decision-making may be a useful tool for defining the aims and objectives of evaluations, something which often jars with the realities of the commissioning process.

Ultimately, however, it is pragmatism's methodological flexibility which allows evaluators to favor it over more stringent methodologies rooted in other ontologies. Its focus on producing actionable insights and meaningful results for a specific setting makes it attractive to those who work with limited resources and under tight deadlines but are animated by the desire to contribute to the improvement of health services through their work. It is the impetus for continuous reflection and learning that pragmatism instils, which underpins successful evaluation work in practice. Embracing a pragmatic ontology in evaluation studies offers a powerful framework for addressing complex, real-world challenges. By focusing on human action and the practical consequences of human decisions, pragmatism transcends traditional philosophical debates and focuses on improving outcomes through effective, context-sensitive healthcare practice. Prioritizing the concept of utility from the patient's perspective permits evaluations to bring about meaningful change that reconciles organizational objectives with the needs of patients.

Critical realism and pragmatism challenge us to question the status quo which has dominated some evaluation practice for so long. They articulate a radically different vision of scientifically produced insights into the performance of health services, moving us beyond narrowly defined organizationally defined efficiency metrics to include patient-generated information about their well-being. Their ontologies ask us to consider the emotional, social, and psychological aspects of health and to investigate health outcomes as the product of an interplay between all stakeholders, including those with less visibility and power in the cacophony of voices.

Pragmatism and critical realism are well aligned with the widely acknowledged need to create personalized services today and tailor them to the individual preferences of patients (Choi et al. 2021). Evaluation as a reflective practice, taking into account the wider societal transformations and changing conversations about health, may use pragmatic and critical realist approaches to incorporate dialogical perspectives between all stakeholders to shape evaluation objectives, benchmarks of success as well as evaluation techniques and tools. The ethical tenets of personal autonomy, equity and access underpin these approaches but need to be renegotiated every day in the heat of the evaluation battle.

3 Epistemology in Health Service Evaluations

In this section, I will explore the epistemological principles emanating from these perspectives and outline how they impact on evaluation work in practice. While ontological viewpoints are intricately linked to epistemological ones, it is worthwhile to note that most researchers and evaluators favor a pragmatic (again, in common parlance) strategy when it comes to selecting their sources of knowledge and facts or which views to promulgate on their validity. This in turn often determines their methods of inquiry which will bring us to the core of evaluation practice, the choice of data collection and data analysis techniques and tools.

Whereas ontology is the ground on which philosophers fight their battles as to what constitutes reality, epistemology relates to the issue of what can be known (Shenhav 2003; Stanley 2012; Kaehne 2016). The nature of knowledge in evaluation however is framed not through the notion of everyday facts of life as perceived by ordinary human beings, but through the lens of science as a method to generate evidence which is intersubjectively acknowledged to be valid (Popper 1992). Science as a regulated activity imposes different constraints and licenses on what may or may not be seen as a fact, and the debate about how scientific procedures produce something different from facts we encounter in our everyday lives has been raging ever since Descartes formulated prescriptive rules for scientific investigations (Weber 1980; Clarke 2009).

In our context, what appears to be important is to recognize that evaluation as a scientific endeavor lays claim to knowledge emanating from its inquiries as *scientific* knowledge. This claim is supported by its increasingly theory-based and theory-led nature. Going back several decades, evaluations would feature significantly less theory content (Cordray and Lipsey 1986). Today, evaluations in all public policy domains rarely lag behind their research project cousins. Epistemologically, this has important implications for evaluation practice, given that the use of theories and concepts provides an element of criticality which hitherto may have been reserved for research. The ascent of logic models and theories of change in evaluations speaks to this increasing research character of evaluations (Douthwaite et al. 2003; Kneale et al. 2015; Wilson et al. 2021), and moves the production of evaluation insights closer to knowledge generated by rule-based, transparent and replicable inquiries, all fundamental attributes of research. In fact, postulating a difference in the scientific nature of evaluation and research inquiry may strike us as odd nowadays as both increasingly converge on a universally accepted concept of scientific, theory-led investigation.

The notions of replicability, transparency and criticality thus now serve as key scientific benchmarks of evaluation as well as research. Their compliance with them influences the validity of knowledge produced in the exercise of either practice. However, as evaluation has moved ever closer to research, it has come to be affected by the same centrifugal tendencies apparent in epistemological debates. What is accepted as a source of knowledge is largely represented by the two diametrically opposing poles of positivism and interpretivism, which either postulate the reliance on observable and measurable evidence often obtained quantitative methods or perceives valid facts to be products of understanding of subjective experiences through qualitative methods such as interviews and focus groups (Hollis 1994; Fraser and Robinson 2004; Lee 2012).

I have already articulated the opportunity open to all evaluators of adopting a pragmatic stance with regard to the different epistemological options and views on what constitutes knowledge. In that sense, evaluators (and indeed researchers) often only sketch tenuous links between the ontology they espouse and the epistemological standpoint they adopt. Yet, it may be important to stress that it is perfectly possible to subscribe to the need for a purist alignment between ontology, epistemology and methods. In such a worldview, ontological disagreements are thought to extend to epistemological dissent and disputes about methodological tools and techniques.

The more practical discussion about what constitutes valid knowledge is originally tethered to the notions of observations, their role in research and evaluation and the idea of generalizable evidence (Harmon et al. 2013; Schwarz et al. 2019). Generalizability often serves as a touchstone of validity for researchers, although this has been challenged by those propagating a more constructivist view of reality (Adcock and Collier 2001; Berry 2011). Again, seeing this intractable disagreement through the pragmatic lens, we may use the concept of *context* as a catalyst for softening the lines of discord. Even the most battle-hardened researcher tying scientific work to generalizability often recognizes that knowledge to be valid is influenced by the context in which individuals operate (Paparini et al. 2021). This discovery of the role of context has led to significant changes in how complex interventions in medicine and healthcare are being researched and evaluated (Skivington et al.

2021), often broadly accepting the view that knowledge is constructed by individuals interacting with their environment which, in turn, inserts a context dependency into research findings.

The wider recent approximation or convergence between research and evaluation is mirrored in the fluidity and flexibility of evaluators when it comes to selecting their methods of reasoning in their work. Two methods of inquiry have long been postulated as mutually exclusive, yielding facts of different validity depending on the view of practitioners. Deductive reasoning, which starts with a theory or hypothesis, produces knowledge through testing and validating the theory by collecting data which can prove or disprove it. The inductive way of reasoning offers the opposite image of deductive reasoning, intending to build theories through the analysis of observations and identifying patterns inherent in the data. What makes perfect sense when seen from the vantage point of scientific logic, however, possesses the capacity to be much messier in practice.

As philosophers of science have long pointed out, data do not come in an unmediated fashion to us but are perceived through conceptual frames (Oakeshott 1975). Those frames already contain embryonic theories and notions of how the world works. Strictly speaking, deductive reasoning is a misnomer, a misapprehension of how we perceive and orient ourselves in the world, including the moments when we conduct research or evaluations. Equally, building theories from simply observing data also reflects an epistemological naivety hard to sustain. We do not observe patterns in unordered masses of information simply by fiat. Patterns present themselves to us through mechanisms of recognition which, again, are reflective of prior experiences we may have had (Oakeshott 1975).

Neither deductive nor inductive reasoning can therefore sensibly maintain their purist stance. The work of researchers is much more likely to be marked by an oscillation between the poles of reasoning, drawing pragmatically on either when more likely to yield insights. This may lead us to suggest that flexible pragmatic approaches in ontology may also be of benefit to anybody navigating the epistemological standards of evaluation work. Two implications of such epistemological flexibility are however important to note. First, policy and policymaking often still has strong preferences for deductively produced observational evidence, aligning with the desire to support policy choices through "hard facts" in public debates. Second, the notion of validity of knowledge still remains tied to different types of reasoning which present non-negotiable opposites. The rise of mixed methods approaches in research and evaluation therefore draws on two different validation mechanisms which are incommensurable. No amount of pragmatism by mixed methods scientists can extinguish the fact that there has so far not been any corresponding epistemological position which can meaningfully combine deductive and inductive reasoning in an acceptable way (Creswell and Plano Clark 2018; de Haan et al. 2021).

For the purpose of comprehensiveness, it is important to note that reductionism and reductive reasoning has occupied an ever increasing role in social sciences and left their mark on healthcare evaluations too (Paley 2010; Duryan et al. 2012). In a simplified way, reductive reasoning may be defined as breaking down complex phenomena into constituent parts or components to understand the whole. The underlying assumption is that a complex system is a sum of its parts. Yet this assumption has come under scrutiny as we are gaining a better understanding of complex systems including the role of feedback loops, and phenomena such as emergence which go beyond simplified reductionist approaches. While complexity as a scientific approach may come to be applied increasingly in health service research, reductive reasoning will still have its place and underpin some of the initial analysis of programs and interventions. Theories of change and logic model development are some of the more reductionist tools to make sense of interventions in healthcare which are often used to identify active ingredients of programs (May et al. 2016; Malley et al. 2022).

Sketching the directions of reasoning used in reductive and inductive thought may reveal some of their fundamental differences and illustrate their complementary role in health service evaluations. While reductionism may involve analyzing single components of service activity, such as allocated resources or staffing, and ascertain the impact they have on service outcomes, inductive analysis would seek to identify patterns of service activity which may indicate a generalizable order of things. Once patterns have been formulated as general principles of (organizational or individual) behavior using theories, they can be tested. Reductive reasoning thus tries to understand the whole by analyzing its parts, while inductive reasoning attempts to develop general principles from specific observational data. The former has an analytical and deconstructive thrust, whereas the latter is synthetic and generative in nature. The Achilles heel of reductive reasoning remains the possibility that programs or service interventions have emergent features, i.e. are more than the sum of their parts, a phenomenon which complexity theory tries to describe and explain.

The remainder of this chapter will outline some of the key developments of health service evaluations which have marked the direction of change over the last decade or so. The purpose of this ultimate part of the chapter is not to provide a comprehensive overview of the multitude of modifications, theoretical or otherwise, in the practice of evaluation, but to demarcate the main lines of methodological changes which define healthcare evaluation at present. Some of those changes have taken place slowly and incrementally, while others have been rapid and profound. In fact, one may argue that the current dynamic pace of change in evaluation studies in healthcare research may be a combination of all transformative movements in the field. Let's look at them one by one and then draw them together in the last section.

4 Diversity of Methods

The field of evaluation in health services is still young but has already seen a significant diversification in methods and methodologies. In part, this may be simply because of the diversity of purposes for which evaluations are used. At times, commissioners of evaluations may be interested in the cost-effectiveness of programs, while at other times, it is the wider impact of an intervention which is in their sight.

This methodological pluralism has been a strength of evaluations but also makes it difficult at times to synthesize findings across studies which have utilized different research methods or theoretical approaches, an issue which specialists of evidence synthesis are addressing through novel integrative techniques (Pawson et al. 2004; Movsisyan et al. 2020).

One unmistakable trend however has been the increasing use of theories in evaluation. In particular, social sciences have been a prolific source of theories to evaluation practitioners. This has clearly brought about richer debates about key issues in evaluation such as causality, context and complexity (Pawson 2024). It has also led to a re-appraisal of study designs, and a resurgence or recognition of the utility of non-experimental designs over more traditional research designs such as randomized controlled trials or controlled cohort studies. This diversity of methods and its resultant methodological pluralism can only be of benefit to the practice of evaluation even though it has sparked sometimes heated debates amongst practitioners about the validity and advantage of different approaches, especially as the stakes were higher than normal during the recent pandemic (Pawson 2019).

Overall, however, diversity should be taken as a strength, addressing the discomfort we sometimes have as evaluators with approaches favoring a one-size-fits-all perspective. Arguably, healthcare is too complex to be adequately analyzed through exclusively one approach. Yet methodological pluralism also offers evaluators more choice, which empowers them to select the most appropriate approaches for unique environments or settings and, thus, possibly also to create a better fit of methodological apparatus to the phenomena to be investigated. It is this flexibility produced by choice which gives evaluators a toolkit that can be tailored to fit specific evaluation needs in particular circumstances.

In addition, it seems to me that healthy methodological pluralism also encourages innovation through more debate about which methods align best with the programs we assess. Where singular and narrow methods may be suitable for confined analyses, investigations of large programs have to contend with uncertain circumstances, the interplay of multiple program components and unforeseen complexities. Uniform methodological approaches are unlikely to succeed under these conditions. The concept of impact itself is likely to be a compound of different program aspects, often involving clinical or nonclinical effects in healthcare services.

As we come to recognize the interdependence of program components and their context, we have also learned to increasingly acknowledge the importance of transferring insights from one program to another through carefully calibrated evaluation methods. This transfer may include program or organizational learning but also often comprises the advantage of using specific innovative evaluation tools in certain situations (Mann et al. 2004; Belling et al. 2014). It thus extends from empirical insights to methodological knowledge transfer across evaluation practices. In my mind, this should be considered a win for everyone willing to embrace methodological pluralism.

5 From Value-Free to Value-Conscious Perspectives

Anybody who has attended a presentation by Canadian or Australian colleagues is bound to notice a preamble presenters usually read out to the effect that they acknowledge the rights of indigenous people on whose territory they are working and living. The preambles vary in content, but their intent is similar: to recognize that our lives are built on foundations which have often been laid by force and coercion in times past. To some listeners, these preambles may sound strange, but it is hard not to recognize the good intent as well as the fundamental shift of attitudes these preambles signal, to be cognizant of harm done in times past. Moreover, the preambles are an indication that researchers are increasingly aware of the role of trauma, individual or collective, which shapes our present and is inscribed into human behavior and social problems. It is this awareness which altered evaluation practice to some extent over the last decade or so and to which I would like to turn now.

Seeing research or evaluation as investigative practices which produce value-free insights has been a touchstone of scientific endeavors for a long time. Science started under the auspices of the Enlightenment and was animated by the desire to eliminate religious or non-rational interpretations of reality. This aspiration is written into the DNA of all modern research, ushering in a strong preference for empirical and observational methods. Durkheim's notion of sociological investigations widened the radius of observational concepts to social and economic forces as agents of change but retained its strong empirical impetus. Max Weber added sophisticated considerations about the value-free and value-bound nature of science and tried to steer a middle path through these opposing poles of empiricist, materialist and theory-informed knowledge.

But in practice, what resembled a value-free paradigm came to prevail in some research, especially data science and statistics, which have extended their appeal and attraction into evaluation studies. The preambles of the rights of indigenous people about which we hear so often now are only a culmination of a shift from the premise of value-free research to a more subtle understanding of the role of value in our work. While the notion of complete objectivity still has its proponents, Weber's work prepared the ground for a long-term adjustment to the idea that values inform the way in which we view and perceive healthcare, its users and the organizations that deliver it (Weber 1980; Clarke 2009).

In fact, whereas the ambition to conduct research ethically was previously conceived to be a form of "value-free" investigation, we now understand the interplay between values and healthcare in a much more sophisticated way which contributes to novel ideas of what constitutes ethical integrity of evaluation work. The inspiring impetus for this shift from value-free to the value-conscious perspective is the belief that the latter leads us to assess and design health services which will meet the needs of individual and communities with their unique needs. By recognizing the values underpinning our work, arguably, we become more sensitive to the contexts in which people use health services. We understand much better what people care about when they enter a hospital and why, at times, they deliberately opt not to take up healthcare offers.

Our handbook offers several examples of value-informed and value-based health service evaluation practices, so there is no need to describe them here in more detail. Yet it is noteworthy that a fundamental justification and conceptual exploration of this shift and its implications is still lacking. While value-based healthcare has received a sound and articulate foundation (Porter and Teisberg 2006; Zipfel et al. 2019), the slow yet noticeable shift from the vision of value-free science to value-cognizant research still awaits a thorough philosophical defense. For now, the preambles we hear from our Canadian and Australian colleagues are signs of a universally welcome shift to more culturally sensitive evaluations which hopefully result in more responsive health service for communities experiencing societal and organizationally rooted discrimination and neglect. But they remain statements of intent whose ontological and epistemological implications remain mainly unarticulated.

This brings us to a critical development which complements the recognition of the role of values in our work. It is the role of leadership in evaluations which has, so far, received short shrift from observers and methodologists. Initially, I will discuss this through the lens of the role of evaluators in defining the scope of evaluations. This perspective offers us a unique angle to explore how evaluators have to navigate, amongst others, the Scylla and Charybdis of time and resource limitations.

6 Evaluators as Leaders

There can be little doubt that the role of evaluators is integral to the success of the evaluation. Often, this manifests itself through collaboratively defining the scope of the evaluation through proactive discussions with all stakeholders. But not all evaluations are co-produced in scope and reach. In fact, oftentimes evaluations are commissioned "after the fact" when service directors or managers are trying to establish the effect and impact of a service. The role of evaluation leaders involves, amongst other things, to ensure that their study is methodologically sound, ethically responsible and of course that findings are relevant to stakeholders, including program beneficiaries or service users, regardless of their involvement in designing the evaluation (or indeed the program or service). In essence, it is the task of evaluation leaders to act as a catalyst for positive change through delivering meaningful and effective assessments of health services.

I have deliberately spoken here of evaluation leaders, rather than simply of evaluation or project leads. What do I mean by this? I would like to distinguish between evaluators as technical experts (project leads) and evaluators as advocates for positive change (leaders). Both roles comprise different sets of tasks, and in this last section of the chapter, I want to illustrate the importance of moving from an understanding of evaluators as executors of technical knowledge to a deeper understanding of our role in bringing about societal change.

The first notion of evaluators as technical experts still enjoys wide support. Its justification arguably comes from the fact that evaluators are often called late to the party, with services or programs already underway when they arrive at the scene. This leaves them little room for maneuver when it comes to influencing the design of the intervention or the way in which data are generated to assess its effects or impact. The desire to be of help and assistance which motivates evaluators when conducting their work comes from a good place and, ostensibly, often involves critical thought enabled by the real-time delay between what program designers do and program evaluators do. Yet, the problem with a largely reactive role of evaluators is encapsulated in the often-heard adage that evaluators are a "taxi for hire," a vehicle to reach a predefined destination.

In contrast, evaluators as *leaders* carry out activities which question the conventional sequence of design, implementation and evaluation. Evaluators as leaders demonstrate conduct which does not ground criticality of evaluation work solely in the deployment of suitable methods and techniques. Evaluation leaders are attempting to (re-)negotiate the scope or ambition of programs or interventions by introducing a wider horizon of relevance into stakeholder discussions. They do not focus exclusively on selecting the best available methods to evaluate a service but try to embed the evaluation aims and objectives in the broader ambit of societal change and the needs of affected communities. It is a vision of utility (of evaluations) for the purpose of societal relevance and social change. In this perspective, evaluations are a means to an end, not an end in themselves. This may be surprising given that evaluators normally have little influence over program design. But the intention to use evaluations to improve health services for populations is not an absolutist normative principle, it is a guide which prompts us to highlight critical aspects of health service use which may have been overlooked or were not considered when stakeholders originally shaped the outlines of their service.

Tenets of equity and inclusion may serve as a good example. Evaluators can advocate for the inclusion of both principles in the evaluation and thus increase the opportunity to ask important questions which address service access for underserved communities. Through this, they may also be able to spark conversations about social determinants of health which hitherto may have flown below the radar of program makers. This is how proactive evaluation leadership aligns with value-based health services discussed above and moves notions of patient-centered healthcare and community empowerment into sharper focus.

There is little doubt that evaluation leaders are constrained by several factors when advocating for evaluations responsive to wider social change. Evaluations are post hoc investigations; they cannot change the thrust of programs carved into them at the time of design. Evaluation leaders also need to set realistic goals which can be operationalized through effective evaluation techniques such as data collection, data analysis and synthesis of findings. Ultimately, evaluations are supposed to produce actionable recommendations, not flights of right-thinking fancy.

Yet, programs rarely consist of singular points of authority but instead are likely to contain a diverse range of stakeholder interests. Evaluators require leadership skills to navigate different priorities amongst them, and they may find this an opportunity to inject awareness of the need to include marginalized or underrepresented populations through (re-)defining the scope of the evaluation. Often, strategic objectives of health organizations also provide space and opportunity to ask questions about inclusivity or value of programs to specific communities. Aligning evaluation aims with wider organizational strategic goals may help advocating for policy change even within the confines of existing services (McAnaney and Wynne 2016; Vize 2017).

It is this ethical and value-based influence that evaluators can exercise which has often been underestimated in the pressurized environment of evaluation practice. The notion of societal leadership I have articulated above challenges our often narrow conception of the evaluator role. It formulates a more expansive task of evaluators as leaders, which, in turn, requires capacity, capabilities and skills as our chapter in this handbook demonstrates. In short, leadership qualities are integral to the work of evaluators in health services where resources are limited and the field of resource allocation is contested between powerful interest groups arguing their corner. We may have to get used to evaluators as advocates for principles of equity, social justice and fairness rooted in cultural competencies and sensitivity. Of course, the flag for social change is not carried by evaluators alone, nor is it a call which overrides sensible, reasonable and well-established practices of evaluation. But as we demonstrate with this handbook, evaluations can no longer be "taxies for hire" if they want to stay relevant in our rapidly changing world and strive to empower people and build evaluation capacity and ownership collaboratively with the communities served by health services.

References

Abma TA, Broerse JEW (2010) Patient participation as dialogue: setting research agendas. Health Expect 13(2):160–173. https://doi.org/10.1111/j.1369-7625.2009.00549.x

Adcock R, Collier D (2001) Measurement validity: a shared standard for qualitative and quantitative research. Am Polit Sci Rev 95:529–546. https://doi.org/10.1017/S0003055401003100

Bartlett CW, Ray WC (2021) Are the organisational management characteristics of healthcare organisations distinguishable from other professional organisations? J Health Manag 23:1–9. https://doi.org/10.1177/09720634211050445

Belling R et al (2014) The effect of organisational resources and eligibility issues on transition from child and adolescent to adult mental health services. J Health Serv Res Policy 19(3):169–176

Berry TR (2011) Qualitative researchers as modern day Sophists? Reflections on the qualitative–quantitative divide. Qual Res Sport, Exerc Health 3(3):324–328. https://doi.org/10.1080/2159676X.2011.607176

Birken SA et al (2023) Toward a more comprehensive understanding of organizational influences on implementation: the organization theory for implementation science framework. Front Health Serv 3:1–10. https://doi.org/10.3389/frhs.2023.1142598

Bonifanti-Romanelli AM (2018) Understanding the lived experiences of parents of disabled children regarding their child's education., dissertation abstracts international section a: humanities and social sciences. ProQuest Information & Learning, Harrow. https://liverpool.idm.oclc.org/login?url=http://search.ebscohost.com/login.aspx?direct=true&db=psyh&AN=2017-19719-242&site=ehost-live&scope=site

Buntinz W (2008) The logic of relations and the logic of management. J Intellect Disabil Res 52(7):588–597. http://www.wiley.com/bw/journal.asp?ref=0964-2633&amp
Caffrey L, Wolfe C, McKevitt C (2016) Embedding research in health systems: lessons from complexity theory. Health Res Policy Syst 14(1):54. https://doi.org/10.1186/s12961-016-0128-x
Calnan M (2020) Health policy, power and politics. Emerald Publishing, Bingley
Choi H, Jung Y-I, Kim H (2021) Implementation fidelity of the Systems for Person-Centered Elder Care (SPEC): a process evaluation study. Implement Sci 16(1):1–13. https://doi.org/10.1186/s13012-021-01113-3
Chou Y-C et al (2014) Working but not employed: mothers of adults with intellectual disability as hidden workers. J Intellect Develop Disabil 39(4):353–363
Clarke C (2009) Paths between positivism and interpretivism: an appraisal of Hay's via media. Politics 29(1):28–36
Collins M, Halliday E (2020) Public engagement in health research. In: Handbook of theory and methods in health research. Questions, methods, and choices. Edgar Elgar, Cheltenham, pp 323–340
Cordray DS, Lipsey MW (1986) Program evaluation and program research. In: Evaluation studies: review annual, vol 11. Sage, Newbury, pp 17–44
Coulter A (1991) Evaluating the outcomes of health care. In: Gabe J, Calnan M, Bury M (eds) The sociology of the health service. Routledge, London, pp 115–139
Creswell JW, Plano Clark VL (2018) Designing and conducting mixed methods research, 3rd edn. Sage Publications, Thousand Oaks
De Brún A, McAuliffe E (2020) Identifying the context, mechanisms and outcomes underlying collective leadership in teams: building a realist programme theory. BMC Health Serv Res 20(1):261. https://doi.org/10.1186/s12913-020-05129-1
de Haan M, van Eijk-Hustings Y, Vrijhoef HJM (2021) Using mixed methods in health services research: a review of the literature and case study. J Health Serv Res Policy 26(2):141–147. https://doi.org/10.1177/1355819620955223
de Souza DE (2013) Elaborating the context-mechanism-outcome configuration (CMOc) in realist evaluation: a critical realist perspective. Evaluation 19(2):141–154. https://doi.org/10.1177/1356389013485194
De Waele I et al (2005) Quality of life versus quality of care: implications for people and programs. J Policy Pract Intellect Disabil 2(3–4):229–239. https://doi.org/10.1111/j.1741-1130.2005.00035.x
Douthwaite B et al (2003) Impact pathway evaluation: an approach for achieving and attributing impact in complex systems. Agric Syst 78(2):243–265. https://doi.org/10.1016/S0308-521X(03)00128-8
Durand F, Fleury MJ (2021) A multilevel study of patient-centered care perceptions in mental health teams. BMC Health Serv Res 21(1):1–8. https://doi.org/10.1186/s12913-020-06054-z
Duryan M et al (2012) System dynamics modeling for intellectual disability services: a case study. J Policy Pract Intellect Disabil 9(2):112–119
Feather JL (2018) Developing programme theories as part of a realist evaluation of a healthcare quality improvement programme. Int J Care Coord 21(3):68–72. https://doi.org/10.1177/2053434518779753
Fraser S, Robinson C (2004) Paradigms and philosophy. In: Fraser S et al (eds) Doing research with children and young people. Sage and Open University Press, London, pp 59–77
Fulop N et al (2013) Innovations in major system reconfiguration in England: a study of the effectiveness, acceptability and processes of implementation of two models of stroke care. Implement Sci 8(1):1–10. https://doi.org/10.1186/1748-5908-8-5
Galbraith J (1973) Designing complex organizations. Addison-Wesley Publishing, Reading
Galbraith J (1977) Organization design. Addison-Wesley Publishing, Reading
Geyer R (2012) Can complexity move UK policy beyond "evidence-based policy making" and the "audit culture"? Applying a "complexity cascade" to education and health policy. Polit Stud 60(1):20–43

Gillibrand S et al (2024) "We might not have been in hospital, but I were frontline workers in the community": a qualitative study exploring unmet need and local community-based responses for marginalised groups in Greater Manchester during the COVID-19 pandemic. BMC Health Serv Res 24(1):1–13. https://doi.org/10.1186/s12913-024-10921-4
Greenhalgh T (2003) How to read a paper. The basics of evidence based medicine, 2nd edn. BMJ books, London
Gualandi R et al (2021) What does the patient have to say? Valuing the patient experience to improve the patient journey. BMC Health Serv Res 3:1–12
Gunn IP (2000) Patient safety and human error: the big picture. CRNA 11(1):41–48
Hammermeister KE et al (1994) Continuous assessment and improvement in quality of care—a model from the Department-of-Veterans-Affairs Cardiac-Surgery. Ann Surg 219(3):281–290. https://doi.org/10.1097/00000658-199403000-00008
Harmon KG et al (2013) American Medical Society for Sports Medicine position statement: concussion in sport. Br J Sports Med 47(1):15–27
Hollis M (1994) The philosophy of social science. An introduction. Cambridge University Press, Cambridge
Kaehne A (2016) Complexity in programme evaluations and integration studies: what can it tell us? J Integr Care 24(5/6):313–320. https://doi.org/10.1108/JICA-10-2016-0041
Kaehne A (2017) Integration as a scientific paradigm. J Integr Care 25(4):271–279. https://doi.org/10.1108/JICA-07-2017-0023
Kaehne A (2022) Integrated care. Reflections on change in health services. Emerald Publishing Limited, Bingley. https://doi.org/10.1108/9781801179782
Kaehne A, Catherall C (2012) Co-located health and social care services in Wales: what are the benefits to professionals? Int J Healthc Manag 5(3):164–172. https://doi.org/10.1179/2047971912Y.0000000014
Kaehne A et al (2017) Bringing integration home policy on health and social care integration in the four nations of the UK. J Integr Care 25(2):84–98. https://doi.org/10.1108/JICA-12-2016-0049
Kaehne A, Beacham A, Feather J (2018) Co-production in integrated health and social care programmes: a pragmatic model. J Integr Care 26(1):87–96. https://doi.org/10.1108/JICA-11-2017-0044
Karimi Madjid EMJ (2015) Exploration of racial and ethnic disparities in health care transition and quality for youth with intellectual and developmental disabilities: analysis of 2009--2010 National Survey of Children with Special Health Care Needs. Dissertation Abstracts International: Section B: The Sciences and Engineering, vol 75(8)
Kelly LM (2020) Three principles of pragmatism for research on organizational processes. Methodol Innov 13(2):1–20. https://doi.org/10.1177/2059799120937242
Kelly LM, Cordeiro M (2020) Three principles of pragmatism for research on organizational processes. Methodol Innov 13:723
Kneale D, Thomas J, Harris K (2015) Developing and optimising the use of logic models in systematic reviews: exploring practice and good practice in the use of programme theory in reviews. PLoS One 10(11):1–26. https://doi.org/10.1371/journal.pone.0142187
La Placa V, McNaught A, Knight A (2013) Discourse on wellbeing in research and practice. Int J Wellbeing 3:116–125. https://doi.org/10.5502/ijw.v3i1.7
Laurant M et al (2018) Nurses as substitutes for doctors in primary care. Cochrane Database Syst Rev 7(7):CD001271. https://doi.org/10.1002/14651858.CD001271.PUB3
Lee CG (2012) Reconsidering constructivism in qualitative research. Educ Philos Theory 44(4):403–412. https://doi.org/10.1111/j.1469-5812.2010.00720.x
Lewis RQ et al (2021) Integrated care in England—what can I learn from a decade of national pilot programmes? Int J Integr Care 21(4):1–10. https://doi.org/10.5334/ijic.5631
Ly S, Runacres F, Poon P (2021) Journey mapping as a novel approach to healthcare: a qualitative mixed methods study in palliative care. BMC Health Serv Res 21:1–9
Lynch EA et al (2018) "There is nothing so practical as a good theory": a pragmatic guide for selecting theoretical approaches for implementation projects. BMC Health Serv Res 18:857. https://doi.org/10.1186/s12913-018-3671-z

MacLeod MLP et al (2023) Exploring the intersection of hermeneutics and implementation: a scoping review. Syst Rev 12(1):1–21. https://doi.org/10.1186/s13643-023-02176-7
Malley J et al (2022) Theory-based evaluation of three research-practice partnerships designed to deliver novel, sustainable collaborations between adult social care research and practice in the UK: a research protocol for a layered' contributions analysis and realist evaluation. BMJ Open 12(11):1–10. https://doi.org/10.1136/bmjopen-2022-068651
Maniatopoulos G et al (2020) Large-scale health system transformation in the United Kingdom: implementing the new care models in the NHS. J Health Organ Manag 34(3):325–344. https://doi.org/10.1108/JHOM-05-2019-0144
Mann P, Pritchard S, Rummery K (2004) Supporting inter-organizational partnerships in the public sector. Public Manag Rev 6(3):417–439
Martínez-García M et al (2019) Novel methods of qualitative analysis for health policy research. Health Res Policy Syst 17(1):1–13. https://doi.org/10.1186/s12961-018-0404-z
May CR, Johnson M, Finch T (2016) Implementation, context and complexity. Implement Sci 11(1):1–12. https://doi.org/10.1186/s13012-016-0506-3
McAnaney DF, Wynne RF (2016) Linking user and staff perspectives in the evaluation of innovative transition projects for youth with disabilities. J Intellect Disabil 20(2):165–182. https://doi.org/10.1177/1744629516633574
McCarthy S et al (2016) An integrated patient journey mapping tool for embedding quality in healthcare service reform. J Decis Syst 25:354–368. https://doi.org/10.1080/12460125.2016.1187394
Melder A et al (2022) Integrating the complexity of healthcare improvement with implementation science: a longitudinal qualitative case study. BMC Health Serv Res 22(1):1–12. https://doi.org/10.1186/s12913-022-07505-5
Morgan G (2006) Images of organizations. Sage Publications, Thousand Oaks
Movsisyan A, Rehfuess E, Norris SL (2020) When complexity matters: a step-by-step guide to incorporating a complexity perspective in guideline development for public health and health system interventions. BMC Med Res Methodol 20(1):1–13. https://doi.org/10.1186/s12874-020-01132-6
Mukumbang FC et al (2018) Unearthing how, why, for whom and under what health system conditions the antiretroviral treatment adherence club intervention in South Africa works: a realist theory refining approach. BMC Health Serv Res 18(1):1–15. https://doi.org/10.1186/s12913-018-3150-6
Nelson EC, Batalden PB, Godfrey MM (2007) Quality by design. A clinical microsystems approach. John Wiley & Sons, San Francisco
Oakeshott M (1975) On human conduct. Oxford University Press, Oxford
Paley J (2010) The appropriation of complexity theory in health care. J Health Serv Res Policy 15(1):59–61. https://doi.org/10.1258/jhsrp.2009.009072
Paparini S et al (2021) Evaluating complex interventions in context: systematic, meta-narrative review of case study approaches. BMC Med Res Methodol 21(1):1–22. https://doi.org/10.1186/s12874-021-01418-3
Pawson R (2018) The realist foundations of evidence-based medicine: a review essay. Evaluation 24(1):42–50. https://doi.org/10.1177/1356389017746718
Pawson R (2019) The shrinking scope of pragmatic trials: a methodological reflection on their domain of applicability. J Clin Epidemiol 107:71–76. https://doi.org/10.1016/j.jclinepi.2018.11.020
Pawson R (2020) The relevance of realism in the pandemic. The Denial of Complexity, London. https://www.ramesesproject.org/media/WP3_-_Denial_of_complexity.pdf
Pawson R (2024) How to think like a realist. A methodology for social science. Edward Elgar, Cheltenham
Pawson R et al (2004) In: E. R. M. Programme (ed) Realist synthesis: an introduction, Working paper series. ESRC, London
Peck B, Mummery J (2017) Hermeneutic constructivism: an ontology for qualitative research. Qual Health Res 28:104973231770693. https://doi.org/10.1177/1049732317706931

Popper K (1992) The logic of scientific discovery. Routledge, London
Porter ME, Teisberg EO (2006) Redefining health care. Creating value-based competition on results. Harvard Business Review Press, Boston
Raz J, Wallace RJ (2011) The practice of value. https://doi.org/10.1093/acprof:oso/9780199278466.001.0001
Richards DA (2015) The critical importance of patient and public involvement for research into complex interventions. In: Complex interventions in health. An overview of research methods. Routledge, Taylor & Francis Group, London, pp 46–50
Russell J et al (2008) Recognizing rhetoric in health care policy analysis. J Health Serv Res Policy 13:40. https://doi.org/10.1258/jhsrp.2007.006029
Sanderson I (2009) Intelligent policy making for a complex world: pragmatism, evidence and learning. Polit Stud 57(4):699–719
Schwarz UVT, Aarons GA, Hasson H (2019) The value equation: three complementary propositions for reconciling fidelity and adaptation in evidence-based practice implementation. BMC Health Serv Res 19(868):1–10. https://doi.org/10.1186/s12913-019-4668-y
Scott JC (1998) Seeing like a state. How certain schemes to improve the human condition have failed. Yale University Press, New Haven
Sheikh K, Bullock C, Preston SD (2004) Evaluation of quality improvement interventions for reducing adverse outcomes of carotid endarterectomy. Med Care 42(7):690–699. 00005650-200407000-00010 [pii]
Shenhav Y (2003) The historical and epistemological foundations of organization theory: fusing sociological and engineering discourse. In: Tsoukas H, Knudsen C (eds) The Oxford handbook of organization theory. Oxford University Press, Oxford, pp 183–209
Shimmin C et al (2017) Moving towards a more inclusive patient and public involvement in health research paradigm: the incorporation of a trauma-informed intersectional analysis. BMC Health Serv Res 17:539. https://doi.org/10.1186/s12913-017-2463-1
Shortell SM (2016) Applying organization theory to understanding the adoption and implementation of accountable care organizations: commentary. Med Care Res Rev 73(6):694–702. https://doi.org/10.1177/1077558716643477
Siegel A et al (2011) Jahresbericht zur Evaluation der Integrierten Versorgung Gesundes Kinzigtal. Evaluations-Koordinierungsstelle Integrierte Versorgung, Freiburg, p 73
Skivington K et al (2021) A new framework for developing and evaluating complex interventions: update of Medical Research Council guidance. BMJ 374:n2061. https://doi.org/10.1136/bmj.n2061
Slattery P, Saeri AK, Bragge P (2020) Research co-design in health: a rapid overview of reviews. Health Res Policy Syst 18(1):17. https://doi.org/10.1186/s12961-020-0528-9
Stanley L (2012) Rethinking the definition and role of ontology in political science. Politics 32(2):93–99
Strandberg-Larsen M, Krasnik A (2009) Measurement of integrated healthcare delivery: a systematic review of methods and future research directions. Int J Integr Care 9:e01
Temple B (2012) Continuity of care: a multi-site case study of people with intellectual disabilities living in the community. J Intellect Disabil Res 56(7–8)
Vize R (2017) Swimming together or sinking alone: health, care and the art of systems leadership. https://ihm.org.uk/stp-report-swimming-together-or-sinking-alone/
Warner M, Zaranko B, Lumpkin R (2022) NHS funding, resources and treatment volumes. Institute for Fiscal Studies (IFS), London
Weber M (1980) Wirtschaft und Gesellschaft. In: Grundriss der verstehenden Soziologie [1922], 5th revised edn. J.C.B.Mohr, Tübingen
Williams L, Rycroft-Malone J, Burton CR (2017) Bringing critical realism to nursing practice: Roy Bhaskar's contribution. Nurs Philos 18(2):1–11. https://doi.org/10.1111/nup.12130
Willmington C et al (2022) The contribution of benchmarking to quality improvement in healthcare. A systematic literature review. BMC Health Serv Res 22(1):1–20. https://doi.org/10.1186/s12913-022-07467-8

Wilson P, Billings J, Macinnes J et al (2021) Investigating the nature and quality of locally commissioned evaluations of the NHS Vanguard programme: an evidence synthesis. Health Res Policy Syst 19:1–10. https://doi.org/10.1186/s12961-021-00711-3

Zipfel N et al (2019) The implementation of change model adds value to value-based healthcare: a qualitative study. BMC Health Serv Res 19:1–12

Evaluation Models and their Implementation

Walter P. Wodchis, Kaileah McKellar, and Sara Shearkhani

Abstract

This chapter provides a framework for undertaking evaluations and offers advice and specific suggestions regarding the methodologies that are useful in evaluating health services. The chapter begins by identifying key purposes of health service evaluation. An overview of formative, summative, developmental, and other alternative approaches to evaluation are described. A justification for developmental evaluation (DE) leads to a focused discussion on this approach including methods and tactics such as appreciative inquiry, logic models, quantitative measurement and analysis, qualitative methods, as well as approaches to feedback. The themes explored include capacity building for local evaluation, the role of internal and external evaluation, and plans for dissemination and reporting. The purpose of the chapter is to support a model of practice that enables ongoing, embedded evaluation.

Keywords

Program evaluation · Developmental evaluation · Summative evaluation · Comparative effectiveness · Rapid cycle feedback · Logic model

W. P. Wodchis (✉)
Institute of Health Policy, Management and Evaluation, University of Toronto, Toronto, ON, Canada

Institute for Better Health, Trillium Health Partners, Mississauga, ON, Canada
e-mail: walter.wodchis@utoronto.ca

K. McKellar
Institute of Health Policy, Management and Evaluation, University of Toronto, Toronto, ON, Canada
e-mail: kaileah.mckellar@utoronto.ca

S. Shearkhani
Institute of Health Policy, Management and Evaluation, University of Toronto, Toronto, ON, Canada

Michael Garron Hospital, Toronto, ON, Canada
e-mail: sara.shearkhani@tehn.ca

A. Kaehne, J. Feather (eds.), *Handbook of Health Services Evaluation*,
https://doi.org/10.1007/978-3-031-87869-5_2

1 Overview

This chapter provides a framework for undertaking evaluations and offers advice and specific suggestions regarding the methodologies that are useful in evaluating health services. The emphasis here is on practical approaches that can be implemented in most contexts, though a few more advanced techniques and methods are mentioned for more state-of-the-art and well-resourced evaluations. This chapter uses the term "program" to refer to the program, model, or intervention implemented to improve the delivery of health services.

This chapter begins by identifying key purposes of health service evaluation. An overview of formative, summative, developmental, and other alternative approaches to evaluation are described. A justification for developmental evaluation (DE) leads to a focused discussion on this approach including methods and tactics such as appreciative inquiry, logic models, quantitative measurement and analysis, qualitative methods, as well as approaches to feedback. The themes explored include capacity building for local evaluation, the role of internal and external evaluation, and plans for dissemination and reporting. The purpose of this chapter is to support a model of practice that enables ongoing, embedded evaluation.

1.1 Context and Rationale

Evaluation is undertaken in health systems for a variety of reasons: as a requirement and condition for funding specific programs, as an assessment of merit and worth, or as program and organizational improvement. Evaluation may also be undertaken for research purposes (knowledge development) (Mark et al. 2000). It is, however, most helpful when evaluation is undertaken with an intrinsic motivation among health care providers to improve the effectiveness of care. Enabling evaluation is particularly important in the context of health service evaluation, where there is an emerging evidence base and wide variation in the focus and extent of program evaluation and implementation.

2 Approaching Evaluation

2.1 Purpose and Approach of the Evaluation

There may be multiple different purposes for undertaking evaluation, which will directly impact the approach employed for the evaluation. Programs that have been implemented are suitable for formative or summative evaluations. Formative evaluations are typically process-oriented, focusing on program improvement, whereas summative evaluations are assessment-focused and outcome-oriented. For programs in the early days of implementation, developmental evaluation, which shares similarities with quality improvement approaches, may be more suitable. As many programs are new and may benefit from iterative adjustments and improvements, we use the case of developmental evaluation to more fully describe and unpack the necessary activities to undertake effective evaluations. In addition to the stage of development of the intervention, its level of complexity should be considered when selecting an evaluation approach. Developmental evaluation is appropriate to deal with the complexity that characterizes many health service initiatives, particularly those that focus on the health system. Finally, the purpose (e.g., improvement or assessment) and evaluation questions of stakeholders and funders will help to determine the approach. Rosi et al. (1999) suggest evaluators "...determine the purpose of the evaluation by attempting to establish as firmly as possible who wants the evaluation, what they want and why they want it" (p. 39).

2.2 Formative Evaluation

Formative evaluations focus primarily on implementation of the program with the goal of improvement. Questions here can relate to whether the program is achieving intended enrolment and whether the intended activities of the program are being delivered (e.g., patient referral and assessment processes), or what is the patient experience and how this can be improved. Formative evaluations may also identify whether the intended program resources have been acquired and deployed as intended and whether program data collection and reporting are in place. They may also answer questions such as whether the "right" number and type of individuals are enrolled in the program, whether they receive the "right" number and type of services (provided by the "right" individuals), and whether changes might improve the appropriateness. A formative evaluation can also clarify and test whether the program theory or logic is reasonable or whether the rationale behind the program may require some rethinking and adjustments, and even if implemented perfectly, whether the program activities would lead to the desired outcomes. Regardless, formative evaluations require identifying program goals as well as information about program inputs, outputs, and processes. Formative evaluations may lead to recommendations regarding adaptations or program changes, and while some see formative evaluation as a way of stabilizing or standardizing the model, this does not have to be the case. Formative evaluations are less resource-intensive than other forms of evaluation as they only require measurement after the program is implemented, and comparisons either to pre-intervention activity or with other comparators are not necessary.

2.3 Summative Evaluation

Funders and researchers might be interested in whether the program "worked" and achieved the outcomes of interest. This focus is most closely aligned with a summative evaluation. This form of evaluation is best undertaken after a program has implemented with considerable rigor and attention to program fidelity (where fidelity refers to whether the proposed program elements or activities are delivered as intended). Many designs are possible with summative evaluation. The most rigorous form is a randomized controlled trial (RCT); however, an RCT may not be feasible and possibly undesirable because it requires highly artificial control over the setting and activities undertaken, which might be much more variable in a real-world clinic settings of health service improvement initiatives. Pragmatic variations such as stepped-wedge trials allow all participants to enter a trial but in delayed waves of participation. These approaches are most useful for interventions at a practice or group level and allow for deferred participation rather than non-participation for those who would like to receive the intervention, irrespective of its' proven effectiveness in the local context. Most often, summative evaluations are non-experimental and observational or quasi-experimental methods are employed. In this case, having both pre-intervention and post-intervention measurement is necessary to demonstrate that the program had an effect on the outcome(s) of interest. It is also highly recommended for summative evaluations to have a comparator group with comparable measurement from individuals who would be eligible for the program but did not receive the intervention for reasons unrelated to the program (e.g., they live in a similar geography where the program was not implemented). The more closely the comparators are matched to intervention participants, the greater the validity of any conclusions regarding program effectiveness. A comparator is necessary to conclude whether a program was the reason or cause for changes in outcomes. The resulting rigorous summative evaluation has a clearer interpretation as to whether a program works or not.

2.4 Developmental Evaluation

Whereas both formative and summative evaluation are more often singular, time-limited evaluations and are suitable for fully implemented programs, there is growing interest and use of ongoing evaluation that is more associated with quality improvement approaches. Developmental evaluation has similarities to formative evaluation in that it is primarily process oriented but a key distinction is that developmental evaluations are driven by program considerations (Patton 2002, p. 50). Developmental evaluations are implemented with explicit ongoing feedback to the program and generally suited to evaluations generally occurring earlier, before the program has achieved stability, after which, more definitive evaluations can be achieved. Developmental evaluation itself can be an intervention because the ongoing feedback can (and should) lead to adjustments and improvements in the delivery of the program. Optimally, the evaluators in a developmental evaluation become part of the program implementation team, participating in ongoing meetings and providing regular updates as to whether the program implementation is on track; timely feedback is a key principle to developmental evaluation. Because developmental evaluations are undertaken while the program is evolving, the focus and emphasis for the developmental evaluation is also iterative and evolves over time. While sharing similarities with formative evaluation, developmental evaluations should be driven by the program more so than with other approaches (Patton 2002), and co-creation is a key principle of this approach. Developmental evaluation can also be challenging to implement as the evaluators must retain methodological rigor and be clear in their positionality. They must evaluate the program against specified intentions.

2.5 Other Evaluation Approaches

There are multiple other forms of evaluation that could be employed to evaluate health services. We highlight two here that are suitable for programs that emerge in the context of complex adaptive systems and may be particularly useful for programs that are adaptive and emergent.

2.5.1 Realist Evaluation

An increasing emphasis in implementation science has been the use of Realistic or, more simply, Realist evaluation. Realist evaluations are intended to capture a more nuanced view of evaluation that starts from a perception that human and social changes are not biological or entirely mechanistic in that they may have different effects depending on important contextual features. Realist evaluations seek to understand "what works, for whom, under what circumstances" (Pawson and Tilley 1997). These questions are answered by an exploration of mechanisms, which explain why the program activities lead to the program outcomes (intended or unintended) in a given context. Context-Mechanism-Outcome Configurations (CMOCs) are often a primary goal of realist evaluations as they capture how an outcome is achieved under a specific context. For example, adherence to a treatment is increased with higher physical activity levels and better physical health, where patients are more active *because* the individual trusts their nurse coach and therefore is more adherent to their recommendations. In this example, the context is the clinic with a nurse coach, the mechanism is trust, the output is treatment adherence and the outcome could be better blood pressure or more miles walked per day. Mechanisms are typically implied and not explicitly included in a program description or logic model, but they are the reason that the actions taken work to create the effects observed. The realist approach can happen in combination with others, for example, a realist formative evaluation. There are many useful resources available for realist evaluations at the RAMESES website (ramesesproject.org).

2.5.2 Principles-Focused Evaluation

Patton recommends a principles-focused evaluation (P-FE) for innovative programs and initiatives that are adaptive in response to uncertainties and complex systems change (Patton 2002). A P-FE methodology assumes that in the context of complex adaptive systems, programs are developed and innovated by adhering to established principles. P-FE seeks to understand "(1) whether principles are clear, meaningful, and actionable, and, if so, (2) whether they are actually being followed, and if so, (3) whether they are leading to desired results" (Patton 2002). In this approach, the principles underlying a particular program become the focus of evaluation. It seeks to evaluate if the principles that guide a program are guiding, useful, inspiring, developmental, and evaluable (the GUIDE criteria; Patton 2002). This approach to evaluation leads evaluators to identify and evaluate principles that guide organizations and programs. It may be useful in evaluating community-based programs as it supports the creation of a framework that allows for a structured formative evaluation where intervention components may vary but intended to align with program principles.

3 Setting Up the Evaluation

This section outlines practical steps to developing and implementing an evaluation plan. Developing an evaluation plan begins by ensuring agreement on the purpose of the evaluation and the primary evaluation questions. The starting point for evaluation is a clear understanding of the purpose of the program or intervention. This requires gathering foundational knowledge about the program, the elements or components or activities of the program, and the intended outputs and outcomes (and perhaps also potential unintended consequences). Using a logic model is a common and useful way of displaying the most important elements, though greater detail is needed for evaluation purposes. The following steps are similar for all the above-described approaches to evaluation, whereas the information required varies depending on the identified approach. Formative will focus mostly on process measures with little attention to outcomes, while the opposite is true of summative evaluations.

3.1 Understanding the Program

Understanding what is new and different about the program and how this new model is expected to change key outcomes of interest is fundamental to undertaking evaluation. Describing the program in the early stages of an evaluation allows targeted and relevant measurement and findings in the later stages. There should be a clear understanding of the target population or eligibility of individuals or groups who will benefit from the program and practically how individuals will be identified and enrolled in the program. Essential elements of the program and the duration of services should be clearly specified. Communication and understanding of expected roles and responsibilities are useful in assigning activities with resources. Even though these might be flexible and individualized, the selection process and potential basket of services delivered by the program should be stated because it will be necessary to ensure that planned services are available.

The program description should also set out the purpose of the program or the program theory, which can be defined as a description of how the program design expects to achieve the intended outcomes (Brouselle and Champagne 2011). Explicitly linked to the outcomes, there should be a clearly defined set of activities that are newly started or modified that have an apparent relationship to the outcome.

It may also be helpful to identify activities are essential to continue that are also related to the outcome, as well as old activities that are replaced or no longer undertaken.

3.1.1 Determining Program Goals and Outcomes

The overall goal or purpose of the program can be described as the program's impact statement. It might respond to the question of "What does success look like, from each participant's perspective?" Many health and social care systems have adopted the quadruple aim (Sikka et al. 2015) as an overall framework for describing system goals, with several also considering equity. The quadruple aim can, therefore, be a useful framework to position the purpose and goals of the program, where the specific effects of a program on health outcomes, patient experience, provider experience, and health care cost and efficiency are specifically defined for a population of interest that enrolled in the program. This approach enables alignment with overall system goals. For example, a program to improve the integration between acute and post-acute care for individuals who are hospitalized to treat heart failure may include patient improvements in mobility and endurance as well as patient capability to understand and self-manage their heart condition as key patient-reported outcomes. Patient and caregiver experience measures could include feeling heard and supported by the program, while providers might indicate better experience in coordinating care as patients transition from hospital to community. Reductions in hospital days relative to additional community-based resources comprise health system impacts and could be represented as economic measures of interest in the evaluation. It may also be useful to clarify more upstream objectives of the program, for example, improving access and timeliness of a set of services. Whatever the context, organization, or system goals may be, it is useful to consider how the objectives and outcomes of the program are linked to and support the higher-level goals.

Determining outcomes that reflect program goals means making the program goals more specifically measurable. Outcomes specify measurable concepts but naming the outcome (e.g., quality of life) still leaves some choice regarding the specific measurement tools. Outcomes should be measurable and expected to change as a result of implementing the program. They can reflect participants' behaviors, knowledge, skills, or level of health status. Outcomes may include increases in participants' knowledge and self-care actions. While a goal may be broad, such as improving mental health, a related outcome would be something more specific, such as reducing anxiety among youth with complex health and social conditions. Often, in health care evaluations, adverse events such as mortality or unplanned hospitalizations are identified. It can be more difficult to measure things that do not occur, so thoughtful and rigorous data collection and analysis should be implemented. Sometimes hospital or other outcomes that are indicative of breakdowns in preventative programs can be easier to measure.

3.1.2 Describing Program Activities

Program activities refer to specific actions and events that are to occur that represent the delivery of the program or intervention. Activities should be specifically related to an output or outcome. Activities answer the question: "What needs to happen to achieve the desired outcomes? What processes need to be in place?" These may include actions such as intake referrals, participant health and needs assessments, ongoing or follow-up care, case conferences, etc. It should also specify to the extent possible the roles that are responsible for care (e.g., respiratory therapist follow-up within 3 days). All outputs identified should have an accompanying activity and all activities should have an accompanying output/outcome. Activities may include the delivery of workshops, training, or peer-counselling.

3.1.3 Identifying Outputs

Outputs are the direct products of program activities that demonstrate that the program is being implemented according to plan. A set of countable outputs of the program is often helpful to demonstrate the scale of the program in terms of the number of individuals included in the program, the number and types of services delivered to each participant, the number of program activities within care delivery teams (e.g., case conferences and participants). This is particularly important for process-oriented or formative evaluations and answering evaluation questions such as "To what extent is the program being implemented as planned?". Note that in some cases, outputs can be viewed as indicators of activities. The program theory is what links the activities and outputs to outcomes: what elements of care contribute to the overall program goals and outcomes? Often it is easier to proceed with identifying program activities and resources and then to return to assess what outputs will result from the program activities. Outputs may include client participation in workshops, training, peer-counselling.

3.1.4 Program Resources

All resources both human (e.g., staff) and capital (e.g., equipment) necessary to accomplish program activities should be identified. This includes both existing and new or incremental resources. The resources (capital equipment and supplies and personnel) should also be associated with activities to ensure that the resources are available where they are needed and not used where they are not beneficial.

3.2 Putting Together a Program Logic Model

The above elements (resources, activities, outputs, and outcomes) together represent the logic model of the program. A logic model is an evaluation tool that enables an explicit linkage of the four elements. The logic model is a communication tool about the program for both internal and external stakeholders. It should clarify what needs to happen, who does what, and what the connections between activities and outputs and outcomes are. The logic model is embedded in the planning for the implementation of the program. All key stakeholders, including clinicians, patients, staff, and evaluators, should be involved as the program is being formed and the implementation is being planned. This diverse team is crucial for gaining a comprehensive understanding of the program and determining the goals and outcomes of both the program and the evaluation. The logic model is an essential output of the implementation planning. Initial discussions often reveal that team members, who think they have a good grasp of the program, actually hold vastly different ideas about the program and its goals. This highlights the importance of transitioning from "work as imagined individually" to "work as imagined as an interdisciplinary team" and ultimately to "work as done." The process of developing the logic model and engaging relevant stakeholders can have benefits such as fostering collaboration and building consensus.

A challenge in logic model development is striking a balance in the level of detail included. The presentation of a logic model should capture key elements without being over-specified or including too many details. For example, the occurrence of a case conference (and possibly the required timing of that) would be included, but the specific agenda or participants in the case conference need not be included in a logic model. At the same time, the logic model does not need to document each specific activity of each participant. A balance needs to be struck whereby all essential elements of the program are reflected. A logic model can also help to communicate roles and responsibilities among program participants.

There are several approaches to building a logic model; we recommend, one starts with the overall program outcomes, then the activities, which are measured with program outputs. Outputs should be linked to outcomes, activities to outputs, resources to activities. For example, health assessments can lead to program eligibility, team meetings can lead to coordinated care plans, referrals to other agencies for program participants with particular needs can lead to receipt of additional services, etc. Finally, the required resources for each activity should be identified. If there are new care coordinators, how many? If there is new funding for medications, what is the amount? If there are new transportation services, how much is available? One can then link, for example, new transportation services to increased attendance in adult day programming and higher function among program participants, showing how resources, activities, outputs, and outcomes relate to each other. Finally, the logic model should be reviewed for alignment and connection between components.

3.2.1 Example Program Overview and Evaluation Approach

We offer an example of an evaluation approach, logic model (Table 1), and evaluation (measurement) matrix (Table 2) based on a composite program from the authors' experience as evaluators. The program is a collaborative endeavor across several health and social care delivery agencies. One main aim of the programs is to reduce inequities in access by offering additional support to marginalized populations. For this reason, services are organized around historically resource-poor neighborhood. Other program goals are improving patient health, provider experience, and efficient use of resources aligned with the quintuple aim framework. The logic model (Table 1) depicts aspects of the neighborhood-based homecare program.

The overall approach to evaluation was developmental with an emphasis on continuous learning and adjustment. However, the maturity stage of the program dictated the specific approach within a certain time frame. For example, at the planning and early implementation stage, the evaluation was formative. The objectives were set to describe key transformation ideas and understand barriers and facilitators to implementation with a lens to support program improvement. Later in the evaluation, while process questions were still addressed, the emphasis was on outcomes (i.e., a summative approach), including measures relevant to the quintuple aim (Table 1).

4 Undertaking the Evaluation

Once the logic model is created, you can start thinking about the scope and timeline of the evaluation. It is important to note that there is neither a need to evaluate all components of the logic model nor is it always possible to do so. Factors such as the maturity of the program, the capacity (e.g., staff and resources) to conduct the evaluation, external factors (e.g., funding), and data availability might prevent you from conducting a comprehensive evaluation of the program at any given time. For these reasons, evaluation can be effectively structured in stages to ensure thorough and systematic assessment. By establishing an overall evaluation timeline, the process can be broken down into smaller, manageable components with specific timelines that are linked to different components of the logic model. If the program is in development and early stages of implementation, a developmental evaluation may be best suited. For programs that are established, a formative evaluation can be conducted, focusing on particular aims and measures within a defined period. Preparations for future summative evaluations can be made as part of formative or developmental evaluations, such as collecting relevant outcomes data. This phased approach allows for a clear and organized evaluation process, ensuring that all aspects are adequately addressed over time.

To implement the evaluation, relevant measures must be established, data collection must occur, quality assessment of the data must be undertaken, and data must be analyzed and synthesized to create information and interpreted to provide new knowledge about the implementation and/or the effectiveness of the program.

4.1 Measurement

Measurement in evaluation includes both qualitative and quantitative sources. If using the quadruple aim to frame the outcome measurement, it is ideal to have measures that represent each aim and to collect and to clearly identify sources and to report on such measures. When deciding on a measurement approach, resources for the evaluation must be considered. Collecting data automatically or passively is one approach to limiting evaluation costs. Furthermore, considering the evaluation early in the program development or implementation stage can help ensure data collection

Table 1 Example logic model

Resources/inputs	Activities	Outputs	Outcomes	
		What we create How we know we've implemented our plan	*Short term 1–2 years*	*Long term 3–5 years*
What we invest	*What we do*			
Partner organization planning time Patient, family, and caregiver advisors' input Service providers: Community and social care, primary care, home care specialist, community coordinators Expertise: in-home care, evaluation, project management, change management Space: Space in the neighborhoods for shared visits with primary care, clinic service delivery; "touch down" space for providers Technology: new and adapted digital tools	Identify and enroll neighborhood clients Coordinate patient-care 1. Initial assessment 2. Create person-centered care plans 3. Virtual cross-discipline case conferencing and team huddles using a new platform Delivery of services Service (e.g., nursing) Follow-up 1. Follow-up assessment 2. Virtual team huddles 3. Connect to additional community supports Person-centered discharge plan	• No. and characteristics of clients • No. of assessments • No. of care plan created • No. of care plan created with client/family outputs • No. and characteristics of care team member involved • No. of meetings • No. and type of services identified • No. and reason for follow-up assessment • No. and characteristics of team member involved • No. of meetings • No. and reason for updating care plan • No. and type of additional support • No. of discharge plan created • No. and type of supports	Improved equity (reach) Improved client experience (satisfaction, client involvement) Improved provider experience (satisfaction with the new platform, satisfaction with the implementation process) Improved health outcome (perceived health and quality of life) Improved efficiency (shorter length of stay, avoid unnecessary ED visits)	Improved equity (access) Improved client and caregiver experience (care-coordination, communication, transition, cost) Improved provider experience (improved team communication, decreased burnout) Improved health outcomes (improved clinical health outcomes) Improved efficiency (decreased population-level hospital utilization)

is integrated, where possible, with program delivery, and not as an additional step. In this section, we outline measurement considerations for quantitative measurement.

4.1.1 Defining Measures

Measures are important for activity, output, and outcome elements of the program. Defining quantitative measures should be assessed against the SMART criteria (Specific, Measurable, Actionable, Reliable, Timely). A measurement table or evaluation matrix is a valuable tool to connect the evaluation question to measures or approaches. The measurement table can also be aligned with the logic model, including measures throughout the pathway. There are different templates to choose from depending on your design and foci, but overall, they should clearly outline what you are measuring and why. When defining measures, the definition should be clear (e.g., with quantitative data including details on numerator and denominator) as well as their source (e.g., primary data collected through interviews or secondary data from specific databases). The frequency of collecting and reporting is also a relevant consideration here. In this section, we outline measurement considerations for quantitative measurement. Table 2 offers and example of an evaluation matrix, with sample evaluation questions and indicators aligned with the logic model in Table 1.

4.1.2 Individual-Level Quantitative Measurement

In most health systems, providers are required to track patient care for (medico-legal) care documentation, accountability, and payment reasons. These records are generally identified to individuals using health insurance numbers or similar. In social care programs, total counts of services or service recipients may be collected but are often not tracked at the individual client level. For robust evaluation, services should be tracked to the individual level to measure and attribute program activities and outputs to the individuals enrolled in the program. This is particularly important where services are provided in differing quantities and types to different participants and where outcome measurement is collected through a different reporting system than activity and output reporting systems. Individual-level data provides the most robust information for evaluation data analyses.

Countable activities and outputs such as the number of services provided, the number of individuals served, the number of virtual or in-person encounters and who provided that service (or what service was provided) should be fairly standard to collect and track. They can also be summarized from individual-level data. Recording these activities only once and extracting the data from the systems used by the front-line delivery staff is the most straightforward and cost-effective. Raw data can be transformed into indicators. For example, having programs track appointment dates for enrolled clients is standard procedure, but measuring timeliness is often not standard. Recording appointment dates and having evaluation personnel to support indicators such as the proportion of clients meeting expected service times are examples of multiple uses of the same data sources. Similarly, elements of electronic medical records (EMRs) may be used to ensure that individuals accessed care and which elements of a care pathway are activated in the

Table 2 Measurement table/evaluation matrix

Evaluation questions	Indicator	Data source	Timelines	Analysis
Does the program reach its target population (i.e., people living in resource-poor neighbourhoods)	Proportion of participants from specific postal codes	Participant registry	Ongoing data collection upon enrollment. Reported bi-weekly	Descriptive analysis. Geospatial analysis (heat map)
What factors help or hinder program implementation?	Thematic description of barriers and facilitators at the program and system level	Semi-structured interviews with program organizers	During the planning phase and 3 months after implementation	Thematic analysis. Coding using qualitative analysis software. Development of analytical notes
What are the effects of the program on provider experience?	Provider burnout	Provider experience survey	A survey was distributed at 6 months and 1 year. Results were reported following each round	Response frequencies, comparison to baseline and over time
What are the effects of the program on patient experience?	Patient reporting "there is someone who is reliable in responding to any questions or issues that you may have about your home care"	Patient experience survey	A survey was administered on a rolling timeline. Results reported quarterly	Response frequencies, comparison to baseline and over time
What are the effects of the program on patient health outcomes?	Change in health-related quality of life	Administrative databases	Reported at baseline and quarterly	Single summary score of overall health
What are the effects of the program on acute care utilization?	Emergency department visits for conditions best managed elsewhere	Administrative databases	Reported at baseline and quarterly	Monthly averages compared against baseline

treatment of an individual. This can be considered as treatment or intervention adherence or fidelity.

4.1.3 Patient-Reported Data

Another source is the patient's own reporting, which allows the participant's voice to be part of the evaluation. Collecting survey data through mail, telephone, or online surveys is a relatively low-cost approach to capture patient-reported data. This enables the collection and reporting of patient-reported experience and patient-reported outcome measures (both elements of the quadruple aim framework). Patient interviews in person, virtually, or by phone is highly useful but much more resource-intensive way to collect information about patient experience. In health service programs, caregivers and other informal providers of health and social care services may also be involved, and it is recommended to collect information about these individuals' experiences as well. Ethical or quality improvement governance approvals are essential to ensure appropriate individual knowledge and consent to the use of their information (see Sect. 4.4).

4.2 Data Sources and Data Collection

Different data sources have distinct resource impacts, trustworthiness, reliability, precision, and sustainability. Generally, registry databases have the highest quality, with considerable investments and routines to set up the databases and ensure training in the measurement and recording of data. This also makes the infrastructure costs relatively high. Administrative data, including billing and health records, are available for most or all uses of health care services but often have limited data quality processes. Surveys have the opportunity to reach large numbers of individuals but risk selection bias in the distribution and responses. Interviews with clients and staff, as well as direct observations of team interactions or care delivery with clients, will offer detailed insights but are time-consuming and require considerable observer expertise in recording and analyzing observations. While quantitative data should be collected on all program participants, qualitative data provide in-depth understanding but are not intended to be representative. Transparency is an essential trust-building mechanism for evaluation success as measures are defined and data sources identified and reported. Developmental evaluation approaches of engagement with participants throughout the evaluation process provide an important strategy of transparency.

When using existing data or data owned by program participants, access may require the implementation of data-sharing agreements, whereas primary data collection is more expensive, but the data will be fully accessible without restriction to the evaluators.

4.2.1 Document Review

The purpose of document review is to identify a formal description of aspects of the evaluation that could be captured from existing materials. This would reduce the amount and type of information that would need to be captured through interviews or related processes and would capture information that are available for all team members. Documents can also be a good starting place for developing and/or assessing a program logic model.

4.2.2 Using Surveys

We explicitly provide information on the use of surveys, as these are very commonly used in evaluation, though there are strengths and weaknesses in the development and implementation of surveys. Surveys can be useful for collecting information that is not available from other data sources, such as information about participant's attitudes, beliefs, behaviors, or opinions.

It is essential to clearly identify the respondent population: Will the survey be distributed to all program participants or to a sample? Will the sample be representative (either complete or probability sampling) or convenience (e.g., collected one day per week by evaluation/research staff)? In determining the number of surveys that will be collected, it is useful to keep in mind that most statistical testing that relies on Chi-Square or *t*-tests is generally more stable in populations of at least 30 individuals. If quality improvement is the goal, samples of even as few as five or ten respondents may be sufficient. For surveys that are not completed by all (sampled) respondents, it will be important to have basic information about the respondents and non-respondents to be able to assess biases that might result because non-respondents and respondents differ in important characteristics related to the outcomes reported on.

When possible, particularly for patient-reported measures, look for existing and validated tools that measure the elements in the logic model. Common health outcome measures include the EuroQOL-5D-5L (EuroQol Research Foundation 2019), the SF-36 or SF-12 (RAND Corporation n.d.), and the Patient Health Questionnaire 9-item and 2-item (for mental health) (Kroenke et al. 2001). The Patient Reported Outcome Measures Inventory System (PROMIS) is a website with many validated measures (*U.S. Department of Health and Human Services* n.d.). If none are suitable, developing a purpose-built survey is an alternative. In developing a survey, pay attention to the clarity of question wording. Surveys provide useful information when the questions are interpreted by the respondents in the same way that the data are analyzed and reported and when the information requested is specific and familiar to respondents. Once a survey has been developed for use in an evaluation, it is critical that the survey undergo "cognitive testing." Cognitive testing is a process of providing the questionnaire to potential respondents in an interview and asking them to provide feedback on their interpretation of the question and any uncertainty about the meaning (and importance) of the question. Cognitive testing with three to five individuals who are representative of participants is sufficient.

Finally, consider the mode of distributing surveys. Electronic, mail, and telephone-based surveys all have potential biases in the respondents who will participate in each mode. Where costs are a consideration and smaller sample sizes may result, consider whether there are particular populations that you are most interested in. Above all, ensure that you collect the questions that you need to know and that you use the data from the questions that you collect.

4.2.3 Administrative Data

A relatively inexpensive and widely used evaluation data source is administrative or claims data. These data sources are widely collected across health systems from providers to enable activity reporting and payment from health payers. These data include physician encounters, hospital admissions, emergency department care, pharmaceuticals, and sometimes community-based care from home and institutional long-term care. Encounter-based data may be used to determine whether program services are delivered as expected and whether investments are associated with reductions in other health care services. There are common health system standards for data collection and reporting, and many health administrative databases provide valid and reliable data to evaluate health care utilization. Many providers can access and use such standardized data submissions. Most countries also have some form of access to health administrative data for evaluation purposes. An important requirement for using health administrative data is to be able to identify individuals who have received care or been enrolled in a health program or intervention being evaluated. This may be accomplished by creating variables or "flags" in existing health administrative data or creating linkable registries from programs and interventions. These data are essential to track measures of health care use that are commonly requested of health payers when evaluating health system programs and interventions.

4.2.4 Qualitative Data

Qualitative data can serve many useful purposes. It can provide a greater depth of knowledge about participants' experiences, emotions, and beliefs. Interviews can explore critical phenomena and meaning. Qualitative data can support interpretation and explanations for observed and reported behaviors and also provide essential information about participant's understanding of how and why a program works. There are several useful guides to qualitative data collection and analysis (Sangaramoorthy and Kroeger 2020; Creswell and Poth 2016; Hsieh and Shannon 2005; Vindrola-Padros and Johnson 2020).

Individual interviews are most useful when there is a desire to have an in-depth understanding of individual participants' unique perspectives, or there might be power imbalances among participants or when the topic may relate to sensitive topics with perceived social risks. Focus group interviews are an effective and efficient way to collect qualitative data when there is a specific desire to understand how people make sense of a phenomenon in collaboration, when the topic of interest is not particularly sensitive and where the topic is relevant to multiple individuals. Focus groups are also helpful to clarify, extend, qualify, or challenge data collected through other methods.

Qualitative data collection can be highly structured with a fixed set of interview questions to ensure consistent data collection across a range of participants. It can also be entirely unstructured, when there is little preexisting understanding of a phenomenon. For an evaluation, the openness of your approach can be tailored to your evaluation purpose and questions. Semi-structured interviews are common because they will enable an overall structure to a set of interviews that might be collected as part of an evaluation while allowing for individual interviews to probe and expand on topics where the participant may have additional or advanced experience and knowledge. Interview guides should be developed to lead to open-ended discussion, be as neutral as possible, be sensitive to participant vulnerabilities and be direct, clear, and understandable. Adjusting qualitative interview guides may be undertaken as interviews are undertaken and participants reflect on their understanding and interpretation of interview questions.

4.2.5 Using Observations

Formative, developmental, and realist evaluations benefit from methods of direct observation. This approach removes the filter of the intervention participants regarding their perceived activities: the work as done versus the work as imagined (Deutsch 2017). It also allows the evaluation team to observe the extent to which the activities outlined in the logic model are performed as expected or whether there are challenges in the implementation that lead to unintended workarounds. The reason, extent, and effects of such workarounds or alternative approaches are important to codify as a reality check on the actual program activities in effect for the evaluation. Additionally, observations allow evaluators to understand inter-professional teamwork and the different elements of the program that occupy the majority of participants' time as a measure of the issues that are most challenging to implement or overcome. Observations can be done quantitatively or qualitatively and with varying amounts of structure. Recording data from direct observations is an ethnographic activity, which requires training and expertise. The documentation can be simplified by using structured templates that correspond to central activities and themes. Observations may involve shadowing specific members of the team or events such as team case conferences or meetings. Data to collect could include aspects of time allocation to different topics and issues, the nature of communications (open, conflict, appreciative, etc.), decision-making approaches, record-keeping, and information sharing. There may be specific aspects of care coordination or involvement of program clients that are of interest to the program based on the declared program activities and goals. All observations should only be done with the participants' consent/knowledge, and thought should be given to the observer not being seen as intrusive. Observations provide important information on program implementation and fidelity, help inform process-oriented evaluations, identify workarounds and potential impacts, and provide an opportunity to provide specific feedback and coaching to adapt processes.

4.2.6 Participant Journaling

Evaluators or program participants may capture data through structured or unstructured journaling as an additional data source. This enables reflective practice to be included in the evaluation without requiring interviews. It could be viewed as a form of open-ended survey. From an evaluator's perspective, journaling can include perceptions and interpretations that synthesize information across participants and events. Topics such as attitudes, activities, challenges, and decisions regarding coding and analysis can be recorded by the evaluator. Participant journaling can be used to capture experiences, opinions, beliefs, emotions, perceptions, attitudes, or even to identify important program milestones that significantly advanced or impaired change program's implementation. Journaling can also provide self-reflective insights that can be included in team meetings and lead to program adaptations. Journaling can capture insights in real time rather than only through pre-specified data capture times. Journaling can also be time-consuming and unless it is part of participants' daily practice, it is highly recommended that time be set aside during regularly occurring meetings for participants to take time to provide simple reflections. Prompts regarding events or experiences that may accelerate or hinder the program's success are sufficient to organize input.

4.3 Analyses and Reporting

The most important consideration for analyses and reporting is to be clear about the purpose: what questions are being answered by what analyses and what interpretations and conclusions are being drawn. Before starting on analysis, one should also review evaluation questions identified in early planning and engagement stages and, depending on the timelines of the evaluation, even revisit these questions to ensure they are still relevant. Analyses and reporting should be mutually reinforcing and supporting activities. While there may be analyses that are undertaken and not reported, analyses should be undertaken with a specific purpose in order to clearly support the interpretation of results. Guidance on how the results should be used to improve program delivery should be included as part of reporting.

4.3.1 Quantitative Survey Analysis

Survey analysis starts by examining the frequencies of all survey item responses. This can determine response rates, data completeness, and whether a test appears to measure what it is supposed to measure. Comparing responses to two items by developing simple cross-tabulations (e.g., experience ratings by health condition or by respondent sex) can be used to assess patterns in the data. If consistent data were collected at multiple time points, tabulations can be used to examine changes over time. Understanding the type of data you have will determine the analysis or statistical tests used. Ordinal measures refer to an ordered set of categories (e.g., from Strongly Disagree to Strongly Agree), whereas there is no particular ordering to categorical items (such as the use of non-dependent care types such as personal support worker and occupational therapist). Kendall and Chi-square statistics are examples of tests that can determine the degree of association among ordinal or categorical items (respectively), with correlations used for continuous measures.

4.3.2 Quantitative Utilization and Outcome Analysis

Very often, funding and participating organizations in health system innovations that offer new models or services are most interested in substitutions or reductions in other, more costly services, for example, increasing primary health care services to reduce acute services. With only pre-intervention and post-intervention data within a program or target population, the primary analysis is focused on the differences in service utilization and, where possible, patient health outcomes. The appropriate statistical analyses of these differences depends on the measurement characteristics of the service or outcome. Plans for statistical analyses should be reviewed by a statistician prior to data collection to ensure that the correct and sufficient data are collected during the implementation of the intervention. The measurement could be dichotomous (yes/no), ordinal (low, medium, high), count data (number of visits), continuous, or in some cases, entirely categorical where there is no natural ordering of the possible measured outcomes (e.g., primary care, home care, social visits). Statistical testing, therefore, can range from using continuous tests such as *t*-tests to categorical tests such as Chi-Square, or other non-parametric tests for measures that do not conform to statistical assumptions for non-standard data. Special cases such as count data are addressed by using Poisson or negative binomial tests. Sometimes, data are transformed into dichotomous categories to simplify the analysis. Such transformations should be clearly justified by the actual distribution of the observed data. In the ideal case where there is a comparator population, baseline differences in the intervention and comparator data should be the first step. If these are similar, then a difference-in-difference approach can be used where the post-minus pre-intervention data are evaluated in each of the intervention and comparator groups, and then the incremental difference between these two differences is used to measure the incremental effect of the intervention as compared to usual care (as delivered in the comparator population). Where there are substantive differences in the baseline characteristics, advanced statistical techniques such as propensity matching may resolve the biases introduced from differences in risk associated with each group.

4.3.3 Qualitative Analysis of Interviews, Focus Groups, Observations, Journaling

Qualitative analysis can be seen as story-telling with data. The starting point for qualitative analysis, analogous to surveys, begins with reviewing transcripts and becoming familiar with the data. Description is the foundation of qualitative analysis, and interpretation happens when evaluators answer the "why" questions (Patton 2002). A common approach to describing the data and moving to interpretations in evaluation and health services research is thematic analysis (Vaismoradi et al. 2013). This approach follows broad steps of generating initial codes, searching for themes, and then reviewing, defining, and naming these themes (Braun and Clarke 2006). Analysis can be approached deductively, with a predetermining framework used to code or classify trenches of text; inductively, where codes are generated in a ground-up approach; or a combined approach (e.g. classifying into broad deductive codes, then using an inductive approach). The approach to analysis can be tailored to your evaluation question and type and richness of data (e.g., data from open-ended survey questions vs. participant interviews). The value of qualitative work can be capitalized by seeing what emerges from the data and understanding the connections between what might already be known. There are many approaches to analysis, as well as guides (e.g., Goodrick and Rogers 2015), tools, and software, to support this process; however, few prescriptive instructions are wholly applicable. Despite this, the steps of monitoring and documenting the analytical processes are critical to supporting transparency and quality in qualitative analysis.

4.3.4 Reporting

Stakeholder engagement early in evaluation planning will support the development of meaningful reports and promote the use of results. Co-designing the report with input from end users ensures that it meets their specific needs and preferences. By involving stakeholders in the report's development, you can tailor the content and format to resonate with their interests and priorities. A key point of involvement is the interpretation of results. High-level questions such as "What are results telling us?" and "What does this mean for our program?" can guide these conversations. Co-designing the report with input from end users ensures that it meets their specific needs and preferences. By involving stakeholders in the report's development, the content and format can be tailored to resonate with stakeholder interests and priorities.

Build a reporting schedule into the evaluation plan, including opportunities for intermediate data reviews as well as formal reports. When considering the frequency of reporting intervals, not everyone requires updates at the same intervals, and those who are more removed from the evaluation process may require less frequent updates. Tailoring the reporting schedule to the needs of different stakeholders ensures that information is provided efficiently without inundating individuals with irrelevant or excessive updates. When reporting evaluation findings or progress to different stakeholder groups, clarity and conciseness are paramount. Consider the busy schedules of team members, especially clinicians who may have limited time for in-depth analysis. Schedule meetings well in advance.

Central to effective reporting is maintaining a clear purpose. Each report should be guided by a specific evaluation question, providing a focused framework for analysis and communication. Aligning the report with the evaluation question, you ensure that it remains targeted and relevant, fostering meaningful insights and actionable recommendations for the team. Avoiding unnecessary complexity is crucial in facilitating understanding among diverse team members. By prioritizing brevity, simplicity, stakeholder engagement, and clarity of purpose, the effectiveness and impact of reporting on evaluation outcomes are enhanced.

4.4 Ethical Considerations

All evaluations should be undertaken with strict adherence to ethical guidelines. Local organizational requirements must be ascertained prior to beginning the data collection and analysis. However, all evaluations do not need to be reviewed and approved by a formal Research Ethics Board (REB). In many cases, evaluation can be part of Quality Improvement. The guidelines from ARECCI (A Project Ethics Community Consensus Initiative) offer considerable support for deciding whether a project is primarily a research project (and REB is essential), or primarily an improvement project (which leaves REB optional or inappropriate) (Alberta Innovates 2024a). The ARECCI tool can help you decide whether the project is primarily research versus quality improvement (Alberta Innovates 2024b). Much of this decision depends on the central purpose and uses of the evaluation as well as the evaluator's control over the form of the intervention. In either event, where data is collected from individuals (patients, family, providers), all participating individuals should be fully appraised and consent to the proposed uses of the data.

4.5 Build a Timeline for the Evaluation

It is important to have an evaluation work plan with clearly specified time periods for each activity and milestones for the completion of key activities and reports. This plan could be laid out as a Gantt chart format and communicated widely with all program stakeholders.

5 Sustainable Evaluation Capacity

There are many challenges in performing high-quality evaluations. These can stem from capacity, knowledge, and skill as well as resources to support work. From an organizational perspective, evaluation capacity is the structures, processes and human resources that support and promote evaluation thinking in operation and program delivery.

5.1 Building Local Evaluation Capacity

Approaches to evaluation capacity building commonly draw from Preskill's and Boyle's Multidisciplinary Model of Evaluation Capacity Building (Preskill and Boyle 2008). The model proposes strategies to improve evaluation knowledge skills and attitudes and outlines components that lead to sustainable evaluation practice. Strategies for building knowledge skills and attitudes include coaching, training, written materials, technical assistance, involvement in evaluation, and communities of practice. Sustainable evaluation practice is supported by components such as leadership, evaluation policies and procedures, resources dedicated to evaluation, integrated knowledge management evaluation sustainment, and continuous learning about evaluation (Wade and Kallemeyn 2020; Preskill and Boyle 2008).

Building evaluation capacity can be a way to contribute to effective decision-making and add value to the organizations and stakeholders involved in the process, resulting in a better understanding and value of evaluation results for their future decision-making (Bourgeois and Buetti 2019; Janzen et al. 2017).

5.2 Central Supports for Evaluation

There is a strong argument to be made for systemic evaluation supports to be available within health organizations, within local health care delivery systems and supported by the broad health system. There are many alternatives to the structures that can be put in place. In Scotland, the Department of Public Health provides centralized data and analytical support to health and social care partnerships. Similarly, the Department of Health and Social Care (DHSC) in England provides data and analytical support to Integrated Care Partnerships, while Academic Health Science Networks provide evaluation support. In the Netherlands, centers of excellence are supported to provide evaluation and research support according to areas of expertise including long-term care, primary care, and others. In Ontario, Canada, the Ministry of Health provides data, and evaluation support is provided by an academic partner. In all cases, these health systems support robust evaluation that engages with health system partners.

6 Conclusion

Evaluation of health services is an essential role within the health system. Supporting evaluation ensures that health investments are thoughtfully deployed and used to improve health outcomes in the populations of interest. Comprehensive evaluation including qualitative and quantitative measurement provides a broad understanding of the implementation factors that are key to success (or failure) and supports the spread of effective innovations. The most appropriate approach to evaluation depends on the maturity of programs and interventions and the central evaluation questions being pursued. Using rapid cycle feedback with programs enables ongoing adjustments and improvements, while robust comparative effectiveness is able to assert the incremental benefits of programs and interventions. Building local capability for participating in evaluation enables ongoing learning and improvement. Supporting external evaluation from highly skilled research and evaluation groups that engage with local programs enables more comprehensive knowledge and understanding and can be particularly useful in policy development and program scale and spread.

References

Alberta Innovates (2024a) A pRoject Ethics Community Consensus Initiative (ARECCI). https://albertainnovates.ca/strategic-initiatives/a-project-ethics-community-consensus-initiative-arecci/. Accessed 13 Jul 2024

Alberta Innovates (2024b) ARECCI ethics screening tool. https://arecci.albertainnovates.ca/ethics-screening-tool/. Accessed 13 Jul 2024

Bourgeois I, Buetti D (2019) Using action research to build evaluation capacity in public health organizations. J Multidiscip Eval 15(33):81–90

Braun V, Clarke V (2006) Using thematic analysis in psychology. Qual Res Psychol 3(2):77–101

Brouselle A, Champagne F (2011) Program theory evaluation: logic analysis. Eval Program Plann 34:69–78

Creswell JW, Poth CN (2016) Qualitative inquiry and research design: choosing among five approaches. Sage Publications, Thousand Oaks

Goodrick, D., & Rogers, P. J. (2015). Qualitative data analysis. Handbook of practical program evaluation, 561–595. Chicago

Deutsch ES (2017) Bridging the gap between work-as-imagined and work-as-done, vol 14. Pennsylvania Patient Safety Authority, Harrisburg, pp 80–83

Euroqol Research Foundation (2019) EQ-5D-5L user guide. https://euroqol.org/publications/user-guides. Accessed 18 Sep 2024

Hsieh H-F, Shannon SE (2005) Three approaches to qualitative content analysis. Qual Health Res 15:1277–1288

Janzen, R., Ochocka, J., Turner, L., Cook, T., Franklin, M., & Deichert, D. (2017). Building a community-based culture of evaluation. Evaluation and Program Planning, 65, 163–170
Kroenke K, Spitzer RL, Williams JB (2001) The PHQ-9: validity of a brief depression severity measure. J Gen Intern Med 16:606–613
Mark MM, Henry GT, Julnes G (2000) Evaluation: an integrated framework for understanding, guiding, and improving policies and programs. Jossey-Bass, San Francisco
Patton, M. Q. (2002). Qualitative research & evaluation methods. Sage
Pawson R, Tilley N (1997) Realistic evaluation. Sage, London
Preskill H, Boyle S (2008) A multidisciplinary model of evaluation capacity building. Am J Eval 29:443–459
RAND Corporation (n.d.) RAND medical outcomes study: measures of quality of life core survey from RAND Health Care. https://www.rand.org/health-care/surveys_tools/mos.html. Accessed 18 Sep 2024
Rossi PH, Freeman HE, Lipsey MW (1999) Evaluation: a systematic approach. Sage Publications, Thousand Oaks, CA
Sangaramoorthy T, Kroeger KA (2020) Rapid ethnographic assessments: a practical approach and toolkit for collaborative community research. Routledge, London
Sikka R, Morath J, Leape L (2015) The quadruple aim: care, health, cost and meaning in work. BMJ Qual Saf 24:608–610
U.S. Department of Health and Human Services (n.d.) Patient-reported outcomes measurement information system. https://www.healthmeasures.net/explore-measurement-systems/promis. Accessed 18 Sep 2024
Vaismoradi M, Turunen H, Bondas T (2013) Content analysis and thematic analysis: implications for conducting a qualitative descriptive study. Nurs Health Sci 15(3):398–405
Vindrola-Padros C, Johnson GA (2020) Rapid techniques in qualitative research: a critical review of the literature. Qual Health Res 30:1596–1604
Wade J, Kallemeyn L (2020) Evaluation capacity building (ECB) interventions and the development of sustainable evaluation practice: an exploratory study. Eval Program Plann 79:101777

Health Policy Evaluation and the Policy Process

Nicholas Mays and Stefanie Ettelt

Abstract

Health policy evaluation is often seen as a purely technical exercise in data collection and analysis. This chapter will demonstrate that health policy evaluation can be understood better as a component of the wider policy process. It explores the main theoretical lenses for understanding policy-making, locates evaluation within each, and discusses how different policy contexts and interests shape evaluation. The final section considers the role of policy "pilots" since these are where the processes of policy-making and evaluation are expected to work most closely with one another.

Keywords

Policy evaluation · Policy process · Policy pilots · Commissioning of evaluations · Use of evaluation

1 Introduction

Health policy evaluation is often seen as a technical exercise whose results are expected to inform the continuation or revision of policy. In practice, this expectation is often frustrated by the political context of health policy-making in which policy evaluation is embedded. This chapter aims to show how policy evaluation is shaped by politics and the policy process. "Policy" is loosely defined according to Guy Peters as "the set of activities that governments engage in for the purpose of changing their economy and society" (Peters 2015: 1). They do so by navigating the

N. Mays (✉) · S. Ettelt
Department of Health Services Research and Policy, London School of Hygiene & Tropical Medicine, London, UK
e-mail: nicholas.mays@lshtm.ac.uk; stefanie.ettelt@lshtm.ac.uk

A. Kaehne, J. Feather (eds.), *Handbook of Health Services Evaluation*,
https://doi.org/10.1007/978-3-031-87869-5_3

institutions, interests, and ideas that together shape the policy process (John 2012). In this case, the "ideas" stem from the values of policy-makers and the evidence from research, including from evaluation. However, policy evaluation also interacts with institutions and the diverse and often opposing interests that influence health policy-making, as the chapter will demonstrate.

There is an increasing commitment to policy evaluation in the health policy field and in policy-making generally. This is because policy evaluation sits well with demands that policy-making should be better informed and use evidence from research. Despite this, there is little evidence to suggest that health policy entirely "follows the science" when it comes to using evaluation findings. Instead, research widely demonstrates that while evaluation can be influential on occasions in shaping policy decisions, it is only one input to policy among many and is as prone to political entanglement as the other factors that shape policy. In this respect, policy evaluation shares the fate of many efforts of evidence generation that are expected to inform policy, but in practice are not used to their full potential.

2 Evaluation and the Policy Process

Most discussions of theories of the policy process begin with the argument that such theories require a recognition of the nature of power and its distribution in contemporary societies. In this chapter, we focus on pluralist theories anchored in liberal democracies and, within those, the theories that have proven to be most salient (and most frequently used) in health policy analysis. "Pluralist" means that it is assumed that political power is widely, although unevenly, diffused in society and that policy-making is an activity that elected governments do on behalf of the populace. We only briefly touch on policy-making and evaluation in non-democratic or authoritarian regimes.

Most analyses of how public policies come to be made and implemented indicate that evaluation as a source of evidence for policy plays a relatively modest role. Health policy has been something of an exception, at least at the rhetorical level. Appeals to the use of evidence, including from policy evaluation, have been stronger and more consistent in the field of health policy than most other policy arenas, deriving from the "evidence-based medicine" movement which started in the 1980s. However, generally, policy evaluation only occupies a prominent place in highly linear and rational ways of conceptualizing the public policy process, such as the stages model (initially Lasswell 1956; Knott and Wildavsky 1980). While seeming to describe the policy process, this highly normative model depicts the policy process as a sequence of distinct phases that together form recurrent cycles of activity leading to policy improvement. These stages comprise agenda setting—i.e., the recognition of an issue as a policy problem; policy formulation and legitimation (e.g., via legislation); policy implementation; and, finally, evaluation. The findings from the evaluation are then expected to feed into renewed efforts to reformulate and improve the policy in question.

According to this model, evaluation is a distinct phase that sits between policy implementation and policy improvement or policy termination (e.g., Brewer 1974). In its pure form, the stages model is a simplified illustration of an idealized administrative process devoid of internal or external interference, ignoring the possibility of controversy over social values, without competing interests and absent political conflict over the means and ends of policy. It also conceives of governments as acting neutrally in the interest of an uncontested common good rather than being vulnerable to capture by particular powerful interests or explicitly representing a particular section of society. As a theory of the policy process, the stages heuristic represents an optimistic belief in policy-making as a process of social improvement, although arguably as a heuristic tool its main value is to provide a simple structure for policy analysis rather than to act as an explanatory theory. In practice, most real-world policy processes fail to correspond to a clearly defined improvement cycle and the stages model is regularly criticized as being insufficiently cognizant of the political nature of policy-making (Cairney 2023). Despite the extensive critique, the stages model continues to influence more sophisticated forms of policy analysis, often in combination with other theories (Cairney 2013; Howlett et al. 2015; Bozzini and Hunt 2015). It also remains influential in that many policy agencies present their strategies and plans as if the stages model were a realistic approach to the practice of policy.

Other, more sophisticated and empirically grounded ways of explaining the policy process, provide a stronger understanding of where and how evidence, including from policy evaluation, fits into the public policy process. A well-known model of the policy process was developed by John Kingdon, originally to explain how issues get onto the government's policy agenda but now used more extensively to analyze other aspects of policy-making such as local implementation (Kingdon 2013). This model of the policy process concerns itself with the question of why some problems reach the agenda of policy-makers sufficient to be under active consideration by officials while others languish. Kingdon's model stipulates that a topic can only become important enough in the estimation of policy-makers if it is widely recognized to be a legitimate policy problem for the government, if there is a feasible policy solution that is regarded as suitable to address the problem and if there is sufficient political willingness and opportunity to do something about it. Only if all three of these factors are in alignment can policy change begin to be achieved. While the model itself does not entirely explain how political will comes about and how it is influenced or generated, it has created substantial interest in the political nature of policy-making and the role of power and influence in the policy process. Kingdon himself drew attention to the role of "policy entrepreneurs" as drivers of policy change who act as intermediaries between different groups to promote a policy solution to a problem and build political support for action. The possibility to translate political support into policy change is also strongly shaped by institutional factors, i.e., the characteristics of political systems and policy subsystems.

Evaluation is typically not a concern at the point of agenda setting and the concept has no explicit place in Kingdon's model of policy change (Kingdon 2013). However, it is possible to see how it would inform policy within it. Evaluations of previous policies are likely to contribute in particular to the identification of the policy solution(s) in play as well as shedding some light on the nature of the policy problem. Following this line of argument, evaluations contribute to clarifying the content of policy but are also exposed to the politics that shape the policy process. As a consequence, policy evaluation can be used by policy actors, including "policy entrepreneurs," to strengthen support for policy change, but it can also be used in arguments against change (e.g., by suppressing or selectively interpreting its findings).

Sabatier's Advocacy Coalition Framework (ACF) further explores the role of actors and interests in policy-making (Sabatier and Jenkins-Smith 1993). Its main insight is that in a given policy subsystem (such as a country's health policy), policy actors form advocacy coalitions to effect or oppose policy change and that these coalitions are formed around actors' deep core beliefs (i.e., underlying personal values), policy core beliefs (i.e., fundamental policy positions, for example, a preference for certain policy instruments over others) and secondary aspects (such as approaches to policy implementation). Coalitions can therefore be formed of a wide range of actors, including civil servants, politicians, academic researchers, civil society organizations and issue advocates devoted to a cause if they share the same policy core beliefs (Sabatier and Jenkins-Smith 1993; Sabatier and Weible 2007). While the ACF does not explicitly discuss the role of policy evaluation, it emphasizes policy learning as a condition of policy change in the long term.

Policy learning can have many sources which will influence policy beliefs slowly and in the long term (in contrast to external shocks that can be powerful influences in the short term). This is similar to the "enlightenment" use of evidence identified by Carol Weiss (1979) in which the findings of studies do not necessarily influence policy directly or immediately but contribute to a body of thinking which eventually contributes to changing policy positions. Arguably, in the health policy subsystem, the continuous support of an advocacy coalition is crucial for any durable form of policy change. The level of support may also determine whether evaluation is commissioned, whether there is engagement with its findings and whether there is continued interest and investment in the maintenance and further development of a policy. Yet, the ACF also highlights the possibility that policy evaluation can be exposed to contrarian interests and that findings from evaluation are likely to be received differently by policy actors, reflecting the recipients' policy beliefs and wider belief systems. Indeed, policy actors may attach different initial purposes to policy evaluation, even if they are generally supportive of the policy. For example, they may share the same policy beliefs but not necessarily the same views about how those beliefs should be realized in policy terms. From this perspective, evaluation can be understood as a tool used by those on different sides of an argument rather than as contributing to a disinterested exercise in policy improvement. This emphasizes the performative function of evaluation in argumentation and policy discourse (Majone 1989; Pearce et al. 2014; Schlaufer et al. 2018). For example, commissioning an evaluation of a policy initiative is a way of signaling a commitment to evidence-informed policy. However, as a basis for policy learning, evaluation is likely to be more influential in relation to modifications of policy (i.e., addressing secondary beliefs such as changes in the mode of implementation) rather than major changes of policy that would require shifting deep-rooted belief systems. These are unlikely to be shifted by the outcomes of an evaluation.

3 Evaluation in Different Policy-Making Contexts

Whether or not, why, how, and where health policy evaluation takes place and how it relates to the policy process vary by country. Country context matters and there are important differences that shape the role and uptake of policy evaluation: first, in the institutional design of a country's political system that determines how and where policy decisions are taken; and second, in the degree of institutionalization of policy evaluation and whether it is embedded in a political culture and organizational structure that is supportive of evaluation.

In relation to the institutionalization of evaluation, very broadly, there has been explicit promotion of the value of rigorous (external) evaluation of health policies and programs especially in the English-speaking world, starting in Canada and the UK in the 1980s. This does not necessarily mean that evaluations are given greater weight in policy decisions in these countries, but evaluation of a particular type is now seen as highly normative. In parts of Western Europe, such as the Netherlands, a different way of thinking about policy-making and evaluation has emerged (Waardenburg et al. 2020). Rather than extolling the virtues of independent evaluation modelled as far as possible on the paradigm of the clinical trial, there is more of an emphasis on policy experimentation in which the policy itself is undertaken as a continuous process of learning based on pragmatic trial and error using techniques such as rapid prototyping. The emphasis is on creativity and there is a higher tolerance of risk than in more conventional policy development and evaluation processes. In this way, the policy and its evaluation are inseparable, often undertaken by overlapping groups of people.

There is little research on how differences in political systems interact with policy evaluation. There is an assumption that evaluation is part of a political culture that emphasizes accountability and learning and is thus associated with policy-making in liberal democracies. However, this is not necessarily so. For example, studies on policy piloting in the context of health system reform in China have shown that evaluation and experimentation can also be used in autocratic systems and for a range of purposes, including facilitating and managing system change (Wang and Yang 2021; He et al. 2022). Indeed, it can be argued that more authoritarian regimes have more unfettered opportunities to conduct and learn from evaluations (e.g., to undertake large social experiments) than more democratic ones since they do not face criticism from opposition parties or the public if "experiments" go wrong. However, little is known about how such systems use the findings from evaluation and whether this is any different from other countries.

Among liberal democracies, countries also differ in where evaluation takes place within a health policy process, i.e., which organization is responsible and has the authority to commission or conduct policy evaluation. In health policy, the role of evaluation is also shaped by how the interface between political decision-making (e.g., primary and secondary legislation and related mechanisms of accountability) and specialized health system governance is organized. In most countries, health system governance is the ultimate responsibility of the ministry of health, yet the portfolios of health ministries differ, as well as the degree of parliamentary involvement in, and oversight of, health policy decisions. In federated and decentralized systems, health system governance may be largely delegated to regional or provincial levels of government. This means that policy evaluation can take place at regional/provincial or central/federal government level, reflecting the constitutional division of powers and responsibilities between different levels of governance.

A 2020 survey by the OECD showed that most policy evaluation in OECD countries takes place in the executive branch at national level, with government ministries and their agencies being the main commissioners and ostensible users of evaluation (OECD 2020). Evaluations of health policies are mostly commissioned by ministries of health, but there are other potential government "customers" such as ministries of finance and of science and technology. Ministries of finance are more likely to emphasize value for money in an evaluation, while ministries of health may be more focused on effectiveness and equity. In combination, these differences in institutional design create a highly varied picture as to how policy evaluation is organized within the political apparatus. For example, as the UK's public health care system is paid for from general tax revenues, the Treasury frequently requires the ex ante and ex post evaluation of major spending proposals related to the National Health Service. By contrast, in the federal USA, evaluation at national level requires the use of legislative waivers to allow new policies to be introduced experimentally for a defined period of time and thus enable their evaluation (Haynes et al. 2013). Legislated, time-limited experiments are virtually unheard of in the UK.

Depending on how government is organized, there may be incentives or disincentives which help or hinder policy evaluation. For example, Varone et al. (2005) argue that the fact that governments are typically formed by four to six political parties in Belgium's proportional electoral system creates an environment in which policy-makers are reluctant to commission evaluation. Their main concern is to avoid giving veto power to evaluators and providing fresh ammunition to the opposition which might endanger the stability of the government in a system that is already prone to volatility. The same reluctance to evaluate can occur for completely different reasons, for example, where a government enjoys a large parliamentary majority and thus may not need to concede an evaluation in order to secure support for a new policy.

There are few examples of parliaments being the main commissioners and thus "customers" of policy evaluation. Switzerland is an exception. Bundi (2017) demonstrates that policy evaluation is well established in its cantonal parliaments (these also have authority over a substantial part of health policy). However, the same study also shows that evaluation is often deployed strategically to provide support or encourage opposition to a policy introduced in parliament rather than to provide unbiased evidence to inform policy-making. For that reason, members of parliament are often more interested in requesting evaluation than in using its findings. Indeed, it is frequently the case in settings where the use of evidence-informed policy rhetoric is the norm that announcements of the commissioning of an evaluation are more valuable politically than the use of their eventual findings since the latter can turn out to be embarrassing to the original proponents of a policy.

Mavrot and Pattyn (2022) argue that the degree of institutionalization of evaluation is usually weaker in the legislature than in the executive. Typically, the executive has far more resources routinely available to commission or undertake evaluative research though the legislature can demand an evaluation from the executive. In some countries, the requirement for evaluation is embedded in important pieces of legislation (e.g., Denmark, Germany, the Netherlands, New Zealand). In such instances, parliament retains the authority to request or require evaluation and to act upon its findings, although the responsibility for the commissioning and conducting of evaluation rests with the government of the day. For example, the Organ Donation (Deemed Consent) Act 2019 in England included the requirement that an evaluation of the implementation and impacts of the Act be commissioned by the executive to assuage the concerns of those parliamentarians who were skeptical of the merits of the law change (Williams et al. 2024).

Countries also differ in the degree of embeddedness (i.e., institutionalization) of policy evaluation in the executive and the extent to which evaluation is seen as a routine element of the policy process. The degree of institutionalization varies greatly but there have been efforts in many countries to establish more effective evidence ecosystems or national infrastructures to encourage evaluation and evidence use in policy. The 2020 OECD study found that all 42 participating governments were committed to policy evaluation but most of them faced significant challenges in promoting policy evaluation across government organizations. They also found that about two-thirds of the countries surveyed had a legal or policy framework in place for policy evaluation, while a few countries also referred to evaluation in their constitutions (OECD 2020).

A comparison of 19 OECD countries based on a survey of evaluation experts found different degrees of maturity with regard to the 9 indicators of the extent and use of evaluation (Jacob et al. 2015). These included, for example, evaluation taking place in many policy domains, a sufficient supply of domestic evaluators covering different disciplines and a supportive national discourse concerning evaluation. The authors noted that while the interest in evaluation and maturity of evaluation cultures had increased over time, differences between countries remained. Other studies have shown that having policies in place requiring or enabling policy evaluation can help in building a culture of evaluation and support evaluation use (Mark and Hart 2022). An example would be a requirement that new resource-intensive policies have to be reviewed within a specified time, thereby creating a demand for ex post evaluation. Such an evaluation culture benefits from involving many different policy actors and can productively contribute to capacity building both within and outside government. However, it has also been observed that evaluation policy "will have little to no effect on capacity building if the organization lacks a culture that supports making evaluation strategic and useful" (Al Hudib and Cousins 2022:

243). Thus, an effective evaluation ecosystem requires both a supportive institutional structure and an evaluation culture.

While it is tempting to assume that more evaluation is always a good thing in terms of increasing the likelihood of effective policy-making, the opportunity costs of routinizing policy evaluation have to be borne in mind. In addition, the institutionalization of evaluation can lead to unrealistic expectations being placed on evaluation. For example, some policies lack detail or are aspirational and many are introduced universally across an entire jurisdiction making certain forms of rigorous evaluation impossible.

4 The Interests and Power Relations That Shape Policy Evaluation

Evaluation is often portrayed as a neutral activity. However, evaluations of health policy almost always affect a range of policy actors whose interests and positions on any given subject can be diverse and often conflicting. These actors are also equipped with different resources and wield different levels of influence over the policy process. Policy actors within government are politicians and civil servants who usually have major influence over the policy process. Actors outside the government may have less direct control over the process but may have their own power base because the health system depends on the goods and services they provide. These include health professionals, payers/insurers (if they are separate from the government), provider organizations and businesses (e.g., the pharmaceutical industry or manufacturers of medical devices) and others such as advocacy and other civil society organizations whose interests are affected by the policy in question. Health policy evaluations "implicate power relationships at various steps of the process" (Mavrot and Pattyn 2022: 4) and are, therefore, almost always political (Tayler 2005).

Politicians and their advisers are not always keen for their policies to be evaluated, especially not by external researchers with a degree of independence unless they are confident of positive findings. In practice, many policy evaluations are undertaken by policy agencies themselves more or less informally. Over the last decades, however, calls for evidence-informed policy have become louder and, in many jurisdictions, external policy evaluation is now the expected standard for significant policy changes (WHO 2021). In some instances, the requirement for external evaluation may be written into the policy (or related legislation). In such cases, the stated aim of policy evaluation may be to increase the transparency of the state of policy implementation, to inform policy adjustments or termination and to ensure accountability and value for money. Research has shown that policy-makers often seek confirmation of a policy direction either consciously or implicitly (Ettelt et al. 2015b). This does not exclude them from seeking opportunities for policy learning, although this can be limited by a desire to avoid the risk of the limitations of their policy becoming apparent. As Donald Campbell, the doyen of learning from policy experimentation and evaluation, put it

> If the political and administrative system has committed itself in advance to the correctness … [or] efficacy of its reforms, it will find it hard to tolerate learning of failure. ….. This predicament, abetted by public apathy and by deliberate corruption, may prove in the long run to permanently preclude a truly experimental approach to social amelioration. (Campbell 1969: 410).

In other words, health policies are rarely, if ever, introduced in the state of "equipoise" advocated by clinical triallists; however, much proponents of evidence-informed policy would desire it to be otherwise (Petticrew et al. 2013). Policy-making is a creative, forward-looking, value-driven enterprise which requires considerable political support to be enacted. As such, especially for democratic governments, it reduces governments' commitment to evaluation in practice as opposed to their commitment in principle and provides an incentive to influence how evaluation is conducted as well as to take into account the outcomes and insights it can produce. Sometimes, governments even suppress or try to prevent the results of evaluations being published (though this can backfire by drawing attention to a study). As commissioners, policy-makers can determine the scope and questions to be analyzed and they have control over budget and timelines, which gives them powerful instruments of influence without directly influencing the outcomes of an evaluation. Generally, elected politicians dislike policy evaluations which directly or indirectly lead to comparing their policies with those of their political rivals.

Those affected by the policy or those tasked with implementing the policy may have an entirely different set of interests at stake, resources at hand and ways of interacting with policy evaluation. For example, a lack of support from specific groups can undermine evaluation efforts, as evaluation usually relies on the active participation of implementers and their contribution to data collection. Health professionals, for example, often act as gate keepers to study participants, especially patients, without whom an evaluation might not be meaningful (Der Spiegel 2015). Policy implementers, such as local system managers, may also wish to see their efforts rewarded and reflected positively in the evaluation findings. Irrespective of the extent to which they identify with the policy, they may well need to devote scarce administrative resources to enable an external evaluation to take place.

In contrast, patients and service users may have less influence on health policy evaluation and therefore their interests may be more easily overlooked. Many health policy evaluations include patients as research participants whose role is to provide insight into the user experience. But this typically does not extend to their involvement in the design of the evaluation when evaluation questions and research design options are being discussed or its conduct (Tayler 2005). What is possible or not is also highly dependent on context. In some contexts, it is permissible (or for some even seen as desirable) to link access to a new service to study participation (e.g., in a randomized controlled trial or a staged roll-out by region), while in other contexts, restrictions to access to services for the purpose of such research would be unthinkable. Patient participation in evaluation, therefore, raises a number of ethical questions and there is increased emphasis on other forms of engagement and participation that go beyond study participation. For example, in the UK, an increasing number of funders of health research, including policy evaluations, now insist on lay, patient/service user, and informal carer involvement throughout studies, including, on some occasions, requiring members of the public to become full members of the research team.

Evaluators themselves are not usually seen as policy actors, but as producers of evidence for policy; however, they do have interests in relation to policy evaluation (e.g., a bias toward more and more elaborate evaluative research) and they usually have some, limited influence on the policy process, though rarely over the origin and design of the policy itself to be evaluated. Policies are rarely specified primarily with evaluation and the needs of evaluators in mind. Evaluators may also have formed their own professional and personal views ex ante of the desirability and likely performance of policies in their area of expertise. Accordingly, evaluators are encouraged to be aware of and reflect on the nature of their biases and assumptions, especially if they are recruited to provide an "independent" assessment of the benefits and costs of a policy. Hanberger (2022) found that evaluators do use different types of power, including power delegated to them by evaluation commissioners during the design and implementation phases of evaluations, while also using (epistemic) power to interpret findings and to resist pressure from commissioners to adjust their conclusions. For academic evaluators, there are reputations and scientific credibility at stake if an evaluation is obviously influenced by the commissioners or policy clients. For similar reasons, academics also tend to resist the labelling of "evaluation" as distinct from "research," arguing on scientific and ethical grounds that it should be governed and judged the same as any other research activity. In some countries, such as the UK, guidance exists on the relationships between policy-makers and policy evaluators, although practices vary by government department (HM Treasury 2020).

In health policy, in the UK, there is a strong emphasis on the scientific independence of evaluators, and a higher share of evaluations is contracted to academics than in other fields of public policy, perhaps because of the origins of health services research in medical schools in the UK starting in the 1960s. In other countries, such contracts are mostly given to private firms and consultancies, or internal evaluation takes place conducted by analysts within policy agencies. There are also differences in the level of competence and experience of evaluators which tend to reflect the degree of institutionalization and long-term support for policy evaluation in a given country. A culture of evaluation may not only shape the expectations of policy-makers vis-à-vis evaluators but also help to build capacity among the professional communities and disciplines (e.g., statistics, economics, sociology) that deliver evaluations and contribute to the evidence base for policy.

5 The Role of Policy Experiments and Pilots

Policy piloting has become an increasingly common practice in policy-making in many countries, normally with evaluation built in. "Piloting" means testing a policy over a limited period of time and usually at a smaller scale than full implementation, for instance, on a population subgroup or within a number of selected organizations or geographic locations. In some countries, piloting has come to prominence under the banner of evidence-informed policy-making. This alignment typically comes with a set of assumptions about the purpose of piloting and the preferred approaches to evaluation, particularly in relation to measuring outcomes. Policy piloting assumes that policy-makers will embrace findings from evaluation and that these will be used to inform further policy refinement in a fairly simple linear manner. However, empirical analysis suggests that there are many different types of pilots at play that are highly context-dependent and that the purpose of policy pilots can be contested and open to interpretation (Ettelt et al. 2015b).

There are many potential benefits from policy piloting. Most often, the stated objectives of a policy pilot are to test whether a policy delivers according to its objectives and to learn how best to implement it to inform a future roll-out if successful (if "success" can be agreed upon and defined). However, there can be other motivations to initiate pilots, such as a strategic consideration to reduce resistance to the full implementation of a policy by doing it at a smaller scale initially, or simply because money to support the full implementation is currently unavailable. Policy-makers may wish to seek ways to initiate implementation without the risk of the policy failing at full scale. From these perspectives, policy piloting can be seen as a method for managing policy risks. Research has also shown that piloting can indeed have the effect of convincing other, perhaps more skeptical, audiences, of the merits of a policy proposal and can expand the policy network in support of a policy (McFadgen and Huitema 2018).

The actors involved in a policy pilot may interpret the purpose of the pilot very differently. For example, policy officials and evaluators may aim to find out "what works best" in the spirit of evidence-informed policy. This assumes that there is a realistic option of discontinuing the policy if the evaluation shows that it is inferior to, say, previous approaches. By contrast, local managers who have invested time and effort in implementing the pilot and changing local practices may understandably be vested in a continuation of the policy that is piloted. For them, seeing that the policy pilots that they have worked hard to implement do not produce the expected effects can be difficult. They may wish to adjust the implementation to increase the odds of the policy "working" rather than adhering to a binary conception of the pilot as either "working" (cost-effectively) or not. Lastly, evaluators will be interested in conducting evaluation in a way that conforms with their professional norms and standards, which may mean that they prefer some study designs over others. In consequence, a given policy pilot may be serving different purposes in the eyes of different groups of stakeholders (Ettelt et al. 2015a, b). The idealized scenario of evidence-informed policy-making which defines the purpose of the pilot as being to generate evidence to inform a policy decision about the future roll-out of the policy may not be shared by all those involved.

A different set of purposes relates to using the pilot to learn how to improve implementation of the policy. This typically means that the decision whether to pursue the policy has already been taken, explicitly or otherwise. This set of purposes can be distinguished as follows:

- Early implementation for (local) innovation—to stimulate diversity in implementation by local managers, "letting a hundred flowers bloom"—a common approach to stimulate activity and change, but where it is unclear how evaluation can contribute knowledge that is actionable or informative for future implementation.
- Identifying the best route to implementation (literally expressed in terms such as "pathfinder", "pioneer", or "trailblazer"), starting from a position of uncertainty with regard to feasibility and acceptability, but potentially also conscious of the diversity of contexts in which a policy will be implemented and that effectively influence, even change, how the policy will operate in practice.
- Demonstrating to others how best to implement the policy (as expressed in terms like "demonstrator" or "beacon") and thereby create momentum for more widespread implementation.

There is clearly scope for conflict and confusion given these different purposes and especially between those who approach a pilot as an outcome-focused experiment versus those who wish to emphasize learning for subsequent (better) policy implementation. For example, this leads to different preferences for the focus and design of evaluations (e.g., at the simplest between an emphasis on process or outcome evaluation) (Ettelt et al. 2022). However, there are also differences in the assumptions relating to knowledge utilization, the possibilities of policy innovation and approaches to implementation.

Policy piloting is sometimes used as a synonym for "policy experiments" or "social experiments." However, this can lead to further confusion since the term "experiment" means different things to different research and policy communities. In an important contribution to clarification, Ansell and Bartenberger (2016) developed a typology of policy experimentalism, distinguishing three distinct types of policy "experiments" related to different conceptions of policy learning:

- "Controlled," of which the RCT is a paradigmatic example, focused on establishing causality; this form of experimentation emphasizes the role of evaluation as a scientific study. This usually implies that a policy has to be codified in detail such that it becomes a clearly defined, potentially reproducible "intervention," capable of being compared with an unexposed population in a controlled study. This also includes a clear separation between policy as intervention and the context in which it operates.
- "Darwinian" in which as many different approaches as possible are pursued in a process of "trial and error" in order to see which prove useful and which less so. Such experiments may involve evaluation, but trial and error could also be a by-product of a wider effort to roll out the policy so that it can be seen whether it is capable of being more or less successfully implemented in different places. Darwinian experimentation stipulates that the best or perhaps most suitably adjusted pilots survive while others fall by the wayside. This approach is more akin to innovation cycles in the private sector.

- "Generative," described as "a process of generating and iteratively refining a solution concept (an idea, innovation, design, policy, program, etc.) based on continuous feedback" (Ansell and Bartenberger 2016: 68). This approach to policy experimentation is more akin to ideas of continuous learning in public management, including learning from failure. Understanding piloting as generative may also be a matter of perspective as it is easier to see the long-term trajectory of a policy in retrospect. There is a question as to whether "generative" approaches to policy change and to experimentation can be planned and under which circumstances. However, the approach certainly requires a degree of continuity, long-term vision and a tolerance of failure at least in the short term. A generative approach can accommodate many different roles for evaluation, for example, emphasizing process learning through qualitative methods as well as outcome-oriented approaches using predominantly quantitative methods, but the main emphasis would be on producing formative feedback for improvement.

There is also the question of the timing of an evaluation of a policy pilot: when should a pilot evaluation be conducted for the evaluation to be useful in a given policy process? Arguably, if the evaluation is organized too early, the implementation of the pilot may still be incomplete and there may be little to observe in terms of outcomes (Ogilvie et al. 2011). In such instances, the evaluation will not be able to assess effectiveness, but will most likely only be able to capture activities and assess intermediary outputs. While such a process evaluation can provide valuable insight into the state of implementation of a pilot, it may not produce the type of definitive findings to which policy-makers aspire if they seek to find out whether or not the pilot "delivers." However, if the pilot is evaluated at a later stage, when the policy is more fully implemented, it may be too late for findings to be useful in policy decisions because policy commitments to roll-out may already have been made and it may be difficult to reverse course if outcomes are suboptimal. Policy piloting and related evaluations also take a considerable amount of time, so there is a risk that policy-makers lose interest and the pilot becomes irrelevant along with its evaluation (Sanderson 2002).

From a policy stages perspective, piloting sits somewhere between policy formulation and policy implementation. If the stated aim is to ensure policy learning, piloting aims to inform policy formulation, while pilots also (by necessity) involve implementation, sometimes to the point that the purpose of piloting is to drive implementation rather than testing with a view to improve or discard a policy. Also, as with policy evaluation more generally, intentions and motivations at the start of pilots can vary significantly from their actual use and impact on policy-making (Greenberg and Mandell 1991). Even the best laid plans and most rigorously designed evaluations are no guarantee that the policy context at the end of a pilot is the same as when it started.

6 Commissioning Policy Evaluation

The role of the commissioner is central to policy evaluation since, unlike other forms of health services research which can be investigator-driven, evaluations are almost always initiated by policy agencies. Commissioners determine the scope of the evaluation, the principal evaluation questions to be addressed, the conditions under which the evaluation is to be conducted and, to varying degrees, the broad approach to be taken to the evaluation. They often specify the methods to be applied to collect and analyze data, though academics generally expect to determine more of these themselves. Commissioners can also have an important role in supporting the evaluation. For example, cooperating with an evaluation team is often a precondition for a local site to take part in a pilot program. At the very least, commissioners can facilitate access to research participants by providing a letter of support which sets out the purpose of the evaluation and encourages local implementers to assist the evaluators. Most policy evaluations will be commissioned by the government or other state agencies such as government research bodies, although, in principle, policy evaluation can also be commissioned externally, for example by third-sector organizations with a stake in a policy area. However, in the field of health policy, since many countries have a version of a publicly funded health care system, policy evaluations are frequently commissioned by governments one way or another. In countries dependent to varying degrees on external donors, bilateral and multi-lateral donors pay for, and commission evaluations of, their programs. Receipt of funding is normally dependent on cooperating fully with evaluators. This can be hugely advantageous when undertaking ambitious evaluations.

Commissioning policy evaluation typically involves collaboration with different professionals within government, including policy officials and analysts, research managers specialized in dealing with policy-related research, and procurement and contract staff who ensure compliance with commissioning standards (e.g., to ensure fair competition for contracts based on quality and price if the evaluation is outsourced). Multiple requirements need to be served and balanced (Cox and Barbrook-Johnson 2021). For example, policy officials may require specific timelines to be observed to ensure findings can contribute to a decision within an electoral cycle. Policy officials and research managers may have different preferences for evaluation designs and data collection methods. These expectations can pull in different directions. Typically, trade-offs are needed between methodological rigour (especially in relation to measuring outcomes which may only be measured validly in the longer term) and pragmatism (such as having some findings available to inform a decision on whether to extend or vary a program). The more a policy agency commissions evaluations, assuming a capacity for institutional "memory," the more its processes should improve as commissioners and providers of evaluations become more familiar with the requirements and limits of what is feasible, and learn to manage each other's expectations. Commissioning also benefits from an established culture of evaluation in a policy agency such that thinking about policy evaluation is integral to the policy process. A continuous investment in evaluation also helps to build capacity among policy officials to become effective commissioners and users of evaluation, and evaluators to deliver high-quality, relevant, and timely evaluations (Huckel Schneider et al. 2016).

There is an important distinction to make between evaluation undertaken externally and internally, the latter by members of the same organization initiating the policy (Weiss 1993). There are advantages and disadvantages to both practices: evaluators on the inside of an organization may have more knowledge of the nuances of a policy and better access to routine administrative information. If they are policy-makers, they may even have the capacity to act on their findings. However, they are more likely to be vested in the success of the policy than external evaluators and therefore have greater incentives to suppress unfavorable results, defeating the purpose of evaluation (Schoenefeld and Jordan 2017). As employees, they may be under pressure to "spin" the interpretation of their data in ways favorable to the agency and its political leadership. There is also less likely to be an ex ante guarantee that the findings will be published. In contrast, external evaluators are more likely to be granted a greater degree of independence. As a result, the distance between evaluators and policy-makers will be greater if evaluation is externally commissioned, and, therefore, the evaluators will be less exposed to direct political influence. On the other hand, there are reports from various countries of policy-makers attempting to lean on evaluators, irrespective of the formal contractual arrangements (Pleger and Sager 2018). External evaluators may also temper their conclusions for fear that they are less likely to win future research contracts.

Commissioning an evaluation can be by open competition or tendered selectively from a list of preferred providers. In most countries, competitive tendering has become the norm to ensure that the most suitable proposal and team is selected.

However, organizing open competitions is resource-intensive for the commissioner and incurs significant costs for the research community which have ultimately to be recouped or providers go out of business. There are also different types of professionals who act as evaluators, such as academic researchers and consulting firms, which reflect the availability of expertise in different settings. There are also cultural differences as to whether health policy evaluation is regarded as bona fide research and thus an academic pursuit that is sufficiently well regarded to build a university career around, or a service that is contracted to private businesses, perhaps with some involvement of academics as paid advisers.

At the commissioning stage, the scope of the policy evaluation, the requirements for robustness, and the range of data collection and stakeholder perspectives are defined, usually in the form of an invitation to tender or research specification. Sometimes a preliminary study is required at this stage to identify more precisely how the policy is being implemented to develop a "theory of change" (that is, a conceptual model of the causal pathways by which the policy's planned outcomes are to be achieved) and thus identify the appropriate evaluation questions (Anderson et al. 2008). Basic design choices such as whether the evaluation should focus mostly on demonstrating activity by examining implementation processes (process evaluation) or attempt to measure effectiveness (outcome evaluation) will reflect the main purpose of the evaluation, for example, whether it is needed to ensure accountability, reinforce legitimation, or support policy learning and improvement. A tender invitation will also make further stipulations on design and research methods, although evaluators will be expected to go into more detail in their proposals to convince commissioners that they are capable of delivering the evaluation. In some settings, there are guidelines and standards that communicate the expectations placed on evaluators, such as the OECD Framework for Regulatory Policy Evaluation (OECD 2014), the UK Treasury's *Magenta Book* (HM Treasury 2020) and the Better Regulation Toolbox developed by the European Commission (EC 2023).

Last but not least, commissioners will determine the budget available and timelines. Both are crucial ingredients for evaluation. If the budget is too small and the timeline too short, the ability of evaluators to examine the policy in a meaningful way will be limited which can undermine the purpose of the evaluation. Tight budgets are also likely to limit the ability to develop new approaches to evaluation and methods of data collection (Cox and Barbrook-Johnson 2021). If evaluation is only planned as an afterthought to policy implementation, it may not be possible to collect the type of data required for robust outcome evaluation (e.g., a baseline and potentially a control group). In an ideal scenario, evaluation would always be considered alongside policy development, particularly if the policy is being piloted.

7 Use of Evaluation in Policy-Making

The assumption behind taking care with the commissioning of health policy evaluation is that this will increase the odds that the findings will be useable and used to shape policy in the future. This begs the question as to what is meant by the "use" of evaluation. The classic analysis by Weiss (1979) identified four common ways in which evidence is used in policy: instrumental, symbolic, enlightening, and strategic. This typology has largely stood the test of time insofar as recent analyses merely further elaborate Weiss' approach. Thus Vedung (2000) identifies the following contemporary uses of evaluation:

- Instrumental—this is the direct, linear use of evaluation findings that corresponds to the rational ideal of the policy process toward which proponents of evidence-informed policy adhere.
- Conceptual—this refers to the gradual enlightenment contribution of evaluation findings to the stock of knowledge and, more importantly, ideas pertaining to a policy issue.
- Legitimizing—the use of evaluation findings selectively to confirm pre-existing convictions.
- Tactical—the use of findings to gain a political advantage.
- Discursive—the use of evaluation and its findings to foster dialogue between policy actors.

All the above uses are broadly "strategic" in Weiss' terminology in that they are intimately tied to politics except perhaps the instrumental use. Whether they are seen as good or bad depends on the position of each interest group involved in the specific policy area. It is also the case that the same evaluation's findings can be used differently over time depending on the political context. Thus, an evaluation can be ignored initially but later heavily used when a policy-making "window of opportunity" (in Kingdon's terms) opens. The evaluation literature is replete with barriers and facilitators of evaluation use, and it is clear that the precise combination of factors shaping use will vary between topic areas and institutional settings (Dobrow et al. 2006; Morrato et al. 2008). However, recent rigorous research on the use of in-house evaluations in the Dutch Ministry of Foreign Affairs highlighted the importance of policy makers' interest in the evaluation itself and their engagement in the evaluation process for the uptake of findings (Pattyn and Bouterse 2020). Other positive factors were whether the evaluation produced novel knowledge affecting the relevant policy and its timing. Findings were especially likely to be used if their availability coincided with the drafting of new policy documents. One factor that had been hypothesized to encourage the use of findings but which seemed neither to increase nor reduce the odds of use was the political salience of the issue. While this may seem surprising given the acknowledged political nature of evaluation, an explanation is that political salience is driven by wider political forces and is not under the direct influence of policy officials. Indeed, the more politically salient an issue, the more strongly it is likely to be shaped by debates about values and policy priorities which are not necessarily amenable to empirical resolution.

8 Conclusion

The commitment to policy evaluation is especially strongly held and articulated in the field of health policy. This tends to obscure the fact that policy evaluation is always entwined in politics since policy-making is shaped by values as well as evidence. As a result, evaluators cannot determine the goals of policy or tell policymakers what they should be doing. It can only inform them of the likely consequences of pursuing their chosen goals using their chosen means.

References

Al Hudib H, Cousins JB. (2022) Evaluation policy and organizational evaluation capacity building: a study of international aid agency evaluation policies. *Evaluation Policy 173*:29–48 https://doi.org/10.1002/ev.20494

Anderson S, Allen P, Peckham S, Goodwin N (2008) Asking the right questions: scoping studies in the commissioning of research on the organization and delivery of health services. Health Res Policy Syst 6:7. https://doi.org/10.1186/1478-4505-6-7

Ansell CK, Bartenberger M (2016) Varieties of experimentalism. Ecol Econ 130:64–73

Bozzini E, Hunt J (2015) Bringing evaluation into the policy cycle. Eur J Risk Regul 6(1):57–67

Brewer GD (1974) The policy sciences emerge: to nurture and structure a discipline. Policy Sci 5(3):239–244

Bundi P (2017) Parliamentarians' strategies for policy evaluations. Eval Program Plann 69:130–138

Cairney P (2013) Standing on the shoulders of giants: how do we combine the insights of multiple theories in public policy studies? Policy Stud J 41(1):1–21

Cairney P (2023) What does policymaking look like? Public Policy Design Blog. https://publicpolicydesign.blog.gov.uk/2023/02/09/what-does-policymaking-look-like/

Campbell D (1969) Reforms as experiments. Am Psychol 24:409–429

Cox J, Barbrook-Johnson P (2021) How does the commissioning process hinder the update of complexity-appropriate evaluation? Evaluation 27(1):32–56

Der Spiegel (2015) Deutsche Vorzeigestudie wird abgebrochen. https://www.spiegel.de/gesundheit/diagnose/prostatakrebs-prefere-studie-wird-abgebrochen-a-1124534.html

Dobrow MJ, Goel V, Lemieux-Charles L, Black NA (2006) The impact of context on evidence utilization: a framework for expert groups developing health policy recommendations. Soc Sci Med 63:1811–1824

EC (2023) Better regulation toolbox, 2023 edn. European Commission, Brussels. https://commission.europa.eu/system/files/2023-09/BR%20toolbox%20-%20Jul%202023%20-%20FINAL.pdf

Ettelt S, Mays N, Allen P (2015a) Policy experiments: investigating effectiveness or confirming direction? Evaluation 21(3):292–307

Ettelt S, Mays N, Allen P (2015b) The multiple purposes of policy piloting and their consequences: three examples from national health and social care policy in England. J Soc Policy 44(2):319–337

Ettelt S, Williams L, Mays N (2022) National policy piloting as steering at a distance: the perspective of local implementers. Governance 35:385–401. https://doi.org/10.1111/gove.12589

Greenberg DH, Mandell MB (1991) Research utilization in policymaking: a tale of two series (of social experiments). J Policy Anal Manage 10(4):633–656

Hanberger A (2022) Power in and of evaluation: a framework of analysis. Evaluation 28(3):265–283

Haynes L, Service O, Goldacre B, Torgerson D (2013) Test, learn, adapt. Developing public policy with randomised controlled trials. Cabinet Office, Behavioural Insights Team, London

He AJ, Fan Y, Su R (2022) Seeking policy solutions in a complex system: experimentalist governance in China's healthcare reform. Policy Sci 55(755):776

HM Treasury (2020) Magenta Book: Central Government guidance on evaluation. https://www.gov.uk/government/publications/the-magenta-book

Howlett M, McConnell A, Perl A (2015) Streams and stages: reconciling Kingdon and policy process theory. Eur J Polit Res 54:419–434

Huckel Schneider C, Milat AJ, Moore G. (2016) Barriers and facilitators to evaluation of health policies and programs: Policymaker and researcher perspectives. *Eval Program Plann 58*:208–215. https://doi.org/10.1016/j.evalprogplan.2016.06.011

Jacob S, Speer S, Furubo J-E (2015) The institutionalization of evaluation matters: updating the International Atlas of Evaluation 10 years later. Evaluation 21(1):6–31

John P (2012) Analyzing public policy, 2nd edn. Routledge, London/New York

Kingdon J (2013) Agendas, alternatives and public policies. Update edition with an epilogue on health care. Pearson New International Edition, 2nd edn. Pearson, Longman Classics, London

Knott J, Wildavsky A (1980) If dissemination is the solution, what is the problem? Knowl Creat Diffusion Util 1(4):537–578

Lasswell DH (1956) The decision process: seven categories of functional analysis. University of Maryland Press, College Park

Majone G (1989) Evidence, argument, and persuasion in the policy process. Yale University Press, New Haven, CT

Mark MM, Hart NR (2022) The future of evaluation policy. N Dir Eval 2022:117–124

Mavrot C, Pattyn VE (2022) The politics of evaluation. In: Lander A, Sager F (eds) Handbook of the politics of public administration. Edward Elgar, Cheltenham, pp 244–255. Available online at view (universiteitleiden.nl)

McFadgen B, Huitema D (2018) Experimentation at the interface of science and policy: a multi-case analysis of how policy experiments influence political decision-makers. Policy Sci 51(2):161–187

Morrato E, Elias M, Gericke C (2008) Using population-based routine data for evidence-based health policy decisions: lessons from three examples of setting and evaluating national health policy in Australia, the UK and the USA. J Public Health 29(4):463–471

OECD (2014) OECD framework for regulatory policy evaluation. OECD, Paris. https://read.oecd-ilibrary.org/governance/oecd-framework-for-regulatory-policy-evaluation_9789264214453-en#page1

OECD (2020) How can governments leverage policy evaluation to improve evidence informed policy making? Highlights from an OECD comparative study. https://www.oecd.org/gov/policy-evaluation-comparative-study-highlights.pdf

Ogilvie D, Cummins S, Petticrew M, White M, Jones A, Wheeler K (2011) Assessing the evaluability of complex public health interventions: five questions for researchers, funders, and policymakers. Milbank Q 89(2):206–225

Pattyn V, Bouterse M (2020) Explaining use and non-use of policy evaluations in a mature evaluation setting. Hum Soc Sci Commun 7:85. https://doi.org/10.1057/s41599-020-00575-y

Pearce W, Wesselink A, Colebatch H (2014) Evidence and meaning in policy making. Evid Policy 10(2):161–165

Peters G (2015) Advanced introduction to public policy. Edgar Elgar Publishing, Cheltenham

Petticrew M, McKee M, Lock K, Phillips G (2013) In search of social equipoise. BMJ 346:f4016. https://doi.org/10.1136/bmj.f4016

Pleger L, Sager F. (2018) Betterment, undermining, support and distortion: A heuristic model for the analysis of pressure on evaluators. *Eval Program Plann, 69*:166–172. https://doi.org/10.1016/j.evalprogplan.2016.09.002

Sabatier PA, Jenkins-Smith H (1993) Policy change and learning: an advocacy coalition approach. Westview Press, Boulder, CO

Sabatier PA, Weible CM (2007) The advocacy coalition: innovations and clarification. In: Sabatier PA (ed) Theories of the policy process. Westview Press, Boulder, CO, pp 189–220

Sanderson I (2002) Evaluation, policy learning and evidence-based policy making. Public Adm 80(1):1–22

Schlaufer C, Stucki I, Sager F (2018) The political use of evidence and its contribution to democratic discourse. Public Adm Rev 78(4):645–649

Schoenefeld J, Jordan A (2017) Governing policy evaluation? Towards a new typology. Evaluation 23(3):274–293

Tayler D (2005) Governing through evidence: participation and power in policy evaluation. J Soc Policy 34(4):601–618

Varone F, Jacob S, de Winter L (2005) Polity, politics and policy evaluation in Belgium. Evaluation 11(3):253–273

Vedung E (2000) Evaluation research and fundamental research. In: Stockmann R (ed) Evaluationsforschung. Grundlagen und ausgewählte Forschungsfelder. Leske + Budrich, Opladen, pp 103–126

Waardenburg M, Groenleer M, De Jong J (2020) Designing environments for experimentation, learning and innovation in public policy and governance. Policy Polit 48(1):67–87. https://doi.org/10.1332/030557319X15586040837640

Wang S, Yang DY (2021) Policy experimentation in China: the political economy of policy learning. Working paper. National Bureau of Economic Research, Cambridge. https://www.nber.org/papers/w29402

Weiss CH (1979) The many meanings of research utilization. Public Adm Rev 39(5):426–431

Weiss CH (1993) Where politics and evaluation research meet. Eval Pract 14(1):93–106

WHO (2021) Evidence, policy, impact: WHO guide for evidence-informed decision-making. World Health Organization, Geneva. 9789240039872-eng.pdf (who.int). Accessed 24 May 2024

Williams L, Bostock J, Noyes J, McLaughlin L, O'Neill S, Al-Haboubi M, Boadu P, Mays N (2024) Why did England change its law on deceased organ donation in 2019? The dynamic interplay between evidence and values. Health Econ Policy Law 19:353. https://doi.org/10.1017/S1744133124000112

Ethical Principles Guiding Health Services Evaluation

Judith Brown and Jeremy Brown

Abstract

This chapter provides an ethical framework that protects the evaluator and the participants whilst adding rigor and credibility to evaluations. We explore how a project that is process-driven can facilitate joint expectations from the outset and allow reflection and review. We argue that if commissioners and evaluators follow processes and regularly review expectations, then transparency, a key requirement of ethical evaluations, will follow. The chapter concludes by reflecting on the wider context of how evaluations that embed ethical principles can improve policy-making in health care.

Keywords

Ethics · Autonomy · Consent · Co-production · Trust · Transparency

1 Introduction

Embedding ethical principles into evaluation is important as it guides people's decision-making. This chapter will provide a framework for policy-makers, commissioners, and evaluators at every stage of the project process (from evaluation project conception and design to dissemination and ultimately influencing policy change). This will enhance the knowledge and understanding of ethical principles and

J. Brown
The National Autistic Society, London, UK
e-mail: judith.brown@nas.org.uk

J. Brown (✉)
Edge Hill University, Ormskirk, Lancashire, UK
e-mail: brownjm@edgehill.ac.uk

A. Kaehne, J. Feather (eds.), *Handbook of Health Services Evaluation*,
https://doi.org/10.1007/978-3-031-87869-5_4

provide an ethical framework that protects the evaluator and the participants adding rigor and credibility to an evaluation.

This chapter will consider the relationship between ethical principles, policy-making, and evaluation practice. We recognize that each evaluation has its own individual context, and each profession or country may have its own guidance on ethical practice, for example, the Canadian Evaluation Society (2020) and the Asia Pacific Evaluation Association (2023). Throughout we will use generic terminology that is applicable and transferable to any context. We will not refer directly to governance processes related to gatekeeping, permissions, and sponsorship of projects.

1.1 The Context of Ethics in Health Services Evaluation

Ethics is a philosophical concept about moral principles and societal rights and wrongs (Cambridge Dictionary 2023). However, "ethics" can be interpreted in different ways causing confusion. Many understand "ethics" as a colloquial term for the process of permission to begin a study. In this chapter, when referring to "ethics" in the context of health services evaluation, we focus on the moral duty to prioritize the well-being of all involved. Ethics in Health Services Evaluation is so important. Evaluating health services directly impacts patients and healthcare providers making ethical integrity essential.

Ethical principles should underpin and drive all evaluations, this concept aligns with the values of the World Health Organization (WHO). "Our Values, Our DNA" (WHO 2024) is the WHO's charter, striving for excellence, collaboration, trust, care, and integrity. This amplifies the message that we have a moral duty to protect commissioners, evaluators, and participants throughout the evaluation process.

The following five values of the WHO demonstrate how important it is to reflect on the altruistic nature of evaluation and the integral ethical principles that can contribute to providing high-quality evidence to influence policy change and improving health outcomes.

Trusted to serve public health at all times (We put people's health interests first; our actions and recommendations are independent; our decisions are fair, transparent, and timely.)

Professionals committed to excellence in health (We uphold the highest standards of professionalism across all roles and specializations; we are guided by the best available science, evidence, and technical expertise; we continuously develop ourselves and innovate to respond to a changing world.)

Persons of integrity (We practice the advice we give to the world; we engage with everyone honestly and in good faith; we hold ourselves and others accountable for words and actions.)

Collaborative colleagues and partners (We engage with colleagues and partners to strengthen impact at the country level; we recognize and use the power of diversity to achieve more together; we communicate openly with everyone and learn from one another.)

People caring about people (We courageously and selflessly defend everyone's right to health; we show compassion for all human beings and promote sustainable approaches to health; we strive to make people feel safe, respected, empowered, fairly treated and duly recognized.)
(Source: https://www.who.int/about/values)

To evaluate something is to weigh up the pros and cons. When considering it in a formal context, it is about measuring the impact of an activity. The World Health Organization (WHO) specifies that:

> *An evaluation is an assessment, as systematic and impartial as possible, of an activity, project, programme, strategy, policy, topic, theme, sector, operational area, "institutional performance* (...)" (United Nations Evaluation Group 2012).

Ethics is important, not only in evaluations but any work that involves the participation of patients. Arguably, ethics may convey negative undertones for some and can be perceived as being a complex process that has to be undertaken in academia. In the context of academic study, ethical approval is necessary for a study to move on to the next stage, and quite often it is seen as a tokenistic exercise, something that you have to do, rather than an understanding and appreciation that embedding ethical principles will improve the project. The difficulty with ethical approval is it can be seen as an academic endeavor.

When it comes to evaluations, ethical consideration can be engulfed by responsibility, accountability, and legislation. What if something goes wrong? Who takes the blame? However, this is a distraction from the reality that everyone has a responsibility to protect the welfare and safety of all participants and evaluators.

Evaluations are usually time sensitive to align with funding which exacerbates the tendency to focus on legality rather than considered ethical risks and mitigations. For anyone wanting to elicit the genuine opinions of the people at the center of any evaluation, it is of paramount importance that their well-being is embedded into the design of the project from inception to dissemination. Participants and the evaluators should be equally protected from any harm, protecting those that are going to be involved and also those that are conducting the piece of work. Ensuring participants' safety is more complicated when the evaluation involves babies, children, young people, vulnerable adults, those with an intellectual disability or other minority or hard-to-reach groups. Communication differences can create barriers and informed consent can be compromised unless accessibility of information is prioritized. This should not prevent evaluations from taking place with these individuals as it is essential that their voice is heard in relation to their education, health, care, and well-being. The challenge is with the evaluator.

The context of the evaluation is important. An evaluation can be conducted in any situation where the impact of something is to be measured. It is not possible to cover all evaluation contexts as they can take place in any organization or setting. However, examples provide a flavor of their complexity and diversity. Rarely are they conducted purely in one context and usually there are multiple stakeholder groups involved. Evaluations that are solely conducted in an academic environment will follow university procedures and processes which may or may not include ethical review.

Practitioners, whether focused on clinical, medical, healthcare, educational, or social care, may be involved in an evaluation of a program, service, intervention, or activity. Sometimes the lead of the evaluation team may be an academic. This creates a partnership between a university and another setting. There are various funding bodies that regularly request submissions of proposals that will then be peer-reviewed with successful applications being awarded the funding. However, each university will have its own governance procedures related to evaluations; some will require ethical scrutiny and some will not, for example, if evidence of legal responsibility for the conduct of the evaluation is provided by the commissioner.

If there are small-scale in-house evaluations completed in clinical, medical, healthcare, educational, or any social care settings, these are less likely to follow robust ethical guidelines, but safeguarding and risk assessments should still be an integral part of any participation. There will be safeguarding guidelines and policies that must be adhered to within these settings, but there may or may not be specific ethical guidance.

Those conducting pieces of work outside universities (or organizations with ethical review mechanisms) are often aware of the term "ethics" but do not necessarily think that they can factor it into what they are doing. For example, a clinician or teacher might want to measure the impact the work they do has on the users. Naturally, this can become an element of their day-to-day work and is a relatively informal process, and they may conduct a survey or chat with those involved in the activity to gain some insight and opinions about the impact. This is unlikely to be a robust process and there may be a concern that conducting a formal evaluation will trigger the need for ethical approval. This reluctance means that practitioners may avoid formal evaluations. In these cases, despite not being able to conduct a full ethical review, evaluators can still adhere to general ethical principles to ensure the safety of all evaluation participants.

2 Best Practice: Ethical Considerations in Health Services Evaluations

It is a fact that all evaluations require ethical consideration. However, the myth that all evaluations have to go through ethical scrutiny or be approved by a committee is limiting good-quality evaluations from being undertaken. In this chapter, we explore how ethical principles can be embedded into the design and implementation of any health service evaluation in any context. There are three influential reference documents that have informed professional codes of ethics, internationally: the Nuremberg Code of Ethics (1947), the Declaration of Helsinki (1964, revisions up to 2008) and the Belmont Report (US Department of Health and Human Services 1979).

Six ethical principles that underpin evaluations and enquiry are drawn from these key texts. They are:

- Informed consent (Autonomy).
- Best interests of the participants (Beneficence).
- Maximizing benefits for the evaluation and minimizing risks to the evaluation participants (Non-maleficence).
- Fairness and equity (Justice).
- Protecting the identity of participants (Confidentiality).
- Trust and honesty (Veracity).

Each of these principles must be integrated into any evaluation. In practical terms, this means that actions are taken to ensure that everyone involved in the process knows what they are agreeing to, the best interests of each person are taken into consideration, any risks to well-being are identified and mitigated, the process is fair and equitable, there is trust developed via honesty and steps are taken to protect the identity of participants.

The way that the principles are written down in general ethical guidance is formal and academic. This chapter will consider what each of these principles means in practice so that we can then illustrate with real-life examples. Understanding what the ethical principles mean in practice helps identify the ethical challenges that evaluators face, and then best practice examples provide solutions to remove those barriers, prevent harm and protect well-being.

2.1 "Autonomy" in Practice

When we talk about autonomy in an evaluation we are emphasizing the importance of informed consent. Providing potential participants with clear information to make an informed choice about taking part is of great importance. This is not just to ensure autonomy but it also adds to the credibility of the evaluation findings. If participants feel pressurized in any way to participate in an evaluation, it immediately raises questions regarding bias and the integrity of the data collected.

Informed consent can be a complex process. This can be particularly challenging in health care settings. Every evaluator should consider potential participants vulnerability and how information about the project is provided ahead of any consent process. This may be related to how project information sheets and consent forms are formatted in different ways, for example, language needs, or information by audio or braille. Where an adult is incapable of giving consent, evaluators may consider consulting with those who have a duty of care toward that individual.

Evaluations where children are participants should be undertaken with appropriate assent or consent for the age and abilities of the child. Assent is given by a child who may not be legally in a position to give consent but can be involved in the decision-making process. This can be done by receiving personalized information which aligns with their capacity. Assent, in most cases, is in addition to the consent from a parent or guardian.

Coercion must not be a part of recruitment. To ensure this does not happen, there must be distance between the evaluator and the potential participant, at the point of invitation. For example, a participant must not be "put on the spot" and pressured to decide about their involvement. They should be allowed adequate time to process the information about the study. To facilitate genuine informed consent, it is important that the process allows time, space, and distance to decide about taking part or not. Potentially there can be hidden power dynamics that influence decision-making and this can lead to perceived coercion. If evaluations are introduced to potential participants in a face-to-face situation, it is good practice to provide at least a 24-h gap between invitations to participate and actual recruitment. If any method of incentive is used, for example, a voucher or gift, the study design should ensure that there is a possibility that this can be seen as a coercive method of recruitment. It again brings into question the motivations for participation and the integrity of the data collected. It can be seen as good practice to offer a voucher or gift after data has been collected as a token of thanks rather than offering it up front as an incentive.

If the informed consent process is thorough and transparent, it will add rigor to the evaluation findings. As well as providing information on the aims and objectives of the evaluation, it is usual practice to outline what participants will be asked to do and the time commitment involved in their participation. Other information could include withdrawal mechanisms and how data collected will be used by the evaluator(s).

People will usually remember to gain consent when they are including people in their data collection. However, they may not consider consent in the context of the dissemination of the findings and conclusions. It is important to remember that dissemination can impact participant well-being. How does the participant influence what they say is accurately interpreted? How can they ensure they are truly represented?

To summarize, informed consent for evaluations should include three elements. Firstly, information about the evaluation and the participant's involvement is shared to allow for an informed decision to be made about whether to take part or not. Secondly, processing time and distance from the recruiter are provided before deciding whether to take part or not. Finally, the decision to take part is entirely voluntary.

2.2 "Beneficence" in Practice

Beneficence means taking into consideration the best interests of the participants. For an evaluation to genuinely consider everyone's best interests, then the evaluation should be co-designed and co-produced. Evaluations need to be non-biased, whether commissioned by a funder or by a third party that's interested in knowing the impact of an activity. The way to make sure that your evaluation is robust is to ensure that those who are affected or impacted by the activity that you are evaluating are part of the design. This could be through the setting up of a steering group or a project board where participants are involved right from the outset so that they are influencing the design of the project.

2.3 "Non-maleficence" in Practice

When we talk about non-maleficence in an evaluation, we are wanting to ensure that we are maximizing the benefits of the evaluation and minimizing risks to the evaluation participants and the evaluation team. What is good for a participant might not be good for the commissioner. Benefits for those who are impacted by the activity should drive the evaluation. The priorities in terms of outcomes must come from the participant in co-design so that the evaluator knows what the priorities of those involved are. Your evaluation will be driven by their priorities, not your own priorities and not those of the commissioners. However, in the real world, commissioners may have their own drivers which have to be acknowledged and recognized. In these cases, evaluators need to guide commissioners and ensure that the evaluation is user-centered.

2.4 "Justice" in Practice

When we talk about justice, we are thinking of ways to ensure fairness and equity. Everyone involved in an evaluation should be treated equally. Paying participants for their time in co-production ensures that both evaluators and participants are equal. Barriers to accessing information can cause inequality and the study must be designed taking this into consideration. It is expected that those conducting the evaluation will ensure that their project is accessible to anyone with any difference. Fairness and equity bring into question power dynamics, and any participant or evaluator can be vulnerable compared to the power of the commissioner.

2.5 "Confidentiality" in Practice

Confidentiality means that we must protect the identity of participants. This is not simply the action of removing names from data; it is far more complex than anonymity. Successful evaluations are when participants are fully absorbed in the evaluation process. Participants informing the process is as important as recruiting participants to the study, and if fully absorbed in the project, their input may be recorded and transcribed at any point in the evaluation process. It is important from the outset that participants know what will happen to that data. There must be a clear process in place to reassure participants that they will not be able to be identified in any form of dissemination of the findings. For example, if there is a small sample of participants, individuals may be identifiable just by the fact that they are the only male and only professional or that they are linked to a certain organization. It's important therefore to think more holistically about anonymity, and it is much easier to promise anonymity than confidentiality.

Safeguarding guidance means that if any information is shared by a participant that may compromise their safety or the safety of others, then this has to be recorded and reported and it is essential that participants know the confidentiality clause from the outset before they volunteer to take part.

2.6 "Veracity" in Practice

Veracity in any evaluation refers to the importance of trust and honesty. Not all ethical considerations are addressed straight away at the outset of the project. You can build up trust by ensuring informed consent and throughout the process of data collection, but in reality, the evaluator does not demonstrate full trust and honesty until they have written up the findings and have disseminated them into the public domain, in whatever format that might be, presentation, report, or publication.

Trust and honesty are something that really brings the evaluation timeline to life. Co-design and co-development of the evaluation provides an honest and equal relationship between evaluator and participant, facilitates trust. The participant being involved in every stage of the process, from design to dissemination, means that the evaluator develops a relationship with the co-design participants. Having participants co-design means that the recruited participants will trust the process far more in the knowledge that their voice has been represented. For example, an evaluation of a service developed to support autistic people must be designed by autistic people so that the autistic service users have trust in the process. There will be more trust in the findings if the study is shaped by participants and you can evidence how you have created your evaluation based on the participants.

3 Ethical Challenges in Health Services Evaluations

In this section, we identify potential ethical challenges that evaluators, stakeholders, commissioners and policy-makers face and how to mitigate these risks or challenges.

As with any project that involves multiple stakeholders, it is important to ensure positive and constructive working relationships. These relationships have to be maintained throughout but can naturally be tested at various points during the duration of a project. A specific test point often occurs during the interpretation of the evaluation findings and conclusions. For example, the results of the evaluation may be perceived as being disappointing to the commissioners (or any other party within the team). It takes strength, determination, and honesty for an evaluator to remain uncompromised and independent when there is pressure to edit drafts to display the findings differently. Open communication with commissioners from an early stage to manage their expectations is important.

When an evaluation is reliant on stakeholders working together and following processes, it makes it challenging to estimate timings and follow a scheduled time plan. This is particularly the case when working within settings where there are immense service pressures, for example, health service provision. Governance processes and gaining the necessary permissions to undertake evaluations can have an immediate impact on timeframes and can delay the initial start date. For example, in health service evaluations, permissions may be required across multiple sites with different governance gatekeepers and requirements causing significant delays. From our experience of undertaking evaluations, there are usually set timeframes with tight deadlines. The evaluation may be driven by the need for policy-makers or organizations to find the answers urgently. For example, important decisions on whether to continue or discontinue a specific health service may need to be made within months.

Drafting and editing the report can delay proceedings as often there are multiple stakeholders involved in the process. Waiting for feedback, managing, and making amendments based on others' comments are something that can easily slow the end stages of an evaluation. This can often set challenges that have not been built into evaluation timelines. Time is often underestimated when it comes to incorporating peer review feedback and finalization. From our experience of working in the National Health Service in the United Kingdom, commissioners are reliant on their own approval processes before completion.

Evaluators can be placed under enormous pressure to write reports that are tailored to commissioners' preconceived ideas and expectations. An evaluation must present the findings accurately and without bias. This means that the impact data gathered as part of the evaluation may reveal negative findings rather than fully supporting the service or activity being evaluated. There is always a risk that negative findings may have consequences. Independent evaluators can be placed in difficult situations where key stakeholders are not happy with the evaluation findings and recommendations in the report. Adherence to independence can place immense pressure on working relationships.

Reflection throughout the evaluation process can sometimes lead to the initial evaluation aims needing amends. It is often at the final stage of a project that commissioners realize what they really want to know. Sometimes this can lead to additional requests being made of the evaluators which change the original purpose and objectives. Dealing with any requests for changes slows down the process and can add costs that have not been accounted for.

All evaluations that collect empirical data rely almost entirely on those in the study populations who are willing and prepared to participate. Evaluators want genuine engagement and uncoerced participation. This cannot always be guaranteed but is a relevant issue for any study. When evaluation recruitment is poor and there is a lack of engagement, this creates challenges for policy-making decisions. Evaluation recruitment is challenging in health services where demands on staff are high and pressurized. Ethical recruitment must not be compromised even under the most challenging circumstances.

4 The Integration of Ethics into Health Service Evaluation

To ensure an impactful evaluation protects the wellbeing of participants and evaluators it is essential to embed the six ethical principles into the design of the project. A project that is process-driven will facilitate joint expectations from the outset and allow reflection and review of these throughout the duration of the entire project. If processes are followed and expectations reviewed, then transparency will follow.

Transparency links to communication and the importance that must be placed on the accessibility of information and reporting on every single aspect of the evaluation. Co-designing an evaluation from inception to dissemination allows the voices of the participants to shape the evaluation and the impact measures, adding value, independence, and validity. In short, process, expectations and transparency are key to a successful evaluation that is based on clear ethical foundations.

It is essential to plan for potential ethical challenges when designing and conducting an evaluation. Embedding processes that can mitigate those challenges will lead to a successful evaluation that is grounded in ethical principles. The evaluation must include a protocol. This should include clearly set out study aims, objectives, recruitment processes, risks and mitigation, data collection, and analysis methods, genuine participation and co-production, and a proposed timeline. Agreement should be reached with key stakeholders that the protocol is thorough, realistic and achievable and is recognized as a reference point for all. The protocol should be detailed enough so that it is transferable; for example, someone outside of the evaluation team can use the protocol to undertake the project based on the information it provides. Any subsequent meetings should focus on the agreed protocol to review progress.

A communication plan should also accompany an evaluation protocol. This should include a document outlining roles and responsibilities and ways of working. The evaluation lead, chair of meetings and the main point of contact should be clearly set out. A schedule of meetings should be outlined from inception to dissemination. These regular meetings for all stakeholders are planned to discuss progress, raise issues, answer questions and make joint decisions, and identify opportunities to discuss early findings. Each meeting should have a clear agenda that includes methods of reporting regular updates and progress to complement these meetings. The communication plan should also outline a way of recording early discussions and creating agreed action plans.

A Gantt chart or time schedule will also be needed to initially estimate an agreed timeline presented clearly and visually. Details should include project milestones, realistic time estimates for governance processes, user participation, recruitment, data collection, analysis, drafting and editing, final write-up, and dissemination of the evaluation report.

An assessment identifying potential risks to the evaluation and ways of mitigating these risks also can pre-empt potential problems later on in the project. Outlining a drafting and editing plan also helps all stakeholders to remain aligned throughout the project and mitigate any potential delays in agreed timeframes. This aspect of how commissioners and stakeholders can review first drafts and how evaluators finalize the report is often neglected. From experience, this can be quite a long, drawn-out process that can involve unplanned, unfunded, and hidden work for evaluators. A simple process for draft, review, editing, and finalizing can be agreed at the inception meeting. This element of the evaluation must be factored into the time plan.

Reflective practice should also be actively encouraged for all stakeholders involved in evaluation. Reflection must be an integral part of update meetings. Evaluators need to consider their own support mechanisms from their own employer. The well-being of participants includes the evaluators themselves.

Thinking ahead to how potential disagreements with stakeholders are dealt with is worth consideration from the outset. A complaints process can be drafted to accompany the protocol and supporting documents. This could include a named independent person that any member of the evaluation team can approach. Information for all stakeholders can be shared to signpost to legal, insurance support if there is conflict of opinion especially over presenting the findings.

Finally, a user participation plan can demonstrate how users will lead or co-produce the evaluation. This could include terms of reference for their involvement. Another aspect to consider is providing evidence that there is an equal partnership between the evaluator and the service users in designing, shaping, and executing the evaluation.

5 A Step-by-Step Approach to Embedding Ethical Principles into Health Service Evaluation

The process below is a step-by-step approach to embedding ethical principles into any health service evaluation, whatever the context or the activity. Each activity within an evaluation project is outlined as a step. This chronological list of activities has ethical underpinning, and by noting the "ethical rationale," we can demonstrate how ethical principles are embedded throughout every step of an evaluation.

Throughout the duration of the project, the evaluation should be based on (https://www.who.int/about/values) and evaluators must ensure that:

- People's health and well-being come first.
- Actions and recommendations are independent.
- Decisions are fair, transparent, and timely.
- Highest standards of professionalism are maintained.
- Guided by the best available expertise.
- Engage with everyone honestly.
- Hold ourselves and others accountable.
- Engage with colleagues and partners.
- Recognize the power of diversity to achieve more together.
- Communicate openly with everyone and learn from one another.

- Show compassion for all human beings.
- Strive to make people feel safe, respected, empowered, fairly treated and recognized.

Step 1

Activity: Complete a literature/rapid review of published research, practice guidelines and lived experience on the topic area.

Ethical rationale: Make use of existing evidence to avoid duplication.

Step 2

Activity: Risk analysis (and mitigation).

Ethical rationale: This helps to maximize the benefits of the evaluation and minimize the risks to the evaluation participants and the evaluation team. What is good for a participant might not be good for the commissioner.

Step 3

Activity: Recruit user-led steering group/co-production group including: agreed terms of reference, information about the study, advertising and recruitment plan, ongoing support, and reimbursement.

Ethical rationale: A user-led steering group will ensure genuine participation right from the outset so that they are influencing the design of the project. Evaluation should be co-designed and co-produced if it is to genuinely consider everyone's best interests and increase the credibility of the findings. Evaluations need to be independent, whether commissioned by a funder or by a third party that's interested in knowing the impact of an activity. Ensuring that those who are affected or impacted by the activity that you are evaluating are part of the design increases independence. Paying participants for their time in co-production ensures that both evaluators and participants are equal. Successful evaluations are when participants are fully absorbed in the evaluation process. Participants informing the process is as important as recruiting participants to the study process. The participant being involved in every stage of the process, from design to dissemination, means that the evaluator develops a relationship with the co-design participants. This can increase trust.

Step 4

Activity: Hold an inception meeting with steering/co-production group and all stakeholders. At this meeting, a draft protocol will be discussed, refined and agreed. A plan and project summary document will be signed which sets out expectations, roles, responsibilities, and communication arrangements. A time plan will be verified. Benefits for those who are impacted by the activity should drive evaluation.

Ethical rationale: The priorities in terms of outcomes must come from the participants in co-design so that the evaluator knows what the priorities of that population of people are. Evaluation will be driven by their priorities, not your own priorities and not those of the commissioners. Fairness and equity bring into question power dynamics, any participant or evaluator can be vulnerable compared to the power of the commissioner. Establishing roles at the start sets equality. Having participants involved in the co-design of the evaluation means that the recruited participants will trust the process far more in the knowledge that their voice has been represented. For example, an evaluation of a service developed to support autistic people must be designed by autistic people so that the autistic service users have trust in the process.

Step 5

Activity: A stakeholder meeting to develop a participant recruitment plan. A draft information sheet and consent forms, advertising plans and recruitment options will be discussed and refined with input from users to ensure accessibility. An equality framework should be used to plan for recruitment from hard-to-reach groups.

Ethical rationale: Confidentiality means that we must protect the identity of participants. This is not simply the action of removing names from data; it is far more complex than anonymity. It is important from the outset that participants know what will happen to that data. There must be a clear process in place to reassure participants that they will not be able to be identified in any form of dissemination of the findings; for example, if there is a small sample of participants, individuals may be identifiable just by the fact that they are the only male and only professional or that they are linked to a certain organization. Safeguarding guidance means that if any information is shared by a participant that may compromise their safety or the safety of others, then this has to be recorded and reported and it is essential that participants know the confidentiality clause from the outset before they volunteer to take part.

Clear and accessible information is needed to ensure participants can make an informed choice about taking part. As well as providing information on the aims and objectives of the evaluation, it is usual practice to outline what participants will be asked to do and the time commitment involved in their participation. Other information could include withdrawal mechanisms and how data collected will be used by the evaluator(s). Barriers to accessing information can cause inequality and the study must be designed with this in mind. It is expected that those conducting the evaluation will ensure that their project is accessible to anyone with any difference.

Step 6

Activity: Recruit participants following a recruitment plan that considers accessibility of information, processing time of at least 24 h, incentive methods, recruitment distance between the evaluator and the potential participant, at the point of invitation.

Ethical rationale: If participants feel pressurized in any way to participate in an evaluation, it immediately raises questions regarding bias and the integrity of the data collected. For example, a participant must not be "put on the spot" and pressured to decide about their involvement. Participants should be allowed to process the information about the study. If the informed consent process is thorough and transparent, it will add rigor to the evaluation findings. The recruitment process must allow time, space, and distance so that participants can decide about taking part or not. Potentially there can be hidden power dynamics that influence decision making and this can lead to perceived coercion. If evaluations are introduced to potential participants in a face-to-face situation, it is good practice to provide at least a 24-h gap between invitations to participate and actual recruitment. If any method of incentive is used, for example, a voucher or gift, it brings into question the motivations for participation and the integrity of the data collected. It can be seen as good practice to offer a voucher or gift after data has been collected as a token of thanks rather than offering it up front as an incentive. An honest and equal relationship between evaluator and participant facilitates trust.

Step 7

Activity: Co-production workshop 1—to discuss data collection methods (reaching target audiences and accessibility requirements).

Ethical rationale: Providing potential participants with clear information to make an informed choice about taking part is of great importance to ensure autonomy but also to add credibility to the evaluation findings. If participants feel pressurized in any way to participate in an evaluation, it immediately raises questions regarding bias and the integrity of the data collected.

Step 8

Activity: Data collection.

Ethical rationale: Data collection methods must be accessible to all participants. This can be led by the co-production group.

Step 9

Activity: Data analysis.

Ethical rationale: More than one person analyzing the data creates greater reliability and guards against questions related to the integrity of the findings and mitigating the risk of individual bias and subjectivity.

Step 10

Activity: Co-production workshop 2 (discussing and verifying findings).

Ethical rationale: By discussing the findings with those who use the service, it adds an additional layer of validity and develops an honest and equal relationship between evaluator and participant. It facilitates trust.

Step 11

Activity: Write up findings—draft report and infographics.

Step 12

Activity: Co-production workshop 3—discuss and verify draft report.

Ethical rationale: an honest and equal relationship between evaluator and participant. It facilitates trust.

Step 13

Activity: Amend and finalize the report.

Ethical rationale: The final version of the report needs to address the actions generated from the co-production workshop and further embed the honest and equal relationship between evaluator and participant. It further facilitates trust.

Step 14

Activity: Develop a comprehensive and meaningful dissemination plan and then disseminate findings.

Ethical rationale: Consent in the context of the dissemination of the findings and conclusions. It is important to remember that dissemination can impact participant well-being. How does the participant influence what they say is accurately interpreted? How can the evaluation ensure they are truly represented? Not all ethical considerations are addressed straight away at the outset of the project. You can build up trust by ensuring informed consent and throughout the process of data collection, but in reality, the evaluator does not demonstrate full trust and honesty until they have written up the findings and have disseminated it into the public domain, in whatever format that might be, presentation, report, or publication.

6 Evaluations: Influencing Change

It is important to refer back to the WHO's values that were outlined at the start of this chapter. Good quality and ethically successful evaluations are challenging to undertake. Difficulties can be mitigated by ensuring that there are clearly defined aims, objectives, a realistic time schedule, clear roles and responsibilities, and excellent communication channels. Genuine participation and co-production, led by users, are essential in all evaluations to ensure the findings are meaningful and purposeful to health service organizations and policy-makers.

We must reflect on how we ensure that evaluation is maximized by health service organizations and policy-makers. Evaluation should never be viewed as an add-on or tick-box exercise. It should be an integral design element of all programs, models, interventions and services. Evaluators and users should be part of early discussions to help scope out impact measures.

Evaluations can only influence change in policy-making by aligning with the values outlined by the World Health Organization. Priority must be given to independence, fairness, transparency, excellence, professionalism, best available expertise, integrity, accountability, partnership, and communication. These values along with the ethical principles outlined in this chapter are not solely for evaluators but for everyone involved in the evaluation process from commissioning, design, and dissemination.

References

Asia Pacific Evaluation Association (2023) Code of ethics for evaluation in the Asia Pacific Region. https://asiapacificeval.org/wp-content/uploads/2023/09/Code-of-Ethics-for-the-Asia-Pacific-Region_Sep_23.pdf

Cambridge Dictionary (2023). https://dictionary.cambridge.org/dictionary/english/ethic

Canadian Evaluation Society (2020). https://evaluationcanada.ca/career/ethical-guidance.html

Declaration of Helsinki (2008). https://www.wma.net/what-we-do/medical-ethics/declaration-of-helsinki/
Nurnberg Military Tribunals Indictments Cases 1-12 (1947) [Nuremberg: Office of Military Government for Germany US, to 1948] [pdf]. Retrieved from the Library of Congress. https://www.loc.gov/item/2011525463/
UNEG (2012) Norms for evaluation in the UN system. United Nations Evaluation Group, New York, NY. (http://www.uneval.org/papersandpubs/documentdetail.jsp?doc_id=21. Accessed 24 Oct 2024) as cited in World Health Organization (2013) WHO Evaluation Practice Handbook. https://iris.who.int/bitstream/handle/10665/96311/9789241548687_eng.pdf;sequence=1
US Department of Health and Human Services (1979) Belmont report. https://www.hhs.gov/ohrp/regulations-and-policy/belmont-report/read-the-belmont-report/index.html
World Health Organisation (2024) Our values, our DNA. https://www.who.int/about/values

Evaluation Theory and Methods

Principles-Focused Evaluation of Health Services

Amy Salmon, Ihoghosa Iyamu, M. Elizabeth Snow, and Mai Berger

Abstract

Principles-focused evaluation (PFE) is an emergent approach to evaluation in health care. It is useful for evaluating health services where principles guide implementations and adaptations across different contexts, in complex situations, and when preparing to scale a program or intervention up or out. Unlike evaluation approaches emphasizing standardized performance indicators, outputs, and outcomes, PFE examines the meaningfulness of principles guiding the program, how the principles are enacted, and associated outcomes.

In this chapter, we discuss the process of conducting a PFE, including developing evaluation questions and effectiveness principles and designing methods to collect, analyze, and interpret data. We describe characteristics of health services that make them amenable to PFE and those that do not, as well as the strengths and limitations of this evaluation approach.

Keywords

Principles-focused evaluation · Developmental evaluation

A. Salmon (✉) · I. Iyamu · M. Elizabeth Snow
Centre for Advancing Health Outcomes, University of British Columbia, Vancouver, BC, Canada

School of Population and Public Health, University of British Columbia, Vancouver, Canada
e-mail: asalmon@advancinghealth.ubc.ca; miyamu@cheos.ubc.ca; bsnow@cheos.ubc.ca

M. Berger
First Nations Health Authority, Vancouver, BC, Canada
e-mail: mai.berger@fnha.ca

A. Kaehne, J. Feather (eds.), *Handbook of Health Services Evaluation*,
https://doi.org/10.1007/978-3-031-87869-5_5

1 Introduction

Principles-focused evaluation (PFE) is an emerging evaluation approach that has gained relevance in health systems and services settings. In these settings, program planners, system decision-makers, and clinicians frequently adopt principles to guide actions and decisions towards overarching goals. Such principles draw on the health services' beliefs, experiences, norms, knowledge, and identity (Norman 2023; Wolfe 2020). This is especially relevant for health care initiatives that are implemented within or across multiple, differing contexts. While the goals of a health service may remain the same across contexts, adaptation to each context will be necessary for success. Principles help guide the health service's thinking toward the specified goals of the initiatives while acknowledging differences in implementation required across contexts. The principles may be articulated initially as mission statements, guiding principles, values, or other variants of the term. Whatever their form, principles become the critical wayfinder in defining collaborations and designing and implementing constituent plans in alignment with contextual realities. They indeed become a stable way and inspiration to achieve desired results despite the surrounding complexity (Bailie et al. 2022; Norman 2023; Patton 2018).

Herein lies the power of PFE, especially in services that already use "principles" either formally or intuitively to make decisions about how to plan, implement, and assess their work (Patton 2021). Rather than evaluating the health service as is traditionally done, PFE focuses on the principles as the evaluand (Patton 2018). A PFE examines the clarity, meaningfulness, and actionability of principles used to guide a health service; the extent to which principles are adhered to; and the outcomes that result from adhering to the principles (Patton 2018). PFE was originally seen as a type of developmental evaluation but evolved to become an evaluation approach in its own right. It can be applied in developmental, formative (process), and summative (outcome) evaluations. It provides useful data to support evaluative thinking to provide an added sense of direction in such complex contexts.

It is important to highlight our definition of principles, given their varied use in diverse contexts. The Oxford Dictionary defines principles as "*a fundamental truth or proposition that serves as the foundation for a system of belief or behavior or for a chain of reasoning*" (Hornby 1995). An astute observer will identify various principles at play in the world around them. For example, natural principles explain how the natural world works. Other principles might guide how we interact with others around us and with our environment (Patton 2018). For example, moral principles guide our understanding of what actions are right or wrong. Contrastingly, effectiveness principles tell us how to think/act to achieve a desired outcome, based on norms, values, and knowledge (Patton 2018). Effectiveness principles do not prescribe a specific course of action, rather they provide a framework for thinking and acting in specific contexts (Patton 2018). Rules, on the other hand, provide precise prescriptions on what to do in specific situations. They do not allow a person or an agent to make decisions about the situation.

For PFEs, effectiveness principles (EP) become the evaluands and the hypotheses that are tested (Patton 2018). This offers advantages to an evaluator in complex contexts, because the effectiveness principles are a stable definition of the "intervention," regardless of the diversity of activities and inputs required to implement the service in different contexts (Casey et al. 2023; Patton 2021). In a PFE, these principles can be evaluated in terms of their design (are the principles clear, meaningful, and actionable?), the process (was the principle followed?), and the outcome (was the intended result accomplished when the principle was followed?).

PFE has particular utility when supporting decision-making in initiatives that are situated within complex dynamic systems. Complex dynamic systems are defined by multiple conditions. These include *non-linearity* (meaning that the addition of individual constituents of the program, initiative, or service (hereafter referred to as health service) does not sufficiently describe the whole), *feedback and interconnection* (in which changes in one aspect of the system may result in unintended and sometimes unpredictable changes in other parts of the system through their mutual interactions), *temporal flexibility* (meaning that time and space affect the parts and their relations differently), and *flexible negotiated boundaries* (where the limits of the system are fuzzy or can change over time based on the perception of the actors within the system) (Ladyman et al. 2013; Norman 2023).

In such complex systems, an additional challenge to evaluators rests in the recognition that cause and effect cannot necessarily be ascribed linearly (Patton 2018; Turner and Cromhout 2020). For example, in a traditional formative or summative evaluation, we might elucidate our understanding of a health service by drawing on an "if-then" logic. We may suggest that under a set of assumptions or conditions, *if* specific activities are implemented using specific inputs, *then* we expect specified outputs that lead to specified outcomes, which in turn lead to the health service's anticipated outcomes (Savaya and Waysman 2005). These propositions are commonly articulated as a logic model or a theory of change. The implied understanding is that there is a stepwise sequence of events that we can logically elucidate to determine cause and effect. However, in complexity contexts, other mediating factors typically have a substantial influence on outcomes, and these mediators are often well outside the implementers' locus of control. These factors may also mediate how an intervention is implemented and, therefore, must be accounted for when assessing if something was implemented as planned. In contemporary health systems and services evaluations, this is often found to be the case. Delivering healthcare today involves numerous interacting elements, including people, technologies, policies, natural and built environments, supply chains, social determinants of health, and the broader economic, cultural, and political contexts in which needs for care are determined and responded to; all of these are continuously in flux and influence one another in ways that evolve over time and in ways that are often not under the direct control of a health system, service, or program. This interconnectedness and constant change create a landscape where outcomes and processes are often unpredictable and require adaptive response strategies. It is here where PFE can be a useful tool for evaluators working with health systems and care providers.

In this chapter, we describe the utility of PFE in health services and pre-requisite contexts for a successful PFE. We also describe our perspectives on the process for conducting a PFE of health services, including creating EPs, collecting appropriate data to evaluate EPs, and approaches to evaluate the data. We have drawn on our experiences implementing PFEs of health services to highlight these steps at a high level. However, this chapter is neither intended to be an exhaustive account of PFEs of health services nor is it intended to be prescriptive. We have constrained our discussion to an overview of what evaluators might encounter in a PFE. Readers may consult Patton's (2018) *Principles-Focused Evaluation: The Guide* for more detail.

2 PFE of Health Services and Systems

Recently, health services have begun to move toward adopting principles to guide their attempts to transform their delivery of care within complex health systems (Iyamu et al. 2021). Common examples of such principles promoting person-centered care, trauma-informed care, evidence-informed practice, and ensuring equity, accessibility, anti-racism, and social justice in healthcare systems (Iyamu et al. 2021; Wolfe 2020). Many of these health services are scaled up (or intended for scale-up) across varied contexts and implemented by multiple different partners where adaptation to the local context is essential (Casey et al. 2023; Iyamu et al. 2021). These health services are often implemented in complex, dynamic, and interconnected contexts where the implementers must adapt based on pre-specified principles (Patton 2021). Therefore, these programs and initiatives can exhibit obvious differences despite being created based on similar principles. As a result, a straight line cannot necessarily be drawn between an observed cause and observed effect, with a great deal of complexity inherent in the change. It is in these cases where PFE is particularly useful, as it provides a flexible framework to help assess the meaningfulness and relevance of the principles implementers rely on, the extent to which they adhere to the principles, and the results observed when these principles are followed. These PFEs are designed, conducted, and reported with the intention that the results can be used, as that feedback from the evaluation will frequently inform subsequent adaptations to the principles or to the process for implementing the principles (Iyamu et al. 2021; Patton 2021). This aligns with the well-established practice of continuous quality improvement within health services and systems. There are examples of PFEs in mental health, long-term care (Iyamu et al. 2021), and integrated community care (Vandensande 2020).

2.1 Pre-requisite Conditions for PFE of Health Services

Not all principles-guided programs or initiatives may be amenable to a PFE. It is important to begin a PFE with an initial assessment of the program or initiative to ensure that a PFE will likely be successful in generating the evidence required. Here we provide an overview of pre-requisite conditions to be met before considering a PFE. This list is based on our reflections from our practice and is in no way exhaustive. However, we would recommend careful consideration of the appropriateness of a PFE approach if any of these conditions are not present.

1. *Collaborators' commitment to promoting and implementing their program or initiative based on principles*: to evaluate the design, process, and outcomes of principles in a program, it must be clear that there is a shared commitment among the collaborators to those principles. Commonly, programs or initiatives may have principles listed as part of their promotional materials or marketing, but their implementation may not necessarily account for these principles. For a PFE to be successful, it should be apparent that the principles are promoted and considered across the design, implementation, and evaluation of the program or initiative.
2. *Alignment of program or initiative principles with the GUIDE criteria or collaborators' openness to adapt the principles to these criteria if necessary*: assess the existing principles using Patton's GUIDE criteria. In many cases, the principles may not be aligned to all the criteria, especially in terms of their evaluability. Where this occurs, assess how open collaborators are to adapting the existing principles. Also, assess how committed they are to using the new principles in their practice. This applies mainly in a developmental evaluation context.
3. *Flexibility of the program or initiative to allow program strategies and activities to be adapted to the local context based on the principles*: this is important for large-scale health programs and initiatives implemented across various sites. These sites may have different contexts and serve different populations. Principles may need to be applied differently in each context. However, the reasoning and methods supporting the local adaptations must be apparent. It is also important to clarify that the reporting systems are aligned with the principles.
4. *Buy-in from collaborators (including funders) about the utility of PFE to their processes*: PFE is a relatively new approach of which not all evaluation partners, collaborators, or funders may be aware. This might become challenging in cases where collaborators do not see its utility for their work. It is important to clarify that there is a shared understanding of what a PFE is, and how it might contribute to their understanding of their program or initiative.

3 Conducting a PFE

3.1 Creating Effectiveness Principles

We have described effectiveness principles as the evaluand in PFEs. To begin a PFE, an evaluator should identify or co-create effectiveness principles using the GUIDE framework (Patton 2018). This means that effectiveness principles should provide clear **G**uidance about actions in the program, be **U**seful for informing decisions and actions, be **I**nspirational, be **D**evelopmental or adaptable to each context, and be **E**valuable (Fig. 1). Patton describes a ten-step process (Patton 2018), summarized in Fig. 1.

Our four-step process summarizes the process in a systematic way. It has been described in detail elsewhere (Iyamu et al. 2021).

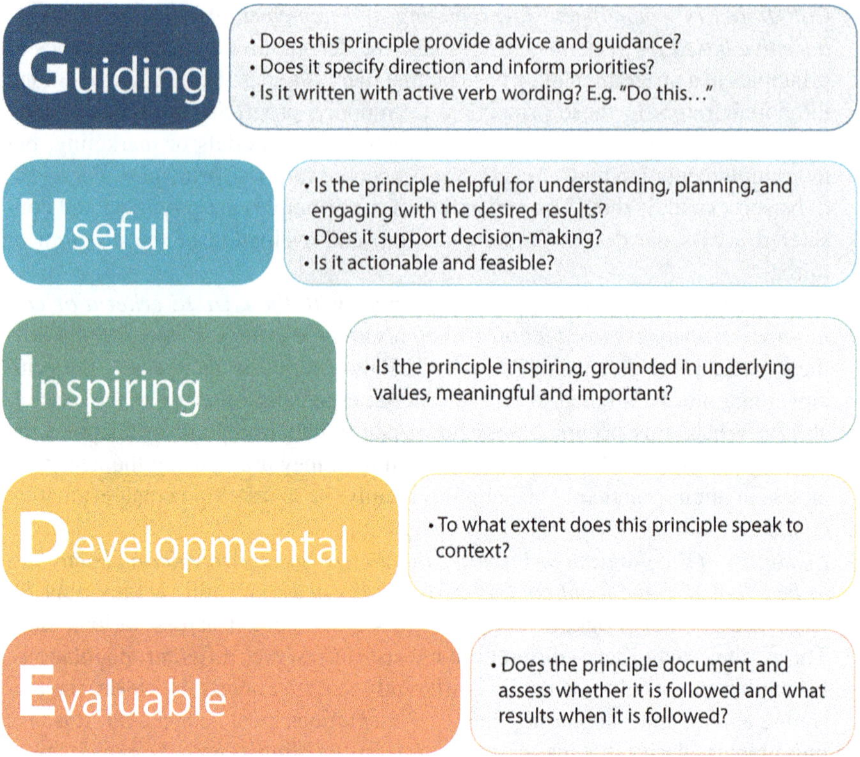

Fig. 1 GUIDE acronym and mnemonic. GUIDE indicates that an effectiveness principle must (**a**) provide Guidance, (**b**) be Useful, (**c**) Inspire, (**d**) support ongoing Development, and (**e**) be Evaluable. (Figure adapted from Patton 2018)

1. *Engaging partners and collaborators for a PFE*: identifying and engaging all relevant partners and collaborators is ideally the first step of most evaluations. For PFE, the evaluator will need to clarify this approach and its focus on principles as the evaluand. The utility and flexibility of the approach must be emphasized in this case. As described in the previous section, the goal is to achieve a shared understanding of the value of the PFE. Through engagement, existing principles (if any) may be reviewed to see if they need to be adapted to the GUIDE criteria. In such cases, careful engagement may be required to ensure all understand the need to reframe the principles and commit to the new versions.
2. *Reviewing underlying theories, values, and evidence*: to create effectiveness principles, underpinning values that guide or inspire decisions and actions must be understood. This process helps to get at "how health programs or initiatives are being implemented" (Balmer et al. 2023; Iyamu et al. 2021). It involves reviewing program documents, theories on which the programs or initiatives are built, and potentially collecting data through surveys, interviews, and observations (Balmer et al. 2023). All these activities aim to explore principles expressed in the program or initiative. Some evaluators describe using storytelling

approaches where they encourage implementers to describe successes in their program while focusing on "how things were done" (Casey et al. 2023). Even when principles are already laid out in the program or initiative, this process can help to identify unspoken values that influence decision-making, as well as the ways in which different principles might be interrelated or mutually reinforcing.

3. *Drafting effectiveness principles*: the effectiveness principles are usually drafted collaboratively. The draft principles should be made with close consideration of the GUIDE framework and should draw on the output from stage 2. Consider the interrelation and interdependence of the principles during the process. In situations where there are already existing principles, the drafting process may involve reframing the principles to be more in line with the GUIDE framework and more connected to the evidence from stage 2. This may also be the opportunity to add principles that reflect the unspoken values identified in previous stages or those that ensure the principles are exhaustive for the context (Casey et al. 2023).
4. *Reviewing and finalizing effectiveness principles using the GUIDE criteria*: The draft principles must be reviewed in collaboration with all parties to the evaluation. Commonly, this may be done as a workshop or any other shared discussion where initial evidence and experiences are reviewed in comparison with the list. The GUIDE criteria can be used to achieve a consensus that the effectiveness principles meet the criteria from all perspectives and can now be deployed in the program or initiative. This process could also include a prioritization process to help the evaluator determine how much resources may be allocated to each effectiveness principle during the evaluation (Casey et al. 2023).

3.2 Choosing the Evaluation Design and Methods for a PFE

There are three types of assessment involved in PFEs. These include evaluating the meaningfulness and usefulness of EPs, determining the degree to which the EPs are being adhered to, and assessing how adhering to the EPs may be associated with achieving certain outcomes or impacts (Patton 2018; Casey et al. 2023). Regardless of the assessment type, there is no standard or preferred method for conducting a PFE (Patton 2018). The methods used to collect, analyze, and interpret data will depend on various factors such as the evaluation questions, the purpose and goals of the evaluation, and the attributes of the intervention (e.g., What data is available for collection?).

For the first type of assessment, evaluators may assess the EPs themselves by applying the GUIDE criteria and refining them using processes similar to those described in step 4 of creating EPs. In addition to using workshops and other collaborative strategies, evaluators may interview or conduct surveys about the meaningfulness or usefulness of EPs using the GUIDE criteria. An interview guide used for this purpose would contain open-ended questions based on the GUIDE criteria, and collaborators would be asked to evaluate each EP based on this framework.

Similarly, a survey used for this purpose may ask respondents to rate each EP against the GUIDE criteria.

For the other two types of assessment, evaluators may create an evaluation matrix with indicators for each EP that can be measured quantitatively and/or qualitatively as well as options for evidence to collect and analyze. The matrix can provide guidance on measuring how well these EPs are adhered to or the results or impact of adherence. The matrix may be developed collaboratively, as demonstrated by Casey et al. (2023) who used a World Café approach to craft indicators for each of their principles. The indicators should be specific, measurable, and linked to the EPs. To avoid evaluation fatigue and maximize the output of data collection efforts, it is recommended that evaluators make note of existing and practical data sources (such as routinely collected data) in their matrix whenever possible. It is also important to note that while an evaluation matrix can help standardize the evaluation process across different sites, the development of shared indicators may also limit the flexibility and applicability of the evaluation (as noted by Casey et al. 2023).

After creating the evaluation matrix and corresponding indicators, evaluators need to identify or develop data collection tools to assess the specific EPs that are being examined. For qualitative assessment, evaluators may create an interview or focus group guide that includes questions directly related to each of the EPs. Another approach might be to interview participants about their experiences and reflections on a program or intervention and then analyze (or code) the data for evidence of the principles being adhered to impacting outcomes (Patton 2018). For quantitative indicators, evaluators may identify and measure variables that align with each EP using established, valid, and reliable measurement instruments. Should such instruments be unavailable or inappropriate for the study context, evaluators may develop their own. For instance, Casey et al. (2023) designed a survey instrument for practitioners to self-assess whether they were implementing and actively using the EPs. In PFEs, it is essential that data collection procedures align with the principles being evaluated. For example, Bailie et al. (2022) conducted a PFE using an inductive qualitative approach that was appropriate for Indigenous settings and for addressing questions that had little prior research.

As in the case with data collection, data analysis procedures should also be tailored to align with EPs. To gain a comprehensive understanding, we encourage evaluators to use a mixed-method approach to data collection and analysis. For qualitative analysis of PFEs, data is generally coded systematically to identify recurring themes and patterns that are directly related to the EPs. Framework analysis, as demonstrated by Bailie et al. (2022), can be useful for this purpose as it allows for the systematic coding of data as they relate to specific EPs. For quantitative data, statistical techniques should assess the extent to which the principles have been implemented and their impact on desired outcomes. Findings should be contextualized within the specific EPs being assessed, and broader contextual factors that may influence the extent to which principles are adhered to should be considered, such as external political or economic factors, organizational culture, and/or resource constraints.

Table 1 provides a sample of a short evaluation matrix linked to the effectiveness principles, drawn from a PFE our team completed in a long-term care home setting in Canada (Salmon et al. 2023). In this PFE, we worked with the team to identify effectiveness principles and the anticipated outcomes evaluation partners expected to see as a result of following those principles. Then, our team identified measures and data sources from existing administrative data sets (the Inter-RAI MDS), standardized tools (the McGill Quality of Life Questionnaire), clinical records (e.g., care planning documents, resident health assessments), and needs for additional qualitative data collection that mapped onto each dimension of the matrix.

3.3 Strengths and Limitations of PFE

In this section, we review the strengths and limitations of PFE, drawing on insights from our own experience and those documented in the literature. By understanding both its advantages and constraints, evaluators can make informed decisions when applying PFE to their contexts.

3.3.1 Strengths

- *Applicable across multiple sites*: One of the main strengths of PFE is its adaptability across diverse and complex settings. PFE enables evaluators to assess interventions operating in different sites that may share common principles yet vary in contextual features.
- *Identification of shared effectiveness principles*: PFE enables the identification of shared EPs among various organizations or stakeholders. This can foster a common understanding of values and standards within a community or setting. For instance, Casey et al. (2023) identified common EPs for sexual violence prevention practitioners in their various communities of practice.
- *Collaborative and empowering approach*: The process of identifying EPs can empower practitioners by drawing on their wisdom, expertise, and values. This makes evaluation efforts more practice-centered and engaging. As highlighted by Casey et al. (2023), practitioners felt more empowered through the process of developing EPs. Additionally, involving individuals with diverse expertise such

Table 1 Sample PFE evaluation matrix (Salmon et al. 2023)

Guiding	Does the principle provide guidance and advice? Does it specify direction and inform priorities? Is it written using active verbs? E.g. "Do this…"
Useful	Is the principle helpful for understanding, planning, and engaging with desired results? Does it support decision-making? Is it actionable and feasible?
Inspiring	Is the principle inspiring, grounded in underlying values? Is it meaningful and important?
Developmental	To what extent does this principle speak to context?
Evaluable	Does the principle enable one to document and assess whether it is followed? What are the anticipated results of following the principle?

as implementation, research, evaluation, policy, etc., can contribute to the development of EPs that are comprehensive and grounded in local and cultural contexts. This is evident in Balmer et al., where a range of expertise contributed to comprehensive EPs.

- *Flexibility and adaptability*: PFE allows for flexibility in the evaluation approach by tailoring EPs based on emergent feedback, making it suitable for adapting to changing contexts and program needs. This adaptability is seen in Balmer et al., where guiding principles were revised based on feedback.
- *Potential for integration with existing QI and evaluation measures*: PFE can complement existing quality improvement and evaluation measures, as demonstrated by Balmer et al.

3.3.2 Limitations

- *Dependent on buy-in*: Successful PFE implementation depends on the support and buy-in of leadership and funders who are committed to working within a PFE approach. Bailie et al. emphasized the importance of buy-in in their Indigenous evaluation context. In publicly funded health systems contexts, buy-in can be challenged if government requirements for evaluations orient assessments toward pre-determined performance metrics that may not align meaningfully or appropriately with EPs.
- *Complexity in formulating principles*: Identifying, formulating, and defining high-quality EPs can be challenging, which can affect the successful application of a PFE. Duncan et al. discussed this as part of their experience using PFE.
- *Potential bias*: In contexts where the same group that created the principles assesses their relevance and usefulness, there is a potential for bias as practitioners may be reluctant to critique their own work. This is particularly challenging if the evaluation shows adhering to EPs does not lead to intended outcomes. Casey et al. acknowledged this potential bias.
- *Resource constraints*: The time and resource-intensive nature of PFE can be a challenge, particularly for organizations with limited resources or tight timelines. Balmer et al. highlighted resource constraints in their implementation of PFE, especially due to the need for continuous focus on the EPs.

4 Conclusion

PFE is an emergent, flexible, and innovative approach to evaluating principles-driven programs and initiatives that are embracing complexity at scale. Like any evaluation approach, PFEs must be carefully constructed and implemented. Considering the utility of EPs in the evaluation context and identifying the presence of necessary prerequisite conditions that can support success, are critical when planning a PFE in any context, including health systems and services evaluations. Following a PFE approach also presents unique methodological considerations for data collection and analysis.

References

Bailie J, Cunningham F, Abimbola S, et al. Methodological pluralism for better evaluations of complex interventions: lessons from evaluating an innovation platform in Australia. Health Res Policy Syst. 2022;20(1):14. https://doi.org/10.1186/s12961-022-00814-5

Balmer DF, Anderson H, West DC (2023) Program evaluation in health professions education: an innovative approach guided by principles. Acad Med 98(2):204–208. https://doi.org/10.1097/ACM.0000000000005009

Campbell R, Munford A, Moylan CA, PettyJohn ME, Schweda K, Fedewa T, Rosen H, Ferguson MA, Beal J, Buchanan NT (2023) Creating a university strategic plan to address relationship violence and sexual misconduct (RVSM): an application of principles-focused evaluation at Michigan State University. Violence Against Women 29(1):3–34. https://doi.org/10.1177/10778012221130106

Casey EA, Vanslyke J, Beadnell B, Tatiana Masters N, McFarland K (2023) The process of applying principles-focused evaluation to the sexual violence prevention field: implications for practice in other social services fields. Am J Eval 44(3):374–393. https://doi.org/10.1177/10982140211056935

Hornby AS (1995). Oxford Advanced Learner's Dictionary of Current English [by] A.S. Hornby. In: Jonathan C (ed). Oxford, England: Oxford University Press

Iyamu I, Berger M, Ono E, Salmon A (2021) Creating effectiveness principles for principles-focused developmental evaluations in health-care initiatives: lessons learned from three cases in British Colombia. Can J Program Eval 36(1):64–81. https://doi.org/10.3138/cjpe.70804

Ladyman J, Lambert J, Wiesner K (2013) What is a complex system? Eur J Philos Sci *3*(1):33–67. https://doi.org/10.1007/s13194-012-0056-8

Norman C (2023) Systems and complexity: implications for evaluation. Censemaking: the innovation cafe. https://censemaking.com/2022/08/10/systems-and-complexity-implications-for-evaluation/

Patton MQ (2018) Principles-focused evaluation: the GUIDE. Guildford Press, New York

Patton MQ (2021) Principles-focused evaluation for agroecology. Elementa Sci Anthropocene 9(1):00052. https://doi.org/10.1525/elementa.2021.00052

Salmon A, Iyamu I, Easterbrook A, Sawatsky R, Zhang W, Guh D (2023) Protocol for the evaluation of home for us and providence living at the views. Centre for Advancing Health Outcomes, Vancouver, BC

Savaya R, Waysman M (2005) The logic model: a tool for incorporating theory in development and evaluation of programs. Adm Soc Work 29(2):85–103. https://doi.org/10.1300/J147v29n02_06

Turner RE, Cromhout PB (2020) Case study used to guide the development of effectiveness principles for principles-focused evaluation. Afr Eval J 8(1):1–6. https://doi.org/10.4102/aej.v8i1.416

Vandensande T (2020) Starting the transition towards integrated community care 4all. Int J Integr Care 20(2):18. https://doi.org/10.5334/ijic.5553

Wolfe SM (2020) Using a principles-focused evaluation approach to evaluate coalitions and collaboratives working toward equity and social justice. New Dir Eval 165:45–65. https://doi.org/10.1002/ev.20404

Realist Evaluation of Health Services: Principles, Processes, and Potential

Julie Feather

Abstract

Realist evaluation is a theory-driven approach that has gained increasing popularity in recent years, particularly for evaluating complex healthcare programs. This chapter provides an overview of its application in health service evaluation. It begins with a description of the underlying principles that shape realist evaluation followed by a detailed discussion of the various stages within the evaluation cycle and its practical use in assessing health services. The chapter concludes by examining the strengths and limitations of this methodology, along with its broader contribution to health service evaluation.

Keywords

Realist evaluation · Healthcare program · Theory-driven evaluation · Program development · Program implementation

1 Introduction

Realist evaluation originated from the work of British sociologists Ray Pawson and Nick Tilley. In 1997, they published their seminal work *Realistic Evaluation* in which they introduced the approach and provided a theoretical and methodological framework for evaluators to use (Pawson and Tilley 1997). Pawson and Tilley (1997) developed realist evaluation as an alternative to the prevailing positivist approach, which focuses on understanding the world through objective facts, and scientific observations, as well as the experimental evaluation paradigm which

J. Feather (✉)
Evaluation and Policy Analysis (EPA) Unit, Edge Hill University, Ormskirk, UK
e-mail: featherj@edgehill.ac.uk

A. Kaehne, J. Feather (eds.), *Handbook of Health Services Evaluation*,
https://doi.org/10.1007/978-3-031-87869-5_6

focuses on understanding the world through controlled experiments and observation (Wong et al. 2017). Pawson and Tilley (1997) urged evaluators to move beyond the traditional experimental evaluation approach, which assumes a positivist understanding of cause and effect, to a realist account of causation which attempts to understand the underlying mechanisms and contextual factors that influence program outcomes. Over recent years, realist evaluation has gained increasing popularity as it provides a deeper understanding of healthcare programs and interventions, focusing not only on whether they are effective but also on why and how they work within specific contexts.

Realist evaluation is a theory-based approach as opposed to an outcomes-focused approach. This means it aims to understand why programs succeed or fail (Astbury and Leeuw 2010). Program theory is used to guide the evaluation from beginning to end. Realist evaluation's distinguishing feature is its application of realist thinking to its evaluation design (Westhorp 2014). Using a model of generative causation, which focuses on understanding the processes that lead to outcomes, realist evaluation—guided by critical realism—seeks to explain how and why programs work, for whom, and in what circumstances (Astbury 2013). Realist evaluation structures program theory around three fundamental realist concepts: context, mechanisms, and outcomes. It brings these three concepts together to form context-mechanism-outcome configurations (CMOc) which are used to guide the evaluation process. Definitions of key realist concepts discussed throughout this chapter are included in Table 1. The underlying principles of realist evaluation and realist concepts are described in more detail in Sect. 2.

Realist evaluation's understanding of the relationship between context, mechanisms, and outcomes makes it a good fit for the evaluation of health services due to the complex nature of healthcare programs and the complex social systems in which they are implemented. Healthcare programs are often made up of multiple components, such as various treatment modalities, organizational changes, or behavioral

Table 1 Definitions of realist concepts used in realist evaluation

Context	Features of the situation into which programs are introduced that affect how the program's mechanisms work. Features of contexts may include social, material, psychological, economic, organizational, and technical aspects
Mechanism	Mechanisms consist of the interaction between resources offered by the program and the interpretations and actions of participants to those resources
Outcome	Outcomes are the intended, unintended, or unexpected outcomes from the program
Context-mechanism-outcome configuration (CMOc)	A heuristic framework used to display program theories and explain what works, for whom, under which circumstances, and how
Program theory	The theoretical underpinning of a program which explains how the program works to produce outcomes. Program theories can alternatively be presented as "if-then-because" propositions

Source: http://ramesesproject.org/Standards_and_Training_materials.php#re_training

strategies, which interact in intricate ways (Skivington et al. 2021). They are highly context-dependent, and their outcomes are shaped by the context in which they are implemented. Approaches to evaluating healthcare programs should account for such complexity. Realist evaluation stands out as a useful approach to the evaluation of complex healthcare programs for several reasons. Firstly, it embraces the complexity of healthcare programs by examining the interactions between program components and contextual factors, moving beyond simplistic cause-and-effect relationships (Skivington et al. 2021). Secondly, it recognizes the critical role of context in shaping program outcomes, aiming to uncover how mechanisms existing within a program interact with specific contexts to produce outcomes (Pawson and Tilley 1997). Thirdly, it focuses on identifying the causal mechanisms that drive program outcomes, offering valuable insights into how and why healthcare programs achieve their outcomes (Skivington et al. 2021). Finally, it enables evaluators to gain a deeper understanding of the logic behind healthcare programs and the environments in which they are implemented, through the development of program theories. The advantages of using realist evaluation to evaluate healthcare programs are discussed in more detail in Sect. 4.

This chapter offers readers an introductory exploration of the realist evaluation approach. While the chapter provides an overview of the process involved in undertaking a realist evaluation, it is important to note that it is not a comprehensive "how to do it" guide and it does not offer step-by-step instructions for conducting a realist evaluation. Instead, it provides an overview of key foundational principles underpinning realist evaluation (Sect. 2) and practical examples of how it has been applied when evaluating healthcare programs (Sect. 3). It further highlights some of the strengths and limitations of realist evaluation (Sect. 4). Readers are encouraged to consult additional sources particularly Pawson and Tilley's (1997) *Realistic Evaluation* and Emmel et al.'s (2018) *Doing Realist Research*.

2 Understanding How Realist Evaluation Works

This section explores the mechanisms of realist evaluation, offering the reader a clearer insight into how it helps us understand how healthcare programs create change. It delves into the fundamental principles that guide realist evaluation including how it conceptualizes healthcare programs and how it investigates the causes behind program outcomes. It introduces the reader to key realist concepts including "mechanisms," "contexts," "outcomes," and "CMOc."

2.1 How a Realist Evaluation Approach Allows the Evaluator to See Beyond the Surface

The realist evaluation approach focuses on why and how programs produce their outcomes. It recognizes the enormous amount of work that happens within programs to produce resulting outcomes, and it seeks to understand the deeper layers of programs uncovering the hidden mechanisms that shape their outcomes. This way of viewing programs is particularly useful in a healthcare context as it can help evaluators to better understand the complexities of healthcare programs and identify how they work, for which groups of patients, and under what circumstances.

Realist evaluation draws on critical realism to offer an understanding of how programs produce their outcomes. Critical realism is a philosophical perspective that suggests there is more to reality than what we can directly see or observe (Sayer 2010; de Souza 2014).

According to Bhaskar (1978), a prominent figure in critical realism, reality consists of three interconnected levels: the real, the actual, and the empirical. This is illustrated in Fig. 1. Bhaskar (1978) suggests that the "real level" contains structures and mechanisms which shape the outcomes that we observe at the "empirical level." These structures and mechanisms are not visible to the human eye; however, they exist and act independently of human knowledge and experience, and the outcomes they generate (Bhaskar 1978). When triggered in the right conditions, these structures and mechanisms set off a series of events at the "actual level" (Pawson 2013; de Souza 2014). These events happen whether we notice them or not and may differ from what we directly observe (Fletcher 2017). This is because our observations are influenced by how we interpret and experience things (Fletcher 2017). So, what we see and experience in our everyday lives makes up the empirical level (de Souza 2014) as seen in Fig. 1.

At this stage you may be thinking "but how does this relate to realist evaluation and the way in which it conceptualizes healthcare programs?" Let's look at this aspect in more detail. Realist evaluation conceptualizes healthcare programs as complex systems with hidden mechanisms that exist within the "real level." Although these mechanisms are not always visible, they are "real" and are crucial

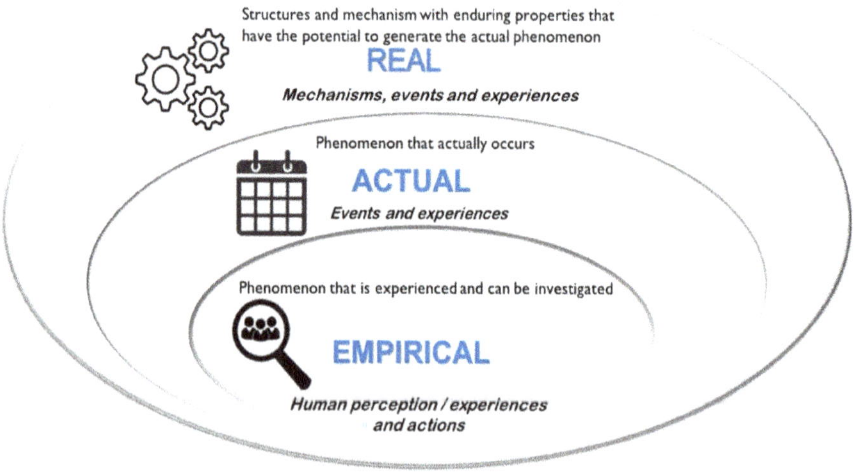

Fig. 1 Ontological positions of realist philosophy (Mukumbang et al. 2019, p. 489)

for understanding how programs work. Realist evaluators seek to uncover these underlying mechanisms to provide insights into what causes program outcomes. However, the realist approach requires an evaluator to be sensitive to context (Greenhalgh et al. 2015) and suggests that mechanisms are conditioned by the context in which programs operate (Pawson and Tilley 1997). It is within the "actual level" that this interaction occurs. For realist evaluation, program outcomes which are observed at the "empirical level" are produced by the mechanisms that exist within programs which are shaped by external contextual factors. Realist evaluation thus aims to unpack programs to provide insights into the mechanisms and contexts through which programs produce their outcomes. So, what are these so-called "mechanisms," "contexts," and "outcomes," and how are they described in realist evaluation?

2.2 Understanding Mechanisms in Realist Evaluation

Understanding mechanisms is crucial in realist evaluation because they help to explain how and why changes happen (Pawson 2006). However, defining and identifying mechanisms has been reported as one of the most problematic areas in realist evaluation research (Wong et al. 2017) (see Sect. 4 on limitations of realist evaluation). Different authors have provided various definitions of "mechanisms," and there is a lack of consistency in how "mechanisms" are operationalized across the literature. Despite this, it is important to ensure that any definition used aligns with the fundamental realist explanation of "mechanisms" (Westhorp 2018). Mechanisms are hidden and operate beneath the surface of a program, shaping the outcomes they produce (Westhorp 2018). As they may not be visible, the role of the evaluator is to delve deeper into the inner workings of the program to uncover them (Pawson and Tilley 1997).

According to Pawson and Tilley (1997), mechanisms further involve a combination of the resources provided by the program and the reasoning of recipients. In other words, programs offer opportunities and resources to individuals (Wong et al. 2017), who then decide whether to use them based on their reasoning. Identifying mechanisms in realist evaluation involves a process of weaving together these resources and reasoning (Pawson and Tilley 1997; Dalkin et al. 2015). Dalkin et al. (2015) offer a helpful framework for identifying mechanisms by separating resources and reasoning and considering the role of context (see Fig. 2). They suggest that intervention resources are introduced in a context, which influences changes in reasoning and ultimately leads to outcomes (Dalkin et al. 2015). This framework provides a structured approach for evaluators to follow when identifying mechanisms.

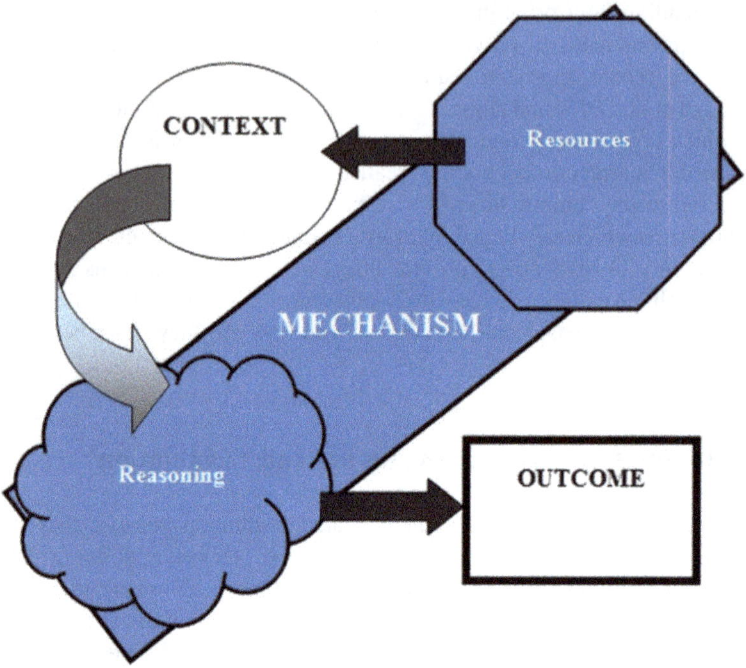

Fig. 2 A CMOc framework (Dalkin et al. 2015)

2.3 Context Matters

Having a good understanding of context is similarly important in realist evaluation because it shapes how mechanisms work and influences the outcomes of programs. According to Pawson and Tilley (1997), the environment in which a program operates (i.e., context) affects how its mechanisms function, meaning that the success of programs depends on factors in the environment that influence mechanisms. Pawson and Tilley (1997) point out that programs are always introduced into existing social contexts, and social conditions play a big role in explaining the successes and failures of programs. Resources provided by the RAMESES II project describe context as the features of situations where programs are introduced, which affect how program mechanisms work. Contexts can include social, material, psychological, economic, organizational, and technical aspects (RAMESES II). Contexts can also interact with each other at different levels of the system which can influence how programs function and the outcomes produced. While some contexts may facilitate the activation of specific mechanisms, other contexts may act to hinder activation of mechanisms (De Weger et al. 2020).

Pawson's (2006, 2013) 4 I framework provides a structured way for evaluators to identify different aspects of the context within a system. The framework includes four layers: the individual layer, interpersonal relationships, institutional settings, and infrastructure.

1. **Individual layer**: This layer focuses on the individual characteristics and capacities of key stakeholders in a program.
2. **Interpersonal relationships**: This layer focuses on the relationships and interactions between stakeholders involved in a program.
3. **Institutional settings**: This layer examines the broader institutional context surrounding a program, including the norms, customs, and rules within organizations.
4. **Infrastructure**: This layer encompasses the wider economic, social, and cultural setting in which a program operates.

This framework serves as a helpful tool for identifying and analyzing features of program context.

2.4 Exploring Outcomes in Realist Evaluation

"Outcomes" are the final component in realist evaluation's CMO model. Pawson and Tilley (1997) suggest that outcomes are always linked to mechanisms operating within specific contexts. There may be multiple mechanisms operating across different contexts which can result in what Pawson and Tilley (1997) call "mixed outcome-patterns." These outcome-patterns encompass both intended and unintended consequences of programs (Pawson and Tilley 1997).

2.5 Context-Mechanism-Outcome Configurations (CMOc) in Realist Evaluation

The three main analytical components in realist evaluation Context, Mechanism, and Outcome (CMO) are brought together to form Context-Mechanism-Outcome Configurations (CMOc). CMOc represent the theories behind programs known in realist evaluation as program theories. They demonstrate which mechanisms and contexts are thought to lead to which outcomes (Pawson and Tilley 1997). CMOc further show how contexts, mechanisms, and outcomes interact, demonstrating their interconnectedness and contingent relationship (Pawson 2013; Emmel et al. 2018). CMOc are testable hypothesis (Pawson 2013), and by collecting empirical data, program theories represented as CMOc are tested and refined, leading to the presentation of refined CMOc as the evaluation's findings (Pawson and Tilley 1997).

While many realist studies continue to report their findings using Pawson and Tilley's (1997) original CMOc framework, different variations of the CMOc have been used (De Weger et al. 2020). These include the Intervention-Context-Actor-Mechanism-Outcome (ICAMO) heuristic which incorporates interventions and actors as additional explanatory factors (see Mukumbang et al. 2018). Mukumbang et al. (2018) suggest that the ICAMO heuristic allows for a more detailed analysis by firstly considering aspects of the intervention, which in a healthcare context are often complex containing multiple components which need to be differentiated between.

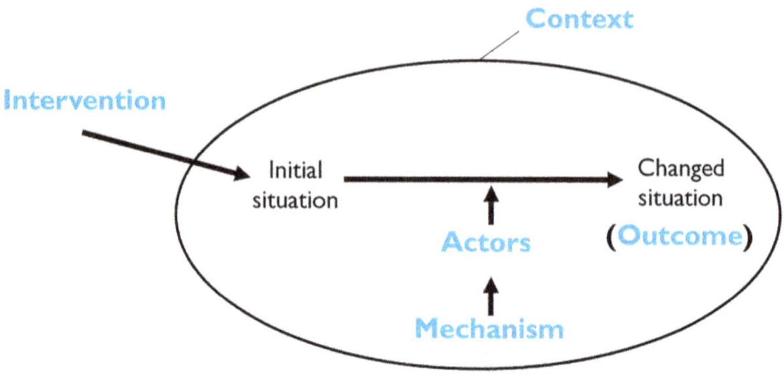

Fig. 3 The Intervention-Context-Actor-Mechanism-Outcome heuristic tool (Mukumbang et al. 2018)

The inclusion of actors acknowledges that people are not passive recipients of programs but instead active participants (Mukumbang et al. 2018). This tool may be particularly useful when evaluating different aspects or components of programs as it can help to provide a more nuanced explanation of the causal links between these elements (De Weger et al. 2020). The ICAMO heuristic is illustrated in Fig. 3.

Evaluators may choose to use any heuristic tool to analyze and present their program theories or to adapt an existing tool that fits the needs of their evaluation. However, configurations must explain the causal link between context, mechanism, and outcome, and when reporting findings, evaluators should be transparent stating what tool they used and providing examples of configurations (De Weger et al. 2020).

This section has provided an overview of realist evaluation, offering insights into its underlying principles and defining key realist concepts. The next section explores how realist evaluation can be conducted in a healthcare context by drawing on practical examples from the author's own work.

3 How to Conduct a Realist Evaluation of a Healthcare Program

This section describes the different stages involved in undertaking a realist evaluation. It demonstrates how the realist evaluation cycle can be effectively applied to evaluate healthcare programs by drawing on the author's own experiences in health service evaluation. Practical examples are used to illustrate each stage.

Realist evaluation consists of three main stages: formulating a program theory, testing program theory, and refining program theory (Pawson and Tilley 1997). The objective of the first stage is to elicit an initial program theory that reflects the assumptions of how the program is expected to work and for whom (Westhorp 2014). Program theory is then tested in the second stage through empirical investigation to see if it holds (Manzano 2016). The final stage of realist evaluation involves analysis and interpretation to refine the program theory and address the initial research

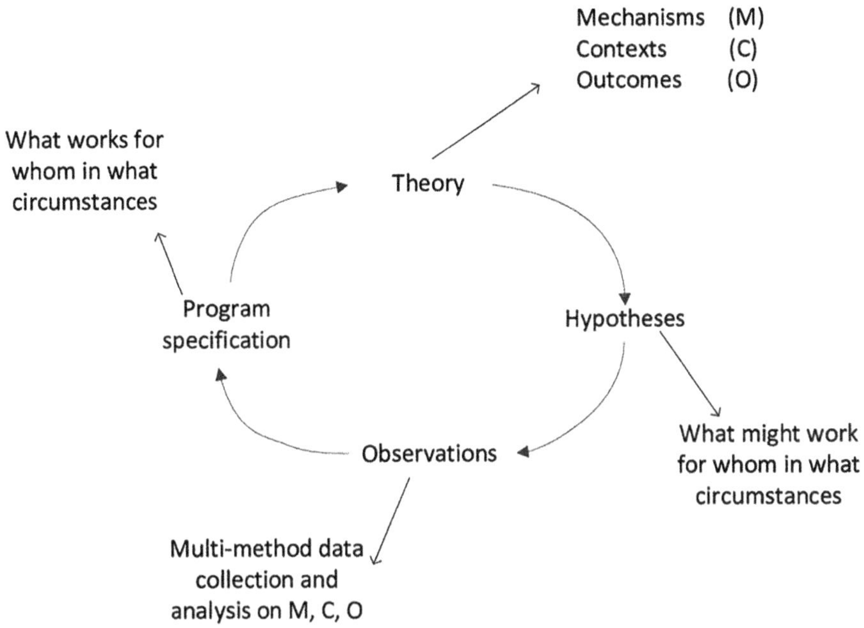

Fig. 4 The realist evaluation cycle (Pawson and Tilley 1997)

question of "what works, for whom, under what circumstances, why and how?" (Jagosh et al. 2015). This iterative cycle of theory development, empirical testing, and theory refinement allows evaluators to generate actionable insights which can be used to adapt and improve healthcare programs and their implementation. The realist evaluation cycle developed by Pawson and Tilley (1997) is shown in Fig. 4.

3.1 Developing the Initial Program Theory (IPT)

The starting point when undertaking a realist evaluation is to develop an Initial Program Theory (IPT) which encompasses the ideas and assumptions about how the healthcare program is expected to work, for whom, and in what conditions (Dalkin et al. 2017). The IPT is developed based on previous research or the insights, knowledge, and experience of program designers, policy-makers, and stakeholders. Realist evaluators use various qualitative and quantitative data collection methods to develop IPTs and often combine these in an iterative process (Marchal et al. 2018). Examples of methods used to develop IPTs in health program evaluations include analysis of program documents (Feather 2018), stakeholder consultations or interviews (Shearn et al. 2017), and realist synthesis of empirical and non-empirical literature (Jagosh et al. 2022). There is no exact formula for the development of IPTs (Rycroft-Malone et al. 2013). However, they must reflect a realist understanding of causation and include key components of contexts, mechanisms, and outcomes (Wong et al. 2017). Logic models can also be used to guide IPT development by separating program components and activities from program mechanisms (see Feather 2018). The IPT acts as a theoretical framework that evaluators can use to guide their evaluation.

3.2 Generating Context-Mechanism-Outcome Configurations (CMOc)

In realist evaluation, IPTs are expressed as Context-Mechanism-Outcome Configurations (CMOc) or "if-then-because" statements. A CMOc is a testable hypothesis or a proposition that states which mechanisms and contexts lead to which outcomes (Pawson 2013). Configuring contexts, mechanisms, and outcomes to demonstrate the causal relationship between components is essential. The propositional function of the CMO configuration is often misunderstood by evaluators when undertaking a realist evaluation (see section on limitations). "If-then-because" statements can be used as an alternative option to articulate the relationship between contextual factors (C), underlying mechanisms (M), and observed outcomes (O) (Mukumbang et al. 2018).

An example of an "if-then-because" statement taken from the author's own work is provided in Box 1. The author used "if-then-because" statements to display IPTs in a realist evaluation which investigated the implementation of a person-centered transition program for adolescents and young adults (see Feather 2022). The evaluation explored how pediatric healthcare professionals implemented the transition program and considered the broader organizational behavior influences (see Feather et al. 2024). The evaluation developed four IPTs by undertaking semi-structured interviews with program designers and document analysis.

The IPT displayed in Box 1 theorized that pediatric healthcare professionals who are motivated, committed, and open to organizational change will be more inclined to adopt and implement the transition program. "Motivation," "commitment," and "receptiveness" of healthcare professionals to organizational change were contextual factors thought to be essential to a successful implementation of the program which was the predicted outcome. "If" was used to represent the contextual factors while "then" represented the expected outcome resulting from the interaction between the contexts and mechanism. In this case, the mechanism through which successful implementation would be achieved was theorized to be the ability to adapt the new transition program and use it flexibly alongside existing processes to cater to different patient group' needs. In doing so, healthcare professionals would see the benefit that the use of the new transition program would bring to their patients and the wider services in which they worked. "Because" was used to represent the mechanism triggered in response to the different contextual factors.

Box 1 Example of "If-Then-Because" Statement Used in a Realist Evaluation (Author's Own Work)

IF pediatric healthcare professionals are motivated and committed to improving transition **(C)** and receptive to organizational change **(C)**,

THEN the transition program is more likely to be adopted and implemented by pediatric healthcare professionals **(O)**,

BECAUSE pediatric healthcare professionals can use the transition program flexibly alongside existing transition processes to meet the needs of different patient groups. Pediatric healthcare professionals see the benefit that implementation of the transition program has to young people and the services in which they work **(M)**.

In line with Pawson and Tilley's (1997) realist evaluation cycle (Fig. 4), this IPT (expressed as an "if-then-because" statement) was then exposed to a process of testing and refinement through empirical data collection. The process for undertaking this stage of a realist evaluation is described in the section below.

3.3 Testing and Refining the Program Theory (PT)

Once IPTs have been developed, the next step in a realist evaluation is to test IPTs using the best available evidence (RAMESES II). Realist evaluation is not prescriptive in the types of evidence that should be collected. Much depends on what an evaluator considers to be the most reliable and relevant information that can be accessed to understand how the program is working in practice. Manzano (2016) suggests that evaluators should purposely choose the most effective tools, which will help reveal patterns and regularities about the program. As realist evaluation is method-neutral, evidence can come from a range of sources. These may include qualitative interviews with key stakeholders, surveys, observations, service level data and innovative methods such as diaries, photographs, vignettes and social media (see Renmans and Castellano Pleguezuelo 2023). Theory testing should follow an iterative process (Manzano 2016) to allow for evaluators to refine or modify IPTs as the evaluation progresses.

This connects with the third stage of realist evaluation "program theory refinement" which involves gradually revising IPTs to produce a final program theory or set of program theories at the end of the evaluation cycle (Pawson 2013). Program theory refinement involves searching for semi-predictable patterns across the data, also known as demi-regularities in the realist evaluation literature (Gilmore et al. 2019). This involves a careful examination of the data to identify prominent themes or relationships between contexts, mechanisms, and outcomes. To support program theory refinement, realist evaluators often draw on existing explanatory theories from various disciplines such as the social sciences, behavioral sciences, and policy sciences. Explanatory theories can offer deeper insights into the contexts, mechanisms, and outcomes that may exist within a program (Leeuw and Donaldson 2015) and facilitate a deeper understanding of what works, for whom, in what circumstances, and why. For more detailed information on how to undertake data analysis in realist evaluation, see Gilmore et al. (2019).

Once program theories have been refined, they are presented using either the CMOc heuristic or "if-then-because" statements as the findings of the evaluation. The author again draws on an example from her own work mentioned earlier in this chapter. Box 2 is an example of a final program theory (displayed using the CMO heuristic) which was tested and refined through an iterative process of data collection and analysis. The data collected to test the IPT (shown in Box 1) provided partial support for its validity. However, the IPT did not fully consider the full range of contextual factors required to support program implementation or the unsupportive contextual factors which triggered a different mechanism and resulting outcome. The final program theory thus shows two different program outcomes resulting from different mechanisms that were shaped by either supportive or unsupportive contextual features.

Box 2 Example of a Final Program Theory from a Realist Evaluation (Author's Own Work)

Context: Implementation of the transition program is supported by existing, well-established transition processes that are similar to the newly developed pathway and inter-organizational commonalities between pediatric and adult services. Existing transition processes, inter-organizational differences, and healthcare professionals' perceptions of transition also act as barriers to program implementation.

Mechanism: Pediatric healthcare professionals use their professional autonomy and agency when making implementation decisions based on perceived individual needs and the value implementation brings to patient quality of care. Where the context is unsupportive, pediatric healthcare professionals experience feelings of "self-defeat."

Outcome: Pediatric healthcare professionals adapt and use the transition program flexibly to meet individual patient needs. Where the context is unsupportive and professionals experience feelings of "self-defeat," there is an acceptance that nothing more can be done to change transition within services.

This section has outlined the three key stages of realist evaluation: developing an IPT, testing it through empirical investigation, and refining the IPT based on analysis and interpretation. By drawing on practical examples from the author's own work, it demonstrates how this iterative cycle of theory development, testing, and refinement can generate actionable insights to improve healthcare programs by understanding what works, for whom, under what circumstances, and why. The next section explores some of the advantages and limitations of using realist evaluation in real-world practice.

4 Strengths and Limitations of Realist Evaluation

This final section provides a critical examination of the strengths and limitations of applying realist evaluation in real-world practice. It considers the value of using a realist evaluation approach to evaluate complex healthcare programs while also acknowledging the difficulties and challenges in operationalizing the method.

Realist evaluation can provide rich and nuanced explanations of how and why complex interventions work, across different contexts and for different groups of individuals (Greenhalgh and Manzano 2022). It can help to capture the complexity and dynamism of rapidly changing health service delivery models (Jagosh et al. 2022) through its focus on understanding the complexity of social systems and mechanisms of change (Duncan et al. 2018). By identifying mechanisms of change within interventions and the contextual conditions needed to enable such mechanisms, realist evaluation supports healthcare managers and policymakers in making informed decisions about which interventions are likely to be most effective across different contexts.

Realist evaluation can also be used to inform program design and implementation. It provides important understandings of the underlying logic and assumptions of healthcare interventions, and how interventions can be adapted and delivered by frontline practitioners and healthcare policymakers (Greenhalgh et al. 2015). It offers valuable insights into contextual influences and the conditions that are needed for program mechanisms to work, and an understanding of why certain interventions work in particular contexts and not in others. Findings can be used by program developers and healthcare policymakers to personalize and tailor existing interventions to better suit different patient groups and healthcare settings (Duncan et al. 2018; Feather 2018). When used to evaluate the implementation of complex healthcare programs, realist evaluation can shed light on the contextual conditions needed for successful implementation which can be used by healthcare managers and policymakers to inform future program development and implementation strategies (see Feather et al. 2024).

Realist evaluation is not prescriptive when describing the types of evidence sources and data collection methods to be used by evaluators (Duncan et al. 2018). Instead, it offers a flexible approach to data collection with evaluators often utilizing mixed methods approaches to collect and analyze data (Haynes et al. 2017; Lane et al. 2021). This level of flexibility allows evaluators to choose from a wide range of data collection methods which can provide a more comprehensive understanding of how and why complex healthcare programs work or fail to work.

Resulting program theories represented as CMO configurations further offer detailed understandings of "what works, for whom, in what contexts, and how" that are transferable and can be used to better inform the development and evaluation of social programs and policies (Astbury and Leeuw 2010; Westhorp 2014). Realist evaluation has the ability to generate middle-range theories that are generalizable and transferable across different settings and situations (Greenhalgh and Manzano 2022). Evaluation findings therefore have broader relevance and can be used by policymakers to inform healthcare policy and practice beyond the immediate context of the evaluation.

Nevertheless, it has its limitations and there are several practical challenges that arise when applying realist evaluation in a healthcare context. Firstly, realist evaluation can be time-consuming and resource intensive due to the complexity of data analysis (Quintans et al. 2020) and the iterative nature of theory development (Jagosh et al. 2022). Undertaking a realist evaluation can be complex as it involves multiple data collection methods, data sources, and analytical steps. This requires significant time, effort, resources, and expertise from evaluators.

Operationalizing and applying realist evaluation in practice further presents a significant challenge (Duncan et al. 2018; Greenhalgh and Manzano 2022). The absence of clear methodological and practical instructions on implementing realist evaluation can create difficulties for evaluators (Feather 2022). Quality and Reporting Standards for Realist Evaluation developed as part of the RAMESES II project (Wong et al. 2017) offer some direction. However, they lack specific guidance on how to operationalize the approach in practice, particularly on how to analyze data using the CMO framework (Feather 2018).

Defining and analyzing the mechanisms and contexts involved in a program can be problematic. There is a risk that evaluators may oversimplify or overcomplicate the causal relationships between contexts and mechanisms (Greenhalgh and Manzano 2022), which can impact the findings generated. Evaluators may find a paper by Dalkin et al. (2015) to be useful if faced with this challenge. In their paper on "What's in a mechanism?," Dalkin et al. (2015) reconceptualize Pawson and Tilley's original CMOc framework by disaggregating mechanisms into resource and reasoning. Using this model as a guide can help evaluators to differentiate mechanisms from contexts. For more information on how this can be used to support the process of data analysis, see Feather (2022).

The propositional function of the CMO configuration used in realist evaluation has also been significantly misinterpreted by various authors engaged in realist research (Pawson and Manzano-Santaella 2012; Pawson 2013). In some instances, CMOs have been analyzed as isolated and disconnected entities (Pawson 2013). This can be problematic as the main purpose of CMO configurations is to provide an explanation of the social processes underpinning the program (Pawson and Manzano-Santaella 2012). Using an alternative way to represent the relationship between contexts, mechanisms, and outcomes can be helpful and can act to simplify data analysis. "If-then-because" statements can be used to represent interconnected mechanisms, contexts, and outcomes (see Mukumbang et al. 2018). "If" is used to represent the context in which a program operates, while "then" represents the expected outcome arising from the interplay of context and mechanism, and "because" signifies the mechanism activated in response to various contextual factors. The use of "if-then-because" statements can support evaluators to convey complex information in a clear and accessible way (Pearson et al. 2015).

The complexity of healthcare programs and the dynamic nature of healthcare environments must also be considered when using realist evaluation (Feather 2018). Healthcare environments are continuously evolving due to changes in technologies, practices, and policy. Initial program theories generated through a realist evaluation may therefore become outdated or irrelevant as the context evolves (Jagosh et al. 2022). Evaluators need to continuously monitor their approach and be flexible to account for and capture changes in the healthcare environment over time.

In summary, realist evaluation can be particularly helpful in providing a more in-depth understanding of how and why complex healthcare programs work, for whom, and in what contexts. It can be used to inform program design and implementation and offers evaluators a flexible approach to data collection and use of evidence sources. However, realist evaluation currently lacks prescriptive guidelines, posing challenges in operationalizing the method particularly when it comes to data analysis.

5 Conclusion

In conclusion, this chapter has provided a comprehensive overview of realist evaluation, emphasizing its growing importance in evaluating healthcare programs. By delving into its underlying principles and describing the different stages involved in undertaking a realist evaluation, the chapter illustrates how the approach offers valuable insights into program implementation and effectiveness. Realist evaluation's unique focus on understanding the mechanisms underlying program outcomes and the contexts in which they operate makes it a useful approach for evaluators working in the healthcare sector who wish to design more effective programs and implementation strategies.

References

Astbury B (2013) Some reflections on Pawson's science of evaluation: a realist manifesto. Evaluation 19(4):383–401. https://doi.org/10.1177/1356389013505039

Astbury B, Leeuw FL (2010) Unpacking black boxes: mechanisms and theory building in evaluation. Am J Eval 31(3):363 381. https://doi.org/10.1177/1098214010371972

Bhaskar R (1978) A realist theory of science. Harvester Press, Sussex

Dalkin SM, Greenhalgh J, Jones D, Cunningham B, Lhussier M (2015) What's in a mechanism? Development of a key concept in realist evaluation. Implement Sci 10(1):49. https://doi.org/10.1186/s13012-015-0237-x

Dalkin S, Lhussier M, Williams L, Burton CR, Rycroft-Malone J (2017) Exploring the use of soft systems methodology with realist approaches: a novel way to map programme complexity and develop and refine programme theory. Evaluation 24(1):84–97. https://doi.org/10.1177/1356389017749036

de Souza DE (2014) Culture, context and society—the underexplored potential of critical realism as a philosophical framework for theory and practice. Asian J Soc Psychol 17(2):141–151. https://doi.org/10.1111/ajsp.12052

De Weger E, Van Vooren NJE, Wong G, Dalkin S, Marchal B, Drewes HW, Baan CA (2020) What's in a realist configuration? Deciding which causal configurations to use, how, and why. Int J Qual Methods 19:160940692093857. https://doi.org/10.1177/1609406920938577

Duncan C, Weich S, Fenton S-J, Twigg L, Moon G, Madan J, Singh SP, Crepaz-Keay D, Parsons H, Bhui K (2018) A realist approach to the evaluation of complex mental health interventions. Br J Psychiatry 213(2):451–453. https://doi.org/10.1192/bjp.2018.96

Emmel N, Greenhalgh J, Manzano A, Monaghan M, Dalkin S (2018) Introduction: doing realist evaluation, synthesis and research. In: Emmel N, Greenhalgh J, Manzano A, Monaghan M, Dalkin S (eds) Doing realist research. Sage Publications Ltd, London, pp 1–13

Feather JL (2018) Developing programme theories as part of a realist evaluation of a healthcare quality improvement programme. Int J Care Coord 21(3):68–72. https://doi.org/10.1177/2053434518779753

Feather J (2022) Implementing a transition pathway developed to improve services for young people with long-term conditions moving between children's and adult health care services: a realist evaluation. Thesis. https://research.edgehill.ac.uk/files/47874315/clean_version_of_final_thesis_pdf.pdf. Accessed 9 Apr 2024

Feather J, Kaehne A, Kiernan J (2024) Evaluating the implementation of a person-centred transition programme for adolescents and young adults with long-term conditions: the role of context and organisational behaviour. J Health Organ Manag 38(1):112–128. https://doi.org/10.1108/JHOM-03-2023-0095

Fletcher AJ (2017) Applying critical realism in qualitative research: methodology meets method. Int J Soc Res Methodol 20(2):181–194. https://doi.org/10.1080/13645579.2016.1144401

Gilmore B, McAuliffe E, Power J, Vallières F (2019) Data analysis and synthesis within a realist evaluation: toward more transparent methodological approaches. Int J Qual Methods 18:160940691985975. https://doi.org/10.1177/1609406919859754

Greenhalgh J, Manzano A (2022) Understanding 'context' in realist evaluation and synthesis. Int J Soc Res Methodol 25:1–14. https://doi.org/10.1080/13645579.2021.1918484

Greenhalgh T, Wong G, Jagosh J, Greenhalgh J, Manzano A, Westhorp G, Pawson R (2015) Protocol—the RAMESES II study: developing guidance and reporting standards for realist evaluation: Figure 1. BMJ Open 5(8):e008567. https://doi.org/10.1136/bmjopen-2015-008567

Haynes A, Brennan S, Redman S, Williamson A, Makkar SR, Gallego G, Butow P (2017) Policymakers' experience of a capacity-building intervention designed to increase their use of research: a realist process evaluation. Health Res Policy Syst 15(1):99. https://doi.org/10.1186/s12961-017-0234-4

Jagosh J, Bush PL, Salsberg J, Macaulay AC, Greenhalgh T, Wong G, Cargo M, Green LW, Herbert CP, Pluye P (2015) A realist evaluation of community-based participatory research: partnership synergy, trust building and related ripple effects. BMC Public Health 15(1):725. https://doi.org/10.1186/s12889-015-1949-1

Jagosh J, Stott H, Halls S, Thomas R, Liddiard C, Cupples M, Cramp F, Kersten P, Foster D, Walsh NE (2022) Benefits of realist evaluation for rapidly changing health service delivery. BMJ Open 12(7):e060347. https://doi.org/10.1136/bmjopen-2021-060347

Lane R, D'Souza S, Livanou M, Jacob J, Riches W, Ullman R, Rashid A, Singleton R, Wheeler J, Fuggle P, Bevington D, Deighton J, Law D, Fonagy P, Hindley N, White O, Edbrooke-Childs J (2021) A mixed-methods realist evaluation of the implementation and impact of community forensic CAMHS to manage risk for young people with forensic and mental health needs: study protocol. Front Psych 12:697041. https://doi.org/10.3389/fpsyt.2021.697041

Leeuw FL, Donaldson SI (2015) Theory in evaluation: reducing confusion and encouraging debate. Evaluation 21(4):467–480. https://doi.org/10.1177/1356389015607712

Manzano A (2016) The craft of interviewing in realist evaluation. Evaluation 22(3):342–360. https://doi.org/10.1177/1356389016638615

Marchal B, Kegels G, Van Belle S (2018) Theory and realist methods. In: Emmel N, Greenhalgh J, Manzano A, Monaghan M, Dalkin S (eds) Doing realist research. Sage Publications Ltd, London, pp 79–89

Mukumbang FC, Marchal B, Van Belle S, van Wyk B (2018) Unearthing how, why, for whom and under what health system conditions the antiretroviral treatment adherence club intervention in South Africa works: a realist theory refining approach. BMC Health Serv Res 18(1):343. https://doi.org/10.1186/s12913-018-3150-6

Mukumbang FC, Marchal B, Van Belle S, van Wyk B (2019) Using the realist interview approach to maintain theoretical awareness in realist studies. Qual Res 20(4):146879411988198. https://doi.org/10.1177/1468794119881985

Pawson R (2006) Evidence-based policy: a realist perspective. Sage, London

Pawson R (2013) The science of evaluation. SAGE, London

Pawson R, Manzano-Santaella A (2012) A realist diagnostic workshop. Evaluation 18(2):176–191. https://doi.org/10.1177/1356389012440912

Pawson R, Tilley N (1997) Realistic evaluation. SAGE, London

Pearson M, Brand SL, Quinn C, Shaw J, Maguire M, Michie S, Briscoe S, Lennox C, Stirzaker A, Kirkpatrick T, Byng R (2015) Using realist review to inform intervention development: methodological illustration and conceptual platform for collaborative care in offender mental health. Implement Sci 10(1):134. https://doi.org/10.1186/s13012-015-0321-2

Quintans JR, Yonekura T, Trapé CA, Soares CB (2020) Realist evaluation for programs and services in the health area: an integrative review of the theoretical and methodological literature. Rev Lat Am Enfermagem 28:e3255. https://doi.org/10.1590/1518-8345.3933.3255

ramesesproject.org (n.d.) The RAMESES project. http://ramesesproject.org/Standards_and_Training_materials.php#re_training. Accessed 12 Apr 2024

Renmans D, Castellano Pleguezuelo V (2023) Methods in realist evaluation: a mapping review. Eval Program Plann 97:102209. https://doi.org/10.1016/j.evalprogplan.2022.102209

Rycroft-Malone J, Seers K, Chandler J, Hawkes CA, Crichton N, Allen C, Bullock I, Strunin L (2013) The role of evidence, context, and facilitation in an implementation trial: implications for the development of the PARIHS framework. Implement Sci 8(1):28. https://doi.org/10.1186/1748-5908-8-28

Sayer A (2010) Realism and social science. Sage Publications, Los Angeles

Shearn K, Allmark P, Piercy H, Hirst J (2017) Building realist program theory for large complex and messy interventions. Int J Qual Methods 16(1):160940691774179. https://doi.org/10.1177/1609406917741796

Skivington K, Matthews L, Simpson SA, Craig P, Baird J, Blazeby JM, Boyd KA, Craig N, French DP, McIntosh E, Petticrew M, Rycroft-Malone J, White M, Moore L (2021) A new framework for developing and evaluating complex interventions: update of Medical Research Council guidance. BMJ 374(1):n2061. https://doi.org/10.1136/bmj.n2061

Westhorp G (2014) Key messages a methods lab publication realist impact evaluation an introduction. https://odi.cdn.ngo/media/documents/9138.pdf. Accessed 12 Apr 2024

Westhorp G (2018) Understanding mechanisms in realist evaluation and research. In: Emmel N, Greenhalgh J, Manzano A, Monaghan M, Dalkin S (eds) Doing realist research. Sage, London, pp 41–57

Wong G, Westhorp G, Greenhalgh J, Manzano A, Jagosh J, Greenhalgh T (2017) Quality and reporting standards, resources, training materials and information for realist evaluation: the RAMESES II project. Health Serv Deliv Res 5(28):1–108. https://doi.org/10.3310/hsdr05280

Value-Based Healthcare in Health Service Evaluations

Paulus Torkki, Laura J. Pitkänen, and Kristiina Patja

Abstract

This chapter discusses the evaluation of health services from a value-based health care (VBHC) perspective. First, we introduce the key principles of VBHC. Second, as the healthcare systems vary worldwide, we discuss the main system-level factors affecting value-based approaches. A system-wide approach is essential, as the long-term sustainability relies on shared goals across the entire health system. As an example, payment models, government regulations, and digital infrastructure may support or hinder the development of value-based care.

The sections in this chapter will consider the evaluation of health services focusing on key VBHC goals: maturity of VBHC, outcomes, and costs. We introduce various perspectives, methods, and tools for both internal and external evaluation of health services. Finally, we discuss the challenges related to VBHC.

Keywords

Value-based healthcare · Outcomes · Costs · Cost-effectiveness · Quality registers

P. Torkki (✉)
Faculty of Medicine, University of Helsinki, Helsinki, Finland

Jyväskylä University, Jyväskylä, Finland
e-mail: paulus.torkki@helsinki.fi

L. J. Pitkänen. K. Patja
Faculty of Medicine, University of Helsinki, Helsinki, Finland
e-mail: laura.pitkanen@gov.fi; kristiina.patja@helsinki.fi

A. Kaehne, J. Feather (eds.), *Handbook of Health Services Evaluation*,
https://doi.org/10.1007/978-3-031-87869-5_7

1 Introduction

This chapter discusses the evaluation of health services from a value-based health care (VBHC) perspective. First, we introduce the key principles of VBHC from service providers' point of view. Second, as the healthcare systems vary worldwide and they may have a significant impact on both the implementation of VBHC and health service provision, we discuss the main system-level factors affecting value-based approaches in health services. A system-wide approach is essential because the long-term sustainability of any single organization's efforts to improve patient value depends on the alignment of all industry stakeholders around this common goal. As an example, national health system components, such as payment models, government regulations, and digital infrastructure, may support or hinder the development of value-based care (Larsson et al. 2023).

The following sections will consider the evaluation of health services focusing on key VBHC goals: maturity of VBHC, outcomes, and costs. We introduce various perspectives, methods and tools for both internal and external evaluation of health services. Finally, we discuss the challenges related to VBHC approach in health services.

2 Key Principles of Value-Based Healthcare

VBHC has evolved from an intriguing concept to a global movement in the 17 years since Michael Porter and Elizabeth Teisberg introduced the term. It emphasizes delivering meaningful health outcomes to patients for a given cost across the entire care cycle. Emphasizing the patient-relevant outcomes, the role of patient-reported outcome measures (PROMs) has been increasing in addition to the clinical measures (Porter 2010; Larsson et al. 2023; Torkki et al. 2023).

The costs should cover the services required to achieve the improvement in outcomes. According to the principles of VBHC, value is created only when there is an effect on a person's health outcomes, and efforts that focus only on cost reduction are incomplete (Teisberg et al. 2020).

VBHC originally focused on health service production rather than the health of a population or the performance of a healthcare system (Torkki et al. 2023). The aim is that the service providers will measure outcomes for each important medical condition in a standardized way to enable comparison of outcomes and costs worldwide (Porter et al. 2016).

Since its establishment, VBHC has gained much attention both internationally and nationally with development of patient-reported outcomes and experience measures (ICHOM 2020) and state-level initiatives on national quality registries. Healthcare providers worldwide have started measuring patient outcomes and associated costs, using this data to identify best practices and improve patient results. Mjåset et al. suggested that "in a value-based health system, patient value becomes what evolutionary biologists call the "selection principle" against which the contribution and performance of all institutions in the system, as well as the effectiveness of health-system reform initiatives, are assessed and evaluated" (Mjåset et al. 2020).

VBHC not only focuses on the measurement of value but also encourages service providers to organize care around medical conditions over the full cycle of care and delivering into integrated practice units (IPUs) and developing value-based reimbursement systems and incentives (Fig. 1). This often requires investments on IT systems and databases as enablers (Larsson et al. 2023). The aim of VBHC has been seen as shifting care from supply-centric to patient-centric (The Economist 2016).

When evaluating health services from a VBHC perspective, the overall aim is to evaluate the value (outcomes and costs) of the services. In addition, understanding the explaining factors, the evaluation can include (1) system level: drivers, enablers, and barriers for VBHC, (2) the maturity of VBHC in health service providers and (3) outcomes and cost measurement systems, e.g., international comparisons or national quality registers.

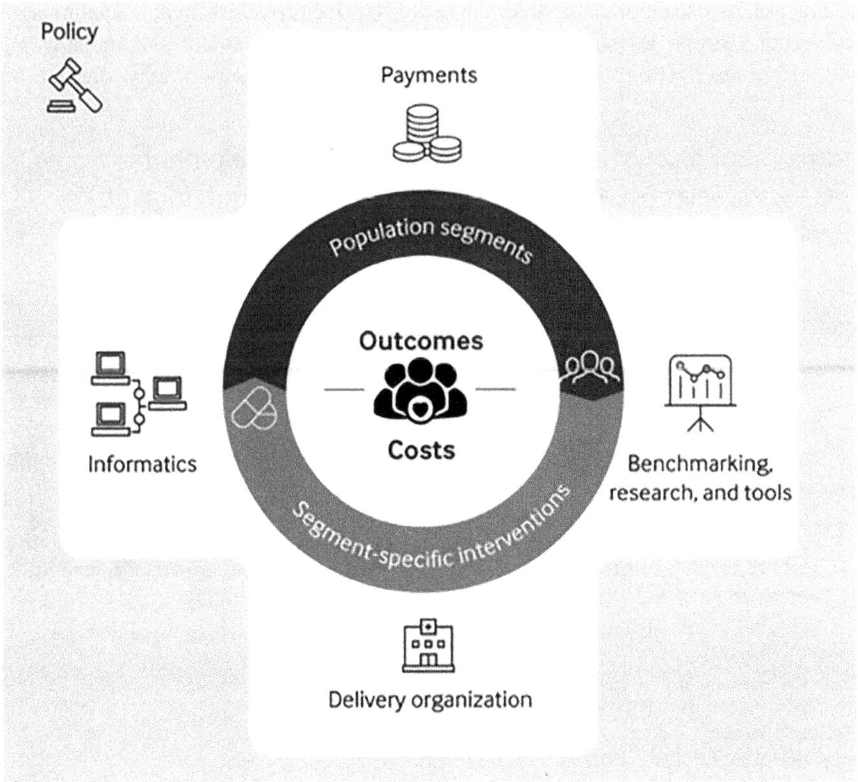

Fig. 1 A conceptual framework for a value-based health system (Larsson et al. 2023)

3 Evaluating the System-Level Drivers for VBHC

The constituents of health systems vary between countries and this also has an impact on how VBHC is interpreted. It is important to include the system level as a context description to understand the role of service providers in the complex service system. A system-wide approach is necessary as the efforts of any single organization to improve value delivered to patients will only be sustainable in the long term if all stakeholders align their efforts around this shared goal and if the various components of national health systems are designed explicitly to support value-based approaches to care (Larsson et al. 2023).

At the system level, the evaluation may focus on enablers and barriers for VBHC. Earlier evaluations of the healthcare systems have found that VBHC functions better in some healthcare systems compared to others (see Fig. 2) (Mjåset et al. 2020). In addition, the conceptualization and interpretation of VBHC may have high variation between health systems and health service providers. Some of them may focus only on the measurement of value as some use the broader concept including incentives and organizing principles (Kokko and Kork 2021; van Staalduinen et al. 2022; Eijsink et al. 2023). The system-level evaluation can follow the original VBHC agenda (Porter and Lee 2013).

The policy instruments that steer the health service providers include elements of regulation through legislation, economic means (reimbursement and incentives), and information (Pitkänen et al. 2021). Thus, the evaluation may consist of

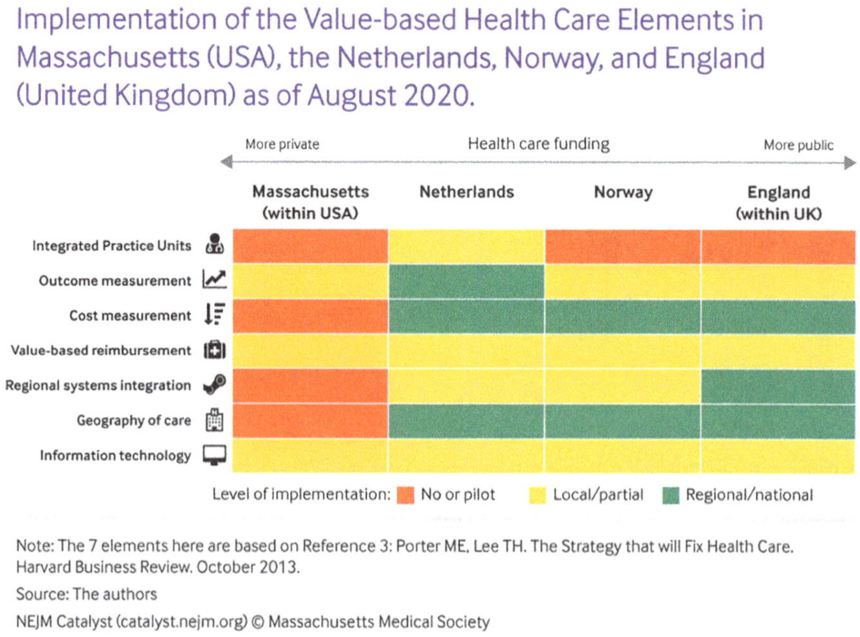

Fig. 2 Implementation of the value-based health care elements (Mjåset et al. 2020)

qualitative analysis of how these instruments support or hinder the VBHC agenda consisting of literature and document analysis, surveys, or interviews. In the following, we give some examples of how the system-level drivers can affect VBHC at the service level.

The reimbursement principles specifically, e.g., fee-for-service vs. bundled payments, play a crucial role in shaping the goals of a health service provider. Many countries are experimenting with value-based payment models, such as pay-for-performance bonuses, bundled payments, and capitation and other forms of risk-based contracting for specific population segments. There are many ways to design a value-based payment model (Cattel and Eijkenaar 2020), and it is unclear how exactly to design a successful one (Damberg et al. 2014). Either way, reimbursement principles provide financial incentives for commissioners and service providers, and thus the alignment (or lack thereof) of these incentives with value-based care is essential.

In addition, legislation creates boundaries, enablers and barriers for the service provider. For example, in Finland, in the context of residential care of the elderly, the number of nurses per resident has been a subject of strict legislation. The objective of the legislation has been to ensure quality of care, yet this has resulted in slowing down of development and use of technology, as the number of nurses (and thus the main cost driver) is constant.

Another notable factor is whether the health system is national, regional, or insurance-based without certain coverage of the population and how the service provision is shared between public and private service providers. All these factors influence the incentives of the service commissioners and providers to focus on outcomes. For example, if a commissioner or provider has wide-ranging responsibility for their population, they have an incentive to minimize future cost of care by focusing on long-term population health—on the other hand, if a provider receives a fee-for-service type of reimbursement, they are incentivized to produce outputs instead of outcomes.

Although there has been significant advancement in the adoption of VBHC, it has been characterized by fragmentation and disparities across countries and medical conditions. Similarly, the extent of engagement from various stakeholders within the healthcare sector has varied. This will be elaborated more in the following sections. Even countries leading in specific areas may lag in other areas.

4 Evaluating the Maturity of VBHC

4.1 Maturity of Organizations

Implementing VBHC requires extensive and time-consuming organizational and cultural changes in the way care is delivered. There have been numerous examples of early adopters of VBHC, but they have been mostly small service providers or focusing on a single disease. VBHC is still in its infancy and requires, e.g., investments on systematic measurement of outcomes and costs, paradigm shift among professionals and service providers, and the environment promoting the learning and adoption of best practices between physicians and providers.

Healthcare providers that are implementing value-based healthcare often start with the measurement of clinical outcomes. However, there remains a disconnect between measuring outcomes that are important to patients and employing rigorous methodological approaches to measure financial outcomes. The primary obstacles to achieving a more replicable value-based healthcare agenda seem to be technological limitations and a need for a cultural shift in management toward embracing change (Zanotto et al. 2021). Technological challenges are related to the whole information management process covering the collection of the outcomes data including patient-reported outcomes, analyzing and interpreting the outcomes information in a meaningful way to patients, and delivering the information to various levels of decision-making.

Implementing outcomes in healthcare provider quality management is seen as a straightforward consequence of measuring outcomes. However, this step is a major change for healthcare providers. A true shift from volume to patient value requires a change in the culture and way of working of healthcare professionals.

Even inside a single health service provider organization, the different units or specialties may define the concepts and even the measures (outcomes or effectiveness) in a different way. Stakeholders' perspectives on effectiveness can vary, with some emphasizing economic or productivity-related measures, others focusing on societal outcomes, and yet others prioritizing clinical outcomes. Also, the health professionals working closer to the care process may have a different view even on the goals and key concepts compared to the high-level managers (Rosen 2000; Axelsson and Engström 2001).

In evaluating the organizations' management, capabilities, processes, culture, technology, etc., one approach has been the development of maturity models as assessment frameworks or tools. Maturity models have typically been developed for specific evaluation purposes such as data and information management or business process management. The European University Hospital Alliance has suggested starting VBHC implementation by setting up a strategic plan for the implementation of VBHC, including evaluation and follow-up of the maturity and readiness to transform toward VBHC (Cossio-Gil et al. 2022).

Currently, there is no one established framework or model to assess the capacities or maturity of VBHC of the health service providers, and dimensions vary between models.

The maturity of VBHC has been evaluated utilizing the strategic agenda of Michael Porter as a framework for evaluation, including (1) organizing into integrated practice units, (2) measuring outcomes and costs, (3) moving to bundled payments, (4) integrating across separate facilities, (5) expanding across geography and (6) building an information platform (Mjåset et al. 2020; Vijverberg et al. 2022). Various questions and scales have been utilized to evaluate the progress of these dimensions.

The BCG (Boston Consulting Group) maturity-assessment framework has been used for health systems and it utilizes four success factors ("clinical engagement", "national infrastructure," 'data quality," and "outcomes-based initiatives") to evaluate a country's progress toward value-based healthcare on two broad dimensions: (1) data quality and use and (2) national enablers.

Rural Health Value has developed a tool to assess healthcare organization's capacities (resources, processes, infrastructure, etc.) to deliver value-based care. Value-based care refers to healthcare that concurrently improves clinical quality/ patient safety, advances community health and lowers per capita cost. The dimensions of the tool are (a) governance and leadership, (b) care coordination, (c) clinical care, (d) community health, (e) patient and family engagement, (f) performance improvement and reporting, (g) health information technology and (h) financial risk management. The questions per dimension vary between 8 and 13.

Example of a maturity assessment tool for VBHC: *Value-Based Health Care Strategic Planning Tool*, V3 (source: Rural Health Value, University of Iowa, https://ruralhealthvalue.public-health.uiowa.edu/)

The strategic Planning Tool will assess your healthcare organization (HCO) capacities (resources, processes, infrastructure, etc.) to deliver value-based care (VBC). Value-based care refers to healthcare that concurrently improves clinical quality/patient safety, advances community health, and lowers per capita cost.

The Strategic Planning Tool guides an assessment of 80 specific capacities or best practices categorized under eight topic headings. The topic headings are interrelated and codependent; thus, capacities may fit under more than one topic heading.

For each capacity, please rate the degree to which the capacity is developed *and* deployed in your HCO. Alternately, some capacities may be better assessed by the degree of adoption (alternate response in parentheses). The six response options are:

- Fully developed and deployed: The VBC capacity is fully developed and deployed throughout the HCO. (The HCO has fully adopted this capacity.)
- Developed, incompletely deployed: The VBC capacity is developed, but incompletely deployed throughout the HCO. (The HCO has nearly adopted this capacity.)
- In development: The VBC capacity is in development but has not been deployed in the HCO. (The HCO has partially adopted this capacity.)
- In discussion: The VBC capacity has been discussed within the last 2 years, but no development activity is occurring at the HCO. (The HCO is considering adopting this capacity.)
- Not applicable: The VBC capacity has been discussed by the HCO in the last 2 years, but was determined to be not applicable. (The HCO does not plan to adopt this capacity.)
- Not considered: The VBC capacity has not been considered by the HCO in the last 2 years. (The HCO has no plans for this capacity.)

The evaluations have focused either on single organizations or on the specific comparison groups in academic studies. In addition, as VBHC is closely linked to knowledge management, some knowledge management maturity models have been modified for VBHC evaluation purposes.

4.2 Professional Level

Health service is a complex and interconnected collection of individual agents posing some freedom to act in ways that are not predictable, and an environment where one agent's actions change the context for the other agents (Plsek and Greenhalgh 2001). Capability to produce value is directly dependent on the quality of performance of professionals in professional teams to produce positive change for individuals' functional capacity, objective and subjective health and coping with disabilities (Fig. 3). Most decisions leading to value in the health systems are produced by individuals, i.e., patients, by compliance with treatments and ability to change their behaviors (Derksen et al. 2020). Therefore, one of the core elements of value-based healthcare is professional performance, which has been later added to some quality frameworks, like the Triple Aim, which has thus become the Quadruple Aim (Berwick et al. 2008; Bodenheimer and Sinsky 2014).

Professional performance is based on staff competencies. Professional competencies are a sum of the elements of abilities (knowledge, skills, and attitudes)

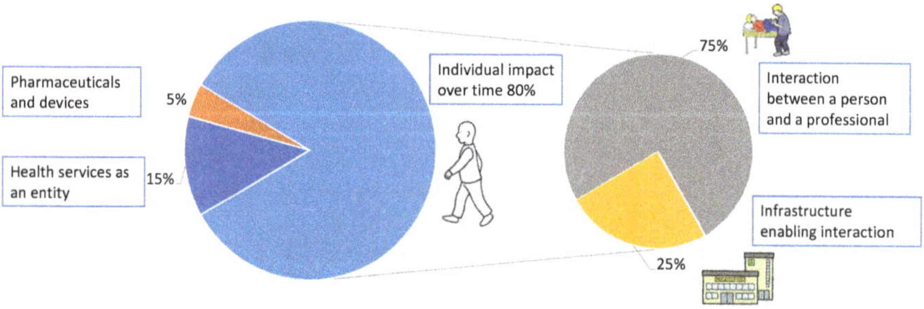

Fig. 3 Pathway to healthcare outcomes leading to improvements in functional capacity, objective and subjective health and coping with disabilities. (Formulated from source: https://assets.kingsfund.org.uk/f/256914/x/6d1d122b88/inequalities_life_expectancy_2015.pdf original publication are McGinnis JM, Williams-Russo P, Knickman JR (2002). "The case for more active policy attention to health promotion." Health Affairs, vol 21, no 2, pp 78–93. and Canadian Institute of Advanced Research, Health Canada, Population, and Public Health Branch. AB/NWT 2002, quoted in Kuznetsova D (2012). Healthy places: councils leading on public health. London: New Local Government Network))

needed in effective and safe patient work (Cooke et al. 2006). Competencies are most relevant when they are defined in the context of the clinical environment as they develop and vary over time and setting (Ten Cate and Billett 2014) to global frameworks practice specific competency descriptions are useful.

Organizational learning theories, like expansive learning theory, see organizational learning as a collaborative process rather than individual performance (Engeström 2014). Effective education leads to a change in professional behaviors and, therefore, development needs arise from clinical work. There is a large body of methodology and tools in both formative assessment (Van Der Vleuten and Schuwirth 2005) and summative assessment (Kogan et al. 2009) both within the profession and in interprofessional education (Rogers et al. 2017). Quality assessment systems should be directly attached to Continuing Professional Development (CPD) programs through system assessment. Thus, understanding of the interrelationships between components of process and outcomes would increase among health professionals, and understanding of system-wide thinking needed for more mature VBHC will emerge (Bodenheimer and Sinsky 2014).

When improving organizational capacity to produce value, professional competencies and performance define limits for implementing any investment, policy, and technology. Competency management in assessing value-based strategic planning has been recognized (Van Der Vleuten and Schuwirth 2005), but only few studies have demonstrated the linkage between CPD with quality and cost in a single care pathway (Moriates et al. 2014). Data for advanced competency management and value calculations exist. Care units produce, e.g., data on process flows, timing, responses, safety data or complaints, not to mention the patient outcome data. Personnel resources have data on investment in education, continuous education, e-learning usage or personal assessments. Equally, data exists for assessing variation in individual staff appraisals and specialist training programs that would allow to also assess the assessors (Apramian et al. 2016).

Competency evaluations can be integrated into value-based healthcare in several ways (Fig. 4). Most known are individual competency standards like recertification and/or performance metrics (e.g., UK revalidation process for physicians) or target setting for continuous professional development. More advanced methods include enhancement to adapt to evolving care models, technological advancements and changing patient needs utilizing more outcome-based metrics integrating measures of the impact on patient outcomes, safety metrics, cost reduction, patient satisfaction and adherence to quality metrics. This outcome-based evaluation reinforces the importance of competency in achieving value-based care goals. Technology enables this at a professional level but also at a team-based level (Fig. 5). There is a possibility to build feedback loops and improvement initiatives with regular feedback mechanisms and performance reviews to assess the competency needs for implementation of value-based care.

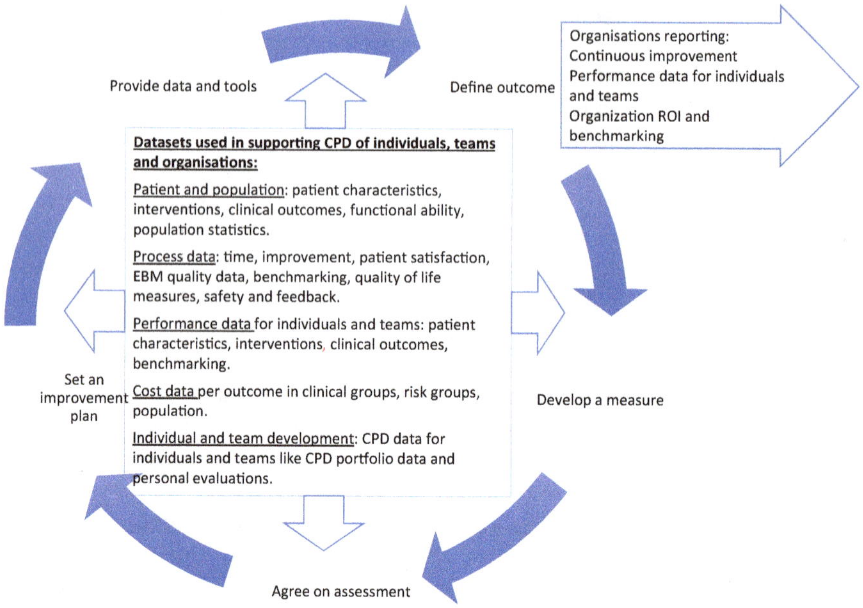

Fig. 4 Professional development cycle and its link to big data analytics in healthcare and examples of data sources which could be used in providing data for physicians, organizations, and society

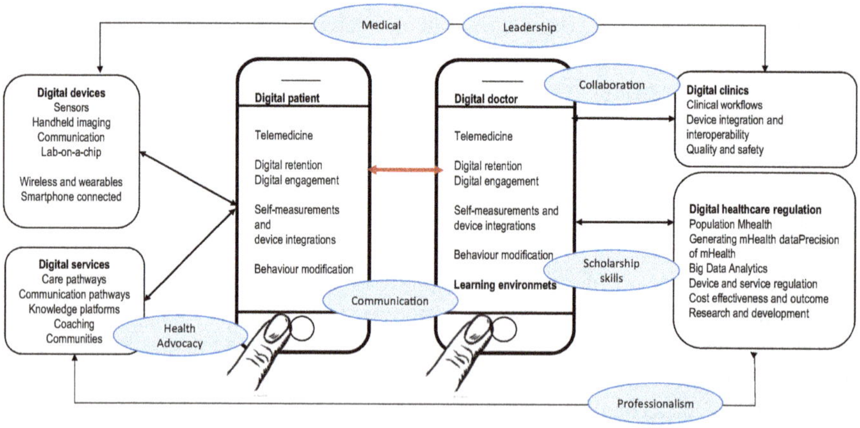

Fig. 5 Digital working environment of doctors with CanMEDS competencies relevant to targets in healthcare. (Modified from Bhavnani SP, Narula J, Sengupta PP. Mobile technology and the digitization of healthcare. Eur Heart J. 2016 May 7;37(18):1428–38 and CanMEDS 2015)

5 Evaluating the Outcomes of Health Services

To fully harness the potential of value-based healthcare for driving improvements, there must be a significant acceleration in outcomes measurement. This entails a commitment to measuring a comprehensive set of outcomes for all major medical conditions. Furthermore, standardizing these outcome sets on a national and global scale is imperative (Porter et al. 2016).

Practically, the evaluation of outcomes means comparison from (1) international, (2) national or (3) internal perspectives. Standardized measurement frameworks or quality registers are essential as the comparison of outcomes requires employing well-defined data collection methods, long-term efforts to collect high-quality data with high coverage and enabling effective risk adjustment. We present the most common ways to evaluate outcomes of health services.

5.1 International Evaluations

5.1.1 International Consortium for Health Outcomes Measurement (ICHOM)

ICHOM is a North American non-profit organization, founded in 2012 by Professor Porter, Dr. Stefan Larsson (of Boston Consulting Group) and Professor Martin Ingvar (of the Karolinska Institutet in Stockholm, Sweden), with a mission to standardize healthcare outcomes measurement. ICHOM builds on the framework developed by Porter and Teisberg (2006), aiming to bring the ideas to practice. Enabling international evaluations is at the heart of ICHOM.

Toward this end, ICHOM develops Standard Sets: disease-specific sets of metrics for standardizing the measurement of outcomes. ICHOM has released 45 Standard Sets to date, covering over 60% of the global disease burden. Each set is developed by a multi-professional team and patients to ensure that patient-relevant metrics are included. Each set includes patient characteristics, clinical measures, and patient-reported measures. Typically, after the acute phase, questionnaires are repeated annually for 5 years—or indefinitely, in case of a non-curable condition.

VBHC creates substantial job demands and resources for different professionals. It is a developing concept, and its next phase needs to include professionals, their capacities and communication strategies into the eq. A recent review stated that currently several job demands are triggered by an unsupportive organizational environment rather than executing VBHC. Professionals need to see the value of measuring value in their everyday lives (van Engen et al. 2022). This is important for reducing ineffective care without impacting on quality of care. We have a promising example for modifying care with improved outcomes (O'Donnell et al. 2023), but implementation throughout the system requires professionals to unlearn poor quality practices.

ICHOM has been developing an international benchmarking platform and some pilot programs have been launched (Dias et al. 2017; García-Lorenzo et al. 2024), but this is still a work in progress, and many questions remain. When the same outcomes are measured in different healthcare units in different countries, their comparison is theoretically simple. Yet, for the data to be comparable, it must be defined in a very detailed manner. For example, at what time point precisely should heart rate be recorded for a coronary artery disease patient—at hospital arrival, immediately prior to procedure, etc. Comorbidities, risk factors and variables of condition severity must be recorded meticulously to be able to compare patient-mix.

Another question is whether analysis should be performed on-site (based on shared specifications) or centrally. The latter would often be preferable, but it would necessitate sharing patient-level data, which is problematic from the point of view of data protection.

ICHOM Standard Sets yield a wide array of data, which translates into laboriousness for the patient. In addition to chronically multi-morbid patients, patients experiencing a series of episodic diseases (say, a stroke, then an AMI) on top of a chronic condition will find themselves filling out several sets of questionnaires for years to come. As different sets have been developed in silos of independent professionals, they may record the same symptom with different questionnaires—and many sets record the same symptoms: pain, depression, etc. Also, the choice of a generic PROM varies widely between sets. This means that the burden of filling in the questionnaires adds up. ICHOM has been working on aligning the generic PROMs across sets.

One way to tackle the problem of overlapping questionnaires would be using PROMIS measures (https://www.healthmeasures.net/explore-measurement-systems/promis), which are symptom-specific instead of condition-specific. Especially when using Computer Adaptive Tests (CAT), PROMIS measures minimize the number of items asked per patient. However, this approach has not been widely embraced by ICHOM, although some PROMIS short forms are used in some ICHOM Standard Sets.

So far, although initiatives have been launched (Dias et al. 2017; García-Lorenzo et al. 2024), systematic and ongoing international benchmarking based on ICHOM Standard Sets is still not being done.

5.1.2 Other International Evaluations

National registers are often useful in estimating the effectiveness of the service system as a whole. If reliable registers are available for causes of death and age at death, then PYLL (Potential Years of Life Lost) can be calculated. YLD (Years Lost due to Disability) calculations require data on the prevalence of conditions, indicators on the severity of conditions and QALY valuations for each condition. An often-referred source for QALY valuations is the Global Burden of Disease study (GBD; https://www.healthdata.org/research-analysis/gbd) by the Institute for Health Metrics and Evaluation (IHME), which can be used if national valuations are unavailable. For benchmarking purposes, the indicators of condition severity should be agreed upon to ensure comparability. Likewise, interpretation of prevalence must be defined precisely: for example, if a patient has a diagnosis for diabetes type 1 at any time point, they should be considered to be a patient with diabetes indefinitely. How about a trauma diagnosis—for how long should that be considered relevant?

PYLL and YLD are system-level outcome indicators, and changes in them from 1 year to the next can be seen as an indicator of effectiveness of the national health system—although it must be noted that they reflect genetics, health policies, etc., in addition to the effectiveness of the health service system. Despite this limitation vis-a-vis health services evaluation, these kinds of system-level outcome indicators are key, as they indicate results regarding the ultimate goal: population health and well-being. They also highlight the importance of health policy: a lion's share of health and well-being are being produced outside of the healthcare services sector, and if health is not considered in all policies (nutrition, exercise, smoking, etc.), then all that can be done in healthcare services is minimize the damage and treat the illnesses caused.

Comparisons of healthcare expenditure and crude markers of effectiveness (such as life expectancy) have been conducted in academic studies (Papanicolas et al. 2018). However, ongoing benchmarking is still not known to be happening. Some countries do have initiatives for healthcare data standardization and exchange to facilitate benchmarking, such as the Nordic Interoperability Project (https://nordicinteroperability.com/) and the OMOP Common Data Model (https://www.ohdsi.org/data-standardization/).

5.2 National or "Internal" Evaluations

5.2.1 Quality Registers

Quality registers have traditionally been established and utilized by clinicians primarily for research purposes, and their use for systematic benchmarking and process improvement has gained more attention in recent years (Santos and Eriksson 2014).

A quality register is a collection of patient-level data that includes patient characteristics, interventions, and outcomes. Hence, the "quality" in quality registers is to be understood as a wide concept which includes effectiveness. National quality registers are quality registers that are steered and funded by the government. Some trailblazers for national quality registers include Sweden (over 100 registers), Denmark (80) and Norway (54) (Jonsson et al. 2019).

While quality registers are often the only source of nation-level comparable outcome data, there are some noteworthy limitations. Firstly, quality registers are based on patient segments defined by diagnosis or intervention. While this is congruent with VBHC, this means that their scope is limited and will never encompass the entire population. However, by choosing to start with the most significant patient segments (based on patient volume, health services expenditure, disease severity, etc.), the problem of limited coverage can be minimized. In the Nordics, first national quality registers have usually been focused on cancer, cardiovascular disease and artificial joints.

Especially problematic are multimorbid patients, whose proportion of the population is ever-increasing due to ageing. Comorbidities are often recorded in quality registers, but the focus is on a single diagnosis instead of the holistic health state of the patient.

Another limitation is that quality registries often require that data be input separately into the registry and the electronic medical record, thus creating administrative burdens on the professionals. Whenever possible, double documentation should be avoided and integrations between systems utilized.

As quality registers are typically maintained and developed by specialists, choice of outcome metrics may become a source of disagreement. Different specialties often have deep-rooted traditions for using a particular metric, while management or government officials often need a more generic metric in order to allow for inter-segment comparison. These needs need to be mediated in a way that allows quality register data to be used effectively for development and benchmarking, while satiating the needs of the specialists, on whose continued contributions the system heavily lies. Where opinions on, e.g., choice of generic PROM questionnaire differ, the balancing of views cannot be done by including both (or all) questionnaires, as that would create an unnecessary burden on the patient filling out the questionnaires. Increased patient burden often leads to lower compliance in filling out the questionnaires.

As patient-centeredness has been on the rise for the last few years equally, national quality registers have taken a step in that direction. VBHC has influenced the development, and so the emphasis on patient-reported measures has become more prominent. Sweden, Norway, and Denmark all mandate that PROM data be included in every national quality register. Some countries also involve patients in choosing the metrics. PREMs are also increasingly seen as a valid part of quality registers, even though they are not as widely used as PROMs are. Using PREMs could strengthen the patient's perspective.

The mere existence of national quality registers does not bring forward change—as is the case with any collection of data. Reporting and utilization of data are key. When analyzing outcomes data, it soon becomes evident that the choice of metrics alone does not guide us in reporting them. For example, we record pain on visual analogue scale (VAS) before and after a procedure—how do we evaluate the results? Average pain before vs. average pain after? Average change? Or the portion of patients whose pain has been alleviated? Reporting is as much of a multi-disciplinary group effort as is the choice of metrics.

Benchmarking is often the only way to determine what is a good result, and what is a reasonable target level. At the very least, results of analysis must be made available to the participating clinics, so that they can benchmark their results against each other. For benchmarking to be effective, though, the availability of the results is not enough: a forum for discussion is also needed. It is necessary for participants to discuss the results and the underlying reason for their differences so that best practices can be recognized. An understanding of the practices explaining the results is a prerequisite for change.

Figure 6 illustrates HbA1c levels in Finnish DM1 patients per region, as analyzed by the Finnish national quality register for diabetes. Finnish regions gather twice annually to discuss the results; decide on development areas, such as patient-centered improvements to the urine sample collection process in order to increase the coverage of kidney function screening, and present practical examples of how each region has utilized the results and what sorts of best practices underlie the results.

In addition to clinic-level benchmarking, many countries use the results of quality registers for national steering of the healthcare system. Furthermore, patient

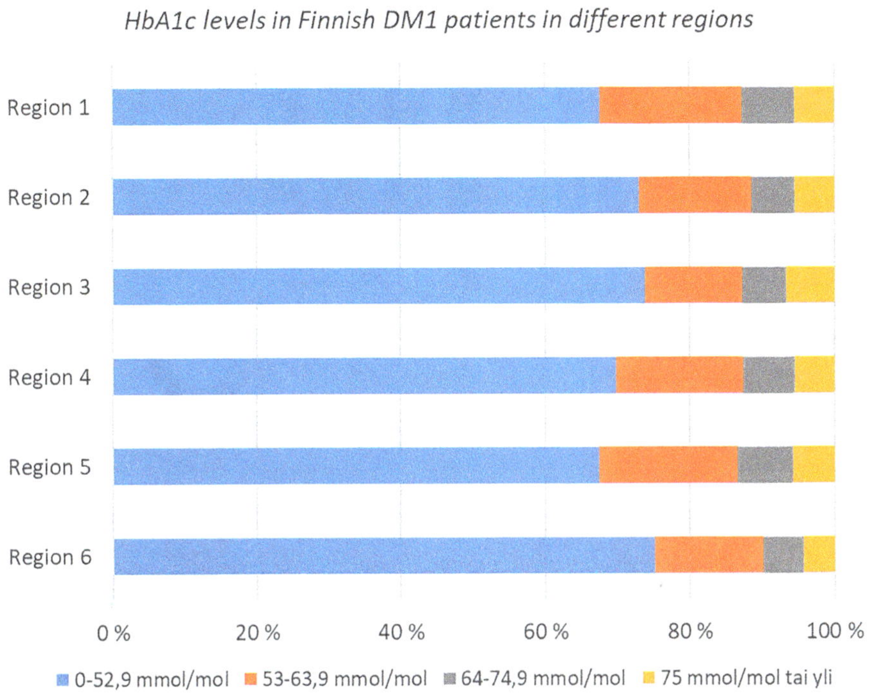

Fig. 6 HbA1c levels in Finnish DM1 patients in different regions. (Source: Finnish Institute of Health and Wellbeing)

freedom of choice can be supported by providing understandable information on treatment results in different facilities to the wider public.

5.2.2 Other Evaluations

As noted before, quality registers are defined as including patient-level data about patient characteristics, treatments, and outcomes. While other registers typically lack some of this data, they may still be useful in estimating the effectiveness of the service system as a whole. As described earlier, PYLL and YLD can be used within a nation as well. Depending on the national legislature, the effect of general health policies may be diminished in national comparisons as compared to international ones—the health policies may be similar in different regions. Even so, genetics and environmental factors still play a role.

It must be noted that when using health economics indicators for comparisons, the units of comparison should be healthcare service commissioners (e.g., regions or insurance companies/schemes) that have an overall responsibility for the health services of their population.

ICHOM Standard Sets have also been utilized for national comparison, e.g., for stroke outcomes benchmarking in Estonia (https://www.ichom.org/nordic-healthcare-group/visual-dashboard-to-benchmark-outcomes-and-costs-between-hospitals/) (Fig. 7) The dashboard is not a clinical evaluation tool but rather aiming

Fig. 7 Example of value-based dashboard enabling evaluation of outcomes and costs

at evaluating the processes and practices to enable improvement of the services enabling learning.

Some groups of private hospitals have utilized VBHC and benchmarking to evaluate and improve results within the group. In many instances, such as in the famous example of the Dutch Santeon hospitals, this has resulted in notable improvements. In the long run, though, unless external benchmarks are also used, the drive to improve may run out as all hospitals within the group reach the level of the best-performing hospital.

6 Evaluating Costs

Evaluating the costs of the health services following the VBHC principles is a challenging task. First, the cost accounting principles are different in almost every organization. Second, the cost should cover the full cycle of care, and single service providers are typically covering only a part of the value chain. Moreover, healthcare services are typically an investment of society not only focusing on better health but also aiming to avoid other societal costs which may be important to include in cost evaluations. Third, especially international comparisons are difficult, although there are instruments (e.g., Purchasing Power Parity) aiming at making the costs comparable across countries. The challenge mostly relates to different salary levels between countries.

The essential question in cost measurement is determining the perspective from which costs are measured and which costs are considered. Costs can be divided into direct costs related to treatment or service and indirect costs related to other aspects of illness or care. Direct costs include items like consultation, hospitalization, or diagnostic costs, while indirect costs may encompass disability-related expenses.

From a cost-effectiveness perspective, there's a risk of sub-optimization if only direct costs are evaluated. For instance, focusing solely on unit production costs may lead to increased service utilization, longer wait times, and potentially higher costs for patients or society, which could diminish overall cost-effectiveness. For example, in Finland, total costs of cancer treatment increased by 4.4% annually from 2004 to 2014, while indirect costs increased by 0.6% annually, resulting in a decrease in total costs per patient when considering inflation and the number of patients (Torkki et al. 2018). The VOICE initiative assessed only direct costs: "Since no standard set on economic outcomes was available for breast cancer, an ad hoc set of resource use was designed following the patient care pathway designed by the VOICE research team, the healthcare centre perspective and the health economics literature on healthcare utilization" (García-Lorenzo et al. 2024).

The central goal in the context of cost-effectiveness is measuring individual patient costs rather than just unit costs. However, the commonly used approach first estimates unit costs for each activity and then combines them based on individual patient utilization of activities within a service chain. This type of cost calculation is commonly referred to as activity-based costing, where episodic costs are thought to arise from the consumption of each activity (service) based on the cost causality principle. Often, a simpler time-based activity-based costing model is used, where service costs are estimated based on the time and resource unit costs used to produce the service. Such an analysis may be possible using data extracted from patients' charts (case notes) or an administrative database.

The evaluations should include (1) total costs per patient, (2) use of services and (3) unit prices of services separately to increase transparency of the cost comparisons and to understand the most significant cost drivers and their effects. Table 1 shows the illustrated differences between two hospitals in a same patient group, and it can be quite easily noticed that the differences in costs relate mostly to differences in service use in inpatient days and sick leaves.

Table 1 Example of cost comparison between two hospitals

	Hospital A			Hospital B		
Service	Service costs	Service use	Unit cost	Service costs	Service use	Unit cost
Outpatient	520 €	2 visits	260 €	480 €	2 visits	240 €
Inpatient	2880 €	4 days	720 €	4080 €	6 days	680 €
Rehabilitation	1200 €	5 visits	240 €	440 €	2 visits	220 €
Sick leaves	1800 €	6 days	300 €	2400 €	8 days	300 €
Total costs	6400 €			7400 €		

Then the question is whether we are evaluating the costs of specific health services or the costs over patient's episode of care. The first one may be useful in evaluating the efficiency or productivity of a health service provider but the latter is required to understand the total costs, thus enabling the assessment of the value. For instance, patients' travel expenses are costs both from the patient's perspective and from society's perspective but aren't considered a cost from the Ministry of Health's viewpoint. Conversely, workers' compensation payments represent a cost for the government paying them, a benefit for the recipient patient, and are neutral in terms of society's costs and gains. Economists refer to these monetary transfers that don't reflect resource usage as transfer payments, and while there are administrative costs associated with them, these aren't measured by the payment amounts themselves. Therefore, the chosen perspective is a critical factor in determining which costs are considered relevant.

7 Challenges of VBHC

No system or framework comes without limitations and challenges. VBHC has emerged as a center of health systems. This has made it possible to examine value from two perspectives for a single patient or treatment pathway, perceived and measured. Both contain significant challenges in terms of healthcare and society. The most of health is however produced outside of health systems, and at least at the population level or when looking at the formation of the value of patient groups, a broader review should be included. Limitations of VBHC relate to its extensions out of its original aim looking at value produced in healthcare. Thus, being complicated, it is limited to individuals with disease and/or treatment, leaving out the population level with the socio-ecological model determining health (Sallis et al. 2008).

Using PREMs has strengthened the patient perspective, but what is the right balance between PROMS and PREMS for different patient groups? Our perception of health is on the one hand a communal and cultural concept and on the other hand a very individual one. Society's expectations and the possibilities of living environments to make up for functional deficits have a significant impact on the experience of health. Health system differences will obviously produce methodological challenges, but transforming scales between languages and cultures may support comparability across countries (Tietschert et al. 2018).

The future does not look bright at present. It has been argued that some health technology trends have been biased toward technology adoption, even with modest benefits, rather than investing in social care or patient support even when showing strong evidence (Lewis 2022). This trend is accelerating with wearable technologies measuring physiological data and functional capacity. Precision medicine and understanding of genetics and genomics enable tailoring medical diagnostics, treatment, and interventions to individual characteristics and lifestyles, but at what cost-benefit? Improved treatments for, e.g., cancer lead to more effective and less invasive treatments, but higher costs. What is then defined as value? How do we compare the perceived value between groups of patients and non-patients? Biotechnological innovations and advances in regenerative medicine hold promise for revolutionizing treatments for various diseases and injuries. The question of value also depends on the unit of analysis—whether we consider value at the level of populations, patient groups, or individual patients. Do we consider value for people, patient groups or individuals? There is a real threat of continuing medicalization for producing less value for people with more resources. Comparison over different patient groups should be better assessed in VBHC, e.g., ensuring requirement of same generic measure(s) in all standard sets.

Noncommunicable diseases are rarely single diagnoses, but a group of diseases produced by the same pathological process and risk factors. VBHC at organizational level can enhance the effectiveness of chronic disease treatment, but at the individual level, it is the ability for health behavior changes that determines the outcomes and risks. There are real positive options for improvement in using healthcare data and digital health wearable devices, health apps, and health tracking technologies helping people to prevent, improve care and support in coping with personalized health management. However, this requires new types of metrics that can be used to assess the ability for change of professionals and their system-wide ability.

Most resources in healthcare are nowadays used for long-term complex conditions. Applications to those patient groups have revealed that the outcome measures must be standardized to allow evaluation of specific conditions at an aggregated level, but they must also be sensitive enough to capture each patient's individual needs and goals. However, this is challenging in fragmented healthcare systems and for multi-morbid patients with long-term needs. It is also difficult to decide which part of the cycle of care should be evaluated in terms of value-based healthcare (Elf et al. 2017). In addition, as the standard sets are designed for specific single health conditions, the measurement efforts may be too complicated and also lack relevance if trying to follow each specific condition instead of evaluating the overall health of those patients.

8 Summary

Evaluating health services from a VBHC perspective involves assessing value, including outcomes and costs. This evaluation can encompass system-level factors; the maturity of VBHC in healthcare providers; outcomes and costs measurement systems; international, national, and internal comparisons; and performance evaluation.

System-level drivers for VBHC, such as payment models and legislative frameworks, significantly influence their success in different healthcare systems. The maturity of VBHC within organizations requires organizational and cultural changes, with a focus on measuring outcomes and shifting from volume to patient value. Evaluating outcomes involves international comparisons, national quality registers and internal benchmarking, while cost evaluation is complex, considering various perspectives and cost components.

VBHC is a transformative approach to healthcare delivery emphasizing patient value, outcomes and costs. Evaluating health services through a VBHC lens involves assessing a range of factors to enhance healthcare delivery and value for patients and society.

VBHC examines the production of value from the point of view of the producer organizations. It is a significant addition to evaluating healthcare systems' resilience for adaptation and mitigation in the climate crisis. Healthcare produces indirect and direct emissions hazardous to the climate and nature diversity. Ineffective treatments should be abandoned as they merely form waste in the system. VBHC has primarily focused on generating value within treatment processes, optimizing operational models and managing costs, particularly within specific disease groups (Falivena and Palozzi 2020). To achieve comprehensive sustainability, VBHC may need to incorporate broader determinants of health, such as socio-ecological models, to improve healthcare effectiveness (Sallis et al. 2008).

References

Apramian T, Cristancho S, Watling C, Ott M, Lingard L (2016) "Staying in the game": how procedural variation shapes competence judgments in surgical education. Acad Med 91(11). Association of American Medical Colleges learn serve lead proceedings of the 55th annual research in medical education sessions, p S37. /pmc/articles/PMC5578755/. Accessed 30 Nov 2023

Axelsson L, Engström AK (2001) The concept of effectiveness—a blind alley? A study of different interpretations in a Swedish county council. Int J Health Plann Manag 16(1):61–71. https://onlinelibrary.wiley.com/doi/full/10.1002/hpm.610. Accessed 30 Nov 2023

Berwick DM, Nolan TW, Whittington J (2008) The triple aim: care, health, and cost. Health Aff (Project Hope) 27(3):759–769. https://pubmed.ncbi.nlm.nih.gov/18474969/. Accessed 30 Nov 2023

Bodenheimer T, Sinsky C (2014) From triple to quadruple aim: care of the patient requires care of the provider. Ann Fam Med 12(6):573–576. https://pubmed.ncbi.nlm.nih.gov/25384822/. Accessed 30 Nov 2023

Cattel D, Eijkenaar F (2020) Value-based provider payment initiatives combining global payments with explicit quality incentives: a systematic review. Med Care Res Rev 77(6):511. /pmc/articles/PMC7536531/. Accessed 27 Jun 2024

Cooke M, Irby DM, Sullivan W, Ludmerer KM (2006) Medical education: American medical education 100 years after the flexner report. N Engl J Med 355(13):1339–1344. +1306

Cossio-Gil Y, Omara M, Watson C, Casey J, Chakhunashvili A, Gutiérrez-San Miguel M, Kahlem P, Keuchkerian S, Kirchberger V, Luce-Garnier V, Michiels D, Moro M, Philipp-Jaschek B, Sancini S, Hazelzet J, Stamm T (2022) The roadmap for implementing value-based healthcare in European University Hospitals—consensus report and recommendations. Value Health 25(7):1148–1156. http://www.valueinhealthjournal.com/article/S1098301521031806/fulltext. Accessed 25 Nov 2023

Damberg CL, Sorbero ME, Lovejoy SL, Martsolf GR, Raaen L, Mandel D (2014) Measuring success in health care value-based purchasing programs: findings from an environmental scan, literature review, and expert panel discussions. Rand Health Q 4(3):9. /pmc/articles/PMC5161317/. Accessed 27 Jun 2024

Derksen FA, Hartman TO, Lagro-Janssen T (2020) The human encounter, attention, and equality: the value of doctor–patient contact. Br J Gen Pract 70(694):254–255. https://bjgp.org/content/70/694/254. Accessed 30 Nov 2023

Dias AG, Roberts CJ, Lippa J, Arora J, Lundström M, Rolfson O, Tonn ST (2017) Benchmarking outcomes that matter most to patients: the globe programme. Eur Med J: 42–49. https://www.mendeley.com/catalogue/5e8c0b97-e4f7-3efe-8fac-5984e22516fa/. Accessed 30 Nov 2023.

Eijsink JFH, Fabian AM, Vervoort JPM, Al Khayat MNMT, Boersma C, Postma MJ (2023) Value-based health care in Western countries: a scoping review on the implementation of patient-reported-outcomes sets for hospital-based interventions. Expert Rev Pharmacoecon Outcomes Res 23(1):1–13. https://www.tandfonline.com/doi/abs/10.1080/14737167.2023.2136168 . Accessed 25 Nov 2023

Elf M, Flink M, Nilsson M, Tistad M, Von Koch L, Ytterberg C (2017) The case of value-based healthcare for people living with complex long-term conditions. BMC Health Serv Res 17(1):1–6. https://link.springer.com/articles/10.1186/s12913-016-1957-6. Accessed 1 Dec 2023

Engeström Y (2014) Learning by expanding: an activity-theoretical approach to developmental research, 2nd edn. Orienta-Konsultit, Helsinki, pp 1–299. https://www.cambridge.org/core/books/learning-by-expanding/6D0648C3DEDE20157B359E464AFDB8C1. Accessed 30 Nov 2023

Falivena C, Palozzi G (2020) Value-based healthcare paradigm for healthcare sustainability. In: Accounting, finance, sustainability, governance and fraud. Springer, Berlin, pp 133–153. https://art.torvergata.it/handle/2108/244025. Accessed 30 Nov 2023

García-Lorenz B, Gorostiza A, Alayo I, Castelo Zas S, Cobos Baena P, Gallego Camiña I, Izaguirre Narbaiza B, Mallabiabarrena G, Ustarroz-Aguirre I, Rigabert A, Balzi W, Maltoni R, Massa I, Álvarez López I, Arévalo Lobera S, Esteban M, Fernández Calleja M, Gómez Mediavilla J, Fernández M, Del Oro Hitar M, Del Carmen Ortega Torres M, Sanz Ferrandez MC, Manso Sánchez L, Serrano Balazote P, Varela Rodríguez C, Campone M, Le Lann S, Vercauter P, Tournoy K, Borges M, Oliveira AS, Soares M, Fullaondo A, VOICE Study Group, González N, Lerma IV, Irazabal IA, de Larrinoa Santamaría AF, Capanaga AF, Cacicedo J, Elorduy EV, Acaiturri-Ayesta T, Gómez-Inhiesto E, Danesi V, Gentili N, Roncadori A, Alarz FH, Iraola KI, Adam V, De Rijck H, Everaert E, Barreira E, Medeiros P, Barros E (2024) European value-based healthcare benchmarking: moving from theory to practice. Eur J Pub Health 34(1):44–51. https://doi.org/10.1093/eurpub/ckad181 Accessed 30 Nov 2023

Jonsson, P. M., Pikkujämsä, S., & Heiliö, P. L. (2019). Kansalliset laaturekisterit sosiaali-ja terveydenhuollossa: Toimintamalli, organisointi ja rahoitus. (In Finnish)

Kogan JR, Holmboe ES, Hauer KE (2009) Tools for direct observation and assessment of clinical skills of medical trainees: a systematic review. JAMA 302(12):1316–1326. https://pubmed.ncbi.nlm.nih.gov/19773567/. Accessed 30 Nov 2023

Kokko P, Kork AA (2021) Value-based healthcare logics and their implications for Nordic health policies. Health Serv Manag Res 34(1):3–12. https://journals.sagepub.com/doi/10.1177/0951484820971457. Accessed 30 Nov 2023

ICHOM (2020)– International Consortium for Health Outcomes Measurement. www.ichom.org. https://www.ichom.org. Accessed 30 Nov 2023

Larsson S, Clawson J, Howard R (2023) Value-based health care at an inflection point: a global agenda for the next decade

Lewis S (2022) Value-based healthcare: is it the way forward? Future Healthc J 9(3):211. /pmc/articles/PMC9761467/. Accessed 30 Nov 2023

Mjåset C, Nagra NS, Feeley TW (2020) Value-based health care in four different health care systems

Moriates C, Mourad M, Novelero M, Wachter RM (2014) Development of a hospital-based program focused on improving healthcare value. J Hosp Med 9(10):671–677. https://pubmed.ncbi.nlm.nih.gov/24980982/. Accessed 30 Nov 2023

O'Donnell MT, Lewis S, Davies S, Dinneen SF (2023) Delivering value-based healthcare for people with diabetes in a national publicly funded health service: lessons from Ireland and Wales.

J Diabetes Investig 14(8):925–929. https://pubmed.ncbi.nlm.nih.gov/37203299/. Accessed 30 Nov 2023

Papanicolas I, Woskie LR, Jha AK (2018) Health care spending in the United States and other high-income countries. JAMA 319(10):1024–1039. https://pubmed.ncbi.nlm.nih.gov/29536101/. Accessed 30 Nov 2023

Pitkänen LJ, Leskelä RL, Tolkki H, Torkki P (2021) A value-based steering model for healthcare. Front Health Serv 1:709271

Plsek PE, Greenhalgh T (2001) The challenge of complexity in health care. BMJ 323(7313):625–628. https://www.bmj.com/content/323/7313/625. Accessed 30 Nov 2023

Porter ME (2010) What is value in health care? N Engl J Med 363(26):2477–2481. http://www.nejm.org/doi/abs/10.1056/NEJMp1011024. Accessed 29 May 2021

Porter M, Lee T (2013) The strategy that will fix health care. Harv Bus Rev 91(10):50–70. https://hbr.org/2013/10/the-strategy-that-will-fix-health-care. Accessed 27 Jun 2024

Porter ME, Teisberg EO (2006) Redefining health care: creating value-based competition on results. Harvard Business Press, Boston

Porter ME, Larsson S, Lee TH (2016) Standardizing patient outcomes measurement. N Engl J Med 374(6):504–506

Rogers GD, Thistlethwaite JE, Anderson ES, Abrandt Dahlgren M, Grymonpre RE, Moran M, Samarasekera DD (2017) International consensus statement on the assessment of interprofessional learning outcomes. *Med Teach* 39(4):347–359. https://pubmed.ncbi.nlm.nih.gov/28024436/. Accessed 30 Nov 2023

Rosen R (2000) Applying research to health care policy and practice: medical and managerial views on effectiveness and the role of research. J Health Serv Res Policy 5(2):103–108. https://pubmed.ncbi.nlm.nih.gov/10947544/. Accessed 30 Nov 2023

Sallis JF, Owen N, Fisher EB (2008) Ecological models of health behavior. In: Glanz K, Rimer BK, Viswanath K (eds) Health behavior and health education, 4th edn. John Wiley & Sons, San Francisco, pp 465–485

Santos, M., & Eriksson, H. (2014). Making quality registers supporting improvements: a systematic review of the data visualization in 5 quality registries. Quality Management in Healthcare, 23(2), 119–128

Teisberg E, Wallace S, O'Hara S (2020) Defining and implementing value-based health care: a strategic framework. Acad Med 95(5):682. /pmc/articles/PMC7185050/. Accessed 30 Nov 2023

Ten Cate O, Billett S (2014) Competency-based medical education: origins, perspectives and potentialities. Med Educ 48(3):325–332. https://onlinelibrary.wiley.com/doi/full/10.1111/medu.12355. Accessed 30 Nov 2023

The Economist (2016) A report from The Economist Intelligence Unit value-based healthcare: a global assessment findings and methodology

Tietschert MV, Angeli F, Van Raak AJA, Ruwaard D, Singer SJ (2018) Cross-cultural validation of the patient perception of integrated care survey. Health Serv Res 53(3):1745–1776. https://pubmed.ncbi.nlm.nih.gov/28726236/. Accessed 30 Nov 2023

Torkki P, Leskelä RL, Linna M, Mäklin S, Mecklin JP, Bono P, Kataja V, Karjalainen S (2018) Cancer costs and outcomes in the Finnish population 2004–2014. Acta Oncol 57(2):297–303. https://pubmed.ncbi.nlm.nih.gov/28696797/. Accessed 30 Nov 2023

Torkki P, Leskelä R-L, Mustonen P, Linna M, Lillrank P, Paulus D, Torkki TP, Fi H (2023) How to extend value-based healthcare to population-based healthcare systems? Defining an outcome-based segmentation model for health authority. BMJ Open 13(11):e077250. https://bmjopen.bmj.com/content/13/11/e077250. Accessed 30 Nov 2023

Van Der Vleuten CPM, Schuwirth LWT (2005) Assessing professional competence: from methods to programmes. Med Educ 39(3):309–317. https://pubmed.ncbi.nlm.nih.gov/15733167/. Accessed 30 Nov 2023

Van Engen V, Bonfrer I, Ahaus K, Buljac-Samardzic M (2022) Value-based healthcare from the perspective of the healthcare professional: a systematic literature review. Front Public Health 9:800702. https://pubmed.ncbi.nlm.nih.gov/35096748/. Accessed 30 Nov 2023

Van Staalduinen DJ, Van Den Bekerom P, Groeneveld S, Kidanemariam M, Stiggelbout AM, Van Den Akker-Van Marle ME (2022) The implementation of value-based healthcare: a scoping review. BMC Health Serv Res 22(1):1–8. https://link.springer.com/articles/10.1186/s12913-022-07489-2. Accessed 25 Nov 2023

Vijverberg JRG, Daniels K, Steinmann G, Garvelink MM, Van Der Voort MBVR, Biesma D, Bos WJW, Van Merode F, Van Der Nat P (2022) Mapping the extent, range and nature of research activity on value-based healthcare in the 15 years following its introduction (2006–2021): a scoping review. BMJ Open 12(8):e064983. https://bmjopen.bmj.com/content/12/8/e064983. Accessed 25 Nov 2023

Zanotto BS, Etges APBDS, Marcolino MAZ, Polanczyk CA (2021) Value-based healthcare initiatives in practice: a systematic review. J Healthc Manag 66(5):340. /pmc/articles/PMC8423138/. Accessed 26 Nov 2023

Complex Intervention Research: What, Why, and How

Walter Sermeus

Abstract

Healthcare is dealing with a series of challenges such as chronic conditions, aging populations, climate change, staff shortages, stringent legislations, and financial constraints. It is well accepted that these challenges require complex responses, generally called "complex interventions." However, to be effective, they need a specific research and evaluation approach. In this chapter, we will describe what makes an intervention complex and why we study them in a different way. We will describe various complex intervention frameworks which complements the discussion of evaluation frameworks and theories in chapter "Evaluation of Implementation: A Taxonomy of Implementation Science Theories, Models and Frameworks" in this handbook. We will discuss the development of complex interventions, pilot and feasibility testing for complex interventions, and several evaluation and implementation strategies, mainly applicable in organizational change and practice change evaluations.

Keywords

Health services research · Complex intervention research · Implementation research · Effectiveness · Efficacy · Research designs

W. Sermeus (✉)
Healthcare Management, Department of Public Health and Primary Care, Leuven Institute for Healthcare Policy, KU Leuven, Leuven, Belgium
e-mail: Walter.sermeus@kuleuven.be

A. Kaehne, J. Feather (eds.), *Handbook of Health Services Evaluation*,
https://doi.org/10.1007/978-3-031-87869-5_8

1 What Is a Complex Intervention?

Although intuitively a complex intervention (CI) can be well understood, it is not so easy to define. Complexity in this context refers to the number of components, range of behaviors, number of groups, settings, and levels targeted, expertise and skills required, as well as the permitted level of flexibility (Skivington et al. 2021). As the focus is mainly on the totality of components and not solely on the contribution of one single component, it is not always clear what the contribution is of every single component on the overall effect. And often the effect is produced by the interaction between the various components. Effects might be even more broadly engendered as the intervention may interact with the context that is conditional for the success of an intervention. Complex interventions are now generally considered as "events in systems" (Skivington et al. 2021).

Some argue that all interventions are complex. This is partially true. The pathway for introducing a new drug is indeed complicated as it goes through years of in vitro and animal studies. When bringing the new drug to the market, success is dependent not only on the efficacy of the drug but also on acceptability, availability, reimbursement, and a wide range of subjective elements. If indeed a drug is not prescribed or taken, there is no effect. However, introducing a new drug is strictly not defined as a complex intervention because the pathway on how the drug is working is fully understood and described. There is a clear difference between the efficacy of the drug in ideal conditions and the effectiveness in real life. When arguing that the introduction of a new drug is complex, the argument is mainly about the behavioral aspects originating with prescribers and patients.

Essential for complex interventions is that the process is indeed not fully understood and under control. Moreover, the efficacy of the intervention cannot be strictly separated from effectiveness as creating the ideal conditions for implementation is part of the intervention from the very beginning. To give an example: stroke units cannot be studied under laboratory conditions.

2 Why Study Complex Interventions Differently from Other Types of Interventions?

A major question is why we should study complex interventions differently from other interventions. The main reason is that a complex intervention cannot be separated from its context and implementation. This is problematic when performing a traditional RCT, which is the gold standard of research. The Medical Emergency Team (MET) trial (Hillman et al. 2005) is a good example in showing what can go wrong. In the mid-1990s, there was evidence that inpatients resuscitated outside intensive care units have a low probability of survival. However, early warning signs for cardiac arrest are present in a large percentage of patients and would allow to bring expert clinicians (rapid response teams or MET teams) to the bedsides of deteriorating patients to prevent cardiac arrest. All evidence came from observational studies, pre-post trials, seen as low evidence. At the beginning of the 2000s, a cluster RCT was conducted to finally prove that the intervention was effective (Hillman et al. 2005). Twenty-three hospitals in Australia agreed to participate, of which 11 were randomized into the control group and 12 into the intervention group. The result was however inconclusive which led to three different hypotheses: (1) the intervention itself is not effective; (2) the implementation is not effective; (3) the evaluation design is not the proper design to evaluate this kind of intervention. What came out of the analysis (Berwick 2008) is that all hospitals that volunteered to participate were eager to be in the intervention group. Which means that half of them were disappointed to be in the control group. They were expected to give usual care, but with their raised awareness of good practice, they struggled to avoid to provide improved quality of care, leading to a reduction of the rate of cardiac arrests and unexpected deaths in both groups from baseline. Although in the intervention group the incidence of calling MET was doubled, it was still only 30% of the optimal incidence related to the calling criteria. The reason was a high variability in the implementation of the intervention between hospitals. The intervention itself was organizational in nature: collaboration between clinical staff at the bedside and the MET-teams, calling the MET-team when needed, MET-teams getting there in time in response to urgency and other factors. What we observed is that some MET-teams were called too early (leading to false positives) or too late (false negatives) and perceptions of mutual disrespect, e.g., "why do you have called so late?" Clinical staff felt uneasy to call the MET-team as they felt being accused of not being able to stabilize their patients themselves. Some hospitals were better in managing this type of reaction than others. But these important factors, which we identify as "confounders" or "context," were probably the key vital elements of the intervention and were not well managed or documented. Berwick concluded that, most likely, the design was not fit to evaluate this type of intervention.

3 An Overview of Complex Intervention Frameworks

Similar observations as described above were leading to research failures by always applying the same methodologies that were so successful in biomedical research, while showing to be less effective in other research areas (Chalmers and Glasziou 2009). This led to a new framework for development and evaluation of RCTs for complex interventions to improve health (MRC 2000). The model is a copy of the five stages of clinical trials with five phases, starting from theory (phase 0), modeling of the intervention (phase 1), an exploratory trial (phase 2) until the definitive RCT (phase 3) and long-term implementation (phase 4). For each of the phases, different approaches were suggested. But the main critique to the framework was that it was too general and not evidence-based.

In turn, this prompted a revision of the MRC complex intervention framework in 2008 (Craig et al. 2008). The main differences from the original framework were that phase 0 and I (theory and modeling) were grouped together and that the model went from a linear (going through the different phases) to a circular approach. This means that a complex intervention might follow a continuous process of improvement where the start can be at any point in the process, and going back and forth in the model is not only possible but even expected. A major improvement of the revision is that much more examples and evidence were provided.

The latest revision was made in 2021 (Skivington et al. 2021), jointly commissioned by the UK Medical Research Council (MRC) and the National Institute for Health Research (NIHR), taking recent developments in theory and methods into account. One area of progress is the greater attention to the role of context. In the original definition of a CI, an intervention was considered complex because of properties of the intervention itself: the number of components, range of behaviors targeted, and level of permitted flexibility. In the new definition "CI as events in systems," more emphasis is given to the context and the conditions needed to implement the intervention in the real world and to maximize impact. A second change is that the simple focus on effectiveness is broadened to other dimensions such as acceptability, cost-effectiveness, and transferability. This requires the involvement of key stakeholders such as citizens, patients, practitioners, and policy makers much earlier in the process.

The current MRC framework on complex interventions defines four different phases and a list of core elements that have to be considered in all of the four phases (Fig. 1).

Phase 1 is developing (or identifying) the intervention. It is the crucial and most important phase. When we compare it with the development of a drug, this phase is the development of the drug itself. When there is no active component in the drug, there is no need to test it. The same with a complex intervention. But the difficulty is that the intervention is often seen as a black box, in which the active component is not always clear. This phase consists of systematic reviews on determining the efficacy of each of the components in the intervention, to model carefully how the intervention might work. A useful approach here is to create a program theory (Funnell and Rogers 2011) which articulates the key components of the intervention and how they interact, describing the mechanisms of the intervention and all conditions that are influential.

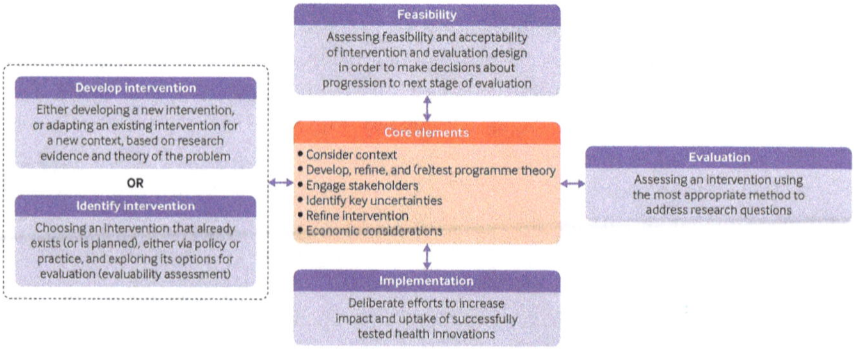

Fig. 1 MRC complex intervention framework (Skivington et al. 2021)

Phase 2 is testing the feasibility and piloting the intervention. Phase 2 is often underdeveloped and underestimated. There is a key difference between feasibility and piloting. Piloting is the full study on a small scale to determine initial responses to the study such as incidence/prevalence of the targeted outcome, response rates, missing data, and sample size. Feasibility studies on the other hand focus on all sorts of research questions dealing with key uncertainties in the intervention. An example is the acceptability of the intervention to practitioners. A proper research design that can be used to test feasibility can be a qualitative study to interview a series of practitioners on the barriers and enablers for adapting the intervention. Embedding this knowledge in the implementation strategy might improve acceptability. Phases 1 and 2 often interact, reducing the number of possible uncertainties in the intervention via small feasibility studies.

Phase 3 is the evaluation of the intervention. It is the main part of the study. A full range of designs has been developed in dealing with complex interventions. A popular design is a cluster RCT in which the intervention is randomized into a control and intervention group. Key in the evaluation is that there is some variability within and between groups, as this might give useful information on conditions and contextual factors. Often, blinding is not possible when organizational or behavioral change is required. This might cause bias as organizations, practitioners, or patients participating in the trial might be aware of being in the experimental or control arm of the study. They may not be willing to participate if they are not in the experimental arm. As a solution, often a stepped-wedge design is proposed in which every organization is implementing the intervention but at a different (randomized) moment in time. The time before implementing the intervention is considered to be the control group. The time after implementation is considered as intervention group. There is general agreement that a purely quantitative approach is not enough and should be combined with a qualitative approach such as a process evaluation. A cost-effectiveness evaluation is often recommended as a measurement of efficiency.

Phase 4 of implementation is the last phase. There is some consensus that implementation questions should be considered in all previous phases. Yet phase 4 goes beyond the study phase into the issue of transferability of the intervention into other settings, its policy impact by giving policy recommendations on education, legislation, financing, and management to create the right conditions for adoption and normalization of new practices.

Based on the MRC framework (mainly the first three phases), a framework called 13 Criteria for Reporting the Development and Evaluation of Complex Intervention Research in Healthcare has been formulated as a guide for research (CReDECI) (Möhler et al. 2015) (Fig. 2).

We will discuss these four phases of the model in depth using three cases of complex intervention studies. In all three cases (CADET: collaborative practice, EQCP: care pathway, and QIP: quality improvement program), the intervention is very general, similar to a black box. Secondly, all three have taken about 10 years to move from initial development to evaluation and policy recommendations.

First stage: Development	
1	Description of the intervention's underlying theoretical basis
2	Description of all intervention components, including the reasons for their selection as well as their aims / essential functions
3	Illustration of any intended interactions between different components
4	Description and consideration of the context's characteristics in intervention modelling
Second stage: Feasibility and piloting	
5	Description of the pilot test and its impact on the definite intervention
Third stage: Evaluation	
6	Description of the control condition (comparator) and reasons for the selection
7	Description of the strategy for delivering the intervention within the study context
8	Description of all materials or tools used delivery the intervention
9	Description of fidelity of the delivery process compared the study protocol
10	Description of a process evaluation and its underlying theoretical basis
11	Description of internal facilitators and barriers potentially influencing the delivery of the intervention as revealed by the process evaluation
12	Description of external conditions or factors occurring during the study which might have influenced the delivery of the intervention or mode of action (how it works)
13	Description of costs or required resources for the delivery of the intervention

Fig. 2 CReDECI criteria for reporting the development and evaluation of complex intervention research in healthcare (Möhler et al. 2015)

CADET trial (Bower et al. 2006; Chew-Graham et al. 2007; Coupe et al. 2014; Gilbody et al. 2003, 2006; Green et al. 2014; Richards et al. 2006, 2008, 2009, 2013, 2016; Simpson et al. 2008).

The Collaborative Depression Trial (CADET) was running from 2009 until 2013, although the study was already started in 2006 via a meta-analysis until 2016 as a Health Technology Assessment. The main issue is depression, as a large cause of global disability. The proposed intervention is "collaborative care," which is a complex combination of clinician and patient education, consultation liaison between primary and secondary care clinicians, and case management. Phase 1 was done by extensive literature review. Feasibility studies were performed between 2006 and 2008. The phase 3 evaluation was done using a cluster RCT involving 51 primary care practices in the UK involving 276 participants in the experimental (collaborative care) group and 305 participants in usual care. Mean depression scores were significantly lower in the experimental group at 4 months and at 12 months. The researchers conducted a qualitative study understanding barriers in implementation and a cost-effectiveness study.

EQCP-COPD trial (Deneckere et al. 2012, 2013; Lodewijckx et al. 2011, 2012, 2013; Seys et al. 2016, 2018; Vanhaecht et al. 2010a, b).

The European Quality of Care Pathway study (EQCP) consists of two studies, one studying on patients with a proximal femur fracture (PFF) and the other on patients with chronic obstructive pulmonary disease (COPD). We focus here on the COPD arm of the study. The study started in 2012, in building an evidence-based care pathway via a systematic review and a Delphi study. The evaluation was done using a cluster RCT in 22 hospitals in 3 countries (Belgium, Italy, Portugal) involving 174 patients in the intervention group and 168 patients in the control group. The 30-day readmission rate was significantly lower in the intervention group. They found no difference after 6 months. Performance on process indicators and adherence to guidelines was monitored. Adherence to guidelines and teamwork was mainly mediating the effect of the care pathway on reduced 30-day admission.

QIP-DM2 trial (Borgermans et al. 2008, 2009; Goderis et al. 2009a, b, 2010). The Quality Improvement Program (QIP) for Type 2 Diabetes Mellitus (DM2) aims to improve the adherence to evidence-guidelines on diabetes in primary care physicians. The study was initiated in Belgium in 2008. In 2009, an observational study was conducted on type 2 diabetic patients among 120 general practitioners. It showed that metabolic control in primary care was acceptable with major room for improvement in the use of statins and blood pressure control. A feasibility study on barriers and facilitators was conducted in 2009. An evaluation was performed using an 18-month cluster RCT. One hundred twenty general practices were randomized in an Advanced QIP (AQIP) experimental group ($N = 1577$ patients) and a Usual QIP (UGIP) control group. In both groups, endpoints on HbA1C, systolic blood pressure (SBP), and low-density lipoprotein cholesterol levels (LDL-C) improved significantly. However, there was no difference between the groups. More in-depth analysis of the use of interdisciplinary diabetes care teams operating on the interface of primary and secondary care was performed.

4 Phase 1: Development and Modeling of a Complex Intervention

Phase 1 is probably the most important one but at the same time the least understood element of developing a complex intervention. A first element is unraveling the "black box" and putting together all active ingredients which are proven to work. Potential questions to ask in this phase may be: the complex intervention as a whole might indeed generate an overall significant effect, but is it the best intervention possible? Can it be optimized? A third aspect to investigate is the linkage between implementation and context. It may be that the intervention is working in organization A but not in B. The conclusion is that we should integrate implementation and context/conditions right from the beginning.

4.1 Modeling the Complex Intervention

Campbell et al. (2000) noted that intervention models should describe all active components in the intervention, how they work and which effect they may produce, how they relate and interact with each other, including all important mediators and moderators. The model should describe the right outcome measures to evaluate the effect of the intervention. The model should also describe all theories underpinning these relationships and effects.

Important work in this field has been done by Judea Pearl, an Israeli-American computer scientist and philosopher. His most famous book is *The Book of Why: The New Science of Cause and Effect* (Pearl and MacKenzie 2018) describing the causal pathway from intervention to outcomes and the role of mediators, moderators, confounders, and covariates. These causal models can be drawn into causal diagrams or directed acyclic graphs (DAGs) and imported directly into statistical software such as R, SAS, and other Structural Equation Modeling software.

As the understanding of the intervention is key, it is important to describe the evidence. In all three cases, the components are evidence-based. In the case of the CADET study, they were based on a literature review, a meta-analysis, and a meta-regression in which key components of the interventions were identified. In the EQCP-COPD study, a long list of evidence-based interventions was defined based on a literature review. This list was presented to a large international interdisciplinary panel of 35 experts from 15 countries not involved in the study. They were selected because of their role in international associations or being first authors in leading publications in this domain. In the QIP-DM2 study, the list of interventions was mainly based on theory, based on the classification scheme from Shojania and colleagues (2006), who defined eleven distinct categories of quality improvement interventions adapted from the Cochrane Effective Practice and Organization of Care (EPOC) group (Grimshaw et al. 2001). In none of the three cases, however, interaction effects, mediators, or moderators were modeled.

4.2 Optimizing the Complex Intervention

Complex interventions are a package of components rather than a singular intervention. The package is evaluated but not the specific constellation of components. In our three cases, the CADET trial is rather simple, focusing on case management and a series of five key components. In the EQCP-COPD trial, the care pathway is more complex and consists of 38 evidence-based key interventions. In the QIP-DM2 trial, 26 different interventions on the level of the patient, the professional (GP), and the organization were defined. Although all 38 or 26 might be relevant and evidence-based, the implementation of all these components together at the same time seems to be rather impossible. But which activities are key to the effect and essential? If you had to make a choice, what would be your pick?

There are different approaches. One was developed by Linda Collins and colleagues (2005) and is probably the "golden" way, which is called the multiphase optimization strategy (MOST). Collins and colleagues are defining three phases: a screening phase, a refining phase, and a confirming phase. The screening phase is based on the existing research literature as described before. The main objective is to explore which intervention components are contributing to positive outcomes and should therefore be included in the intervention. It is what most authors do. The main difference is that in MOST trials, decisions to include components are taken based on the results (estimated effect size, costs) of randomized experiments and not on the basis of subjective decisions. To do this, they use a factorial design in which the different components are randomly allocated simultaneously. If only a few components are evaluated simultaneously, then a full factorial design can be used. If many components need to be evaluated (e.g., 6 which would lead to 2^6 or 64 different combinations), a fractional factorial design might be more appropriate.

Collins et al. (2005) demonstrate how a full 6-factor factorial design with 64 combinations can be redesigned in a fractional factorial design with 16 combinations, with the capability to provide main effects estimates for each of the six independent variables and to provide estimates for the selected interactions. The screening phase results in a draft version of the intervention with a selection of the most effective components. The next phase, called the refining phase, is evaluating the optimal dose of any of the intervention components. Again, a factorial design strategy can be used. At the end of this phase, the investigator has identified the optimized final draft of the intervention with a set of active components at their best dose. The term "dose" is used here in correspondence to the Bradford Hill criteria for causation that were established in 1965 by the English epidemiologist Sir Austin Bradford Hill (1965). He proposed a set of nine criteria to prove epidemiological evidence of a causal relationship between a presumed cause and an observed effect. One of these criteria is the dose-response relationship as a function of exposure (or dose) to the magnitude of a response.

In the last confirming phase, the optimized intervention as a whole can then be evaluated in a standard RCT. Although I see these approaches work when few components are discussed, such as in losing weight interventions, the question remains: should I focus on diet, exercise, or both. In more difficult settings, as in our three cases, it is difficult to see a factorial design being used. In the EQCP-COPD trial, it would lead to 2^{38} or 275 billion different combinations. Many of the components are also based on the needs of patients and clients, which cannot be randomized, for example, when giving controlled oxygen therapy for hypoxemic patients when a patient is admitted for exacerbation.

A few other approaches have been suggested. The Delphi approach used in the EQCP-COPD study provides a good support base for the decision, but also leads to some priority setting (Lodewijckx et al. 2013). In the EQCP-COPD study, an importance-performance matrix analysis (IPMA) is used for priority setting (Slack 1994). The importance of a certain component is assessed by a Delphi approach. The performance is a pre-test assessment of performing each of the components of the intervention. The analysis shows which "important" components have poor performance and should be improved or require urgent action. These components will then get somewhat higher priority on the action list. Again, what we learn from this is that the intervention, although standard in its theoretical conception, will lead to a different action plan for each individual organization.

4.3 Linking the Intervention to Context and Implementation

The earlier elements were mainly focusing on those aspects of the health intervention which we can rationalize: what is working and what is not? What are the active components and are they interrelated? But the degree of acceptance, willingness for change, and required effort are also important factors to take into account when designing a multi-component intervention. From Six Sigma, we learn the change effectiveness eq. ($E = Q \times A$) which indicates that the effectiveness (E) is the result of the quality (Q) of the intervention multiplied by its acceptance (A). So even when the quality of the intervention is theoretically high, the effect might be quite low if the acceptance by practitioners is low. In the EQCP-COPD trial, one of the underperforming components was smoking cessation in active smokers among the group of COPD patients being admitted to the hospital with an exacerbation. Only 2.6% of smokers were invited to a smoking cessation program. It is obvious that this intervention is highly relevant for this patient group. In-depth analysis showed that task allocation was not clear: whose job is it to recruit smokers into the program? Moreover, recruitment is not an easy job with a group of inveterate smokers. Nurses argued that they did not have the right skill set to do so. A solution advocated by several hospitals was to hire tobaccologists for this intervention. In the experimental group, the frequency of this component of smoking cessation for this target group increased to 36%, a significant improvement. But it is clear from this example that each component would require significant resources and expertise (Berry et al. 2009).

5 Phase 2: Feasibility and Piloting

Feasibility testing is directly connected with the development phase, relating to mainly the context and implementation element. Again, this phase is not always well understood and often skipped altogether. The CADET study performed two different feasibility studies before starting with the trial: one study investigating the views of stakeholders (patients, GPs, mental health workers) as well as the acceptability and barriers to the collaborative care model, interviewing 11 patients and 38 professionals. A second study interviewed 13 patients who received collaborative care during a phase II platform trial. Findings from both trials were used to improve the protocol for the final multi-center Cluster RCT. The QIP-DM2 trial also performed semi-structured interviews with GPs on the barriers and facilitators of the QIP program. But they performed this during and not before the main trial, which didn't afford them the possibility to embed it in the protocol for the main trial.

Pilot testing is the final rehearsal before the play is coming to the stage. All elements are in place and prepared to enter the final trial. The CADET study had an interesting question for the pilot: Can we run it as an RCT where patients are randomized or do we have to run it as a cluster RCT where primary practices are randomized? Therefore, they undertook a phase II patient-level RCT, nested within a cluster RCT. They found evidence of substantial contamination between the intervention and the patient-randomized control participants, which would indicate that a cluster RCT in the main trial should be favored. It is a good example of why a pilot is useful: one can test out last design options, determine effect sizes, as well as gauge response rates used for final sample size calculations. And at the same time, the protocol can be refined for maximum effect in the main trial.

6 Phase 3: Evaluation

The piece de resistance in the development of complex interventions is the evaluation phase. In the three selected cases, all three make use of a cluster RCT. Sometimes a stepped wedge design is used. Both designs definitively are the gold standard in complex intervention research, not only because of the nature of the intervention (which is often organizational), but more importantly because of the large variability in context and implementation at the different sites. We see three different elements in running these types of trials: the flexibility in the intervention, evaluating adherence to the protocol, and assessing the dose of the intervention and process evaluation.

6.1 The Adaptation of the Intervention

What we learn from implementation research (Damschroder et al. 2009) is that the intervention as described in the protocol has some core components that are the heart of the intervention and should not be changed. At the same time, each intervention has an "adaptable periphery" in the way in which core components are put in practice leading to local adaptation. This local adaptation is a function of the individuals (patients as well as professionals) involved, the inner and outer setting, or the context and the process of implementation. It finally leads to an adapted version of the intervention that is different in every site. Understanding this adaptation is a key feature of implementation which is often the most difficult element in getting approval by institutional review boards where they expect that the intervention should be standardized in line with the strict research conditions in exploratory trials.

The degree of adaptation and the methodological pragmatism required can vary, however. Green et al. (2019) described a series of hybrid effectiveness-implementation designs. Type 1 are studies where the program is largely designed by the research team. Type 2 are those where the program is co-created by researchers in clinical settings and populations, while type 3 are studies where the program is primarily designed by the clinical program sites and the researchers act more as consultants. Along these types, evaluation is moving from quantitative and summative evaluations to mixed methods and more formative evaluations as well. But it should be noted that adaptation of the intervention to local needs and requirements is an essential element of acceptability and implementation. A recommendation would be to include a detailed description of the intervention as performed in the study. It is very difficult to understand the findings without a clear understanding of what actually happened in the experimental and control group. Reporting guidelines or checklists such as the Template for Intervention Description and Replication (TIDieR) tool (Hoffmann et al. 2014) might be helpful when doing this.

In the CADET trial, differences in delivery and receipt of the intervention were described in general but not specifically for the different sites. It described that case managers provided collaborative care for a mean of 27.6 participants. The range was however wide. Some case managers were taking care of only a few number of participants. But some case managers were taking care of a high number of participants with 46 participants the highest number reported. Although the protocol indicates that each of these managers should have 6–12 contacts with the participants over 14 weeks, the mean number of sessions was 5.6, varying from 0 to 15. Fifteen percent (15%) of the participants did not attend any session. Only 62% had more than 4 contacts. All data showed significant underperformance. In the EQCP-COPD trial, five key components (arterial blood gas measurement, referral to pulmonary rehab, nutritional assessment according to BMI, overweight, underweight) were selected which had significant impact on 30-day readmission. Average adherence to the protocol in the intervention group was only 47% against 25% in the control group. This means that an important improvement was detectable, while at the same time significant underperformance was seen too. In the QIP-DM2 trial, no information was given on the specifics of the actual implementation of the intervention.

6.2 Adherence to the Protocol and Assessment of the Dose

It is quite obvious that underperformance and low adherence to the protocol have an impact on the study results. The CADET trial leads to significant results, but effect size (Cohen's d) was small to medium ($d = 0.26$ after 4 months; 0.28 after 12 months). In the cost-effectiveness analysis, collaborative care offered a mean incremental gain of 0.02 quality-adjusted life-years (QALY), which was not statistically significant. The QIP-DM2 saw some significant results between the post-test (T1) and the pre-test (T0) for both groups, but no differences between intervention (AQIP) and control (UQIP) group. One of the reasons might be that the control group was not offered usual care but rather a "light" version of the intervention. One of the main components of the intervention "involving the interdisciplinary Diabetes Care team" was available for both groups and was used for 14% of the patients in the AQIP group and for 9% in the UQIP group. This leads to serious underperformance of the experiment (AQIP) group and, consequently, a limited contrast to the control group. In the EQCP-COPD trial, the analysis showed that adherence and teamwork mediated the effect of care pathway implementation and reduced 30-day readmissions.

The current practice in these circumstances is to compare the average performance in the experimental group with the average performance in the control group.

It is possible to do this if the intervention is standard. But when the nature of intervention and the adherence or degree of implementation are variable, the dose of the intervention should be taken into account in the statistical analysis. An interesting solution could be to calculate the "dose" of the intervention for each of the clusters. One could expect that the cluster where the "dose" is high and closer to the protocol better results will be produced. In clusters where the "dose'" is low or where the implementation in fact didn't take place, we may not expect any effect. Only in the EQCP-COPD trial do we find data on the variability of adherence to the guidelines (Seys et al. 2016) in the pre-test. Adherence to the protocol varied between 0% and 86% on a patient level. On average, patients received 41% of the recommended care. But at the same time, a large variation between hospitals was reported, ranging from 19% up to 59% adherence. In the other cases, the variability in "dose" for the different sites was not available.

6.3 Process Evaluation

Beyond the fact that the dose is a mediating variable that should be taken into account, it would be interesting to understand why some hospitals have a much higher adherence than others. Process evaluations are a good mechanism to do this. They describe in detail the implementation process (training, resources, fidelity, dose, adaptations, reach), the mechanisms of impact (participant responses to the intervention, possible mediators, unexpected pathways, and consequences), contextual factors that affect implementation, intervention mechanisms, and outcomes. These elements are evaluated in the process evaluation described by Moore et al. (2015). An interesting model for describing the uptake of a new way of working is also the Normalization Process Theory (NPT) (May 2013) or what Carl May calls normalization. In the model, four dimensions have been defined:

- Interactional workability: How is the intervention affecting their work? The main question would be whether or not their work/life is the same or different.
- Relational integration: What is the relation to existing knowledge and relationships? How does the complex intervention influence the relationship between people?
- Skill-set workability: What is the effect on the current division of labor?
- Contextual integration: What is the relation to the organization? Does it have any impact on resources and capacity?

It seems plausible to assume that when the impact of the new way of working on the daily life of people is high, the resistance to change might be high too. This, in turn, would then require much more effort to implement the change. As well as in the CADET trial as the QIP-DM2, the division of labor between GPs and other health professionals was key. In the CADET trial, researchers noted a limited understanding of the Collaborative Care model by GPs, leading to organizational and communication barriers. In the QIP-DM2 trial, the main barriers were the communication between GPs and consulting specialists, especially with diabetes educators and dieticians. In both trials, communication and understanding were main factors for the limited effect of the intervention.

7 Phase 4: Implementation

"Implementation" is probably not always the right term to use in this context as implementation is already occurring in all previous phases. In fact, this phase goes beyond the nominal study duration. It tackles the question of what happens next? Traditionally, research stops when the findings of the study are published. But the complex intervention framework is going one step further in formulating recommendations for practice and policy while also monitoring long-term impact and effect. For further monitoring, the RE-AIM framework (Glasgow et al. 1999) is often used. It has five domains (Reach, Effectiveness, Adoption, Implementation, and Maintenance) and is evaluating in which way the intervention is in fact practiced, whether or not it has a measurable effect, is well adopted by organizations and providers, has a good compliance rate, and is well integrated in the health system. If the intervention is not widely spread or not well used in practice, a root cause analysis could be useful to evaluate the bottlenecks for implementation and to revise the intervention to get a better acceptability. The CADET trial performed a 36-month follow-up of the trial. Participants of both groups greatly improved in terms of depression, anxiety, and the quality of their mental health. It is useful to see how well an intervention was adopted and implemented by the wider healthcare community.

Key in this phase is closing the gap between research and policy/practice. The clinical evidence is obviously required but so is also the cost-effectiveness. The CADET study performed a cost-effectiveness study, but small program benefits resulted in a high cost per QALY. Both of the other studies didn't perform or report any cost-effectiveness of the intervention which is likely to hamper adoption.

Although there is now an emphasis on evidence-based policy making, the reality is that influencing policy making is hard. Let us consider the evidence of our three cases. The CADET trial shows some limited effect that even disappears after 36 months of follow-up. The EQCP-COPD trial shows only an effect on reducing 30-day readmission rates, and QIP-DM2 doesn't show any effect. If you are a clinician, manager, or a policy maker, are these studies providing you with enough information to make a decision? Insufficient or insufficiently robust evidence leaves policy makers with the only option to make decision on the basis of opinion, experience, expertise, or subjective judgment. Values, available resources, habits and traditions, pragmatics, and contingencies also play a role when deciding on organizational change, as do lobbyists and pressure groups, media attention, or adoption of programs by other organizations and countries as described by Philip Davies during his Jerry-Lee Lecture in Washington DC (Davies 2004). A way to deal with the dilemma of insufficient evidence is to write a policy brief that is written in lay language (Lavis et al. 2010). It starts with a clear problem statement and the available evidence. It might formulate several options with their benefits and drawbacks. It can reveal how decisions are based on various opinions or prevented by barriers. It may point out key implementation issues while also proposing a series of recommendations and a roadmap on how to get there.

8 Conclusion

The nature of complex interventions requires some essential adaptations to research design and analysis. The fact that context is an integral part of complex interventions requires us to handle it as a confounding variable which has to be included in the model. Efficacy and effectiveness can often not be distinguished, as implementation is becoming an essential part of the intervention. During the analysis phase, adherence to the protocol (or "dose" of the intervention) should be treated as an important mediator. Still many researchers present their complex intervention as a black box, and this should no longer be accepted as good practice. The intervention should be described in as many details as possible. Uncertainties are inevitable but should be identified and explicitly articulated where possible. In addition, evaluations require quantitative as well as qualitative approaches. Recommendations for later implementation should not only be focused on the intervention and its effectiveness in the strict sense but extend to the broader context. All these elements are making complex intervention research more challenging yet interesting, and a key factor in our learning to accomplish our ambition to produce better and more rigorous findings.

References

Berry SA, Doll MC, McKinley KE, Casale AS, Bothe A (2009) ProvenCare: quality improvement model for designing highly reliable care in cardiac surgery. Qual Saf Health Care 18(5):360–368

Berwick DM (2008) The science of improvement. JAMA 299(10):1182

Borgermans L, Goderis G, Van Den Broeke C, Mathieu C, Aertgeerts B, Verbeke G, Carbonez A, Ivanova A, Grol R, Heyrman J (2008) A cluster randomized trial to improve adherence to evidence-based guidelines on diabetes and reduce clinical inertia in primary care physicians in Belgium: study protocol [NTR 1369]. Implement Sci 3(1):42

Borgermans L, Goderis G, Van Den Broeke C, Verbeke G, Carbonez A, Ivanova A, Mathieu C, Aertgeerts B, Heyrman J, Grol R (2009) Interdisciplinary diabetes care teams operating on the interface between primary and specialty care are associated with improved outcomes of care: findings from the Leuven Diabetes Project. BMC Health Serv Res 9:179

Bower P, Gilbody S, Richards D, Fletcher J, Sutton A (2006) Collaborative care for depression in primary care: making sense of a complex intervention: systematic review and meta-regression. Br J Psychiatry 189:484–494

Campbell M, Fitzpatrick R, Haines A, Kinmonth AL, Sandercock P, Spiegelhalter D, Tyrer P (2000) Education and debate framework for design and evaluation of complex interventions to improve health. BMJ 321:694–696

Chalmers I, Glasziou P (2009) Avoidable waste in the production and reporting of research evidence. Lancet 374(9683):86–89

Chew-Graham CA, Lovell K, Roberts C, Baldwin R, Morley M, Burns A, Richards D, Burroughs H (2007) A randomised controlled trial to test the feasibility of a collaborative care model for the management of depression in older people. Br J Gen Pract 57:364–370

Collins LM, Murphy SA, Nair VN, Strecher VJ (2005) A strategy for optimizing and evaluating behavioral interventions. Ann Behav Med 30(1):65–73

Coupe N, Anderson E, Gask L, Sykes P, Richards DA, Chew-Graham C (2014) Facilitating professional liaison in collaborative care for depression in UK primary care; a qualitative study utilising normalisation process theory. In: BMC family practice, vol 15(1). BioMed Central Ltd, London

Craig P, Dieppe P, Macintyre S, Michie S, Nazareth I, Petticrew M (2008) Developing and evaluating complex interventions: new Medical Research Council guidance. BMJ 337:a1655

Damschroder LJ, Aron DC, Keith RE, Kirsh SR, Alexander JA, Lowery JC (2009) Fostering implementation of health services research findings into practice: a consolidated framework for advancing implementation science. Implement Sci 4(1):1–15

Davies P (2004) Is evidence-based government possible?

Deneckere S, Euwema M, Lodewijckx C, Panella M, Sermeus W, Vanhaecht K (2012) The European quality of care pathways (EQCP) study on the impact of care pathways on interprofessional teamwork in an acute hospital setting: study protocol: for a cluster randomised controlled trial and evaluation of implementation processes. Implement Sci 7(1):47

Deneckere S, Euwema M, Lodewijckx C, Panella M, Mutsvari T, Sermeus W, Vanhaecht K (2013) Better interprofessional teamwork, higher level of organized care, and lower risk of burnout in acute health care teams using care pathways: a cluster randomized controlled trial. Med Care 51:99–107

Funnell SC, Rogers PJ (2011) Purposeful program theory: effective use of theories of change and logic models. Jossey-Bass, San Francisco

Gilbody S, Whitty P, Jeremy Grimshaw M, Ruth Thomas F (2003) Educational and organizational interventions to improve the management of depression in primary care: a systematic review. JAMA 289(23):3145–3151

Gilbody S, Bower P, Fletcher J, Richards D, Sutton AJ (2006) Collaborative care for depression: a cumulative meta-analysis and review of longer-term outcomes. Arch Intern Med 166:2314–2321

Glasgow RE, Vogt TM, Boles SM, Glasgow E (1999) Evaluating the public health impact of health promotion interventions: the RE-AIM framework. Am J Public Health 89(9):1322–1327

Goderis G, Borgermans L, Heyrman J, Van Den Broeke C, Grol R, Boland B, Mathieu C (2009a) Type 2 diabetes in primary care in Belgium: need for structured shared care. Exp Clin Endocrinol Diabetes 117(8):367–372

Goderis G, Borgermans L, Mathieu C, Van Den Broeke C, Hannes K, Heyrman J, Grol R (2009b) Barriers and facilitators to evidence based care of type 2 diabetes patients: experiences of general practitioners participating to a quality improvement program. Implement Sci 4(1):41

Goderis G, Borgermans L, Grol R, Van Den Broeke C, Boland B, Verbeke G, Carbonez A, Mathieu C, Heyrman J (2010) Start improving the quality of care for people with type 2 diabetes through a general practice support program: a cluster randomized trial. Diabetes Res Clin Pract 88(1):56–64

Green C, Richards DA, Hill JJ, Gask L, Lovell K, Chew-Graham C, Bower P, Cape J, Pilling S, Araya R, Kessler D, Bland JM, Gilbody S, Lewis G, Manning C, Hughes-Morley A, Barkham M (2014) Cost-effectiveness of collaborative care for depression in UK primary care: economic evaluation of a randomised controlled trial (CADET). PLoS One 9(8):e104225

Green BB, Coronado GD, Schwartz M, Coury J, Baldwin LM (2019) Using a continuum of hybrid effectiveness-implementation studies to put research-tested colorectal screening interventions into practice. Implement Sci 14(1):53

Grimshaw JM, Shirran L, Thomas R, Mowatt G, Fraser C, Bero L, Grilli R, Harvey E, Oxman A, O'Brien MA (2001) Changing provider behavior an overview of systematic reviews of interventions. Med Care 39(8 Suppl 2):2–45

Hill AB (1965) The environment and disease: association or causation? Proc R Soc Med 58(5):295–300

Hillman K, Chen J, Cretikos M, Bellomo R, Brown D, Doig G, Finfer S, Flabouris A (2005) Introduction of the medical emergency team (MET) system: a cluster-randomised controlled trial. Lancet 365:2091–2097

Hoffmann TC, Glasziou PP, Boutron I, Milne R, Perera R, Moher D, Altman DG, Barbour V, Macdonald H, Johnston M, Kadoorie SEL, Dixon-Woods M, McCulloch P, Wyatt JC, Phelan AWC, Michie S (2014) Better reporting of interventions: template for intervention description and replication (TIDieR) checklist and guide. BMJ 348:g1687

Lavis JN, Permanand G, Oxman AD, Lewin S, Fretheim A (2010) SUPPORT tools for evidence-informed health policymaking (STP) 13: preparing and using policy briefs to support evidence-informed policymaking. Chin J Evid Based Med 10(5):507–513

Lodewijckx C, Sermeus W, Panella M, Deneckere S, Leigheb F, Decramer M, Vanhaecht K (2011) Impact of care pathways for in-hospital management of COPD exacerbation: a systematic review. Int J Nurs Stud 48(11):1445–1456

Lodewijckx C, Sermeus W, Panella M, Deneckere S, Leigheb F, Decramer M, Vanhaecht K (2012) Impact of a care pathway for exacerbation of chronic obstructive pulmonary disease: a cluster randomized controlled trial. Int J Care Pathways 16(2):41

Lodewijckx C, Sermeus W, Panella M, Deneckere S, Leigheb F, Troosters T, Boto PA, Mendes RV, Decramer M, Vanhaecht K (2013) Quality indicators for in-hospital management of exacerbation of chronic obstructive pulmonary disease: results of an international Delphi study. J Adv Nurs 69(2):348–362

May C (2013) Towards a general theory of implementation. Implement Sci 8(1):1

Möhler R, Köpke S, Meyer G (2015) Criteria for reporting the development and evaluation of complex interventions in healthcare: revised guideline (CReDECI 2). Trials 16(1):204

Moore GF, Audrey S, Barker M, Bond L, Bonell C, Hardeman W, Moore L, O'Cathain A, Tinati T, Wight D, Baird J (2015) Process evaluation of complex interventions: Medical Research Council guidance. BMJ 350:h1258

MRC (2000) A framework for development and evaluation of RCTs for complex interventions to improve health. Medical Research Council, Swindon

Pearl J, MacKenzie D (2018) The book of why: the new science of cause and effect. Basic Civitas Books, New York

Richards DA, Lankshear AJ, Fletcher J, Rogers A, Barkham M, Bower P, Gask L, Gilbody S, Lovell K (2006) Developing a U.K. protocol for collaborative care: a qualitative study. Gen Hosp Psychiatry 28(4):296–305

Richards DA, Lovell K, Gilbody S, Gask L, Torgerson D, Barkham M, Bland M, Bower P, Lankshear AJ, Simpson A, Fletcher J, Escott D, Hennessy S, Richardson R (2008) Collaborative care for depression in UK primary care: a randomized controlled trial. Psychol Med 38(2):279–287

Richards DA, Hughes-Morley A, Hayes RA, Araya R, Barkham M, Bland JM, Bower P, Cape J, Chew-Graham CA, Gask L, Gilbody S, Green C, Kessler D, Lewis G, Lovell K, Manning C, Pilling S (2009) Collaborative depression trial (CADET): multi-centre randomised controlled trial of collaborative care for depression—study protocol. BMC Health Serv Res 9:188

Richards DA, Hill JJ, Gask L, Lovell K, Chew-Graham C, Bower P, Cape J, Pilling S, Araya R, Kessler D, Bland JM, Green C, Gilbody S, Lewis G, Manning C, Hughes-Morley A, Barkham M (2013) Clinical effectiveness of collaborative care for depression in UK primary care (CADET): cluster randomised controlled trial. BMJ 347(7922):f4913

Richards DA, Bower P, Chew-Graham C, Gask L, Lovell K, Cape J, Pilling S, Araya R, Kessler D, Barkham M, Bland JM, Gilbody S, Green C, Lewis G, Manning C, Kontopantelis E, Hill JJ, Hughes-Morley A, Russell A (2016) Clinical effectiveness and cost-effectiveness of collaborative care for depression in UK primary care (CADET): a cluster randomised controlled trial. Health Technol Assess 20(14):1–192

Seys D, Bruyneel L, Decramer M, Lodewijckx C, Panella M, Sermeus W, Boto P, Vanhaecht K (2016) An international study of adherence to guidelines for patients hospitalised with a COPD exacerbation. COPD: J Chron Obstruct Pulmon Dis 14:1–8

Seys D, Bruyneel L, Sermeus W, Lodewijckx C, Decramer M, Deneckere S, Panella M, Vanhaecht K (2018) Teamwork and adherence to recommendations explain the effect of a care pathway on reduced 30-day readmission for patients with a COPD exacerbation. COPD: J Chron Obstruct Pulmon Dis 15(2):157–164

Shojania KG, Ranji SR, Mcdonald KM, Grimshaw JM, Sundaram V, Rushakoff RJ, Owens DK (2006) Effects of quality improvement strategies for type 2 diabetes on glycemic control: a meta-regression analysis. JAMA 296(4):427–440

Simpson A, Richards D, Gask L, Hennessy S, Escott D (2008) Patients' experiences of receiving collaborative care for the treatment of depression in the UK: a qualitative investigation. Ment Health Fam Med 5(2):95–104

Skivington K, Matthews L, Simpson SA, Craig P, Baird J, Blazeby JM, Boyd KA, Craig N, French DP, McIntosh E, Petticrew M, Rycroft-Malone J, White M, Moore L (2021) A new framework for developing and evaluating complex interventions: update of Medical Research Council guidance. BMJ 374:n2061

Slack N (1994) The importance-performance matrix as a determinant of improvement priority. Int J Oper Prod Manag 14(5):144–3577

Vanhaecht K, Sermeus W, Peers J, Deneckere S, Lodewijckx C, Leigheb F, Panella M (2010a) The European Quality of Care Pathway (EQCP) study: history, project management and approach. Int J Care Pathways 14(2):52–56

Vanhaecht K, Sermeus W, Peers J, Lodewijckx C, Deneckere S, Leigheb F, Decramer M, Panella M (2010b) The impact of care pathways for exacerbation of chronic obstructive pulmonary disease: rationale and design of a cluster randomized controlled trial. Trials 11(1):111

Evaluation of Implementation: A Taxonomy of Implementation Science Theories, Models, and Frameworks

Per Nilsen

Abstract

Implementation science is key to understanding how interventions, programs, and other practices are integrated into routine practice across diverse settings. This chapter presents a taxonomy that categorizes five types of theoretical approaches used in evaluating the implementation of health service practices: process models, determinant frameworks, classic theories, implementation theories, and evaluation frameworks. Process models guide the stages of translating evidence into practice, while determinant frameworks highlight factors that influence outcomes. Classic theories from other disciplines and implementation theories developed within the field explain causal mechanisms of change. Evaluation frameworks identify aspects of implementation that should be assessed to determine success. These approaches are crucial for evaluating health service interventions and programs, providing structured methods to operationalize and measure factors influencing implementation success.

Keywords

Implementation science · Theories · Models · Evaluation · Health services · Measures · Determinant frameworks

P. Nilsen (✉)
Linköping University, Linköping, Sweden

Halmstad University, Halmstad, Sweden
e-mail: per.nilsen@liu.se

A. Kaehne, J. Feather (eds.), *Handbook of Health Services Evaluation*,
https://doi.org/10.1007/978-3-031-87869-5_9

1 What Is Implementation Science?

Implementation science is a burgeoning interdisciplinary field focused on how evidence-based practices, such as health interventions and programs, are integrated into routine practice in healthcare and other settings. This research aims to identify barriers and facilitators for implementing various practices and to develop, apply, and evaluate implementation strategies that overcome these barriers and/or enhance the facilitators to increase the uptake of interventions, programs, and other practices (Bauer and Kirchner 2020). Implementation strategies can be defined as activities to enhance the adoption, implementation, sustainment, and scale-up of practices (Proctor et al. 2013).

The field of implementation science has been defined as "the scientific study of methods to promote the systematic uptake of research findings and other evidence-based practice into routine practice and, hence, to improve the quality and effectiveness of health services" (Eccles and Mittman 2006, p. 1). The definition emphasizes that research in this field investigates how implementation of evidence-based practices can be supported, implying that evidence in and of itself does not guarantee successful implementation. The term "methods" in the 2006 definition has since come to be referred to as "implementation strategies" (or merely "strategies"). While the term "implementation interventions" is sometimes used to denote these methods, this term can cause confusion with clinical and other interventions directed at patients and other clients.

Implementation science prioritizes "evidence-based" practices while also exploring interventions, programs, and other practices that, despite lacking robust evidence, show promise for advancing goals like improved healthcare quality. For example, some policies may not have been extensively researched, yet they are supported by logical reasoning that suggests they could enhance efficiency or cost-effectiveness. Additionally, studies are conducted to generate evidence for new practices alongside investigating their implementation; these are known as hybrid studies (Curran et al. 2012).

2 A Taxonomy of Theories, Models, and Frameworks in Implementation Science

Theories in implementation science aim to explain the causal mechanisms of implementation. Models in implementation science are commonly used to describe and/or guide the process of translating research into practice rather than to predict or analyze what factors influence implementation outcomes. Determinant frameworks in implementation science often have a descriptive purpose by pointing to factors believed or found to influence implementation outcomes.

In general, models can be described as theories with a more narrowly defined scope of explanation; a model is descriptive, whereas a theory is explanatory as well as descriptive (Frankfort-Nachmias and Nachmias 1996). A model typically involves a deliberate simplification of a phenomenon or a specific aspect of a phenomenon. Models need not be completely accurate representations of reality to have value (Carpiano 2006; Cairney 2012). A framework usually denotes a structure,

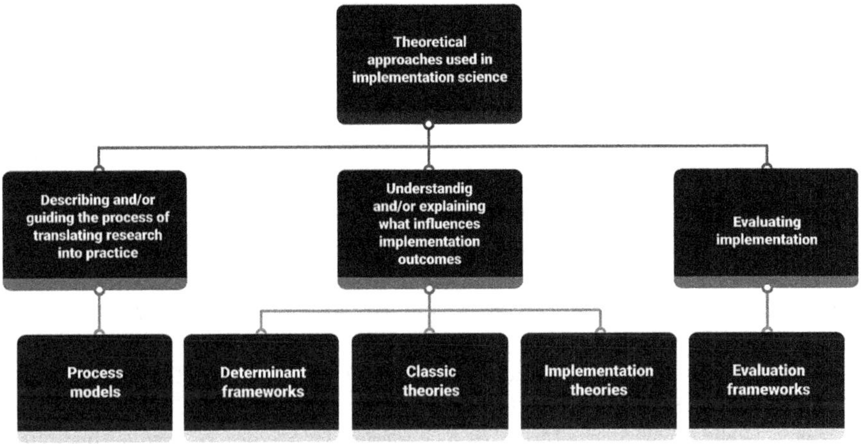

Fig. 1 Three aims of the use of theoretical approaches in implementation science and the five categories of theories, models, and frameworks

overview, outline, system, or plan consisting of various descriptive categories, for example, concepts, constructs, or variables, and the relations between them that are presumed to account for a phenomenon (Sabatier 1999).

A key difference between models and frameworks in implementation science is that models recognize a temporal sequence of implementation efforts, whereas frameworks do not explicitly take a process perspective of implementation. However, the terms "theories," "models," and "frameworks" are not used consistently in the field; they are often used interchangeably (Estabrooks et al. 2006; Kitson et al. 2008; Rycroft-Malone and Bucknall 2010).

Three overarching aims of the use of theories, models, and frameworks in implementation science can be identified:

- Describing and/or guiding the process of translating research into practice.
- Understanding and/or explaining what influences implementation outcomes.
- Evaluating implementation.

Based on descriptions of their origins, how they were developed, what knowledge sources they drew on, stated aims and applications in implementation science, theoretical approaches that aim at understanding, and/or explaining influences on implementation outcomes (i.e., the second aim) can be further broken down into:

- Determinant frameworks
- Classic theories
- Implementation theories

Thus, five categories of theoretical approaches used in implementation science can be delineated, as shown in Fig. 1. This five-category taxonomy has been referred to as "Nilsen's Taxonomy" (KTDRR 2022) and "Nilsen's Schema" (Washington University 2022).

3 Descriptions of the Five Categories

3.1 Process Models

Process models specify steps (stages, phases) in the process of translating research into practice, including the implementation and use of research. The aim of process models is to describe and/or guide the process of translating research into practice. An action model is a type of process model that provides practical guidance in the planning and execution of implementation efforts and/or implementation strategies to facilitate implementation. The terms "mode/l" and "framework" are both used, but the former appears to be the more common.

Examples of process models include models by Landry et al. (2001), Davis et al. (2007), and Majdzadeh et al. (2008). Other examples are the CIHR (Canadian Institutes of Health Research Model of Knowledge Translation (Canadian Institutes of Health Research 2014), the K2A (Knowledge-to-Action) Framework (Wilson et al. 2011), the Stetler Model (Stetler 2010), the ACE (Academic Center for Evidence-Based Practice) Star Model of Knowledge Transformation (Stevens 2013), the Knowledge-to-Action Model (Graham et al. 2006), the Iowa Model (Titler et al. 1994), the Ottawa Model (Logan and Graham 1998), and the Quality Implementation Framework (Meyers et al. 2012).

3.2 Determinant Frameworks

Determinant frameworks specify types (also known as classes or domains) of determinants and individual determinants, which act as barriers and enablers (independent variables) that influence implementation outcomes (dependent variables). Some frameworks also specify relationships between some types of determinants. The overarching aim is to understand and/or explain influences on implementation outcomes.

Examples of determinant frameworks include EPIS (Exploration-Preparation-Implementation-Sustainment) (Aarons et al. 2011), i-PARIHS (integrated-Promoting Action on Research Implementation in Health Services) (Harvey and Kitson 2016), PARIHS (Promoting Action on Research Implementation in Health Services) (Kitson et al. 1998), Active Implementation Frameworks (Blase et al. 2012), Understanding-User-Context Framework (Jacobson et al. 2003), Conceptual Model (Greenhalgh et al. 2005), framework by Grol et al. (2005), framework by Cochrane et al. (2007), Ecological Framework by Durlak and DuPre (2008), CFIR (Consolidated Framework for Implementation Research) (Damschroder et al. 2009), framework by Gurses et al. (2010), Theoretical Domains Framework (Michie et al. 2014), and TICD (Tailored Implementation for Chronic Disease) (Flottorp et al. 2013).

3.3 Classic Theories

Classic theories are a label used for theories that originate from fields external to implementation science (e.g., psychology, sociology, and organizational theory) that can be applied to provide understanding and/or explanation of aspects of implementation. These theories have been referred to as "classic" (or "classic change") theories to distinguish them from research-to-practice models (Graham et al. 2009). An important example is the Theory of Diffusion (Rogers 2003), but there are also countless individual-level, group-level, and organizational-level theories and concepts.

3.4 Implementation Theories

Implementation theories are theories that have been developed by implementation researchers (from scratch or by adapting existing theories and concepts) to provide understanding and/or explanation of aspects of implementation. Examples include Absorptive Capacity (Zahra and George 2002), Organizational Readiness (Weiner 2009), COM-B (Capacity Opportunities Motivation—Behaviour) (Michie et al. 2011), and Normalization Process Theory (May and Finch 2009).

3.5 Evaluation Frameworks

Evaluation frameworks specify aspects of implementation that could be evaluated to determine implementation success. Two prime examples are RE-AIM (Reach Effectiveness—Adoption Implementation Maintenance) (Glasgow et al. 1999) and the outcome framework developed by Proctor et al. (2010). RE-AIM has evolved over time and is not only used for evaluation purposes.

It is important to emphasize that theories, models, and frameworks from the other four categories can also function as "evaluation frameworks" because they identify concepts and constructs that may be evaluated. For instance, the Theoretical Domains Framework (e.g. Fleming et al. 2014; Phillips et al. 2015) and Normalization Process Theory (McEvoy et al. 2014) and COM-B (e.g., Connell et al. 2015; Praveen et al. 2014) have all been widely used as evaluation frameworks. Furthermore, many theories, models, and frameworks have spawned instruments that serve evaluation purposes, for example, tools linked to PARIHS (Estabrooks et al. 2009; McCormack et al. 2009), CFIR (Damschroder and Lowery 2013), and the Theoretical Domains Framework (Dyson et al. 2013). Other examples include the Evidence-Based Practice (EBP) Implementation Scale to measure the extent to which EBP is implemented (Melnyk et al. 2008) and instruments to operationalize theories such as Implementation Climate (Jacobs et al. 2014) and Organizational Readiness (Gagnon et al. 2011).

4 Evaluation in Implementation Science

Differentiating implementation science from the evaluation of clinical interventions, programs, etc. is critical for clarity. Implementation science specifically focuses on studying and testing strategies to enhance the adoption, integration, and sustainability of practices such as the use of brief interventions for alcohol prevention or motivational interviewing for mental health issues. It goes beyond assessing the effectiveness of interventions or programs themselves and examines how to ensure these practices are put into routine practice. A key aspect of implementation science is its use of theories, models, and frameworks to analyze and explain the mechanisms, processes, and outcomes of implementation efforts (Weiner et al. 2023). Consequently, the focus of implementation science is not to determine the impact of a practice, such as the health effects of a clinical intervention or program, but rather to identify and address the factors affecting its uptake into routine use.

In addition, understanding different types of implementation approaches is vital for health service evaluation because these theories, models, and frameworks provide distinct structures for analyzing how interventions, programs, and other practices are successfully integrated into routine practice. Health service contexts are often complex, involving multiple stakeholders, varying professional and organizational cultures, and intricate patient care pathways. Different implementation theories, such as Diffusion of Innovations or Normalization Process Theory (May and Finch 2009), highlight diverse aspects of how new practices become adopted or embedded within healthcare settings. For instance, Diffusion of Innovations may focus on how a new clinical practice spreads among clinicians, while Normalization Process Theory might explore how the practice becomes part of daily clinical routines. By leveraging different theories, models, and frameworks, health service evaluators can adopt a tailored approach that aligns with the specific mechanisms influencing health service delivery, ensuring that their evaluations are nuanced and context-sensitive.

Moreover, the use of different implementation theories, models, and frameworks in health service evaluations can imply distinct roles for evaluation depending on the theoretical approach chosen. For example, theories focused on individual behavior change guide evaluations toward assessing how healthcare providers' capabilities, opportunities, and motivations affect the implementation of new clinical practices. In contrast, determinant frameworks like the CFIR may direct the evaluation toward organizational and environmental factors (i.e., determinants) that affect the implementation of practices such as leadership support and resources. Understanding the diversity of these theories, models, and frameworks helps health service evaluators select appropriate approaches, methods, and metrics, ultimately improving the precision of their evaluations.

5 How and When to Use Implementation Models, Frameworks, and Theories in Evaluation?

The use of implementation theories, models, and frameworks is essential in evaluating the implementation of interventions, programs, and other practices because they provide structured guidance for understanding and interpreting complex processes. These tools help health service evaluators systematically assess which factors contribute to the success or failure of implementation efforts. By employing a theoretical approach, evaluators can ensure that their assessments are not ad hoc or narrowly focused but instead rooted in robust implementation science knowledge. This makes the evaluation more rigorous and capable of providing insights into the causal mechanisms driving implementation outcomes. Without such theoretical grounding, evaluations risk being superficial, focusing merely on outcomes without understanding the pathways and influences that led to those outcomes.

Choosing the appropriate theory, model, or framework depends on the specific goals of the evaluation. Process models, for instance, are particularly useful when evaluators are seeking to understand the stages of implementation or provide guidance on how to facilitate the implementation process. Determinant frameworks, on the other hand, help identify and categorize factors that influence implementation outcomes, making them suitable when the evaluation explains why certain barriers or facilitators impacted success. Theories, whether classic or implementation-specific, offer a deeper explanatory power, allowing evaluators to explore causal mechanisms or predict future implementation success. These approaches are typically used at different phases of an evaluation: models can guide the initial planning and process tracking, frameworks can be applied to diagnose influencing factors prior to or during the implementation, and theories can help explain outcomes and inform improvements in future implementation efforts. Thus, the decision of when to use a particular theory, model, or framework is contingent upon the stage of the implementation being evaluated and the specific questions being addressed.

6 Concluding Remarks

The early phases of implementation science were marked by a trial-and-error approach, often lacking a solid theoretical foundation for selecting and applying specific implementation strategies (Eccles et al. 2005). Many studies did not provide a theoretical rationale for their chosen strategies, leading to mixed results in achieving EBP across various settings. This inconsistency was frequently attributed to a limited theoretical basis (Kitson et al. 1998; Davies et al. 2003; Eccles et al. 2005; Michie et al. 2005; Sales et al. 2006). The absence of robust theoretical underpinnings complicates our understanding of the mechanisms that contribute to both successful and unsuccessful implementation. Consequently, this gap hinders the identification of predictive factors for implementation success and limits the development of more effective strategies to enhance the implementation process.

Despite its empirically driven beginnings, implementation science has increasingly embraced a theoretical foundation. There is now broad recognition of the importance of establishing theoretical bases for implementation strategies to better understand the mechanisms behind practice change. However, the proliferation of theories, models, and frameworks has led some researchers to express concerns about the challenges of selecting the most appropriate one (ICEBeRG 2006; Godin et al. 2008; Mitchell et al. 2010; Rycroft-Malone and Bucknall 2010; Cane et al. 2012; Martinez et al. 2014). These theories, models, and frameworks are crucial for evaluation, as they define concepts and constructs that can be operationalized and measured effectively.

The proposed taxonomy identifies five categories of theoretical approaches in implementation science, though there is significant overlap among some of these categories. Determinant frameworks, classic theories, and implementation theories can all serve to guide implementation efforts by acting as process models. They help identify potential barriers and enablers that are crucial to address during implementation. Some frameworks combine determinant framework and process model characteristics, thus aiming to both provide guidance for the implementation process and identify potentially important determinants. A good example of such a framework/model is EPIS; it highlights four temporal phases in the process of implementation, providing information to guide this process (i.e., a process model trait), and it identifies a number of determinants that may be relevant to consider in these four phases (i.e., a determinant framework trait) (Aarons et al. 2011; Moullin et al. 2019).

Despite the overlap between different theories, models, and frameworks used in implementation science, knowledge about the five categories of theoretical approaches is important to identify and select relevant approaches in various situations. Most determinant frameworks provide limited "how-to" support for carrying out implementation efforts because the determinants may be too generic to provide sufficient detail for guiding users through an implementation process. Conversely, the relevance of addressing barriers and enablers to translating research into practice is mentioned in many process models, yet these models do not identify or systematically structure specific determinants associated with implementation success.

The five categories of the taxonomy are not always recognized as separate types of approaches in the literature. For instance, systematic reviews and overviews by Graham and Tetroe (2007), Mitchell et al. (2010), Flottorp et al. (2013), Meyers et al. (2012), and Tabak et al. (2012) have not distinguished between process models, determinant frameworks, or classic theories because they all deal with factors believed or found to have an impact on implementation processes and outcomes. However, what matters most is not necessarily how an individual approach is labelled, but it is important to recognize that these theories, models, and frameworks differ in terms of their assumptions, aims, and other characteristics that have implications for their use.

References

Aarons GA, Hurlburt M, Horwitz SM (2011) Advancing a conceptual model of evidence-based practice implementation in public service sectors. Adm Policy Ment Health Ment Health Serv Res 38:4–23. https://doi.org/10.1007/s10488-010-0327-7

Bauer MS, Kirchner JE (2020) Implementation science: what is it and why should I care? Psychiatry Res 283(112):376. https://doi.org/10.1016/j.psychres.2019.04.025

Blase KA, Van Dyke M, Fixsen DL, Bailey FW (2012) Implementation science: key concepts, themes and evidence for practitioners in educational psychology. In: Kelly B, Perkins DF (eds) Handbook of implementation science for psychology in education. Cambridge University Press, Cambridge, pp 13–34. https://doi.org/10.1017/CBO9781139013949.004

Cairney P (2012) Understanding public policy: theories and issues. Palgrave Macmillan, Basingstoke. https://doi.org/10.1007/978-0-230-35699-3_1

Canadian Institutes of Health Research (CIHR). About knowledge translation. http://www.cihr-irsc.gc.ca/e/29418.html. Accessed 18 Dec 2014

Cane J, O'Connor D, Michie S (2012) Validation of the theoretical domains framework for use in behaviour change and implementation research. Implement Sci 7:37. https://doi.org/10.1186/1748-5908-7-37

Carpiano RM (2006) A guide and glossary on postpositivist theory building for population health. J Epidemiol Community Health 60:564–570. https://doi.org/10.1136/jech.2004.031534

Cochrane LJ, Olson CA, Murray S, Dupuis M, Tooman T, Hayes S (2007) Gaps between knowing and doing: understanding and assessing the barriers to optimal health care. J Contin Educ Health Prof 27:94–102. https://doi.org/10.1002/chp.106

Connell LA, McMahon NE, Redfern J, Watkins CL, Eng JJ (2015) Development of a behaviour change intervention to increase upper limb exercise in stroke rehabilitation. Implement Sci 10:34. https://doi.org/10.1186/s13012-015-0223-3

Curran GM, Bauer M, Mittman BS, Pyne JM, Stetler CB (2012) Implementation science: a hybrid approach to the study of implementation strategies. Implement Sci 7:1

Damschroder LJ, Lowery JC (2013) Evaluation of a large-scale weight management program using the consolidated framework for implementation research (CFIR). Implement Sci 8:51. https://doi.org/10.1186/1748-5908-8-51

Damschroder LJ, Aron DC, Keith RE, Kirsh SR, Alexander JA, Lowery JC (2009) Fostering implementation of health services research findings into practice: a consolidated framework for advancing implementation science. Implement Sci 4:50. https://doi.org/10.1186/1748-5908-4-50

Davies P, Walker A, Grimshaw J (2003) Theories of behavior change in studies of guideline implementation. Proc Br Psychol Soc 11:120

Davis SM, Peterson JC, Helfrich CD, Cunningham-Sabo L (2007) Introduction and conceptual model for utilization of prevention research. Am J Prev Med 33(1 Suppl):S1–S5. https://doi.org/10.1016/j.amepre.2007.04.004

Durlak JA, DuPre EP (2008) Implementation matters: a review of research on the influence of implementation on program outcomes and the factors affecting implementation. Am J Community Psychol 41:327–350. https://doi.org/10.1007/s10464-008-9165-0

Dyson J, Lawton R, Jackson C, Cheater F (2013) Development of a theory-based instrument to identify barriers and levers to best hand hygiene practice among healthcare practitioners. Implement Sci 8:111. https://doi.org/10.1186/1748-5908-8-111

Eccles MP, Mittman BS (2006) Welcome to implementation science. Implement Sci 1:1. https://doi.org/10.1186/1748-5908-1-1

Eccles MP, Grimshaw J, Walker A, Johnston M, Pitts N (2005) Changing the behavior of healthcare professionals: the use of theory in promoting the uptake of research findings. J Clin Epidemiol 58:107–112. https://doi.org/10.1016/j.jclinepi.2004.09.002

Estabrooks CA, Thompson DS, Lovely JJ, Hofmeyer A (2006) A guide to knowledge translation theory. J Contin Educ Health Prof 26:25–36. https://doi.org/10.1002/chp.48

Estabrooks CA, Squires JE, Cummings GG, Birdsell JM, Norton PG (2009) Development and assessment of the Alberta Context Tool. BMC Health Serv Res 9:234. https://doi.org/10.1186/1472-6963-9-234

Fleming A, Bradley C, Cullinan S, Byrne S (2014) Antibiotic prescribing in long-term care facilities: a qualitative, multidisciplinary investigation. BMJ Open 4:e006442. https://doi.org/10.1136/bmjopen-2014-006442

Flottorp SA, Oxman AD, Krause J, Musila NR, Wensing M, Godycki-Cwirko M et al (2013) A checklist for identifying determinants of practice: a systematic review and synthesis of frameworks and taxonomies of factors that prevent or enable improvements in healthcare professional practice. Implement Sci 8:35. https://doi.org/10.1186/1748-5908-8-35

Frankfort-Nachmias C, Nachmias D (1996) Research methods in the social sciences. Arnold, London

Gagnon M, Labarthe J, Légaré F, Ouimet M, Estabrooks CA, Roch G et al (2011) Measuring organizational readiness for knowledge translation in chronic care. Implement Sci 6:72. https://doi.org/10.1186/1748-5908-6-72

Glasgow RE, Vogt TM, Boles SM (1999) Evaluating the public health impact of health promotion interventions: the RE-AIM framework. Am J Public Health 89:1322–1327. https://doi.org/10.2105/AJPH.89.9.1322

Godin G, Bélanger-Gravel A, Eccles M, Grimshaw J (2008) Healthcare professionals' intentions and behaviours: a systematic review of studies based on social cognitive theories. Implement Sci 3:36. https://doi.org/10.1186/1748-5908-3-36

Graham ID, Tetroe J (2007) Some theoretical underpinnings of knowledge translation. Acad Emerg Med 14:936–941

Graham ID, Logan J, Harrison MB, Straus SE, Tetroe J, Caswell W et al (2006) Lost in knowledge translation: time for a map? J Contin Educ Health Prof 26:13–24. https://doi.org/10.1002/chp.47

Graham ID, Tetroe J, KT Theories Group (2009) Planned action theories. In: Straus SE, Tetroe J, Graham ID (eds) Knowledge translation in health care: moving from evidence to practice. Wiley-Blackwell/BMJ, Chichester, pp 185–195

Greenhalgh T, Robert G, Bate P, Macfarlane F, Kyriakidou O (2005) Diffusion of innovations in service organisations: a systematic literature review. Blackwell, Malden, MA. https://doi.org/10.1002/9780470987407

Grol R, Wensing M, Eccles M (2005) Improving patient care: the implementation of change in clinical practice. Elsevier Butterworth Heinemann, Edinburgh

Gurses AP, Marsteller JA, Ozok AA, Xiao Y, Owens S, Pronovost PJ (2010) Using an interdisciplinary approach to identify factors that affect clinicians' compliance with evidence-based guidelines. Crit Care Med 38(8 Suppl):S282–S291. https://doi.org/10.1097/CCM.0b013e3181e69e02

Harvey G, Kitson A (2016) PARIHS revisited: from heuristic to integrated framework for the successful implementation of knowledge into practice. Implement Sci 11:33. https://doi.org/10.1186/s13012-016-0398-2

ICEBeRG. (2006) Designing theoretically-informed implementation interventions. Implement Sci 1:4. https://doi.org/10.1186/1748-5908-1-4

Jacobs SR, Weiner BJ, Bunger AC (2014) Context matters: measuring implementation climate among individuals and groups. Implement Sci 9:46. https://doi.org/10.1186/1748-5908-9-46

Jacobson N, Butterill D, Goering P (2003) Development of a framework for knowledge translation: understanding user context. J Health Serv Res Policy 8:94–99. https://doi.org/10.1258/135581903321466067

Kitson AL, Harvey G, McCormack B (1998) Enabling the implementation of evidence based practice: a conceptual framework. Qual Saf Health Care 7:149–158. https://doi.org/10.1136/qshc.7.3.149

Kitson AL, Rycroft-Malone J, Harvey G, McCormack B, Seers K, Titchen A (2008) Evaluating the successful implementation of evidence into practice using the PARiHS framework: theoretical and practical challenges. Implement Sci 3:1. https://doi.org/10.1186/1748-5908-3-1

KTDRR (Center on Knowledge Translation for Disability and Rehabilitation Research) (2022) The rise of implementation science. https://ktdrr.org/products/kt-implementation/rise-of-implementation-science.html. Accessed 20 Jul 2022

Landry R, Amara N, Lamari M (2001) Climbing the ladder of research utilization: evidence from social science research. *Sci Commun* 22:396–422. https://doi.org/10.1177/1075547001022004003

Logan J, Graham ID (1998) Toward a comprehensive interdisciplinary model of health care research use. Sci Commun 20:227–246. https://doi.org/10.1177/1075547098020002004

Majdzadeh R, Sadighi J, Nejat S, Mahani AS, Gholami J (2008) Knowledge translation for research utilization: design of a knowledge translation model at Tehran University of Medical Sciences. J Contin Educ Health Prof 28:270–277

Martinez RG, Lewis CC, Weiner BJ (2014) Instrumentation issues in implementation science. Implement Sci 9:118. https://doi.org/10.1186/s13012-014-0118-8

May C, Finch T (2009) Implementing, embedding, and integrating practices: an outline of normalization process theory. Sociology 43:535–554. https://doi.org/10.1177/0038038509103208

McCormack B, McCarthy G, Wright J, Coffey A (2009) Development and testing of the Context Assessment Index (CAI). Worldviews Evid-Based Nurs 6:27–35. https://doi.org/10.1111/j.1741-6787.2008.00130.x

McEvoy R, Ballini L, Maltoni S, O'Donnell CA, Mair FS, Macfarlane A (2014) A qualitative systematic review of studies using the normalization process theory to research implementation processes. Implement Sci 9:2. https://doi.org/10.1186/1748-5908-9-2

Melnyk BM, Fineout-Overholt E, Mays MZ (2008) The evidence-based practice beliefs and implementation scales: psychometric properties of two new instruments. Worldviews Evid-Based Nurs 5:208–216. https://doi.org/10.1111/j.1741-6787.2008.00126.x

Meyers DC, Durlak JA, Wandersman A (2012) The quality implementation framework: a synthesis of critical steps in the implementation process. Am J Community Psychol 50:462–480. https://doi.org/10.1007/s10464-012-9522-x

Michie S, Johnston M, Abraham C, Lawton R, Parker D, Walker A (2005) Making psychological theory useful for implementing evidence based practice: a consensus approach. Qual Saf Health Care 14:26–33. https://doi.org/10.1136/qshc.2004.011155

Michie S, Stralen MM, West R (2011) The behaviour change wheel: a new method for characterising and designing behaviour change interventions. Implement Sci 6:42. https://doi.org/10.1186/1748-5908-6-42

Michie S, Atkins L, West R (2014) The behaviour change wheel: a guide to designing interventions. Silverback, London

Mitchell SA, Fisher CA, Hastings CE, Silverman LB, Wallen GR (2010) A thematic analysis of theoretical models for translational science in nursing: mapping the field. Nurs Outlook 58:287–300. https://doi.org/10.1016/j.outlook.2010.07.001

Moullin JC, Dickson KS, Stadnick NA, Rabin B, Aarons GA (2019) Systematic review of the exploration, preparation, implementation, sustainment (EPIS) framework. Implement Sci 14:1. https://doi.org/10.1186/s13012-018-0842-6

Phillips CJ, Marshall AP, Chaves NJ, Lin IB, Loy CT, Rees G et al (2015) Experiences of using Theoretical Domains Framework across diverse clinical environments: a qualitative study. J Multidiscip Healthc 8:139–146. https://doi.org/10.2147/JMDH.S78458

Praveen D, Patel A, Raghu A, Clifford GD, Maulik PK, Abdul AM et al (2014) SMARTHealth India: development and field evaluation of a mobile clinical decision support system for cardiovascular diseases in rural India. JMIR Mhealth Uhealth 2:e54. https://doi.org/10.2196/mhealth.3568

Proctor E, Silmere H, Raghavan R, Hovmand P, Aarons G, Bunger A et al (2010) Outcomes for implementation research: conceptual distinctions, measurement challenges, and research agenda. Adm Policy Ment Health Ment Health Serv Res 38:65–76. https://doi.org/10.1007/s10488-010-0319-7

Proctor EK, Powell BJ, McMillen JC (2013) Implementation strategies: recommendations for specifying and reporting. Implement Sci 8:139. https://doi.org/10.1186/1748-5908-8-139

Rogers EM (2003) Diffusion of innovations, 5th edn. Free Press, New York
Rycroft-Malone J, Bucknall T (2010) Theory, frameworks, and models: laying down the groundwork. In: Rycroft-Malone J, Bucknall T (eds) Models and frameworks for implementing evidence-based practice: linking evidence to action. Wiley-Blackwell, Chichester, pp 23–50
Sabatier PA (1999) Theories of the policy process. Westview Press, Boulder, CO
Sales A, Smith J, Curran G, Kochevar L (2006) Models, strategies, and tools: theory in implementing evidence-based findings into health care practice. J Gen Intern Med 21(Suppl 2):S43–S49. https://doi.org/10.1111/j.1525-1497.2006.00362.x
Stetler CB (2010) Stetler model. In: Rycroft-Malone J, Bucknall T (eds) Models and frameworks for implementing evidence-based practice: linking evidence to action. Wiley-Blackwell, Chichester, pp 51–82
Stevens KR (2013) The impact of evidence-based practice in nursing and the next big ideas. Online J Issues Nurs 18(2):4. https://doi.org/10.3912/OJIN.Vol18No02Man04
Tabak RG, Khoong EC, Chambers DA, Brownson RC (2012) Bridging research and practice: models for dissemination and implementation research. Am J Prev Med 43:337–350. https://doi.org/10.1016/j.amepre.2012.05.024
Titler MG, Kleiber C, Steelman V, Goode C, Rakel B, Barry-Walker J et al (1994) Infusing research into practice to promote quality care. Nurs Res 43:307–313. https://doi.org/10.1097/00006199-199409000-00009
Washington University (2022) Pick a theory, model or framework. https://impsciuw.org/implementation-science/research/frameworks/. Accessed 20 Jul 2022
Weiner BJ (2009) A theory of organizational readiness for change. Implement Sci 4:67. https://doi.org/10.1186/1748-5908-4-67
Weiner BJ, Lewis CC, Sherr K (2023) Introducing implementation science. In: Weiner BJ, Lewis CC, Sherr K (eds) Practical implementation science. Springer, New York, pp 1–22
Wilson KM, Brady TJ, Lesesne C, On Behalf of the NCCDPHP Work Group on Translation (2011) An organizing framework for translation in public health: the knowledge to action framework. Prev Chronic Dis 8:A46
Zahra SA, George G (2002) Absorptive capacity: a review, reconceptualization, and extension. Acad Manag Rev 27:185–203. https://doi.org/10.2307/4134351

Instruments and Techniques of Evaluation

Evaluability Assessment and Its Use in Health Service Evaluation

Tamara M. Walser and Michael S. Trevisan

Abstract

This chapter describes the evolution and expanded uses of evaluability assessment (EA) from its 1970s beginnings as a pre-evaluation activity for determining if a program is ready for productive outcome evaluation to its flexible use across a variety of health service contexts. Current uses include, for example, formative evaluation, evaluation capacity building, and maximizing limited evaluation resources. The authors outline EA as a threefold check on program plausibility, program reality, and professional evaluation standards and provide examples from a brief review of recent EA publications in health services. They end with related recommendations for unlocking the potential of EA to improve health service evaluation and programs.

Keywords

Evaluability assessment · Program theory · Exploratory evaluation

1 Background

This is an exciting time for those involved with assessing the evaluability of programs, services, and policies. Evaluability assessment (EA), introduced in the 1970s, is being used across disciplines and around the world (Trevisan and Walser 2015). Originally developed as a pre-evaluation activity to determine the readiness

T. M. Walser (✉)
University of North Carolina Wilmington, Wilmington, NC, USA
e-mail: walsert@uncw.edu

M. S. Trevisan
Washington State University, Pullman, WA, USA
e-mail: trevisan@wsu.edu

A. Kaehne, J. Feather (eds.), *Handbook of Health Services Evaluation*,
https://doi.org/10.1007/978-3-031-87869-5_10

of programs for productive outcome evaluation, its use has expanded over the decades as evaluators have developed novel applications to address the complex needs of programs and their communities (Walser and Trevisan 2023).

The history and evolution of EA parallels the history and evolution of evaluation. The 1970s saw the expansion of evaluation as an enterprise. There were several large-scale, multimillion-dollar outcome evaluations of federal programs in the USA. Unfortunately, the results of most of these evaluations showed no impact. This frustrated members in congress, some of whom championed these programs that were in part financed to benefit their constituents. The evaluations could not be used to bolster the argument for continued support of these programs, programs that people believed were important for the well-being of citizens. Consequently, evaluation as an enterprise was called into question (Trevisan and Walser 2015).

In response, EA was born. Often, these programs had no clear goals and objectives nor theory of operation that was agreed on by program personnel. In short, the lack of structure, inconsistent use of viable strategies to achieve outcomes, and poor oversight impacted the utility of evaluation (Craig and Campbell 2015; Trevisan and Walser 2015). Observing the limitations, Wholey (1979) and his colleagues at the Urban Institute in the USA developed EA to determine whether a program was ready to be productively evaluated for outcomes; and, if not, program modification could be recommended. EA has since grown in use across multiple disciplines and contexts, such as public health, health and social services, education, criminal justice, international development, and public administration (Craig and Campbell 2015).

2 Understanding Evaluability Assessment

There are many definitions and models for EA. A common definition used by development agencies (Davies 2013) is provided by the Organization for Economic Co-operation and Development: "The extent to which an activity or project can be evaluated in a reliable and credible fashion" (Glossary of Key Terms in Evaluation and Results Based Management n.d.). Davies (2013) noted that while there are several available EA frameworks, it is impossible to make recommendations for using one over another. Regardless, all frameworks should include identification of program or project boundaries and expected outputs, review of documentation, engagement with stakeholders, development of recommendations, and reporting to a variety of stakeholders.

Although the aforementioned definition of EA is a concise, practice-oriented definition that has helped organizations carry out EA work, we offer a definition that elaborates what EA is and how it is applied: EA is the systematic investigation of program characteristics, context, activities, processes, implementation, outcomes, and logic to determine:

- The extent to which the theory of how the program is intended to work aligns with the program as it is implemented and perceived in the field—a *reality check*.

- The plausibility that the program will yield positive results as currently conceived and implemented—a *plausibility check*.
- The feasibility of and best approaches for further evaluation of the program—a *standards check* (Trevisan and Walser 2015, p. 14).

This definition articulates EA as a threefold check on key aspects of a program that are central to evaluability. The reality check focuses on the extent to which the program conceptually is aligned with the program in reality: How well does the theory of how the program is intended to work align with the reality of how the program is implemented and understood? The plausibility check determines if the program is structured in such a way that it can reasonably be expected to produce positive impact as intended—i.e., the likelihood of achieving desired outcomes. The standards check gauges the feasibility of and best approaches for evaluating the program using professional evaluation standards as guidance, such as the 30 *Program Evaluation Standards* (Yarbrough et al. 2011), which fall into categories of evaluation utility, feasibility, propriety, accuracy, and accountability. Note that the word, *program*, is used broadly to encompass projects, policies, strategies, or a collection of regional partnerships, to name a few possibilities.

As mentioned, there are many different approaches to conducting EA, beginning with Wholey's (1979) model. Often-cited EA models and their historical contributions are summarized in Table 1.

The most recent book on EA (Trevisan and Walser 2015) builds on the work of previous EA scholars and practitioners and introduces a four-component EA model that streamlines the intent of prior models: (a) focusing the EA, (b) developing an initial program theory, (c) gathering feedback on program theory, and (d) using the EA (see Fig. 1). Instead of EA steps, the four components are nonlinear to reflect common application of EA where components may be revisited and overlap in practice.

In addition, Trevisan and Walser (2015) consider program theory and stakeholder engagement central to EA. Program theory is the understanding of a program, including its components, activities, and outcomes, and the assumptions or logic underlying how it is intended to work. It is often represented visually as a logic model, theory of change, or theory of action. Although developing and representing program theory is common in evaluation, EA is distinct, because in addition to developing a program theory, it includes collecting feedback data in relation to the program theory for reality, plausibility, and standards checks. EA can address questions about program context, program implementation, the research base for the program, and methodological scoping (e.g., data access and quality, methodological options). Data collection methods commonly include document review, individual and group interviews, observation, surveys, and literature review.

Engaging stakeholders in EA, including intended beneficiaries of the program, can increase the utility, feasibility, propriety, and accuracy (see Yarbrough et al. 2011) of the EA and subsequent evaluation work. It can also support additional purposes and uses of EA, such as evaluation capacity building, addressing program complexity, understanding program context, and culturally responsive evaluation

Table 1 Often-cited evaluability assessment models (Sources: Rutman 1980; Smith 1989; Thurston and Potvin 2003; Trevisan and Walser 2015; Wholey 1979)

Wholey (1979)	Rutman (1980)	Smith (1989)	Thurston and Potvin (2003)
Steps of EA Models			
– Define the program to be evaluated – Collect information on the intended program – Develop a program model[a] – Analyze the extent to which stakeholders have identified measurable goals, objectives, and activities – Collect information on program reality – Synthesize findings to determine the plausibility of program goals – Identify options for evaluation and management – Present conclusions and recommendations to management	– Prepare a program document model – Prepare a program manager's model – Find out what is really happening – Prepare an evaluable program model based on previous steps – Determine key evaluation questions and information needed to answer them – Determine the feasibility of evaluation procedures	– Determine purpose, secure commitment, identify work group members – Define boundaries of program to be studied – Identify and analyze program documents – Develop/clarify program theory – Identify and interview stakeholders – Describe stakeholder perceptions of program – Identify stakeholder needs, concerns, and differences in perceptions – Determine plausibility of program model – Draw conclusions and make recommendations – Plan specific steps for utilization of EA	– Develop program logic model and evaluation plan – Reach agreement to proceed with evaluation – Identify and assess time and other resources required for evaluation
Key Contributions			
– Original EA – Focused on information needs of managers	– First published book on EA – Focused on methodological, evaluation design – Could determine if one or more program components are ready for evaluation – Could use results to enhance a program's evaluability (formative use)	– Second published book on EA – Focused on EA as a process – Stakeholders are important users of EA findings and should be included in conducting the EA – EA could be used for program modification (formative use)	– Focused on expanded uses of EA—e.g., facilitating social change, stakeholder empowerment – EA as ongoing participatory evaluation – EA could occur at any or multiple points in a program's lifecycle

[a] Refers to program theory models, similar to a logic model or theory of change

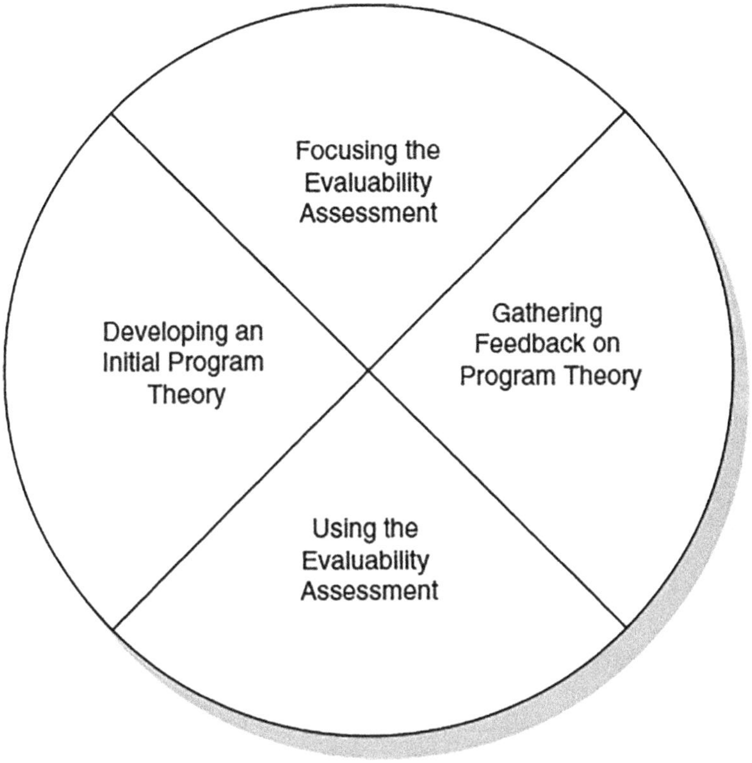

Fig. 1 Trevisan and Walser evaluability assessment model. (Source: Trevisan and Walser 2015)

(Trevisan and Walser 2015). Common EA activities, organized by the four components of the model, are listed in Table 2.

3 Applying Evaluability Assessment

There is a lack of publications in the peer-reviewed literature on EA; therefore, EA practice has seemingly outpaced what is known broadly from the literature. The innovations in EA that have been documented were developed by evaluation professionals problem-solving under organizational and contextual constraints to meet the needs of program clients and communities. Catching up to this work is challenging, and yet, doing so is vitally important to advance sound EA practice. There is a strong desire on the part of many organizations and professionals for information about EA, the relative merits of different strategies within EA, and how these are being applied in a variety of contexts. The available reviews of the EA literature provide a picture of the strengths and challenges of EA practice over time (e.g., Trevisan 2007; Lam and Skinner 2021).

Table 2 Common EA activities (Source: Trevisan and Walser 2015)

Focusing the EA
• Select an EA evaluator • Develop a formal agreement for the EA work • Identify the purpose(s) of the EA • Establish protection of EA participants • Determine stakeholder engagement • Establish procedures for communication • Facilitate effective collaboration and teamwork
Developing Initial Program Theory
• Review and analyze program documents • Gather and analyze stakeholder input • Develop or update a program theory model (e.g., logic model, theory of change)
Gathering Feedback on Program Theory
• Summarize results of analysis (e.g., reality, plausibility, and standards checks) • Answer EA questions • Develop initial EA findings and recommendations
Using the EA
• Finalize EA findings and recommendations • Develop EA reports, presentations, and/or other mechanisms for dissemination and use of findings and recommendations

Trevisan (2007) conducted a review of peer-reviewed literature on the use of EA from 1986 to 2006 and found an upward trend. In addition, EA was being used across a variety of disciplines, around the world, and for purposes that expand the original use of EA. They also identified ambiguity in concept; that is, it was often challenging to determine where an EA started and ended, particularly if the EA was conducted as part of a larger evaluation.

As a follow-on to the review by Trevisan (2007), Lam and Skinner (2021) conducted a scoping review of the literature from 2008 to 2018, focusing on EA case studies, including peer-reviewed and gray literature. A total of 59 EA studies met inclusion criteria, with 61% being peer-reviewed articles. Most of the studies were conducted in the fields of public health (44%) and education (27%). The authors (2018) noted a threefold increase in the number of EAs published, compared to the number found by Trevisan (2007), and similarly noted ambiguity in concept, such as blurred EA boundaries. Four common purposes of the EAs were observed: (a) to determine the extent to which programs are ready for evaluation, (b) to support evaluation planning, (c) to identify promising interventions for evaluation, and (d) to support program development (pp. 528–529). Recommendations for EA practice included: engaging stakeholders; discussing the EA with stakeholders; assessing program understandings, plausibility, and practicality; and considering cross-cutting themes of the program, such as gender equity (p. 535). These recommendations reinforce the value of engaging stakeholders in the EA process, as well as intentional reality, plausibility, and standards checks as part of EA.

Two notable areas of growth in the use of EA are public health (Ogilvie et al. 2011; Leviton et al. 2010b; Craig and Campbell 2015) and international development (Davies 2013; Craig and Campbell 2015). Leviton et al. (2010b) contributed an often-cited article describing and advocating the use of EA in public health. They identified EAs conducted in public health, healthcare, and social services across 160 US organizations at the national, state, and local levels. Characterizing EA as a cost-effective exploratory evaluation activity that provides rapid feedback and is a useful precursor to both quantitative and qualitative evaluation, they identified five ways EA can benefit public health:

- Serving the core public health functions of planning and assurance.
- Building evaluation capacity.
- Navigating federal performance measurement requirements.
- Translating evidence-based research models into practice.
- Translating practice into research by identifying promising practices (p. 214).

Unique benefits of EA cited by Leviton et al. (2010b) are translating research to practice and practice to research. They write:

> As practitioners implement an evidence-based intervention or program, evaluability assessment can test assumptions about the program's operation in new settings for a reasonably low cost and in real time. Where adjustments are indicated, the method can guide adaptation to real-world considerations. (p. 228)

Thus, EA serves as an efficient way to test the external validity of programs as they are implemented in different contexts.

Translating practice into research is described as using EA to screen for promising programs that are ready for evaluation. This is exemplified by the systematic screening and assessment (SSA) method, a strategy used widely by the U.S. Centers for Disease Control and Prevention to "cast a wide net for promising innovations, then screen these innovations systematically" to identify programs that are likely to be effective and ready for evaluation (Leviton et al. 2010b, p. 229). Lam and Skinner (2021) noted this type of "screening" use of EA in their recent scoping review, and an issue of *New Directions for Evaluation* is devoted to the SSA method (Leviton et al. 2010a).

Leviton et al. (2010b) further noted expanded uses of EA, including program improvement, providing a guide for program development, clarifying assumptions underlying a program, and informing the selection of a variety of possible evaluation questions and methods. They also suggest the possibility of EA replacing a more thorough evaluation in some cases, particularly when budgets are limited. EA results could indicate a need to revise goals or activities, the program theory, or program implementation, for example.

In addition, Ogilvie et al. (2011) describe the benefit of using EA in public health where interventions are often complex, there is high demand for evaluation, and resources are limited. Craig and Campbell (2015) similarly describe EA and its benefits, promoting its use for evaluating public health and other service programs in Scotland. They also underscore the centrality of program theory and stakeholder engagement as part of EA.

Craig and Campbell (2015) further noted a pattern of increased use of EA stemming from its application in international development and aid programs. In 2013, Davies produced an often-cited report on the use of EA by development organizations, such as the Department for International Development in the United Kingdom, the organization that commissioned the report. In reviewing the literature, including organizational reports that he was able to obtain, Davies (2013) found: (a) a substantial increase in the number of EAs being conducted in development agencies; (b) EAs were being applied to portfolios of projects or activities, policy initiatives, and regional partnerships, in addition to individual projects; and (c) EAs were used to address issues and challenges with program design, availability of information, and institutional context. Further, over the last 10-plus years the authors of this chapter have engaged in informal discussions with evaluation professionals from a number of development agencies, including the Austrian Development Agency, the United Nations Population Fund, and the United Nations World Food Program, and there is every indication that EA continues to be integrated within international development agencies throughout the world.

4 Recent Examples of Evaluability Assessment in Health Service Evaluation

For a deeper dive into current EA practice in health services, we identified a sample of EA articles and reports published since 2015. They were located through library database and internet searches using keywords such as health services evaluation and health services evaluability assessment, as well as branching techniques to identify additional references. Similar to the results of the review conducted by Lam and Skinner (2021) and the trends observed by Craig and Campbell (2015), most of the EAs were of public health programs, with fewer from other areas of health services such as health workforce development (Taylor et al. 2018) and integrative cancer care (Hilton et al. 2018).

To address health inequalities, a community-based educational training program, *Health Issues in the Community*, was implemented throughout Scotland (Belford et al. 2017). EA was used as a strategy to develop a logic model of the program theory and determine related evaluation design options. The authors outlined a six-step EA model they used, however, did not specify the model's author(s). Document review and individual interviews with nine program stakeholders resulted in a draft logic model that was refined with input from a workshop with a subsample of those interviewed. The workshop also supported subsequent evaluation design.

A key limitation voiced by Belford et al. (2017) was the lack of involvement by program participants in the EA process, largely due to challenges in obtaining needed permissions. Nevertheless, this study provides an example of how an EA plausibility check could occur in practice, by triangulating document review and stakeholder input to develop and refine a logic model. It also exemplifies a standards check, which included stakeholder engagement in a workshop focused on the logic model and related evaluation design options.

Embry et al. (2022) used EA to support revisions to *Wise Guys: The Next Level*, a promising community-based, practitioner-developed sexual violence prevention program for young men in the southeastern USA. The goal was to revise the curriculum and develop observation and fidelity protocols to ready the program for rigorous evaluation. Although the authors reference Leviton et al. (2010b) and Trevisan and Walser (2015) when describing EA, they did not identify an EA model that they used in their work.

In collaboration with program leadership and staff, they (Embry et al. 2022) conducted curriculum review, literature review, observations, and fidelity checks. This resulted in a standardized yet flexible curriculum that aligned with the reality of how the program was delivered, and observation and fidelity protocols. Through this novel use of EA, the evaluators engaged reality and standards checks. Their close partnership with stakeholders contributed to the utility, accuracy, and credibility of the work and supported evaluation capacity building. In addition, this work provides an example of the translation of practice to research benefit of EA articulated by Leviton et al. (2010b).

Hamilton-West et al. (2019) discuss two EAs of social prescribing programs in southeast England, *The Community Wellbeing Service and Encompass SP Service*, which help healthcare workers connect patients who have social, emotional, and practical needs to community-based resources. They used an EA process based on the work of Wholey (1987) and Leviton et al. (2010b) that included the use of EA scoring criteria to determine readiness for outcome evaluation and related recommendations. They conducted interviews with program teams to refine initial logic models and understand program reality and reviewed existing documents and data. Due to the early stage of implementation and data availability, full evaluation was not recommended at the time of the EA. However, evaluators provided recommendations for design and implementation, as well as for future evaluation.

Both EAs included reality, plausibility, and standards checks. The authors (Hamilton-West et al. 2019) highlight the use of EA to strengthen programs and broaden considerations of evaluation designs to include process, mixed methods, and realistic evaluation approaches, which may align better with social prescribing schemes than outcome evaluation.

Hilton et al. (2018) developed an EA approach that included aspects of theory-driven evaluation, rapid assessment, and appreciative inquiry to build clarity and understand the evaluation capacity of *InspireHealth*, an integrative cancer care center with three sites in British Columbia. Although they described their Claim Assessment Profile approach, they did not describe or reference other EA models. They collected a broad range of data from two established sites, including site visits with observations and mind mapping exercises with stakeholders, individual and group interviews, and surveys. Several stakeholder groups were represented, including patients. This resulted in descriptive logic models supplemented by explanatory path models to specify causal assumptions.

Findings provided a "snapshot" description of *InspireHealth*, an understanding of the centers' claims and logic in practice and assessment of whether claims could be researched in the field (Hilton et al. 2018, p. 108). This work provides an example of all three EA checks: reality, plausibility, and standards. It further highlights the value of and ways in which diverse stakeholders can be included in EA.

Spencer et al. (2016) illustrated the benefits of using EA for evaluation and improvement of *Medway Council's Healthy Weight* programs, implemented in southeast England. Seven of 27 programs were prioritized for EA, and in close collaboration with the program team, evaluators conducted EAs of the selected programs. They outlined a six-step iterative EA process based on the work of Wholey (1987) and Leviton et al. (2010b). Document review and interviews with program team members led to development of logical frameworks, followed by draft and final logic models for each of the seven programs.

Through the logic models, they worked to understand program intention and reality, assess plausibility, gauge access and quality of current data and monitoring systems, and develop a checklist and scorecard to summarize results across programs (Spencer et al. 2016). They also made formative recommendations for improvement, in addition to recommendations for subsequent evaluation design. Thus, this work is an example of all three EA checks: reality, plausibility, and standards. It further reinforces the value of engaging stakeholders as EA collaborators and using EA for formative improvements and capacity building.

Taylor et al. (2018) provided results of an exploratory EA survey for the *Area Health Education Centers* workforce development initiative in the USA, which supports access to primary care through education and training in rural and other medically underserved communities. The authors characterize health workforce development as distinct from public health and as a type of health service lacking in research and evaluation. The survey was intended as a first step in an incremental EA process to gauge the evaluation capacity and processes of centers before launching a comprehensive EA. No specific EA models were applied or described by the authors.

Findings provided a foundation for comprehensive EA and subsequent evaluation, and an information resource regarding evaluation structures and processes at the centers (Taylor et al. 2018). Limitations include a low survey response rate and the use of self-report data. In an area where previous research and evaluation are limited and evaluation resources are lacking, this study served as an initial standards check using exploratory, incremental EA to maximize current and future resources for evaluation. The study also highlights the variety of health service contexts in which EA can be applied.

This small sample of EAs provides a window into expanded and novel applications of EA in health service evaluation across continents and diverse contexts. All the programs were multi-site and often served historically marginalized and underserved populations. EAs ranged from an initial exploratory survey to more robust data collection and stakeholder engagement. Although most authors referenced EA models and literature that informed their process, none directly used one of the models presented in Table 1.

Most of the EAs reinforced the centrality of program theory and stakeholder engagement in EA, with some using a participatory EA process. Maximizing limited resources was a common driver for and benefit of EA. Expanded uses of EA included formative evaluation and evaluation capacity building. Similar to the conclusion of Craig and Campbell (2015) based on their rapid scoping review, this snapshot of recent EA use in health services characterizes EA as a "sufficiently flexible method to be used in a wide variety of settings" that is "likely to be especially useful in cases where either the goals or design of an intervention are unclear, or where evaluation needs to be dovetailed with an ongoing program of implementation and monitoring" (p. 3).

5 Recommendations

This chapter provided an overview of the development, evolution, and current applications of EA, particularly in health service evaluation. The intent was to deepen understanding of EA and promote its use among health service practitioners, researchers and evaluators, policymakers, and funders to improve evaluation quality and health service. We offer four interrelated recommendations.

5.1 Disseminate EA Work Broadly

Although there is evidence that interest in and use of EA have grown, authors have nevertheless observed a lack of peer-reviewed and accessible reports of EA use. This was noted by Smith (2005), Trevisan (2007), and Lam and Skinner (2021) broadly about EA; Leviton et al. (2010b) concerning EA in the context of public health policies, programs, and practices; and Davies (2013) and the Evaluability Assessments in Austrian development cooperation Guidance Document (2022) with respect to international development work. Reasons include the fact that professional evaluators are typically focused on the conduct of EA as per the terms of reference, and not on dissemination of results outside the network of stakeholders for which the EA was conducted. In addition, EAs conducted within large agencies such as international development organizations may see the work as somewhat proprietary and reluctant to make the work available to people interested in the contextual, inner workings of EA. And, as Leviton et al. (2010b) argue, much of the EA work found in the peer-reviewed literature are summaries of the work, lacking detail that could be of benefit to others considering EA. The actual detail of a particular EA is often found in the gray literature, such as reports and other internal documents, which are often challenging to locate.

Trevisan (2007) also mentioned that most EAs published in the peer-reviewed literature lacked clarity with respect to the model used; data collected relative to specific components of the model; and when used in conjunction with an evaluation, lacked detail as to when the EA started and ended, and when the evaluation was initiated. Lam and Skinner (2021) found these same issues present in their recent review. The sample of recent health service EAs we discussed in the previous section similarly demonstrates lack of clarity regarding EA models used or rationale for modified models and processes. However, the issue of blurred boundaries was not observed given the articles reported focused solely on the EAs.

We recommend broad dissemination of health service EA work so that others can benefit from the experiences and insights of those conducting EA, particularly in areas outside of public health where literature is most lacking. Further, we recommend seeking peer-reviewed publication in widely read practitioner-oriented health services journals and prominent academic journals in health services to enhance the knowledge base, use, credibility, and rigor of EA within the health services sector.

5.2 Center Program Theory

As mentioned, developing (or revisiting) an initial program theory and gathering feedback data on that theory (see Fig. 1) distinguishes EA from other evaluation work that includes program theory and provides the foundation needed for reality, plausibility, and standards checks as part of a systematic, comprehensive EA process. The centrality of program theory to EA is underscored across commonly cited EA models (see Table 1). Often represented as a logic model or theory of change, program theory was key in most of the recent health service EAs described in the previous section. Researchers include similar recommendations about the critical role of program theory to EA (see Walser and Trevisan 2016; Lam and Skinner 2021). In fact, a criticism of the SSA method used by the U.S. Centers for Disease Control and Prevention is that the method does not include development of program theory, which would improve its utility (Lam and Skinner 2021).

Figure 2 provides a depiction of a simple logic model, which is a useful way to represent program theory, particularly when focused on implementation and service delivery (Weiss 1997). For complex programs, which are common in health services, beginning with a simple logic model and evolving it into a theory of change or theory of action can serve as a scaffolded approach towards more fully describing a program including the conditions and logic of intended change (Walser and Trevisan 2021). When program theory is articulated and represented as a logic model or otherwise, it provides the foundation for EA and a roadmap for subsequent evaluation.

5.3 Engage Stakeholders

In addition to program theory, stakeholder engagement is a central part of EA, as well as evaluation in general, as it supports many of the *Program Evaluation Standards* (see Yarbrough et al. 2011). Stakeholders are those who have a stake in the program, including the intended beneficiaries. In evaluation, stakeholders are often included as study participants—i.e., we collect data from and about them. However, there is also an expectation that they are engaged collaboratively in the work of the evaluation. This can range from gaining support and input from a few key stakeholders at specific points in the evaluation to a participatory approach

Inputs➔	➔Activities➔	➔Outputs➔	➔Outcomes
Resources used to implement the program—e.g., program staff, facilities, equipment, funding, curricula	Services delivered by the program—what most people think of as the "program"	Immediate "products" of the activities, often described as counts—e.g., number of participants who attended training	Benefits of the program—changes in knowledge, skills, dispositions, or conditions
Used to carry out the activities	Intended to lead to outputs and outcomes	Intended to lead to outcomes	Can be categorized as initial to longer-term with initial leading to longer-term

Note: Descriptions of program inputs, activities, outputs, and outcomes are based on *Measuring Program Outcomes: A Practical Approach*, by United Way of America (1996).

Fig. 2 Common components of a simple logic model (Source: Trevisan and Walser 2015)

where the evaluator supports a program team to collaboratively conduct the evaluation (Walser and Trevisan 2021).

Stakeholder engagement played an important role in the recent health service EAs described in the previous section, with all of them mentioning the value of collaboration and many of the EAs serving evaluation capacity building purposes. Researchers include similar recommendations about the critical role of stakeholders to EA (see Davies 2013; Craig and Campbell 2015; Walser and Trevisan 2016; Lam and Skinner 2021). Further, engaging stakeholders productively requires facilitation and interpersonal skills. Trevisan and Walser (2015) suggest the use of EA work groups or advisory groups. Strategies for developing a stakeholder engagement plan and ideas for effective stakeholder interactions are also available (see Trevisan and Carey 2020; Walser and Trevisan 2021).

In addition, stakeholder engagement and honoring practitioner knowledge is part of the "translation of practice to research," identified by Leviton et al. (2010b) as an expanded purpose of EA in public health. The idea is to ground the EA in context and generate more realistic goals and objectives for the intervention from program staff or other practitioners who know the context and understand what could be achievable.

5.4 Use EA to Support Equity and Culturally Responsive Evaluation

EA provides an opportunity to support equity and cultural responsiveness throughout the EA process, such as when focusing on the EA, developing program theory, gathering feedback on program theory, and using the EA (see Table 2). Equity can be intentionally addressed through reality, plausibility, and standards checks, and EA can provide a foundation and build capacity for culturally responsive evaluation. The recent EAs discussed in the previous section were focused on health service programs that were intended to benefit historically marginalized and underserved populations; however, little or no direct emphasis on equity and culturally responsive evaluation was apparent from the details of the articles and reports.

Although stakeholder engagement, which is important for supporting equity and cultural responsiveness, was valued and intentional across the EAs; for the most part, those involved collaboratively in the EA process were program leaders and staff, not program participants or the program community. It is not clear from the articles whether equity was considered as part of program plausibility or reality checks, and if assessing the feasibility of and best approaches for further evaluation (standards checks) included intentional focus on culturally responsive evaluation methods. Hamilton-West et al. (2019) suggested broadening evaluation approaches and methods to consider designs that better align with social prescribing schemes, but they do not connect this to equity or culturally responsive evaluation.

Lam and Skinner (2021) similarly noted a lack of consideration of social equity in the EA cases they reviewed with any work in this area limited to determining availability of disaggregated data, by gender for example. They reference the United Nations Women (2015) and United Nations Evaluation Group (2014) in stating that integrating human rights and gender equality into a program means "asking whether gender and social differentiated data are available, whether attention was given to social equity in the program theory, and whether the context (e.g., social, political, cultural) in which the program is situated is conducive to the advancement of social equity" (p. 533). An example of this sort of integration is provided by Wretman et al. (2021) who describe an EA process combined with a social justice framework that they used for an anti-human trafficking program. Their work is helpful in considering how to use EA to support equity and culturally responsive evaluation.

Pre-dating the aforementioned work is the use of EA for social change. Thurston et al. (2003) and Thurston and Potvin (2003) offer a social justice framework for EA in what the authors refer to as a participatory tool for planning evaluations that focus and foster social change. An example was provided using a project that addressed the mental health of recent immigrants to Calgary, Alberta. Cultural competence among practitioners in addressing mental health concerns of recent immigrants was a priority for this work and thought to be central for social change. In this mental health context, EA was offered as an important tool that could be used at any point in the lifecycle of a program. Stakeholder engagement, particularly in the development of program theory is an important component of this approach.

6 Conclusion

As societies develop knowledge about effective health services, EA is being embraced throughout the world as an essential strategy to enhance promising programs and projects ready for a productive evaluation. From community-based programs to country-specific health policies, EA is central to the development of practitioner-based and evidence-based health service programming, identified and validated through the evaluation process. The examples provided in this chapter illustrate the wide-ranging contexts and ways EA is being used. This provides the means to advance health services evaluation and, therefore, the knowledge base for effective health service programs throughout the world.

References

Belford M, Robertson T, Jepson R (2017) Using evaluability assessment to assess local community development health programmes: a Scottish case-study. BMC Med Res Methodol 17(1):70. https://doi.org/10.1186/s12874-017-0334-4

Craig P, Campbell M (2015 Evaluability assessment: a systematic approach to deciding whether and how to evaluate programmes and policies. http://whatworksscotland.ac.uk/wp-content/uploads/2015/07/WWS-Evaluability-Assessment-Working-paper-final-June-2015.pdf

Davies R (2013) Planning evaluability assessments: a synthesis of the literature with recommendations. DFID working paper 40

Embry V, Macy RJ, Moracco KE, Scheffey K, Moore A, McCort A, Taraskiewicz L (2022) From 'homegrown' to researchready: converting an existing practitioner-developed violence prevention intervention into an evaluable intervention. Carolina Digital Repository (University of North Carolina at Chapel Hill). https://doi.org/10.17615/y0f1-wy88

Evaluability Assessments in Austrian Development Cooperation Guidance Document (2022). https://www.entwicklung.at/fileadmin/user_upload/Dokumente/Evaluierung/GL_for_Evaluability_Assessments.pdf

Glossary of Key Terms in Evaluation and Results Based Management (n.d.). https://www.genderportal.eu/sites/default/files/resource_pool/2754804.pdf

Hamilton-West K, Gadsby E, Zaremba N, Jaswal S (2019) Evaluability assessments as an approach to examining social prescribing. Health Soc Care Commun 27(4):1085–1094. https://doi.org/10.1111/hsc.12726

Hilton L, Elfenbaum P, Jain S, Springel M, Jonas WB (2018) Evaluating integrative cancer clinics with the claim assessment profile: an example with the InspireHealth clinic. Integr Cancer Ther 17(1):106–114. https://doi.org/10.1177/1534735416684017

Lam S, Skinner K (2021) The use of evaluability assessments in improving future evaluations: a scoping review of 10 years of literature (2008-2018). Am J Eval 42(4):523–540. https://doi.org/10.1177/1098214020936769

Leviton LC, Kettle Khan L, Dawkins N (2010a) The systematic screening and assessment method: finding innovations worth evaluating. N Dir Eval 125

Leviton LC, Khan LK, Rog D, Dawkins N, Cotton D (2010b) Evaluability assessment to improve public health policies, programs, and practices. Annu Rev Public Health 31(1):213–233. https://doi.org/10.1146/annurev.publhealth.012809.103625

Ogilvie D, Cummins S, Petticrew M, White M, Jones A, Wheeler K (2011) Assessing the evaluability of complex public health interventions: five questions for researchers, funders and policymakers. Milbank Q 89(2):206–225

Rutman L (1980) Planning useful evaluations: evaluability assessment. SAGE, Beverly Hills, CA

Smith MF (1989) Evaluability assessment: a practical approach. Kluwer Academics, Boston, MA

Smith MF (2005) Evaluability assessment. In: Mathison S (ed) Encyclopedia of evaluation. SAGE, Thousand Oaks, CA, pp 136–139

Spencer S, Gadsby E, Ogilvie J, Elliott S (2016) Evaluability assessments as part of an approach to supporting healthy weight. Br J Healthc Manag 22(10):510–517. https://doi.org/10.12968/bjhc.2016.22.10.510

Taylor J, Forsell G, Perweiler E, Sienkiewicz M (2018) Longitudinal evaluation practices of health workforce development programs: an incremental approach to evaluability assessment. Eval Program Plan 69:68–74. https://doi.org/10.1016/j.evalprogplan.2018.04.007

Thurston WE, Potvin L (2003) Evaluability assessment: a tool for incorporating evaluation in social change programmes. Evaluation 9(4):453–469

Thurston WE, Graham J, Hatfield J (2003) Evaluability assessment. Eval Health Prof 26(2):206–221. https://doi.org/10.1177/0163278703026002005

Trevisan MS (2007) Evaluability assessment from 1986 to 2006. Am J Eval 28(3):290–303

Trevisan MS, Carey JC (2020) Program evaluation in school counseling: improving comprehensive and developmental programs. Routledge, London

Trevisan MS, Walser TM (2015) Evaluability assessment: improving evaluation quality and use. SAGE, Thousand Oaks, CA

United Nations Evaluation Group (2014) Integrating human rights and gender equality in evaluations. https://www.uneval.org/document/detail/980

United Nations Women (2015) UN women evaluation handbook: how to manage gender-responsive evaluation. https://www.unwomen.org/

United Way of America (1996) Measuring program outcomes: a practical approach. United Way of America, Alexandria, VA

Walser TM, Trevisan MS (2016) Evaluability assessment thesis and dissertation studies in graduate professional degree programs: review and recommendations. Am J Eval 37(1):118–138

Walser TM, Trevisan MS (2021) Completing your evaluation dissertation, thesis, or culminating project. SAGE, Thousand Oaks, CA

Walser TM, Trevisan MS (2023) Transformative evaluability assessment: engaging local, cultural, and contextual knowledge to understand a program's story. In: Professional development workshop presented at the American evaluation association annual conference, Indianapolis, IN

Weiss CH (1997) Theory-based evaluation: past, present and future. In: Rog DJ, Fournier D (eds) New directions for evaluation: perspectives on theory, practice, and methods, vol 76. Jossey-Bass, San Francisco, pp 41–55. https://doi.org/10.1002/ev.1086

Wholey JS (1979) Evaluation: Promise and performance. Urban Institute, Washington, DC

Wholey JS (1987) Evaluability assessment: developing program theory. New Dir Eval 33:77–92. https://doi.org/10.1002/ev.1447

Wretman CJ, Macy RJ, Stylianou AM, Teekah AS, Ebright EN, Kim J, Luo J, Rizo CF (2021) Study protocol for an evaluability assessment of an anti-human trafficking program. Int J Equity Health 20:234. https://doi.org/10.1186/s12939-021-01573-5

Yarbrough DB, Shulha LM, Hopson RK, Caruthers FA (2011) The program evaluation standards: a guide for evaluators and evaluation users. SAGE, Thousand Oaks, CA

Social Value in Health Services Evaluation

Kathryn Ashton, Liz Green, and Mariana Dyakova

Abstract

The need to capture the social, economic, and environmental value of health services is imperative to enable sustainable, people-centered systems. This is evident in the face of global health challenges, resulting in deteriorating population health, growing pressure on services and widening health gaps. Historically, "value for money" approaches, such as cost-effectiveness, have driven decision-making and budget allocation, taking into account only the direct financial returns of a service. Looking forward, it is essential to capture the "added" social value, including benefits to individuals, the wider community and the planet.

This chapter introduces the concept of measuring social value, through Social Return on Investment (SROI). The main stages of the SROI methodology are outlined and its applicability alongside other evaluation and assessment processes and frameworks is discussed.

Keywords

Social value · Value-based · Public value · Economic · Environmental · Wider determinants

K. Ashton (✉) · L. Green · M. Dyakova
Policy and International Health, WHO Collaborating Centre on Investment for Health and Well-being, Public Health Wales, Wales, UK
e-mail: kathryn.ashton2@wales.nhs.uk; liz.green@wales.nhs.uk; mariana.dyakova@wales.nhs.uk

A. Kaehne, J. Feather (eds.), *Handbook of Health Services Evaluation*,
https://doi.org/10.1007/978-3-031-87869-5_11

1 Introduction

The need to consider and measure the wider (social, economic, and environmental) value of health services is becoming ever more urgent to enable sustainable, resilient, people-centered value-based health systems. This is evident in the face of global health threats and budgetary constraints, resulting in deteriorating population health, growing pressure on health and social services, and widening health gaps (World Health Organization 2023). Traditional "value for money" approaches, such as cost-effectiveness and cost-benefit analyses, have been driving decision-making, budget allocation and prioritization, taking into account only the direct financial returns of a service. For the future of health care and public health services and interventions, it is essential to capture the "added" social and public value, including co-benefits to individuals, their families, the wider community and economy, and the planet.

Historically, "value for money" has been the overriding factor that determined all public sector procurement decisions, taking into account only the financial or monetarized costs of productivity and outputs of an intervention (Neumann et al. 2008). There is a relatively broad and well-documented evidence base which has illustrated the Return on Investment (ROI) (which includes financial returns and quantifiable health gains) and value for money of public health interventions across the life course (Edwards et al. 2016; Dyakova et al. 2017; Masters et al. 2017).

In recent years, the measurement of social value in evaluations and impact assessments has become an important and increasingly well-established concept in all sectors of the economy (Crown Commercial Service 2023; Salford Social Value 2023). There has been an increasing recognition that organizations need to move away from a traditional "value for money" approach, to find ways to present and measure the full range of their outcomes and impacts (Banke-Thomas et al. 2015). This is of particular importance in the health and social care sectors due to the interdependence with a wide and diverse range of social, economic, and environmental factors (determinants) that impact on people's health and well-being positively or negatively (Dahlgren and Whitehead 2021). These factors are influenced by the distribution of power and resources which shape the conditions of people's daily lives and determine whether individuals and communities have the resources they need to live their lives to the fullest potential be it health, mental, and social well-being, economically or environmentally. Addressing the wider determinants of health also has a key role to play in reducing health inequalities, which is a key objective of public health practice (Graham 2004; Andermann 2016).

It is also important to acknowledge the increasing role and application of Value-Based Health Care (VBHC) methods, approaches, and tools, which try to measure wider patient outcomes and value and improve health services towards being more patient (person)-centered and integrated.

This book chapter provides a definition of social value, how it can be measured using a Social Return on Investment (SROI) method, the strengths and challenges around capturing social value, and how SROI can be used alongside other evaluation and impact assessment methodologies, for example, Health Impact Assessment

(HIA). It also promotes a value-based approach to public health services and interventions.

2 What Is Social Value?

The concept of health can be interpreted in many different ways, and is dependent on local contexts, values, and beliefs. It is defined by not only the individual but also that of society, other key stakeholders, legislators, and policy-makers (Winkler et al. 2021; Green 2023). The concept of social value is interpreted differently dependent on the context, resulting in many definitions of the term (Social Value UK 2012; Box 1). In general, there are three different levels of assessing social value: organizational level; program or intervention level; or contract level through commissioning and procurement (Box 1). We will focus on capturing "social value," which includes social, economic and environmental outcomes and impacts, at the program or intervention level (Number 3, Box 1).

Box 1 Different Levels of Social Value Definitions

1. Organizational-level accounting and reporting.

This is where organizations account for their social, economic, and environmental impacts at an organizational level. In many cases, these approaches attempt to align with wider social and environmental goals, such as the UN Sustainable Development Goals (SDGs) (United Nations 2017) and global climate targets.

2. Contract-level commissioning and procurement.

This is the area where social value is most commonly used and focuses on the social, economic and environmental impacts of commissioning goods or services. This links with the following concepts where social value measurement can be used as a tool to measure the impact of procurement contracts on the wider economy:

- Foundational Economy—the foundational economy is part of our economy that creates and distributes goods and services which we rely on for everyday life, which includes health and care services (NHS Confederation 2020; Welsh Government 2023).
- Anchor Institutions—these are large organizations that make a significant contribution to their local area by supporting health and well-being and tackling health inequalities through, for example, procurement and employment (The Health Foundation 2019).

3. Investment, program, or project level through forecasting and evaluation.

This is the context in which frameworks capturing social value, such as Social Return On Investment (SROI), are most widely used. At this level, social value can be defined as "the quantification of the relative importance that people place on the changes they experience in their lives" (Social Value UK, n.d.), which accounts for the broader intangible human and societal factors which result from an intervention and the wider determinants of health. For example, the value individuals experience from increasing their confidence or from living next to a park in a community.

Social value is the shared positive or negative value that is created from an intervention. These things may be important to individuals, but are not commonly expressed or measured in the same way that financial value is, but may have a major impact on the economy, society, health, and the environment. Therefore, focusing on measuring and capturing social value can have vast potential for improving health and reducing health inequalities in society (Banke-Thomas et al. 2015).

3 How Can Social Value Be Captured and Measured at the Program or Intervention Level?

There is a growing body of evidence that illustrates the wider value of public health programs through the use of methods and techniques, which capture and measure any social, economic, well-being and environmental outcomes and benefits (returns) of investing in public health (Banke-Thomas et al. 2015; Hutchinson et al. 2018). For example, such impacts can include on inequalities, local employment, mental health and well-being, community development, social capital, environmental sustainability and others. When social value is considered at the core of a program/service/project, the emphasis in measurement is usually on the change that is created by the intervention to all stakeholders. Some form of "theory of change" model is likely to be used, in which measurable inputs (people, resources, finance) generate activities that lead to measurable outputs and outcomes (Jackson 2013).

Originally developed by the United States philanthropic sector, *Social Return on Investment (SROI)* is an established mixed-method framework and process which is used to assess the range of health, well-being and wider outcomes and impacts of different public policies, services, and interventions across different stakeholder groups. Pioneered within the non-profit or third sector, the SROI framework aims to capture the social value created and maximize benefits to people and society (Social Value UK 2012).

SROI is the predominant tool used to assess the wider value of policies or programs by identifying and evaluating "soft" outcomes which have traditionally been difficult to measure when compared to other more traditional tools or processes such as Cost Effectiveness or Cost Benefit Analysis (New Economics Foundation 2013) which capture "harder" financial and health outcomes. The SROI process consists of a framework for measuring a much broader concept of value by measuring the changes which matter to stakeholders by considering the triple bottom line (economic, social, and environmental) of investments whilst improving health and well-being in doing so. The framework aims to bring about consistency in the way that social value is captured and measured, whilst recognizing that value will mean very different things to different people in different situations and contexts.

SROI takes a broad perspective by accounting for all resources and investment into an intervention or service (known as inputs) and places a monetary value on outcomes determined not conventionally measured by other economic methods (known as outputs) (Social Value UK 2012).

It is important as an approach because it not only demonstrates the economic return of activities but also highlights their wider social and environmental value. As a result, the use of the framework can help organizations move away from purely financial accounting towards a more comprehensive accountability of value created through an inclusive process of stakeholder and public engagement and involvement (Laing and Moules 2017)—something which is increasingly being asked for in democracies across the world (Welsh Government 2015).

SROI is about demonstrating and capturing value, not solely monetary impact. As money is a common unit, it is a useful and widely accepted way to demonstrate social value. As a participatory, stakeholder-led approach, the SROI framework enables the ratio of costs to benefits to be calculated. An example of this would be for every £1 invested in an intervention, £4 of social value has been created.

There are two types of SROI: *forecast* and *evaluative*. A *forecast* SROI is *prospective or ex-ante and starts before* and continues during the delivery of an activity or intervention to predict the social value which will be generated. These can be particularly useful at the planning stage of an intervention or service, where they can help to illustrate how a particular investment can maximize value and impact and help plan for process evaluation throughout the entirety of the project. In general, forecast SROIs tend to be less detailed and time-consuming than an evaluative SROI.

An *evaluative* form of SROI is *retrospective and conducted once the activity is completed* by capturing what outcomes have been achieved and evaluating how much social value has been generated (or unintentionally destroyed) as a result of the activity. An evaluative SROI can be time-consuming, but this is dependent on the availability of existing outcomes data on the service being analyzed and the availability of key stakeholders.

Both of these types of SROIs can be carried out either internally by an organization as an "in-house" exercise or be commissioned to be led by an external contractor.

SROI is based on seven principles which underpin how it should be applied. These are described below:

- Involve stakeholders: stakeholders are best placed to describe a change experienced from an activity or service. Stakeholders should be involved at all stages of the SROI process to help inform the analysis and how outcomes are identified, analyzed, and measured.

- Understand what changes: it is important to demonstrate how change is created and recognize both positive and negative changes, as well as intended and unintended outcomes.
- Value the things that matter: financial proxies are used to give a value to outcomes which aren't traditionally captured in economic analysis but which matter to the stakeholders affected.
- Only include what is material: only include information in an SROI analysis which provides a true and fair picture of changes and value creation.
- Do not over-claim: only claim the value for which a particular activity is responsible for creating.
- Be transparent: demonstrate all aspects of the analysis and assumptions made throughout the process.
- Verify the result: ensure the final SROI report is quality assured by an external assessor.

A mixed set of skills and knowledge are required to undertake an SROI analysis. For example, in undertaking a valid SROI, experience of facilitation of stakeholder engagement and participation, knowledge and experience of outcomes measurements and basic accounting are needed. These skills can be developed on the job for example, "learning by doing," or acquired through specialist training in SROI.

4 The Six Main Stages of an SROI

The SROI process consists of six main stages (Social Value UK 2012). These can have several sub-steps within them and are articulated below.

4.1 Stage 1: Establish the Scope of Your SROI and Identify the Key Stakeholders

Before the SROI analysis begins, it is important there is clarification around the purpose of the SROI, what is going to be measured and how, and why this analysis is being undertaken and what will be done with it. One aim of this stage is to establish the scope and parameters of what is being considered and what is feasible to be achieved with regard to available time and resources. There are several things which are important to be considered at this step which include the purpose of the SROI, the audience, the background, resources available to carry out the SROI, consider who will be involved in carrying it out, the period of time the SROI will cover and the type of SROI to be conducted (forecast or evaluative).

The identification of stakeholders is also important at this stage. Stakeholders can be defined as individual people or organizations who experience change as a result of an activity or are involved in the activity itself (Petkovic et al. 2020). This change can be positive or negative. Stakeholders can be identified through a stakeholder mapping process. These may be, for example, patients/service users, health clinicians, relatives of patients, local community or volunteers. However, not all identified stakeholders must be included in the SROI analysis. Stakeholders should only be included in the analysis if they are perceived to have experienced material change(s) as a result of the intervention or service being assessed.

There are several ways and time points which stakeholders can be involved in an SROI analysis. Ideally, the involvement should be direct with the identified stakeholders themselves, for example, one-to-one interviews, focus groups, workshops, and surveys. However, time or resource may mean some information will come from existing collated resources, for example pre-existing data.

4.2 Stage 2: Mapping Outcomes

This stage involves the development of an Impact Map which maps out the changes expected to happen as a result of an activity or service. It also shows the relationship between the inputs, the outputs and the outcomes.

The inputs of a service or intervention are defined as the investment that is needed in order to deliver a program. It is important that investments from all stakeholders are accounted for at this stage. This includes both financial inputs (for example, monies invested from a contract) and non-financial inputs which will need to have a value assigned to them (for example, volunteer time).

The outputs can be defined as the quantitative summary of the activity or service being analyzed. For example, a service could be providing flu vaccinations. The output would be successfully vaccinating 50 people with the vaccine.

SROI is an outcomes-based measurement tool and looks at what will happen as a direct consequence or result due to a particular intervention. Using the example above, the outcome of the flu vaccination program would be preventing people from contracting flu. It is important to not only include direct health outcomes but indirect outcomes which may impact an individual's or a population's health. For example, a long-term outcome of a flu vaccination program would be reduced sickness absence as less people would take sick leave for contracting the virus. Running a local flu vaccination clinic in a community center would also potentially have an impact on the environment, with less people having to use a form of carbon dioxide emitting transport to get to the clinic. It is also essential to not confuse outputs with outcomes. *A theory of change* is an important tool to ensure that you are measuring the right things. When deciding which outcomes to include in the analysis, it is important stakeholder views are considered and that outcomes are related to the correct stakeholder.

4.3 Stage 3: Valuing and Evidencing Outcomes

This stage involves developing indicators for each of the identified outcomes. The indicators can then be used to collect evidence of change related to each outcome and assess their value by assigning financial proxies.

First, outcome indicators need to be developed. Indicators are a way of knowing whether a particular change has happened. In an SROI analysis, indicators need to be related to outcomes to show whether a change has occurred and by how much. They are often expressed using terms like "increased" or "less." For example, there was an increased level of mental well-being after the intervention had occurred. Stakeholders are important in helping with the identification of indicators. Once indicators have been identified, it is necessary to ensure they can be measured. For example, via a quantitative questionnaire, existing statistical records or by qualitative interviews with key stakeholders. Ideally you will need to know whether the number of the indicators has change, through collected number of indicators before and after the activity. All indicators need to be measurable and they need to be able to be measured within the scope and resource of your analysis.

Outcome data will need to be collected from stakeholders to create both a baseline of data before the intervention or service was implemented but also to monitor and measure the indicators to show the change experienced. This can either be through new primary research or using existing data. Examples of primary research are one-to-one interviews, focus groups, workshops, and surveys. The sample size of stakeholders engaged with to obtain this information is dependent on the scope and resource within the SROI project.

The duration of the impact of some outcomes will last longer than others—some will be short term and some may be longer term. As a result, SROI analysis accounts for the benefit period. For example, some outcomes will depend on the length of the activity or service. If it is believed that the outcome will continue to generate value once the activity has stopped, this needs to be accounted for. The benefit period can be identified either through stakeholder engagement or from existing data including peer-reviewed evidence and statistical analysis.

The final step at this stage is to apply a financial value to all outcomes using financial proxies and estimates, sometimes referred to as monetization because a monetary value is assigned to things which do not often have a market price. The purpose of valuation is to show the value of individual outcomes and illustrate the importance of them in relation to the value of other outcomes. In *SROI, financial proxies and estimates are used* to estimate the social value of non-market goods to different groups of stakeholders.

For some outcomes, it will be relatively simple to assign a financial proxy to show the value created, for example, for an outcome of improved physical health, it may be decided to use the cost of attending an appointment with a General Practitioner as the proxy. Any outcomes which are identified as more challenging to value can be assessed using one or several techniques available which allow for proxies to be created:

- Stated preference/contingent valuation: also known as "willingness to pay," this type of valuation asks stakeholders how they value things either relative to other things or how much they would be willing to pay to have or avoid something.
- Revealed preference: this takes the value of something from the prices of market-traded goods.

4.4 Stage 4: Establishing Impact

This stage of the SROI process provides methods for a way of estimating how much of an outcome would have happened anyway, and what proportion of the outcome happened *solely as a result* of a particular service or intervention. This is important as it reduces the risk of making unsubstantiated claims of program impact and increases the credibility of the findings. This stage involves working out what proportion of change would have happened anyway (referred to as deadweight) if the activity or service didn't happen. Displacement is an assessment of how much of the outcome is displaced by other outcomes. Attribution should also be accounted for, which is an assessment of how much of the outcome is caused by something else aside from the intervention or service being analyzed. Drop-off is used to account for how the impact of the outcome reduces in future years. For example, an outcome of 100 that lasts for 3 years but drops by 10% each annum would be 100 in the first year, 90 in the second year and 81 in the third year.

4.5 Stage 5: Calculate the SROI

This stage is about summarizing the information collected over the course of the SROI program or intervention analysis by calculating the monetary value of the social value created by the investment in it. Discounting occurs at this stage, which allows for the net present value of costs and benefits paid or received in different time periods to be added up. For the public sector, the basic rate recommended for discounting is 3.5% in the United Kingdom (UK Government 2023).

The SROI ratio is calculated by using the following formula:

$$\left(\text{Total financial value of outcomes}\right)-\left(\text{Attribution}+\text{Deadweight}\right)/$$
$$\text{Total financial value of inputs}$$

A *sensitivity analysis* can also be carried out after the ratio has been produced. This enables an understanding of how results would change if some of the assumptions made at previous stages were changed and which changes would have a significant impact on the ratio.

4.6 Stage 6: Reporting, Using, and Embedding SROI

This stage involves developing a meaningful report which focuses on the change and value created, not by just focusing on the ratio but the amount of value created against each outcome. It is an opportunity to demonstrate the accuracy and robustness of the analysis and allow findings to be shared with stakeholders.

5 Strengths of Measuring Social Value in Health Service Evaluations Using Frameworks Such as SROI

There are a number of benefits to capturing the wider (social) value of health services and interventions. SROI can be used to help inform and influence strategic decision-making, service planning and improvement, and spending/investment allocation and prioritization. It can support the communication of impact and help to attract funding and resources. Demonstrating in monetary terms the wider social, well-being, economic and environmental value and impact can facilitate strategic discussions by allowing a better understanding of the amount of positive change and specific "soft" outcomes an investment or service is creating, moving away from a narrow output-based approach. It can also help to target appropriate resources to manage any unexpected outcomes. Measuring social value can also help to identify common ground and mutual understanding between all stakeholders, including investors (budget holders), practitioners, and the intended target audience (patients/population groups/service users). It also allows stakeholders to be meaningfully involved in service design, planning, and evaluation.

Frameworks such as SROI can also enable the articulation of the wider value of health and social care services and systems as anchor institutions (The Health Foundation 2019), and their role in contributing to the creation of sustainable local foundational economies (NHS Confederation 2020). It does this by capturing not only any health gain (or loss) but by highlighting the wider value of services and interventions, for example, reduced sickness absenteeism and increased productivity, resulting in increased economic outputs.

The SROI approach itself has many benefits. It applies a pragmatic approach which can be used prior to, or after, an intervention and allows for the underlying methodology to be adapted and tailored to the scope of each individual SROI, dependent on factors such as resources and timeframes. It can be used to inform decisions prospectively or evaluate and learn from existing or delivered interventions. It allows value creation to be measured through the lens of the wider determinants of health, which cannot be captured through existing health economic methodologies. SROI can also be viewed as complimentary to other evaluation methods and is a useful way of understanding stakeholder perspectives of an intervention's impact and value to them.

Due to the flexible nature of SROI, it can be integrated into other methodologies to provide additional value. For example, if an outcome evaluation was already being planned on a service or intervention, Stages 3, 4, and 5 of the SROI process could be undertaken to assign financial proxies to the already identified outcomes. There is the potential for the SROI framework to be used alongside other processes in tandem to add value to any analysis being undertaken. A specific example of this is the Health Impact Assessment (HIA). HIA is commonly defined as "a combination of procedures, methods and tools by which a policy, intervention or service may be judged as to its potential effects on the health of a population, and the distribution of those effects within a population" (European Centre for Health Policy 1999). Using the lens of the social determinants of health, it is an evidence-based approach which allows health and well-being to be considered across all policy areas and influence and inform decision-making processes (Collins and Koplan 2009). It considers health impacts through a holistic lens, including health behaviors, living and working conditions, social and community networks, and socio-economic and environmental conditions (Green et al. 2020, 2021), which is of great importance when trying to demonstrate value. The HIA process also identifies particular population groups who will be affected by the intervention, for example, those on low incomes or age groups. It is based on mixed methodology evidence collection, directly involving stakeholders who are affected by the program or policy which is being assessed (Tamburrini et al. 2011; Negev et al. 2013). Outcomes and impacts in HIA are obtained from stakeholder engagement traditionally through methods of participatory workshops, interviews, and focus groups, to aid decision-making. It focuses not only on capturing the potential positive impacts and opportunities for health and well-being but also any unintended consequences which may occur as a result of the specific planned action. HIAs can be carried out prospectively, concurrently, or retrospectively and can follow a comprehensive or rapid format, depending on the scope of the HIA (Winkler et al. 2021).

Although HIA is a recognized robust methodology, existing evidence suggests that impact assessments could potentially benefit from methods to quantify the effect of social and economic outcomes (Veerman et al. 2005; Ashton et al. 2020). A wide range of sectors are considering how to measure social value through economic analysis in order to aid and inform decisions. For example, capturing and understanding social value (such as the value created to individuals, families, communities, and the environment) in relation to the built environment and infrastructure development. The methodological processes of HIA and SROI have synergies and cross-over in their approaches. Combining the two methodologies, running them alongside one another, or using HIA as a platform to build on can have an added value to both processes and provide useful additional information for decision-makers (Ashton et al. 2020).

Both methods apply an inter-sectoral cross-cutting approach, which allows impact assessment to be performed by involving society and key stakeholders (those directly affected by the assessed policy, service, or intervention) in a participatory way. In addition, both HIA and SROI aim to capture the holistic (social, economic and environmental) value and maximize benefits to people and society. Applying these methodologies provides a direct route and useful evidence for including and considering health and equity in health and non-health sector decision-making, prioritization, and investment processes, thus contributing to the "Health in all Policies" agenda and reducing health inequity (Green 2023).

6 Current Challenges Around Measuring Social Value Using Frameworks Such as SROI

Although SROI is an established framework for capturing social value, it has mainly been used within the third sector, with limited use in the health (public) services sector. A key limitation is that of standardization. Although it is promoted as a flexible and pragmatic tool, a significant challenge with SROI is that it does not encourage comparisons between interventions and ratios. This is due to the different contexts and the subjectivity of the stakeholder input in defining outcomes; each service or intervention will have a different impact on the different groups of people who are experiencing the change. Also, different financial proxies can be used to value same/similar outcomes.

An additional challenge is that it is not appropriate to compare the SROI ratios alone, due to the opinions of different stakeholders and the different environments and regulatory backgrounds in which services or interventions are delivered. It is important that all of the SROI findings are read and understood to allow budget holders and commissioners to make decisions.

Another limitation of the SROI framework is the use of well-being valuation approaches to identify financial proxies, for example, valuation of outcomes, which can place more weight on the beneficial outcomes perceived by richer individuals in comparison to poorer individuals. If SROI ratios are taken at face value, then this runs the risk of resources being allocated in line with this issue, either diverting funds away from where they are more needed or else less in collaboration with those who most need them. An improvement would be to limit the use of such methods when valuing outcomes within SROI and clearly highlighting where and when they have been used (and even disaggregating this value from the rest of the social value that is being communicated).

7 Potential Future Developments

Although SROI is an established economic evaluation framework and approach within the third sector, research indicates areas for future development within the field of the public sector, specifically health services. Awareness of the importance of measuring social value and using an SROI approach within the health and social care sectors should be promoted and expanded, and the results of such work should be reported. This could be achieved by aligning and embedding SROI alongside other evaluation processes, health economics and impact assessments such as HIA (Ashton et al. 2020), to add value and help validate the findings.

Subsequently, a relatively simple but major opportunity for the SROI framework would be the standardization of methods and proxies, even if only agreed at an organizational level (Hutchinson et al. 2018).

8 Conclusion

At a time of increasing global threats and resource pressures on health, well-being, and equity, as well as on economies, societies, and the planet, capturing social value is becoming ever more essential to inform strategic and investment decisions. Moving beyond a narrow cost-saving financial return, evidence of programs and services is required to help achieve more sustainable value-based national, local, and organizational policies, budgets and plans. Measuring social value in addition to return on investment approaches to inform decision-making can be an important way of redefining current and future health and social care delivery, which is person-centered, more integrated and long-term oriented. SROI is one of the key and well-established tools to do this, and it is a useful and pragmatic way to identify the wider social, economic, and environmental value of the policies, services, and intervention under consideration.

References

Andermann A (2016) Taking action on the social determinants of health in clinical practice: a framework for health professionals. CMAJ: Canad Med Assoc J 188(17–18):E474–E483. https://doi.org/10.1503/cmaj.160177

Ashton K et al (2020) Health impact and social value of interventions, services, and policies: a methodological discussion of health impact assessment and social return on investment methodologies. Front Public Health 8, 8. https://doi.org/10.3389/fpubh.2020.00049

Banke-Thomas AO et al (2015) Social Return on Investment (SROI) methodology to account for value for money of public health interventions: a systematic review. BMC Public Health 15(1). https://doi.org/10.1186/s12889-015-1935-7

Collins J, Koplan JP (2009) Health impact assessment: a step toward health in all policies. JAMA 302(3):315–317. https://doi.org/10.1001/jama.2009.1050

Crown Commercial Service (2023) Social value in procurement—procurement Essentials. Available at: https://www.crowncommercial.gov.uk/news/social-value-procurement-ccs. Accessed: 20 Nov 2023.

Dahlgren G, Whitehead M (2021) The Dahlgren-Whitehead model of health determinants: 30 years on and still chasing rainbows. Public Health 199:20–24. https://doi.org/10.1016/j.puhe.2021.08.009

Dyakova M et al (2017) Investment for health and well-being: a review of the social return on investment from public health policies to support implementing the sustainable development goals by building on health 2020. Available at: http://www.ncbi.nlm.nih.gov/books/NBK453553/. Accessed: 6 Feb 2019.

Edwards PRT, Bryning L, Lloyd-Williams H (2016) Transforming young lives across Wales: the economic argument for investing in the early years. Bangor University

European Centre for Health Policy (1999) Health impact assessment: main concepts and suggested approach (Gothenburg Consensus Paper). Available at: https://web.archive.org/web/20061007033923/http:/www.who.dk/document/PAE/Gothenburgpaper.pdf. Accessed: 16 Feb 2023.

Graham H (2004) Social determinants and their unequal distribution: clarifying policy understandings. Milbank Q 82(1):101–124. https://doi.org/10.1111/j.0887-378X.2004.00303.x

Green L (2023) Health Impact Assessment (HIA) as a tool to mobilise 'health in all policies'. Doctoral thesis. Maastricht University. Available at: https://cris.maastrichtuniversity.nl/en/publications/health-impact-assessment-hia-as-a-tool-to-mobilise-health-in-all-.

Green L et al (2020) Process, practice and Progress: a case study of the health impact assessment (HIA) of Brexit in Wales. Int J Environ Res Public Health 17(18). https://doi.org/10.3390/ijerph17186652

Green L et al (2021) Using health impact assessment (HIA) to understand the wider health and well-being implications of policy decisions: the COVID-19 "staying at home and social distancing policy" in Wales. BMC Public Health 21(1):1456. https://doi.org/10.1186/s12889-021-11480-7

Hutchinson CL et al (2018) Valuing the impact of health and social care programmes using social return on investment analysis: how have academics advanced the methodology? A protocol for a systematic review of peer-reviewed literature. BMJ Open 8(12):e022534. https://doi.org/10.1136/bmjopen-2018-022534

Jackson ET (2013) Interrogating the theory of change: evaluating impact investing where it matters most. J Sustain Financ Invest 3(2):95–110. https://doi.org/10.1080/20430795.2013.776257

Laing CM, Moules NJ (2017) Social return on investment: a new approach to understanding and advocating for Value in healthcare. J Nurs Adm 47(12):623–628. Available at:. https://doi.org/10.1097/NNA.0000000000000557

Masters R et al (2017) Return on investment of public health interventions: a systematic review. J Epidemiol Community Health 71(8):827–834. https://doi.org/10.1136/jech-2016-208141

Negev M et al (2013) Stakeholder participation in health impact assessment: a multicultural approach. Environ Impact Assess Rev 43:112–120. https://doi.org/10.1016/j.eiar.2013.06.002

Neumann PJ, Jacobson PD, Palmer JA (2008) Measuring the value of public health systems: the disconnect between health economists and public health practitioners. Am J Public Health 98(12):2173–2180. https://doi.org/10.2105/AJPH.2007.127134

New Economics Foundation (2013) Economics in policy-making 4. Social CBA and SROI. NEF. Available at: https://www.nefconsulting.com/wp-content/uploads/2014/10/Briefing-on-SROI-and-CBA.pdf. Accessed: 12 Mar 2019

NHS Confederation (2020) Health as the new wealth | NHS Confederation. Available at: https://www.nhsconfed.org/publications/health-new-wealth. Accessed: 19 Jan 2023.

Petkovic J et al (2020) Protocol for the development of guidance for stakeholder engagement in health and healthcare guideline development and implementation. Syst Rev 9(1):21. https://doi.org/10.1186/s13643-020-1272-5

Salford Social Value (2023) Measuring and evaluating social value, Salford social value. Available at: https://www.salfordsocialvalue.org.uk/social-value-toolkit/measuring-and-evaluating-social-value/. Accessed: 20 Nov 2023.

Social Value UK (2012) A guide to social return on investment 2012—Social Value UK. Available at: https://socialvalueuk.org/resource/a-guide-to-social-return-on-investment-2012/. Accessed: 9 Jan 2023.

Social Value UK (n.d.) What is social value?, Social Value UK. Available at: http://www.socialvalueuk.org/what-is-social-value/. Accessed: 12 Mar 2019.

Tamburrini A-L, Gilhuly K, Harris-Roxas B (2011) Enhancing benefits in health impact assessment through stakeholder consultation. Impact Assess Proj Apprais 29(3):195–204. https://doi.org/10.3152/146155111X12959673796281

The Health Foundation (2019) Building healthier communities: the role of the NHS as an anchor institution—The Health Foundation. Available at: https://www.health.org.uk/publications/reports/building-healthier-communities-role-of-nhs-as-anchor-institution. Accessed: 19 Jan 2023.

UK Government (2023) The Green Book (2022), GOV.UK. Available at: https://www.gov.uk/government/publications/the-green-book-appraisal-and-evaluation-in-central-government/the-green-book-2020. Accessed: 15 Apr 2024.

United Nations (2017) Transforming our world: the 2030 agenda for sustainable development. In: A new era in global health. Springer, New York. https://doi.org/10.1891/9780826190123.ap02

Veerman J, Barendregt J, Mackenbach J (2005) Quantitative health impact assessment: current practice and future directions. J Epidemiol Community Health 59(5):361–370. https://doi.org/10.1136/jech.2004.026039

Welsh Government (2015) Well-being of Future Generations (Wales) Act 2015. Available at: https://www.legislation.gov.uk/anaw/2015/2/contents/enacted. Accessed: 16 Feb 2023.
Welsh Government (2023) A Healthier Wales foundation economy programme | GOV. WALES. Available at: https://www.gov.wales/healthier-wales-foundation-economy-programme. Accessed: 9 Aug 2023
Winkler M et al (2021) Health impact assessment international best practice principles. Special publication series no. 5.. Available at: https://www.researchgate.net/publication/352573139_Health_impact_assessment_international_best_practice_principles_International_Association_for_Impact_Assessment. Accessed: 15 Feb 2023.
World Health Organization (2023) WHO releases the largest global collection of health inequality data. Available at: https://www.who.int/news/item/20-04-2023-who-releases-the-largest-global-collection-of-health-inequality-data. Accessed: 28 Nov 2023.

Qualitative Causal Mapping in Evaluations

Fiona Remnant, James Copestake, Steve Powell, and Melanie Channon

Abstract

What explains variation in use of health services and perception of health outcomes? Answering such causal questions is hard to do credibly and cost-effectively. This chapter presents the Qualitative Impact Protocol, an approach to impact evaluation based on collecting narrative data directly from stakeholders about the changes they perceive to be most important in explaining outcomes across multiple domains relevant to an intervention's goals. The chapter demonstrates how data can be coded and visualized using causal mapping. Findings can contribute both to developing and to testing theories about the causal mechanisms explaining people's behavior.

Keywords

Causal mapping · Qualitative research · Causal pathways · Impact evaluation · Health

F. Remnant (✉)
Bath Social & Development Research Ltd, Bath, UK
e-mail: fiona@bathsdr.org

J. Copestake · M. Channon
University of Bath, Bath, UK
e-mail: j.g.copestake@bath.ac.uk; m.d.channon@bath.ac.uk

S. Powell
Causal Map Ltd, Bath, UK
e-mail: steve@causalmap.app

A. Kaehne, J. Feather (eds.), *Handbook of Health Services Evaluation*,
https://doi.org/10.1007/978-3-031-87869-5_12

1 Introduction

Understanding why and how people access and deliver health services and what they perceive to be barriers or drivers to improved health behavior and outcomes are crucial parts of any health services evaluation, but doing so in a credible and cost-effective way is challenging. This chapter presents the Qualitative Impact Protocol or QuIP (Copestake et al. 2019b), a qualitative approach to data collection and analysis of complex interventions pioneered in the field of international development and since used in a variety of settings, including in the health sector. Previous applications include evaluating the impact of sexual and reproductive health services, of international volunteer inputs into medical training, graduate training of midwives, vaccination programs, and multifaceted interventions aiming to improve early childhood care and nutrition.

This approach uses narrative accounts from a combination of focus groups and in-depth interviews with intended service users and other stakeholders about changes they regard as important in predefined "outcome" domains relevant to an intervention's goals. Identified outcomes provide the starting point for discussion of how and why these changes have taken place. The narrative data is then coded and synthesized using causal mapping (Powell et al. 2023b).

Findings can be used both to (dis)confirm previously formulated "theories of change" about how a particular intervention is expected to work, and in a more exploratory manner to understand the causal processes at play. It is particularly useful for surfacing new, emerging, and unexpected causal factors and possible links between them.

The chapter demonstrates how rich narrative data from carefully selected sources can then be coded, aggregated, reviewed at different levels of detail, and visualized using causal qualitative data analysis and causal mapping. This approach to analysis, combined with innovative developments in data collection methods, helps to make rich narrative data more transparent and accessible. The aim is to provide an independent "reality check" that can complement other forms of evaluative practice, including process tracing, contribution analysis, realist enquiry, statistical inference based on quantitative data, and process evaluation.

2 Overview and Context

The Qualitative Impact Protocol was originally developed as a credible and affordable alternative to large-scale experimental evaluations, specifically for development organizations working in diverse, complex, and rapidly changing contexts (Copestake et al. 2019b). In the decade since its original development, it has been applied to evaluations in a wide range of contexts, and there is scope to extend the approach further in healthcare service evaluations. The person-centered approach to the data collected, with a focus on learning from personal experiences, lends itself well to a better understanding of variation in what helps and hinders access to and use of health services by different people, as well as how, and why. It can help unpick the full continuum of access to healthcare from the perception of need, through seeking healthcare, reaching, obtaining, and fully realizing the benefits from both the population and provider perspectives (Levesque et al. 2013).

QuIP focuses on what people report as changes (and causes of changes) which are most important to them—providing a "reality check" on expected benefits. It is good for understanding impact in complex and fast-changing situations, including unanticipated causes and unintended effects. In contrast, it is not designed to elicit information about the magnitude of changes, nor to generate precise estimates of average "treatment" effects, although it can usefully complement more quantitative approaches and can inform quantitative modeling and simulation.

In contrast to purely quantitative methods, the QuIP sets out to generate case-by-case evidence of impact based on narrative statements collected directly from stakeholders, without the need to interview a control group. Evidence of causal contributors to outcomes is elicited from respondents by using an interview style which prompts them to share their experiences and perceptions of the causal processes underpinning reported changes—"what do you think has changed in this area of your life, and why do you think that change has happened?" This overtly causal approach to data collection and analysis relies on language-based direct perception of causation, and so contrasts with methods that rely on statistical inference based on variable exposure to an intervention to estimate causal effects.

QuIP usually collects evidence of people's perceptions of what has changed compared to a specified time period *before* an intervention. For example, the two following sentences are rich in information about drivers of change (and no change), using a "previous time" anchor of 1 year ago:

> I have been happier and more confident since I joined a local community gardening group. Sometimes I didn't see people for weeks at a time but now I talk to people at least once a week.

> I don't think that my fitness has changed much in the last year, I tried doing an outdoor fitness group, but I didn't like it when it was wet, and I haven't found anything else that I can afford to do, gym classes are too expensive.

In other instances, respondents may implicitly compare an outcome, such as prolonging breastfeeding, with what they would otherwise have done—e.g. if they had not been encouraged to do so by a health worker.

Asking people directly about change requires thinking carefully about credible ways to address potential response biases, particularly confirmation bias. The concern that people will tell you what they "think you want to hear" is a common criticism of relying on self-reported narrative data in evaluation, so tackling this head on in the design is important to the credibility of this approach. As a result, QuIP interviews rely mainly on open-ended questions which are as far as possible posed in a "goal-free" manner, with no reference to the intervention at any point in the interview; indeed, in many contexts it is possible for researchers to conduct the interviews without themselves knowing any or many details of the program being evaluated. This both reduces the possibility of pro-intervention or confirmation bias and helps to collect a broader range of information about activities and drivers of change since respondents' comments are not framed or limited to a specified intervention.

Unprompted reference to cause and effect is particularly important when relying on the "latent counterfactuals" embedded in everyday speech to identify what causes change (or not). So, the example responses above are *not* elicited by asking about how useful the community gardening group has been as a mental health initiative, or the subsidized outdoor exercise classes as an obesity reduction initiative. Rather they are elicited by asking "How has your sense of well-being and happiness changed over the past year?" and "How has your fitness changed compared to this time a year ago?" Whether the initiatives are mentioned, and in relation to which outcomes cannot be planned or guaranteed—the stories of change will depend on what is significant in the minds of the selected respondents in the context of the question asked.

Stories of change collected in this way are analyzed using *causal qualitative data analysis* (Powell et al. 2023b), identifying and connecting reported cause and effect factors in the narrative statements. The analytical challenge is to be able to summarize and present key findings from relatively large sets of qualitative data—usually focused on whether the evidence explicitly or implicitly confirms or undermines the causal *theory* underpinning the intervention. The creation of *empirical* causal maps can be compared with the theories of change that informed the intervention, as well as to compare the experiences and perceptions of different stakeholder groups—e.g., men and women, or junior and senior healthcare staff.

QuIP is the product of a pragmatic and eclectic approach to methodological development that borrows from several other theory-based approaches, notably Realist Evaluation, Contribution Analysis, Most Significant Change, Outcome Harvesting and Process Tracing.[1] It is particularly useful to highlight its affinity with Realist Evaluation (RE), with its emphasis on how causal processes are shaped by the way people think and feel, and on understanding "what works, for whom, in what respects, to what extent, in what contexts, and how?" (Pawson and Tilley 1997). Answering these questions depends firstly on acknowledging and understanding the complexity of the real world; the *context* which surrounds and drives our thoughts and actions, including the complexity of program interventions. Often messy context influences the causal *mechanisms* through which decisions are made, and change does or doesn't happen for different people in the form of *outcomes*. The QuIP's approach to identifying multiple and distinct pathways linking cause and effect bears much similarity to RE's approach to identifying multiple and distinct context-mechanism-outcome (CMO) configurations.

QuIP collects people's perceptions of causal pathways in an explicit attempt to unpack how resilient structural and cultural features of society affect the cognitive,

[1] A detailed comparison of QuIP and other approaches to evaluation can be found in Chapter 2 of the QuIP Casebook (Copestake et al. 2019b).

internal "mechanisms" by which we engage with the world and a particular program or intervention. It does not seek universal laws in respondents' responses but does assume that our experiences and opinions are likely to be important. QuIP is therefore ideally placed to provide detailed information on mechanisms in mixed methods evaluations, whether concurrent, sequential, or more complex (Copestake 2023). Pawson (2013:19) suggests that "as a first approximation... mining mechanisms requires qualitative evidence, observing outcomes requires quantitative [data] and canvassing contexts requires comparative and sometimes historical data".

Where QuIP differs from other approaches to RE is in its indirect approach to interviews and focus group discussions by structuring these around broad "outcome domains" and letting respondents elaborate unprompted on the causes of identified changes. Realist interviewing and focus group discussions tend instead to be more open and explicit in reciprocal exchange of causal theories of researchers and respondents (Manzano 2016, 2022). Another key difference is that QuIP, like other approaches that use causal mapping, is designed to capture information about a wide variety of causal links in an open-ended way rather than focusing on a small number of high-stakes causal "hotspots," as is the case with RE and process tracing. This broader approach is relevant to the most recent Medical Research Council guidance on evaluating complex interventions, which highlights the importance of theorizing impact mechanisms, understanding interactions with changing contexts, and identifying all the impacts of an intervention (Skivington et al. 2021).

One potential limitation of reliance on self-reported evidence of impact is that it is limited by what respondents know and what they regard as most important. Purposive sampling is important to QuIP to increase the likelihood that respondents have relevant experience to share and to maximize the prospects for revealing differences in understanding of causal processes among users and between users and staff. For this reason, QuIP studies are better understood as a form of case study research (Copestake 2021b). Woolcock summarizes how case-based approaches can help an evaluation, "(i) identify causal mechanisms to open the black box processes connecting causes and outcomes; (ii) elicit how processes of change unfold; (iii) explain the circumstances under which causal mechanisms are or not triggered; and (iv) helping to determine whether a particular intervention could work in other contexts" (Woolcock 2022: 30).

3 Planning and Designing a QuIP Study

This section presents practical advice on planning and carrying out a QuIP evaluation, and what different elements of the methodology can be adapted to meet the requirements of a specific evaluation. It covers the timing and staging of a QuIP study, sample selection, interview design and logistics, and analysis and use of the data.

3.1 Timing and Sequencing with Other Studies

Deciding when to schedule a QuIP depends on the purpose of the evaluation and the role of the QuIP in relation to other data being collected for the evaluation. This corresponds to the emphasis on timing, weight and purpose in Guest and Fleming's review of mixed methods research (2015: 8).

- Early in the design phase, QuIP can be used as a diagnostic tool for identifying existing drivers of change in a context without a specific intervention. However, the approach to collecting stories of "change" may need to be adapted to ensure that the data collected contains sufficient causal connections. Rather than relying only on people's lived experiences of change it is possible also to ask hypothetical perceptions, such as "what do you think would cause change in this context?"
- Early or mid-way through a project, QuIP can be used as a "deep dive" or "reality check" to find out what stakeholders perceive to have changed, or not, with time for course correction. This can be particularly useful if you have real-time monitoring data which raises questions, for example, if certain groups/interventions/areas are positive or negative deviants. These groups can be purposively sampled to help understand what is different about their experiences, what are the enabling factors or barriers to success which could help with any program adaptation.
- In an ex-post evaluation QuIP can inform reflection on what worked and why (including the relevance, sufficiency and reliability of assumptions and theory underpinning the project). It is particularly useful when there isn't a baseline or control group to aid impact evaluation through statistical comparisons.

Timing may also depend on its conjunction and weighting with other data. QuIP studies can be carried out concurrently with quantitative studies as part of "quant-led" mixed-method impact evaluation (Copestake 2023). More often it falls into or combines the two sequential approaches included in Creswell and Plano Clark's (2011) classification of six major design types:

Explanatory Sequential research starts with a quantitative survey, which in many cases can be used to help identify a smaller sub-sample for the "deep dive" qualitative work. The QuIP data analysis can then be used to help explain the initial and any subsequent quantitative results, particularly in relation to certain groups where there were questions (e.g., positive or negative deviants).

Exploratory Sequential research starts with qualitative data collection and can then be used to help design and/or refine a quantitative survey. The results of the quantitative data collection can then be used to test or generalize initial findings from the QuIP study.

3.2 Sample Selection

Qualitative samples are not designed to be statistically representative of a wider population but to reveal as much as possible (within constraints of time and money) about the range of causal processes experienced within it. This entails carefully justified purposive selection of cases for interview, taking advantage of what is already known about variation in the characteristics of respondents, context (including exposure to the specified intervention) and (ideally) outcomes (Copestake 2021b). Sampling starts with identifying "clusters" of respondents who are likely to have experienced broadly similar outcomes (e.g., based on their socio-economic characteristics and where they live). This provides a good starting point for identifying different groups, some of which can be further subdivided (e.g., between age groups, by sex or across different treatments). For each clearly defined cluster, QuIP studies aim to interview 24 discrete respondents as independent sources to talk (mainly) about their own personal experience (hence 24 discrete cases). This is often complemented with sex and age-specific focus groups through which participants can discuss experiences of change by "people like them." A cluster of 24 interviews plus four focus groups has proven to be a useful (if somewhat arbitrary) benchmark for a cost-effective and timely evaluation, corresponding to a level of data collection that is usually achievable within a week by a team of two researchers and allows for data collection in at least two contrasting clusters. Larger studies can be designed on the basis of multiples of this benchmark, e.g., 48 interviews + 8 FGDs. The decision to scale up in this way depends on the scope of the study, expected heterogeneity of users' experiences, and budget/timing constraints.

Deciding on overall sample and subsample sizes is a matter of judgment which depends partly on whether the study is primarily exploratory or confirmatory as explained below.

> [QuIP] Sample selection is based on two overlapping criteria, one more exploratory and the other more confirmatory. Thematic saturation is concerned with ensuring that enough data is collected to identify the most important causal processes arising from the project, expected or otherwise. Bayesian updating, in contrast, seeks evidence to reinforce or undermine prior theory about the causal processes triggered by the project. Both criteria favor samples that capture as much heterogeneity as possible in relation to characteristics of respondents likely to affect impact. Consequently, case selection can benefit from being informed by close knowledge of context, project implementation and characteristics of the intended beneficiaries. But there is also a need for transparency about how the selection is made in order to guard against the risk of "cherry picking" or other forms of bias. (Copestake 2021b:6).

When considering healthcare evaluations, in addition to the recipients of an intervention, it may also be useful to sample a more diverse set of stakeholders, especially those involved in delivery and development as they may provide perspectives related to health systems, institutions, and providers that intervention recipients are not aware of. This could be done by including clusters of different stakeholder groups within the sampling framework, using adapted questionnaires for each group.[2] Other possibilities include adding key informant interviews or focus groups with different stakeholders.

[2] This approach was recently used by MannionDaniels where QuIP formed part of an evaluation of the impact of UK government support of the Nepalese healthcare system. Different stakeholder groups interviewed included provincial and local government officers, health facility staff and NGO staff. Each group provided their perspective of a different part of the healthcare system. These perspectives can be combined to provide a bigger picture view.

Box 1 introduces an example case study which will be used throughout this chapter; various projects delivered by Save the Children to improve health outcomes for pregnant mothers and infants. Box 1 focuses on sampling, and more aspects of the evaluation design will follow.

Box 1 Case Study Example—Sampling

Context: Save the Children has used the QuIP approach on a number of projects designed to promote improved health and nutrition amongst pregnant and lactating women, and better feeding practices for babies and young children in rural, agricultural communities in Africa. This sampling example uses the Linking Agriculture & Nutritional Outcomes project (LAN) in Mozambique.

Sample design: Four communities were selected in total from four districts where the intervention was active in Mozambique. The communities were purposively selected based on having had a similar length of project implementation, similar (high) number of project components started, and providing a diversity of geographic contexts. In each community 12 individual households were interviewed, 48 in total. As women and mothers are the key LAN target group, more women were interviewed than men (7:5 in each community), but both were sampled since the theory of change assumes more participation from men in the households. Changes in breastfeeding practices and child nutrition were central to the research questions, so researchers only interviewed households with children under 5.

Beneficiary lists were drawn up to meet these criteria, with those who were part of more than one intervention (out of four possible groups they could have been part of), and a range of types of groups prioritized at the top of lists given to researchers to help collect a wider range of experiences relevant to the interventions. (Researchers did not know why respondents were in the order they were in.) Of the respondents who participated, 26 were part of more than one intervention group and 12 were part of three groups. 19 respondents were logged as having participated in the model mothers' groups; 23 respondents as members of the farming groups; 25 as part of the savings groups; and 19 as gender dialogue participants.

Individual interview sampling breakdown

Households with children under 5 years old and part of at least one intervention group				
Province	District	Community	Gender	Total
A	1	Nhg	7 women + 5 men	12
	2	Nhs	7 women + 5 men	12
B	3	Bra	7 women + 5 men	12
	4	Mgw	7 women + 5 men	12
				Overall: 48

In addition to the individual interviews, eight focus group discussions (FGDs) were conducted, typically with around eight participants each. The FGDs were divided by intervention type in order to facilitate deeper discussion about the different activities, with participants known to have participation in that group; farmer groups, model mother groups (based on nutrition), savings and loans groups, and gender transformation groups. For Group D—Gender, FGDs were only conducted within single-sex groups, due to the gender-sensitive nature of the discussion.

Focus Group Discussion sampling breakdown

Group type	Province A	Province B	Total
A—Agriculture	1	1	2
B—Nutrition	1	1	2
C—Savings	1	1	2
D—Gender	1	1	2
			Overall: 8

3.3 Data Collection

QuIP interviews can be conducted with individuals and/or focus groups. The aim of these interviews is to collect stories of change which focus on intended outcomes from a project-specific theory of change. Collecting and documenting data of this sort requires skilled interviewers who can put a respondent at ease and who have the patience to pursue a conversation of around an hour, teasing out details of cause and effect, without leading the respondent in a particular way. Researchers need to be very aware of their own biases which they bring to interviews and trained how to mitigate and control for these where possible. The less they know about the intervention being evaluated, the easier it is for them to probe for details of causal connections without (even unconsciously) driving responses in a particular direction (see more on "blindfolding" later in this section). The ideal balance to be achieved is to allow respondents to select what *they* think is important to share as stories of change, but for the interviewer to ensure that sufficient detail is captured about exactly how that change happened—including why behaviors changed and what or who influenced that. This requires lots of practice and pilot interviews so that the flow of a questionnaire can be tested, and feedback on the interview style can be provided to researchers.

Interviews are structured around domains which are preselected, typically based on the expected *outcomes* of an intervention (if there is a theory of change)—**not** the inputs or outputs. See Box 2 for an example of how such "domains" are developed. Questions are designed to stimulate discussion; researchers are trained to let the respondent lead with what they consider to be the important stories relating to that domain, using supplementary question prompts to sustain and deepen conversations about changes observed by the respondent and the reasons behind them. These supplementary questions enable the use of more targeted questions should these not be volunteered after the initial question. The example of question C given in Box 2 relating to the food consumed by women and children is an illustration of how some questions can be made more specific if more details are required, but most questions would remain shorter and less specific.

In QuIP, open-ended discussion of a domain is usually followed by a closed question asking about how positive the described changes were for the respondent, overall. These kinds of closed questions are a useful way of drawing discussion to an end before moving onto the next domain and offer the respondent the opportunity to summarize their sentiment about changes in a domain, rather than this be inferred and interpreted by an analyst later. Closed questions may also cover what the respondent considers to be the *main* overall reason for the changes. Stories of change can often be complex and include both positive and negative change; disentangling what that means for the respondent overall is a task which should not be attempted by anyone other than the respondent themselves.

Box 2 Case Study Example—Questionnaire Development

This section outlines the broad domains and some example questions used in various Save the Children projects. The domains take account of the different interventions which are part of a comprehensive approach to improving the nutritional status of women and children in communities considered to be poor in the local context. The interventions relate to improving access to clean water, better sanitation and hygiene practices, training on balanced nutrition—particularly for infants and young children, agricultural programs which aim to improve the range of foods grown in kitchen gardens as well as income from crop sales, support with savings groups, and gender awareness programs for all members of the community. The outcomes particularly focus on pregnant women, mothers, infants, and young children but interventions take a holistic approach—working with the wider household and community on multiple related interventions which are mutually reinforcing in their outcomes.

QuIP outcome domains:

- Health and hygiene.
- Farming.
- Income.
- Food consumption (for all members of the household).
- Relationships within the household and in the community.
- Overall well-being.

The interviews were designed to be broad and open-ended to allow the respondents to speak freely about what they believed to be significant changes in their lives. Researchers were trained to let the respondent answer the broader main question first and then, if necessary, use the additional prompts (in italics) to probe further and ensure that the interviewers establish what the perceived drivers of these changes were. Closed questions were also used at the end of each domain to capture overall perceptions of change in some specific areas.

Example questions:

A. Please tell me how the health of your household has changed over the last year; do you feel that things are different compared to a year ago?

- *Do you and your family get sick more or less often than you used to? Why do you think this is?*
- *Have you changed anything you are doing in your day-to-day life to stay healthy, and if so, what?*
- *Has this been different for different members of the household (males/females; adults/children)? Why do you think this is?*

Overall, how has the health of your family changed over the past year?
Improved, Got worse, No change, Not sure.
What is the main reason for any change?

B. Please tell me about whether the food your household eats has changed over the last year.

- *Are you eating more or less of anything; if so, why? Are you eating anything new; if so, why?*
- *Has food consumption during lean/hungry times of the year changed? How and why?*
- *Have you changed how you process or store your food for the hungry period? If so, why?*
- *Has the type or amount of food you purchase from markets changed? Why is this?*
- *Has the type or amount of wild food you collect changed?*

C. Please tell me about how what the women and children in your household eat has changed over the last year.

If you have been looking after a **young baby (<6 months)** during the last year:

- *Do/did they eat anything except for breast milk for the first 6 months and if so, what?*
- *Has this changed from either a previous baby or the way babies were fed before last year and if so, why?*

- *What are the number of meals and types of food eaten by pregnant or breastfeeding mothers in your household? Has this changed and if so, why?*
- *Are these changes good or bad in your opinion?*

If you have been looking after an **older baby (6 months–2 years)** during the past year:

- *Do/did they eat anything except for breast milk and if so, what?*
- *How many meals and snacks do they eat per day?*
- *Has this changed from previous babies and if so, why?*

If you have been looking after an **older child (over 2 years)** during the past year:

- *What different types and combinations of food are children over two years old eating? Is this different for boy or girl children in your household? Has this changed and if so, why?*

At the end of the interview respondents were asked to list the most important organizations or institutions they had interacted with who had positively impacted their family. This provided further information about which organizations and individuals are at work in the community and their relative importance to respondents.

An evaluation commissioner will need to consider the extent to which details of the program being evaluated are shared with the researchers who will undertake the interviews. This approach can be termed "blindfolding" (or double blindfolding), indicating that some or all of the details are temporarily withheld from the interviewer, interviewee, or both. Inclusion of opportunities for subsequent "unblindfolding," participatory sensemaking and reflective debriefing with interviewers can yield further insights and are also ethically important.[3] This approach can help to reduce the risk of pro-project bias and hence enhance the credibility of findings, but the extent to which it is used will depend on the aims and the context of the study.

- Double blindfolding is only possible by involving a third party, in order that the interviewers can be recruited, trained, and supported without knowing the identity of the organization implementing the project or commissioning the study.

[3] See this blog for more on efforts to incorporate more transparency into evaluations https://bathsdr.org/whose-voice-why-we-must-change-our-tcs/

- Partial blindfolding is most often used as it is easier to gain ethical clearance for a study and is usually sufficient to encourage unprompted responses. A trusted team of researchers might be recruited directly by a commissioner, or they may need to know the identity of the commissioner to gain approved access to the respondents, but they do not need to be given detailed information about the intervention being assessed.
- In some cases, it is impractical, unethical, or dangerous to blindfold either interviewers or respondents. It is still possible to focus on designing an open-ended and exploratory questionnaire, positioning the study in a broader context, and encouraging respondents to refer to this broader context when thinking about drivers of change. A trusted team of researchers may be able to obtain more detailed and relevant information about an intervention without using blindfolding; their professional expertise and integrity may be more than sufficient to ensure they are impartial and do not prompt respondents to respond to questions in line with prior understanding and interests.

4 Analysis and Use of QuIP Data

4.1 Coding and Analysis of Causal Data

A common issue with qualitative research and impact assessment is how to organize and make sense of large quantities of textual data, and to do so in a way that is transparent, so that generalizations drawn from it can be peer reviewed. The aim is to recommend a process of analysis which is rigorous, replicable, relatively parsimonious, (and therefore) fast, and which leads to the consolidation of complex data into digestible visual summaries of reported causal pathways to change, whilst not losing the rich detail which sits behind each link.

QuIP coding is based on the concept of causal mapping (Ackermann and Eden 2004; Axelrod 1976; Eden et al. 1992; Hodgkinson and Clarkson 2005; Laukkanen and Wang 2016; Powell et al. 2023a, b), where a *causal map* is defined very broadly as a diagram in which nodes are joined by directed arrows ("links"). In this example diagram, a link from factor C and D to factor E means that C and D have both in some way causally influenced E, according to some source S.[4] The aim of coding and visualizing data this way is to make rich narrative data more accessible to readers, without making broad generalizations which it is difficult for a reader to substantiate. The approach advocated here retains a connection between the visual summaries and the original coded text which enables easy verification of causal claims (Fig. 1).

[4] Note in general, causal maps encode "a" causal *influence* of C (and D) on E and only in special cases encode *total or exclusive* causation such that C (and D) entirely determines E or is "the" cause of E.

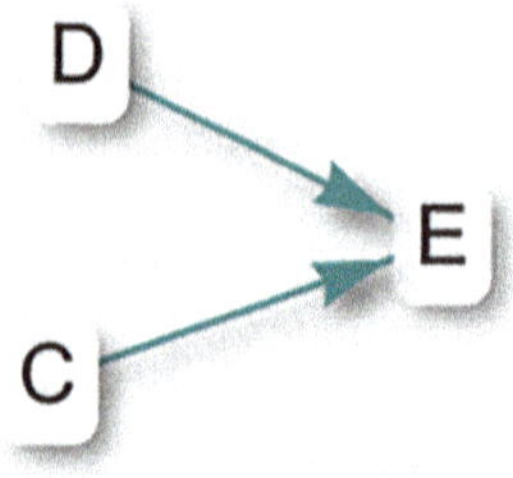

Fig. 1 Example causal diagram

Different forms of causal mapping have a long history in the social sciences; this approach is specifically useful when seeking to document perceptions of what has worked, for whom and why, as elaborated by Powell et al. (2023b).

> Causal mapping and most related approaches share the basic idea that causal knowledge—whether generalized or about a specific case or context—can be at least partially captured in small, relatively portable "nuggets" of information (Powell 2018: 52). These can be assembled into larger models of how things worked, or might work, in some cases (Powell et al. 2023b:3).

The process of coding QuIP data needs to be "natively causal" at the point of coding—that is to say while you are coding, rather than after the fact as would usually be the case with, for example, thematic qualitative data analysis where separate factors can be linked later. QuIP data coding always involves pairs, or longer chains, of factors—cause and effect, one factor leads to another (and perhaps another). The data must, therefore, contain causal claims, reinforcing the need to follow the guidelines laid out in the previous section when collecting data. Reports of change with no causal explanation will prove harder to code with this approach.

The approach to coding data does not rely on very large datasets or very sophisticated ways of differentiating types of causal claims. The analyst is looking for phrases such as "X changed because I started/stopped doing Y", "Since Y happened, we are seeing more/less of X", "Our yields went down because of X, but Z helped them improve", etc. These causal "nuggets" enable the analyst to link X to Y (and Z) in some way, denoting a positive or a negative connection. These links are one piece of evidence that someone claims that in their experience X is causally linked to Y, and this claim may be repeated (and elaborated upon) many times across a dataset. The coding is parsimonious because usually *only* causal claims are coded. Any additional information which describes the status quo is not coded. This may be of interest in other types of qualitative data analysis which seek to document how people live, but QuIP is specifically interested in what has changed, and why. If there is no evidence of change, the lack of any such links in a map is an indication that the project's own "theory of change" (Connell and Kubisch 1998) is not working in practice.

QuIP text analysis is mainly "inductive"; codes and labels are created based on the data in front of the analyst rather than starting with a predetermined codebook. It's important to note that the analyst is not blindfolded in any way and knows details of the theory of change and the interventions in order to be able to flag up any

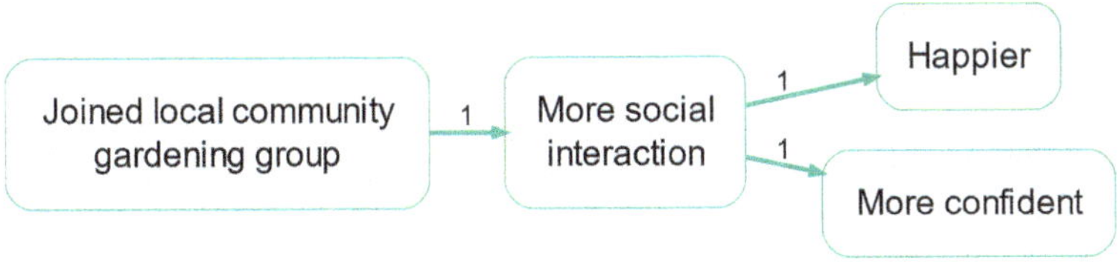

Fig. 2 Example causal map from text

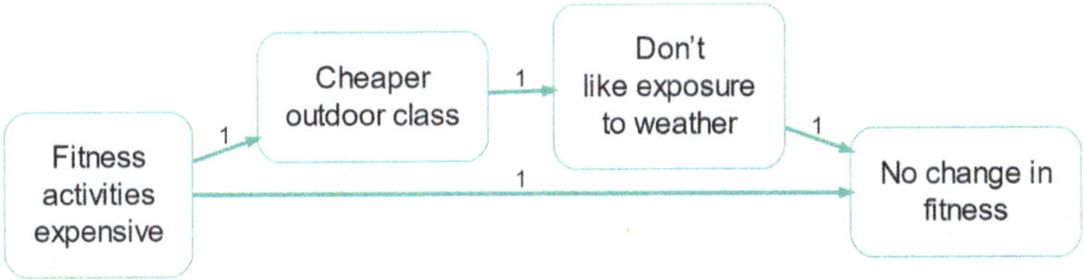

Fig. 3 Example causal map from text

causal pathways attributable to the intervention. However, the analyst bears a responsibility to use this information *only* to guide the analysis in relation to research questions and must think carefully about the risks of their own positionality in relation to coding the data—as with any qualitative data analysis (Copestake et al. 2019a).[5] Simply using the narrative statements provided as they are, the analyst should be able to identify repetition and patterns in the dataset and gradually harmonize labels to consolidate similar causal claims across different interviews.

Links must contain two-factor labels:

- Driver of change/influence.
- Outcome/consequence.

Using the previous examples of single narrative statements in Sect. 1, we can see how these translate into pairs of factors (Figs. 2 and 3).

> I have been happier and more confident since I joined a local community gardening group. Sometimes I didn't see people for weeks at a time but now I talk to people at least once a week.

> I don't think that my fitness has changed much in the last year, I tried doing an outdoor fitness group, but I didn't like it when it was wet and I haven't found anything else that I can afford to do, gym classes are too expensive.

This allows for limitless linked driver-to-outcome pairs to be classified: one driver leading to an outcome, which in turn drives another outcome, or one driver leading to multiple outcomes simultaneously.

[5] See Chap. 2 of the edited volume for more on 'The challenge of positionality in data coding and analysis'.

Although coding is mainly an inductive process, analysis will often be more "deductive"—comparing findings to an explicit project "theory of change" (Powell et al. 2023a), or establishing the specific impact of particular interventions. To this end, it can be helpful to add "attribution" labels to factors which indicate, for example, that they explicitly refer to an intervention activity, or that they refer to a particular thematic area of interest. These can be helpful when it comes to filtering causal maps, e.g., searching for all outcomes downstream of drivers which are part of the program's activities, or all activities which relate to "Health & Hygiene."

It is important to remember that causal maps derived from QuIP data are not causal models in a formal sense, they are representations of *perceptions* or *experiences* of change collected from respondents, "their constituent parts are about beliefs or evidence, not facts" (Powell et al. 2023b: 6). QuIP interviews are deliberately designed to elicit stories of change which articulate the respondents' ideas about causal relationships, which allows us to create "causal maps" from the narrative data. Researchers are specifically looking for respondents' reasoning about what they experienced, what actually happened, not their ideas or theories of "what causes what" in general; in this sense, the meaning of an arrow from C to E in a causal map means that "someone claims that C causally influences E". This is as opposed to other causal diagrams where C → E may simply mean "C causally influences E", and this is assumed to be true. The approach to QuIP data collection is what sets this type of causal mapping apart, relying as it does so critically on respondents' own experiences and their retelling of those experiences.

This should not detract from their usefulness, indeed comparing this kind of epistemic map of change with a theory of change can often be the main aim in a QuIP study. Consider the map below, taken from a QuIP evaluation for Save the Children. As a reminder, this was a health and nutrition program with many interlinked interventions aiming to improve health outcomes for families. The following map is taken from a dataset of 48 interviews in one country and is filtered based on the question "what is linked to the outcome *More balanced/varied food consumption*?"—both drivers and outcomes, with links made by four or more people. The summary map shows us the range of what respondents *think* have caused change in their diet, what they think the causes of those causes are, and, for 10 people (out of 48), that eating a more varied diet has led to an improvement in their health. The numbers above the links tell us how many different sources (people) made that connection (unprompted). The searched-for factor has a highlighted border to indicate the search used in the filter.

The number of people making a claim does not in and of itself have any statistical meaning, since this is not a statistically representative sample. Furthermore, in qualitative studies every story is relevant and important in some way, so some "outlier" individual stories may also be represented in maps as case studies of particular causal pathways. Higher numbers simply indicate that more people reported this connection in this context.[6] Rubrics to help define what level and quality of evi-

[6] For more on the tension between text and numbers see the Bath SDR guidance paper 'From narrative text to causal maps' available at: https://bathsdr.org/wp-content/uploads/2021/10/From-narrative-text-to-causal-maps-QuIP-analysis-and-visualisation.pdf

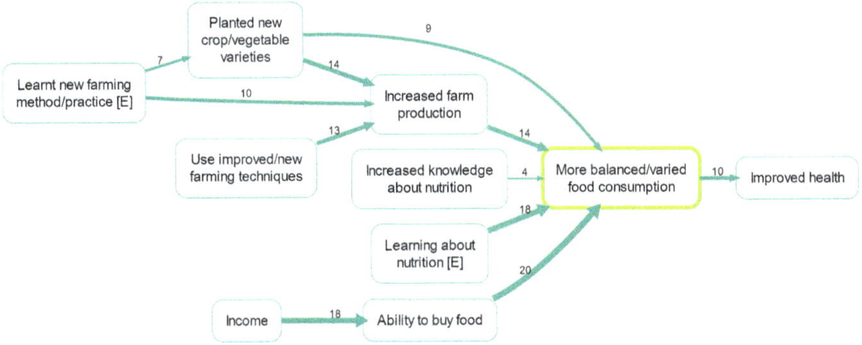

Fig. 4 Causal map showing drivers and outcomes of more varied food consumption

dence is sufficient to establish the success or otherwise of an intervention should be agreed with the commissioner and will be unique to the context of the intervention and evaluation (Fig. 4).[7]

Note that the [E] used in the factor labels for learning about nutrition or farming methods denotes that these claims were explicitly linked to Save the Children's intervention, differentiated from other similar factors where statements did not specify that the learning was via the intervention activities. This type of "flag" is useful at the point of analysis if you need to establish the impact of an intervention relative to other drivers, and mitigating factors. Further investigation can help to understand which combination of links are made by the same people, and whether there are any patterns to those combinations based on what we know about them.

Various qualitative analysis software packages can be used for this approach. Microsoft Excel is one simple way to connect factor labels to portions of text; data can then be exported into visualization software to create maps. Since there was no dedicated causal mapping software available which enabled both qualitative coding and visualization of causal data, the non-profit organization Bath Social & Development Research has invested in the creation of a web application for coding and analysis of causal pathways, www.causalmap.app. This software requires a subscription for data coding but is free to use for visualization and analysis of data for those who wish to upload data already coded elsewhere, e.g., using Excel.

4.2 Using Causal Pathways to Make Evaluative Judgments

Filtering and analyzing maps from a fully coded dataset enables exploration of which factors are reported as contributing to the outcomes cited, the extent to which these are related to the intervention, and what other factors may be mitigating or aiding their success. This approach is particularly useful in contexts where a variety

[7] See Aston and Apgar 2023 for more on Quality-of-Evidence rubrics: https://www.evaluation.org.uk/app/uploads/2023/12/Quality-of-Evidence-Rubrics-2.0-Final.pdf

of factors that are hard to disentangle are known to be likely to influence the intended outcomes of an intervention. This can help to avoid a tendency to exaggerate the role that an intervention plays in a complex system—often providing a "reality check." Questions to ask at the point of analysis:

- Is there evidence that the program is having the expected effect on intended beneficiaries, if so via which causal pathways?
- Did other, non-program, factors affect expected outcomes?
- Were there reports that the program had any unanticipated effects, positive or negative?
- What patterns can be identified that could inform future program design?
- Are there significant differences between the maps as seen by different age groups, sex, location, wealth etc.?

The data analysis described above can be adapted and taken further in numerous ways. Summary tables and maps are typically incorporated into a written report that also pulls out quotes from the source data to illustrate and elaborate on key findings. However, use of findings does not have to rely on written outputs, indeed if used as jumping off point, it can help to add more evidence to explain anomalies or unexpected causal pathways. Interactive maps can be used to structure feedback meetings with project staff, beneficiary communities and other stakeholders. QuIP analysis takes its cues about which outcomes are important from the respondents themselves, so it is logical to involve them in triangulation workshops, enabling those attending to challenge, corroborate, and complement findings. This both serves a quality assurance function and deepens understanding of what changes took place for whom, how, and why.

Key interpretive questions include:

- To what extent are findings consistent with both transmission mechanisms and intended outcomes set out in the theory of change?
- What evidence of processes and outcomes is generated that is not consistent with the original theory of change, and how can these be explained?
- What scope is there for generalizing reasonably from findings to the whole project, taking into account characteristics of the whole sample of intended beneficiaries and of the sample of those interviewed?
- What explains differences in intended and observed processes and outcomes of the project and what are the implications for future activities?
- Is the data consistent or at odds with quantitative monitoring data, as well as data collected from other sources (including meetings with project staff)? How can differences and similarities best be interpreted?

The question of whether this is the right approach for a particular evaluation will depend on the question of what evidence is needed, and what purpose the evaluation serves. Is it primarily to check and demonstrate which past actions worked or to identify specific ways to improve ongoing activities? Is it more important to quantify the magnitude of impact, or to explain why this varied from person to person or from place to place? How credible does the evidence have to be for different audiences, and what level of expenditure can be justified? QuIP can be used as the qualitative component in a mixed methods design, or even offer a faster and much cheaper alternative to a quantitative impact assessment in some contexts where collecting quantitative data is difficult, unaffordable, or unlikely to be very useful. Quantitative ways to assess impact can be rigorous and precise, but they can also be expensive and slow, emphasize average effects, and say relatively little about how change takes place.

Also relevant to the decision to use QuIP or not is being clear about what QuIP studies cannot do:

- Provide results that are statistically representative of all intended beneficiaries. QuIP studies are designed to gain a deeper insight into changes occurring in purposively selected groups and to permit cautious generalization across the wider population.
- Guarantee to answer very specific questions about the impact of certain project activities. If the activity is considered important by respondents in a well-being domain covered in the interview (and not simply taken for granted), then the QuIP should pick up unprompted references to these project-related drivers. However, if project activities are relatively marginal to respondents' lives, then a more direct and targeted line of questioning is required.
- Measure the magnitude of impacts or provide detailed quantitative data. The QuIP focuses on the nature of impact rather than its magnitude. Some quantification of drivers of change and outcomes can be generated to summarize and visualize patterns and themes across the sample, but the data is not statistically representative. It may be useful to inform modeling that can simulate the magnitude of change, but other data will be needed with which to calibrate such models.
- Score or weight the overall success or failure of a project. Whilst the visualization of coded qualitative data can make the evidence easier to digest and highlight patterns and outliers, commissioners need to be prepared to engage with the data, and where possible triangulate with evidence from other sources to make an overall assessment of the project and draw out recommendations for future action.

In contexts where it *is* possible to compromise on any of the above, using a qualitative, causal approach to evaluation such as QuIP can offer a range of benefits, not least of which is a more in-depth understanding of intended beneficiaries' *perceptions* of change and their understanding of why these changes have happened. We have outlined possible ways to reduce the risk of pro-project bias in the collection of such experiences, through careful design of exploratory interviews and incorporation of an appropriate level of blindfolding. Judicious, purposive sampling can help to reveal variation in causal pathways across different populations and different groups of stakeholders (e.g., health facility staff and government policymakers), and to understand the extent to which they overlap. Presenting the data in a digestible and visual format can enable and encourage program staff to use and engage with narrative, causal data which can assist in confirming or refuting the theory (of change) behind interventions.

References

Ackermann F, Eden C (2004) Using causal mapping: individual and group; traditional and new. In: Pidd M (ed) Systems modelling: theory and practice. Wiley, Chichester, pp 127–145

Axelrod R (1976) Structure of decision: the cognitive maps of political elites. Princeton University Press, Princeton

Connell JP, Kubisch AC (1998) Applying a theory of change approach to the evaluation of comprehensive community initiatives: progress, prospects, and problems. New Approaches to Evaluating Community Initiatives 2(15–44):1–16

Copestake J, Davies G, Remnant F (2019a) Generating credible evidence of social impact using the Qualitative Impact Protocol (QuIP): the challenge of positionality in data coding and analysis. In: Clift B, Gore J, Bekker S, Costas Batlle I, Chudzikowski K, Hatchard J (eds) 2019, Myths, methods, and messiness: insights for qualitative research analysis: edited proceedings of 5th Annual Qualitative Research Symposium. University of Bath

Copestake J, Morsink M, Remnant F (2019b) Attributing development impact: the Qualitative Impact Protocol case book. Practical Action Publishing

Copestake J (2021a) Briefing note: case selection for QUIP studies. BathSDR working paper. https://bathsdr.org/wp-content/uploads/2021/10/Sample-selection-for-QUIP-studies-briefing-note.pdf

Copestake J (2021b) Case selection for robust generalisation: lessons from QuIP impact evaluation studies. Dev Pract 31(2):150–160. https://doi.org/10.1080/09614524.2020.1828829

Copestake J (2023) Mixed methods impact evaluation in international development: distinguishing between 'quant-led' and 'qual-led' approaches. BathSDR working paper. https://bathsdr.org/wp-content/uploads/2023/10/Copestake-2023-Mixed-methods-impact-evaluation-pre-publication-version.pdf

Creswell J, Plano Clark V (2011) Designing and conducting mixed methods research, 2nd edn. Sage, Thousand Oaks

Eden C, Ackermann F, Cropper S (1992) The analysis of cause maps. J Manag Stud 29(3):309–324

Guest G, Fleming P (2015) Mixed methods research. SAGE Publications, Inc. https://doi.org/10.4135/9781483398839

Hodgkinson GP, Clarkson GP (2005) What have we learned from almost 30 years of research on causal mapping? Methodological lessons and choices for the information systems and information technology communities. In: Causal mapping for research in information technology. Idea Group Publishing, Hershey, pp 46–80

Laukkanen M, Wang M (2016) Comparative causal mapping: the CMAP3 method. Routledge, London

Levesque J-F, Harris MF, Russell G (2013) Patient-centred access to health care: conceptualising access at the interface of health systems and populations. Int J Equity Health 12(18):1–9

Manzano A (2016) The craft of interviewing in realist evaluation. Evaluation 22(3):342–360

Manzano A (2022) Conducting focus groups in realist evaluation. Evaluation 28(4):406–425

Pawson, R., Tilley, N., (1997). Realistic Evaluation. United Kingdom: SAGE Publications.

Pawson R (2013) The science of evaluation: a realist manifesto. Sage, London

Powell S (2018) The book of why the new science of cause and effect. Pearl, Judea, and Dana Mackenzie. Hachette: Journal of Multidisciplinary Evaluation 13:47–54

Powell S, Larquemin A, Copestake J et al (2023a) Does our theory match your theory? Theories of change and causal maps in Ghana. In: Simeone L, Drabble D, Morelli N et al (eds) Strategic thinking, design and the theory of change. A framework for designing impactful and transformational social interventions. Edward Elgar Publishing, Cheltenham, pp 232–250

Powell S, Copestake J, Remnant F (2023b) Causal mapping for evaluators. Evaluation 0(0):100. https://doi.org/10.1177/13563890231196601

Skivington K, Matthews L, Simpson SA, Craig P, Baird J, Blazeby JM et al (2021) A new framework for developing and evaluating complex interventions: update of Medical Research Council guidance. BMJ 374. https://doi.org/10.1136/bmj.n2061

Woolcock M (2022) Will it work here? Using case studies to generate 'key facts' about complex development programs. In: Widner J, Woolcock M, Nieto DO (eds) The case for case studies: methods and applications in international development. Cambridge University Press, Cambridge, pp 87–116
View examples of how QuIP has been used at. www.bathsdr.org/resources

Save the Children have made three of their reports available:

Malawi QuIP report (2024). https://resourcecentre.savethechildren.net/document/cash-plus-for-nutrition-and-child-development-in-malawi-maziko-midterm-qualitativeevaluation/
Mozambique QuIP report (2019). https://resourcecentre.savethechildren.net/document/mid-term-evaluation-of-the-linking-agribusiness-and-nutrition-lan-project-in-mozambique-a-qualitative-impact-protocol-quip-study-september-2019/
Zimbabwe QuIP report (2021). https://resourcecentre.savethechildren.net/document/the-garden-trust-project-evaluation-in-zimbabwe-2021

Using the Standardized Patient Method in the Evaluation of Health Services

Jack C. Collins, Wei Wen Chong, Rebekah J. Moles, and Carl R. Schneider

Abstract

The standardized patient method has often been used to covertly observe and document behaviors in the healthcare setting, through the eyes of a "service user." A trained person acts as the standardized patient (simulated patient, mystery shopper, pseudopatient, among other terms) and covertly enacts a standardized scenario in the setting of interest. This chapter provides an overview of the standardized patient method, its application in health services evaluation, and practical tips and considerations for designing and conducting evaluations using this method.

Keywords

Standardized patient · Mystery shopper · Evaluation · Patient simulation · Health services · Mystery shopping

1 Introduction

A challenge often encountered by those wishing to evaluate "experiential" aspects of health services is how to capture relevant data practically and reliably. While it is possible to use methods such as self-reports of provider behavior or exit surveys of service users, it is often difficult to evaluate the service from the perspective of a

J. C. Collins (✉) · R. J. Moles · C. R. Schneider
The University of Sydney School of Pharmacy, The University of Sydney, Sydney, Australia
e-mail: jack.c.collins@sydney.edu.au; rebekah.moles@sydney.edu.au; carl.schneider@sydney.edu.au

W. W. Chong
Faculty of Pharmacy, National University of Malaysia, Kuala Lumpur, Malaysia
e-mail: weiwen@ukm.edu.my

A. Kaehne, J. Feather (eds.), *Handbook of Health Services Evaluation*,
https://doi.org/10.1007/978-3-031-87869-5_13

service user ("consumer") in a standardized manner. The standardized (simulated) patient method, commonly used in service-based industries such as retail and banking where it is typically known as "mystery shopping" or "secret shopping," can be employed as an effective technique to allow evaluation of health services through the lens of a service user. This method has the advantages of allowing the evaluation of services through the use of standardized scenarios, which can be augmented to suit the needs and purpose of the evaluation in the setting of interest.

This chapter will provide an overview of the standardized patient method, a brief history of its use, how and when this method can be used to evaluate health services, and practical pointers and considerations for designing, and conducting evaluations of health services using standardized patients. This chapter is designed to be a practical guide to assist both novices and those with more experience alike. Although standardized patients are commonly used in healthcare education, this practice has its own nuances and considerations and is not covered in this chapter.

1.1 Overview of the Standardized Patient Method

The use of standardized patients has become a popular choice for those wishing to conduct observational studies to observe behaviors, particularly in the provision of health and related services. In this method, a trained individual (the standardized or simulated patient (SP); see "Sect. 1.3 Nomenclature") presents to a practice site and enacts a predetermined scenario. The approach is designed such that the SP is indistinguishable from a regular service user, thereby enabling covert observation and evaluation in the natural setting.

The covert nature of the method presents several advantages over other observational methods, notably reducing the impact of the Hawthorne Effect (also known as the observer effect or observer reactivity), whereby people's behavior changes when they know they are being observed (Chen et al. 2015, Mccambridge et al. 2014). Due to the limitations posed by comparable methods, such as direct observation ("fly on the wall"), the SP method can be considered the "gold standard" when it comes to observing behavior in a natural setting (Luck and Peabody 2002). The method also presents the advantage of giving those conducting evaluations the opportunity to adjust numerous aspects of the SP and the scenario to best suit their key aims and objectives, which will be addressed throughout this chapter. This level of control affords a high degree of internal validity. Furthermore, the method has been demonstrated to be acceptable to practitioners (Watson et al. 2009; Kinnersley et al. 2005; Xu et al. 2012a).

The SP method can be employed for a variety of purposes. These include audits against expected practice standards such as provider compliance with protocols, evaluation of clinical and affective skills, measuring the effects of interventions such as training of providers or changes to operating procedures, or measuring other aspects of the service user experience such as wait times, costs, accessibility, and assessment of the environment. Findings from such evaluations can be used to identify areas which may not meet expected standards and subsequently drive quality improvement initiatives.

1.2 Brief History of the Standardized Patient Method

The use of trained actors being employed to covertly evaluate service provision is not unique to the healthcare setting, and predominantly has its origins in retail and customer-oriented settings such as grocery stores and banks, where it has been used since the 1940s (Xu and He 2014). This practice continues today in many similar settings as a means to test key aspects of service provision through the experience of a consumer (Pinar et al. 2009; Wiele et al. 2005).

In the healthcare sector, SPs made their way into medical training programs in the early 1960s, where their value as an educational tool was identified, initially as a means of more authentic assessment (Barrows and Abrahamson 1964). In this classroom context, SPs can authentically enact scenarios with numerous clinical and emotional situations and interact with both students and clinical equipment with a high degree of consistency between students. SPs were progressively woven into medical training programs in the decades that followed (Gliva-Mcconvey et al. 2020), and SPs now form part of health curricula in both teaching and assessment across numerous disciplines worldwide (Plaksin et al. 2016).

The first widely reported study of using SPs in a healthcare practice setting was in 1973 when Rosenhan sent eight SPs to present to mental healthcare facilities enacting a scenario where they were hearing voices (a symptom of schizophrenia) (Rosenhan 1973). This study demonstrated a departure from using the SP method as an educational tool or as a research method in social psychology toward health services evaluation. All but one of the eight SPs were subsequently diagnosed with schizophrenia and admitted for psychiatric treatment. The SPs were so successful in their covert approach that none of them were identified as being disingenuous by any of the practitioners involved (Rosenhan 1973). The findings of this study generated a lot of controversy at the time, generating discourse around the study design itself, but also the clinical competence of the practitioners involved. A similar study was then conducted in psychiatric facilities in Australia by Winkler (1974), who then extended the method to the general practice setting (Owen and Winkler 1974). The method was promptly adopted in developing countries, where it was used to investigate the prescribing habits of doctors in Iran (Amidi et al. 1975).

In the decades following Rosenhan's pivotal study, the SP method has been broadly expanded into numerous healthcare settings, including general practitioner (family physician), clinics (Campbell et al. 2013), outpatient settings (Das et al. 2015), hospitals (Xie et al. 2020), public clinics (Kohler et al. 2017), pharmacies (Collins et al. 2018b), and optometry services (Theodossiades et al. 2012). Of particular note is the increased use of the SP method to evaluate healthcare services in developing countries (Kwan et al. 2019).

1.3 Nomenclature

A challenge for the SP method is the variety of nomenclature used. The following terms have been used in relation to this method: "standardized patient", "simulated patient", "pseudopatient", "standardized client", "mystery shopper", and "secret shopper", among others (Björnsdottir et al. 2020; Xu et al. 2012b). However, these terms, while used interchangeably by authors, may also have some nuanced differences. A search of the PubMed database for these terms during writing of this chapter identified that "standardized patient" and "simulated patient" are the most common terms used to describe the method. It is worth noting that the National Library of Medicine Medical Subject Heading (MeSH) term is "Patient Simulation," which was first introduced as a term in 1992 (United States National Library of Medicine 2023). None of the other commonly used terms appear as MeSH terms.

In a paper by Churchouse and McCafferty on the definition of these terms when used in medical education, distinct features of both terms are provided (Churchouse and Mccafferty 2012). They say that, in contrast to simulated patients, standardized patients are not actors or role-playing, i.e., they are presenting their own "personal, physical, social, and psychological history," which they present *consistently* on multiple occasions. In contrast, simulated patients are acting out a scenario, however, they are not necessarily required to act out a *consistent* scenario (Churchouse and Mccafferty 2012). Accordingly, standardized patients may be useful in comparison between health services through the use of a consistent measure, whereas simulated patients may be useful for evaluation of a single service using a variety of scenarios. In the latter situation, one or more simulated patients may be employed. However, this clear separation is not borne out in the literature for health services evaluation. Accordingly, the following definitions are proposed for use for this chapter, in which features are distinct, yet not mutually exclusive:

A *standardized patient* is a person, who may or may not be an actor, which presents a standardized personal, physical, social, and psychological history to health services.

A *simulated patient* is an actor which presents a personal, physical, social, and psychological history, which may, or may not be standardized, to health services.

Recently, the term *standardized simulated patient* has been used to incorporate both features of acting out a scenario in a consistent manner (Das et al. 2022) and may be considered the preferred term moving forward.

2 What Can the Standardized Patient Method Evaluate and When Is It Suitable?

Standardized patient methods are appropriate to use when one is trying to measure more functional and/or behavioral aspects of a service. Prior to embarking on an SP activity, it is important to be clear of your objectives and consider the best techniques to use to collect data. The SP method can be a particularly useful method when trying to gauge service user experience, measuring affective aspects of service, observing protocol or guideline adherence, observing whether an intervention impacts service provision and as a quality assurance technique. Some may elect to investigate multiple aspects of service provision as markers of overall quality (Sylvia et al. 2015; Daniels et al. 2017; Nie et al. 2020). Some of these scenarios are further discussed in the following sections. A summary of the potential outcome measures and measurement tools that can be used in SP evaluation is shown in Table 1. Further details regarding what can be measured and the logistics of evaluation are addressed later in this chapter.

Using the micro-, meso-, and macro-level systems approach to stratify the healthcare system, the SP method has application across all three levels. At the micro (individual) level, the method can be used to capture individual provider behavior as well as the experiences and factors relating to the service user. At the meso (organizational) level, the SP could examine aspects of the experience of the health service relating to the environment, such as cleanliness or infrastructure. Finally, at the macro (system) level, it could be possible to explore the interplay of different components of the healthcare system, such as evaluation of care transitions. For the most part, SPs are typically employed at the micro level—looking at the individual aspects of a single episode of care. Due to the nature of the SP method and the level of deception and sophistication required to progress further through the experience of a service user, it is challenging to progress to the macro level and track patient journeys across transitions of care.

2.1 Where Can a Standardized Patient Visit Take Place?

Most commonly, SP visits have occurred in a variety of healthcare settings as a face-to-face consultation. Typically, these scenarios entail an initial presentation/first episode of care of a patient at that setting, to preserve the "covert" nature of the presentation. However, it may be theoretically possible for an SP to experience an entire patient journey (longer or multiple episodes of care) within one or more settings, and so long as the true identity of the patient remains covert across the settings and visits and the anticipated need for invasive tests or procedures is limited, this technique could provide a valid surrogate measure of healthcare providers' "typical" practice behaviors rather than just a single snapshot in time. To overcome the issue of investigating only a single encounter, researchers have conducted repeated visits within a practice setting through the use of multiple SPs presenting over several weeks in order to gain a more comprehensive picture of clinical care provided while preserving the covert nature of the presentations by not repeating the same SP (Collins et al. 2017a). The regulatory and ethical considerations of the SP method are discussed in Sect. 3.1.

Although the majority of SP studies have taken place in a face-to-face context, other settings that could be considered, including online and telehealth scenarios, as well as email or social media correspondence. For example, telephone calls were

Table 1 Examples of outcome measures and measurement tools that can be employed in the standardized patient method

Outcome measures	Examples of measurement tools	Examples of studies
Quality of care		
Adherence to clinical guidelines and protocols Care management Quality of diagnosis (e.g., appropriate diagnostic measures such as laboratory testing) and treatment (e.g., appropriateness of prescriptions)	Clinical/disease-specific checklists Score sheets Rating scales	Burger et al. 2020 Daniels et al. 2019 Sylvia et al. 2015
Clinical skills assessment		
Accuracy of diagnoses Appropriateness of treatment plans Interviewing/history-taking Physical examination Counselling practices Clinical problem-solving Other competencies (e.g., risk assessment)	Checklists Structured questionnaire Assessment rubrics Rating scales Score sheets Documents (e.g., prescriptions, referral or visit notes)	Amini et al. 2016 Hammad et al. 2022 Wilhite et al. 2019
Service user experience		
Access (e.g., waiting time, appointment availability) Visit flow Interaction with provider/clinic staff Patient satisfaction Bias/inequity	Feedback surveys Satisfaction surveys SP post-visit checklist SP post-visit interviews/ transcripts Open-ended text responses Rating scales Audiovisual transcripts	Altshuler et al. 2023 Collins et al. 2021b Wisniewski and Walker 2020 Zolezzi et al. 2019
Communication behavior and skills		
Patient-centered communication Empathy Confidence Level of interaction	Checklist Rating scores Communication assessment tools/coding systems	Chang et al. 2017 Chong et al. 2014
Resources		
Cost (charge per visit) Time spent (length of interaction) Number of diagnostic tests/procedures ordered Insurance coverage	Receipts/invoices Stopwatches Data collection sheets	Guo et al. 2022 Parwani et al. 2020 Si et al. 2023
Others		
Acceptability of SP experience	Interviews or questionnaires	Hammad et al. 2022

used to explore the current knowledge of pharmacists regarding the use of salbutamol in elite athletes (Greenbaum et al. 2023), and an after-hours telehealth triage program was evaluated using SPs (Montalto et al. 2010). When using non-face-to-face techniques, the anonymity of the SP may be easier to conceal, and multiple assessments of one practitioner at one setting may be able to be undertaken by one SP without the true identity of the SP being revealed.

There are, however, times where an SP's true identity may not be covert. The first of these scenarios is in a "training session" or through the use of clinical vignettes. In these scenarios, participants are aware that the SP is indeed enacting a scenario and that this is not a "real" presentation. These "role-plays" can also be performed in a clinical setting, and while the setting may add some authenticity and validity to the observation of the healthcare provider's skills within the scenario, these types of activities are measuring performance at a lower level of competence according to Miller's hierarchy of competence (Miller 1990). Another time that the true identity of the SP may be revealed is when the health practitioner identifies that the person enacting the scenario is indeed "acting." While the frequency of this occurring is not often reported to be high (Rethans et al. 2007), it is always a risk and highlights the importance of ensuring SPs are adequately trained and scenarios are designed in such a manner so as to not arouse suspicion (see Sects. 3.3 and 3.4). Where an SP is identified as such, the validity of measurement may be diminished and data from these encounters may need to be excluded.

As discussed in Sect. 3.1, regarding the ethical principles that surround SP techniques, there are many times when it is appropriate to pre-consent the individuals (and authorized representatives from the practice location) who will be participating in the SP observational study. When this is the case, the risk of potential identification of the SP may be heightened.

2.2 What Can Be Measured?

2.2.1 Service User Experience

Using SPs, it is possible to assess aspects of the quality of care from the service user's perspective. These simulations enable one to gauge various aspects of the service user experience, such as practitioner communication skills, empathy, rapport, and the overall patient-provider interaction. Many of the aspects that can be measured using these techniques can be inherently difficult to measure using alternative mechanisms. For example, the affective aspects of communication can be challenging to measure without direct observation. Such assessments could include the ability to listen actively, use of appropriate non-verbal communication, provide clear instructions and convey empathy. Aspects of communication such as the content and nature of what is said during the interaction, as well as other aspects of communication such as tone and sentiment, can be captured (Chong et al. 2014; Collins et al. 2021b). Additional aspects of the service user experience that may be evaluated include accessibility, timeliness, and how the busyness of the health service may be associated with variation of care. For example, it has been demonstrated that as the busyness in a care setting increases, the level of patient assessment via questioning decreases in Kenyan health clinics (Kwan et al. 2019). Conversely, the relationship between busyness and appropriate provision of care was not demonstrated in Australian pharmacies (Schneider et al. 2009).

2.2.2 Guideline and Protocol Adherence

Standardized patient techniques offer a powerful tool for assessing adherence to protocols and guidelines in various professional fields, including healthcare. By using trained actors enacting standardized scenarios, specific situations where adherence to protocols is crucial can be replicated. These simulations enable evaluators to observe how individuals or teams respond to complex or critical scenarios while following established guidelines. For example, the guideline-compliant supply of medicines from pharmacies (Schneider et al. 2013) or management of sexually transmitted infections in clinics (Kohler et al. 2017). This approach allows for a detailed analysis of whether protocols are correctly and consistently followed, identifying areas of improvement, and potential deviations from best practices (De Almeida Neto et al. 2001). Feedback (either immediate or delayed) obtained from SP assessments can aid in refining protocols, enhancing training programs and ensuring that professionals adhere to established guidelines, ultimately improving the quality and safety of services across different industries.

2.2.3 Clinical Skills Assessment

In healthcare, SPs are commonly used to evaluate the clinical skills of healthcare professionals. This is arguably one of the more straightforward outcome measures associated with the use of SPs. These simulations can assess the accuracy of diagnoses, the appropriateness of treatment plans and the overall quality of patient care. By observing how healthcare providers interact with SPs, organizations can identify areas that need improvement and ensure that quality standards are met. Markers of quality of clinical skills will vary considerably depending on the outcomes of interest. For example, it can be used to determine whether appropriate advice is given (Brata et al. 2019) or if correct diagnoses and associated treatment are provided (Su et al. 2021) against pre-determined criteria. However, it should be noted that the range of scenarios is limited to those that do not involve physical signs or symptoms to be assessed, or any form of invasive procedure (Aujla et al. 2021). However, provision of prior imaging or laboratory results may be used (Gottschalk et al. 2020).

2.2.4 Healthcare Equity

The SP approach provides a method that allows for evaluation of several parameters of health care equity. A key parameter of health equity is that healthcare is accessible and affordable. The use of SPs allows one to evaluate inequity in the accessibility of health services (Rankin et al. 2022). Accessibility could range from the ability to make contact with a healthcare provider (Tenner et al. 2023; Kyle et al. 2021), as well as variation in the accessibility to healthcare services based on sociodemographic factors or SP's racial background (Elmore et al. 2023; Wisniewski and Walker 2020). Another option with standardized patients is to explore the variation in care provided by healthcare providers. For example, one can measure the effect of implicit bias on the communication of health care providers to SPs from different racial groups (Collins et al. 2021b). Similarly, it is possible to evaluate the variation in care associated with variation in socioeconomic factors (Gottschalk et al. 2020).

2.2.5 Financial Aspects

SP studies can provide valuable insights into the financial aspects of a service by assessing various elements of cost-effectiveness, resource utilization and revenue generation. For example, SPs can help evaluate how resources are utilized during service delivery (Mcleod et al. 1997; Si et al. 2023). SPs can measure the time spent by healthcare professionals on each patient encounter, the number of diagnostic tests or procedures ordered and the utilization of medical supplies. By quantifying resource utilization, organizations can identify areas of potential waste and inefficiency, leading to cost-saving opportunities. Furthermore, SPs can also highlight areas of operational inefficiency that have financial implications. By evaluating the ease of service access, waiting times and the flow of service processes, organizations can identify bottlenecks or areas that may need streamlining to reduce operational costs and improve service quality. Direct costs to SPs for services received may also be documented (Su et al. 2021). Furthermore, financial aspects not directly related to the provision of the service, such as the SP's insurance status and how this impacts the provision of care, could also be investigated (Parwani et al. 2020).

2.2.6 Quality Assurance and Continuous Improvement

SP assessments can support a culture of continuous improvement. By regularly measuring performance using SPs, organizations can identify trends, emerging issues and areas for ongoing enhancement, ultimately raising the overall quality of services. Therefore, feedback from SPs provides crucial insights into areas needing improvement, allowing healthcare organizations to refine their services and enhance patient satisfaction. Moreover, these techniques facilitate the evaluation of both clinical and non-clinical aspects of care, ultimately contributing to a more comprehensive understanding of the service user experience within the healthcare system. For example, covert SPs visits have previously been implemented at scale in community pharmacies as part of the quality assurance process for ensuring practice sites meet expected standards (Benrimoj et al. 2007).

3 How to Design and Implement an Evaluation Using the Standardized Patient Method: A Guide

This section of the chapter guides the reader through numerous facets of the design and implementation of the SP method in health services evaluation. While there is not a strict order that should be followed, many of these aspects are closely interrelated and an iterative approach to the design of the evaluation may be required.

3.1 Regulatory and Ethical Considerations

Before using the SP technique, it is necessary to ensure compliance with ethical requirements. In most cases, obtaining ethical approval from the ethics committee or institutional review board of a research institution is necessary if findings are intended to be disseminated publicly. However, some people contend that ethical approval for SP studies is unnecessary if it is done in the wider public interest (King et al. 2019). If applicable, it may also be necessary to obtain permission from national or provincial departments of health, for example, if the plan is to conduct work in public health sector healthcare facilities (Burger et al. 2020). Where an evaluation has been commissioned, it would be prudent to ensure that any regulatory requirements are met and that the subjects of the evaluation are not likely to experience adverse outcomes as a result of the evaluation.

Regulatory requirements differ between jurisdictions, and expert advice should be sought where evaluators are uncertain of their legal obligations. Common examples of aspects to consider include the legality of any audio or video recordings conducted as part of the evaluation (e.g., in some locations it is not permissible to record conversations without the consent of all parties), fraudulent use of government or insurer-funded health services, the use of false identities, disclosing names or images of people without their consent and conducting audits and evaluations in private businesses. Some of these issues (such as fraudulent access to funded services) may present as a barrier to the SP accessing care for evaluation purposes which may result in necessary modifications to the planned evaluation while others may be overcome through obtaining consent from involved parties at an organizational or individual level depending on legal and ethical requirements.

Several ethical considerations are associated with the SP method. Obtaining informed consent from health practitioners before the SP visits is an important consideration, as the method is usually employed covertly (Sylvia et al. 2015). In addition to participation consent, additional consent may be required to record the SP interactions or to have the data entered into a research registry or database (Wilhite et al. 2019). To mitigate the potential influence of the Hawthorne effect, it may be suitable to apply for a consent waiver or leave a period of time between obtaining consent and conducting the actual visits without disclosing the exact timing of the visit or topics of interest (Collins et al. 2021a).

Another ethical concern is the level of deception. It is necessary to determine in advance when to reveal the SP's identity to participants and what behavior or findings will be disclosed to third parties, such as illegal activity to an authority or poor work performance to an organizational representative (Collins et al. 2020b). Regardless, SPs should always be reminded to maintain participants' anonymity and ensure data confidentiality unless otherwise instructed.

Finally, it is imperative to consider the burden of conducting SP research on individual subjects and the healthcare system (Steinman 2014). Ethical justification may need to be considered since resources, such as time, may be diverted from actual patients who require urgent care from a busy general practice or emergency department.

3.2 Measuring Outcomes of Interest in Standardized Patient Studies

As previously discussed, the SP method is a useful approach for gaining comprehensive insights into aspects of the patient journey across varied healthcare settings. Once desired outcomes have been identified, it is necessary to determine how to measure them, who will be responsible for the measurements and when the measurements should be taken.

When measuring the desired outcomes, evaluators should take into consideration the specific nature and types of outcomes they want to measure. They may need to define the appropriate responses before developing data collection tools. This can be informed by existing literature, treatment or practice guidelines, professional standards, or expert consultations (Sylvia et al. 2015; Burger et al. 2020; Daniels et al. 2019). Depending on the nature of the outcome, it is possible to choose from different measurement or scoring tools such as checklists, rating scales, score sheets, structured questionnaires or other applicable methods. For instance, to measure the quality of care or clinical skills of providers, individuals conducting SP studies usually rely on predetermined checklists or rating scales. To obtain more comprehensive feedback about patients' experiences, interviews may be conducted with SPs (Altshuler et al. 2023). Communication skills and behaviors of practitioners can be assessed using communication tools or quantitative coding systems (Chong et al. 2014), such as the Roter Interaction Analysis System (RIAS) (Roter and Larson 2002; Roter et al. 1997). Financial aspects can be determined through documentation such as invoices and receipts. Table 1 provides examples of different types of outcome measures and how they can be measured.

Regarding the individuals responsible for measurements, most studies use SPs to report their interactions and clinical encounters using data collection forms. However, in some cases, audio or visual recordings of the visits may be reviewed to assess the desired outcomes. The timing of measurement can vary, with some measurements taking place immediately after the visits and others after a specific interval.

3.3 Development of Case Scripts and Scenarios

The design of case scenarios and scripts plays an important role in ensuring consistent and authentic portrayals of scenarios to healthcare practitioners. The choice and number of scenarios that are needed depend largely on the outcomes of interest and subject matter. The level of detail and information to be included in the scripts must be determined to ensure that they are fit for purpose. Scripts typically comprise information about disease symptoms and a comprehensive background story that includes details about health history (e.g., medical conditions, medications, lifestyle behaviors such as smoking status and alcohol use), life circumstances, family and socioeconomic situations and any other relevant information (such as insurance coverage) (Daniels et al. 2019). The scripts are usually developed based on existing literature and reviewed by clinical experts to ensure content validity.

When designing case scripts, it is necessary to determine the opening statement, i.e., what initial information the SP should provide at the beginning of the interaction. This could include whether the SP requests a specific provider, product or service, or if the opening statement is broader. Again, this depends largely on the intended purpose of the SP visits and the outcomes of interest. For example, if the outcome of interest is whether a particular service is offered to the SP, then it would be less appropriate to directly request this service in the opening statement. Additionally, the scripts should outline responses to anticipated follow-up questions from practitioners. If the scenario requires detailed prompts for the practitioner or any visual cues (such as a prescription, referral, written notes or empty medication packaging), these elements should be incorporated into the scripts (Chong et al. 2014; Zolezzi et al. 2019).

It is also necessary to consider whether SPs need to purchase specific products prescribed or recommended during the interaction or pay additional fees charged by the healthcare provider, should these aspects be relevant to the scenario. To test and refine the scripts, a training session or pilot study can be conducted to ensure their effectiveness and accuracy.

3.4 Recruitment and Training of Standardized Patients

SPs from various backgrounds may be recruited. They can be members of the evaluation team, trained actors, actual service users or people from the local community (Watson et al. 2006; Björnsdottir et al. 2020). The choice of SPs is driven by the outcome measures and scenario being investigated. Consequently, SPs can either be healthy individuals or individuals with lived experience of the illness, such as patients or survivors.

The selection process for SPs typically considers several key factors, including demographic match to disease cases, to increase the authenticity of portrayal. Prior experience as an SP or in acting may also be considered, as individuals with this experience may require less training. SPs may also be assessed for their suitability for the specific tasks outlined in the scenarios and scripts. For instance, in cases where a particular clinical test may be performed, it is necessary to ensure that the SP will return the result that is desired.

The number of SPs recruited can vary depending on the scenarios, but at least two are usually recruited to facilitate interactions and data collection (Watson et al. 2006). It is important to be aware that various characteristics of the SPs may impact the provision of health services. Where the intention is to be as standardized as possible, i.e., these differences are not being deliberately exploited to elicit differences between SP characteristics, it is necessary to ensure that the SPs are as similar as possible in characteristics. Key aspects to consider when choosing SPs include gender, race/ethnicity, accent, dress, indicators of socioeconomic status (e.g., expensive accessories or jewelry), physical attributes, etc.

Training is essential for SPs before they begin their visits. The length and method of training can vary depending on the number of SPs and the complexity of their roles. It is important to brief the SPs on their role expectations, such as whether they are only required to enact scenarios or also collect data through observation or provide performance feedback to practitioners (Collins et al. 2021a). A crucial aspect of their training should be how to portray the case scenarios assigned to them accurately and follow scripts. This may include how to respond to situations where the practitioner goes "off script" (see Sect. 3.5). This will ensure consistency and authenticity in their case portrayal. The SPs can rehearse their interactions repeatedly through role-plays.

For those involved in data collection, it is important to train them on how to record observations and findings using data collection forms and/or equipment such as recording devices. This will ensure that assessments are valid and reliable. For example, the SPs can be guided on how to score checklist items (Amini et al. 2016). For studies involving performance feedback, the SPs may need to be trained on how to provide effective feedback (Collins et al. 2017b). Additionally, SPs should be instructed on the visit process, including how to approach participants and how to respond to being identified. A small-scale pilot is recommended to evaluate the training, review case fidelity and assess the usability of the data collection forms.

3.5 Visit Logistics

Several sampling considerations are important during the design phase of the evaluation. These considerations include defining the unit of measurement (whether it is the practice sites (meso), individual practitioners (micro), or program participation (macro)), establishing the target sample size, and determining the sampling strategy. Additionally, it is necessary to define the sampling frame and establish eligibility criteria for potential participants. These factors will be largely determined by the nature of the evaluation, for example, commissioned versus research.

As part of the recruitment process, it is also necessary to determine the level of detail to provide to potential participants. This includes considerations such as divulging information about the intended scenarios, objectives, and the timing of visits (see also Sect. 3.1). In some cases, it may also be relevant to have potential participants complete data collection forms prior to the commencement of the SP visits to capture additional data such as demographics or details about the practice site, for example, number of patients seen in a day, availability of equipment and facilities, and opening hours.

Before commencing the visits, it is important to consider the logistics involved in planning for the visits. This includes site-specific considerations such as the accessibility of the sites and the optimal timing for the visits. Accessibility can include both getting the SP to the site, i.e., travel, but also access requirements of the site itself, such as opening hours or physical restrictions on access (e.g., availability of ramps or elevators for SPs with limited mobility). The number of visits that are required for each site and who will be involved in the visits needs to be ascertained.

For instance, will it be a single SP, or will a second SP member or member of the team accompany them to observe and collect data? A preliminary pilot study is recommended to assess the feasibility of the visitation process.

During the actual SP visits, the SPs will initiate the process by identifying and approaching the designated study participants. Depending on the specific scenario requirements, there may be instances where SPs must first be registered at healthcare facilities to minimize the risk of detection by clinic staff (Altshuler et al. 2023). Subsequently, they will convey the request or opening statement in a standardized way based on the predetermined script as discussed above to initiate the interaction. Once the request has been made, the SP should follow the script provided and complete the interaction with the practitioner or other staff involved. When preparing the script and how the scenario may play out, it is necessary to consider the different paths or actions practitioners or staff may take. Engaging with practitioners in the area of investigation and conducting an adequate review of literature during the design phase of the script may be useful to inform the script and scenario development. Due to the nature of human interaction, it is not always possible to prepare for every possible outcome. SPs should be briefed on how to respond to unexpected actions and the "hard stops" for when the interaction may need to be terminated. This may include whether physically invasive or potentially hazardous tests or procedures, such as blood tests or X-rays, are required. If there is the potential for a monetary transaction to occur (either the purchase of goods, payment for services or insurance claims) or for identification or other documents to be produced, then it is necessary to consider how this will take place. Bank cards, identity documents and other documentation (for example, referral letters, prescriptions) may impact the covert nature of the visits. A sophisticated and highly authentic SP interaction will need to account for this possibility.

Following the visits, the SP, or alternatively, a member of the team using recorded observations, will usually fill out the assessment form outside the healthcare facility. Subsequently, the SP or team member may return to the healthcare setting and disclose their true identity. If relevant, the SP or team member will also discuss the observations made and offer performance feedback and coaching to participants. Participants may also be invited to share their experiences and views regarding the SP visits (Watson et al. 2009).

3.6 Data Collection

There are different ways to gather data from interactions between SPs and healthcare professionals. In most studies, SPs document their observations immediately after each visit or encounter using a standardized data collection form. Given that this process relies on the SPs' memory and recollection, it is crucial to minimize recall bias. One recommended approach to improve data accuracy is for SPs to record the interactions using concealed devices. This may result in more accurate measurements, without the need to rely solely on the SP's ability to remember details. Despite concerns regarding recall bias, studies comparing SP reports to independently reviewed recordings demonstrate a good level of reliability (Collins et al. 2020a; Luck and Peabody 2002; Werner and Benrimoj 2008).

3.7 Supplementary Approaches

Apart from these primary data collection methods, supplementary approaches can also be used to triangulate data or gain a more comprehensive understanding of the interactions. For example, it is possible to conduct post-visit interviews with the practitioners to gain deeper insights (Collins et al. 2018a), compare "real-life" practice with clinical vignettes (Sylvia et al. 2017; Mohanan et al. 2017) or review documentation, such as clinical notes in patient charts recorded during the visit (Wilhite et al. 2019). Furthermore, the SP method can be combined with immediate feedback and coaching as an intervention to change practitioner behavior (Collins et al. 2017b; De Almeida Neto et al. 2000). Previous work further describing expansion of the method and further detailing its use as a research method may be of interest to those wishing to explore this area further (Collins et al. 2021a).

3.8 Reporting

In the context of reporting and disseminating findings, it is necessary to carefully consider the appropriateness of sharing data reports with relevant stakeholders, including study practitioners and interested parties. For example, data reports may be shared with clinic staff and administrators as a quality improvement measure (Altshuler et al. 2023). Furthermore, the specific methodology details to be included in reports should be taken into account, both for evaluation purposes and to enhance the quality of reporting. These considerations should cover information on the SPs and their training, the development of case scenarios and scripts, data collection process and ethical considerations. To facilitate this process, a checklist known as CRIsP has been developed (Amaratunge et al. 2021). This checklist, designed to complement existing checklists for observational and interventional studies such as CONSORT (Schulz et al. 2010), STROBE (Vandenbroucke et al. 2007) and TIDieR (Hoffmann et al. 2014), offers a structured framework to guide the reporting of studies that use SPs. Additional considerations include whether data are reported as aggregated measurements or whether more granular data are required. It is necessary to consider the ethical implications of individual data as this increases the risk of identification of practitioners.

4 Conclusion

Despite the initial use of SPs to evaluate healthcare services being over half a century prior, it is only in the past decade that the potential of standardized patient methods has been realized. The strength of the method is in reliability and internal validity that allows for the accurate measurement of healthcare services and variation in care. In particular, the use of SPs in LMICs is rapidly increasing, and the method is now regarded as being a "gold standard" in the evaluation of healthcare quality. Despite advancements, there is still room for further expansion and growth of the use of SPs in the evaluation of health services, with the method having considerable untapped potential. Advancements in health services and technology such as personalized medicine and artificial intelligence present both opportunity and challenge for the SP method, and evaluators must leverage such advancements when using the method.

References

Altshuler L, Fisher H, Wilhite J, Phillips Z, Holmes I, Greene RE, Wallach AB, Smith R, Hanley K, Schwartz MD (2023) Comparison of primary care patients' and unannounced standardized patients' perceptions of care. J Patient Exp 10:23743735231158940

Amaratunge S, Harrison M, Clifford R, Seubert L, Page A, Bond C (2021) Developing a checklist for reporting research using simulated patient methodology (CRiSP): a consensus study. Int J Pharm Pract 29:218–227

Amidi S, Solter S, Rashidian B, Zokaian AR, Razmjoian F (1975) Antibiotic use and abuse among physicians in private practice in Shiraz, Iran. Med Care 13:341–345

Amini H, Shakiba A, Sharifi V, Shirazi M, Sadeghi M, Abolhasani F, Hajebi A (2016) Evaluation of the performance of general practitioners in a collaborative care program by employing simulated patients. Soc Psychiatry Psychiatr Epidemiol 51:1311–1319

Aujla N, Chen YF, Samarakoon Y, Wilson A, Grolmusova N, Ayorinde A, Hofer TP, Griffiths F, Brown C, Gill P (2021) Comparing the use of direct observation, standardized patients and exit interviews in low-and middle-income countries: a systematic review of methods of assessing quality of primary care. Health Policy Plan 36:341–356

Barrows HS, Abrahamson S (1964) The programmed patient: a technique for appraising student performance in clinical neurology. Acad Med 39:802–805

Benrimoj SI, Werner JB, Raffaele C, Roberts AS, Costa FA (2007) Monitoring quality standards in the provision of non-prescription medicines from Australian community pharmacies: results of a national programme. Qual Saf Health Care 16:354–358

Björnsdottir I, Granas AG, Bradley A, Norris P (2020) A systematic review of the use of simulated patient methodology in pharmacy practice research from 2006 to 2016. Int J Pharm Pract 28:13–25

Brata C, Schneider CR, Marjadi B, Clifford RM (2019) The provision of advice by pharmacy staff in eastern Indonesian community pharmacies. Pharm Pract 17

Burger R, Christian CS, Gerdtham U-G, Haal K, Hompashe DM, Smith A, Schutte AE (2020) Use of simulated patients to assess hypertension case management at public healthcare facilities in South Africa. J Hypertens 38:362–367

Campbell JL, Carter M, Davey A, Roberts MJ, Elliott MN, Roland M (2013) Accessing primary care: a simulated patient study. Br J Gen Pract 63:e171–e176

Chen LF, Vander Weg MW, Hofmann DA, Reisinger HS (2015) The Hawthorne effect in infection prevention and epidemiology. Infect Control Hosp Epidemiol 36:1444–1450

Chang DT, Mann M, Sommer T, Fallar R, Weinberg A, Friedman E (2017) Using standardized patients to assess hospitalist communication skills. J Hosp Med 12:562–566

Chong WW, Aslani P, Chen TF (2014) Pharmacist–patient communication on use of antidepressants: a simulated patient study in community pharmacy. Res Soc Adm Pharm 10:419–437

Churchouse C, Mccafferty C (2012) Standardized patients versus simulated patients: is there a difference? Clin Simul Nurs 8:e363–e365

Collins JC, Schneider CR, Faraj R, Wilson F, De Almeida Neto AC, Moles RJ (2017a) Management of common ailments requiring referral in the pharmacy: a mystery shopping intervention study. Int J Clin Pharm 39:697–703

Collins JC, Schneider CR, Naughtin CL, Wilson F, De Almeida Neto AC, Moles RJ (2017b) Mystery shopping and coaching as a form of audit and feedback to improve community pharmacy management of non-prescription medicine requests: an intervention study. BMJ Open 7:e019462

Collins JC, Schneider CR, Moles RJ (2018a) Emergency contraception supply in Australian pharmacies after the introduction of ulipristal acetate: a mystery shopping mixed-methods study. Contraception 98:243–246

Collins JC, Schneider CR, Wilson F, De Almeida Neto AC, Moles RJ (2018b) Community pharmacy modifications to non-prescription medication requests: a simulated patient study. Res Soc Adm Pharm 14:427–433

Collins JC, Chan MY, Schneider CR, Yan LR, Moles RJ (2020a) Measurement of the reliability of pharmacy staff and simulated patient reports of non-prescription medicine requests in community pharmacies. Res Soc Adm Pharm 17:1198

Collins JC, Moles RJ, Penm J, Schneider CR (2020b) Ethical considerations for mystery shopper studies of pharmaceutical sales. Bull World Health Organ 98:375–375A

Collins JC, Chong WW, De Almeida Neto AC, Moles RJ, Schneider CR (2021a) The simulated patient method: design and application in health services research. Res Soc Adm Pharm 17:2108–2115

Collins JC, Mackenzie M, Schneider CR, Chaar BB, Moles RJ (2021b) A mixed-method simulated patient approach to explore implicit bias in health care: a feasibility study in community pharmacy. Res Soc Adm Pharm 17:553–559

Daniels B, Dolinger A, Bedoya G, Rogo K, Goicoechea A, Coarasa J, Wafula F, Mwaura N, Kimeu R, Das J (2017) Use of standardised patients to assess quality of healthcare in Nairobi, Kenya: a pilot, cross-sectional study with international comparisons. BMJ Glob Health 2:e000333

Daniels B, Kwan A, Pai M, Das J (2019) Lessons on the quality of tuberculosis diagnosis from standardized patients in China, India, Kenya, and South Africa. J Clin Tubercul Other Mycobact Dis 16:100109

Das J, Kwan A, Daniels B, Satyanarayana S, Subbaraman R, Bergkvist S, Das RK, Das V, Pai M (2015) Use of standardised patients to assess quality of tuberculosis care: a pilot, cross-sectional study. Lancet Infect Dis 15:1305–1313

Das V, Daniels B, Kwan A, Saria V, Das R, Pai M, Das J (2022) Simulated patients and their reality: an inquiry into theory and method. Soc Sci Med 300:114571

De Almeida Neto AC, Benrimoj SI, Kavanagh DJ, Boakes RA (2000) Novel educational training program for community pharmacists. Am J Pharm Educ 64:302–307

De Almeida Neto AC, Kelly F, Benrimoj SI (2001) Shaping practice behaviour: novel training methodology. Int J Pharm Pract 9:203–210

Elmore AL, Patrick SW, Mcneer E, Fryer K, Reid CN, Sappenfield WM, Mehra S, Salemi JL, Marshall J (2023) Treatment access for opioid use disorder among women with medicaid in Florida. Drug Alcohol Depend 246:109854

Gliva-Mcconvey G, Nicholas CF, Clark L (2020) Comprehensive healthcare simulation: implementing best practices in standardized patient methodology. Springer

Gottschalk F, Mimra W, Waibel C (2020) Health services as credence goods: a field experiment. Econ J 130:1346–1383

Greenbaum DH, Mclachlan AJ, Roubin RH, Moles R, Chaar BB (2023) Examining pharmacists' anti-doping knowledge and skills in assisting athletes to avoid unintentional use of prohibited substances. Int J Pharm Pract 31:290–297

Guo R, Hou M, Han Y, Feng XL (2022) Access charge and quality of tele-dermatology e-consults in China: A standardized patients study. Digit Health 8:20552076221407

Hammad EA, Elayeh E, Jaber D, Mustafa IA, Al-Aqeel S (2022) Feasibility of using simulated patients for onsite structured practice feedback in Jordanian community pharmacy settings. Saudi Pharm J 30:225–229

Hoffmann TC, Glasziou PP, Boutron I, Milne R, Perera R, Moher D, Altman DG, Barbour V, Macdonald H, Johnston M (2014) Better reporting of interventions: template for intervention description and replication (TIDieR) checklist and guide. BMJ 348

King JJ, Das J, Kwan A, Daniels B, Powell-Jackson T, Makungu C, Goodman C (2019) How to do (or not to do)… using the standardized patient method to measure clinical quality of care in LMIC health facilities. Health Policy Plan 34:625–634

Kinnersley P, Ben-Shlomo Y, Hawthorne K, Donovan J, Chaturvedi N (2005) The acceptability of simulated patients for studying and assessing general practice consultations in the United Kingdom. Educ Prim Care 16

Kohler PK, Marumo E, Jed SL, Mema G, Galagan S, Tapia K, Pillay E, Dekadt J, Naidoo E, Dombrowski JC, Holmes KK (2017) A national evaluation using standardised patient actors to assess STI services in public sector clinical sentinel surveillance facilities in South Africa. Sex Transm Infect 93:247–252

Kwan A, Daniels B, Bergkvist S, Das V, Pai M, Das J (2019) Use of standardised patients for healthcare quality research in low-and middle-income countries. BMJ Glob Health 4:e001669

Kyle MA, Tipirneni R, Thakore N, Dave S, Ganguli I (2021) Primary care access during the COVID-19 pandemic: a simulated patient study. J Gen Intern Med 36:3766–3771

Luck J, Peabody JW (2002) Using standardised patients to measure physicians' practice: validation study using audio recordings. BMJ 325:679

Mccambridge J, Witton J, Elbourne DR (2014) Systematic review of the Hawthorne effect: new concepts are needed to study research participation effects. J Clin Epidemiol 67:267–277

Mcleod PJ, Tamblyn RM, Gayton D, Grad R, Snell L, Berkson L, Abrahamowicz M (1997) Use of standardized patients to assess between-physician variations in resource utilization. JAMA 278:1164–1168

Miller GE (1990) The assessment of clinical skills/competence/performance. Acad Med 65:S63–S67

Mohanan M, Giardili S, Das V, Rabin TL, Raj SS, Schwartz JI, Seth A, Goldhaber-Fiebert JD, Miller G, Vera-Hernandez M (2017) Evaluation of a social franchising and telemedicine programme and the care provided for childhood diarrhoea and pneumonia, Bihar, India. Bull World Health Organ 95:343

Montalto M, Dunt DR, Day SE, Kelaher MA (2010) Testing the safety of after-hours telephone triage: patient simulations with validated scenarios. Australas Emerg Nurs J 13:7–16

Nie J, Zhang L, Gao J, Li J, Zhou Q, Shi Y, Sylvia S, Congdon N (2020) Using incognito standardised patients to evaluate quality of eye care in China. Br J Ophthalmol 105:311

Owen A, Winkler R (1974) General practitioners and psychosocial problems an evaluation using pseudopatients. Med J Aust 2:393–398

Parwani V, Ulrich A, Rothenberg C, Kinsman J, Duhaime M, Thomas M, Venkatesh A (2020) National assessment of surprise coverage gaps provided to simulated patients seeking emergency care. JAMA Netw Open 3:e206868

Pinar M, Eser Z, Strasser S (2009) Using mystery shopping to compare the service quality of banks in Turkey. Serv Mark Q 31:1–26

Plaksin J, Nicholson J, Kundrod S, Zabar S, Kalet A, Altshuler L (2016) The benefits and risks of being a standardized patient: a narrative review of the literature. Patient—Patient-Centered Outcomes Research 9:15–25

Rankin KA, Mosier-Mills A, Hsiang W, Wiznia DH (2022) Secret shopper studies: an unorthodox design that measures inequities in healthcare access. Arch Public Health 80:1–7

Rethans JJ, Gorter S, Bokken L, Morrison L (2007) Unannounced standardised patients in real practice: a systematic literature review. Med Educ 41:537–549

Rosenhan DL (1973) On being sane in insane places. Science 179:250–258

Roter D, Larson S (2002) The Roter interaction analysis system (RIAS): utility and flexibility for analysis of medical interactions. Patient Educ Couns 46:243–251

Roter DL, Stewart M, Putnam SM, Lipkin M, Stiles W, Inui TS (1997) Communication patterns of primary care physicians. JAMA 277:350–356

Schneider CR, Everett AW, Geelhoed E, Kendall PA, Clifford RM (2009) Measuring the assessment and counseling provided with the supply of nonprescription asthma reliever medication: a simulated patient study. Ann Pharmacother 43:1512–1518

Schneider CR, Emery L, Brostek R, Clifford RM (2013) Evaluation of the supply of antifungal medication for the treatment of vaginal thrush in the community pharmacy setting: a randomized controlled trial. Pharm Pract 11:132

Schulz KF, Altman DG, Moher D, Group C (2010) CONSORT 2010 statement: updated guidelines for reporting parallel group randomised trials. Trials 11:32

Si Y, Bateman H, Chen S, Hanewald K, Li B, Su M, Zhou Z (2023) Quantifying the financial impact of overuse in primary care in China: a standardised patient study. Soc Sci Med 320:115670

Steinman KJ (2014) Commentary: key issues to consider for reviewing and designing simulated patient studies. Int J Epidemiol 43:903–905

Su M, Zhou Z, Si Y, Sylvia S, Chen G, Su Y, Rozelle S, Wei X (2021) Comparing the quality of primary care between public and private providers in urban China: a standardized patient study. Int J Environ Res Public Health 18:5060

Sylvia S, Shi Y, Xue H, Tian X, Wang H, Liu Q, Medina A, Rozelle S (2015) Survey using incognito standardized patients shows poor quality care in China's rural clinics. Health Policy Plan 30:322–333

Sylvia S, Xue H, Zhou C, Shi Y, Yi H, Zhou H, Rozelle S, Pai M, Das J (2017) Tuberculosis detection and the challenges of integrated care in rural China: a cross-sectional standardized patient study. PLoS Med 14:e1002405

Tenner NL, Reddy M, Block AE (2023) Secret shopper analysis shows getting psychiatry appointment in New York City is well kept secret. Community Ment Health J 59:290–293

Theodossiades J, Myint J, Murdoch IE, Edgar DF, Lawrenson JG (2012) Does optometrists' self-reported practice in glaucoma detection predict actual practice as determined by standardised patients? Ophthalmic Physiol Opt 32:234–241

United States National Library Of Medicine (2023) Patient simulation—MeSH [online]. NLM, Bethesda. Available: https://www.ncbi.nlm.nih.gov/mesh/?term=patient+simulation. Accessed 1 Nov 2023

Vandenbroucke JP, Von Elm E, Altman DG, Gøtzsche PC, Mulrow CD, Pocock SJ, Poole C, Schlesselman JJ, Egger M, Initiative S (2007) Strengthening the Reporting of Observational Studies in Epidemiology (STROBE): explanation and elaboration. PLoS Med 4:e297

Watson M, Norris P, Granas A (2006) A systematic review of the use of simulated patients and pharmacy practice research. Int J Pharm Pract 14:83–93

Watson MC, Cleland JA, Bond CM (2009) Simulated patient visits with immediate feedback to improve the supply of over-the-counter medicines: a feasibility study. Family Prac 26:532–542

Werner JB, Benrimoj SI (2008) Audio taping simulated patient encounters in community pharmacy to enhance the reliability of assessments. Am J Pharm Educ 72:136

Wiele TVD, Hesselink M, Iwaarden JV (2005) Mystery shopping: a tool to develop insight into customer service provision. Total Qual Manag Bus Excell 16:529–541

Wilhite JA, Velcani F, Watsula-Morley A, Hanley K, Altshuler L, Kalet A, Zabar S, Gillespie CC (2019) Igniting activation: using unannounced standardized patients to measure patient activation in smoking cessation. Addict Behav Rep 9:100179

Winkler RC (1974) Research into mental health practice using pseudopatients. Med J Aust 2:399–403

Wisniewski JM, Walker B (2020) Association of simulated patient race/ethnicity with scheduling of primary care appointments. JAMA Netw Open 3:e1920010

Xie Y, Mcneil EB, Sriplung H, Fan Y, Zhao X, Chongsuvivatwong V (2020) Assessment of adequacy of respiratory infection prevention in hospitals of Inner Mongolia, China: a cross-sectional study using unannounced standardized patients. Postg Med 132:643

Xu L, He S (2014) Analysis on the survey method of mystery shopping in hospitality management. In: Lee G (ed) E-commerce, E-business and E-service. CRC Press

Xu T, De Almeida Neto AC, Moles RJ (2012a) Simulated caregivers: their feasibility in educating pharmacy staff to manage children's ailments. Int J Clin Pharm 34:587–595

Xu T, De Almeida Neto AC, Moles RJ (2012b) A systematic review of simulated-patient methods used in community pharmacy to assess the provision of non-prescription medicines. Int J Pharm Pract 20:307–319

Zolezzi M, Abdallah O, Kheir N, Abdelsalam AG (2019) Evaluation of community pharmacists' preparedness for the provision of cardiovascular disease risk assessment and management services: a study with simulated patients. Res Soc Adm Pharm 15:252–259

Making a Case for Q Methodology in Health Service Evaluations

Kristiana Ludlow and Kate Churruca

Abstract

Q-methodology enables evaluators, researchers, and health professionals to systematically study subjectivity. It is an adaptable, holistic and rigorous approach to exploring patients', caregivers', and healthcare professionals' perspectives on complex and sensitive topics, making it a method well-suited to health service evaluations. This chapter makes a case for using Q-methodology in health services research by presenting the benefits of the approach, and discussing topics and participant groups that lend themselves to investigation using Q-methodology. It then offers a step-by-step guide to the seven stages of Q-methodology. The chapter concludes with a discussion of methodological considerations and challenges for conducting evaluations using Q-methodology, focusing on study design, data collection, and analysis.

Keywords

Q-methodology · Subjectivity · Mixed-method · Factor analysis · Qualitative · Vulnerable populations

K. Ludlow (✉)
Centre for Health Services Research, The University of Queensland, Brisbane, Australia

Centre for Healthcare Resilience and Implementation Science, Australian Institute of Health Innovation, Macquarie University, Sydney, Australia
e-mail: k.ludlow@uq.edu.au

K. Churruca
Australian Institute of Health Innovation, Macquarie University, Sydney, Australia
e-mail: kate.churruca@mq.edu.au

A. Kaehne, J. Feather (eds.), *Handbook of Health Services Evaluation*,
https://doi.org/10.1007/978-3-031-87869-5_14

1 Introduction to Q-Methodology and Its Application in Healthcare

Q-methodology is a systematic approach to studying subjectivity, that is, people's perspectives, opinions, beliefs, attitudes, experiences, priorities and values (Brown 1997). In doing so, it aims to identify *shared meaning* among groups of people, known as "viewpoints," rather than focusing on the perspectives of individual participants (Watts and Stenner 2005). The research method has two core components, the first being a card sorting activity, where statements about a research topic are placed on cards and sorted (ranked) by participants on a pre-defined grid, called a Q-sort grid (Watts and Stenner 2012). The second component is an inverted or "by-person" factor analysis, known as "Q-factor analysis" (Watts and Stenner 2012). Both components must be present to be considered Q-methodology (Watts and Stenner 2005). The card sorting activity is often accompanied by some form of qualitative data collection, such as post-sorting interviews or questions, post-sorting comments (Churruca et al. 2021), or think-aloud which is where people vocalize real-time decision-making relating to the ranking of cards in situ (Charters 2003). These complementary qualitative methods are described in more depth in the chapter section "Methodological Considerations". Q-methodology is a mixed-method approach (Ramlo 2016), combining the strengths of both qualitative and quantitative methods. It is said to have the rigor expected of quantitative research, thus reducing evaluator bias, while maintaining the richness and depth of qualitative data (Dziopa and Ahern 2009).

Q-methodology originated in psychology and was developed by UK physicist-psychologist William Stephenson. Stephenson presented a form of inverted factor analysis in 1935 (Stephenson 1935) and formally introduced Q-methodology in 1953 (Stephenson 1953). Q-methodology has since been used in other disciplines including environmental sciences (Sneegas et al. 2021), political science (Balch 1982), and healthcare (Churruca et al. 2021). Our scoping review of Q-methodology in healthcare (Churruca et al. 2021) identified Elstein and Van Pelt's "Dimensions in the Perception of Psychiatric Patients by Hospital Staff", published in 1966, as the first study to apply Q-methodology in healthcare (Elstein and Van Pelt 1966). Since then, the publication of such studies in healthcare has steadily increased, totaling 289 by 2019 (Churruca et al. 2021). Our review found that Q-methodology had been applied across 25 healthcare-related topic areas, with the most common topics being health professional education, nursing practice, and mental healthcare (Churruca et al. 2021). To date, there has been limited application of Q-methodology in health service evaluation, despite being well-suited to topics and outcomes that evaluations aim to assess.

2 The Case for Q-Methodology in Health Service Evaluations

Evidence for the application of Q-methodology in health service evaluations has been limited until quite recently; however, this does not necessarily indicate its lack of utility. For starters, Q-methodology more broadly is still a novel and underrecognized approach to studying subjectivity. Although there has been a trend over time of research increasingly using Q-methodology, the 289 articles we found spanning more than 50 years of studies in healthcare (Churruca et al. 2021) represents a small proportion of research compared with the many thousands of survey studies that are published annually. Still, there is reason to believe that Q-methodology may be particularly useful in health service evaluation. By design, Q-methodology is interested in many of the issues and questions we ask in health service evaluations, including people's views on acceptability, satisfaction, and feasibility. Q-methodology can be used to inform implementation evaluations by looking at participants' perceptions of barriers to, and facilitators of, the implementation of interventions or services, as highlighted by Alderson et al. (2018). Findings may then inform areas for improvement, resource allocation, and successful implementation strategies for future roll-out of an intervention.

Q-methodology can also be used to understand end-users' acceptance, satisfaction and experience with a program or service to guide modifications and adaptations for different groups of people (e.g., staff members or patients). For example, in unpublished work by Zoppi, Ludlow and Cobham, adolescents were asked about their experience of using mental health services, ranking a set of statements from what they found most challenging in engaging with youth mental health services to what they found most motivating. The findings informed a set of recommendations to enhance adolescents' active and sustained engagement with youth mental health services.

Another example of how Q-methodology can be used in evaluations comes from Boilson et al. (2019) evaluation of a European Health Data Analytic End User Framework. The authors used Q-methodology to assess end-users' views of platform progress during its implementation, identifying three different perspectives—"technical optimism", "end-user focus", "end-user optimism"—to inform the platform's development. Drawing on examples from health services research more broadly, the following two sections present research topics and participant groups well-suited to examinations using Q-methodology, making a case for greater use of the approach in the field of health service evaluation.

2.1 Research Topics

Q-methodology is concerned with exploring perspectives, opinions, beliefs, values and experiences (Brown 1993). Individuals will often interpret events, health conditions, health service experiences and interactions differently. Q-methodology allows evaluators to identify shared meaning among different groups of people and, therefore, should be employed when a topic of interest is likely to elicit varied opinions and perspectives (Watts and Stenner 2012). This makes it well-suited to the evaluation of contested, complex, and sensitive topics (Farrimond 2017). If an evaluator anticipates that participants are likely to have similar experiences and views, then Q-methodology may have less utility. Contested issues are those that provoke strong polarizing opinions (e.g., vaccinations). While some evaluation tools, such as surveys, may average out opposing views to give a false sense of neutrality,

Q-methodology showcases different perspectives (White et al. 2012; Flurey et al. 2014).

Q-methodology may also be a useful method for evaluating complexity in healthcare (Farrimond 2017). It has been argued that healthcare settings are complex adaptive systems (Plsek and Greenhalgh 2001), comprising diverse organizations, departments, specialties and stakeholders (Braithwaite et al. 2017). In this view, agents are interconnected and interact via networks, hierarchies and continually changing relationships (Braithwaite et al. 2017). Such relationships are dynamic; continuously adjusting and adapting to internal and external changes; for example, new policies and processes, disease outbreaks and fluctuations in team dynamics (Braithwaite et al. 2017). These agents operate under formal rules and regulations (e.g., governance and policies) as well as internalized rules (e.g., social rules, hierarchies, and structures) (Braithwaite et al. 2017). Q-methodology offers a window into the complexities of health services from the viewpoints of those providing, receiving or governing care. Q-methodology can be used to capture the subjective viewpoints of different stakeholders, providing a nuanced understanding of their perspectives, experiences, attitudes, beliefs, or priorities. It can also help identify convergent and divergent patterns in participants' responses that represent contextual factors such as cultural norms and workplace dynamics. Moreover, Q-methodology takes a holistic approach by requiring participants to reflect on the positioning of each statement in relation to every other statement, producing a "wholeness of view" (Honey et al. 2013; Ho and Gross 2015; Farrimond 2017). This commitment to holism is retained throughout the process of data analysis and interpretation because the goal is to identify and narratively summarize a *whole* viewpoint associated with each factor. It involves considering the placement of all of the statements in relation to each other, rather than focusing on their placement in absolute terms or on a few perceived crucial statements (Stenner et al. 2008). A participant's ranking of cards ("Q-Sort") therefore represents a *gestalt*, and like complexity itself, it is more than the sum of its parts (Stainton 1995; Stephenson 1936). By contrast, surveys focus on breaking issues down into constituent parts as each item is treated independently from the last, both in how participants respond to them and in how analysis is conducted (Stephenson 1936; Watts and Stenner 2012). Independence in how participants respond to the items of a survey can further lead to each receiving the same value; for example, all items could be ranked as "high," "most important," or "strongly agree," whereas Q-methodology requires people to rank statements considering the placement of every other statement (Daniels and Kassam 2013). The forced choice nature of the card sorting activity imitates real-world constraints where individuals must consider multiple factors when making decisions (Ludlow et al. 2020b).

Q-methodology can also allow evaluators to compare the views of different groups of stakeholders (e.g., different healthcare professions or patients). While stakeholder comparison is not the primary intention of Q-methodology, comparing the characteristics of participants associated with identified viewpoints may give additional insights into why and how they come to hold a certain viewpoint. In our study of aged care staff members' prioritization of care (Ludlow et al. 2020b), we identified four viewpoints: (1) prioritization of clinical care; (2) prioritization of activities of daily living; (3) humanistic approach to the prioritization of care; and (4) holistic approach to the prioritization of care. By comparing characteristics of participants represented by each viewpoint (e.g., gender, occupation, length of work experience), in addition to interview data, we found that viewpoints largely mapped to participants' occupations and perceived role responsibilities. Viewpoint 1 represented a range of healthcare professionals, with all registered nurses and managers in the sample mapped to this viewpoint. Viewpoint 2 comprised care assistants (personal care workers) only. The two pastoral carers in the sample mapped to viewpoint 3, and four of the five lifestyle and activities officers mapped to viewpoint 4.

Healthcare is rife with sensitive, personal, stigmatizing and taboo concepts. Q-methodology can be a valuable method for evaluations focused on sensitive topics, as it is considered non-confronting and less intrusive than interviews (Butler et al. 2014). By using pre-determined statements on cards, we can avoid directly asking participants to discuss topics that they might find uncomfortable or triggering. For example, Dudley et al. (2009) reasoned that Q-methodology was an appropriate method for their study of people living with psychosis, which looked at their perceptions of the cause of their psychosis, as it is a dynamic tool that allows for non-verbal expression in the exploration of an emotive and potentially distressing topic. Other examples of sensitive topics that have been studied using Q-methodology include the reasons why women with learning disabilities self-harm (James and Warner 2005), causes of distress in burn survivors (Askay et al. 2009), cancer survivors' views on sex and intimacy (Perz et al. 2013), and older adults' views on death and dying (Yeun 2005).

2.2 Participant Groups

Q-methodology can be applied in studies involving diverse ranges of participant groups, including different professions in the healthcare sector, patients and lived experience experts; family and informal caregivers; managers and leaders; and policymakers. There are some participant groups that Q-methodology is particularly well-suited to, while there are also a few groups where Q-methodology might not be the most appropriate research method. As Q-methodology lends itself to sensitive topics, it can be a suitable method for conducting evaluation studies with vulnerable populations, such as trauma survivors (Askay et al. 2009) or people living with mental illness (Dudley et al. 2009; Butler et al. 2014). Q-methodology also only requires a small number of participants (explained in "Conducting Q-methodological Studies: Stage 4") and is therefore suitable for facilitating research with minority groups and hard-to-recruit populations as in Butler et al. (2014) Q-methodology study of mothers in a psychiatric *Mother and Baby Unit*.

Q-methodology is flexible in nature and thus can help facilitate the participation of individuals with various needs, including people living with dementia, those who experience communication difficulties and people with learning or intellectual disabilities (Combes et al. 2004; Forrest 2000; Hill et al. 2017; James and Warner

2005; Merrick and Farrell 2012; Westbrook et al. 2013; Wolfe et al. 2021). Methodological adaptations that can reduce cognitive load and thereby enhance the card sorting activity with these populations include: having a smaller amount of statements to rank (Watts and Stenner 2012); combining statements with clear, simple and familiar images for easy identification (Combes et al. 2004; Ludlow et al. 2021); and breaking down the card sorting activity into smaller steps (Watts and Stenner 2012). For example, in Combes et al. (2004) evaluation of person-centered planning with people with intellectual disabilities, participants were involved in devising 36 cards with representative images. Images of happy, sad and disinterested faces were used to help participants rank the cards, and the card sorting activity was broken down into steps. Participants' support people (e.g., support workers, family, friends) were also involved in the card sorting activity. One participant in this study was non-verbal and was able to use signs to communicate. On the other hand, Q-methodology may not be suitable for some people with cognitive impairment, so evaluators should work with the individual, informal caregivers and, where appropriate, healthcare providers to tailor research methods to participants. In some instances, it may be appropriate for an informal caregiver to support the person living with cognitive impairment to complete the card sorting activity, or for the caregiver to rank the cards from their own perspective (Ludlow et al. 2020a). Where possible, the perspectives of the individual living with cognitive impairment should be sought, in a manner tailored to their needs and preferences.

The ability to adapt the card sorting activity as outlined above makes Q-methodology a suitable method for studying subjectivity with the aged care population, including those with cognitive impairment, functional limitations and sensory impairments. In our study of aged care residents' prioritization of care, a card sorting activity was successfully completed by residents with a variety of functional limitations, including speech impairment, vision loss, hearing loss, mild cognitive impairment, and mobility limitations (Ludlow et al. 2021). For example, one participant in our study was unable to manually move the cards due to limitations with their hand movements, so they told the researcher where to place the cards on the ranking grid (Q-sort grid). Another resident had a severe speech impairment but was able to move the cards on the Q-sort grid and explain (verbally and with hand gestures) the reasons behind her decision-making. During data collection she expressed that people assumed that she was "stupid" due to her speech impairment. This participant would likely have been excluded from studies that involved exclusively qualitative methods (e.g., interviews). The suitability of Q-methodology for people with communication difficulties has also been cited in research with people with head and neck cancer (Merrick and Farrell 2012) and intellectual disabilities (Combes et al. 2004).

At the other end of the lifespan spectrum, studies have shown that Q-methodology can facilitate research with children and adolescents (Jedeloo et al. 2010; Snethen et al. 2001; Ellingsen et al. 2014). Whyte and Smith (1997) described using Q-methodology in their research on healthcare needs of adolescents with cancer, due to its board game-like nature, which they rationalized would make data collection "easy and fun." They found that the card sorting activity was "readily accepted" by adolescents, who approached the study with "interest, care and enthusiasm" (Whyte and Smith 1997, p.67). Q-methodology has also been found to be effective with younger children (Taylor et al. 1994; Størksen et al. 2012). Ellingsen et al. (2014) described Q-methodology as a "child-friendly" approach. They explain that Q-methodology can be adapted for different ages and developmental stages (e.g., by using images); does not require strong vocabulary, reading or verbal skills; and is considered less intrusive and non-threatening, as "participants do not have to verbalize their experiences themselves" (Ellingsen et al. 2014, p.6). This is especially true for research involving sensitive or emotive topics, where some children may not be able to express or verbalize their feelings (Ellingsen et al. 2014).

As Q-methodology is largely a visual tool, it may be less suitable for those with vision loss. Returning to our research with aged care residents (Ludlow et al. 2021), one resident was legally blind and so the card sorting activity was adapted by having the researcher read out each card while the participant verbally expressed the level of priority they assigned each card. However, this proved to be time-consuming and placed a cognitive burden on the participant, as they had to continuously remember the 34 cards being repeatedly read to them. Interviews may be a more appropriate data collection method for some people with visual impairment. A potential adaptation to Q-methodology for people with vision loss is the incorporation of Braille for those able to read it (Huang and Yu 2013). Overall, these varied examples of the use of Q-methodology with diverse population groups demonstrate its inclusive, flexible and adaptive nature. These characteristics, coupled with the approach's focus on holism, ability to systematically assess subjectivity and explore complex issues, make it well-suited for use in health service evaluations.

3 Conducting Q-Methodological Studies

This section provides an overview of the seven stages involved in Q-methodology: (1) identifying the topic, (2) developing the Q-set, (3) piloting, (4) selecting participants, (5) collecting data (Q-sorting), (6) conducting Q-factor analysis, and (7) interpreting factors as viewpoints (Churruca et al. 2021). While not intended as a comprehensive manual, it provides a useful introduction to Q-methodology for individuals new to the method. For those intending to conduct Q-methodology studies, we recommended further reading, including Watts and Stenner (2012), Watts and Stenner (2005), Brown (1993), McKeown and Thomas (2013) and Paige and Morin (2016). Additionally, Churruca et al. (2021) and Dieteren et al. (2023) offer checklists for publishing Q-methodology studies.

3.1 Stage 1: Identifying the Topic

This first stage involves refinement of one's research question(s), ensuring that the topic under study is appropriately addressed through Q-methodology. As explained earlier, Q-methodological studies should be used when an evaluator wants to study subjectivity and when a topic is expected to elicit different viewpoints (Watts and Stenner 2012). This stage includes not only a consideration of the topic and research question but how exactly we want our participants to think about our topic and respond, that is, what instructions and response anchors (e.g., disagree vs agree, low priority vs high priority, barrier vs enabler) they will be provided with in order to rank the cards. The following questions may help evaluators determine if Q-methodology is an appropriate method for their topic and/or research question:

- Does my topic/research question address subjectivity? For example, attitudes, experiences, opinions, values, beliefs.
- Is my topic/research question likely to elicit different opinions? That is, it is unlikely that all participants will have a similar opinion on the topic.
- Are there multiple aspects to my topic/research question, i.e., could I generate different statements related to the topic? If you are asking a very narrow research question, then you likely won't have enough statements for participants to sort.
- Can my research question be answered with the use of a scale that represents a positive and negative spectrum? For example, dislike vs like, disagree vs agree, barrier vs facilitator?

Refer back to the chapter section "Research Topics" for some examples of topics that are well-suited to Q-methodology.

3.2 Stage 2: Developing the Q-Set

In Q-methodology, the Q-set refers to a set of items (commonly statements) that will be ranked during the card sorting activity (Watts and Stenner 2012). Importantly, we want these items to appropriately reflect and represent the breadth of the topic we are investigating. To ensure this, we must first establish the "concourse"; this is a comprehensive collection of items (statements, images, sounds, smells, text, ideas) that relate to, and can therefore be reasonably expressed about, a topic (Paige and Morin 2016). These items can typically be collected (or "sampled" in Q-methodological language) from interviews, focus groups, the literature, media, or via observations, until the point of data saturation (Mckeown and Thomas 2013). Sampling the concourse for representativeness generally yields an array of statements or items far larger than is manageable in a ranking task, so the statements must then be reduced and refined into a manageable Q-set (Watts and Stenner 2012). This is achieved by grouping similar concepts together—akin to grouping codes into categories or themes in qualitative research (Paige and Morin 2016). Numerous approaches can be used for this, for example, mind mapping techniques (Ludlow et al. 2019) or expert review (Paige and Morin 2016). In terms of the target number of statements for Q-sorting, the general rule of thumb is 40–80 statements in a Q-set (Stainton 1995); however, Q-sets may be smaller or larger depending on the topic and the participant group, for example, using smaller Q-sets to reduce cognitive burden (Watts and Stenner 2012). The size of the Q-set should be informed by considerations related to the topic, participants and research question(s).

While not all Q-methodology studies use statements, this is the most common way items are presented. Therefore, there is often a step in which evaluators must transform items into statements that align with the way participants will rank the cards (e.g., by level of agreement). The Q-set is transferred onto a set of cards (Q-sort deck) where each card represents a concept (e.g., statement and/or images). The Q-sort deck may be a physical deck of cards, or a virtual deck (see "Methodological Considerations …"). Examples of Q-set statements from Boilson et al.'s (2019) evaluation of a big data platform (called MIDAS) are presented in Box 1. These statements were developed from semi-structured interviews, the literature and project deliverables. Statements (presented on cards) were sorted by participants in terms of their level of agreement ("agree" to "disagree") with each statement.

Box 1 Example of Q-Set Statements from Boilson et al. (2019)

- There is a discrepancy between developers' and end users' expectations of the final tools and systems required for the MIDAS platform.
- Non-MIDAS professionals (new users / policy makers) should be encouraged to use the platform tools to ensure the tools are widely used.
- The priority of the MIDAS tools should be assisting public health professionals, as opposed to clinicians.

3.3 Stage 3: Piloting

Piloting is a key stage in Q-methodology to ensure that the Q-set is representative of the study topic (i.e., no key concepts missing) and statements are easy to understand (Watts and Stenner 2012). As Q-methodology is likely to be unfamiliar to many participants, piloting is also important to make sure that participants understand the instruction that is presented to them to guide their rank-ordering of the Q-sort deck, for example, "sort these cards from what is least important to you, to what is most important to you," as well as any other instructions for the card sorting activity. Piloting will also provide evaluators with an indication of how long the card sorting activity will take to complete. Ideally, piloting should involve subject matter experts and lay people (Watts and Stenner 2012). Piloting may result in refinements and modifications to the study materials (e.g., Q-set) or sorting instructions (Paige and Morin 2016).

3.4 Stage 4: Selecting Participants (the P-Set)

Purposive sampling should be used in Q-methodology to select participants who have relevant viewpoints on the topic (Watts and Stenner 2012; Stainton 1995).

Typically, Q-methodology should aim to recruit a range of stakeholder perspectives on a topic, unless, of course, the research question is directed at a particular participant group (Watts and Stenner 2012; Stainton 1995). For example, if you wanted to evaluate a new intervention to improve hospital discharge processes, you are likely to want to elicit the perspectives of patients, caregivers, staff members and management.

The participant sample in Q-methodology is known as the "P-set". Unlike quantitative studies, where larger samples are required for statistical power, representativeness and generalizability, large P-sets are not required, nor recommended, for Q-methodology (Watts and Stenner 2012). This is because Q-methodology data are analyzed using Q-factor analysis which is a type of inverted factor analysis or by-person factor analysis, where participants' Q-sorts (their pattern of ranking the cards) are the variables of interest (Watts and Stenner 2012). Furthermore, the goal of Q-methodology is not to generalize findings to the population (Watts and Stenner 2012), but to instead identify and interpret different viewpoints existing within a population. Q-methodology does not aim to make claims about the proportion of individuals in a population that have that viewpoint. Watts and Stenner recommend that Q-methodology studies should consist of around 40–60 participants (Watts and Stenner 2012). Similar to the size of the Q-set, the size of the P-set will depend on the research topic. Some topics will lend themselves to larger P-sets to ensure the perspectives of all relevant stakeholders are sought. For example, an evaluation of end-user experience of a digital education application for people with asthma would require fewer perspectives to be sought (e.g., end-user and caregiver perspectives), than the evaluation of a hospital-wide quality improvement initiative (e.g., clinician, nurse, allied health professional, patient, caregiver and manager perspectives).

3.5 Stage 5: Collecting Data (Q-Sorting)

During the card sorting activity, participants rank the Q-sort deck onto a Q-sort grid (Watts and Stenner 2012). This Q-sort grid can be any shape but is traditionally and commonly a quasi-normal distributed grid (Fig. 1). The middle column of the deck represents "0" or neutrality. Columns to the left of neutrality are given a negative value, and columns to the right of neutrality are given a positive value.

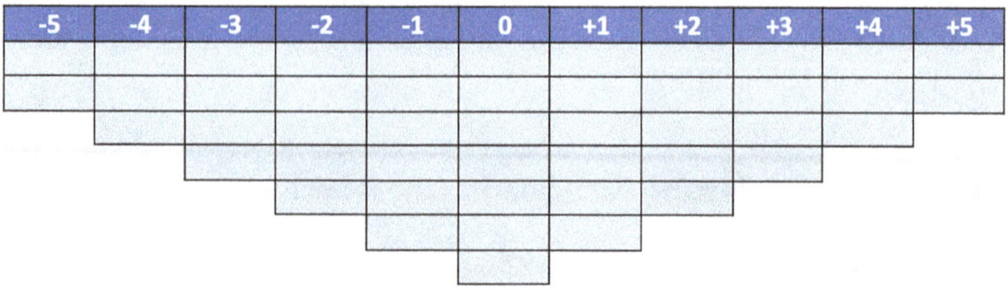

Fig. 1 A Q-sort grid for a Q-sort deck of 47 cards

The Q-sort grid will also be accompanied by response anchors, for example, "disagree most" to "agree most." The number ranking scale (e.g., −5 to +5) and number of cells in each column will depend on the number of cards in the Q-sort deck, for example, a Q-sort deck of 34 may be ranked on a scale from (−4) to (+4), whereas a Q-sort deck of 47, would more likely be ranked on a scale from (−5) to (+5). The forced choice nature of the Q-sort deck reflects the tendency for individuals to have very strong opinions about a small number of statements and less intense views towards a larger number of statements (Watts and Stenner 2012). The shape of the Q-sort grid also circumvents the issue of participants potentially ranking everything as "most important" or "agree most," for example, as can be done in surveys. If a card is placed on the positive side of the grid (e.g., +2), it doesn't necessarily mean that the participant agrees with a statement, but rather, they hold more favorable views of this statement compared with statements placed in cells with lower values than that card (e.g., −5 to +1).

The act of ranking cards on the Q-sort grid is called Q-sorting, and the outcome of this activity is a completed "Q-sort" (Watts and Stenner 2012), whereby each card is placed in an individual cell so that every card is used and every cell is full. It is important to note that each card within a column has an equal value. For example, in Fig. 1 the three cards placed under +4 are valued the same.

Q-sorting is usually broken down into several steps to assist the sorting process and reduce cognitive burden for participants (Watts and Stenner 2012). First, participants are asked to read or view each card and complete a pre-sorting task, where they sort the cards into three piles (e.g., agree/neutral/disagree, or low priority/neutral priority/high priority). Participants are then asked to take the highest ranked pile and rank the cards onto the right side of the Q-sort grid. Once this pile is finished, participants take the lowest ranked pile and rank the cards onto the left side of the Q-sort grid, and then take the neutral pile and place the cards in the remaining spaces. At the completion of the card sorting task, participants should be given the opportunity to review their completed Q-sort and make any changes they wish. As mentioned in the introduction, Q-methodology is often accompanied by additional qualitative data collection methods such as think-aloud, post-sorting comments, or post-sorting interviews or questions.

3.6 Stage 6: Conducting Q-Factor Analysis

Participants' Q-sorts are analyzed via Q-factor analysis (by-person factor analysis) to identify factors that represent shared meaning between participants who sorted their cards in similar ways (Watts and Stenner 2012). The final set of factors is known as the "factor solution." There are several steps in Q-factor analysis: (1) Q-sorts are correlated with all other Q-sorts in a correlation matrix; (2) factor extraction is conducted to identify factors (e.g., groups of participants who ranked their cards similarly and are therefore said to share a similar viewpoint on a research topic); (3) rotation is undertaken to make the factor solution more interpretable without changing the relationship between Q-sorts and factors (i.e., their correlation); (4) correlations between each resulting factor are compared to decide on the final factor solution; and (5) factors are interpreted as viewpoints. This last step constitutes a qualitative analysis in its own right and is described in the next section. For the other four steps, evaluators must make several decisions along the way including the type of factor extraction method they are going to use (e.g., Centroid or Principal Component); what criteria they are going to use to determine a factor; the type of rotation (e.g., varimax or by-hand rotation); how they will handle any correlating factors; and the software they will use to perform the analysis (see "Methodological Considerations ..."). We recommend again Watts and Stenner's user-friendly guide (Watts and Stenner 2012), which walks the reader through each of these decisions.

3.7 Stage 7: Interpreting Factors as Viewpoints

The final stage of Q-methodology is to interpret each factor in the factor solution as a viewpoint. To aid in this, Q-methodology software produces factor arrays (a representative Q-sort for each factor, calculated as a weighted average of the Q-sorts loading on a factor); the amount of study variance explained by each factor (the portion of the variability, expressed as a percentage, that can be attributed to the shared views held by a group of participants, i.e., common variance); consensus statements (cards that do not significantly distinguish between a pair of factors because they are ranked similarly across factors); and distinguishing statements (cards ranked significantly differently in one factor compared to all other factors) (Watts and Stenner 2012). This output can be mapped to crib sheets (organized summaries of key data) to inform the interpretation of factors (Watts and Stenner 2012). Additional qualitative data is of immense value at this stage as it can provide context to decision-making, producing deeper insight into participants' viewpoints. Q-sorts can tell us *how* and *what* participants value, prioritize, like, etc., while the additional qualitative data one might collect during the course of study can explain *why*. The goal is to produce a narrative account of each viewpoint that describes it with supporting data, such as participant quotes, statements, and quantitative data (Watts and Stenner 2012). Figure 2 shows an excerpt from our study of staff members' prioritization of care in residential aged care,[1] to demonstrate how Q-methodology findings are presented as narratives (Ludlow et al. 2020b). In the figure, single quotations reflect the cards, numbers in brackets represent ranking value from the factor array, double asterisks indicate distinguishing statements, and double quotation marks accompanied by italicized text indicate a participant quote.

[1] In an international context, residential aged care refers to nursing homes, care homes, long-term care and aged care facilities.

Viewpoint 1: prioritisation of clinical care: ensuring residents' health and safety

Viewpoint 1 accounted for 23% of study variance and comprised 10 Q sorts from four Care Assistants, three Registered Nurses, one Activities and Lifestyle Officer, and two Managers. Participants who loaded significantly on this viewpoint prioritised clinical aspects of care, as reflected in the cards ranked as most important: 'Monitoring/Safety' (+ 4), 'Medication management' (+ 4), 'Medical condition management' (+ 3), 'Staff knowledge' (+ 3**), and 'Resident information' (+ 3**). The prioritisation of clinical care is reflected in the following quote from Participant 2 (Manager):

"At the end of the day, it's about what is clinically sound ... it is about what is our top priority, which is keeping the residents safe from injury or medical harm and that our staff are knowledgeable about their residents' medical care needs."

Fig. 2 Narrative excerpt from "Staff members; prioritization of care in residential aged care facilities: A Q methodology study." (Source: Ludlow et al. (2020b))

4 Methodological Considerations and Challenges

Several methodological challenges associated with Q-methodology may present themselves for people conducting an evaluation as well as for evaluation participants. In this section, we outline methodological considerations and potential solutions to these challenges.

While Q-methodology is increasingly being used in healthcare (Churruca et al. 2021), many researchers are not familiar with it, with even fewer health practitioners and patients being aware of Q-methodology. The analysis in particular may be daunting for first-time users, given the steps and decision-making required. Q-factor analysis is unique to Q-methodology, with its own rules and procedures that need to be learned (Watts and Stenner 2012). Q-factor analysis is considered a mixed-method; however, there is a strong quantitative component. While prior statistical training is not required, an understanding of traditional factor analysis can be helpful. Several Q-methodology software programs now exist, making the analysis quicker and easier for new users (e.g., Q-Method Software, PQMethod and Ken-Q Analysis). Some of these programs are free, while others require a fee-paid subscription. Some applications, such as PQMethod, require more manual input from a user, while others (e.g., Q-Method Software) are largely automatic.

Due to participants' likely lack of familiarity with Q-methodology, clear instructions or demonstrations should be provided, explaining how to complete the card sorting activity. For example, in our research on care prioritization in residential aged care (Ludlow et al. 2020a, b, 2021), some participants struggled to understand the concept that cards placed in the same column, under the same value (e.g., +3), were weighted the same. In addition to clear instructions, breaking the card sorting activity into smaller steps can assist participants in their understanding of the task. Encouraging participants to think-aloud can help the evaluator to pick up on any confusion related to the card sorting activity. Piloting can ensure that instructions and card statements/images are easy to understand (Watts and Stenner 2012).

One of the most commonly cited challenges associated with Q-methodology is the time it takes to administer the card sorting activity (Yeun 2021). This can be especially problematic for in-person data collection. Evaluators must strike a balance between time burden and data richness. Ideally, Q-methodology is complemented by additional qualitative methods to enhance data richness and the understanding of participants' decision-making. For example, asking participants to think-aloud (Charters 2003) while they are Q-sorting can provide insight into real-time decision-making (Ludlow et al. 2020a, b, 2021). Post-sorting interviews enable an evaluator to clarify participants' decision-making, such as the placement of cards, non-verbal cues, hesitation, and indecision. They may also be used to ask additional questions related to the study topic, for example, participants might be asked what suggestions they have for improving an intervention or program. Many studies opt for post-sorting comments or questions (Churruca et al. 2021), rather than interviews. Post-sorting questions often ask participants about their highest and lowest ranked cards. While eliciting post-sorting comments requires less time than in-depth interviews, it is also true that post-sorting comments capture less data. Additionally, focusing post-sorting questions on the extreme ranks of the Q-sort grid means that the holistic nature of Q-methodology is largely ignored (Watts and Stenner 2012). Post-sorting questions can be an appropriate approach to understanding decision-making for time-poor evaluations. Think-aloud data, interviews and post-sorting questions can be qualitatively analyzed using thematic analysis or content analysis, for example, to help evaluators understand each viewpoint identified by the quantitative component of Q-factor analysis.

Another way in which the time burden of Q-methodology can be reduced is to reduce the number of items in a Q-set. Here there is a trade-off between efficiency and ensuring that the true breadth of a topic is captured (Watts and Stenner 2012). Piloting can help evaluators estimate the time needed to complete a Q-sort. Piloting and expert review can also ensure that a Q-set is comprehensive (Paige and Morin 2016).

Another consideration for conducting evaluations with Q-methodology is the mode of delivery of the card sorting activity. There are several methods to administer a card sorting activity (in-person, online, via mail) (Churruca et al. 2021), each with benefits and drawbacks. In-person administration allows evaluators to verbally explain the card sorting activity to participants, clarify any confusion or answer any questions during the task, and capture think-aloud data (Charters 2003). It also allows evaluators to notice decision-making cues, such as hesitations, confidence in decisions, and indecision, which may be useful for post-sorting questioning and interpretation of data. However, in-person delivery is less flexible than other methods, as there is a need to schedule participants, and in-person data collection may involve an element of travel (Meehan et al. 2022). In-person data collection may be more difficult to conduct with some populations, such as those living in rural/remote communities. Another challenge of in-person data collection is the issue of space. For example, patients in hospitals may not have sufficient space to host a Q-sort grid as well as 60 or more cards. In our research in residential aged care, we transferred the Q-sort grid to a large whiteboard and used magnetic cards (Ludlow et al. 2021). The whiteboard could be placed on beds, on small desks, or held by the researcher.

Online data collection (via Q-methodology software) can circumvent some of the limitations associated with in-person data collection, as it allows participants to complete the activity at a time that suits them, provides anonymity, and does not require physical space for the Q-sort grid (Meehan et al. 2022). It also means that data, which would otherwise be entered manually by the evaluator, is automatically captured by the software. However, online data collection may reduce the richness of data that can be collected via think-aloud and non-verbal cues. A potential alternative would be to ask participants to complete the card sorting activity online, while simultaneously connecting to the evaluator via teleconferencing software or telephone. In our scoping review on Q-methodology, no study described this method (Churruca et al. 2021). Online data collection may also make it harder for participants to understand the card sorting activity without a physical demonstration. Providing video instructions is one way to overcome this barrier.

A less common method of card sorting activity delivery is via mail such as postal service (Churruca et al. 2021). This can be a useful approach for participants with limited digital literacy or poor internet access, while offering the flexibility for participants to complete the task in their own time. Evaluators should make it as easy as possible for participants to return their completed card sorts—for example, supplying pre-paid envelopes or allowing participants to take photos of their completed Q-sort and submit them via email or SMS. Evaluators using mail delivery should also consider how they are going to convey card sorting activity instructions (e.g., through written and visual resources).

5 Conclusions

Q-methodology has been gaining traction in research disciplines outside of its origins in psychology. Despite increased use in healthcare research, little has been published in the way of health services evaluations using Q-methodology. This chapter advocates for Q-methodology as a health service evaluation tool, due to its adaptability, rigor and holistic approach to the study of complex issues and sensitive topics with vulnerable populations and a variety of stakeholders (e.g., healthcare professionals, consumers and caregivers). This chapter provides an introduction to Q-methodology, a step-by-step overview of the method, and recommendations for further reading and additional resources. It discusses research topics and participant groups that are well-suited to Q-methodology in healthcare. Methodological considerations and challenges for conducting Q-methodology in health service evaluations are presented, outlining the benefits and drawbacks of different approaches to help evaluators make informed decisions in line with their evaluation objectives.

References

Alderson S, Foy R, Bryant L, Ahmed S, House A (2018) Using Q-methodology to guide the implementation of new healthcare policies. BMJ Quality Safety 27:737–742

Askay SW, Stricklin M, Carrougher GJ, Patterson DR, Klein MB, Esselman PC, Engrav LH (2009) Using QMethodology to identify reasons for distress in burn survivors postdischarge. J Burn Care Res 30:83–91

Balch G (1982) Political subjectivity: applications of Q methodology in political science. J Mark Res 19:162–163

Boilson A, Gautier S, Connolly R, Davis P, Connolly J, Weston D, Staines A (2019) Q-methodology evaluation of a European health data analytic end user framework. In: Proceedings of the ENTRENOVA—ENTerprise REsearch InNOVAtion Conference, Rovinj, Croatia, 12–14 September 2019. IRENET—Society for Advancing Innovation and Research in Economy, Zagreb, pp 219–231

Braithwaite J, Churruca K, Ellis LA, Long J, Clay-Williams R, Damen N, Herkes J, Pomare C, Ludlow K (2017) Complexity science in healthcare—aspirations, approaches, applications and accomplishments: a white paper. Australian Institute of Health Innovation, Macquarie University, Sydney, Australia

Brown SR (1993) A primer on Q methodology. Operant Subject 16:91–138

Brown SR (1997) The history and principles of Q methodology in psychology and the social sciences. In: British Psychological Society symposium on "a quest for a science of subjectivity: the lifework of William Stephenson". University of London, London

Butler H, Hare D, Walker S, Wieck A, Wittkowski A (2014) The acceptability and feasibility of the Baby Triple P Positive Parenting Programme on a mother and baby unit: Q-methodology with mothers with severe mental illness. Arch Womens Ment Health 17:455–463

Charters E (2003) The use of think-aloud methods in qualitative research an introduction to think-aloud methods. Brock Educ J 12:68

Churruca K, Ludlow K, Wu W, Gibbons K, Nguyen HM, Ellis LA, Braithwaite J (2021) A scoping review of Q-methodology in healthcare research. BMC Med Res Methodol 21:125

Combes H, Hardy G, Buchan L (2004) Using Q-methodology to involve people with intellectual disability in evaluating person-centred planning. J Appl Res Intellect Disabil 17:149–159

Daniels VJ, Kassam N (2013) Impact of personal goals on the internal medicine R4 subspecialty match: a Q methodology study. BMC Med Educ 13:171

Dieteren CM, Patty NJS, Reckers-Droog VT, Van Exel J (2023) Methodological choices in applications of Q methodology: a systematic literature review. Soc Sci Humanit Open 7:100404

Dudley R, Siitarinen J, James I, Dodgson G (2009) What do people with psychosis think caused their psychosis? A Q methodology study. Behav Cogn Psychother 37:11–24

Dziopa F, Ahern K (2009) Three different ways mental health nurses develop quality therapeutic relationships. Issues Ment Health Nurs 30:14–22

Ellingsen IT, Thorsen AA, Størksen I (2014) Revealing children's experiences and emotions through Q methodology. Child Dev Res 2014:910529

Elstein AS, Van Pelt JD (1966) Dimensions in the perception of psychiatric patients by hospital staff. J Consult Psychol 30:213–218

Farrimond H (2017) A typology of vaping: identifying differing beliefs, motivations for use, identity and political interest amongst e-cigarette users. Int J Drug Policy 48:81–90

Flurey CA, Morris M, Pollock J, Richards P, Hughes R, Hewlett S (2014) A Q-methodology study of flare help-seeking behaviours and different experiences of daily life in rheumatoid arthritis. BMC Musculoskelet Disord 15:364

Forrest J (2000) Using Q methodology to assess chronic pain in elderly cognitively intact and Alzheimer's patients. Operant Subject 24

Hill SR, Mason H, Poole M, Vale L, Robinson L (2017) What is important at the end of life for people with dementia? The views of people with dementia and their carers. Int J Geriatr Psychiatry 32:1037–1045

Ho GW, Gross DA (2015) Differentiating physical discipline from abuse: Q findings from Chinese American mothers and pediatric nurses. Child Abuse Negl 43:83–94

Honey S, Bryant LD, Murray J, Hill K, House A (2013) Differences in the perceived role of the healthcare provider in delivering vascular health checks: a Q methodology study. BMC Fam Pract 14:172

Huang C-H, Yu S-C (2013) A study of environmental perception patterns of the visually impaired and environmental design. Indoor Built Environ 22:743–749

James M, Warner S (2005) Coping with their lives—women, learning disabilities, self-harm and the secure unit: a Q-methodological study. Br J Learn Disabil 33:120–127

Jedeloo S, Van Staa A, Latour JM, Van Exel NJ (2010) Preferences for health care and self-management among Dutch adolescents with chronic conditions: a Q-methodological investigation. Int J Nurs Stud 47:593–603

Ludlow K, Churruca K, Ellis LA, Mumford V, Braithwaite J (2019) Understanding the priorities of residents, family members and care staff in residential aged care using Q methodology: a study protocol. BMJ Open 9:e027479

Ludlow K, Churruca K, Ellis LA, Mumford V, Braithwaite J (2020a) Family members' prioritisation of care in residential aged care facilities: a case for individualised care. J Clin Nurs 29:3272–3285

Ludlow K, Churruca K, Mumford V, Ellis LA, Braithwaite J (2020b) Staff members' prioritisation of care in residential aged care facilities: a Q methodology study. BMC Health Serv Res 20:423

Ludlow K, Churruca K, Mumford V, Ellis LA, Braithwaite J (2021) Aged care residents' prioritization of care: a mixed-methods study. Health Expect 24:525–536

Mckeown B, Thomas DB (2013) Q methodology. Sage Publications, Thousand Oaks

Meehan K, Ginart L, Ormerod KJ (2022) Short take: sorting at a distance: Q methodology online. Field Methods 34:82–88

Merrick S, Farrell D (2012) Head and neck cancer patients' experiences of percutaneous endoscopic gastrostomy feeding: a Q-methodology study. Eur J Cancer Care 21:493–504

Paige JB, Morin KH (2016) Q-sample construction: a critical step for a Q-methodological study. West J Nurs Res 38:96–110

Perz J, Ussher JM, Gilbert E (2013) Constructions of sex and intimacy after cancer: Q methodology study of people with cancer, their partners, and health professionals. BMC Cancer 13:270

Plsek PE, Greenhalgh T (2001) Complexity science: the challenge of complexity in health care. BMJ 323:625–628

Ramlo S (2016) Mixed method lessons learned from 80 years of Q methodology. J Mixed Methods Res 10:28–45

Sneegas G, Beckner S, Brannstrom C, Jepson W, Lee K, Seghezzo L (2021) Using Q-methodology in environmental sustainability research: a bibliometric analysis and systematic review. Ecol Econ 180:106864

Snethen JA, Broome ME, Bartels J, Warady BA (2001) Adolescents' perception of living with end stage renal disease. Pediatr Nurs 27(159–61):164–167

Stainton RR (1995) Q methodology. In: Smith JA, Harré R, Langenhove LV (eds) Rethinking methods in psychology. Sage Publications, London, pp 178–192

Stephenson W (1935) Technique of factor analysis. Nature 136:297

Stephenson W (1936) The foundations of psychometry: four factor systems. Psychometrika 1:195–209

Stephenson W (1953) The study of behavior: Q-technique and its methodology. University of Chicago Press, Chicago

Stenner P, Watts S, Worrell M (2008) Q methodology. In: Willig C, Stainton-Rogers W (eds) The SAGE handbook of qualitative research in psychology. SAGE Publications, London, pp 215–239

Størksen I, Thorsen AA, Øverland K, Brown SR (2012) Experiences of daycare children of divorce. Early Child Dev Care 182:807–825

Taylor P, Delprato DJ, Knapp JR (1994) Q-methodology in the study of child phenomenology. Psychol Rec 44:171–183

Watts S, Stenner P (2005) Doing Q methodology: theory, method and interpretation. Qual Res Psychol 2:67–91
Watts S, Stenner P (2012) Doing Q methodological research: theory, method & interpretation. SAGE Publications, London
Westbrook JL, Mcintosh CJ, Sheldrick R, Surr C, Hare DJ (2013) Validity of dementia care mapping on a neuro-rehabilitation ward: Q-methodology with staff and patients. Disabil Rehabil 35:1652–1659
White HK, Corazzini K, Twersky J, Buhr G, Mcconnell E, Weiner M, Colón-Emeric CS (2012) Prioritizing culture change in nursing homes: perspectives of residents, staff, and family members. J Am Geriatr Soc 60:525–531
Whyte F, Smith LN (1997) An exploratory study of the health-care needs of the adolescent with cancer. J Res Nurs 2:59–69
Wolfe SE, Greenhill B, Butchard S, Day J (2021) The meaning of autonomy when living with dementia: a Q-method investigation. Dementia 20:1875–1890
Yeun E (2005) Attitudes of elderly Korean patients toward death and dying: an application of Q-methodology. Int J Nurs Stud 42:871–880
Yeun EJ (2021) Q-methodology: understanding and applying it to nursing and health research. Nurs Health Sci 23:777–781

Social Network Analysis and Its Application in Health Service Evaluation

Janet C. Long, Kate Churruca, and Louise A. Ellis

Abstract

Social network research is a unique method that maps and measures relationships and social processes. It is used in health services evaluation to assess a range of key processes such as robustness of referral networks, reach and inclusiveness of communication, and patterns around seeking advice. Data can be extracted from documents, or collected through observation, survey, or interview. Specialist software can produce engaging maps of the data and compute metrics. These can reveal optimally structured networks, identify gaps in information flows, or key players that perform a special role in the network whose position may require additional support. This chapter outlines how social network analysis can be used in health service evaluations.

Keywords

Social network analysis · Network theory · Communication · Referral · Advice-seeking

1 Overview

Social network research is a unique method that maps and measures relationships and social processes (Borgatti et al. 2013; Scott 2000). It is used in health services evaluation to assess a range of key processes such as robustness of referral networks, reach and inclusiveness of communication, and patterns around seeking advice. Data can be used to diagnose problems, for example, inefficient

J. C. Long (✉) · K. Churruca · L. A. Ellis
Australian Institute of Health Innovation, Macquarie University, Sydney, Australia
e-mail: Janet.long@mq.edu.au; Kate.churruca@mq.edu.au; Louise.ellis@mq.edu.au

A. Kaehne, J. Feather (eds.), *Handbook of Health Services Evaluation*,
https://doi.org/10.1007/978-3-031-87869-5_15

dissemination processes or patchy communication, or evaluate the effect of a new intervention such as baseline and post-implementation assessments. Data on relationships that are used to conduct social network analysis can be extracted from documents or collected through observations, surveys, or interviews. Specialist software can produce engaging maps of the data and can compute parameters of interest that can evaluate or suggest interventions. These can reveal optimally structured networks (Long et al. 2016), identify gaps in information flows (Chan et al. 2016) or key players that perform a special role in the network whose position may require additional support or whose position may be leveraged in the roll-out of an intervention (Hurtado et al. 2018; Long et al. 2013b).

1.1 Background

The delivery of safe, high-quality healthcare is reliant on relationships. Examples include relationships between health professionals within clinical teams sharing information, communicating risks, seeking advice, making referrals; relationships between health professionals and patients and families sharing decision-making, setting goals and planning future management; and relationships between primary, specialist, and acute hospital health professionals and managers planning admission or discharge and appropriate follow up. Relationships can occur face-to-face such as a clinical handover, or consultation, via telephone when booking an appointment in a clinic, written by communicating results of an assessment written in a medical record or via electronic means through online images from an X-ray. We have provided additional examples in Table 1. Problems arise when these relationships are dysfunctional or non-existent as the effectiveness, efficiency, or appropriateness of care can suffer (Sabot et al. 2017). Therefore, it is important for all change programs in healthcare to consider the social relationship dimension.

There are less obvious relationships and social processes which are also important to the delivery of healthcare. There is the social process of *influence* that subtly nudges people to conform to "the way things are done around here", whether that is a good thing (e.g., "everyone here makes a point of checking in with each other") or not such a good thing (e.g., "we don't bother doing that here"). Social influence can be deceptively strong, making it hard to swim against the current. Social influence from line managers, chief executives through communication of organizational priorities and peak bodies through endorsement of guidelines can also be strong. "Trust" and "respect" also play a big role in healthcare relationships and can adversely affect such things as safety culture when missing between health professionals.

Table 1 Some types of relationships encountered by health professionals during the delivery of healthcare (here, on a hospital ward) that impact effectiveness and efficiency

Type of relationship	Mode	Examples
Relationships within teams		
Communication of current situation with other staff	Formal face-to-face	Verbal handover from one shift to the next; consultants' rounds; shared instructions for care
Communication of past situation, event, or incident for the record / other team members	Written/electronic	Archived letter from GP outlining the reason for last admission; test results from previous admission
Safety risks	Formal assessments and communication to team members	Falls risk, pressure injury risk
Advice seeking	Informal face-to-face or telephone	Phoning a pharmacist to check on an appropriate dose to prescribe a patient; checking with a colleague how to do an unfamiliar procedure
Checking practice	Use of online tools	Checking clinical practice guidelines before ordering an assessment
Influence	May be spoken or tacit	Watching how a colleague does their work / explains things to patients / solves problems
Shared decision-making	Formal or informal face-to-face	Multidisciplinary team meeting
Information sharing with other teams		
Referrals to outside agencies	Electronic, fax, written	Formalized referrals (e.g., to rehabilitation services)
Discharge planning	Electronic, fax, written, verbal	Written discharge letter to GP; booking community nurse visits; liaison with family
Test results	Written/electronic	MRI report; X-ray images

2 What Is Social Network Analysis?

2.1 Ties, Nodes, and Boundaries

A social network is a group of people (actors) that have some kind of relationship (tie) between them. Actors in a network can be individuals, or entities such as departments or organizations, and the network has notional boundaries which define who is included and who is not. Sociograms are graphical representations of the data collected where each actor is shown as a node and each relationship a tie (Borgatti et al. 2013; Kadushin 2012; Scott 2000). Figure 1 shows an example of a network.

Relationships (ties) can be based on information exchange ("shares information with"), shared experiences ("attended the same workshop"), an emotive tie ("trusts", "hates") or even a contact network ("who contracted a virus from whom"). Different

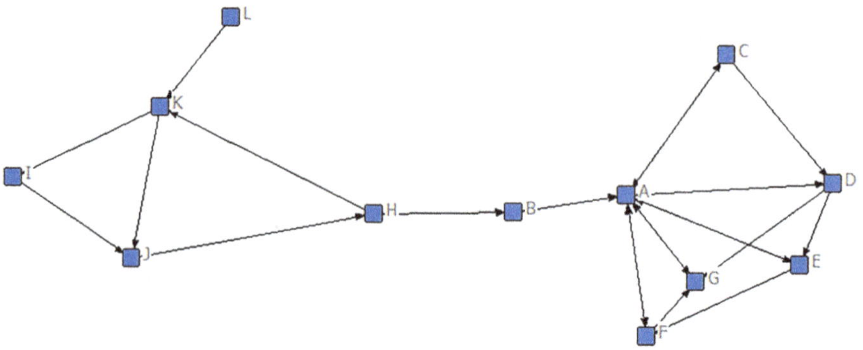

Fig. 1 Sociogram of hospital staff across two wards. Each square (node) is a staff member, and each line (tie) is a relationship. Ward North staff are nodes A through to G, and Ward South are nodes H to L. Node A is a central actor and Node B a broker in the network. This sociogram was generated using UCInet software

ties can result in very different networks; a network consisting of staff on a ward may have a pattern of friendship ties that is very different to their reporting patterns.

Relevant attribute data can be collected about each actor (node) and can contribute to the analysis and understanding of the network. For example, if communication pathways of new patient safety alerts are being mapped and the suspicion is that dissemination practices to out-of-hours staff are not working well, it may be useful to know which nodes are night duty staff and which are day staff to test your hypothesis.

Tie data can be directed, i.e., from one node towards another node, for example, when Node A seeks information from Node B, or undirected where Nodes C and D exchange information or are collaborating on a project. When undirected, ties are depicted in sociograms as just a line linking nodes, while directed ties have an arrow showing the direction as when A seeks information from B, which would have an arrow pointing towards B.

Ties can also be weighted by things such as frequency of contact, e.g., seeking advice from someone every day being a stronger tie than seeking advice once a month; or intensity or importance of the tie, for example, social support that is unimportant compared to social support that is very important to the focal actor.

2.2 Sociograms and Egonets

Sociograms are graphical representations of networks that aggregate empirically collected data on all the ties present between the nodes to show the whole structure (Fig. 1). Each actor in the network is constrained or enabled by their position within the network, in terms of their opportunities, reach, and influence, and algorithms can be used to mathematically compute a range of network parameters relating to this. Sociograms are intuitive structures which can be easily understood by audiences once they have been orientated to the basic conventions of nodes and ties.

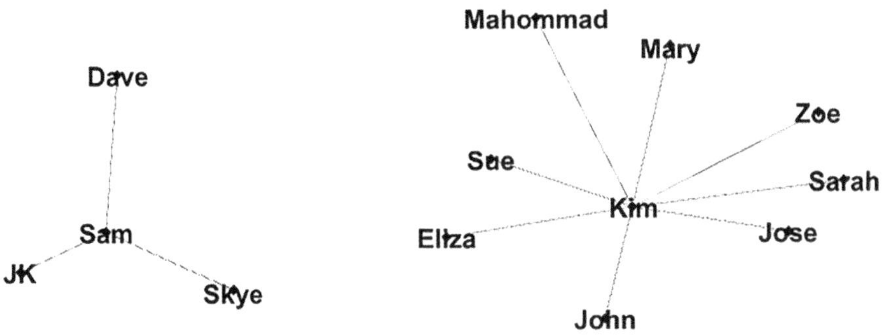

Fig. 2 Egonets of two different patients with cancer, Sam and Kim, mapping the tie: "Who gives you social support in dealing with your cancer?" Sam has named three supporters while Kim has named eight. This egonet was generated using Gephi

While sociograms aggregate data from all the actors in the network, another type of graphic, an egonet, can show data for a single focal actor, the "ego" (Fig. 2). Egonets may depict things such as actors who provide social support for a focal patient, all the specialists that a single GP refers to, or people who have potentially contracted a disease through contact with an index case.

2.3 Network Structure and Actors' Positions

There are several actors' positions within networks that are considered "key player" positions. The first is the central actor. These people are the most interactive with other actors and often hold leadership or coordinating roles. Node A, in Ward North in Fig. 1, is the central actor of that network. The second key player role is a broker. These people are variously called "go-betweens", "boundary spanners" or "bridges" linking up actors in the network that would not otherwise be included (Long et al. 2013a). Node B in Fig. 1 is a broker in that network, linking the staff of the two wards. Another example is the bed manager of a big hospital who coordinates movement of patients (e.g., facilitating transfer of a patient from the Emergency Department to a ward). Here, the bed manager "brokers" the transfer between wards.

3 What Evaluation Questions Can Social Network Analysis Answer?

3.1 Basic Questions

Any service improvement or intervention that changes a socially based process can be usefully evaluated using social network analysis. The data from the social network study can be added to other outcome data such as improved patient outcomes or experience to give a more comprehensive assessment of the intervention.

There are three basic types of evaluation questions that social network studies can address. Firstly, baseline measurements are important to assess how things are currently working and to diagnose and suggest where to intervene. Some examples are communication networks to assess if everyone is being reached or included such as referral networks—are there patients "falling through the cracks" and not receiving help; advice seeking networks—are people in the network all able to find ready advice from others; and integration networks—are patients linked into the right services and are they coordinated and sharing data?

Secondly, social network studies can demonstrate the effectiveness of an intervention. A change from baseline to after the implementation of new technologies or processes are sound evaluation methods. For example, the intervention could include changes to current practice, such as changed communication or referral pathways or processes, changed team structures and responsibilities, or the effectiveness of upskilling and learning on the job. Social network studies can also very clearly evaluate changes in collaboration, such as an intervention that links up formerly siloed teams for better communication and understanding, or increasing holistic care through shared management across services. The target of your assessment may include factors such as shared IT platforms or increased interoperability of patient medical records across providers sharing care of a patient. As well as information pathways, social network analysis could consider a series of patient journeys to demonstrate this linking of services leads to a reduction in duplication of effort (e.g., test requests).

Thirdly, social network studies can evaluate the sustainability of an intervention and be used to target likely future issues or barriers. An example is the identification of key players who may be crucial to the smooth running or coordination of a network. If they retire or leave, the effect may be significant and may threaten the sustainability of the intervention. Putting support around these key players or ensuring their role can be distributed to others in the network may increase the resilience of the intervention. Another use is to identify factors that may be leveraged for future improvements. A successful intervention implemented in one area may be evaluated to determine its appropriateness for implementation in another area.

3.2 Feasibility

Before embarking on a social network analysis, feasibility, and time commitment needs to be considered. If your aim is to map the whole network, the data and accompanying sociogram, like a physical map needs to be as complete as possible. This means that data is ideally collected from all the nodes in the network, not just a sample, i.e., it should be considered a census. Consider the famous London Underground map of stations and train lines. If only a random sample of the stations were included, it would not be useful at all to commuters. Likewise, the structure of the network can only fully be analyzed if data is collected on as many of the actors as possible. Having said that, missing data from key players will have the greatest impact, similar to missing a major interchange like Kings Cross station on the

London Underground map, while actors who are less interactive will have a smaller impact if missing. As a result, a range of methods exist in social network studies, all aimed at capturing those key players.

Social network analyses can vary from a basic, hand-drawn "mud map" to a sophisticated and detailed, computer-generated sociogram with accompanying mathematical insights. The latter will take a significant investment in time, and some methodologic expertise to collect data and then analyze it, while the former may be relatively quick and sufficient to describe the network in question.

4 Data Collection

Social network research requires a number of design decisions to be made before commencing data collection. These decisions include: a clear research question; explication of the relationship of interest; boundaries of the network; and the mode of data collection. These are explored in more detail below.

4.1 A Clear Aim or Research Question

Understanding how relationship data will help you answer a clear question is key to a good social network study. Research questions around the efficiency of information flows, team processes, or presence or absence of actors in a network are good targets as are any issues around advice-seeking. Table 2 shows a number of studies and their research questions.

4.2 Developing the Focal Relationship Question for Self-Reported Ties

Much has been written about how to craft a good social network question that will clearly identify the relationship you are trying to capture. Relationship questions may be perceived as ambiguous by different participants so any wording that makes the tie more concrete is useful to include. "Who do you go to for advice" is an ambiguous question prompting participants to perhaps wonder if it means at work or at home, what type of advice or what does "go to" entail? A better phrasing may be "Thinking about the last 3 months working on Ward 4, from whom did you seek advice if you were uncertain about care for a patient. This includes face-to-face or phone advice." The inclusion of a specific period (last 3 months), a description of the type of advice (uncertain about care for a patient) and mode of communication (face-to-face or on the phone) focuses the question and is more likely to be understood uniformly. Use of a scenario can be useful to focus attention too for example: "A patient has a fall and appears to have injured their arm. After making them comfortable, who is the first person you would communicate this to?" piloting the survey or interview questions with at least 10 people in equivalent roles to your

Table 2 Research questions/aims of social network studies in healthcare improvement projects

Aim or research question	Data collection mode	Reference
To examine the problem-solving, medication advice-seeking and socializing networks of staff working in an Australian hospital emergency department	Whole network, paper-based survey using roster of names	Creswick et al. (2009)
(1) who are the key players of a new translational research network? (2) do they have characteristics in common? (3) are they recognizable as powerful, influential, or well-connected individuals?	Online whole network survey using roster of names	Long et al. (2013b)
To define current hearing health service networks for farming families in a major regional centre in New South Wales, in order to identify approaches that can strengthen local service provision	Whole network survey conducted using email and phone interview	Lower et al. (2010)
To provide an evaluation of the effects of GP network organization on their prescribing behavior	Use of archival data that was routinely collected by local health authority	Fattore et al. (2009)
To use social network analysis to identify champions to facilitate the implementation of a safe patient handling and mobility pilot program	Whole network, paper-based survey using roster of names	Hurtado et al. (2018)

participants, such as staff from another ward not taking part, can be very useful. Asking if the questions made sense or were in any way ambiguous can highlight any problems before the survey is launched.

4.3 Boundaries of the Network: Who's In and Who's Out

Careful consideration needs to be given to who is included in your network and who is not. For example, if your context is staff in a hospital department, will you include temporary staff (e.g., from an agency or seconded from another department) or students on rotation in the network? Will you focus on clinical or patient-facing staff only or include auxiliary staff such as cleaners, catering, or security staff? Without careful consideration of network boundaries, there is the risk that important parts of the system may be omitted.

4.4 Mode of Data Collection

4.4.1 Self-Report Surveys and Interviews

Data pertaining to each node can be collected through self-report survey or interview, observation, or from administrative data (e.g., records of patient referrals). Self-report surveys or interviews ask respondents for their attributes of interest to the study (e.g., role, department) and seek to elicit data about the tie of interest (e.g.,

"Who do you go to for advice?"). Two main methods are used to collect tie data via self-report: the name generator method and the roster method (Kadushin 2012).

A name generator formatted survey or interview asks the participant to list the top five (or whatever number is appropriate) actors with whom they have the focal relationship. For example, for a medication advice network you could ask: "Name up to five staff members who you would trust to give you sound advice on medication issues you were unsure of", or for a referral network question you could ask: "Name the ten specialists that you have referred to the most in the last year".

Instructions should be given for the information you need, to ensure you can identify the named actors as unique nodes in the network. Usually this can be done by asking for first and last names if known, or their role (e.g., Bob, nurse from Ward 4). Using the appropriate number of structured fields labelled "First name, last name and role" rather than a single free text box can ensure meaningful data is collected for each of the actors nominated.

Further questions can be asked around frequency of contact or strength of the relationship. For example, in the medication advice network, the frequency of advice-seeking could be asked for each of the named nodes or the comparative importance or value that each of these people brings to the participant. Name generator surveys work on the assumption that the most interactive nodes in the network are captured by asking for participants' top ties (e.g., top five). This means that not all the network is being mapped, only the most important and active nodes. This method is useful for networks where you are not sure who is included and who is not, as you are letting the participants define it for you. It is also useful for studies that focus on just identifying the key players in certain processes. Downsides of using a name generator are that recall may be imperfect and key people may be forgotten.

Roster-formatted surveys or interviews are more comprehensive but time-consuming. As the name suggests, a roster of names of everyone thought to be in the network is drawn up in the planning stage. For example, all the staff who work in the Emergency Department could be listed. The survey or interview participants then scan the list and answer the same question about each individual (e.g., "In the last week have you exchanged patient information with this person?"). Depending on the number of actors listed, additional questions can be asked. For very large rosters (>100), you can ask participants to skim the list and click on the people they "know" or "work with" as appropriate. Then the focal relationship questions can be answered just for that subset of people.

Roster surveys or interviews rely on maximizing the response rate and should be considered a census not a survey. Sending out reminders or verbally prompting non-responders to do the survey will be important in maximizing the response rate.

Rosters assist participants to remember and consider each network member one by one so they are generally considered more accurate than name generator designs. The problem of identifying actors is largely removed for example where there may be three nurses called Bob on Ward 4 from the earlier example. The design of data collection tool is contingent on the aim or research question and is always a trade-off between meticulously mapping the whole network and mapping the key actors in the network.

Both types of self-report tool can be used to ask the same question at two time points. For example, you could ask about relationships before and after an intervention to assess changes in the structure of the network and the identity of the key players. Longitudinal studies over several years can show changes in networks that develop more slowly, for example, collaborative networks where new partners are slowly added to or leave the network (Festila and Müller 2021).

4.4.2 Ethical Considerations on Survey Design

Using a roster of names on a survey raises some ethical issues around whether those people have consented or not to be included in the network. Several excellent articles discuss this in greater depth (Pomare et al. 2019). Usually, if ethical or research governance approval is likely to be difficult, the name generator design is an acceptable alternative for most research questions.

Gaining the support and sponsorship of senior management for the study can be a useful facilitator for social network studies as the studies are then seen as being conducted under appropriate supervision. If involving senior management, care should be taken to keep those who participate and those who decline confidential so there is no negative perception of being coerced into taking part.

4.4.3 Observation

Collecting data through observation of actors involved in the process of interest (e.g., observing the handing over of patient information from one shift to the next) can be a good design for some research questions. Advantages are that participant effort is limited to consenting to be watched rather than filling out a survey and accurate, real-time data can be assured. This design is useful for describing and evaluating short episodic relationships such as staff handovers, doctor's rounds or team-based meetings such as discharge planning (Benham-Hutchins and Effken 2010; Festila and Müller 2021).

4.5 Analysis and Software

4.5.1 Cleaning Data

Names need to be checked in the name generator model to ensure that each one is identifiable as a unique actor (node) in the network. This may mean deciding if "Bob Smith nurse from ward 4" is the same person as "Bob nurse" or "Robert nurse". Nominated names that cannot be identified because they are vague or ambiguous for example, "nurse on ward 4" may have to be discarded. Decisions also must be made around whether to include surveys with missing data such as blank answers.

Each network member can be given a code before analysis so that confidentiality can be maintained when sharing sociograms, but key actors can be reidentified.

Coding and anonymizing nodes also add some rigor and objectivity to the analysis as expectations of who is a key actor, for example, cannot be tested till after analysis.

4.5.2 Formatting Data

Social network data is usually formatted as a matrix or an edge (tie) list. If mapping by hand, a matrix of names or codes of network members allows collating of data. Table 3 shows a matrix of six nurses who make up the staff of a small outpatient clinic. The network size is six, and all but one (N6) answered the survey asking about "trusted advisors". All the cells need to be filled so no tie present, or missing data is shown as a 0.

The same data can be formatted as an edge list (ego [actor answering the survey], alter [actor they nominate], alter, alter…):

N1 N2 N3 N6
N2 N1 N4
N3 N1 N2
N4 N1
N5 N1 N4
N6

4.5.3 Generating the Sociograms

Two popular and user-friendly social network software packages, UCInet / NetDraw which generates sociograms (Borgatti et al. 2002) and Gephi (Bastian et al. 2009), have excellent supporting documentation and tutorials to explain how to do this in more depth. R may also be used and a range of other software, some requiring a deeper understanding of the algorithms.

Most graphing programs have the facility to show attributes of the nodes—either by color or by shape. For example, for a referral network, clinicians in Service 1 could be colored red and those in Service 2 could be blue; primary care physicians could be shown as circles and specialists as triangles. Think through what features would be best to highlight in the context of your research question. Nodes can be labelled, either as a code, their role, or by name depending on the context of your research. Research done by the service, for the service as an internal quality improvement project, may show the names of the actors if everyone involved is

Table 3 Matrix of tie data for a network of six nurses

From ↓ To →	N1	N2	N3	N4	N5	N6
N1	0	1	1	0	0	1
N2	1	0	0	1	0	0
N3	1	1	0	0	0	0
N4	1	0	0	0	0	0
N5	1	0	0	1	0	0
N6	0	0	0	0	0	0

happy with that. If the results will be shared more widely, it is ethically important to anonymize the data.

4.5.4 Computing Variables

Again, we direct readers to the tutorials of the software package being used to know the commands to compute variables, and more importantly to deeper explanations of the concepts behind them (Borgatti et al. 2009; Kadushin 2012; Valente 2010). We define the main ones here, but note that there are dozens of variables to choose from, depending on the questions. Some are simple measures that can be worked out manually.

Measures pertain to the network as a whole or to individual nodes. Network measures include the size of the network, which is the number of nodes. Individual ties are also usually counted. Density of the network is the ratio of the number of actual ties to the number of possible ties and is usually expressed as a percentage (where 0% is a network where no one has a relationship with anyone else, and 100% means everyone is linked to everyone else, that is, the maximum possible ties). Centralization is a measure of the extent to which a network centers around a key central player. A maximally centralized network would look like a star where every member of the network is tied to a central actor, but no-one else.

Individual measures include the degree of a node (number of ties), centrality (based on degree this can allow ranking of the most interactive and central nodes) and betweenness centrality (a brokerage measure that can be used to identify the key nodes that efficiently link up otherwise separated nodes).

5 Examples of Social Network Studies to Evaluate Health Services

5.1 Evaluation of Lifespan's Strategy of Community and Services Engagement

The LifeSpan suicide prevention intervention was implemented in four regions of New South Wales and involved a whole-of-community approach and engagement of mental health service providers. Key stakeholder groups were invited to complete a social network survey (Long et al. 2022). The introduction to the survey explained that the survey was to help understand how collaboration, communication, and networks were configured in each local area and how the introduction of the LifeSpan intervention had changed these. Using a roster format, survey participants were provided with a list of the key people involved and were asked, for each person on the list, whether they "Met this person through this project" or "Whether they had worked with this person previously". The social network survey was supplemented with a series of focus groups and interviews held in each of the four regions to further understand how the relationships between the community and service providers changed over time.

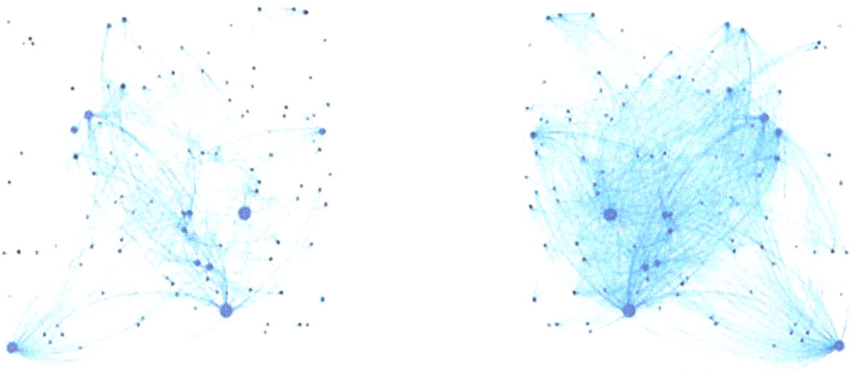

Fig. 3 Before and after the LifeSpan intervention: Ties answering "Who have you worked with previously [before the LifeSpan intervention]" on the left and on the right, showing the collaboration network at the end of the implementation. Size of the node indicates number of ties to other actors. Sociograms generated in Gephi. [unpublished data]

The social network survey was completed by 83 people from three regions; one region was unable to take part due to catastrophic bushfires and COVID-19 response. The results of the social network analysis demonstrated that the collaborative links between community stakeholders increased at each of the three regions after the implementation of LifeSpan. The interviews further explained the benefits of this collaborative approach, such as better communication between groups, identification, and improvement in the integration of priorities, services and activities, and personal support for previously isolated members. LifeSpan coordinators were empirically identified as the key players in the networks and identified as a risk to sustainability if they were to leave (Fig. 3).

5.2 Evaluation of a Translational Research Network (Australian Genomics' Collaborative Learning Strategy)

Australian Genomics was initiated in 2016 as a research alliance involving genetic and medical specialists, scientists, consumers and researchers from across the nation, with the aim of preparing Australia for the implementation of genomics into routine healthcare (Stark et al. 2019). A social network study, using a roster questionnaire was completed by 222 of the 387 members answering the question: "Who is part of your genomic community of practice?" (Long et al. 2019). Additional material in the introduction to the survey explained that we wanted to know how people in the network were learning how to use this new technology—genomic testing—and who were their go-to people. Next, we ranked members by degree (i.e., the number of nominations they received as members of respondents' learning community). We then sequentially removed members starting with the most highly nominated. The idea was to see how important individual "go-to" people were in the

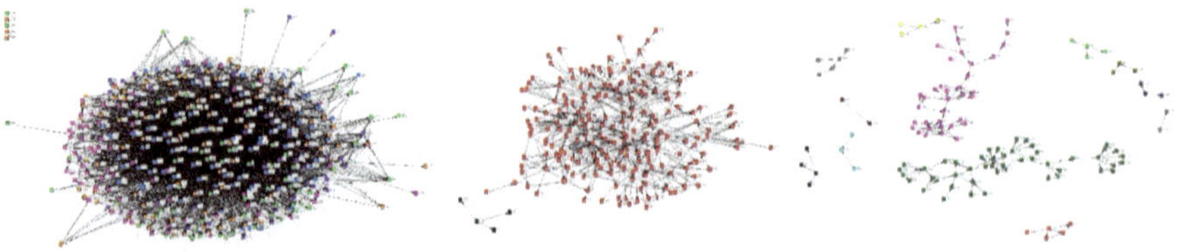

Fig. 4 (**a**) Australian Genomics knowledge exchange network N = 387; (**b**) the same knowledge exchange network with 122 of the most active members removed; (**c**) same network with 208 of the most active members removed. True fragmentation of the network does not happen till (**c**). Generated in UCInet. [unpublished data]

whole network. We observed one or two individual members becoming isolates as more and more nodes were removed but no split-off of distinct components until 122 of the most highly connected members had been removed. Figure 4 shows this graphically. It was not until 208 of the most active members had been removed that the whole network fragmented. This fragmentation analysis shows that the network is cohesive, with many "redundant ties" providing resilience. If one key person leaves, the people to whom they are linked remain part of the network through their links to other members. Cohesion is an important attribute of a learning community, and it can be argued that it is essential for ensuring efficient communication and maintenance of a shared vision and collective goals.

5.3 Evaluating Hidden Costs of Supporting a New Technology

Costs are not always about money. New interventions may have unintended consequences with costs measured in terms of time, resources, and burden on a single actor (Cross and Parker 2004; Long et al. 2013b). A social network study was undertaken to assess the reach and effectiveness of a nationwide referral network, in which pediatric teams from across Australia referred children previously considered untreatable, that met strict criteria to a single research institute in Sydney. A name-generator survey was used to map the advice and consultation network associated with the intervention program. One of the unexpected outcomes was the prominence of one of the Institute's clinicians in the program who had become a key knowledge broker for those referring patients. It was ascertained that this role as informal "go-to" person had increased the workload of the clinician significantly. Moreover, this role was largely invisible to management who still expected their role in everyday service provision to be fulfilled regardless. By providing evidence of this unseen but crucial work, support could be offered to the clinician. Future iterations of the program included use of static website resources such as Frequently Asked Questions and a range of alternative contacts who could give advice. Figure 5 shows the sociogram.

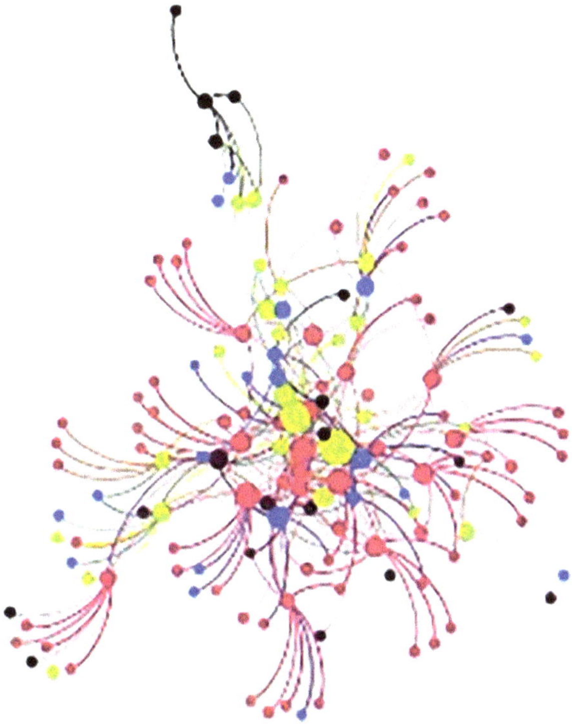

Fig. 5 The advice and consultation network from a new interventional program for children, showing clinicians and scientists involved across three states. The large nodes show key knowledge brokers in the organization running the program. The role is informal and largely invisible to management. Generated in Gephi

6 Comparisons with Other Methods

Why choose social network analysis over a regular survey or observational study, or some other methodology? Here are some of the advantages and disadvantages.

6.1 Advantages

Mapping relationships is a unique way to study an intervention's effect on social processes. Network diagrams are visually and intuitively interesting and great to increase engagement in a project. Everyone wants to know "Where am I in this sociogram? Am I a key player?" In fact, the network diagram may become an intervention in its own right, showing exactly where to intervene or add effort, or throwing up additional areas for exploration or intervention (Borgatti et al. 2009). Social processes are made explicit and invisible networks are identified. People within networks that may be doing unseen work, especially knowledge brokers, may be identified. Empirical evidence from the study can then be used to make a case for support.

6.2 Disadvantages

Social network studies can be time-consuming to set up and to collect data. Specialist software may be needed for larger or more complex networks with the accompanying upskilling needed to become competent.

Aside from feasibility are considerations around appropriateness. Network studies are a snapshot of a dynamic network. Ties are constantly changing with people leaving the network, retiring, learning new skills or changing roles. Results need to be understood as a single point in time. Moreover, network analysis can tell you what ties and nodes exist in the network but not what motivations and intentions those actors have. It is therefore important to include some qualitative work to answer these questions; e.g., interviews with key players to understand how they work, their challenges and barriers (Rice et al. 2014).

7 Conclusion

Social network studies bring a unique perspective to health service evaluations by measuring social relationships and processes. It can reveal hidden work done by key players and suggest areas of improvement. As health care is increasingly delivered by interdisciplinary teams, the need to understand social processes and the best way to structure those teams becomes crucial. The main drawback to using social network analysis is the time commitment and the need for a level of basic methodological expertise.

References

Bastian M, Heymann S, Jacomy M. Gephi: an open source software for exploring and manipulating networks. Presented at the International AAAI Conference on Weblogs and Social Media; 2009.

Benham-Hutchins MM, Effken JA (2010) Multi-professional patterns and methods of communication during patient handoffs. Int J Med Inform 79:252–267. https://doi.org/10.1016/j.ijmedinf.2009.12.005

Borgatti, S.P., Everett, M.G., Freeman, L.C., 2002. UCInet for Windows: software for social network analysis.

Borgatti SP, Mehra A, Brass DJ, Labianca G (2009) Network analysis in the social sciences. Science 323:892–895. https://doi.org/10.1126/science.1165821

Borgatti SP, Everett MG, Johnson JC (2013) Analyzing social networks. SAGE, Los Angeles

Chan B, Reeve E, Matthews S, Carroll P, Long JC, Held F, Latt M, Naganathan V, Caplan G, Hilmer SN (2016) Medicine information exchange networks among health care professionals and prescribing in geriatric medicine wards. Br J Clin Pharmacol 83:1185

Creswick N, Westbrook JI, Braithwaite J (2009) Understanding communication networks in the emergency department. BMC Health Serv Res 9:247. https://doi.org/10.1186/1472-6963-9-247
Cross RL, Parker A (2004) The hidden power of social networks: understanding how work really gets done in organizations. Harvard Business School Press, Boston
Fattore G, Frosini F, Salvatore D, Tozzi V (2009) Social network analysis in primary care: the impact of interactions on prescribing behaviour. Health Policy 92:141–148. https://doi.org/10.1016/j.healthpol.2009.03.005
Festila MS, Müller SD (2021) Information handoffs in critical care and their implications for information quality: a socio-technical network approach. J Biomed Inform 122:103914. https://doi.org/10.1016/j.jbi.2021.103914
Hurtado DA, Dumet LM, Greenspan SA, Rodríguez YI, Heinonen GA (2018) Identifying safety peer leaders with social network analysis. Occup Health Sci 2:437–450. https://doi.org/10.1007/s41542-018-0026-4
Kadushin C (2012) Understanding social networks: theories, concepts, and findings. Oxford University Press, New York
Long JC, Cunningham FC, Braithwaite J (2013a) Bridges, brokers and boundary spanners in collaborative networks: a systematic review. BMC Health Serv Res 13:158
Long JC, Cunningham FC, Carswell P, Braithwaite J (2013b) Who are the key players in a new translational research network? BMC Health Serv Res 13
Long JC, Hibbert P, Braithwaite J (2016) Structuring successful collaboration: a longitudinal social network analysis of a translational research network. Implement Sci 11:19
Long JC, Pomare C, Best S, Boughtwood T, North K, Ellis LA, Churruca K, Braithwaite J (2019) Building a knowledge exchange network in Australian clinical genomics: a social network study of the Australian Genomic Health Alliance. BMC Med 17:44
Long JC, Ruane C, Ellis LA, Lake R, Le Roux A, Testa L, Shand F, Torok M, Zurynski Y (2022) Networks to strengthen community social capital for suicide prevention in regional Australia: the LifeSpan suicide prevention initiative. Int J Ment Health Syst 16:Article 10
Lower T, Fragar L, Depcynzksi J, Fuller J, Challinor K, Williams W (2010) Social network analysis for farmers' hearing services in a rural community. Aust J Prim Health 16:47. https://doi.org/10.1071/PY09043
Pomare C, Long JC, Churruca K, Ellis LA, Braithwaite J (2019) Social network research in health care settings: design and data collection. Soc Netw 69:14–21
Rice E, Holloway IW, Barman-Adhikari A, Fuentes D, Brown CH, Palinkas LA (2014) A mixed methods approach to network data collection. Field Methods 26:252–268. https://doi.org/10.1177/1525822X13518168
Sabot K, Wickremasinghe D, Blanchet K, Avan B, Schellenberg J (2017) Use of social network analysis methods to study professional advice and performance among healthcare providers: a systematic review. Syst Rev 6:208. https://doi.org/10.1186/s13643-017-0597-1
Scott J (2000) Social network analysis: a handbook, 2nd edn. SAGE
Stark Z, Boughtwood T, Phillips P, Christodoulou J, Hansen DP, Braithwaite J, Newson AJ, Gaff CL, Sinclair AH, North KN (2019) Australian genomics: a federated model for integrating genomics into healthcare. Am J Hum Genet 105:7–14. https://doi.org/10.1016/j.ajhg.2019.06.003
Valente T (2010) Social networks and health. Oxford University Press, Oxford

Fidelity in Health Services Research

Raphaëlle Ashley Guerbaai, Daniela Holle, Tina Quasdorf, and Lea Saringer-Hamiti

Abstract

This chapter explores the concept of fidelity in health services evaluation, emphasizing its crucial role in ensuring effective healthcare delivery and improved outcomes for healthcare practices and patient care. Fidelity, in this context, refers to the degree to which healthcare interventions are implemented as intended. This chapter discusses how the dimensions and definitions of fidelity can differ across various conceptual frameworks. Key dimensions contributing to fidelity measures (i.e., treatment protocols, adherence, quality of delivery), which could be considered for assessing fidelity, are identified and discussed. Contextual factors are highlighted as influencers of fidelity as well as the connection between fidelity and intervention results. Practical guidance to incorporate fidelity assessment into healthcare evaluation is provided. This includes ethical considerations and trends, and challenges in fidelity evaluation.

R. A. Guerbaai (✉)
Rehabilitation, Ageing and Independent Living (RAIL) Research Centre, School of Primary and Allied Health Care, Monash University, Frankston, Australia
e-mail: Raphaelle-ashley.guerbaai@monash.edu

D. Holle
Department of Nursing, Midwifery and Therapeutic Sciences, Hochschule für Gesundheit, Bochum, Germany
e-mail: daniela.holle@hs-gesundheit.de

T. Quasdorf
Institute of Nursing, School of Health Sciences, ZHAW Zurich University of Applied Sciences, Winterthur, Switzerland
e-mail: tina.quasdorf@zhaw.ch

L. Saringer-Hamiti
Institute of Nursing Science, Department Public Health, Faculty of Medicine, University of Basel, Basel, Switzerland
e-mail: lea.saringer-hamiti@unibas.ch

A. Kaehne, J. Feather (eds.), *Handbook of Health Services Evaluation*,
https://doi.org/10.1007/978-3-031-87869-5_16

Keywords
Fidelity evaluation · Evaluation · Context · Measures

1 Introduction

1.1 The Concept of Fidelity in the Context of Health Services

Fidelity, also referred to as the delivery, integrity, treatment, intervention, or implementation fidelity, is defined as "the degree to which an intervention or program is delivered as intended" (Breitenstein et al. 2010; Proctor et al. 2011) and is emerging as a critical component of healthcare interventions. The different concepts and underpinnings of fidelity have developed over time. Historically, attention was drawn to the concept of "treatment fidelity" in the field of psychotherapy with issues around the effectiveness of various psychotherapeutic interventions, whereby the extent to which treatment conditions overlapped was overlooked (Eysenck 1952; VandenBos 1980). While the concept of fidelity was mentioned in several social and behavioral studies in the late 1970s and early 1980s (Peterson et al. 1982; Quay 1977), it was in 1991 that an article formally introduced a definition and proposed guidelines for enhancing the concept of treatment fidelity (Moncher and Prinz 1991). The concept of fidelity was indeed focused on whether the treatment was delivered as intended. The concept of treatment fidelity included treatment differentiation, which looked at whether the treatment conditions differed from each other as intended (Moncher and Prinz 1991). Later, the need to assess two additional processes for proper interpretation of study results emerged. Treatment receipt, which involved assessing and optimizing the participant's understanding and ability to use treatment skills, and treatment enactment, which involved assessing and optimizing the participant's application of learned skills in their daily life, were emphasized as important processes to consider (Lichstein et al. 1994).

Fidelity has historically had many applications and uses across different fields; therefore, evaluating fidelity is essential to ensure that interventions are delivered and received as intended. Fidelity evaluation stemmed from the field of health psychology and ensured that prescribed treatments were delivered with minimal variation (Bond et al. 2000; Mars et al. 2013) and adhered to the behavior change theory that informed their design. Fidelity evaluation has become increasingly prominent in implementation science, which is defined as "the scientific study of methods to promote the systematic uptake of research findings (and other evidence-based practices) into routine practice" to enhance the quality and effectiveness of health services and care (Eccles and Mittman 2006). By evaluating fidelity, the aim is to ensure patients receive the intended benefits of an intervention or program, and that healthcare providers can accurately evaluate its effectiveness.

1.2 The Importance of Evaluating Fidelity for Effective Healthcare Delivery and Outcomes

When evaluating a health service intervention, program, or policy, the term "black box" is often used in the literature to indicate a lack of understanding of how these interventions work in daily practice (Grimshaw et al. 2014; Harachi et al. 1999; Wilson et al. 2009). Fidelity evaluation, defined as "the extent to which an intervention or procedure is delivered as intended," is an integral part of assessing the process of a service or intervention (Breitenstein et al. 2012). By ensuring that healthcare interventions adhere to established protocols and guidelines, fidelity evaluation helps maintain treatment integrity and consistency, thereby reducing variability in healthcare delivery. In addition to maintaining treatment integrity, evaluating fidelity enhances treatment effectiveness by allowing healthcare providers to identify and address any deviations or challenges in implementing interventions. By optimizing fidelity, providers can improve the effectiveness of treatments and enhance patient outcomes. Furthermore, fidelity evaluation facilitates the accurate replication of interventions in different settings, enabling researchers, practitioners, and policymakers to measure their impact across diverse populations and contexts (Carroll et al. 2007). This can enhance the generalizability of results and promote the dissemination of evidence-based practices in healthcare.

1.3 Overview of This Chapter's Objectives

This chapter aims to provide an overview of the current landscape of fidelity in health services, including the conceptualization of fidelity, the importance of evaluating and reporting fidelity, and associated challenges. The contents of this chapter are suited to healthcare practitioners, researchers, and administrators who are interested in improving the quality and effectiveness of healthcare interventions, including using fidelity to assess and monitor changes in healthcare delivery services. Real-world examples of organizations or healthcare systems that have successfully evaluated fidelity will be described throughout. The different dimensions of fidelity, including adherence, dose, quality, and program differentiation, will be discussed. This chapter will highlight the challenges associated with measuring fidelity, and how researchers, practitioners, and administrators may address these. Finally, it will explore how healthcare providers can incorporate fidelity assessment into their services and workflows, use fidelity indicators, and utilize technology. The benefits of using fidelity data for continuous quality improvement and evidence-based decision-making are also addressed in this chapter.

2 Understanding Fidelity in Health Services

2.1 Fidelity in the Context of Health Services

A variety of terms are used interchangeably in the literature when referring to fidelity, such as implementation fidelity (Breitenstein et al. 2010; Carroll et al. 2007), treatment fidelity (Fonagy and Luyten 2019), intervention fidelity (Poltawski et al. 2014), and treatment integrity (Gresham 1989). Despite the application of these different terms, fidelity can be contextualized as the extent to which a program, service, intervention, or method of health service delivery is delivered and received as intended. The circumstances relating to the deliverer and receiver for which fidelity relates greatly depend on the setting.

Fidelity is a critical component of health service research and evaluation as it helps to ensure the accurate implementation of a variety of healthcare services (e.g., access to healthcare screening) or interventions and has a significant impact on achieving and maintaining positive outcomes, such as enhancing care quality (Toomey et al. 2020). Currently, health systems are striving to improve individual and population-level health and well-being outcomes to improve the quality of care for an increasingly aging population and to leverage healthcare expenditure (Cristea et al. 2020). As an example, research focusing on health behavior change to encourage the uptake of healthy practices such as smoking cessation, increasing physical activity, and healthier diets are putting a lot of consideration into measuring and evaluating fidelity (Toomey et al. 2020). This is due to reviews underlining that predefined study outcomes were not met, or interventions not sustained in practice, despite well-developed and implemented programs (Flodgren et al. 2017). We took the example of health behavior research; however, similar conclusions were drawn in other fields, such as in prevention medicine, across health and education interventions (Hailemariam et al. 2019; Zurynski et al. 2023). As such, fidelity helps to accurately assess the effectiveness of interventions in health service research, by attributing any observed changes in outcomes to the intervention itself, rather than to other factors such as the surrounding context(s). Studies have shown that interventions with higher fidelity had more significant and consistent effects on outcomes compared to those with lower fidelity (Guerbaai et al. 2023; McNerney et al. 2020; Sprange et al. 2021). For instance, a review evaluating data from more than 500 studies found that when interventions are well implemented, with high fidelity, the magnitude of mean effect sizes is at least 2–3 times higher than when low fidelity of intervention exists (Durlak and DuPre 2008). This highlights the importance of measuring and evaluating fidelity in establishing causal relationships between interventions and their impact on given outcomes.

Fidelity is equally important for the successful implementation of interventions in real-world healthcare settings (Allen et al. 2017). Adhering to fidelity guidelines ensures that interventions are implemented consistently across different healthcare settings, allowing for better evaluation of their effectiveness and potential for successful replication. This consistency is essential for improving the quality and reliability of healthcare services (Allen et al. 2017). When interventions are implemented with a high level of fidelity, patients receive the intended level of exposure to the intervention's components, leading to more significant improvements in their health outcomes. Deviations from fidelity may result in suboptimal dosage or delivery, compromising the effectiveness of the intervention. However, on occasion, findings may demonstrate an inverse relationship, whereby higher adherence to a treatment protocol results in poorer performance. For instance, a study looking at dietitian-delivered health behavior change intervention designed to reduce malnutrition in hospitalized patients demonstrated that higher levels of dietitian adherence to a nutritional plan were associated with significantly poorer patient nutritional status (Beck et al. 2021). Several circumstances such as patient resistance or confrontational provider or patient encounters may affect intervention delivery (Beck et al. 2021; Codern-Bové et al. 2014).

As well as allowing for the identification of effective intervention components in health service research, researchers can determine which specific components contribute to successful outcomes (An et al. 2020; Guerbaai et al. 2023). Monitoring fidelity can enable researchers, administrators, and policymakers to identify the active ingredients of interventions, leading to the refinement and improvement of their effectiveness. This knowledge can inform future intervention adaptations and guide the development of more targeted and efficient healthcare services.

3 Key Dimensions of Fidelity

3.1 Definition and Operationalization of Various Fidelity Concepts

Fidelity encompasses various dimensions that serve to distinguish and operationalize this concept. It is important to note that the specific dimensions of fidelity and their definitions may vary across different conceptual works (Lemire et al., 2022). The following concepts listed below are generally accepted as essential dimensions of fidelity, and they are widely recognized as key elements that define fidelity: (1) adherence to the treatment protocol, (2) dose, (3) quality of delivery, (4) participant responsiveness, and (5) program differentiation.

1. **Adherence to the treatment protocol (or treatment integrity)** refers to whether an intervention is delivered as designed or written (Bellg et al. 2004; Carroll et al. 2007; Dane and Schneider 1998; Dusenbury et al. 2003; Hasson 2010; Mihalic 2004). Sometimes other dimensions of fidelity are included under the concept of adherence: frequency, duration, coverage (which can also be summarized under the concept of dose), and content. Therefore, when assessing adherence, essential and non-essential components of the intervention should be distinguished, and adherence should then be assessed for the essential components (Dusenbury et al. 2003). However, the need for an appropriate relationship between intervention adherence on the one hand and necessary context-related adaptations on the other is increasingly being discussed (Pérez et al. 2016;

Schinckus et al. 2021). Pérez et al. (2016), e.g., provide a modified theoretical framework of implementation fidelity that considers the fidelity-adaptation balance as well. However, Schinckus et al. (2021) point out that the criteria to assess effective adaptations need to be further clarified.

2. **Dose**, also referred to as **dosage or exposure**, pertains to the quantity of the intervention that is administered and received by the intended recipients of the intervention (Carroll et al. 2007; Dane and Schneider 1998; Dusenbury et al. 2003; Mihalic 2004). The specific terms and definitions associated with this concept may vary across different conceptual works on fidelity. In some cases, dose may encompass additional sub-dimensions such as frequency, duration, coverage, and intensity (Carroll et al. 2007; Dusenbury et al. 2003). Other conceptual work refers to these sub-dimensions as stand-alone dimensions (Hasson 2015). A scoping review focusing on the operationalization of the concept of dose highlighted the need for definitions and distinction of associated terms and concepts (Rowbotham et al. 2019).
3. The **quality of delivery**, also known as treatment delivery, pertains to whether an intervention is administered in a manner that aligns with the intentions of the intervention developers (Borrelli et al. 2005; Dane and Schneider 1998; Dusenbury et al. 2003; Mihalic 2004). When the quality of delivery is compromised, it often indicates a lower degree of implementation as well (Carroll et al. 2007). This is because it reflects underlying issues such as poor planning, inadequate resource allocation, insufficient training, and weak monitoring and coordination. If the significance of the intervention delivery is recognized, strategies such as training and education, materials, monitoring and feedback, and other supportive or quality assurance and improvement measures are typically employed to ensure the quality of delivery (Carroll et al. 2007). Structured processes are necessary for implementation studies to assess and improve intervention delivery (Borrelli et al. 2005).
4. **Participant responsiveness** addresses the way the targeted individuals of an intervention respond to and engage with an intervention (Carroll et al. 2007; Dane and Schneider 1998; Dusenbury et al. 2003). This also includes how the target individuals judge the outcomes and relevance of the intervention (Carroll et al. 2007). Borrelli et al. (2005) in this respect further differentiate between the following dimensions:
   - Treatment receipt means whether the target persons understand and apply the intervention while it is being delivered (e.g., during teaching sessions).
   - Treatment enactment means whether the target persons apply the intervention to their daily lives (e.g., between teaching sessions).
5. **Program differentiation** relates to identifying unique elements of interventions and identifying which elements of an intervention are essential to achieve the intended effect (Carroll et al. 2007; Dusenbury et al. 2003). Furthermore, program differentiation comprises avoiding diffusion of treatments or interventions (Dane and Schneider 1998) and ensuring that different interventions differ in the intended way (Borrelli et al. 2005).

3.2 Fidelity Frameworks

The key dimensions described above are organized and prioritized in different ways across various fidelity frameworks (Lemire et al. 2022), which aim to provide a structured basis for understanding and analyzing implementation fidelity. These fidelity frameworks are frequently applied in empirical studies (e.g., Quasdorf et al. 2017; Saarijärvi et al. 2022; En-Nasery-de Heer et al. 2022). An illustration of this variation can be seen in the conceptual framework for implementation fidelity (CFIF) (Carroll et al. 2007). In the CFIF, the key dimensions of implementation fidelity are categorized into dimensions (i.e., categories) related to adherence (i.e., content, coverage, frequency, duration) and dimensions that act as mediators to implementation fidelity (i.e., intervention complexity, facilitation strategies, quality of delivery, participant responsiveness). With their framework, Carroll et al. (2007) emphasize the function of the respective key dimensions regarding the overarching concept of implementation fidelity as well as the relationships between the individual dimensions. In doing so, Carroll et al. (2007) intend to complement earlier work that primarily considered the individual key dimensions isolated from one another. Hasson (2010) adds the key dimensions of context and recruitment as mediators (i.e., moderating factors to implementation fidelity) to the CFIF.

4 Methods for Evaluating Fidelity

4.1 Defining Intervention Components

The evaluation of fidelity implies a comparison of the intervention's actual delivery to the treatment or intervention protocol. Consequently, the intervention and its delivery must be described in detail before the evaluation of fidelity. The template for intervention description and replication (TiDieR) might serve here as reporting guidance and is a 12-item checklist that focuses on reporting details of the intervention element (Hoffmann et al. 2014). The TiDieR focuses on clinical trials but can be applied to all evaluative study designs (Hoffmann et al. 2014).

Moreover, it is important to distinguish between essential and non-essential components of the intervention, as the focus of the evaluation should concentrate on the essential (core) components. Kilbourne et al. (2007) define the core components as the critical elements of the design and intent of the intervention that are thought to be responsible for the intervention's effectiveness. The non-essential components are the mechanism by which they can be operationalized, and which may vary across organizations (Kilbourne et al. 2007). If the core components cannot be identified in advance (e.g., because the intervention is being adapted), it is advisable to consider all intervention components for the evaluation of fidelity (Hasson 2015).

In the case of an RCT or quasi-experimental study, it should be further considered whether fidelity could only be measured for the intervention group or also for the control condition in effectiveness studies, as changes in the fidelity of the control intervention might have also an impact on the observed effects of the clinical trial (Quasdorf et al. 2017).

4.2 Measuring Intervention Components

To achieve a comprehensive picture of fidelity, all the above-mentioned key dimensions of fidelity (e.g., treatment integrity, dose, treatment delivery, participant responsiveness) should be measured (Hasson 2015). This also means that various research methods are required on the continuum between quantitative and qualitative methods to capture the different subcategories of fidelity. In the following paragraph, examples of methods are outlined and illustrated with sample studies. Morello et al. (2017) investigated the program adherence of a nurse-led fall prevention program in Australian hospitals.

In this context, program adherence refers to whether nurses used the individual prevention program as designed by its creators (program content) and whether they delivered the program as frequently and for as long as planned (dose) (Morello et al. 2017). Furthermore, the research team used a combination of structured bedside observations and daily audits of patient care plans to analyze program adherence (Morello et al. 2017). Morris et al. (2019) analyzed adherence to another person-centered fall prevention program in Australian emergency departments. Here, the research team was interested in the intervention clinician's adherence to key program components as well as in the intervention participants' adherence to minimum program requirements (Morris et al. 2019). For the evaluation of the clinician's adherence, the research team used audio recordings of selected intervention sessions, and for the measurement of the patient's adherence, they analyzed the clinician's records (Morris et al. 2019). Observations and audio recordings offer the possibility of obtaining objective information about the actual performance of the intervention participants, although both methods are resource-intensive and thus are only recorded (Morris et al. 2019).

Holle et al. (2019) evaluated the delivery of dementia-specific case conferences (DCC) in German nursing homes. They assessed adherence to the key components of the concept (e.g., defined process and role structures in DCC) through written self-reports from participating trainers, attendance lists, and standardized protocols of the DCC (Holle et al. 2019). Additionally, semi-structured telephone interviews were conducted before and after the DCCs to assess whether a structured pre- and post-preparation of the DCC took place (Holle et al. 2019). Self-reports allow ongoing monitoring of intervention fidelity but might be biased by the participants' self-perception; likewise, focusing solely on interviews offers the risk that practitioners do not reflect on the adaptations they conduct in practice, which might be a limitation of the study of Holle et al. (2019).

Depending on the type of intervention, electronic monitoring systems (e.g., electronic medical records, web log data) can serve as further methods to assess fidelity (Coorey et al. 2021; Dueweke et al. 2024). Chai et al. (2021) analyzed the frequency of a telehealth intervention that focused on child nutrition and weight management through Google Analytics and the Bitly platform to objectively track data on the frequency and pattern of intervention use. As such, the mean number of website visits, the most popular web pages, and resource downloads were evaluated (Chai et al. 2021). The use of electronic monitoring systems might save resources and enable recording the intervention use in real-time.

The timing of data collection is another important aspect that should be considered when evaluating fidelity. Hasson (2015) argues in favor of collecting fidelity data during the entire intervention period since fidelity may change over time (Hasson 2015). In their study on the effectiveness of dementia-specific case conferences, Halek et al. (2020) found that participants adhered to the planned monthly 60-minute case conferences during the first half of the 9-month intervention phase, but several teams reduced both the frequency and duration of the discussions in the second half (Halek et al. 2020). This indicates that the high fidelity at the beginning of the intervention phase is offset by the partial decline in fidelity toward the end of the phase.

In a simulation study, Trutschel et al. (2023) were able to demonstrate that high fidelity is important right at the start of the intervention phase to achieve accurate intervention effect estimates in parallel and stepped-wedge cluster randomized trials (Trutschel et al. 2023). In addition to the duration of the fidelity measurement, its timing is also crucial. While fidelity should ideally be measured concurrently with the implementation of the intervention, a post-hoc analysis conducted after the intervention ends might result in lower-quality data (Gerritsen et al. 2021). If the interval between the implementation of the intervention and the measurement of its fidelity is too long, recall bias can occur, resulting in incomplete or limited memories of the intervention's implementation and thus in lower quality data.

Another challenge discussed in the included literature regarding fidelity evaluation is, if no standard defining the optimal degree of adherence exists (Hasson 2015; Morello et al. 2017). Thus, a high level of fidelity might be defined as delivering intervention components according to the protocol always or most often (Hasson 2015), but this does not guarantee that this definition represents the optimal level of fidelity. This also raises the questions as to whether or how to weigh the fidelity of the different intervention components. As such, whether high fidelity for essential components compensates for low fidelity of less essential components (Hasson 2015).

In summary, methods for evaluating fidelity should be carefully selected considering the specific research question, the type of intervention, and the strengths and weaknesses of the respective methods. Thus, quantitative and qualitative methods have both an important place in measuring fidelity, independently and in combination to capture the different dimensions of fidelity (Moore et al. 2015).

5 Importance of Context

5.1 The Role of Conceptual Factors in Evaluating Fidelity

The role of contextual factors in evaluating fidelity is important as different healthcare settings, cultural considerations, and patient populations can significantly influence fidelity (Joyce et al. 2019). Adapting fidelity measures to different contexts while maintaining the integrity of the intervention requires a fundamental understanding of the context, flexibility in implementation, stakeholder engagement, pilot testing, and data-driven adaptations (Rosas 2017).

Contextual factors play a significant role in evaluating fidelity as they can impact the implementation and outcomes of interventions. Different healthcare settings may have varying resources, policies, and organizational structures that may influence fidelity. Cultural considerations, such as language barriers, beliefs, and norms, can also affect the implementation of interventions (Habitu et al. 2022). Additionally, patient populations may have diverse needs, preferences, and levels of health literacy that should be considered during fidelity assessment. Understanding these contextual factors is essential for adapting fidelity measures appropriately.

5.2 Strategies for Adapting Fidelity Measures to Different Contexts

Ensuring a fundamental understanding of the context in which the intervention is being implemented is one of several strategies for adapting fidelity measures. This involves conducting a thorough assessment of the healthcare setting, including its resources, infrastructure, and organizational culture. Understanding the characteristics and challenges of the context can inform the development of fidelity measures that are relevant and feasible (Ginsburg et al. 2021). Flexibility in implementation is another important strategy for adapting fidelity measures while maintaining the integrity of the intervention (Damschroder et al. 2009). Recognizing that different contexts may require adjustments to the intervention delivery can help ensure that fidelity measures are tailored appropriately and are setting-specific. This flexibility allows for the customization of the intervention to fit the specific needs and constraints of the context, while still adhering to the core components and principles of the intervention, which should be clearly defined beforehand (e.g., clarifying core components and peripheral elements of a given intervention) (Damschroder et al. 2009). While fidelity ensures adherence to core components, the need for adaptability to diverse contexts and populations is equally crucial (Breitenstein et al. 2010). Reaching this equilibrium demands careful consideration—maintaining fidelity to essential components while allowing for appropriate adaptations (Fixen et al. 2013). Rigidity or strictly adhering to core components without the possibility of adapting peripheral elements might hinder intervention uptake or effectiveness in varying settings, yet excessive flexibility risks diluting the intervention's core components, impacting its efficacy (Kendall and Frank 2018). Negotiating this challenge involves defining core components and peripheral elements and discussing important aspects of interventions with participants and end users (U.S. Department of Health and Human Services 2013). Codesigning interventions with adaptable frameworks can help to acknowledge contextual nuances without compromising fidelity, thereby optimizing outcomes across diverse healthcare landscapes (Meyer et al. 2022).

Stakeholder engagement and public and patient involvement are other important strategies for adapting fidelity measures to different contexts and settings (Treichler et al. 2022; Triplett et al. 2022). Involving key stakeholders, such as healthcare providers, administrators, and patients, in the fidelity evaluation process can provide valuable insights and perspectives. These stakeholders can contribute to the adaptation of fidelity measures by sharing their experiences, providing feedback, and suggesting modifications that align with the context (Kirk et al. 2021). Alongside stakeholder engagement, pilot testing is an effective strategy for adapting fidelity measures to different contexts (Glasgow et al. 2019; Knudsen et al. 2020). Conducting small-scale trials or pilot studies allows for the identification of potential challenges and opportunities for adaptation. This process helps refine fidelity measures and ensures that they are feasible, acceptable, and meaningful in the specific context. Pilot testing also provides an opportunity to gather feedback from stakeholders and make necessary adjustments before full-scale implementation.

Data-driven adaptation is another strategy to consider when adjusting fidelity measures while maintaining the integrity of the intervention (von Thiele Schwarz et al. 2021). Monitoring (i.e., regular checks or observations) and analyzing fidelity data can reveal patterns, trends, and areas for improvement. By continuously collecting and analyzing fidelity data, researchers and healthcare professionals can identify contextual factors that may impact fidelity and make informed changes (Bond et al. 2022). This iterative process ensures that fidelity measures remain responsive to the context and contribute to the ongoing improvement of the intervention.

6 Fidelity and Intervention Outcomes

6.1 Impact of Fidelity on Intervention Outcomes

Research has demonstrated a correlation between fidelity and health outcomes across various healthcare domains. For instance, in chronic disease management interventions, high fidelity implementation of structured care plans and medication adherence protocols has shown marked improvements in patient health indicators. Improved outcomes included reduced blood pressure levels in hypertensive patients and better glycemic control in diabetes management programs (Nieuwlaat et al. 2014). Similarly, a study providing a mixed-method approach to the implementation of the INTERCARE nurse-led model in Swiss nursing homes found that high fidelity to the core components of the model was associated with a reduced likelihood of unplanned transfers to hospitals (Guerbaai et al. 2023). These outcomes underscore the key role of fidelity in positively influencing patients' physical health.

In mental health interventions, fidelity has also been associated with enhanced recovery outcomes (Egeland et al. 2017). Studies examining fidelity in psychotherapy interventions show that adherence to evidence-based treatment protocols leads to better patient outcomes, including reduced symptom severity, improved functioning, and increased rates of recovery (Marques et al. 2019; U.S. Department of Health and Human Services 2002). Furthermore, the faithful delivery of specific psychological techniques has been associated with more favorable recovery trajectories for individuals with various mental health conditions, but also in healthy populations to improve cognitive performance (Goodyer et al. 2017).

Fidelity is considered a key factor for patient satisfaction. As such, interventions delivered with high fidelity tend to align more closely with patients' expectations and needs, leading to increased satisfaction levels (Janducci et al. 2023). For instance, in patient-centered care initiatives, adherence to communication protocols and patient engagement strategies positively influences patient satisfaction metrics, fostering trust, perceived quality of care, and overall satisfaction with healthcare services (Bragstad et al. 2019; Forsythe et al. 2019).

6.2 Consequences of Low Fidelity

Low fidelity often undermines the intended effectiveness of healthcare interventions (Miller and Rollnick 2014). Studies across diverse healthcare contexts highlight that deviations from intervention protocols or incomplete implementation compromise the expected outcomes (King and Bosworth 2014; An et al. 2020). For example, in community health programs, when certain components of an intervention are inconsistently delivered or omitted, the anticipated health improvements may not materialize as intended, diminishing the intervention's effectiveness (Breitenstein et al. 2010; Lara et al. 2011).

In addition to compromising outcomes, low fidelity can also result in significant resource wastage (Klaic et al. 2022). When interventions veer off course from their intended protocols and fail to achieve expected results, this leads to inefficient allocation of resources—time, funding, and human resources may be misdirected (De Geest et al. 2020; Swindle et al. 2018).

7 Integrating Fidelity Evaluation into Practice

Intervention fidelity is a crucial aspect in both research and practice settings, encompassing adherence to structured procedures, techniques, and treatment methodologies. To establish a robust framework for fidelity evaluation, it is essential to have a clear understanding of its contextual relevance within the healthcare landscape. This involves defining fidelity's parameters and expectations within the specific intervention or treatment regimen (Peters et al. 2022).

7.1 Challenges in Implementing Evidence-Based Guidelines

Implementing evidence-based guidelines is recognized as vital for improving standards of care and guiding healthcare providers in decision-making (World Health Organization 2018). However, their use in practice can be inconsistent, often due to lack of compliance and inadequate knowledge of the guidelines. Studies have highlighted gaps in provider understanding and compliance across low-income, middle-income, and high-income countries, indicating a significant disparity between knowledge and actual practice in service delivery (Dixon-Woods 2014; Jha et al. 2013; Praveen et al. 2014; Raghu et al. 2015). Various approaches, such as inspection of medical records, patient exit interviews, direct observation of provider-client interactions, standardized patients, and clinical vignettes, have been used to assess the quality of care and compliance with guidelines (Piryani and Piryani 2019; World Health Organization 2018).

7.2 Evaluating Fidelity for Quality Improvement

Evaluating fidelity through interested institutions is often linked with quality improvement structures (World Health Organization 2018). In this internal evaluation process, institutional culture becomes a critical consideration to ensure enthusiastic engagement and avoid fear and resistance. Providers must perceive fidelity evaluation as part of an active learning mechanism to promote the acknowledgment of the need for quality improvement. Several methods, such as peer review, clinical audit, individual feedback, supervision and training, and multidisciplinary learning collaboratives, can be employed to facilitate this mechanism and outline fidelity evaluation (World Health Organization 2018).

8 Ethical Considerations

Considering and maintaining ethical standards is crucial when evaluating fidelity in healthcare. Central to this assessment is respecting participant autonomy and privacy, ensuring informed consent, and safeguarding sensitive data collected during evaluations. Additionally, cultural sensitivity is vital, requiring adaptations to assessment tools to suit diverse contexts. For instance, in the fields of psychotherapy or social care focusing on underserved communities, observing certain practices or rituals may be considered unethical. Ethical considerations regarding attempts to observe mental health practice (Garland et al. 2008) also may interfere with some routine care providers' willingness to utilize this method. On the other hand, Schoenwald et al. (2008) found that most of the community-based mental health clinics serving children used live observation of sessions as part of clinical supervision or employed audio or videotaping, thus suggesting observation of clinical practice is not entirely uncommon in routine care. However, it remains unclear how frequently observations should ideally occur. Evaluators, healthcare professionals, researchers, and other stakeholders involved in fidelity measurements must strike a balance between rigorous assessment and participant well-being, ensuring minimal negative impacts on both participants and healthcare practitioners.

Ethical fidelity evaluation prioritizes constructive feedback for practitioners, fostering an environment of professional growth (Jarden et al. 2021). Transparency in reporting methods and findings ensures integrity, enabling continuous improvement in fidelity assessment while upholding ethical principles in healthcare.

9 Future Directions and Challenges

9.1 Emerging Trends and Future Directions in Fidelity Evaluation

Fidelity evaluation in health services is an evolving field, with promising emerging trends and future directions for advancing its assessment. This includes the development of standardized measures and addressing the digital divide in electronic monitoring. This can be achieved through improvements in how we measure and assess monitoring systems by creating consistent evaluation methods, bridging gaps between different levels of access to technology, and ensuring that methods for evaluating fidelity can be effectively scaled up (Haynes et al. 2016).

Emerging trends in fidelity assessment for health services include the use of innovative technologies such as mobile applications, wearable devices (e.g., smart watches), and electronic health records (Lindauer et al. 2019). These technologies offer opportunities for real-time monitoring and data collection, allowing for more accurate and efficient fidelity assessment (Mason et al. 2022). For example, mobile applications can be used to track intervention delivery, collect patient-reported outcomes, and provide prompts and reminders to healthcare providers (Bonar et al. 2020). Electronic health records can facilitate the integration of fidelity assessment into routine clinical practice, enabling continuous monitoring and feedback (Matthews and Stanhope 2020).

Another emerging trend is the incorporation of patient perspectives in fidelity assessment (Skovlund et al. 2020). Patient-reported outcomes and experiences are increasingly recognized as valuable indicators of intervention fidelity. Including patient perspectives in fidelity assessment can provide insights into the acceptability, feasibility, and impact of interventions from the patient's point of view (Skovlund et al. 2020). This patient-centered approach is essential for ensuring that interventions are aligned with patient needs and preferences, ultimately improving intervention outcomes.

9.2 Ongoing Challenges

Despite the emerging trends, there are ongoing challenges in evaluating fidelity that need to be addressed. One challenge is the development of standardized measures.

Currently, there is a lack of consensus on the most appropriate and comprehensive measures of fidelity (Walton 2024). Developing standardized measures that are valid, reliable, and applicable across different healthcare settings is essential for promoting consistency and comparability in fidelity assessment (Walton et al. 2020). Efforts are needed to establish guidelines and frameworks for fidelity measurement that can be widely adopted in health services research.

Another challenge is the digital divide in electronic monitoring (Matthews and Stanhope 2020). While technology holds great potential for fidelity assessment, not all individuals have equal access to or proficiency in using digital tools (Fareed et al. 2021). This digital divide can result in disparities in the accuracy and representativeness of fidelity assessment data (Fareed et al. 2021). Addressing this challenge requires considering alternative methods for data collection and ensuring equitable access to technology-based fidelity assessment approaches. Additionally, training and support should be provided to healthcare providers and patients to enhance their digital literacy and ensure equal participation in fidelity assessment (Busse et al. 2022).

Ensuring the scalability of fidelity assessment approaches is also a challenge (Stirman 2020). As interventions are implemented in larger healthcare systems or across multiple sites, scalability becomes crucial for effective fidelity assessment (Milat et al. 2020). Implementing fidelity assessment approaches that can be easily replicated, integrated into routine practice, and scaled up is essential for evaluating intervention effectiveness on a broader scale (Greenhalgh and Papoutsi 2019). Technology can play a significant role in addressing this challenge by providing automated and scalable solutions for fidelity assessment, such as remote monitoring systems and data analytics tools. Such systems and tools include access to or development of log-file data, for instance, that enable computer-generated data files containing information about usage patterns, activities, and operations within an operating system to gain an understanding of how a system is operating (Vanacore et al. 2024). Log-file data and technology have been effectively used in the evaluation of fidelity for online learning platforms in a variety of implementation contexts such as within classrooms, with teachers and students (Vanacore et al. 2024).

10 Conclusion

This chapter explored the evaluation of fidelity in health services and highlighted its key dimensions. The lack of consistent definitions, with terms often used interchangeably, can make the operationalization of fidelity assessment challenging for researchers, practitioners, and other stakeholders involved in health services evaluation. Despite these challenges, valuable insights into the different dimensions that contribute to fidelity measures are discussed in this chapter which offers practical recommendations for enhancing fidelity evaluation in health services. Understanding the factors that affect fidelity helps healthcare practitioners make better decisions to enhance patient outcomes. Institutional culture, along with methods like peer review, clinical audits, and multidisciplinary learning collaboratives, plays a crucial role in encouraging active engagement and ongoing learning. These approaches help bridge the gap between what is known and how it is implemented in service delivery.

The chapter also emphasizes the need for scalable solutions in fidelity evaluation, with technology playing a significant role. The integration of technology-driven approaches holds promise for addressing the challenge of fidelity assessment on a broader scale, reflecting the ongoing advancements in healthcare delivery.

References

Allen JD, Shleton RC, Emmons KM, Linnan LA (2017) Chapter 16: Fidelity and its relationship to implementation effectiveness, adaptation, and dissemination. In: Disseminating and implementation research in health translating science to practice, 2nd edn. Oxford University Press, pp 267–284

An M, Dusing SC, Harbourne RT, Sheridan SM (2020) What really works in an intervention? Using Fidelity measures to support optimal outcomes. Am Phys Therapy Assoc 100(5):757–765

Beck AK, Baker AL, Carter G, Robinson L, McCarter K, Wratten C, Bauer J, Wolfenden L, Britton B (2021) Is fidelity to a complex behaviour change intervention associated with patient outcomes? Exploring the relationship between dietitian adherence and competence and the nutritional status of intervention patients in a successful stepped-wedge randomised clinical trial of eating as treatment (EAT). Implement Sci 16(1):46. https://doi.org/10.1186/s13012-021-01118-y

Bellg AJ, Fau BB, Resnick B, Hecht J, Minicucci DS, Ory M, Ogedegbe G, Orwig D, Ernst D, Czajkowski S (2004) Enhancing treatment fidelity in health behavior change studies: best practices and recommendations from the NIH Behavior Change Consortium. Health Psychol 23(5):443–451

Bonar JRM, Wright S, Yadrich DM, Werkowitch M, Ridder L, Spaulding R, Smith CE (2020) Maintaining intervention Fidelity when using technology delivery across studies. Comput Inform Nurs 38(8):393–401. https://doi.org/10.1097/CIN.0000000000000625

Bond GR, Evans L, Salyers MP, Williams J, Kim HW (2000) Measurement of fidelity in psychiatric rehabilitation. Mental Health Service Research 2(2):75–87

Bond L, Simmons E, Sabbath EL (2022) Measurement and assessment of fidelity and competence in nonspecialist-delivered, evidence-based behavioral and mental health interventions: a systematic review. SSM Popul Health 19:101249. https://doi.org/10.1016/j.ssmph.2022.101249

Borrelli B, Sepinwall D, Ernst D, Bellg AJ, Czajkowski S, Breger R, DeFrancesco C, Levesque C, Sharp DL, Ogedegbe G, Resnick B, Orwig D (2005) A new tool to assess treatment fidelity and evaluation of treatment fidelity across 10 years of health behavior research. J Consult Clin Psychol 73(5):852–860. https://doi.org/10.1037/0022-006X.73.5.852

Bragstad LK, Bronken BA, Sveen U, Hjelle EG, Kitzmuller G, Martinsen R, Kvigne KJ, Mangset M, Kirkevold M (2019) Implementation fidelity in a complex intervention promoting psychosocial well-being following stroke: an explanatory sequential mixed methods study. BMC Med Res Methodol 19(1):59. https://doi.org/10.1186/s12874-019-0694-z

Breitenstein SM, Gross D, Garvey CA, Hill C, Fogg L, Resnick B (2010) Implementation fidelity in community-based interventions. Res Nurs Health 33(2):164–173. https://doi.org/10.1002/nur.20373

Breitenstein S, Robbins L, Cowell JM (2012) Attention to fidelity: why is it important. J Sch Nurs 28(6):407–408. https://www.ncbi.nlm.nih.gov/pubmed/23132849

Busse TS, Nitsche J, Kernebeck S, Jux C, Weitz J, Ehlers JP, Bork U (2022) Approaches to improvement of Digital Health Literacy (eHL) in the context of person-centered care. Int J Environ Res Public Health 19(14). https://doi.org/10.3390/ijerph19148309

Carroll C, Patterson M, Wood S, Booth A, Rick J, Balain S (2007) A conceptual framework for implementation fidelity. Implement Sci 2:40. https://doi.org/10.1186/1748-5908-2-40

Chai LK, Collins CE, May C, Brown LJ, Ashman A, Burrows TL (2021) Fidelity and acceptability of a family-focused technology-based telehealth nutrition intervention for child weight management. J Telemed Telecare 27(2):98–109. https://doi.org/10.1177/1357633X19864819

Codern-Bové N, Pujol-Ribera E, Pla M, Gonzalés-Bonilla J, Granollers S, Ballvé JL, Fanlo G, Cabezas C (2014) Motivational interviewing interactions and the primary health care challenges presented by smokers with low motivation to stop smoking: a conversation analysis. BMC Public Health 14:1225. https://doi.org/10.1186/1471-2458-14-1225

Coorey G, Peiris D, Scaria A, Mulley J, Neubeck L, Hafiz N, Redfern J (2021) An internet-based intervention for cardiovascular disease management integrated with primary care electronic health records: mixed methods evaluation of implementation fidelity and user engagement [original paper]. J Med Internet Res 23(4):e25333. https://doi.org/10.2196/25333

Cristea M, Noja GG, Stefea P, Sala AL (2020) The impact of population aging and public health support on EU labor markets. Int J Environ Res Public Health 17(4). https://doi.org/10.3390/ijerph17041439

Damschroder LJ, Aron DC, Keith RE, Kirsh SR, Alexander JA, Lowery JC (2009) Fostering implementation of health services research findings into practice: a consolidated framework for advancing implementation science. Implement Sci 4:50. https://doi.org/10.1186/1748-5908-4-50

Dane AV, Schneider BH (1998) Program integrity in primary and early secondary prevention: are implementation effects out of control? Clin Psychol Rev 18(1):23–45. https://doi.org/10.1016/S0272-7358(97)00043-3

De Geest S, Zuniga F, Brunkert T, Deschodt M, Zullig LL, Wyss K, Utzinger J (2020) Powering Swiss health care for the future: implementation science to bridge "the valley of death". Swiss Med Wkly 150:w20323. https://doi.org/10.4414/smw.2020.20323

Dixon-Woods, M. (2014). Perspectives on context: the problem of context in quality improvement (The health foundation inspiring improvement, Issue).

Dueweke AR, Archer A, Tolliver M, Polaha J (2024) Can the electronic medical record provide reliable indicators of primary care behavioral health fidelity? Comparison of accessibility and productivity indicators assessed through observational coding. Fam Syst Health 42(2):270–274. https://doi.org/10.1037/fsh0000872

Durlak JA, DuPre EP (2008) Implementation matters: a review of research on the influence of implementation on program outcomes and the factors affecting implementation. Am J Community Psychol 41(3–4):327–350. https://doi.org/10.1007/s10464-008-9165-0

Dusenbury L, Brannigan R, Falco M, Hansen WB (2003) A review of research on fidelity of implementation: implications for drug abuse prevention in school settings. Health Educ Res 18(2):237–256. https://doi.org/10.1093/her/18.2.237

Eccles MP, Mittman BS (2006) Welcome to Implementation Science. Implement Sci 1(1):1–3. https://doi.org/10.1186/1748-5908-1-1

Egeland KM, Ruud T, Ogden T, Fardig R, Lindstrom JC, Heiervang KS (2017) How to implement Illness Management and Recovery (IMR) in mental health service settings: evaluation of the implementation strategy. Int J Ment Health Syst 11:13. https://doi.org/10.1186/s13033-017-0120-z

En-Nasery-de Heer S, Uitvlugt EB, Bet PM, van den Bemt BJF, Alai A, van den Bemt PMLA, Swart EL, Karapinar-Çarkit F, Hugtenburg JG (2022 Jul) Implementation of a pharmacist-led transitional pharmaceutical care programme: process evaluation of Medication Actions to Reduce hospital admissions through a collaboration between Community and Hospital pharmacists (MARCH). J Clin Pharm Ther 47(7):1049–1069. https://doi.org/10.1111/jcpt.13645

Eysenck HJ (1952) The effects of psychotherapy, an evaluation. J Consult Psychol 16(5):319–324

Fareed N, Swoboda CM, Jonnalagadda P, Huerta TR (2021) Persistent digital divide in health-related internet use among cancer survivors: findings from the Health Information National Trends Survey, 2003-2018. J Cancer Surviv 15(1):87–98. https://doi.org/10.1007/s11764-020-00913-8

Fixen D, Blase K, Metz A, Van Dyke M (2013) Statewide implementation of evidence-based programs. Except Child 79(2):213–230

Flodgren G, Goncalves-Bradley DC, Summerbell CD (2017) Interventions to change the behaviour of health professionals and the organisation of care to promote weight reduction in children and adults with overweight or obesity. Cochrane Database Syst Rev 11(11):CD000984. https://doi.org/10.1002/14651858.CD000984.pub3

Fonagy P, Luyten P (2019) Fidelity vs. flexibility in the implementation of psychotherapies: time to move on. World Psychiatry 18(3):270–271. https://doi.org/10.1002/wps.20657

Forsythe LP, Carman KL, Szydlowski V, Fayish L, Davidson L, Hickam DH, Hall C, Bhat G, Neu D, Stewart L, Jalowsky M, Aronson N, Anyanwu CU (2019) Patient engagement in research: early findings from the Patient-Centered Outcomes Research Institute. Health Aff (Millwood) 38(3):359–367. https://doi.org/10.1377/hlthaff.2018.05067

Garland AF, McCabe KM, Yeh M (2008) Ethical challenges in practice-based mental health services research examples from research with children and families. American Psychology Association 15(2):118–124

Gerritsen DL, de Vries E, Smalbrugge M, Smeets CHW, van der Spek K, Zuidema SU, Koopmans R (2021) Implementing a multidisciplinary psychotropic medication review among nursing home residents with dementia: a process evaluation. Int Psychogeriatr 33(9):933–945. https://doi.org/10.1017/S1041610219000577

Ginsburg LR, Hoben M, Easterbrook A, Anderson RA, Estabrooks CA, Norton PG (2021) Fidelity is not easy! Challenges and guidelines for assessing fidelity in complex interventions. Trials 22(1):372. https://doi.org/10.1186/s13063-021-05322-5

Glasgow RE, Harden SM, Gaglio B, Rabin B, Smith ML, Porter GC, Ory MG, Estabrooks PA (2019) RE-AIM planning and evaluation framework: adapting to new science and practice with a 20-year review. Front Public Health 7(64):1–9. https://doi.org/10.3389/fpubh.2019.00064

Goodyer IM, Reynolds S, Barrett B, Byford S, Dubicka B, Hill J, Holland F, Kelvin R, Midgley N, Roberts C, Senior R, Target M, Widmer B, Wilkinson P, Fonagy P (2017) Cognitive-behavioural therapy and short-term psychoanalytic psychotherapy versus brief psychosocial intervention in adolescents with unipolar major depression (IMPACT): a multicentre, pragmatic, observer-blind, randomised controlled trial. Health Technol Assess 21(12):1–94. https://doi.org/10.3310/hta21120

Greenhalgh T, Papoutsi C (2019) Spreading and scaling up innovation and improvement. BMJ 365:l2068. https://doi.org/10.1136/bmj.l2068

Gresham F (1989) Assessment of treatment integrity in school consultation and prereferral intervention. Sch Psychol Rev 18(1):37–50

Grimshaw JM, Presseau J, Tetroe J, Eccles MP, Francis JJ, Godin G, Graham ID, Hux JE, Johnston M, Légaré F, Lemyre L, Robinson N, Zwarenstein M (2014) Looking inside the black box: results of a theory-based process evaluation exploring the results of a randomized controlled trial of printed educational messages to increase primary care physicians' diabetic retinopathy referrals. Implement Sci 9(86). https://doi.org/10.1186/1748-5908-9-86

Guerbaai RA, De Geest S, Popejoy LL, Simon M, Wellens NIH, Denhaerynck K, Zúñiga F (2023) Evaluating the implementation fidelity to a successful nurse-led model (INTERCARE) which reduced nursing home unplanned hospitalisations. BMC Health Serv Res 23(1):138. https://doi.org/10.1186/s12913-023-09146-8

Habitu YA, Biks GA, Worku AG, Gelaye KA (2022) Individual and contextual factors affect the implementation fidelity of youth-friendly services, Northwest Ethiopia: a multilevel analysis. PLoS One 17(2):e0263733. https://doi.org/10.1371/journal.pone.0263733

Hailemariam M, Bustos T, Montgomery B, Barajas R, Evans LB, Drahota A (2019) Evidence-based intervention sustainability strategies: a systematic review. Implement Sci 14(1):57. https://doi.org/10.1186/s13012-019-0910-6

Halek M, Reuther S, Muller-Widmer R, Trutschel D, Holle D (2020) Dealing with the behaviour of residents with dementia that challenges: a stepped-wedge cluster randomized trial of two types of dementia-specific case conferences in nursing homes (FallDem). Int J Nurs Stud 104:103435. https://doi.org/10.1016/j.ijnurstu.2019.103435

Harachi TW, Abbott RD, Catalano RF, Haggerty KP, Fleming CB (1999) Opening the black box: using process evaluation measures to assess implementation and theory building. Am J Community Psychol 27(5):711–731. https://doi.org/10.1023/A:1022194005511

Hasson H (2010) Systematic evaluation of implementation fidelity of complex interventions in health and social care. Implement Sci 5(1):67. https://doi.org/10.1186/1748-5908-5-67

Hasson H (2015) Intervention fidelity in clinical trials. In: Richards DA, Rahm Hallberg I (eds) Complex interventions in health: an overview of research methods, 1st edn. Routledge. https://doi.org/10.4324/9780203794982

Haynes A, Brennan S, Redman S, Williamson A, Gallego G, Butow P, team, C. (2016) Figuring out fidelity: a worked example of the methods used to identify, critique and revise the essential elements of a contextualised intervention in health policy agencies. Implement Sci 11:23. https://doi.org/10.1186/s13012-016-0378-6

Hoffmann TC, Glasziou PP, Boutron I, Milne R, Perera R, Moher D, Altman DG, Barbour V, Macdonald H, Johnston M, Lamb SE, Dixon-Woods M, McCulloch P, Wyatt JC, Chan AW, Michie S (2014) Better reporting of interventions: template for intervention description and replication (TIDieR) checklist and guide. BMJ 348:g1687. https://doi.org/10.1136/bmj.g1687

Holle D, Muller-Widmer R, Reuther S, Rosier-Segschneider U, Graf R, Roes M, Halek M (2019) Process evaluation of the context, reach and recruitment of participants and delivery of dementia-specific case conferences (WELCOME-IdA) in nursing homes (FallDem): a mixed-methods study. Trials 20(1):45. https://doi.org/10.1186/s13063-018-3147-9

Janducci AL, Gramani-Say K, da Silva LC, Florido JVB, Novaes ADC, Porcatti LR, Ansai JH (2023) Treatment fidelity and satisfaction with an intervention based on case management for older people with falls history: randomized clinical trial. Geriatr Nurs 52:48–55. https://doi.org/10.1016/j.gerinurse.2023.05.002

Jarden A, Rashid T, Roache A, Lomas T (2021) Ethical guidelines for positive psychology practice (English: version 2). International Journal of Wellbeing 11(3):1–38. https://doi.org/10.5502/ijw.v11i3.1819

Jha AK, Larizgoitia I, Audera-Lopez C, Prasopa-Plaizier N, Waters H, Bates DW (2013) The global burden of unsafe medical care: analytic modelling of observational studies. BMJ Qual Saf 22(10):809–815. https://doi.org/10.1136/bmjqs-2012-001748

Joyce A, Ollis D, Kearney S, Leung L, Foenander E (2019) The influence of contextual factors on implementation fidelity in a whole school approach to prevention of violence against women. Health Promot J Austr 30(2):238–245. https://doi.org/10.1002/hpja.198

Kendall PC, Frank HE (2018) Implementing evidence-based treatment protocols: flexibility within fidelity. Clin Psychol (New York) 25(4). https://doi.org/10.1111/cpsp.12271

Kilbourne AM, Neumann MS, Pincus HA, Bauer MS, Stall R 2007 Implementing evidence-based interventions in health care: application of the replicating effective programs framework. Implement Sci 2(42). https://www.ncbi.nlm.nih.gov/pubmed/18067681

King HA, Bosworth H (2014) Treatment fidelity in health services research. In: Hagermoser Sanetti LM, Kratochwill TR (eds) Treatment integrity: a foundation for evidence-based practice in applied psychology. American Psychological Association, pp 15–33. https://doi.org/10.1037/14275-003

Kirk JW, Nilsen P, Andersen O, Stefansdottir NT, Gronfeldt B, Brodsgaard R, Pedersen BS, Bandholm T, Tjornhoj-Thomsen T, Pedersen MM (2021) Adaptations and modifications to a co-designed intervention and its clinical implementation: a qualitative study in Denmark. BMC Health Serv Res 21(1):1108. https://doi.org/10.1186/s12913-021-07142-4

Klaic M, Kapp S, Hudson P, Chapman W, Denehy L, Story D, Francis JJ (2022) Implementability of healthcare interventions: an overview of reviews and development of a conceptual framework. Implement Sci 17(1):10. https://doi.org/10.1186/s13012-021-01171-7

Knudsen HK, Drainoni ML, Gilbert L, Huerta TR, Oser CB, Aldrich AM, Campbell ANC, Crable EL, Garner BR, Glasgow LM, Goddard-Eckrich D, Marks KR, McAlearney AS, Oga EA, Scalise AL, Walker DM (2020) Model and approach for assessing implementation context and fidelity in the HEALing Communities Study. Drug Alcohol Depend 217:108330. https://doi.org/10.1016/j.drugalcdep.2020.108330

Lara M, Bryant-Stephens T, Damitz M, Findley S, Gavillan JG, Mitchell H, Ohadike YU, Persky VW, Valencia GR, Smith LR, Rosenthal M, Thyne S, Uyeda K, Viswanathan M, Woodell C (2011) Balancing "fidelity" and community context in the adaptation of asthma evidence-based

interventions in the "real world". Health Promot Pract 12(6 Suppl 1):63S–72S. https://doi.org/10.1177/1524839911414888
Lemire C, Rousseau M, Dionne C (2022) A Comparison of Fidelity Implementation Frameworks Used in the Field of Early Intervention. American Journal of Evaluation 44(2): 236–252. https://doi.org/10.1177/10982140211008978
Lichstein KL, Riedel BW, Grieve R (1994) Fair tests of clinical trials: a treatment implementation model. Adv Behav Res Therapy 16(1):1–29
Lindauer A, McKenzie G, LaFazia D, McNeill L, Mincks K, Spoden N, Myers M, Mattek N, Teri LL (2019) Using technology to facilitate fidelity assessments: the Tele-STAR caregiver intervention. J Med Internet Res 21(5):e13599. https://doi.org/10.2196/13599
Marques L, Valentine SE, Kaysen D, Mackintosh MA, Dixon De Silva LE, Ahles EM, Youn SJ, Shtasel DL, Simon NM, Wiltsey-Stirman S (2019) Provider fidelity and modifications to cognitive processing therapy in a diverse community health clinic: associations with clinical change. J Consult Clin Psychol 87(4):357–369. https://doi.org/10.1037/ccp0000384
Mars T, Ellard D, Carnes D, Homer K, Underwood M, Taylor SJ (2013) Fidelity in complex behaviour change interventions: a standardised approach to evaluate intervention integrity. BMJ Open 3(11):e003555. https://doi.org/10.1136/bmjopen-2013-003555
Mason M, Cho Y, Rayo J, Gong Y, Harris M, Jiang Y (2022) Technologies for medication adherence monitoring and technology assessment criteria: narrative review. JMIR Mhealth Uhealth 10(3):e35157. https://doi.org/10.2196/35157
Matthews EB, Stanhope V (2020) A help or a hindrance: the role of electronic health records in implementing new practices in community mental health clinics. Psychiatr Serv 71(10):1065–1068. https://doi.org/10.1176/appi.ps.201900470
McNerney NA, Losensky MJ, Lash MM, Rozaieski KR, Ortiz D, Garcia AN, Rethorn ZD (2020) Low theoretical fidelity hinders the research on health coaching for opioid reduction: a systematic review of randomized controlled trials. PLoS One 15(10):e0241434. https://doi.org/10.1371/journal.pone.0241434
Meyer C, Ogrin R, Golenko X, Cyarto E, Paine K, Walsh W, Hutchinson A, Lowthian J (2022) A codesigned fit-for-purpose implementation framework for aged care. J Eval Clin Pract 28(3):421–435. https://doi.org/10.1111/jep.13660
Mihalic S (2004) The importance of implementation fidelity. Emot Behav Disord Youth 4(4):83–105
Milat A, Lee K, Conte K, Grunseit A, Wolfenden L, van Nassau F, Orr N, Sreeram P, Bauman A (2020) Intervention scalability assessment tool: a decision support tool for health policy makers and implementers. Health Res Policy Syst 18(1):1. https://doi.org/10.1186/s12961-019-0494-2
Miller WR, Rollnick S (2014) The effectiveness and ineffectiveness of complex behavioral interventions: impact of treatment fidelity. Contemp Clin Trials 37(2):234–241. https://doi.org/10.1016/j.cct.2014.01.005
Moncher FJ, Prinz RJ (1991) Treatment fidelity in outcome studies. Clin Psychol Rev 11(3):247–266
Moore GF, Audrey S, Barker M, Bond L, Bonell C, Hardeman W, Moore L, O'Cathain A, Tinati T, Wight D, Baird J (2015) Process evaluation of complex interventions: Medical Research Council guidance. BMJ 350:h1258. https://doi.org/10.1136/bmj.h1258
Morello RT, Barker AL, Ayton DR, Landgren F, Kamar J, Hill KD, Brand CA, Sherrington C, Wolfe R, Rifat S, Stoelwinder J (2017) Implementation fidelity of a nurse-led falls prevention program in acute hospitals during the 6-PACK trial. BMC Health Serv Res 17(1):383. https://doi.org/10.1186/s12913-017-2315-z
Morris RL, Hill KD, Ackerman IN, Ayton D, Arendts G, Brand C, Cameron P, Etherton-Beer CD, Flicker L, Hill AM, Hunter P, Lowthian JA, Morello R, Nyman SR, Redfern J, Smit V, Barker AL (2019) A mixed methods process evaluation of a person-centred falls prevention program. BMC Health Serv Res 19(1):906. https://doi.org/10.1186/s12913-019-4614-z
Nieuwlaat R, Wilczynski N, Navarro T, Hobson N, Jeffery R, Keepanasseril A, Agoritsas T, Mistry N, Iorio A, Jack S, Sivaramalingam B, Iserman E, Mustafa RA, Jedraszewski D, Cotoi C, Haynes RB (2014) Interventions for enhancing medication adherence. Cochrane Database Syst Rev 2014(11):CD000011. https://doi.org/10.1002/14651858.CD000011.pub4

Pérez D, Van der Stuyft P, Zabala M, d. C., Castro, M., & Lefèvre, P. (2016) A modified theoretical framework to assess implementation fidelity of adaptive public health interventions. Implement Sci 11(1):91. https://doi.org/10.1186/s13012-016-0457-8

Peters S, Sukumar K, Blanchard S, Ramasamy A, Malinowski J, Ginex P, Senerth E, Corremans M, Munn Z, Kredo T, Remon LP, Ngeh E, Kalman L, Alhabib S, Amer YS, Gagliardi A (2022) Trends in guideline implementation: an updated scoping review. Implement Sci 17(1):50. https://doi.org/10.1186/s13012-022-01223-6

Peterson L, Homer AL, Wonderlich SA (1982) The integrity of independent variables in behavior analysis. J Appl Behav Anal 15(4):477–492

Piryani RM, Piryani S (2019) Clinical vignette-based interactive discussion sessions: feedback from residents. Adv Med Educ Pract 10:829–833. https://doi.org/10.2147/AMEP.S218157

Poltawski L, Norris M, Dean S (2014) Intervention fidelity: developing an experience-based model for rehabilitation research. J Rehabil Med 46(7):609–615. https://doi.org/10.2340/16501977-1848

Praveen D, Patel A, Raghu A, Clifford GD, Maulik PK, Mohammad Abdul A, Mogulluru K, Tarassenko L, MacMahon S, Peiris D (2014) SMARTHealth India: development and field evaluation of a Mobile clinical decision support system for cardiovascular diseases in rural India. JMIR Mhealth Uhealth 2(4):e54. https://doi.org/10.2196/mhealth.3568

Proctor E, Silmere H, Raghavan R, Hovmand P, Aarons G, Bunger A, Griffey R, Hensley M (2011) Outcomes for implementation research: conceptual distinctions, measurement challenges, and research agenda. Admin Pol Ment Health 38(2):65–76. https://doi.org/10.1007/s10488-010-0319-7

Quasdorf T, Riesner C, Dichter MN, Dortmann O, Bartholomeyczik S, Halek M (2017) Implementing dementia care mapping to develop person-centred care: results of a process evaluation within the Leben-QD II trial. J Clin Nurs 26(5–6):751–765. https://doi.org/10.1111/jocn.13522

Quay HC (1977) The three faces of evaluation. Crim Justice Behav 4(4):341–354

Raghu A, Praveen D, Peiris D, Tarassenko L, Clifford G (2015) Engineering a mobile health tool for resource-poor settings to assess and manage cardiovascular disease risk: SMARThealth study. BMC Med Inform Decis Mak 15:36. https://doi.org/10.1186/s12911-015-0148-4

Rosas SR (2017) Systems thinking and complexity: considerations for health promoting schools. Health Promot Int 32(2):301–311. https://doi.org/10.1093/heapro/dav109

Rowbotham S, Conte K, Hawe P (2019) Variation in the operationalisation of dose in implementation of health promotion interventions: insights and recommendations from a scoping review. Implement Sci 14(1):56. https://doi.org/10.1186/s13012-019-0899-x

Saarijärvi M, Wallin L, Moons P et al (2022) Implementation fidelity of a transition program for adolescents with congenital heart disease: the STEPSTONES project. BMC Health Serv Res 22:153. https://doi.org/10.1186/s12913-022-07549-7

Schinckus L, Van den Broucke S, van der Zanden G, Levin-Zamir D, Mueller G, Riemenschneider H, Hayter VA-O, Yardley L, Schillinger D, Doyle GA-O, Ganahl KA-O, Pelikan J, Chang PA-O (2021) To adapt or not to adapt: the association between implementation fidelity and the effectiveness of diabetes self-management education. Int J Environ Res Public Health 18(8). https://doi.org/10.3390/ijerph18084095

Schoenwald SK, Chapman JE, Kelleher K, Hoagwood KE, Landsverk J, Stevens J, Glisson C, Rolls-Reutz J, Research Network on Youth Mental, H (2008) A survey of the infrastructure for children's mental health services: implications for the implementation of empirically supported treatments (ESTs). Admin Pol Ment Health 35(1–2):84–97. https://doi.org/10.1007/s10488-007-0147-6

Skovlund PC, Nielsen BK, Thaysen HV, Schmidt H, Finset A, Hansen KA, Lomborg K (2020) The impact of patient involvement in research: a case study of the planning, conduct and dissemination of a clinical, controlled trial. Res Involv Engagem 6:43. https://doi.org/10.1186/s40900-020-00214-5

Sprange K, Mountain G, Craig C (2021) Evaluation of intervention fidelity of a complex psychosocial intervention lifestyle matters: a randomised controlled trial. BMJ Open 11(4):e043478. https://doi.org/10.1136/bmjopen-2020-043478

Stirman SW (2020) Commentary: challenges and opportunities in the assessment of fidelity and related constructs. Admin Pol Ment Health 47(6):932–934. https://doi.org/10.1007/s10488-020-01069-4

Swindle T, Selig JP, Rutledge JM, Whiteside-Mansell L, Curran G (2018) Fidelity monitoring in complex interventions: a case study of the WISE intervention. Arch Public Health 76:53. https://doi.org/10.1186/s13690-018-0292-2

Toomey E, Hardeman W, Hankonen N, Byrne M, McSharry J, Matvienko-Sikar K, Lorencatto F (2020) Focusing on fidelity: narrative review and recommendations for improving intervention fidelity within trials of health behaviour change interventions. Health Psychol Behav Med 8(1):132–151. https://doi.org/10.1080/21642850.2020.1738935

Treichler EBH, Mercado R, Oakes D, Perivoliotis D, Gallegos-Rodriguez Y, Sosa E, Cisneros E, Spaulding WD, Granholm E, Light GA, Rabin B (2022) Using a stakeholder-engaged, iterative, and systematic approach to adapting collaborative decision skills training for implementation in VA psychosocial rehabilitation and recovery centers. BMC Health Serv Res 22(1):1543. https://doi.org/10.1186/s12913-022-08833-2

Triplett NS, Woodard GS, Johnson C, Nguyen JK, AlRasheed R, Song F, Stoddard S, Mugisha JC, Sievert K, Dorsey S (2022) Stakeholder engagement to inform evidence-based treatment implementation for children's mental health: a scoping review. Implement Sci Commun 3(1):82. https://doi.org/10.1186/s43058-022-00327-w

Trutschel D, Blatter C, Simon M, Holle D, Reuther S, Brunkert T (2023) The unrecognized role of fidelity in effectiveness-implementation hybrid trials: simulation study and guidance for implementation researchers. BMC Med Res Methodol 23(1):116. https://doi.org/10.1186/s12874-023-01943-3

U.S. Department of Health and Human Services (2002) Finding the balance: Program fidelity and adaptation in substance abuse prevention—a state-of-the-art review (Substance Abuse and Mental Health Services Administration Center for Substance Abuse Prevention, Issue). https://www.csun.edu/sites/default/files/FindingBalance1.pdf

U.S. Department of Health and Human Services (2013) Core components: identifying and operationalizing what makes programs work. https://aspe.hhs.gov/sites/default/files/migrated_legacy_files//139036/rb_CoreIntervention.pdf

Vanacore K, Ottmar E, Liu A, Sales A (2024) Remote monitoring of implementation fidelity using log-file data from multiple online learning platforms. J Res Technol Educ 1-21:706. https://doi.org/10.1080/15391523.2024.2303025

VandenBos, G. R. (1980). Psychotherapy: practice, research, policy. Sage.

von Thiele Schwarz U, Giannotta F, Neher M, Zetterlund J, Hasson H (2021) Professionals' management of the fidelity-adaptation dilemma in the use of evidence-based interventions-an intervention study. Implement Sci Commun 2(1):31. https://doi.org/10.1186/s43058-021-00131-y

Walton H (2024) Towards comprehensive fidelity evaluations: consideration of enactment measures in quality improvement interventions. BMJ Qual Saf 33:78–81

Walton H, Spector A, Williamson M, Tombor I, Michie S (2020) Developing quality fidelity and engagement measures for complex health interventions. Br J Health Psychol 25(1):39–60. https://doi.org/10.1111/bjhp.12394

Wilson DK, Griffin S, Saunders RP, Kitzman-Ulrich H, Meyers DC, Mansard L (2009) Using process evaluation for program improvement in dose, fidelity and reach: the ACT trial experience. Int J Behav Nutr Phys Act 6:79. https://doi.org/10.1186/1479-5868-6-79

World Health Organisation (2018) Delivering quality health services: a global imperative for universal health coverage. World Health Organization, Organisation for Economic Cooperation and Development, and The World Bank, Geneva

Zurynski Y, Ludlow K, Testa L, Augustsson H, Herkes-Deane J, Hutchinson K, Lamprell G, McPherson E, Carrigan A, Ellis LA, Dharmayani PNA, Smith CL, Richardson L, Dammery G, Singh N, Braithwaite J (2023) Built to last? Barriers and facilitators of healthcare program sustainability: a systematic integrative review. Implement Sci 18(1):62. https://doi.org/10.1186/s13012-023-01315-x

Evaluation Themes

Evaluating Digitally Enabled Health Services

Carolyn Steele Gray, Nelson Shen, Quynh Pham, and David Wiljer

Abstract

This chapter provides an overview of how to effectively assess the impact of digital health solutions on core objectives of high-performing health systems at the patient, provider, and system levels. Key measures of impact on patient outcomes and experience, provider experience, system efficiency, and equity related to digitally enabled models of care are outlined to help evaluators understand

C. S. Gray (✉)
Science of Care Institute and Lunenfeld-Tanenbaum Research Institute, Sinai Health, Toronto, ON, Canada

Institute of Health Policy Management and Evaluation, University of Toronto, Toronto, Ontario, Canada
e-mail: Carolyn.SteeleGray@sinaihealth.ca

N. Shen
Digital Mental Health Lab, Krembil Center for NeuroInformatics, Centre for Addiction and Mental Health, Toronto, ON, Canada

Institute of Health Policy Management and Evaluation, University of Toronto, Toronto, Ontario, Canada
e-mail: Nelson.Shen@camh.ca

Q. Pham
Centre for Digital Therapeutics, University Health Network, Toronto, ON, Canada

Institute of Health Policy Management and Evaluation, University of Toronto, Toronto, Ontario, Canada
e-mail: Q.Pham@uhn.ca

D. Wiljer
Institute of Health Policy Management and Evaluation, University of Toronto, Toronto, Ontario, Canada

Education, Technology & Innovation, University Health Network, Toronto, Ontario, Canada
e-mail: David.Wiljer@uhn.ca

A. Kaehne, J. Feather (eds.), *Handbook of Health Services Evaluation*,
https://doi.org/10.1007/978-3-031-87869-5_17

how impact can be measured. To effectively capture this impact, this chapter outlines how commonly used evaluation approaches can be adapted to adequately capture digitally enabled services and highlights the importance of adopting developmental and design thinking to evaluate these types of interventions. The chapter finishes with some guidance on choosing among the different approaches when considering capturing the impact on the quintuple aim.

Keywords
Digital health · Evaluation · Healthcare · Quintuple aim

1 Introduction

Digital health solutions ranging from information communication technologies, remote monitoring systems and devices, and clinical and operations data systems are woven into the fabric of health and social care service delivery globally. For nearly 20 years, the World Health Organization (WHO) has been urging countries to strengthen their digital health implementation efforts and in 2020 released a global strategy in support of this effort (World Health Organization 2021). Digital health technologies, sometimes referred to as health information systems or eHealth technologies, have a myriad of definitions in the wider literature. A 2020 review of the literature identified 95 unique definitions of digital health, finding that central to these definitions was a concern with the provision of healthcare to support population health and individual well-being (Fatehi et al. 2020). Broadly, the dominant uses for digital health in healthcare delivery include: monitoring and tracking of patient health information; enabling communication between providers, patients, and families; collecting, managing, and using health data for system planning and monitoring; advancing diagnosis and treatment; supporting self-management; and ensuring care continuity (Shaw et al. 2017; Abernethy et al. 2022).

In 2019, the Digital Health Action Collaborative in the National Academy of Medicine in the United States developed a helpful visual of the evolving applications of digital technology in health and healthcare, which brings together these different uses of technology linked to specific functions and available applications (see Fig. 1).

2 Impact of Digital Health

Increasingly, global health systems have been adopting the quadruple aim and equity framework to assess the quality of their care services (Strategies for Quality Care 2023; Canadian Institute for Health Research 2023). The quadruple aim of high-performing health systems includes improving patient outcomes, patient experience, provider experience, and efficiency. Recently, equity has been added as an important aim which can be viewed as either a cross-cutting aim (embedded within the other four aims) or as a fifth aim (making it the quintuple aim of high-performing

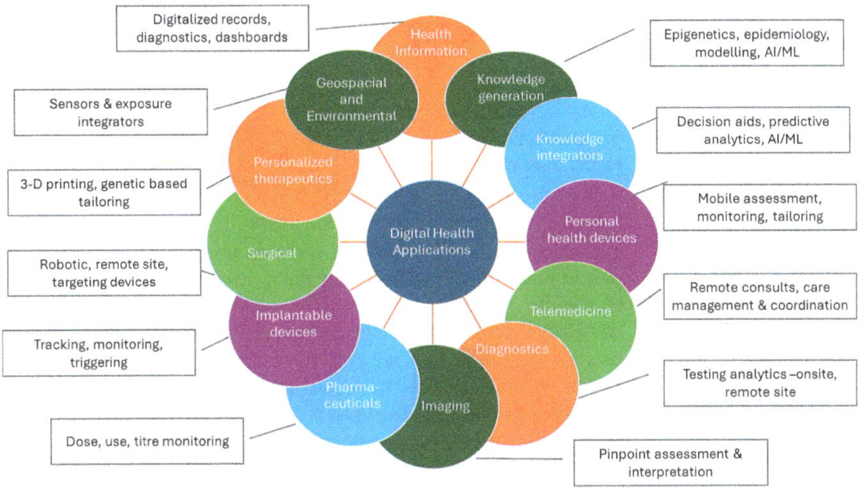

Fig. 1 The evolving applications of digital technology in health and healthcare. Adapted from Abernethy et al. (2022)

health systems). Digital health solutions have been found to have a significant impact on the quintuple aim objectives. This first section of this chapter offers an overview of some of the impacts of digital health tools in relation to the quintuple aim and the types of measures used to assess impact.

2.1 Patient Experience and Outcomes

Often digital health technologies are implemented in order to improve patient outcomes and/or experiences. Evaluations in this field have explored the impact of patient-facing technologies such as patient portals, personal health records, internet-based interventions, and self-management solutions (such as wearables and mobile monitoring applications) (Brands et al. 2022; Zanaboni et al. 2018). As this is a vast and growing literature, many systematic and scoping reviews have been conducted to attempt to quantify the impact of these technologies on patient outcomes and experience. A few of these reviews offer helpful categorization of common patient-related outcomes that have been collected to evaluate the impact of technology (summarized in Table 1).

In a review by Zanaboni et al., it was found that patient access to their records showed some improvement in safety (identification of medication errors), improved self-care, communication, and engagement with clinicians (Zanaboni et al. 2018). While this review finds that these benefits were most noted for patients with specific chronic health conditions, another review by Brands et al. suggested that favorable effects of patient-centered digital health records are mainly experienced among those with a lower disease burden (Brands et al. 2022). These types of mixed results are common in the evaluation of technologies on patient outcomes, with these

Table 1 Patient outcome measures linked to digital interventions (Brands et al. 2022; Zanaboni et al. 2018)

Outcome category	Measures
Health and clinical outcomes	Disease events and complications; vital parameters; laboratory parameters; mortality risk factors; health status; safety and medication management
Patient-reported outcomes	Self-management and self-efficacy, patient engagement, health-related quality of life, treatment adherence
Psychological and behavioral outcomes (can include patient-reported outcomes)	Self-management and self-efficacy; satisfaction; patient activation; patient-provider communication; patient access to information; acceptance or endorsement; health literacy; awareness and knowledge; perceived benefits; concerns (privacy, security); perceived social support; adherence to treatment; empowerment; attitudes; harms (distress, stress, anxiety)
Healthcare utilization	Emergency department visits and hospitalizations; recommended care services; regular workload; outpatient clinic visits; access or wait time; urgent care utilization
Technology-related outcomes	Patient satisfaction; feasibility; acceptability; patient adoption; professional practice; patient utilization; system attributes linked to patient use (usability, utility, personalization, efficiency)

variations often being attributed to outcome effects being moderated by personal factors (ethnicity, education level, health literacy, health status) (Zanaboni et al. 2018).

Some of the outcomes noted in Table 1 also include what would be considered patient experience measures. Patient experience has been captured in multiple ways and is often related to the specific model of care and intervention being studied. Wang et al.'s systematic review of patient experience of digital health identified nine factors that can influence patient experience with digital health (Wang et al. 2022). These factors include patient capability, patient opportunity, patient motivation, intervention technology, intervention functionality, intervention interaction design, organizational environment, physical environment, and social environment. What this review shows is that when assessing patient experience with digital health technologies, it is important to consider how multiple factors, beyond just the technology itself, may influence experience measures like satisfaction and intent to use.

2.2 Provider Experience and Outcomes

Evaluations of digitally enabled models of care will often explore the impact on provider experience, and sometimes (but less often) provider outcomes. Experience-related evaluations and systematic and scoping reviews have sought to understand providers' experience with conducting virtual care visits (Lampickienė and Davoody 2022), remote patient monitoring (Palmieriserrano et al. 2023), clinical decision-support tools (Kimmel et al. 2018), and, perhaps most frequently studied, the use of electronic health and medical records systems (Kruse et al. 2022). Similar to patient measures related to the technology itself, evaluations of provider experience will include technology-related experiences such as usability, utilization, and acceptability. These studies, however, will also include explorations of how technology fits into team and organizational workflows and activities (with an emphasis often on how technology can improve information sharing, communication and efficiency (Hobensack et al. 2022)), impacts on decision-making, and how technology may influence relationships with patients and other providers (Lampickienė and Davoody 2022).

While there are fewer examples, there is an increasing number of studies that look at the impact of technology on provider outcomes. More studies are emerging that assess how technologies can contribute to physician burnout (Yan et al. 2021; Harris et al. 2018; Ehrenfeld and Wanderer 2018), impact professional satisfaction and identity, influence intention to leave (Ehrenfeld and Wanderer 2018; Muhiyaddin et al. 2022; Jussupow et al. 2018), and contribute to cognitive fatigue (Sbaffi et al. 2020). One systematic literature review of the impact of digital health transformation on nursing practice categorized provider experience and outcomes using socio-technical themes outlined in Table 2 (Livesay et al. 2023). This review identified many variables that can be considered when evaluating digital health's impact on providers. In Table 2, we offer potential measures linked to these socio-technical themes identified by Liversay et al.'s review.

2.3 Efficiency and Cost

When considering digitally enabled models of care and intervention, efficiency and cost-related evaluation will often explore organization and system-level impact and measures. In scanning the literature in this field, reviews of evaluations and assessments of digital health's impact on efficiency and cost will tend to focus on specific types of technologies like patient portals (Carini et al. 2021), remote monitoring (Knight et al. 2021), or EMRs (Nguyen et al. 2022; Keasberry et al. 2017), or through exploring the system impacts of particular care pathways like wound care (Shi et al. 2022) or digitally enabled health interventions for patients (Zanaboni et al. 2018).

Some components of efficiency and cost are captured in the above examples around patient and provider outcomes. In particular, measures of healthcare utilization, safety (e.g., errors and adverse events), and workflow measures around clinical efficiency (such as reduced documentation time, using diagnostic aids, and appropriate test orders) will be included in assessments of how digital health tools impact healthcare delivery efficiency (Keasberry et al. 2017). More targeted economic evaluations of digital technologies, like EMRs, have been assessed using cost-benefit analysis, cost studies, impact evaluations, and effectiveness and efficiency analyses that include cost-effectiveness (such as cost per QALY gained), cost efficiency, and productivity analyses (Nguyen et al. 2022; Gentili et al. 2022). Identifying the primary outcomes for the economic analysis is critical and involves engagement with critical stakeholders. Another important challenge in considering cost evaluations with regard to digital health is accounting for the cost of the

Table 2 Example provider-level measures of experience and outcomes linked to socio-technical themes from Livesay et al. (2023)

Socio-technical themes	Considerations	Example measures
Hardware and software computing infrastructure	Technical requirements to ensure smooth and easy access by users (e.g., internet access and quality of connection, appropriate functions to perform clinical tasks)	Availability of reliable internet connection Technology function meets clinical task requirements
Human-computer interface	Usability of technology (e.g., smooth audio and video connection, amount of data entry required)	System Usability Scale (Brooke 1996; Lewis 2018) Amount of time spent entering data Ease of use
Clinical content	Capacity of systems to manage data appropriately (e.g., extracting meaningful insights from data)	Perceived quality or value addition of clinical information to clinician's work
People	Personal characteristics and training needs of system users (e.g., digital literacy, trust in technology, cognitive fatigue). Includes necessary human resources to support the use of technology (e.g., available digital health coach, supportive leadership)	Digital literacy of staff Trust in digital systems Availability of digital supports for staff
Workflows and communication	Technology's ability to support clinical communication needs and workflows (e.g., integration of tools into practice EMRs, communication efficiency)	Availability of data across different systems/clinics Ease of communication between clinicians and patients Technology supports clinical workflow
Internal organizational policies, procedures, and culture	Organizational policies and funding methods related to the use of technology (e.g., reimbursement for services, regulations regarding clinician responsibilities around technology use)	Funding supports available for ongoing use of technology Identified roles and responsibilities related to technology use
External rules, regulations, and pressures	External policy, funding, and regulatory guidelines and laws related to the use of technology (e.g., multijurisdictional licensure and data standards, litigation concerns)	Available data standards for sharing information across platforms Established processes for complying with legal standards
System measurement and monitoring	Processes in place for regular assessment of technology effectiveness and sustainability (e.g., systemic approach to measuring clinician burnout related to technology)	Available digital sources to collect effectiveness and/or efficiency data Process plan for collecting impact data on clinicians and patients

technology itself, which has interacting and evolving features with associated shifts in costs to be considered (Gomes et al. 2022).

2.4 Equity

Debates regarding digital health's ability to support or worsen health equity abound in the literature. The number of potential dangers with adopting digital health solutions without considering the equity impacts was particularly noted during and after the COVID-19 pandemic, where health systems had to quickly adopt solutions to continue to deliver services during lockdowns, but systemic inequities persisted or worsened (2020). Important to recognize with regard to equity as related to digital technologies is the concept of the "digital divide" which can help to understand the relationship between social inequity and technology. Shaw et al. (2021) identify three potential divide "levels": first-level divide being the gap between those who have technologies and those who do not; second level relating to disparities in technology literacy; and third level being around disparities in outcomes related to the use of digital technologies. All three divide levels should be considered when evaluating digital health technologies.

In addition to attending to the digital divide, understanding the relationship between health equity and digital health requires recognizing health equity as both a process and an outcome, a process that seeks to remove systemic barriers in order to reach optional or "full" health for all individuals and communities (Evans et al. 2023). As such, the explorations of digital health in relation to equity have explored measures in both of these domains. In Woolley et al.'s scoping review, digital health equity was assessed in relation to an individual's ability to *access, use, and engage with digital health technologies*, in relation to the PROGRESS PLUS framework, a framework that categorizes factors through which health inequities may be experienced, e.g., place of residence, race, ethnicity, culture, language, occupation, gender and sex, religion, education socioeconomic status, social capital, disability, age and sexual orientation (Woolley et al. 2023). This review found significant inequities with regard to access, use, and engagement with digital health technologies along multiple characteristics from the PROGRESS PLUS framework.

Whiley Wooley et al.'s review focuses on process measures related to digital health, Evans et al. break down both process and outcomes that could be related to equity and digital health (Evans et al. 2023). In the Evans review, process measures of interest included digital and health literacy, where outcome measures included user's self-efficacy, self-management, and self-advocacy, all of which were presumed to increase the health status of communities. In some studies, however, access to technology is considered an outcome as well, exploring issues such as geographic and spatial factors (Cuadros et al. 2023), as well as qualitative explorations of relationships, fear, and trust (Kaihlanen et al. 2022) that can influence individuals' ability to access and ultimately benefit from digital health technologies.

As digital health equity has emerged as a critical issue, multiple frameworks have been developed that can help evaluators to account for individual,

Table 3 Digital environment measurement domains (building on Richardson et al. 2022)

	Levels of influence			
	Individual	Interpersonal	Community	Societal
Digital environment	Digital literacy Digital self-efficacy Technology access Attitudes toward use	Implicit tech bias Interdependence (e.g., shared devices) Patient-tech-clinician relationship	Community infrastructure Healthcare infrastructure Community tech norms Community partners	Tech policy Data standards Design standards Social norms and ideologies Algorithmic bias

organizational, institutional, and environmental factors related to digital health equity. Crawford and Serhal developed the Digital Health Equity Framework in 2020 which brings together social and *digital* determinants of health which includes: access to digital resources, use of digital resources, digital health literacy, beliefs about the potential for digital health, values and cultural norms related to digital resources, and integration of digital resources into the community and health infrastructure. Similarly, Richardson et al. developed a framework for digital health equity which builds from the National Institute on Minority Health and Health Disparities Research Framework to outline the digital environment as a domain of influence for individual health (Richardson et al. 2022). In addition to the important individual and intersectional lens offered by Crawford and Serhal (2020), Richardson et al. (2022) also note how the digital environment can also exert influence at the interpersonal (e.g., patient-tech-provider relationship), community (e.g., community infrastructure), and societal levels (e.g., technology policy and data standards). These frameworks can be useful tools for evaluators who want to ensure they attend to process- and outcome-related equity when assessing digital health technologies.

Table 3 builds on Richardson et al.'s framework to suggest potential measurement domains as aligned to the identified levels of influence related to the digital environment. However, we encourage those engaging in these evaluations to review the full framework and consider how it might be applied.

3 Considering Digital Health in Measuring Impact

When looking across the literature that measures impact of digital technologies, it is helpful to consider the specific set of measures used and required when interpreting findings in the evaluation. As noted above, variables related to the technology itself will often focus on the usability of technology and human-computer interaction factors. Tools like the System Usability Scale (SUS) or the Post-Study System Usability Questionnaire (PSSUQ) can be deployed to capture factors such as learnability, effectiveness, efficiency, and satisfaction of the users as they interact with digital interfaces (Lewis 1992; Lewis 2018). However, in exploring the impact of digital health across quintuple aim factors related to high-performing health systems, we can see that the complexity of micro-, meso-, and macro-level context, process, and outcome measures can be relevant. If we consider this from a socio-technical view of technology, in which digital health tools are seen as actors within complex environments of interacting humans, institutions, and contexts, then we need to situate the technical factors within the relevant context. The following section offers several theoretical frameworks that can offer a useful scaffold to guide evaluations of digitally enabled interventions in health settings.

3.1 Theoretical Frameworks

The literature identifies a confluence of factors that can influence digital health's impact on quintuple aim objectives. Multiple evaluation and implementation frameworks to guide assessment of digital health solutions have emerged that seek to capture micro-, meso-, and macro-level factors. It is important to recognize here that digital health tools are often one factor within large complex adaptive systems, as such simple logic models may not be sufficiently appropriate (Greenhalgh et al. 2017). While this chapter offers multiple evaluation approaches that can be taken to assess the impact of digital health solutions, it is recommended that these evaluations are scaffolded using theoretical frameworks or models that capture the many factors that can influence outcomes.

A recent scoping review found that there were 68 distinct theories, models, and frameworks applied to the evaluation and implementation of digital health interventions (protocol see Soobiah et al. 2020). Among the most common of 68 was the Consolidated Framework for Implementation Research (CFIR). CFIR was found to be the most commonly applied (39 of 85 studies) (Rouleau et al. 2024). Another framework being increasingly used is the Non-Adoption, Abandonment, Scale-Up, Spread, and Sustainability (NASSS) framework which was designed to study and guide the implementation of digitally enabled care in real time (Greenhalgh et al. 2017), but can also be helpful in evaluating these models (Abimbola et al. 2019). Given the complexity of digitally enabled interventions (as outlined above), approaching digital health from a socio-technical perspective can be of value (Herrmann et al. 2022). These three theoretical approaches are briefly described here, including an example of how they can help inform the evaluation process.

3.2 Consolidated Framework for Implementation Research (CFIR) in Evaluating Digital Health

The Consolidated Framework for Implementation Research (CFIR) is a highly cited and often used framework to guide the implementation and assessment of interventions and innovations. CFIR is a deterministic framework built from 20 different theories, models, and frameworks to identify enablers and barriers to implementation. CFIR includes 5 domains and 39 related constructs that occur within these domains. The five domains relate to innovation, individual characteristics, inner setting, outer setting, and implementation process. The model helps to distinguish the innovation (for example, a digital health tool) from the process of putting into practice, suggesting that what persists after the implementation ends is the sustained innovation. Importantly, this framework does not specify relationships between constructs as a model would; however, it can help to generate hypotheses about potential relationships between constructs (Damschroder et al. 2009). CFIR has been found to be useful in implementation-effectiveness studies of digital health technologies like telehealth (Rangachari et al. 2022). CFIR has multiple, accessible tools for evaluators and implementers, including an outcomes addendum, making it a helpful resource (see www.cfirguide.org).

Another notable framework out of the implementation science and evaluation literature is Proctor's implementation outcomes (Proctor et al. 2011). While not as prominently used in relation to digital health as noted in Rouleau et al.'s systematic review (Rouleau et al. 2024), it offers a useful set of potential measures that can readily be applied to the evaluation of digital health tools. Notably, the CFIR set of tools references Proctor as a useful option to identify outcome measures.

3.3 Non-Adoption, Abandonment, Scale-Up, Spread, and Sustainability (NASSS) Framework in Evaluating Digital Health

The NASSS framework includes seven domains related to a digitally enabled model or intervention in health and social care settings. The components of each domain can be understood as being simple, complicated, or complex depending on the number of components and predictability, or the domain in a particular case. As an evaluation tool, NASSS can help offer a sensitizing framework to capture the different micro, meso, and macro factors that influence the implementation of an intervention as related to outcomes of interest. In one example, the framework was used to evaluate an electronic decision support system used in primary care to treat cardiovascular risk (the TORPEDO research program). Using the NASSS framework, researchers were able to uncover problematic assumptions about the technology and intervention, as well as the program's poor fit with the organizational and system contexts which led to less than ideal outcomes for patients (Abimbola et al. 2019). This framework may be particularly helpful when studying complex interventions in which the seven domains are interdependent and unpredictable.

3.4 Socio-technical Intertwinement in Evaluating Digital Health

Another theoretical framework approach that can help those evaluating digital health solutions and digitally enabled models comes from the fields of human-centered design, socio-technical systems, and heuristics, called *sociotechnical* *intertwinement (*Herrmann et al. 2022*)*. This approach recognizes that humans, processes, and technical artifacts are complex and often contingent on each other, leading to intertwinement; meaning we cannot assess one component without considering the others. To unpack this complexity, Herrmann et al. applied a heuristic approach (heuristic mean "rules of thumb for reasoning") to define key components of digital health interventions across six domains: human-computer interaction; computer-supported cooperative work (or "groupware"); process (re)design; socio-technical design; principles of job design; and privacy (Herrmann et al. 2022). Through a review of the literature and validation work with an expert panel, eight heuristics for socio-technical evaluations were identified. The eight heuristics can help guide evaluators to know what questions to ask and which tools to employ when assessing a digital health intervention to ensure attention to the complex environment in which the intervention is deployed (Box 1).

Box 1 Herrmann et al.'s eight heuristics for socio-technical evaluation (Herrmann et al. 2022, Table 10)

1. ***Visibility about task handing and feedback about its success:*** Focused information is continuously offered about the progress of technical processes and, as far as permitted, about collaborative workflows. This helps to understand what further steps are possible or not and why as well as how well the expectations of others are met.
2. ***Flexibility for variable task handling leading to a participatory evolution of the system:*** One can vary options of task handling and can flexibly decide about technology usage, time management, sharing of tasks, etc. Consequently, one can develop a wide range of competencies that support participation in the ongoing evolution of the whole system.
3. ***Communication support for task handling and social interaction:*** By means of technical and spatial support for communication, a person can be reached to an influenceable extent for purposes of task handling and coordination This support is intertwined with negotiating duties and rights of roles, including values, so that reciprocal reliability can be developed.
4. ***Purpose-oriented information exchange for facilitating mental work:*** To support task handling, information is purposefully exchanged via technical means, updated, kept available, and minimized. This implies technical linking of information and the emergence of personal profiles that must be visible and exchanged in compliance with privacy regulations.
5. ***Balance of effort and experienced benefit by organizational structuring of tasks:*** Organizational structuring of tasks supports a proportional balance between individuals' effort and experienced benefit. Tasks are assigned to people, pooled, and technically supported in a way that makes sense and is fun for people. Tasks comply with individuals' technical,

social, and physical competencies while also supporting health. Thus, a sustaining balance of efforts and personal benefits is pursued.

6. ***Compatibility between requirements, development of competencies, and the system's features:*** Technical and organizational features of the system are continuously adjusted to work with each other. Within clarified limits, they meet outside requirements in a way that is based on the development of competencies and proactive help for dealing with changing challenges.
7. ***Efficiency-oriented allocation of tasks for pursuing holistic goals:*** By appropriate sequencing, integration, and distribution of tasks between humans and technology, seamless collaboration is supported. Unnecessary steps or wasting resources are avoided. If needed, an increase in efficiency can be realized.
8. ***Supportive technology and resources for productive and flawless work:*** Technology and further resources support work and collaboration and consider the intertwining of criteria, such as technology acceptance, usability, and accessibility for different users, avoiding consequences of mistakes and of misuse, security, and constant updating.

4 Evaluation Approaches

The WHO Digital Strategy 2020–2025 recommends that countries continuously monitor and evaluate their digital health maturity and its contribution to health system processes, health workforce processes, and meeting individual health needs (World Health Organization 2021). This chapter overviews approaches and methods to evaluating digital health solutions used in health and social care settings. While methods and approaches used in the evaluation of health services can be applied, there are a number of considerations with regard to digitally enabled services that create a unique context which will impact how we measure, analyze, and interpret process and outcome data. Evaluation can be considered as distinct from the WHO conceptualization of monitoring, which focuses on indicators regarding the adoption and use of digital health tools. Here we are focusing on evaluation to assess impact to inform design, implementation, and decision-making regarding digital health tools used in health and social care systems.

Broadly, evaluations can be categorized into two major approaches: ***Formative and developmental evaluations*** are conducted to help *improve* a digital health solution or program, whereas **summative evaluations** set out to *assess* whether a digital health solution or program worked as planned (W.K. Kellogg Foundation 2004). In the following sections, we overview how formative, developmental, and summative approaches might be adapted, introduce how we can integrate implementation and design thinking into our evaluations, offer guidance on how equity considerations can be embedded, and conclude with suggestions on how evaluators might choose among these different approaches.

4.1 Formative and Developmental Evaluations

Formative evaluations are assessments of a project's implementation as it progresses toward its goals (Pan et al. 2014). It is a rigorous assessment process that can help identify the potential and actual influences on the progress, effectiveness, and sustainability of an implementation (Curran et al. 2012). The central tenet of formative evaluations is to *inform* continuous mid-course adjustments and improvements. Formative evaluations can support the development of a project, assess the fidelity of implementation, monitor progress toward key outcomes or impacts, and provide an interpretation of the successes and failures of the implementation (Stetler et al. 2006). These formative evaluation activities are critical as they ensure that a project is feasible, appropriate, and acceptable before it is fully implemented, maximizing the likelihood of program success.[1]

Formative evaluations are particularly valuable during the early stages of a project, where opportunities to influence impact are the greatest (Dehar et al. 1993), especially with the rapid iterative development cycle of digital health innovation. However, formative evaluations should occur throughout a digital health project's lifecycle—from pre-prototype to prototype, pilot, demonstration, scale-up, spread, and sustainability (World Health 2016). While there are variations in definitions and terminology of the different types of formative evaluation, this adopts the Agency for Healthcare Research and Quality definition which suggests it is an evaluation approach that seeks to provide feedback on the effectiveness of an intervention while it is being developed and implemented, by working closely with stakeholders to identify what an intervention is or is not being delivered as planned or having intended effects, with the intention of modifying the intervention (Geonnotti et al. 2013).

Findings from formative evaluations enable decision-makers to establish baseline metrics, measure progress, and proactively strategize to mitigate existing shortcomings and avoid emerging unintended consequences (Catwell and Sheikh 2009). Drawing from the commonalities of existing health informatics evaluation frameworks, the influencing factors of a digital health implementation can be categorized into four dimensions—technology, people, organization, and macroenvironment (TPOM) (Cresswell et al. 2020). Table 4 outlines some example measures for formative evaluations.

Developmental evaluations are similar to formative evaluations, as they both recognize the complexity of implementation and embody the essence of design thinking (Scott et al. 2019; Steele Gray and Shaw 2019). However, the most notable difference is that formative evaluations focus on *improvement* through benchmarks and predetermined goals of the program logic, whereas developmental evaluations focus on *development*, innovation, and adapting within the emerging and dynamic realities of a complex environment (Patton 2006). In digital health environments, developmental evaluation can be used to guide multiple phases of design, usability testing, and implementation stages. Furthermore, this approach can help in

[1] https://www.cdc.gov/std/program/pupestd/types%20of%20evaluation.pdf

Table 4 Examples of formative evaluation measures by technology, people, organization, and macroenvironment (Cresswell et al. 2020; Proctor et al. 2011; Lau et al. 2007; World Health Organization 2016)

Domain	Measure
Technology factors	Usability/effort expectancy/user experience, system quality (functionality, performance, security), information quality (content, availability), data quality (availability, integrity, accuracy), service quality (responsiveness, reliability, connectivity)
People (society/human) factors	Use/adoption/reach (use patterns, self-reported use, intention to use, use at organizational or broader level), user satisfaction, acceptability/appropriateness (perceived usefulness, relative advantage), feasibility (fit with workflow, routines), social influence, awareness, digital literacy, preliminary outcomes (health, behavior, knowledge)
Organizational context	Organizational readiness, training, change management strategy, fidelity with resourcing/inputs and implementation activities, cost
Wider macroenvironment	External stakeholder perceptions, professional groups, funding and economic considerations, legal and regulatory environment, policy context, vendors/supply chain, interoperability

exploratory trials and establishing theories of change related to digital interventions (Steele Gray et al. 2019; Steele Gray et al. 2016; Steele Gray et al. 2020). Additional details regarding the developmental approach can be found in Chap. 2 of this book.

4.2 Summative Evaluation

In contrast to formative and developmental evaluations, summative evaluations are intended to summarize whether a project or program successfully achieves its intended outcomes and objectives. It is a judgment of the overall merit, worth, value, generalizability, and significance of the program (Patton 2011). A summative evaluation describes the outcomes of a digital health program and how the program contributed to those outcomes. It is a form of accountability for the program and supports decision-making; summative evaluations may determine the future of a program (i.e., scaling, spreading, sustaining/discontinuing a digital health program) (Mcdavid et al. 2019).

Summative evaluations are usually conducted at an end-point of an implementation phase or developmental path (Ammenwerth and Rigby 2016). While summative evaluations can also occur throughout a digital health program's lifecycle (Halminen et al. 2021), programs that are more mature and have achieved a level of stability within an environment permit attribution or causality of the program outcomes (Ammenwerth and Rigby 2016; Friedman et al. 2022). Summative evaluation may focus on consequences which include but are not limited to patient-level health outcomes, process or quality measures for an implementation strategy, population-level health status, or an index of system function for an organizational-level intervention (Bernet et al. 2013). Performance or outcome evaluation focuses on measuring the effectiveness of the digital health program on the immediate or intermediate changes in key outcomes such as knowledge, behavioral change, service provision and utilization, and coverage. Impact evaluations focus on the long-term net effects or the impact on health outcomes such as mortality, morbidity, and

Table 5 Digital health service delivery measures adapted from WHO (World Health Organization 2016)

Service delivery dimension	Example measures
Technical Efficiency—measures related to changes as a result of how resources are used during service provision (*World Health Organization* 2023). Technical efficiency provides an indication whether a particular output is obtained with less input (i.e., maximizing resources)	Client: Time savings to access and receive care; utilization of in-person healthcare providers
	Provider—Time allocated to clinical care versus administrative activities; response time to events
	Health system—Cumulative time savings for clinical documentation activities
Quality—Measures related to changes in processes, outcomes, and structure from the user and intervention perspective. The definition of quality should be defined for each project	Client—Client experience, satisfaction, perceived value of services (digital and in-person), perceived quality of care
	Provider—Ability to provide services, knowledge gained, decision-making, responsiveness, patient-centeredness
	Health system—penetrance/integration into care; errors; health information exchange outcomes (Pan et al. 2014); operational logistics
Utilization—Measures related to changes in health service utilization resulting from digital health intervention	Client—Use; utilization patterns; behaviors related to use
	Provider—Meaningful use (e.g., using full capacity of the intervention)
	Health system—Number of users; penetrance; demand; access to services
Cost—Measures related to changes in direct and indirect costs due to the outcomes of the digital health program	Client—Changes in direct (fees paid); indirect (transportation, opportunity costs)
	Provider—Cost due to changes in clinical practice or use of the system
	Health system—Cost of providing care; operational costs; administrative costs

disease risk. In these instances, trial methods, such as randomized clinical trials or pragmatic trials, may be applied. Depending on the health data available, economic evaluations can also be incorporated to determine the program's value by comparing the costs of the program to a common outcome or impact (World Health Organization 2016).

The outcomes of a digital health program could be outlined in its conceptual framework, results framework, theory of change, and logic model (World Health Organization 2016). The outcomes should capture quintuple aim objectives outlined above, and as such need to be measured at each level of the health system (i.e., client level, provider level, health system level) and categorized into two broad categories: service delivery outcomes and health outcomes. Service delivery outcomes tend to be the early to intermediate measures of a program's success, which consist of technical efficiency, quality, utilization, and costs (see Table 5 for example). Improved service delivery may lead to health outcomes specific to the program and its broader system impact (World Health Organization 2016). In addition to outcome measures identified earlier in this chapter, the WHO has identified a number of digital health service delivery outcomes to consider as outlined in Table 5.

4.3 Integrating Implementation and Design Thinking into your Evaluation

While these above methods can be very useful to evaluate digital health technologies in relation to quintuple aim outcomes and processes, what may be most required is ensuring the digital health technologies get adopted so that there is something to evaluate. Digital health technologies are notoriously difficult to implement and sustain, with many studies showing high rates of non-adoption, attrition, and abandonment (Greenhalgh et al. 2010; Solomon and Rudin 2020; Morrison 2015), leading for calls for a stronger focus on implementation in relation to study of digital health technologies (Buis 2019). The tools of implementation science and design thinking can be helpful to include within or alongside evaluations of digital health technologies as a means to better understand how the technology under study may be related to outcomes of interest. Embedding these approaches can also help to improve overall adoption and uptake of the technology, particularly when used alongside developmental and formative approaches.

Design thinking may be another useful tool or approach for evaluators working in the complex space of digital health. Design thinking can be defined as "an analytic and creative process that engages a person in opportunities to experiment, create and prototype models, gather feedback, and redesign" (Razzouk and Shute 2012). While this approach is most often associated with service design and redesign in organizational and industrial engineering (Bender-Salazar 2023), it can also be a useful lens through which to better understand why a technology does or does not get implemented (Shaw et al. 2018). Importantly, these approaches emphasize the importance of understanding the value of a new innovation to the users and the ways that it may be adapted to best achieve that value. This type of thinking can be embedded within evaluation work, in particular developmental evaluation, as a means to provide information to inform adaptation of the intervention. This approach can also provide better insights into the value of a digital health technology needed for decision-makers to make informed choices about whether to sustain or abandon an innovation (Steele Gray and Shaw 2019). This chapter will not go into detail around design thinking and implementation, as these literatures and methods are quite vast. However, evaluators should be encouraged to consider these process-oriented approaches that seek to collect context-rich, value-embedded data that can help to better understand not just the what of digital health evaluation, but also the why and the how. Another chapter in this book around co-production in health services evaluation may be instructive as many of these approaches and methods can similarly support effective design and implementation of digital health interventions.

4.4 Choosing the Right Approach

This chapter has presented a number of evaluation considerations in relation to evaluating digital health technologies. Similar to evaluations in other, non-digital, space,

Table 6 Digital health program maturity and its corresponding stages of evaluation (Halminen et al. 2021)

	Stage of maturity	Evaluation stage	Claim about digital health program
Early	Pre-prototype/prototype	Feasibility Usability	Does it work as intended in a given context? Is it being used as intended by users?
	Pilot—Single deployment to examine whether digital intervention can produce desired effects	Efficacy	Does it work in a controlled setting?
Mid	Demonstration—Deployment at multiple-sites to examine the cost and implementation requirements in new contexts	Effectiveness	Does it work in the real world?
Advanced	Initiative and setting readiness for: Scale-up—Optimized and scaled across regions or population levels	Implementation research	Is the initiative ready to be delivered in a broader setting (e.g., scale, spread, or sustained at an organizational, regional, or national level)?
	Integration/sustainability—Determine how to support impact at large scale and integration in to the broad health-care system		

evaluators should consider a few key things when choosing among different approaches. First, it is critical to understand the maturity of the digital health intervention, its corresponding stage of evaluation, and the appropriate claims to be made based on that stage (World Health Organization 2016). For instance, evaluating for efficacy (e.g., research trial) at an early maturity as the findings may not be meaningful given its instability (Murray et al. 2016). See Table 6.

Second, based on the stage of maturity, what is the intention of the evaluation? Are you seeking to make program decisions after a tool has been put in place or are you seeking to decide whether to continue past a pilot phase? The intention of the evaluation will help to guide which may be the most appropriate method as well as the types of measures to be included in the evaluation. Third, who is the intended audience for the evaluation? As noted above, design thinking and values may be particularly important when seeking to provide feedback to policy makers, whereas impact on workflow and provider processes may be of concern to healthcare organizations that have recently adopted a new health information system. Finally, what can be appreciably changed in response to the evaluation? While it may be of interest to capture usability data as part of a formative assessment, for example, if there are no ways to change the user interface or functionality of the technology, then this data may be of lower value. With so many measures and approaches available, focusing on capturing actionable, meaningful, and valuable information as part of the evaluation can help to reduce unnecessary data collection burden, and ensure evaluation data can serve its intention of intended audience.

If evaluators are not seeking to collect their own data about a digital health technology, but rather are keen to explore the existing evidence on a particular tool, the Evidence in Digital health for EFfectiveness of INterventions with Evaluative Depth (DEFINED) framework offers a rapid rigorous approach to assess clinical value for digital health interventions: https://www.nature.com/articles/s41746-023-00836-5

5 Summary

This chapter offers an overview of how evaluation methods and approaches can be applied and adapted to be used in the assessment of digital health tools and digitally enabled models of care. The overview of the process and context measures that have been typically used in evaluations and assessments of digital health technologies are aligned to the quintuple aim objectives of high-performing health systems: patient outcomes, patient experience, provider experience, efficiency, and equity. These lists of potential measures can be used within the different evaluation approaches presented, depending on the intention and the audience for the evaluation. This chapter also includes several useful theoretical frameworks and approaches that can help provide a conceptual scaffold for these evaluations. Digital health solutions can, and should, be considered a complex intervention, being implemented into a complex environment. Theoretical scaffolds, appropriate approaches and methods, and the right measures of contexts, processes, and outcomes can help ensure evaluation of digital health technologies attends to this complexity, helping leaders to make informed choices.

References

Abernethy A, Adams L, Barrett M, Bechtel C, Brennan P, Butte A, Faulkner J, Fontaine E, Friedhoff S, Halamka J, Howell M, Johnson K, Long P, Mcgraw D, Miller R, Lee P, Perlin J, Rucker D, Sandy L, Savage L, Stump L, Tang P, Topol E, Tuckson R, Valdes K (2022) The promise of digital health: then, now, and the future. NAM Perspect

Abimbola S, Patel B, Peiris D, Patel A, Harris M, Usherwood T, Greenhalgh T (2019) The NASSS framework for ex post theorisation of technology-supported change in healthcare: worked example of the TORPEDO programme. BMC Med 17:233

Ammenwerth E, Rigby M (2016) Evidence-based health informatics. IOS Press, Amsterdam

Bender-Salazar R (2023) Design thinking as an effective method for problem-setting and needfinding for entrepreneurial teams addressing wicked problems. J Innov Entrep 12:24

Bernet AC, Willens DE, Bauer MS (2013) Effectiveness-implementation hybrid designs: implications for quality improvement science. Implement Sci 8(Suppl 1):S2. https://doi.org/10.1186/1748-5908-8-S1-S2. eCollection 2013

Brands MR, Gouw SC, Beestrum M, Cronin RM, Fijnvandraat K, Badawy SM (2022) Patient-centered digital health records and their effects on health outcomes: systematic review. J Med Internet Res 24:e43086

Brooke J (1996) SUS: a "quick and dirty" usability scale. Usability evaluation in industry. Taylor and Francis, Oxfordshire

Buis L (2019) Implementation: the next giant hurdle to clinical transformation with digital health. J Med Internet Res 21:e16259
Canadian Institutes of Health Research (2023) Canadian Institutes of Health Research—Institute of Health Services and Policy Research Strategic Plan 2021–2026 [Online]. Available: https://cihr-irsc.gc.ca/e/52481.html. Accessed 15 Dec 2023
Carini E, Villani L, Pezzullo AM, Gentili A, Barbara A, Ricciardi W, Boccia S (2021) The impact of digital patient portals on health outcomes, system efficiency, and patient attitudes: updated systematic literature review. J Med Internet Res 23:e26189
Catwell L, Sheikh A (2009) Evaluating eHealth interventions: the need for continuous systemic evaluation. PLoS Med 6:e1000126
Crawford A, Serhal E (2020) Digital health equity and COVID-19: the innovation curve cannot reinforce the social gradient of health. J Med Internet Res 22:e19361
Cresswell K, Williams R, Sheikh A (2020) Developing and applying a formative evaluation framework for health information technology implementations: qualitative investigation. J Med Internet Res 22:e15068
Cuadros, D. F., Moreno, C. M., Miller, F. D., Omori, R. & Mackinnon, N. J. 2023. Assessing Access to Digital Services in Health Care–Underserved Communities in the United States: A Cross-Sectional Study. Mayo Clinic Proc: Digital Health, 1, 217–225.
Curran GM, Bauer M, Mittman B, Pyne JM, Stetler C (2012) Effectiveness-implementation hybrid designs: combining elements of clinical effectiveness and implementation research to enhance public health impact. Med Care 50:217–226
Damschroder LJ, Aron DC, Keith RE, Kirsh S, Alexander J, Lowery JC (2009) Fostering implementation of health services research findings into practice: a consolidated framework for advancing implementation science. Implement Sci 4:50–65
Dehar M-A, Casswell S, Duignan P (1993) Formative and process evaluation of health promotion and disease prevenion programs. Eval Rev 17
Ehrenfeld JM, Wanderer JP (2018) Technology as friend or foe? Do electronic health records increase burnout? Curr Opin Anaesthesiol 31:357–360
Evans L, Evans J, Pagliari C, Källander K (2023) Scoping review: exploring the equity impact of current digital health design practices. Oxford Open Digital Health 1
Fatehi F, Samadbeik M, Kazemi A (2020) What is digital health? Review of definition. Integrated Citizen Centered Digital Helath and Social Care
Friedman CP, Wyatt JC, Ash JS (2022) Study planning. In: Evaluation methods in biomedical and health informatics. Springer, Cham
Gentili A, Failla G, Melnyk A, Puleo V, Tanna GLD, Ricciardi W, Cascini F (2022) The cost-effectiveness of digital health interventions: a systematic review of the literature. Front Public Health 10:787135
Geonnotti K, Peikes D, Wang W, Smith J (2013) Formative evaluation: foster real-time adaptations and refinements to improve the effectiveness of patient-centered medical home models. Agency for Healthcare Research and Quality, Rockville
Gomes M, Murray E, Raftery J (2022) Economic evaluation of digital health interventions: methodological issues and recommendations for practice. PharmacoEconomics 40:367–378
Greenhalgh T, Hinder S, Stramer K, Bratan T, Russell J (2010) Adoption, non-adoption, and abandonment of a personal electronic health record: case study of HealthSpace. BMJ 341:c5814
Greenhalgh T, Wherton J, Papoutsi C, Lynch J, Hughes G, A'court C, Hinder S, Fahy N, Procter R, Shaw S (2017) Beyond adoption: a new framework for theorizing and evaluating nonadoption, abandonment, and challenges to the scale-up, spread, and sustainability of health and care technologies. J Med Internet Res 19:e367
Halminen O, Chen A, Tenhunen H, Lillrank P (2021) Demonstrating the value of digital health: guidance on contextual evidence gathering for companies in different stages of maturity. Health Serv Manag Res 34:13–20
Harris DA, Haskell J, Cooper E, Crouse N, Gardner R (2018) Estimating the association between burnout and electronic health record-related stress among advanced practice registered nurses. Appl Nurs Res 43:36–41

Herrmann T, Jahnke I, Nolte A (2022) A problem-based approach to the advancement of heuristics for socio-technical evaluation. Behav Inform Technol 41:3087–3109

Hobensack M, Levy DR, Cato K, Detmer DE, Johnson KB, Williamson J, Murphy J, Moy A, Withall J, Lee R, Rossetti SC, Rosenbloom ST (2022) 25 × 5 symposium to reduce documentation burden: report-out and call for action. Appl Clin Inform 13:439–446

Jussupow, E., Spohrer, K., Heinzl, A. & Link, C. 2018. I am; We are - Conceptualizing Professional Identity Threats from Information Technology. *ICIS 2018*. PRO 8.

Kaihlanen A-M, Virtanen L, Buchert U, Safarov N, Valkonen P, Hietapakka L, Hörhammer I, Kujala S, Kouvonen A, Heponiemi T (2022) Towards digital health equity—a qualitative study of the challenges experienced by vulnerable groups in using digital health services in the COVID-19 era. BMC Health Serv Res 22:188

Keasberry J, Scott IA, Sullivan C, Staib A, Ashby R (2017) Going digital: a narrative overview of the clinical and organisational impacts of eHealth technologies in hospital practice. Aust Health Rev 41:646–664

Kimmel HJ, Brice YN, Trikalinos TA, Sarkar IN, Ranney ML (2018) Real-time emergency department electronic notifications regarding high-risk patients: a systematic review. Telemed e-Health 25:604–618

Knight SR, Ng N, Tsanas A, Mclean K, Pagliari C, Harrison EM (2021) Mobile devices and wearable technology for measuring patient outcomes after surgery: a systematic review. npj Digital Med 4:157

Kruse CS, Mileski M, Dray G, Johnson Z, Shaw C, Shirodkar H (2022) Physician burnout and the electronic health record leading up to and during the first year of COVID-19: systematic review. J Med Internet Res 24:e36200

Lampickienė I, Davoody N (2022) Healthcare professionals' experience of performing digital care visits-a scoping review. Life (Basel) 12

Lau F, Hagens S, Muttitt S (2007) A proposed benefits evaluation framework for health information systems in Canada. Healthc Q 10(112–6):118

Lewis JR (1992) Psychometric evaluation of the post-study system usability questionnaire: The PSSUQ. Human Factors Society 36th Annual Meeting, 1992 Boca Raton, FL

Lewis JR (2018) The system usability scale: past, present, and future. Int J Hum–Comput Interact 34:577–590

Livesay K, Petersen S, Walter R, Zhao L, Butler-Henderson K, Abdolkhani R (2023) Sociotechnical challenges of digital health in nursing practice during the COVID-19 pandemic: National Study. JMIR Nurs 6:e46819

Mcdavid J, Huse I, Hawthorn L (2019) Program evaluation and performance measurement: an introduction to practice, 3rd edn. SAGE

Morrison LG (2015) Theory-based strategies for enhancing the impact and usage of digital health behaviour change interventions: a review. Digital Health 1:2055207615595335

Muhiyaddin R, Elfadl A, Mohamed E, Shah Z, Alam T, Abd-Alrazaq A, Househ M (2022) Electronic health records and physician burnout: a scoping review. Stud Health Technol Inform 289:481–484

Murray E, Hekler EB, Andersson G, Collins LM, Doherty A, Hollis C, Rivera DE, West R, Wyatt JC (2016) Evaluating digital health interventions: key questions and approaches. Am J Prev Med 51:843–851

Nguyen K-H, Wright C, Simpson D, Woods L, Comans T, Sullivan C (2022) Economic evaluation and analyses of hospital-based electronic medical records (EMRs): a scoping review of international literature. npj Digital Med 5:29

Palmieriserrano L, Cmaita K, Ravila F, Atorres-Guzman R, Pgarcia J, Seldaly A, Rhaider C, Lfelton C, Rpaulson M, Jmaniaci M, Jforte A (2023) Benefits and challenges of remote patient monitoring as perceived by health care practitioners: a systematic review. Perm J 27:100–111

Pan E, Byrne C, Damico D, Crimmins M (2014) Guide to evaluating health information exchange projects. Agency for Healthcare Reserach and Quality, Rockville

Patton MQ (2006) Evaluation for the way we work. Nonprofit Q. Online: Nonprofit Quarterly

Patton MQ (2011) Developmental evaluation: applying complexity concepts to enhance innovation and use. Guilford Press, New York

Proctor E, Silmere H, Raghavan R, Hovmand P, Aarons G, Bunger A, Griffey R, Hensley M (2011) Outcomes for implementation research: conceptual distinctions, measurement challenges, and research agenda. Admin Pol Ment Health 38:65–76

Rangachari P, Mushiana SS, Herbert K (2022) A scoping review of applications of the Consolidated Framework for Implementation Research (CFIR) to telehealth service implementation initiatives. BMC Health Serv Res 22:1450

Razzouk R, Shute V (2012) What is design thinking and why is it important? Rev Educ Res 82:330–348

Richardson S, Lawrence K, Schoenthaler AM, Mann D (2022) A framework for digital health equity. npj Digital Med 5:119

Rouleau G, Wu K, Ramamoorthi K, Boxall C, Liu RH, Maloney S, Zelmer J, Scott T, Larsen D, Wijeysundera HC (2024) Mapping theories, models, and frameworks to evaluate digital health interventions: scoping review. J Med Internet Res 26:e51098

Sbaffi L, Walton J, Blenkinsopp J, Walton G (2020) Information overload in emergency medicine physicians: a multisite case study exploring the causes, impact, and solutions in four North England National Health Service Trusts. J Med Internet Res 22:e19126

Scott VC, Alia K, Scaccia J, Ramaswamy R, Saha S, Leviton L, Wandersman A (2019) Formative evaluation and complex health improvement initiatives: a learning system to improve theory, implementation, support, and evaluation. Am J Eval 41:89–106

Shaw T, Mcgregor D, Brunner M, Keep M, Janssen A, Barnet S (2017) What is eHealth (6)? Development of a conceptual model for eHealth: qualitative study with key informants. J Med Internet Res 19:e324

Shaw J, Agarwal P, Desveaux L, Palma DC, Stamenova V, Jamieson T, Yang R, Bhatia RS, Bhattacharyya O (2018) Beyond "implementation": digital health innovation and service design. npj Digital Med 1:48

Shaw J, Brewer LC, Veinot T (2021) Recommendations for health equity and virtual care arising from the COVID-19 pandemic: narrative review. JMIR Form Res 5:e23233

Shi C, Dumville JC, Juwale H, Moran C, Atkinson R (2022) Evidence assessing the development, evaluation and implementation of digital health technologies in wound care: a rapid scoping review. J Tissue Viability 31:567–574

Solomon DH, Rudin RS (2020) Digital health technologies: opportunities and challenges in rheumatology. Nat Rev Rheumatol 16:525–535

Soobiah C, Cooper M, Kishimoto V, Bhatia RS, Scott T, Maloney S, Larsen D, Wijeysundera HC, Zelmer J, Gray CS, Desveaux L (2020) Identifying optimal frameworks to implement or evaluate digital health interventions: a scoping review protocol. BMJ Open 10:e037643

Steele Gray C, Shaw J (2019) From summative to developmental: incorporating design-thinking into evaluations of complex interventions. J Integr Care 27:241–248

Steele Gray C, Wodchis WP, Upshur R, Cott C, Mckinstry B, Mercer S, Palen T, Ramsay T, Thavorn K, Inc QH, P. C. A. T. P. (2016) Supporting goal-oriented primary health care for seniors with complex care needs using Mobile technology: evaluation and implementation of the health system performance research network, bridgepoint electronic patient reported outcome tool. JMIR Res Protoc 5:e126

Steele Gray C, Gravesande J, Hans PK, Nie JX, Sharpe S, Loganathan M, Lyons R, Cott C (2019) Using exploratory trials to identify relevant contexts and mechanisms in complex electronic health interventions: evaluating the electronic patient-reported outcome tool. JMIR Form Res 3:e11950

Steele Gray C, Tang T, Armas A, Backo-Shannon M, Harvey S, Kuluski K, Loganathan M, Nie JX, Petrie J, Ramsay T, Reid R, Thavorn K, Upshur R, Wodchis WP, Nelson M (2020) Building a digital bridge to support patient-centered care transitions from hospital to home for older adults with complex care needs: protocol for a co-design, implementation, and evaluation study. JMIR Res Protoc 9:e20220

Stetler CB, Legro MW, Wallace CM, Bowman C, Guihan M, Hagedorn H, Kimmel B, Sharp ND, Smith JL (2006) The role of formative evaluation in implementation research and the QUERI experience. J Gen Intern Med 21(Suppl 2):S1–S8

Strategies for Quality Care (2023) Quadruple aim: a framework for achieving value-based care [online]. Strategies for quality care: solutions for achieving value-based care goals. Available: https://www.strategiesforqualitycare.com/quadruple-aim. Accessed 15 Dec 2023

W.K. Kellogg Foundation (2004) Logic model development guide. W.K. Kellogg Foundation, Michigan

Wang T, Giunti G, Melles M, Goossens R (2022) Digital patient experience: umbrella systematic review. J Med Internet Res 24:e37952

Woolley KE, Bright D, Ayres T, Morgan F, Little K, Davies AR (2023) Mapping inequities in digital health technology within the World Health Organization's European Region using PROGRESS PLUS: scoping review. J Med Internet Res 25:e44181

World Health Organization (2016) Monitoring and evaluating digital health interventions: a practical guide to conducting research and assessment. World Health Organization, Geneva

World Health Organization (2021) Global strategy on digital health 2020–2025. World Health Organization, Geneva

World Health Organization 2023. Technical efficiency [online]. World Health Organization. Available: https://www.who.int/teams/health-systems-governance-and-financing/economic-analysis/costing-and-technical-efficiency/technical-efficiency. Accessed 15 Dec 2023

Yan Q, Jiang Z, Harbin Z, Tolbert PH, Davies MG (2021) Exploring the relationship between electronic health records and provider burnout: a systematic review. J Am Med Inform Assoc 28:1009–1021

Zanaboni P, Ngangue P, Mbemba GIC, Schopf TR, Bergmo TS, Gagnon M-P (2018) Methods to evaluate the effects of internet-based digital health interventions for citizens: systematic review of reviews. J Med Internet Res 20:e10202

Evaluating Leadership in Health Services

Shibaab Rahman and Helen Dickinson

1 Introduction

Leadership is seen as a crucial component in driving performance in health organizations and is often seen as a normative good. To design an effective evaluation to determine whether leadership is having the impact intended, it is crucial to understand precisely what is expected of leadership activities within given contexts. In this chapter, we explore segments of the vast leadership and evaluation literatures to provide guidance on the sorts of issues and questions that evaluators should consider when designing evaluations of leadership within health services.

The chapter starts by exploring the evaluation literature, arguing that it is important to be clear about what is being evaluated to design the most effective evaluation, to ensure it is meaningful and makes best use of available resources. The next section then moves on to explore some of the various models of leadership found in the health services literature, arguing that each of these requires different approaches to their evaluation. We then set out two case illustrations that explore leadership in health services and the ways these might be evaluated. The first deals with middle managers in hospitals and the second with general practice and its leadership role in communities. The final section signposts some frameworks for evaluation that can help those embarking on the evaluation of leadership in determining their approach. Ultimately, we argue that evaluation is not a one-size-fits-all approach and all evaluations make trade-offs in terms of different factors. This means that evaluation needs careful crafting to the organizational context, the dynamics of leaders' positions, and the outcomes sought.

S. Rahman (✉) · H. Dickinson
UNSW, Canberra, Australia
e-mail: Shibaab.rahman@unsw.edu.au; Helen.dickinson@unsw.edu.au

A. Kaehne, J. Feather (eds.), *Handbook of Health Services Evaluation*,
https://doi.org/10.1007/978-3-031-87869-5_18

2 Evaluating Leadership in Health Services

Over the past 40 years or so the evaluation field has developed and expanded, in part in response to the rise of the evidence-based policy and practice movement (Smith 2013). It is often seen as a highly specialized and technical field, when at its heart we all engage in evaluation activities daily. At its most basic level, evaluation is the "process of determining the merit, worth or value of something, or the product of that process" (Scriven 1991: p. 139). Beyond this broad definition, evaluation involves the "systematic application of social research procedures in assessing the conceptualisation and design, implementation, and utility of social intervention programs". In other words, evaluation research involves the use of social research methodologies to judge and improve the planning, monitoring, effectiveness, and efficiency of health, education, welfare, and other human service programs" (Rossi and Freeman 1985).

While the intention of evaluation is to judge the value of an outcome or process, the methods for doing this have become increasingly complex. There are a variety of different approaches available to evaluate health services. Judgments about their suitability depend on the aims of the services or activities under investigation and the resources (e.g., time, data) available to undertake this process (Dickinson and O'flynn 2016). For example, an *outcome or impact* evaluation might seek to assess the outcomes or wider impacts of a service against its goals. A *process* evaluation typically attempts to support stakeholders to understand the way a service operates, rather than what it produces. *Summative* evaluations aim to help decision-makers to decide whether to continue a particular service, giving an assessment of the effects and efficiency of a service, whereas a *formative* evaluation is more developmental, seeking to give feedback on how to improve a service with evidence about what this service produces and how. A first important step in an evaluation is therefore to establish what is to be evaluated (a process, an outcome, or both) and for what purpose (to judge the impact of a service, to improve a service, or both).

Within these broad evaluation approaches, a range of different methods might be used to collect data. These can vary from highly sophisticated quantitative methods to qualitative methods that seek to elucidate the views of individuals or groups, or a mix of these. In the context of healthcare, there can often be a tendency to give greater weight to more "objective" forms of evidence that are collected quantitatively, but there is no intrinsically superior method in evaluation. Instead, what is more important is being clear about what it is that is being evaluated for what purpose and why the chosen method is most appropriate (Silverman 2013). For instance, a mixed-methods approach, combining quantitative and qualitative data, can often provide the most comprehensive and nuanced understanding of phenomenon being evaluated. It allows for the triangulation of findings, where different types of evidence are used to corroborate and enrich each other, ultimately leading to more robust evaluations. In addition to these methods, other valuable approaches could include case studies, document analysis, surveys, benchmarking, and simulation exercises (Jenkinson 1997). Each of these methods offers unique strengths and limitations, and the choice of approach should be carefully considered bearing in mind the specific evaluation goals and the available resources.

In this chapter, we seek to employ the principles of effective evaluation within the domain of leadership in health services. As we will demonstrate in the following section, leadership is multifaceted seeking to achieve different things in various settings. Leadership can have diverse purposes and impacts across health services, including guiding service delivery, shaping organizational culture, or driving patient outcomes (Zonneveld et al. 2021). Moreover, different models or understandings of leadership focus on various factors as being important in driving activity, such as traits, behaviors, situations, and styles (Day et al. 2014). Effective evaluation of leadership requires a nuanced approach to ensure that it is meaningful and makes the best use of available resources.

3 Leadership in Health Services

In the complex landscape of health services, leadership is an amorphous concept (Armistead et al. 2007) meaning that researchers and practitioners alike have often struggled to define and understand it. One of the most pressing debates relates to the impact or effectiveness of leadership (Amaladas 2019). A key question here is what impact leadership has on health services. In order to determine how to answer this question through evaluation, it is important to consider the purpose of leadership in different health services, what leadership looks like in these different settings, and the type of impact it can create.

Leadership scholarship has often grappled with the notion of leadership effectiveness. While it is often discussed, it is not straightforward and is often contested. Burns (1978) provided an important contribution arguing that leadership effectiveness centers on creating *real* change among those who need it: "the ultimate test of practical leadership is realization of intended real change that meets peoples enduring needs" (Burns 1978, p. 461). What this means is the true measure of effective leadership lies in its ability to instigate and bring about genuine transformation. Leadership, according to Burns, is not merely about maintaining the status quo or making incremental adjustments; it is about realizing substantial and enduring change. This change is directed towards addressing the fundamental and persistent needs of individuals and groups, particularly those who are most affected by the issues at hand. Within contemporary scholarship, the notion of creating "real change" has been interpreted in a number of ways, from evaluating the impact leadership can have on organizational performance (Ng 2017) to supporting and improving employee outcomes (e.g., well-being) (Top et al. 2015). The latter of these aligns with what Burns (2004) identifies as *enduring needs*, meaning leadership has to serve the basic needs of people (i.e., food, education) but also higher needs, such as respect, dignity, justice, and the pursuit of happiness.

Often leadership is interpreted as a virtuous endeavor and this resonates with the types of qualities that have been the cornerstone of the medical profession. Virtues such as compassion, empathy, and commitment to the well-being of patients have long been proposed as the guiding principles of the medical profession (Schweller et al. 2017). Research on leadership in health services has often embodied this in attempting to identify links between leadership and patient care outcomes (Sarabi Asiabar et al. 2019; Willcocks 2012). However, a singular focus on this type of leadership effectiveness ignores the transformation health services have undergone in general, particularly in relation to the emphasis on management and performance. For example, as the quest for enhanced hospital performance gains momentum, medical and clinical leaders find themselves increasingly called upon to extend their roles beyond direct patient care. For example, healthcare professionals are being required to exercise leadership in the managerial realm, for example, their role in resource allocation within organizations. This evolving landscape demands they cultivate collaboration with executive boards and undertake tasks that encompass a broader spectrum of responsibilities (Denis and Van Gestel 2016). In considering evaluation of leadership in health services, this means we may not simply need to consider just clinical excellence but also operational and performance considerations and these will vary in emphasis across roles and health service settings.

In any evaluation, it is important to gain clarity on what is being evaluated. This is not always an easy thing to achieve when it comes to leadership as there are various perspectives on what leadership effectiveness means. Earlier we drew on Burns who argues that leadership effectiveness is about real change, but Rost (1991) offers a different perspective arguing that this can be attained even in instances where tangible outcomes might not be realized. Rost believes that leadership "happens when leaders and followers enter into relationships that intends real changes" (Rost 1991). This suggests that leaders only have to have the intention to produce the change and then act on that intention. While this may initially appear radical, it opens a pathway for contemplating the conceptual role of leadership and, importantly, directs attention towards scrutinizing the process of leadership enactment. Rost's perspective asks us to acknowledge that leadership effectiveness not only entails evaluating outcomes but also underscores the significance of dissecting *how* leadership is put into practice. This broader perspective prompts a shift towards holistic assessment, where the interplay between intention, action, and process assumes importance.

The leadership literature is replete with different leadership models, each offering distinct prescriptions for how leadership should be embodied and practised. Some of these include models, such as transformational leadership (Bass and Riggio 2006), authentic leadership (Avolio and Gardner 2005), and servant leadership (Greenleaf 1977). These models each prescribe a unique set of competencies, characteristics, and ways of interaction that have found credence and been widely adopted in organizations as solutions to leadership problems (Eva et al. 2019). It is not surprising to see these models transposed to the health sector, predicted to achieve diverse sets of outcome such as work performance (Curado and Santos 2022) and also forms of justice (Yasir and Jan 2023).

These different models of leadership come with various underpinning assumptions, often molded by the dynamics of leader–follower relationships and the organizational structures prevalent in non-health sectors. It is important to recognize these paradigms might not comprehensively encapsulate the intricate structural complexities inherent to health services. For example, health care services have become increasingly interconnected, giving rise to a burgeoning necessity to work across organizational boundaries. This can include the establishment of collaborative care teams for patients with complex medical conditions. In such cases, patients often require the expertise of multiple healthcare specialists, including physicians, nurses, social workers, therapists, and more. These structural conditions prompt reconsideration of leadership approaches, shifting focus to emerging notions of collaborative or distributed leadership (Fitzgerald et al. 2013). These perspectives represent a departure from traditional hierarchical and individualized models to leadership as a shared responsibility that spreads across various levels and roles within a healthcare organization or multiple organizations. It emphasizes collaboration, mutual support, and the active involvement of multiple team members, including doctors, nurses, administrative staff, and even patients.

For example, collaborative leadership considers fostering interdependency among various healthcare professionals, whereas distributed leadership relies on the "concertive" action of different leaders situated in different levels of a healthcare setting (Currie and Lockett 2011). Here, the structural properties of health services may drive leadership behavior that fosters collective decision-making and effective communication among multidisciplinary teams to optimize organizational and patient outcomes (Chreim et al. 2010). Below, we have summarized (Table 1) a list of popular mainstream leadership approaches and associated outcomes that have found the currency in broader healthcare research.

A key message of this section is that there is a danger that in a health service setting leadership can mean everything to all people. In an evaluative sense, this is challenging as it can be difficult and expensive to interrogate this range of factors and impacts. When evaluating leadership what needs to be established is what that particular leadership approach can reasonably be expected to deliver and to identify the types of indicators and data that will tell us if that has been successful. Leadership to drive clinical engagement will need to be evaluated in a different way to that intended to drive team or organizational efficiency, much as leadership to drive engagement of service users will require another approach. It is important that we understand what it is that leadership is intended to achieve and how we will know if it is successful before we are able to evaluate it.

In the following section, we present two case illustrations that present distinctive factors that shape leadership's impact within various health service settings. In introducing the two cases, we want to emphasize that health services leadership is not a monolithic concept; it varies significantly depending on context. In our first case, we examine the "caught in the middle" phenomenon experienced by hospital middle managers, emphasizing the need for a multifaceted evaluation approach that balances outcome-based and process-based assessments. In the second case, we explore the collective leadership of general practitioners (GPs) engaging with diverse communities, highlighting the limitations of individualistic models and the importance of considering social determinants of health. By examining these contrasting contexts, we aim to equip practitioners with a nuanced understanding of

Table 1 Summary of mainstream leadership models in health[a]

Leadership style	Key focus	Leader competencies	Outcomes	Notable works
Servant leadership	Revolves around putting the needs of others first and helping people reach their full potential	Empathy; active listening; self-awareness; persuasion; stewardship; foresight	Organizational climate; employee well-being and job satisfaction; patient satisfaction; improving patient health outcomes	Silver and Martin (2022), Wong et al. (2023), Neubert et al. (2016)
Transformational leadership	Leadership style focused on inspiring and motivating followers to achieve exceptional performance and embrace change within an organization	Visionary thinking; inspiration; tolerance for intelligent risk; empowering others; entrepreneurial	Organizational change; innovation; innovative behavior; work performance	Raoush (2023), Curado and Santos (2022), Weintraub and McKee (2019)
Ethical leadership	Involves guiding individuals and teams with integrity, fairness, and moral fortitude. Ethical leaders prioritize patient Well-being, adhere to professional codes of conduct, and foster a culture of trust, empathy, and respect among staff	Integrity; empathy; respect; transparency; accountability; fairness; courage	Employee voice; safety compliance	Enwereuzor et al. (2020), Islam et al. (2018)

(continued)

Table 1 (continued)

Leadership style	Key focus	Leader competencies	Outcomes	Notable works
Authentic leadership	Centers on genuine, transparent, and self-aware leadership practices that cultivate trust, respect, and empathy within the healthcare environment	Self-awareness; transparency; ethical decision-making; balanced processing; compassion; empathy	Employee Well-being; safe organizational climate; patient care quality; employee work–life balance	Alsalmi and Alilyyani (2023), Mrayyan et al. (2022), Puni and Hilton (2020)
Adaptive leadership	Focuses on navigating complex challenges and fostering innovation within the ever-evolving healthcare landscape	Emotional intelligence; integrity; life-long learning; collaboration	Addressing complex challenges such as pediatric health disparities, life sustaining therapy, chronic illness	Raphael (2013), Randolph et al. (2022)
Collective/ distributed leadership	Leadership that is not confined to a single individual but is a shared responsibility spread across various levels and roles within a healthcare organization or across multiple organizations	Shared decision-making; mutual accountability; collaborative problem-solving	Delivering integrated health services; service delivery improvement in health systems	Fitzgerald et al. (2013), Chreim et al. (2010)

[a]This is not an exhaustive list of leadership models found in healthcare research and is not derived from comprehensive review of the literature. Rather, the authors compiled this table relying on their expertise on leadership and health-related research

leadership diversity, enabling them to develop contextually relevant and practically applicable evaluation strategies to enhance leadership effectiveness across health-care settings.

4 "Caught in the Middle": Evaluating the Leadership of Middle Managers Roles in Hospitals

In this section, we set out a case illustration of leadership of middle managers in a hospital setting. Before proceeding, we acknowledge there is larger debate that merits drawing distinctions between managers and leaders, the former being attributed to activities such as setting goals, organizing, and monitoring results, while the latter has been primarily argued to deal with change, communicating vision, and inspiring others (Kotter 1990). However, in recent scholarship, there is revival of the seminal views of Mintzberg (1971) who argues that leadership is one of the many roles undertaken by managers, the lines between the two are blurred (Fernandez et al. 2010) and everyday leadership in organizations is enacted at least in part through the mundane and routine work of managers (Alvesson and Sveningsson 2003; Cox and Hassard 2018). We believe this view emphasizes more contemporary notions of leadership, in that it is not tied to any single organizational position; anyone may engage in it. In that same spirit, the following case illustration sees middle managers as occupying an intermediate position in an organizational hierarchy with an inherent capacity to exercise leadership from their position.

Middle manager roles in hospitals operate in a space where they are expected to respond to top-down demands as well as to bottom-up needs (Carlström 2012). This means that they need to fulfil functions of middle managers that may relate to activities associated with cost efficiencies and control, human resources management, compliance, and responsibilities leaning toward broader management, and financial objectives of the hospital that generally bear down on them from the top. At the same time, they also engage in activities that relate to patient care and outcomes, such as resources allocation, staff management, patient care coordination, and supporting and meeting the expectations of frontline workers delivering health services that generally come from the so-called bottom. Middle managers in healthcare are often described as being "caught in the middle," balancing the guidance and expectations of senior leadership with the needs and requests of their staff and patients. Some have also described it as "extreme jobs" characterized by long hours, high pressure, and significant responsibilities, leading to potential issues, such as fatigue, stress, and compromised patient care quality (Buchanan et al. 2013). In the following paragraphs, we elaborate on the nature of the work middle managers engage in and the implication this has for their leadership with a view to offering considerations for evaluation.

4.1 The Various Roles of Hospital Middle Managers

The work of middle managers is particularly complex due to the duality of their roles defined by their responsibility to respond to top-down directives while also translating those directives and managing clinical needs from the bottom-up. For example, middle managers are entrusted with implementing and sometimes even formulating policies and strategies that align with broader strategic objectives of the hospital. For instance, middle managers might be tasked with finding ways to reduce costs, engage with quality improvement initiatives, track performance metrics, and ensure staff development (Carlström 2012). Tending to such demands from the top is sometimes described as "managing upwards" (O'toole 2015) and entails a type of managerial leadership (Holmberg and Tyrstrup 2010). This generally entails implementing and being accountable for management priorities set by senior leadership of hospitals. For example, in response to expectations of financial constraints set by senior management, middle managers might take measures to ensure cost-efficiency by identifying areas of optimization and propose strategies to reduce operational costs. Hartviksen et al. (2018) suggest that leadership in this regard generally entails middle managers relying on effective communication to rationalize and communicate the potential benefits of cost-saving measures and, crucially, engage in persuasive tactics to convince senior management how their measures align with the hospital's financial goals. Evaluating these forms of leadership could tend towards summative and outcome evaluations.

Contrasting upward responsibilities, middle managers are also deeply engaged in responding to bottom-up needs. This means some middle managers also have to consider patient care, support frontline healthcare workers, allocate resources judiciously, and continually improve quality of care (Daly et al. 2014; Jeon et al. 2010). For instance, in practice, middle managers overseeing a hospital ward will have responsibility to support and ensure patient care. This involves engaging with clinical staff to understand their challenges and needs. The middle manager may regularly meet with clinical teams to discuss patient care plans, address any issues or bottlenecks in the care process, and gather feedback on how to enhance patient outcomes. Beyond this, middle manager downward managerial responsibilities also may include thoughtfully allocating resources, such as ensuring adequate staffing, medical supplies, and equipment to provide optimal care. Evaluating these forms of leadership activities may lean more towards formative and process evaluations.

4.2 Leadership from the Middle

The health leadership literature points to several leadership approaches that may assist middle managers in navigating the various roles and responsibilities discussed above. For example, Curado and Santos (2022) drawing on transformational approaches suggest that the ability to inspire, motivate, and communicate a compelling vision that emphasizes patient care can positively impact staff, helping them find meaning in their work and which ultimately can lead to better patient outcomes. Willcocks (2012), however, suggests that a genuine desire to "serve" the team and patients (often associated with servant leadership approach) can help in addressing the needs of nursing staff, doctors, and clinicians. In particular, middle managers' ability to embody trust, integrity, empathy, and support can be crucial in prioritizing team activities, ensuring they have the necessary resources and support to deliver excellent care.

In addition to influencing staff and patient outcomes, there is also growing recognition that middle managers lead change processes within their scope of work, such as driving innovation that contributes to continuous quality improvement in their departments (Gutberg and Berta 2017). For example, middle managers, within directives provided by senior management, may lead quality improvement initiatives, encouraging staff to participate in identifying and implementing better practices to enhance patient care. Birken et al. (2012) highlight a key leadership role for middle managers in this regard, noting that they serve as pivotal intermediaries between top-level strategic goals and the innovation implementation realities experienced by frontline staff. They highlight that middle managers act as a bridge, aligning the organization's high-level strategic objectives with the practical, day-to-day tasks performed by frontline staff. For instance, they take a strategic goal of reducing waiting times and translate that into actionable steps that involve introducing technologies or redesigning workflows to optimize patient flow. In implementing such change, middle managers, along with other competencies, need to demonstrate effective communication for the purposes of translating strategy to practice, justifying and "selling" the implementation of innovation, and convincing employees of the value such innovation brings.

In summary, the leadership of middle managers in healthcare is a multifaceted endeavor, necessitating a delicate balance between top-down directives and bottom-up needs. Evaluating their leadership might encompass both outcome-based assessments, such as improved patient outcomes, cost-efficiency gains, and successful quality improvement initiatives, and process-based evaluations, focusing on their behaviors, competencies, and leadership approaches. The detail of any designs will be dependent on the particular priorities and activities that are seen as most important within that particular organizational context. There is no singular way to evaluate the success or failure of middle managers, and this must align with organizational expectations, priorities, and available resources.

For practitioners, Table 1 offers some guidance for evaluating the leadership of middle managers. Whether adopting transformative or servant leadership styles, we recommend that evaluators particularly pay attention to the type of outcomes that any type of middle manager may be responsible or accountable for and consider the competencies that may be more relevant or aligned as we suggested in the table. It is worth nothing that all competencies and outcomes may not be applicable to a single position but would depend on the nature of the middle manager being evaluated and the broader organizational context which they are embedded in.

5 Evaluating Leadership in Primary Care: General Practice and Community Engagement

In the last case, we showed that evaluating leadership of middle managers in a tertiary setting can be particularly complex, given their contextual realities of being "caught in the middle." In this section, we present another case illustration, this time focusing on a primary healthcare setting to emphasize the need for greater consideration of context and circumstances when evaluating leadership in healthcare.

Primary healthcare settings are often the first point of contact for citizens, providing comprehensive, continuous, and coordinated care with a workforce that generally includes general practitioners, nurses, practice staff, pharmacists, opticians, and others (Swanwick and Varnam 2019). We focus on the leadership role of general practitioners (GPs). The leadership landscape of general practitioners has traditionally been characterized by a dual focus: one, rooted in clinical expertise, where leadership is expressed through medical knowledge and decision-making; and two, from a managerial perspective, encompassing administrative tasks essential for the smooth operation of their practice (Spehar et al. 2017). Within such a context, the emphasis often leans towards individualist type of leadership, particularly the scrutiny of how GPs motivate and inspire their staff towards better health outcomes for patients and also, sometimes, fostering a sense of performance-oriented dedication (Chreim et al. 2010). Moreover, being emotionally intelligent and empathetic, especially when dealing with patients, is also seen as an essential leadership quality (Coskun et al. 2018).

Being embedded within such duality requires GPs to strike a balance between the rigors of medical expertise and the nuances of relational aspects of leadership. For instance, they are not only diagnosing illnesses but also nurturing trust and confidence in their team as well as their patients. However, this individualist approach, while valuable, often lacks a broader contextual understanding (Fitzgerald et al. 2013). In this evolving landscape, understanding the complexities of community dynamics, integrating the diverse skills of the healthcare team, and adapting leadership styles according to the specific needs of the patient population are becoming increasingly vital aspects of GP leadership (Swanwick and Varnam 2019). As healthcare dynamics shift, the leadership role of GPs has required nuanced understanding of both the clinical intricacies and the social fabric they operate within to be able better evaluate their leadership. This case specifically focuses on evaluating leadership of GPs in community engagement.

5.1 Community Engagement and General Practice

The purpose of "being in the service of the health needs of the community" has long imbued the work of primary healthcare organizations, but it has not always translated well in terms of practical precision until recently. For example, Rowe et al. (2019) states the notion of community engagement continues to lack clarity within general practice, especially in terms of how it can be operationalized and the role GPs can play in the process. This issue is particularly pertinent given that pockets of evidence suggest community engagement can bring about beneficial health outcomes, such as increased health activity and outcomes that GPs value (e.g., screening targets), addressing obesity in communities, and improving healthcare access for disadvantaged populations (Cyril et al. 2015; Wolfenden et al. 2014). There are varied examples of initiatives that can contribute to such outcomes, such as active involvement in community organizations, running initiatives for specific groups like youth and low-income individuals, and even engaging grandmothers for contraceptive education (Rowe et al. 2019). Schiavo (2017) argues that examples of these types of engagements not only help address medical needs but also social and environmental factors that contribute to diseases. Here, the emphasis is on prevention, health promotion, and addressing the social determinants of health (Erku et al. 2023).

5.2 Collective Leadership for Effective Community Engagement

In the above context, the limitations of solitary, individualistic leadership, as we explored previously, become apparent, particularly since effective community engagement for substantive health outcomes may require a "collective" approach to understanding diverse patient needs and critically understanding interconnective issues, such as socioeconomic status and being responsive to sociocultural sensitivity. Following emerging views on leadership within the healthcare sector (Silva et al. 2022), we propose that evaluators may find it more constructive to focus on forms of "collective leadership" particularly in evaluating leadership of GPs in community engagement. Collective leadership[1] is often used as an umbrella term to refer to "multiple individuals assuming (and perhaps divesting themselves) of leadership roles over time in both formal and informal relationships" (Eva et al. 2021). Silva et al. (2022) contextualize this within healthcare and suggest that collective leadership "involves all staff members and patient, where everyone shares responsibility for the success of patient care and the healthcare service." In the case of GPs pursuing community engagement for the purposes of achieving health outcomes that are inherently interconnected in nature, collective leadership can be a promising approach. In particular, the approach acknowledges the intricate interplay of factors that determine health outcomes at the community level and accordingly promotes collaboration, synergy, and a comprehensive understanding of community health dynamics (Silva et al. 2022). Given the relevance of collective leadership in community engagement by GPs, we elaborate on what evaluators may seek in assessing impact in terms of leadership outcomes and processes.

GPs embedded within diverse communities can be expected to achieve various outcomes through community engagement that go beyond traditional health metrics, such as enhancing health literacy, enabling informed decisions, support for community mental health, preventive care such as addressing obesity and diseases, and of course contributing to overall patient outcomes and satisfaction (Cheng et al. 2015; Erku et al. 2023; Swanwick and Varnam 2019; Milton et al. 2012). The list can indeed be long and can be counterproductive if evaluators seek to explore all aspects. Instead, what we advise is to take cues from a "community-needs" approach and evaluate leadership on the basis whether it address priorities and needs of the community that are identified (Schiavo 2017). In light of this, we provide examples of how this may be in two instances.

First, we draw on the empirical work of Rowe et al. (2019) to discuss community engagement of primary health services in Māori communities in Aotearoa New Zealand and highlight collective leadership elements (Friedrich et al. 2016). The community engagement initiative had a multifaceted approach, aimed at achieving some general outcomes, such as health literacy within the community, empowering individuals to make informed decisions about their health, and offering vital support

[1] Collective leadership as an umbrella term encapsulates concepts such as shared, distributed, and collaborative leadership.

and resources for psychological well-being. Beyond these, there were also community expectations, for example, timely and high-quality care, a desire for health services to be delivered in a culturally sensitive manner, fostering strong and respectful patient–doctor relationships, and addressing health disparities between Māori and non-Māori populations.

In delivering such a complex set of objectives and outcomes, evaluators should seek out foundational collective leadership behaviors that can underpin effectiveness. Following Friedrich et al. (2016), we broadly categorize these under network development, communication, and sharing of leadership. For example, in terms of communication, GP initiatives in such settings may demonstrate behaviors that relate to collaboration and consultation. Collaboration, for instance, can allow GPs to understand the unique needs of the community, include diverse perspectives, and allow for different expertise to emerge that help contribute to addressing the various outcomes that are identified; consultation can mean holding open dialogues for community members to voice their concerns, preferences, and suggestions, ensuring that GPs, through community engagement, are leveraging collective wisdom in achieving health outcomes.

Supporting the above, network development as a collective leadership approach is crucial. In this case, we see the process of engagement encompassing the fostering of connections with the community, ensuring the free flow of information, and providing a platform for voices to be heard. And last, in terms of sharing of leadership, leadership roles may not be confined to singular entity, such as the GP, but widely distributed, ensuring the Māori population became a protagonist in their healthcare narrative.

In a similar case, Cheng et al. (2015) discuss primary health community engagement to address the challenges faced by newly arrived refugees in Afghan communities in Australia. Among others, a key aim for leadership was to enhance accessibility and strengthen the Afghan community's ability to engage with healthcare services, which proved difficult for new arrivals. Here, collective leadership and the elements identified above may be something that evaluators may seek out when evaluating leadership in such a scenario. For example, through network development, GPs can reach out to Afghan communities to build partnerships such as setting up of Afghan community advisory groups as Cheng et al. (2015) discuss.

In conclusion, evaluating leadership of general practitioners in community engagement necessitates a nuanced approach rooted in the specific context of each community. Evaluation may focus less on outcomes initially given the time it might take to develop deep and meaningful relationships with communities and for this to develop into action that delivers change in social determinants of health. Evaluators should prioritize outcomes that align with community priorities, emphasizing the contextual relevance of initiatives, all the while being mindful that successful achievement of outcomes identified above can be contingent on factors beyond the scope of what leadership can achieve. Thus, in such case, the evaluation process must be flexible, acknowledging the diverse needs of communities and the multifaceted aspects of collective leadership that include actors beyond health service providers, such as recipients.

The juxtaposition of the two cases is intended to provide insights that evaluation practitioners may leverage and develop evaluation approaches that are tailored to the specific roles and responsibilities of leaders in different health service settings. For middle managers, this might involve a combination of performance metrics, 360-degree feedback, and qualitative assessments of their ability to balance competing priorities. For GPs engaged in community work, evaluation could focus on collective leadership behaviors, community engagement outcomes, and the impact on social determinants of health. Ultimately, a nuanced understanding of leadership context can allow evaluators to evaluate leadership that is contextually relevant and practically impactful.

6 Frameworks for Evaluation

Our case illustrations have shown that evaluation of leadership can be complex, requiring a thorough understanding of the organizational context, dynamics of leaders' position within the organization, the nature of their work, and the outcomes that are expected of them. These aspects are likely to differ between contexts and it is through careful consideration of the nuances that evaluations can be usefully undertaken. There is no single or natural evaluation approach that can be used to evaluate leadership and if the approach is to be meaningful it needs careful crafting.

The leadership models presented in Table 1 can serve as guidelines for evaluators interested in understanding leadership processes and dimensions in association with identified outcomes. Beyond this, it is also worth noting that practice-focused frameworks can also serve as helpful tools for evaluating leadership in real-world contexts. These practice-focused frameworks, often the product of health organizations, can provide tangible, actionable insights on leadership effectiveness and leadership processes that we highlighted previously. These frameworks, often based on academic discourse on leadership, can serve as practical frameworks that are grounded in the reality of leadership tasks, making them highly applicable for assessing leaders' effectiveness in their given roles. By incorporating these frameworks into evaluations, evaluators can move beyond conceptual ideals and grasp the practical implications of leadership within their unique settings. In the following sections, we elaborate on two such frameworks collected from different health jurisdictions.

6.1 New South Wales (NSW) Health Leadership and Management Framework

This framework was developed by the Health Education and Training Institute under the NSW government in Australia. It evaluates leadership across six domains, achieving outcomes; developing and leading self; engaging people and building relationships; partnering and collaborating across boundaries; transforming the system; managing for now and the future. It represents somewhat of a holistic approach to evaluating leadership, one that not only focuses on outcomes or driving change but also mechanisms that help in the achievement of these ends, such as leader competencies, relationship, and collaboration. Underlying this model is the emphasis on both individual and collective leadership, recognizing the leadership effectiveness occurs at different levels and by anyone capable within health organizations. In doing so, it integrates leadership and management competencies that allow evaluators to assess leadership on task-oriented management actions but also relational, change-oriented leadership behaviors. In matching this framework to earlier discussions on leadership, we note that this framework in particular pays attention to transformational and collaborative leadership practices and so can be particularly useful when considering outcomes, such as change, innovation, or delivering integrated services (Fig. 1).

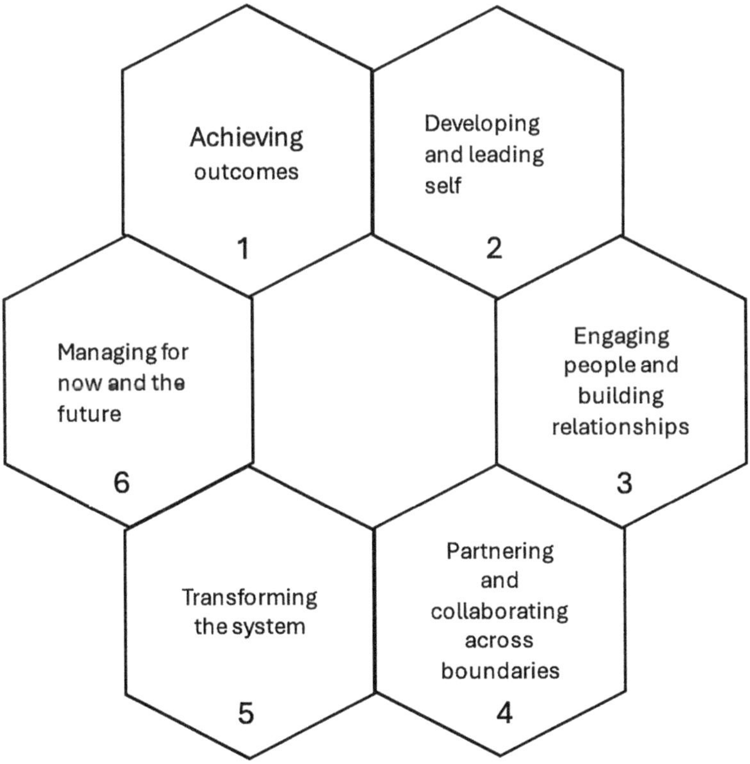

Fig. 1 NSW Health Leadership and Management Framework (HETI 2020). Note: this is the authors' illustration of original framework

6.2 NHS Medical Leadership Competency Framework

The Medical Leadership Competency Framework (MLCF) by the NHS is grounded in the philosophy of collective/distributed leadership, transcending designated roles to foster a collective sense of responsibility for organizational success. It promotes a broad understanding of leadership, encouraging acts of leadership from any member of the organization, focusing on group achievements rather than individual accomplishments. Unlike the previous framework, the MLCF is centered on the delivery of services as its primary outcome and doctors as leaders. It identifies five domains crucial for doctors' leadership competence. These domains encompass personal qualities, collaboration, service management, service improvement, and engagement in medical leadership. It serves as a comprehensive guide for evaluating leadership of doctors in the delivery of health services (Fig. 2).

While the above frameworks provide valuable structures for evaluating leadership, caution is paramount when applying them to diverse healthcare contexts. For example, the intricacies of leadership in community health settings often involve multifaceted challenges that may not be fully encapsulated by standardized frameworks. Community healthcare leadership demands a nuanced understanding of

Fig. 2 NHS Medical Leadership Competency Framework (NHS 2010). Note: this is the authors' illustration of original framework

local dynamics, cultural considerations, and community engagement, which may not be exhaustively addressed by generic competency models. Moreover, the priorities in community healthcare, such as preventive care, social determinants of health, and community collaboration may not align perfectly with the domains and competencies outlined in broader frameworks. Therefore, while these frameworks offer valuable insights, evaluators should exercise discretion, adaptability, and a keen awareness of the unique demands of healthcare contexts to ensure a more nuanced and contextually relevant evaluation of leadership effectiveness.

In addition to these frameworks assisting practitioners, it can also be helpful if a broader set of guiding questions are considered while navigating the complex practice of evaluating leadership in health services. As we have discovered, leadership is not a one-size-fits-all concept; health contexts vary widely, and sometimes, rigid frameworks might overlook critical nuances. Moreover, no evaluation can assess every facet of leadership and needs to make trade-offs between different factors and depth and breadth of analysis. In such cases, we recommend practitioners consider the following set of guiding questions to help them determine the most appropriate evaluation approach:

- What is the purpose of the evaluation (e.g., formative, summative, developmental, etc.)? What is it you are trying to do with the evaluation? What are the opportunities for impact of the evaluation?
- What is the role of leadership within the team/organization/service and what is it trying to achieve?
- Is there a theory of change and associated leadership framework/theory that might explain how leadership is supposed to be enacted and for what purposes?
- Are there a set of leadership competencies/processes that is being evaluated? If so, what are they?
- How will the impact of leadership be assessed/understood or in some cases, measured?

These questions serve as navigational beacons, allowing practitioners to delve into the intricacies of contextual specificities, diversity of leadership practices, and evolving health landscapes. Careful consideration of these questions can help in aligning leadership evaluations with unique healthcare settings. For instance, questioning the purpose of the evaluation enables practitioners to tailor strategies based on whether it is formative, summative, or developmental and to identify potential leadership impacts. Evaluators can explore the role of leadership and its intended achievements, ensuring a thorough understanding of how leadership competencies contribute to the overall healthcare outcomes. In essence, these questions promote contextually attuned evaluation of leadership and leadership impact on varied healthcare settings.

7 Conclusion

The evaluation of leadership in health services is a nuanced endeavor that demands a comprehensive and contextual approach. Our case illustrations have underscored the complexity of leadership, emphasizing the need for evaluative frameworks that go beyond the one-size-fits-all mentality. While structured frameworks offer valuable guidance, the inclusion of broader guiding questions becomes imperative, aligning leadership assessments with the diverse tapestry of healthcare settings. In short, we recommend a balanced approach of the evaluation of leadership in health services, one that draws on extant leadership knowledge but is tempered with context-sensitive evaluations, revealing more holistically the factors that shape effective leadership.

References

Alsalmi M, Alilyyani B (2023) The role of authentic leadership in nurses' stress and burnout in emergency departments. Leadership in Health Services. ahead-of-print
Alvesson M, Sveningsson S (2003) Good visions, bad micro-management and ugly ambiguity: contradictions of (non-) leadership in a knowledge-intensive organization. Organ Stud 24:961–988
Amaladas S (2019) Leadership effectiveness and the problem of social action: continuing the conversation between Burns and Rost. Leadership 15:517–534
Armistead C, Pettigrew P, Aves S (2007) Exploring leadership in multi-sectoral partnerships. Leadership 3:211–230
Avolio BJ, Gardner WL (2005) Authentic leadership development: getting to the root of positive forms of leadership. Leadersh Q 16:315–338
Bass BM, Riggio RE (2006) Transformational leadership. Lawrence Erlbaum Associates Inc., Mahwah
Birken SA, Lee S-YD, Weiner BJ (2012) Uncovering middle managers' role in healthcare innovation implementation. Implement Sci 7:1–12
Buchanan D, Parry E, Gascoigne C, Moore C (2013) Are healthcare middle management jobs extreme jobs? J Health Organ Manag 27:646–664
Burns J (1978) Leadership. Harper & Row, New York
Burns JM (2004) Transforming leadership: a new pursuit of happiness. Grove Press
Carlström ED (2012) Middle managers on the slide. Leadersh Health Serv 25:90–105
Cheng I-H, Wahidi S, Vasi S, Samuel S (2015) Importance of community engagement in primary health care: the case of Afghan refugees. Aust J Prim Health 21:262–267
Chreim S, Williams BE, Janz L, Dastmalchian A (2010) Change agency in a primary health care context: the case of distributed leadership. Health Care Manag Rev 35:187–199
Coskun O, Ulutas I, Budakoglu II, Ugurlu M, Ustu Y (2018) Emotional intelligence and leadership traits among family physicians. Postgrad Med 130:644–649
Cox JW, Hassard J (2018) From relational to relationist leadership in critical management education: recasting leadership work after the practice turn. Acad Manag Learn Edu 17:532–556
Curado C, Santos R (2022) Transformational leadership and work performance in health care: the mediating role of job satisfaction. Leadersh Health Serv 35:160–173
Currie G, Lockett A (2011) Distributing leadership in health and social care: concertive, conjoint or collective? Int J Manag Rev 13:286–300

Cyril S, Smith BJ, Possamai-Inesedy A, Renzaho AM (2015) Exploring the role of community engagement in improving the health of disadvantaged populations: a systematic review. Glob Health Action 8:29842

Daly J, Jackson D, Mannix J, Davidson PM, Hutchinson M (2014) The importance of clinical leadership in the hospital setting. J Healthcare Leadersh:75–83

Day DV, Fleenor JW, Atwater LE, Sturm RE, Mckee RA (2014) Advances in leader and leadership development: a review of 25years of research and theory. Leadersh Q 25:63–82

Denis J-L, Van Gestel N (2016) Medical doctors in healthcare leadership: theoretical and practical challenges. BMC Health Serv Res 16:158

Dickinson H, O'flynn J (2016) Evaluating outcomes in health and social care. Policy Press, Bristol

Enwereuzor IK, Adeyemi BA, Onyishi IE (2020) Trust in leader as a pathway between ethical leadership and safety compliance. Leadersh Health Serv 33:201–219

Erku D, Khatri R, Endalamaw A, Wolka E, Nigatu F, Zewdie A, Assefa Y (2023) Community engagement initiatives in primary health care to achieve universal health coverage: a realist synthesis of scoping review. PLoS One 18:e0285222

Eva N, Robin M, Sendjaya S, Van Dierendonck D, Liden RC (2019) Servant leadership: a systematic review and call for future research. Leadersh Q 30:111–132

Eva N, Cox JW, Herman H, Lowe KB (2021) From competency to conversation: a multi-perspective approach to collective leadership development. Leadersh Q 32:101346

Fernandez S, Cho YJ, Perry JL (2010) Exploring the link between integrated leadership and public sector performance. Leadersh Q 21:308–323

Fitzgerald L, Ferlie E, Mcgivern G, Buchanan D (2013) Distributed leadership patterns and service improvement: evidence and argument from English healthcare. Leadersh Q 24:227–239

Friedrich TL, Griffith JA, Mumford MD (2016) Collective leadership behaviors: evaluating the leader, team network, and problem situation characteristics that influence their use. Leadersh Q 27:312–333

Greenleaf RK (1977) Servant leadership: a journey into the nature of legitimate power and greatness. Paulist Press, New York

Gutberg J, Berta W (2017) Understanding middle managers' influence in implementing patient safety culture. BMC Health Serv Res 17:1–10

Hartviksen TA, Sjolie BM, Aspfors J, Uhrenfeldt L (2018) Healthcare middle managers' experiences developing leadership capacity and capability in a public funded learning network. BMC Health Serv Res 18:433

HETI (2020) The NSW health leadership and management framework. Health and Education Training Institution, NSW Health, Sydney

Holmberg I, Tyrstrup M (2010) Well then-what now? An everyday approach to managerial leadership. Leadership 6:353–372

Islam T, Ahmed I, Ali G (2018) Effects of ethical leadership on bullying and voice behavior among nurses: mediating role of organizational identification, poor working condition and workload. Leadersh Health Serv 32:2–17

Jenkinson C (1997) Assessment and evaluation of health and medical care: a methods text. McGraw-Hill Education (UK)

Jeon Y-H, Glasgow NJ, Merlyn T, Sansoni E (2010) Policy options to improve leadership of middle managers in the Australian residential aged care setting: a narrative synthesis. BMC Health Serv Res 10:1–11

Kotter JP (1990) What leaders really do. Harv Bus Rev 68:103–111

Milton B, Attree P, French B, Povall S, Whitehead M, Popay J (2012) The impact of community engagement on health and social outcomes: a systematic review. Commun Dev J 47:316–334

Mintzberg H (1971) Managerial work: analysis from observation. Manag Sci 18:B-97-B-110

Mrayyan MT, Al-Atiyyat N, Al-Rawashdeh S, Algunmeeyn A, Abunab HY (2022) Nurses' authentic leadership and their perceptions of safety climate: differences across areas of work and hospitals. Leadersh Health Serv 35:372–389

Neubert MJ, Hunter EM, Tolentino RC (2016) A servant leader and their stakeholders: when does organizational structure enhance a leader's influence? Leadersh Q 27:896–910

Ng TWH (2017) Transformational leadership and performance outcomes: analyses of multiple mediation pathways. Leadersh Q 28:385–417
NHS (2010) Medical leadership competency framework: enhancing engagement in medical leadership. In: NHS Institute for Innovation and Improvement and Academy of Medical Royal Colleges, Coventry
O'toole, L. J. (2015) Networks and networking: the public administrative agendas. Public Adm Rev 75:361–371
Puni A, Hilton SK (2020) Dimensions of authentic leadership and patient care quality. Leadersh Health Serv 33:365–383
Randolph SD, Johnson R, Mcgee K, Adimora A, Ramirez C, Bailey JDE, Holt L, Koch A, Mcmillian-Bohler JM, Ritchwood T, Relf MV (2022) Adaptive leadership in clinical encounters with women living with HIV. BMC Womens Health 22:217–217
Raoush A (2023) Transformational leadership impact on innovative behaviour as perceived by healthcare workers in private hospitals in Jordan. Cogent Bus Manage 10:2265606
Raphael JL (2013) Observations from the balcony: directions for pediatric health disparities research and policy. J Appl Res Child 4
Rossi PH, Freeman HE (1985) Evaluation: a systematic approach. Sage, Newbury Park
Rost JC (1991) Leadership for the twenty-first century. Greenwood, New York
Rowe N, Keenan R, Lack L, Malloy N, Strasser R, Lawrenson R (2019) Community engagement in general practice: a qualitative study. J Prim Health Care 11:146–151
Sarabi Asiabar A, Kafaei Mehr MH, Arabloo J, Safari H (2019) Leadership effectiveness of hospital managers in Iran: a qualitative study. Leadersh Health Serv 33:43–55
Schiavo R (2017) Turning clinicians into community leaders: perspectives from a recent trip in Cuba and beyond. Taylor & Francis
Schweller M, Ribeiro DL, Celeri EV, De Carvalho-Filho MA (2017) Nurturing virtues of the medical profession: does it enhance medical students' empathy? Int J Med Educ 8:262
Scriven M (1991) Evaluation thesaurus. Sage, Newbury Park
Silva JAM, Mininel VA, Agreli HF, Peduzzi M, Harrison R, Xyrichis A (2022) Collective leadership to improve professional practice, healthcare outcomes and staff well-being. Cochrane Database Syst Rev
Silver R, Martin M (2022) Servant leadership and its association with an environment of empathic care: an empirical analysis of the perspectives of mid-level practitioners. Leadersh Health Serv 35:116–136
Silverman D (2013) Doing qualitative research: a practical handbook London. Sage
Smith K (2013) Beyond evidence-based policy in public health: the interplay of ideas. Palgrave Macmillan, Basingstoke
Spehar I, Sjøvik H, Karevold KI, Rosvold EO, Frich JC (2017) General practitioners' views on leadership roles and challenges in primary health care: a qualitative study. Scand J Prim Health Care 35:105–110
Swanwick T, Varnam R (2019) Leadership development and primary care. BMJ Leader 3:59–61
Top M, Akdere M, Tarcan M (2015) Examining transformational leadership, job satisfaction, organizational commitment and organizational trust in Turkish hospitals: public servants versus private sector employees. Int J Hum Resour Manag 26:1259–1282
Weintraub P, Mckee M (2019) Leadership for innovation in healthcare: an exploration. Int J Health Policy Manag 8:138
Willcocks SG (2012) Exploring leadership effectiveness: nurses as clinical leaders in the NHS. Leadersh Health Serv 25:8–19
Wolfenden L, Wyse R, Nichols M, Allender S, Millar L, Mcelduff P (2014) A systematic review and meta-analysis of whole of community interventions to prevent excessive population weight gain. Prev Med 62:193–200
Wong LY, Sendjaya S, Wilson S, Rixon A (2023) Evidence behind the exhortation? A rapid review of servant leadership's influence and claims in healthcare over the last decade, vol 8. BMJ Leader, p 88

Yasir M, Jan A (2023) Servant leadership in relation to organizational justice and workplace deviance in public hospitals. Leadersh Health Serv 36:164–185
Zonneveld N, Pittens C, Minkman M (2021) Appropriate leadership in nursing home care: a narrative review. Leadersh Health Serv 34:16–36

Evaluation in the Context of a Learning Health System

Anna Perry and Douglas Easterling

Abstract

Learning Health Systems (LHS) leverage a health system's patient data and internal and external research to enhance quality, safety, efficiency, and equity. The LHS paradigm has been adopted by local, regional, and national systems. Evaluation plays a crucial role across all. This chapter defines LHS, specifies its operational elements, and explores how evaluation supports LHS. It focuses specifically on the types of evaluation that LHS calls for, the roles that evaluators play and the skills they should have in order to optimize their contributions. This chapter presents the first analysis of how evaluators can support a healthcare system in being an LHS. The LHS paradigm can elevate the use of evaluation in healthcare, but this will require new skills and roles for evaluators and support from system leaders.

Keywords

Healthcare evaluation · Health service evaluation · Learning health system · Learning healthcare system · Embedded evaluation · Evaluation approaches

A. Perry (✉)
Milken Institute School of Public Health, George Washington University, Washington, DC, USA
e-mail: annap@gwu.edu

D. Easterling
Department of Social Sciences and Health Policy, School of Medicine, Wake Forest University, Winston-Salem, NC, USA
e-mail: dveaster@wakehealth.edu

A. Kaehne, J. Feather (eds.), *Handbook of Health Services Evaluation*,
https://doi.org/10.1007/978-3-031-87869-5_19

1 Introduction

As demonstrated throughout this volume, evaluation is an essential function in ensuring that healthcare organizations deliver high-quality care efficiently and equitably. In this chapter, we will introduce a paradigm for improving healthcare service delivery, called "Learning Health Systems" (LHS), which calls for healthcare organizations (and larger "health systems") to use structured learning, analysis of clinical data and translation of evidence into improved practice. LHS calls for health systems to place a much greater emphasis on evaluation and, more specifically, calls for evaluation processes that are more comprehensive than what health systems have traditionally put in place. This chapter serves as an introductory exploration of the LHS paradigm, its implications for the practice of evaluation within the context of healthcare systems, and the interplay between these two facets of healthcare improvement.

It should be noted that this chapter is written from the United States (US) perspective, where a "health system" is a corporate entity involved in the delivery of healthcare services, as well as related activities such as medical education, residency training, population health management and research. Any given health system might contain multiple outpatient clinics, hospitals, primary care facilities and patient information sharing, all unified under a single provider name, a single Chief Executive Officer (CEO) and a single board of directors. This structure ensures shared leadership, financial resources and operations across these entities.

2 What is a Learning Health System (LHS)?

An LHS is a paradigm designed to encourage healthcare organizations and health systems to continuously improve the quality of the care they deliver through deliberate learning, which integrates internal and external research, ongoing analysis of clinical care, and feedback from patients and other stakeholders. The term, "learning health system," has two distinct interpretations. First, the health system has centered learning as a core function to improve patient care and patient outcomes. Second, learning is conducted in an ongoing, structured, cyclic fashion. Or in other words, the health system has put "learning systems" in place to capture, analyze, interpret, and act on data.

The idea of a LHS assumes that a health system can learn through iterative processes and knowledge transfer among research, policy, and practice. Thought leaders in the health industry are promoting LHS as a means of accelerating both the translation of research into practice and the development of interventions that will improve patient care and patient outcomes (Agency for Healthcare Research and Quality n.d.; NCATS 2014). The LHS concept calls for healthcare organizations to be more systematic and data-driven in generating and utilizing knowledge to improve the quality and value of the care they deliver, while also stimulating innovation (Psek et al. 2015).

2.1 Origins of the Concept

The LHS concept was initially framed as "learning *healthcare* systems" when it was discussed at a 2006 workshop organized by the Institute of Medicine (IOM) (McGinnis et al. 2007). IOM's emphasis on LHS reflected several factors including:

- Increased recognition and reporting of shortcomings in clinical care that impact patient outcomes (e.g., hospital-borne infections, medical errors, poor transitions in care following hospitalization).
- Frustration that treatments found to be effective in clinical trials are not being adopted in a widespread or timely fashion.
- Increased focus on evidence-based policy decisions.
- New opportunities for discovery stemming from the transition to electronic health records, combined with the advances in computing power and analytic sophistication.
- Increased costs for health services.

The summary publication from this workshop introduced the LHS concept to the larger field. It defined LHS as a model to "generate and apply the best evidence for the collaborative healthcare choices of each patient and provider; drive the process of discovery as a natural outgrowth of patient care, and ensure innovation, quality, safety and value in health care," (page *ix*). This definition has evolved over time. In 2015, IOM's successor, the National Academy of Medicine (NAM), released its current definition: "In a learning healthcare system, science, informatics, incentives and culture are aligned for continuous improvement and innovation, with best practices seamlessly embedded in the delivery process, patients and families as active participants in all elements, and new knowledge captured as an integral by-product of the delivery experience" (IOM 2015, p. 136).

Although LHS first gained traction in the United States, the concept has resonated with healthcare systems worldwide, including the Netherlands, United Kingdom, Australia, and Singapore. The adaptability and broad appeal of the LHS concept show in its global adoption. Additionally, the LHS concept can be applied at various levels, from an individual healthcare delivery clinic to a national health system. IOM purposely defined LHS in broad terms so that it could be applied in many different contexts (McGinnis et al. 2007).

2.2 A More Detailed Framework

This lack of specificity means that any health system that adopts LHS faces the challenge of determining what exactly this will mean in terms of the new work that is expected. To guide health system leaders in meeting that challenge, our team conducted a scoping review of 79 scientific publications outlining current or recommended work that health systems are carrying out, or should be carrying out, under the rubric of LHS (Easterling et al. 2022).

The publications we reviewed pointed to 25 different activities that could or should occur within an LHS. We organized these into the following five "bodies of work,": (1) organizational learning and continuous quality improvement; (2) translating knowledge and evidence into practice; (3) building new knowledge and evidence; (4) analyzing clinical data for learning; and (5) engaging clinicians, patients and other stakeholders. These five bodies of work are interconnected and each support the overall goal of improving the quality, value, safety, and equity of patient care. This is reflected in the Learning Health System Consolidated Framework (LHS-CF), which is presented in Fig. 1.

LHS-CF also points to four "enabling conditions" that need to be in place within a health system to support the implementation of the LHS paradigm: (1) employees have the expertise to carry out LHS research; (2) clinical data are stored and managed electronically, and the health system has the informatics infrastructure that

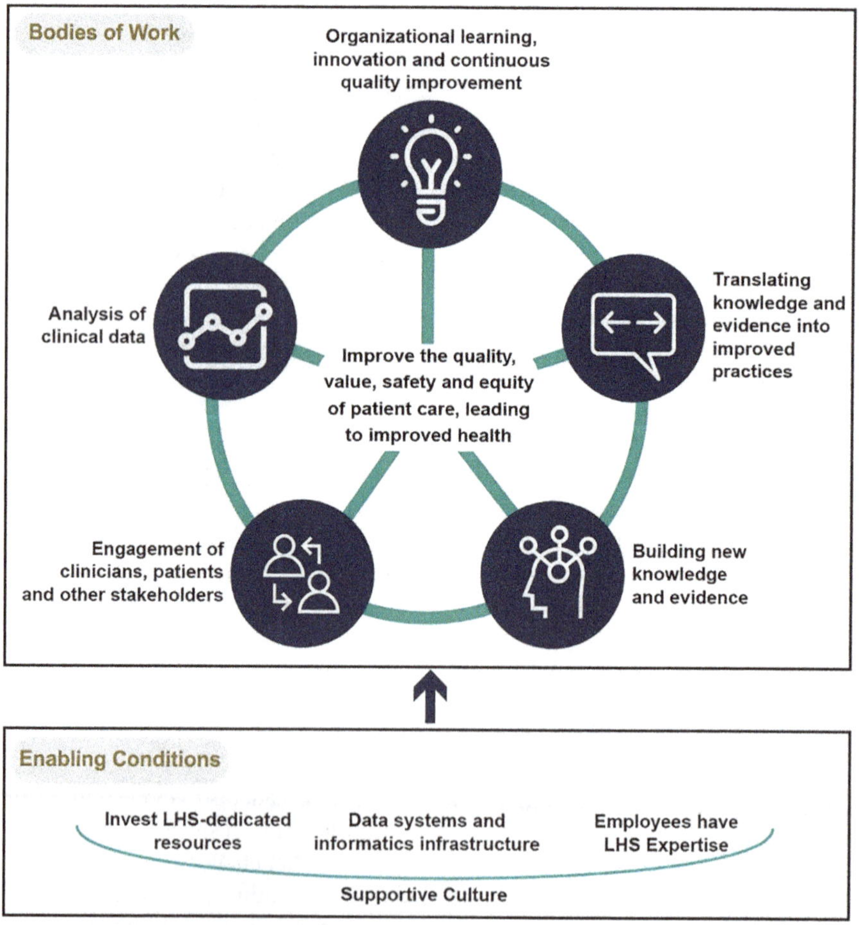

Fig. 1 Learning health systems consolidated framework (LHS-CF) (Easterling et al. 2022)

allows clinicians and researchers to access those data for learning purposes; (3) health system leaders invest sufficient resources for LHS work; and (4) the organization's culture reinforces the importance of LHS and supports LHS work. A supportive organizational culture underlies the other three conditions and is one of the most frequently cited elements of LHS in the literature.

2.3 What Work Happens in a LHS?

As mentioned earlier, LHS is defined in broad terms which makes it challenging to identify the work that health systems are expected to carry out under the paradigm. LHS-CF divides that work into five "bodies," and specifies more concrete "forms" of work within each. Table 1 lists specific forms of work that were cited in at least 10 of the 79 articles included in the scoping review.

The first body of work, *organizational learning, innovation, and continuous quality improvement*, involves the creation and use of intentional learning processes that allow the healthcare organization and its employees to become smarter in organizing and delivering services that affect patient outcomes. This body of work is supported by models such as Charles Friedman's Learning Cycle (Guise et al. 2018) and rapid-cycle learning (Etheredge 2014). In addition, some publications pointed to broader concepts such as "systems science" (Lessard et al. 2017; Boes et al. 2018) and "positive deviance" (McLachlan et al. 2018, 2019), which provide an orientation to thinking, learning, and innovation. Sixteen of the publications specifically noted collaborative or team-based learning as being more fruitful than individually oriented learning.

A critical first step in carrying out high-payoff organizational learning is for leaders to determine and identify a limited number of issues that are critical to the health system's performance and effectiveness. These issues might involve improvements to quality of care delivered by specific service lines, high rates of hospital-acquired infections, disparities in health outcomes, high readmission rates, or clinician burnout and turnover. Once these priorities are established, leaders develop a "learning agenda" defined by specific learning questions, specific methods to answer those questions, assignment of roles and responsibilities, and mechanisms for sharing and acting on what is learned.

The second body of work is *translation of knowledge and evidence* into improved practice by researchers, clinicians, and other stakeholders. "Knowledge" and "evidence" are global terms that cover a wide range of information such as findings from clinical trials, reports on the effectiveness of innovative procedures, empirical analyses of disease processes, and descriptions of the risk factors facing a particular patient population. Knowledge and evidence can be generated both inside and outside the organization.

Knowledge and evidence have the potential to improve care, but those pay-offs require deliberate searching, critical assessment and smart approaches to implementation. As such, translating knowledge and evidence into improved practice involves identifying research findings and other knowledge that have the potential to improve

Table 1 Forms of work practiced within an LHS

Body of work	Specific forms of work mentioned in the literature (all work is oriented toward improving patient care and outcomes)
Organizational learning, innovation, and continuous quality improvement	• Structured learning processes are integrated into operations and clinical practice with the explicit intent of improving quality, safety, and value of care, and to enhance efficiency of operations • Quality improvement processes, including continuous quality improvement and rapid-cycle learning, are routinely employed throughout the organization • The organization uses learning models that are informed by systems science and that link data, knowledge and performance • Collaborative or team-based learning is practiced
Translating knowledge and evidence	• Relevant internal and external research findings are identified and translated into treatments and practices that improve patient outcomes and organizational performance • The organization systematically adopts and implements evidence-based treatments • Principles of implementation science are used in selecting, adopting, adapting, implementing, and sustaining new practices • Ineffective or sub-optimal practices are systematically de-implemented
Building new knowledge and evidence	• The organization conducts LHS research to answer questions that relate directly to the organization's goals and issues regarding patient care. (over and above any basic science or investigator-initiated studies that might also be conducted within the health system) • The LHS research conducted within the institutions emphasizes cost-effectiveness, practicality, and quick turnaround, while still adhering to the standards of science • The organization conducts rigorous research (especially extramurally funded research) that addresses critical questions regarding health and health care that are important at a more general level (beyond the health system's own issues) • Interventions found to be promising through quality improvement processes are investigated through more systematic research • Findings from research are strategically shared/disseminated internally within the organization • Generalizable findings are also disseminated to external audiences through publications and scientific presentations
Analysis of clinical data in support of organizational learning and knowledge generation	• Patient data are captured and organized into an information system in ways that they can be analyzed for research, quality improvement and other forms of learning • Clinical and/or informatics data are used in diagnosing and treating individual patients • Clinical decision support systems are in place and routinely used • Clinical data are analyzed to support personalized treatment and/or precision medicine • Clinical data are analyzed to develop research questions, design studies and carry out studies • Clinical data are shared with other institutions and/or networked • Employees throughout the organization routinely access and analyze clinical data for research and learning (e.g. to identify patterns in how patients are treated and in treatment outcomes)

(continued)

Table 1 (continued)

Body of work	Specific forms of work mentioned in the literature (all work is oriented toward improving patient care and outcomes)
Engagement of clinicians, patients, and other stakeholders	• Employees from throughout the organization (including practicing clinicians) are directly engaged in all aspects of learning, generating knowledge and translating knowledge into practice • Patients and family members are actively engaged in clinical decision making • Patients and family members play a substantive role in the organizational learning process, identifying research questions, translating knowledge into practice, etc. • The organization reaches out to external partners with a stake in improving patient care and provides meaningful forums for influencing the learning agenda

patient care, and then critically assessing and appropriately applying that knowledge in ways that lead to uptake and then better outcomes for the health system's patients. Adopting evidence-based practices is central to this translation. Learning health systems are intentional in selecting the practices that are most relevant and beneficial to their patient population.

The field of implementation science offers a variety of tools, methods, and theories to support the translation of knowledge into practice. Interestingly, only 3 of the 79 publications in our literature review explicitly mentioned the term, "implementation science" (Moffatt-Bruce et al. 2018; Forrest et al. 2018; Kilbourne et al. 2019), but several others pointed to key concepts from implementation science, such as systematic approaches to implementation and adaptation of interventions to the local context (McGinnis et al. 2011b, c; Maddox et al. 2017).

The third body of work is *building knowledge and evidence* with the potential to improve health. This is work that goes beyond individual and organizational learning. It produces generalizable knowledge (e.g. research findings, tests of interventions, new theories) that various audiences can use to improve health care and health outcomes.

The definitive approach to building knowledge and evidence is scientific research. More than one-third of the publications in our sample included "conducting research" within their conceptualization of LHS, but they generally referred to "practical" rather than the sort of "scientific" research carried out by academic institutions. The predominant view among the publications is that the research conducted within an LHS should answer questions directly related to issues facing the health system and its patients. This emphasis on immediate usability of the findings means that at least some of the research conducted within the organization prioritizes efficiency and practicality over applying rigorous scientific methods, especially randomized clinical trials.

The fourth body of work is the *analysis of clinical data in support of organizational learning and knowledge generation* that lead to improved patient care. One of the most prominent streams of innovation around the LHS concept has involved optimizing the informational value of electronic health records, especially regarding assessing patterns and trends that can only be seen when data are pooled across hundreds or thousands of patients. When a health system is operating as an LHS, those data are routinely accessed and analyzed by employees throughout the organization. Those analyses support research, quality improvement projects and other forms of organizational learning that lead to improved treatments and patterns of practice. In addition, clinicians take advantage of the higher functionality of clinical data systems to provide care that is personalized to the patient's physical condition, genetics, and disease characteristics. This deliberate analysis of clinical data is one of the most important features that distinguish an LHS from healthcare organizations that operate in a more traditional fashion.

The fifth body of work is the *engagement of clinicians, patients, families and other stakeholders* in learning, translation, and knowledge generation. Just over half the publications in our sample included patient engagement in their conceptualization of LHS. This form of engagement extends beyond shared decision making in individual patient care. Nearly half of these publications described patient engagement in terms of the learning process (e.g. contributing to the development of research questions, interpreting data). It is not only patients who have a substantive role to play within LHS work. Patient advocacy groups and community-based organizations also have a stake in how health systems deliver care, and thus a role to play in the learning process. In addition, payers and policy makers might be engaged to align incentives with the adoption and delivery of evidence-based care.

2.4 What Work Enables a LHS?

The LHS-CF also specifies the enabling conditions needed to support these bodies of work. Table 2 provides a top-level view of what aspects have been emphasized in the literature (elements cited in at least 10 articles in the scoping review).

Three of these enabling conditions involve specific forms of capacity and resources that are needed to carry out effective LHS work across the organization: expertise, data systems and informatics infrastructure, and investment of LHS-dedicated resources. The fourth enabling condition—an organizational culture supportive of LHS—is an essential overarching requirement which ensures that the other three conditions are in place.

The first enabling condition is that the organization has a critical mass of *employees with the skills and knowledge necessary for LHS work*. This includes the ability to access clinical data, submit queries and run analyses (Forrest et al. 2018; Deans et al. 2018). Skills in research design and statistics are also important within an LHS. Health systems such as Kaiser Permanente have deployed "embedded researchers" who can support clinicians in developing and answering clinically relevant research questions (Gould et al. 2020). Some of this capacity can be built through the training of existing employees (Wysham et al. 2016), but most healthcare organizations will need to hire new employees with specialized

Table 2 LHS enabling conditions

Condition	Specific enabling factors frequently mentioned in the literature
Expertise	• Employees throughout the organization have the skills and knowledge to engage in structured learning, quality improvement, data analysis, etc. • Organization provides training to employees on LHS competencies (e.g. quality improvement, research methods, and analysis of clinical data)
Data systems and informatics infrastructure	• Appropriate informatics technology and resources are in place within the organization • Clinical data systems are designed strategically (anticipating the questions that investigators will bring and the analyses to be conducted) • Clinical data systems and repositories meet rigorous standards, especially privacy, quality, and reliability
Investment of LHS-dedicated resources	• Organizational policies incentivize LHS activities
Supportive culture	• Organizational leaders are active, visible champions of LHS principles and practices • The organization has norms that encourage and support learning, translation of evidence into practice, building knowledge and patient engagement • Organizational policies and culture promote transparency, integrity, and trust-building • Collaboration and/or team-based learning is valued

skills in research methodology, clinical informatics and/or implementation science.

Data systems, informatics technology and resources are in place within the organization to support analyses of clinical data that address the organization's learning questions. In particular, clinical data systems need to be structured in ways that a variety of users can access the data and submit queries of varying levels of complexity (McGinnis et al. 2011a). The records in those data systems need to meet standards around quality, completeness, reliability, and privacy (Lessard et al. 2017; Lowes et al. 2017).

The *organization invests resources* that are sufficient to carry out the different bodies of LHS work. This includes major investments in the clinical data system and informatics infrastructure, as well as hiring professionals with the skills to carry out the wide array of tasks that go along with being an LHS (Morain et al. 2017). It also means making dedicated investments in research that addresses the issues and questions that health system leaders have identified as priorities (Psek et al. 2015). In other words, LHS requires healthcare organizations to dedicate a portion of their budget to staff who are primarily involved in the process of learning, analysis, and building knowledge—under the assumption that this will result in improvements in quality, effectiveness, and efficiency, which in turn will bring about a positive return on investment.

The fourth enabling condition, *supportive culture*, is at the root of what it takes for a healthcare organization to be successful at LHS work (Moffatt-Bruce et al.

2018; Menear et al. 2019). One indication of a supportive culture is that leaders of the organization are active, visible champions of LHS principles and practices (Morain et al. 2017). Similarly, institutional policies should incentivize LHS work. LHS publications also make a point of calling out transparency, integrity, collaboration, and trust as values that the culture needs to reinforce and reward (Moloney et al. 2016).

As indicated above, significant new investment accompanies the transition to an LHS. These costs may be substantial, covering infrastructure, technology upgrades and the training of personnel. There are significant cost advantages associated with larger health systems undertaking these initiatives, as they are better equipped to manage the substantial new expenses involved in becoming an LHS. Smaller healthcare organizations would likely face considerable challenges (e.g. financial burden) in undertaking LHS activities and in attempting to fully utilize their data to enhance clinical practices.

Even greater economies of scale are possible with government-operated health systems that operate throughout the country. Their size and centralized data structures would enable LHS work across the whole system. This operational scale may offset some of the financial requirements associated with transitioning to LHS work, making government-run health systems particularly well-suited to make this change.

3 New Expectations and Implications for Evaluators

When a healthcare organization adopts the LHS paradigm, the focus on learning, analysis, and translation will increase the demand for evaluators. But it is important to recognize that LHS requires evaluators with specific skill sets. The starting point here are the competencies that the American Evaluation Association has specified in the areas of methodology, planning and management, context, and interpersonal and professional practice (American Evaluation Association 2018). At the same time, it is important to point out that that the LHS paradigm calls for evaluators who have a broader set of skills than has been typically expected within the evaluation field.

As in any organization that conducts or contracts for evaluation, an LHS needs evaluators who have a high level of proficiency in working with data. This includes data collection, management, analysis, and interpretation. These evaluators should be comfortable using statistical tools, data visualization and other software used to make sense of large datasets.

In addition, LHS evaluators need to be skilled in a variety of evaluation methods, including both quantitative and qualitative approaches. They should be able to collect, analyze, and interpret data from diverse sources. This could include, but is not limited to, patient outcomes, clinical processes and stakeholder feedback. When multiple methods have been used to evaluate a particular intervention, the evaluator needs to present findings in tandem to provide a more comprehensive understanding of the data and, when possible, produce triangulated conclusions.

3.1 Key Evaluation Methods

The specific methodological skills required within any given LHS will depend in large part on the types of studies the organization uses for learning and building knowledge. Our review of LHS in practice points to seven research methodologies which are applied at different stages in developing and testing new interventions. These methods include:

1. Quality improvement (QI): a tool to continuously track how well healthcare processes are performing. Regularly collecting and analyzing data allows healthcare teams to identify patterns and trends. These data can be mapped onto key performance indicators and can help clinicians gauge whether they are moving in the right direction and achieving their, and the health systems, goals.
2. Formative evaluation of new intervention models: gathering information and feedback while the program or project is still ongoing, rather than at the end.
3. Pragmatic trials: interventions in natural, or "real-world" settings. Evidence is applicable and relevant as the intervention will more closely resemble routine clinical practice.
4. Multi-site clinical trials: a research study that takes place at more than one location simultaneously, allowing for larger and more diverse samples.
5. Analysis of EHR data: identifying predictors of patient outcomes, to assess whether natural variation in intervention strategies (e.g., based on provider preference) leads to differential outcomes, to identify patients eligible for studies, to create comparison groups for case-control studies, etc.
6. Implementation evaluations: assessing how well an intervention is being implemented according to its intended design and whether adjustments are needed to increase effectiveness.
7. Stakeholder-engaged research: emphasizing collaboration and active participation of stakeholders throughout the process. Stakeholders include patients, community members, advocates, clinicians, policymakers, etc.

These methods involve distinct orientations and approaches to all phases of the evaluation process, including question formation, engagement with stakeholders, data collection/extraction, analysis, and learning. As such, evaluators tend to specialize in only a subset of the methods and develop their competencies accordingly. Table 3 shows specific examples of evaluation competencies associated with each method.

Table 3 Evaluator competencies required for LHS evaluation methods

Evaluation method	Required competencies
QI studies	Learning cycles, tailored data collection, quick turnaround
Formative evaluation	Process evaluation, qualitative methods, delivering feedback, interactive process design
Pragmatic trials/multi-site trials	Research design, statistical analysis, analytic modelling, power analysis
Analyzing electronic health records	Informatics
Implementation evaluation	Implementation science, process evaluation
Stakeholder-engaged research	Community-based participatory research (CBPR)

3.2 Expanding Beyond Methodological Competencies

In addition to these competencies related to evaluation methodologies, LHS evaluators will also need to understand how to work effectively within a dynamic healthcare environment. They will need to know enough about the organization and delivery of clinical care to use appropriate methods and measures for evaluating the implementation of interventions. While evaluators with expertise in specific methodologies remain valuable, roles within the LHS may need an interdisciplinary orientation that enables them to communicate and collaborate appropriately with researchers, clinicians, administrators, and other stakeholders. They will need to excel at translating evidence into actionable recommendations that align with evolving priorities of local healthcare systems. Accomplishing this balancing act will require competencies such as the following:

1. Clinical understanding: LHS evaluators will require a true understanding of clinical practices, medical terminology, and patient care processes. This knowledge will allow them to assess and interpret the impact of findings and interventions within the clinical context more effectively. Given that most evaluators will not have the specialized knowledge that comes with medical education, they need to be active listeners and curious learners (Xiao et al. 2021).
2. Systems thinking: They will need a strong understanding of the interconnectedness of various components within LHS. This involves not merely assessing individual elements in isolation but rather understanding how these elements interact within the broader healthcare ecosystem. Evaluators must appreciate and navigate the complexities between data collection, research outcomes, clinical practices, and patient outcomes. They will need to be able to see the health system from a holistic perspective, rather than focusing narrowly on specific clinical services (Williams and Imam 2007).
3. Collaborative communication skills: Because LHS evaluators focus on the usability of their studies, they need to have strong working relationships with their clinical colleagues. This requires a willingness and ability to spend time at the outset of a project, learning about the rationale and context for whatever interventions are being evaluated, as well as the specific questions that clinicians and health system leaders want to have answered. Once the data have been collected and analyzed, the evaluator needs to know which results are most relevant to share and have the language that allows users to understand the implications of those results (Baumbusch et al. 2008).
4. Change facilitation: A main goal of LHS is to drive continuous improvement. Evaluators working in this space should be adept at change facilitation for their teams. This includes guiding discussions, feedback sessions and workshops that help the teams understand the purpose of evaluation and evaluation results (Sweeney et al. 2022). This will hopefully lead to stronger collaboration when implementing changes. The evaluator should be excited to help foster a culture of learning and innovation with the LHS.

5. Ability and willingness to adapt: An evaluator should approach all projects and processes with the ability to adapt. This means being capable of adjusting evaluation approaches in response to changing priorities, unexpected insights and the evolving needs of the group. According to Ghere et al. (2006), this is a competency that evaluators typically build at a later stage of their development.

3.2.1 Skilled in Translating Research Knowledge Into Practice

One specific function emphasized in an LHS is the efficient translation of research into practical application. This will require evaluators who not only conduct research but also aid in interpretation, learning, and facilitating translation within the healthcare setting. Learning and translation do not happen as a natural matter of course when studies are collected. Clinicians, administrators, and other "users" of the research findings need to be engaged fully in the learning process, paying attention to the potential implications for improving patient care.

By connecting evaluation to everyday healthcare, LHS encourages clinicians to use this ongoing flow of information to make changes and improve decision-making based on this evidence. This integration can help bridge the gap between theory and practice, allowing clinicians to make decisions based on experience, but also emerging evidence on the local patient level, resulting in more patient-centered care. This can be a complex process in practice, beginning with problem assessment, then identifying potential remedies, then pilot testing (using QI methods), then refining and re-testing, and eventually stabilizing and possibly scaling to additional settings. The field of implementation science is extremely well suited for training evaluators with the ability to adapt, implement, and scale interventions that have been shown to effectively address patient care issues of importance to the health system (Leeman et al. 2017; Rapport et al. 2018).

3.2.2 Developmental Evaluation

One evaluation paradigm that is particularly relevant for this integration process is "developmental evaluation" (DE) (Patton 2011). Within this paradigm, evaluation findings are translated into actionable recommendations through close engagement with stakeholders, promoting collaboration and communication. This dissemination of knowledge and best practices across the LHS ensures the application of valuable insights for continuous improvement in patient care. DE expects the evaluator to play a central and proactive role in fostering and encouraging learning, providing continuous feedback and assessing practices.

DE is well suited to address LHS's emphasis on local learning and improving health in the local context. One of the key elements of DE is that it applies to situations where the intervention being evaluated is assumed to always be "under development," as opposed to more traditional scientific paradigms where the goal is to design and show effectiveness for a "fixed" intervention which can be scaled and replicated in multiple settings. DE is particularly sensitive to the unique context-dependent factors that determine an intervention's effectiveness and thus focuses on tailored evaluation approaches. Moreover, conditions within the organization or the policy context can change over time, which may necessitate a shift in strategy in order to maintain effectiveness. (See text box for an example.)

DE offers a dynamic and iterative approach to evaluation, providing real-time feedback and data to inform decision-making on an ongoing basis. Acting as a collaborator within the team, a DE evaluator enables proactive course corrections based on emerging findings and trends. This "living" evaluation process ensures that the LHS can adapt and respond to evolving needs, maximizing its potential to achieve optimal outcomes in care delivery.

In order to achieve this sort of ongoing, context-specific learning, a developmental evaluator needs to be able to work closely with program designers, clinicians, patients, and other stakeholders to understand organizational dynamics and clinical issues surrounding the intervention and its implementation. The evaluator must also be skilled in engaging relevant stakeholders in interpreting findings and determining implications for ongoing implementation and possible refinement. These interpersonal and strategic skills are just as important as technical competency in the data-collection and analysis methods typically associated with evaluation. Essential to the effectiveness of DE is a commitment on the part of leaders to engage the evaluator over the long run, especially in supporting clinicians and managers in making data-informed improvements to the intervention and testing effectiveness in an iterative manner.

Case Study of Developmental Evaluation

Bailie et al. (2020) present an example of developmental evaluation in the healthcare space, focusing on an innovation platform called CRE-ICI. The aim of the evaluation was to support the formation, functioning, and outcomes of the platform, while embracing the complexity of Indigenous primary care in Australia. The evaluation process aimed to encourage continuous learning, adaptation, and innovation. This case study highlights the value of a developmental evaluation approach within healthcare innovation.

Background: CRE-IQI is an innovative platform that promotes the sharing of ideas and practices among healthcare professionals within Australian indigenous primary care.

Evaluation approach and methods: The evaluation adopted a developmental approach, using iterative cycles of development and testing similar to continuous quality improvement (CQI) methods. This approach allowed for continuous reflection, learning, and adaptation for the project team. Instead of sitting external to the team, evaluation actively participated in the development of the platform and facilitated rapid adaptations as needs and insights emerged. This allowed the evaluation team to engage multiple perspectives and to consider relationships and interactions among stakeholders.

The evaluation team held bi-annual meetings for stakeholders to identify emerging issues and propose modifications to the platform. Feedback from these meetings led to collaborative change decisions that were recorded in evaluation logs and project records, to ensure transparency and accountability. Additionally, evaluators engaged in document review, year 2 and year 4 reviews, and interviewed key stakeholders to provide a more comprehensive understanding of the platform's progress and impact.

Conclusion: The evaluation of CRE-IQI provided continuous feedback, facilitated adaptations and fostered a learning culture within the platform. By embracing complexity, engaging multiple perspectives and actively involving stakeholders, the evaluation process enabled the platform to address the unique challenges of indigenous primary healthcare effectively. This case study serves as a compelling example of how developmental evaluation can contribute to positive change and innovation in the healthcare space, ultimately leading to improved healthcare outcomes for indigenous communities.

4 What Do Health Systems Need to Do to Support LHS Evaluators?

To effectively support LHS evaluators, health systems must first have a strong commitment to the LHS paradigm. As outlined in the earlier discussion of LHS-CF (especially Table 2), our literature review identified four enabling conditions that promote the effective adoption and implementation of the LHS paradigm:

- Expertise
- Data systems and informatics infrastructure
- Investment of resources in LHS work
- Supportive culture

All four of these enabling conditions apply directly to the question of how health systems can support LHS evaluators. First, the health system needs to hire and maintain a workforce with the appropriate skills and knowledge for evaluation within a dynamic healthcare landscape. Second, investing in robust data systems and informatics infrastructure becomes critical to ensure the seamless flow and analysis of information for evaluation processes. Third, health system leaders need to dedicate resources toward LHS initiatives. This includes not only high-priority studies but also resources for training and compensation for doing this type of work. Finally, cultivating a supportive culture within the health system, one that encourages collaboration, innovation, and a commitment to continuous improvement, serves as the cornerstone for enabling successful LHS evaluation practices.

One of the essential and obvious implications of adopting the LHS paradigm is that the health system will need to expand the number of staff members who focus on evaluation and learning. Evaluation, once limited to focusing on the assessment of process and outcomes, now extends to quality improvement, knowledge translation and stakeholder engagement (Laycock et al. 2019). This expansion of responsibilities necessitates the allocation of additional human, financial, and technological resources within the health system. Most of this growth in evaluation staff will come through new hires. However, there may also be chances for current staff to transition into evaluation roles, provided they possess the necessary skills or are willing to acquire them. In either case, the health system will incur new expenses associated with becoming an LHS.

For leaders to make these investments, they will need to be able to see direct benefits from LHS work—in terms of improved patient outcomes, more efficient processes, reductions in avoidable readmissions, lower turnover among staff, etc. This analysis applies not only to the overall decision of whether to adopt the LHS paradigm but also the more specific question of where to focus LHS work. For LHS to be a cost-effective proposition, leaders need to efficiently prioritize the issues, problems, and questions where they will dedicate their LHS resources. As the role of evaluation broadens within the LHS framework, health systems will be compelled to allocate resources strategically to ensure the effective implementation of evaluation initiatives.

A key practical question facing health systems is whether they should hire evaluators with general or specialized expertise. Diverse studies within the context of an LHS may require varying sets of analytic and methodological skills, making it impractical for a single evaluator to possess all the required expertise. Rather than relying on individual evaluators to encompass all necessary skills, a more effective strategy may be to assemble a cohort of evaluators whose collective knowledge and expertise span the full spectrum of required skills. In doing this, health system leadership can help promote a knowledge-sharing environment where evaluators can collaborate, learn from each other, and continuously advance the quality of evaluation processes within the LHS paradigm.

One of the key structural questions facing health system leaders is how to position evaluators on the organizational chart. On the one hand, LHS evaluators are typically embedded within clinical units and provide targeted support for the testing of specific interventions. This would suggest that evaluators are accountable to leaders within those clinical units. On the other hand, LHS evaluators are also serving a higher-order function of ensuring that the organization as a whole does better at learning, translating evidence into practice and achieving metrics related to patient care. This would suggest that evaluators should report centrally to health system leaders, possibly through the strategic planning unit. In either case, it will be essential that the health system have leaders who are well-versed enough in evaluation methods and theories to provide appropriate supervision.

5 Conclusion

The concept of LHS revolutionizes healthcare delivery by prioritizing continual evaluation and learning for ongoing improvement. LHS emphasizes the utilization of acquired knowledge to enhance patient care and system performance, focusing on local impact and relevance. Evaluators within LHSs play a crucial role in facilitating this learning process and delivering actionable recommendations. By better integrating evaluators and evaluation approaches into LHSs, healthcare organizations can better drive improvements in healthcare delivery, quality, equity, and patient outcomes.

The evolving role of evaluators within LHSs presents challenges and opportunities. Health systems will need to decide whether to bring in new evaluators or upskill existing staff. The skill sets for evaluators working in an LHS differ from those focused on specific methodologies. They require a diverse skillset that spans traditional approaches and emerging data analytics, as well as proficiency in data management and clinical understanding. In addition to their technical skillset, abilities to collaborate with diverse stakeholders within the clinical and research space will be vital. Additionally, adaptability and a commitment to continuous learning become essential traits for evaluators in the dynamic setting of the LHS paradigm. To succeed as an evaluator within the LHS context requires expanded competencies—both in the breadth of methodologies that can be brought to bear in any given learning task and in the more general ability to diagnose, engage a broad range of stakeholders, think critically and adapt to whatever presents itself in the situation.

Given the unique requirements of an LHS, there may be a need for further development and refinement of evaluation approaches tailored to continuous learning. This could include exploring real-time feedback mechanisms or the more adaptive evaluation frameworks. Additionally, structural questions, such as the placement of evaluators within health systems, require further exploration. A future focus could involve assessment of different organizational models and leadership structures to identify best practices in supporting a continuous learning environment.

Acknowledgements The authors gratefully acknowledge the use of the services and facilities of the Wake Forest University Clinical and Translational Science Institute, funded by the National Center for Advancing Translational Sciences (NCATS), National Institutes of Health, through Grant Award Number UL1TR001420.

References

Agency for Healthcare Research and Quality (n.d.) Learning health systems. Available https://www.ahrq.gov/learning-health-systems/index.html

American Evaluation Association (2018) The 2018 AEA evaluator competencies. Available https://www.eval.org/Portals/0/Docs/AEA%20Evaluator%20Competencies.pdf

Bailie J, Laycock AF, Peiris D, Bainbridge RG, Matthews V, Cunningham FC, Conte KP, Abimbola S, Passey ME, Bailie RS (2020) Using developmental evaluation to enhance continuous reflec-

tion, learning and adaptation of an innovation platform in Australian indigenous primary healthcare. Health Res Pol Syst 18(1):1–11
Baumbusch JL, Kirkham SR, Khan KB, McDonald H, Semeniuk P, Tan E, Anderson JM (2008) Pursuing common agendas: a collaborative model for knowledge translation between research and practice in clinical settings. Res Nurs Health 31(2):130–140
Boes S, Mantwill S, Kaufmann C, Brach M, Bickenbach J, Rubinelli S, Stucki G (2018) Swiss learning health system: a national initiative to establish learning cycles for continuous health system improvement. Learn Health Syst 2(3):e10059
Deans KJ, Sabihi S, Forrest CB (2018) Learning health systems. Semin Pediatr Surg 27(6):375–378
Easterling D, Perry AC, Woodside R, Patel T, Gesell SB (2022) Clarifying the concept of a learning health system for healthcare delivery organizations: implications from a qualitative analysis of the scientific literature. Learn Health Syst 6(2):e10287
Etheredge LM (2014) Rapid learning: a breakthrough agenda. Health Aff 33(7):1155–1162
Forrest CB, Chesley FD Jr, Tregear ML, Mistry KB (2018) Development of the learning health system researcher core competencies. Health Serv Res 53(4):2615–2632
Ghere G, King JA, Stevahn L, Minnema J (2006) A professional development unit for reflecting on program evaluator competencies. Am J Eval 27(1):108–123
Gould MK, Sharp AL, Nguyen HQ, Hahn EE, Mittman BS, Shen E, Alem AC, Kanter MH (2020) Embedded research in the learning healthcare system: ongoing challenges and recommendations for researchers, clinicians, and health system leaders. J Gen Intern Med 35:3675–3680
Guise JM, Savitz LA, Friedman CP (2018) Mind the gap: putting evidence into practice in the era of learning health systems. J Gen Intern Med 33:2237–2239
IOM (2015) Integrating research and practice: health system leaders working toward high-value care: workshop summary. The National Academies Press, Washington
Kilbourne AM, Braganza MZ, Bowersox NW, Goodrich DE, Miake-Lye I, Floyd N, Garrido MM, Frakt AB, Bever CT Jr, Vega R, Ramoni R (2019) Research lifecycle to increase the substantial real-world impact of research: accelerating innovations to application. Med Care 57(10):S206
Laycock A, Bailie J, Matthews V, Bailie R (2019) Using developmental evaluation to support knowledge translation: reflections from a large-scale quality improvement project in indigenous primary healthcare. Health Res Pol Syst 17(1):1–11
Leeman J, Birken SA, Powell BJ, Rohweder C, Shea CM (2017) Beyond "implementation strategies": classifying the full range of strategies used in implementation science and practice. Implement Sci 12:1–9
Lessard L, Michalowski W, Fung-Kee-Fung M, Jones L, Grudniewicz A (2017) Architectural frameworks: defining the structures for implementing learning health systems. Implement Sci 12:1–11
Lowes LP, Noritz GH, Newmeyer A, Embi PJ, Yin H, Smoyer WE, Tidball A, Love L, Schmidt J, Golias J (2017) 'Learn from every patient': implementation and early results of a learning health system. Dev Med Child Neurol 59(2):183–191
Maddox TM, Albert NM, Borden WB, Curtis LH, Ferguson TB Jr, Kao DP, Marcus GM, Peterson ED, Redberg R, Rumsfeld JS, Shah ND (2017) The learning healthcare system and cardiovascular care: a scientific statement from the American Heart Association. Circulation 135(14):e826–e857
McGinnis JM, Aisner D, Olsen L (eds) (2007) The learning healthcare system: workshop summary. National Academies Press, Washington
McGinnis JM, Olsen L, Goolsby WA, Grossmann C (eds) (2011a) Engineering a learning healthcare system: a look at the future: workshop summary. National Academies Press, Washington, pp 1–25
McGinnis JM, Powers B, Grossmann C (eds) (2011b) Digital infrastructure for the learning health system: the foundation for continuous improvement in health and health care: workshop series summary. National Academies Press, Washington
McGinnis JM, Saunders RS, Olsen L (eds) (2011c) Patients charting the course: citizen engagement and the learning health system: workshop summary. National Academies Press, Washington

McLachlan S, Potts HW, Dube K, Buchanan D, Lean S, Gallagher T, Johnson O, Daley B, Marsh W, Fenton N (2018) The Heimdall framework for supporting characterisation of learning health systems. J Innov Health Inform 25(2):77–87

McLachlan S, Dube K, Kyrimi E, Fenton N (2019) LAGOS: learning health systems and how they can integrate with patient care. BMJ Health Care Inf 26(1):e100037

Menear M, Blanchette MA, Demers-Payette O, Roy D (2019) A framework for value-creating learning health systems. Health Res Policy Syst 17:1–13

Moffatt-Bruce S, Huerta T, Gaughan A, McAlearney AS (2018) IDEA4PS: the development of a research-oriented learning healthcare system. Am J Med Qual 33(4):420–425

Moloney RM, Tambor ES, Tunis SR (2016) Patient and clinician support for the learning healthcare system: recommendations for enhancing value. J Comp Effect Res 5(2):123–128

Morain SR, Kass NE, Grossmann C (2017) What allows a health care system to become a learning health care system: results from interviews with health system leaders. Learn Health Syst 1(1):e10015

National Academy of Medicine (n.d.) Learning health system homepage. Available https://nam.edu/programs/value-science-driven-health-care/learning-health-system-homepage/. Accessed 1 December 2020

NCATS (2014) Clinical and translational science award (U54): RFA-TR-14-009. Available https://grants.nih.gov/grants/guide/rfa-files/RFA-TR-14-009.html

Patton MQ (2011) Developmental evaluation. Guilford Press, New York

Psek WA, Stametz RA, Bailey-Davis LD, Davis D, Darer J, Faucett WA, Henninger DL, Sellers DC, Gerrity G (2015) Operationalizing the learning health care system in an integrated delivery system. EGEMS 3(1):1122

Rapport F, Clay-Williams R, Churruca K, Shih P, Hogden A, Braithwaite J (2018) The struggle of translating science into action: foundational concepts of implementation science. J Eval Clin Pract 24(1):117–126

Sweeney SM, Baron A, Hall JD, Ezekiel-Herrera D, Springer R, Ward RL, Marino M, Balasubramanian BA, Cohen DJ (2022) Effective facilitator strategies for supporting primary care practice change: a mixed methods study. Ann Fam Med 20(5):414–422

Williams B, Imam I (2007) Systems concepts in evaluation: an expert anthology. EdgePress of Inverness, Point Reyes

Wysham NG, Howie L, Patel K, Cameron CB, Samsa GP, Roe L, Abernethy AP, Zaas A (2016) Development and refinement of a learning health systems training program. EGEMS 4(1):1236

Xiao Y, Sesto M, Zern SC (2021) Working with experts from non-clinical fields. In: Comprehensive healthcare simulation: improving healthcare systems. Springer, Cham, pp 211–216

Healing Practices: Evaluating Trauma-Informed Health Services

Monika Sanchez and Lisa Schafer

Abstract

There is growing recognition of how trauma affects health and wellbeing. To support the populations they serve, some public health and healthcare organizations are introducing trauma-informed approaches, and there are several frameworks describing key principles. Programs vary in how trauma-informed health services are implemented, affecting evaluation approach, tool development, and reception. Evaluating trauma-informed programs is also nascent, with metrics and approaches still being tested. Additionally, evaluation has historically perpetuated trauma by operating in a top-down way, using data punitively, or not sharing results with participants. This tendency emphasizes the importance of evaluating trauma-informed programs in a trauma-informed manner. This chapter provides an overview of the research on evaluating trauma-informed programs and describes the principles of trauma-informed approaches and their application to trauma-informed evaluation of health services.

Keywords

Trauma · Trauma-informed care · Evaluation

M. Sanchez · L. Schafer (✉)
Center for Community Health and Evaluation, Seattle, WA, USA
e-mail: monika.a.sanchez@kp.org; lisa.m.schafer@kp.org

A. Kaehne, J. Feather (eds.), *Handbook of Health Services Evaluation*,
https://doi.org/10.1007/978-3-031-87869-5_20

1 Introduction

Trauma-informed care is an evidence-informed approach growing in use in various service delivery settings, including healthcare, social services, education, and criminal justice (Center for Substance Abuse Treatment. SAMHSA/CSAT Treatment Improvement Protocols 2014). Trauma-informed health care and health services recognize the widespread impact of trauma on individuals and understand the potential pathways for healing. It involves assessing and potentially modifying every aspect of care to acknowledge and respond to how trauma affects the lives of those seeking healthcare services. More and more, it is seen as a central part of providing holistic, whole-person, patient-centered health services across the lifespan (Mahon 2022).

Implementing trauma-informed care can be challenging in healthcare systems that are traditionally paternalistic and designed to focus on medical diagnoses and deficits with an emphasis on standardized assessments and treatments. Trauma-informed care requires centering individual patients and attempting to understand their lives. This exercise requires practice and culture changes at both clinical and organizational levels (Raja et al. 2015). It involves people and systems working differently than—and sometimes in opposition to—their original training or design. This long-term, sometimes emotional work, necessitates a shift in orientation to patients and families from "What is wrong with you?" to "What happened to you?"

Evaluation of trauma-informed care is critical given the complex and long-term work of changing practice and culture. Developing evaluation methods that support and document the systems and culture changes needed for successfully integrating trauma-informed care into healthcare settings is essential for widespread implementation, which can improve care delivery for patients and families and create better work environments for health care providers and staff (Bosk 2023). However, employing traditional evaluation approaches can be traumatic for some. Relatively common top-down practices include (1) funders imposing an evaluation process on grant recipients and (2) requirements that extract data from people and communities that are either not reported back or are used punitively against them, for example threatening to withhold funding if expected outcomes are not met. Evaluators could also present findings without contextualization, participant engagement or a lens of learning and improvement. Evaluators of trauma-informed care programs are responsible for avoiding re-traumatization of evaluation participants (e.g., patients, families, health care providers, and staff). This chapter describes effective methods for trauma-informed program evaluations aligned with the core principles of trauma-informed care practice.

2 Background on Trauma and Trauma-Informed Organizations

This section is in two parts. Part 1 provides an overview of trauma, including its impact on health and wellbeing and the evolution of trauma care. Part 2 is more relevant to this chapter's proposed evaluation approach focusing on organizations' implementation of trauma-informed programs and defines and describes a "trauma-informed organization" (TIO) as one whose approach to providing services (e.g., healthcare, social services, education) emphasizes the role of trauma and how it impacts patients. This approach is "trauma-informed care" (TIC). We also summarize the best practices of a TIO.[1] This section does not detail, nor do the evaluation methods focus on, the efficacy of trauma-informed care approaches on patients' outcomes.

2.1 Trauma: Definition, Impacts, and Attitudes

The United States' Substance Abuse and Mental Health Services Administration (SAMHSA) has a widely used definition of trauma: "trauma results from an event, series of events, or set of circumstances that is experienced by an individual as physically or emotionally harmful or threatening and that has lasting adverse effects on the individual's functioning and physical, social, emotional, or spiritual wellbeing" (Menschner and Maul 2016). Trauma can affect people of every race, ethnicity, age, sexual orientation, gender, psychosocial background, and geographic region. A traumatic experience can be a single event, a series of events, or a chronic condition (e.g., childhood neglect or domestic violence).

In their systematic review, Fernandez et al. cite evidence linking trauma exposure to many adverse outcomes, including health risk behaviors, social and psychological impairment, reduced work functioning, major causes of death, and an overall reduction in life expectancy. Research has indicated that when trauma is intense or repeated throughout time, it can exhaust our physiological stress response. Exposure during sensitive developmental periods (i.e., childhood) can have functional and structural consequences on our neurobiology (Fernández et al. 2023).

Early accounts of traumatic stress described the effects of battle conditions on soldiers during the American Civil War, e.g., "soldier's heart."[2] The advent of heavy explosives in World War I led to the attribution of symptoms to "shell shock," giving a more physiological description of the effects. Even with this more physical explanation of traumatic stress, a prevailing attitude remained that the traumatic stress response was due to a character flaw. Trauma care approaches were limited to talk therapy until the post–Vietnam War era when the United States Department of Veterans Affairs (then called the Veterans Administration) developed group therapy for post-traumatic stress disorder (PTSD).

---

[1] Note on literature and sources: The information in Sect. 2.1 draws heavily on documents from the United States' Center for Substance Abuse treatment. SAMHSA/CSAT Treatment Improvement Protocols (2014), which has played an important role in synthesizing the evidence around trauma care and TIOs. Evidence presented in Sect. 2.2 comes from a scan of systematic reviews of TIC/TIOs.

[2] The description of the evolution of trauma care and health system attitudes toward trauma draws directly from Appendix C of the SAMSHA Report Center for Substance Abuse Treatment. SAMHSA/CSAT Treatment Improvement Protocols (2014).

The publication of the American Psychiatric Association's (APA's) Diagnostic and Statistical Manual of Mental Disorders, Third Edition (DSM-III) in 1980 marked the introduction of PTSD as a diagnosis for both military and civilian populations. Over time, national studies began to demonstrate the prevalence of traumatic experiences. Research, including the Adverse Childhood Experiences and the Women, Co-Occurring, and Violence studies, clearly demonstrated the pervasive long-term impact of trauma. Patients' rights movements in the United States called for humane treatment and involvement in the treatment process. These events prompted government agencies and national organizations to promote the need for trauma-informed policies and care.

2.2 Trauma-Informed Care and Trauma-Informed Organizations: Overview of Principles and Evidence

The widespread presence of trauma and its impact on health and wellbeing have caused it to become a central focus of many health and human service organizations, including educational institutions and the criminal justice system. Trauma-informed organizations (TIOs) provide trauma-informed care (TIC), which occurs when every part of a service is assessed and potentially modified to include a basic understanding of how trauma impacts the life of an individual seeking services (Raja et al. 2015). SAMHSA emphasizes the "4 R's" in moving toward becoming a TIO: A program, organization, or system that is trauma-informed *realizes* the widespread impact of trauma and understands potential paths for recovery; *recognizes* the signs and symptoms of trauma in clients, families, staff, and others involved with the system; *responds* by fully integrating knowledge about trauma into policies, procedures, and practices; and seeks to actively *resist re-traumatization* (Huang et al. 2014).

Experts have developed several principles and frameworks to provide concrete guidance to organizations moving toward becoming trauma informed. Many of these were for the context of behavioral health organizations where trauma is at the center of the work and is more comprehensively understood and addressed. Organizations in other settings, including healthcare services, have been working to adapt and modify as appropriate.

Becoming a TIO requires administrative guidance and support across all levels of an agency. One frequently used framework is outlined in a report prepared by SAMHSA's Trauma and Justice Strategic Initiative and includes ten domains of organizational change that have appeared both in the organizational change management literature and among models for establishing TIC (Huang et al. 2014). Table 1 summarizes the ten domains drawn from that work.

A growing number of health and human service organizations have recognized the importance of incorporating trauma awareness into their work and are taking concrete steps to become TIOs. While we did not conduct a systematic inquiry of evidence regarding implementation of TIC in organizations, review articles showed

Table 1 Domains of organizational change for trauma-informed organizations

Domain	Description
Governance and leadership	Leadership supports and invests in implementing and sustaining a trauma-informed approach, with an identified point of responsibility to lead the work
Policy	Written policies and protocols establish a trauma-informed approach as essential to the organizational mission
Physical environment of the organization	The organization ensures that the physical environment promotes safety and collaboration
Engagement and involvement of people in recovery	People in recovery, trauma survivors, and people receiving services have significant involvement, voice, and meaningful choice at all levels and in all areas of organizational functioning
Cross-sector collaboration	Collaboration across sectors is built on a shared understanding of trauma and the principles of a trauma-informed approach
Screening, assessment, and treatment services	Trauma screening and assessment are an essential part of the work. Trauma-specific interventions are acceptable, effective, and available for individuals and families seeking services
Training and workforce development	Ongoing training on trauma and peer support for all health service workers is essential. The organization's human resource system incorporates trauma-informed principles in hiring, supervision, and staff evaluation
Progress monitoring and quality assurance	There is ongoing assessment, tracking, and monitoring of trauma-informed principles and effective use of evidence-based trauma-specific screening, assessments, and treatment
Financing	Financing structures support a trauma-informed approach, including staff training resources and appropriate and safe facilities
Evaluation	Measures and methodologies used to evaluate service or program implementation and effectiveness reflect an understanding of trauma and use relevant trauma-oriented research instruments

that empirical evidence is scarce on how TIC is implemented effectively within organizations and the impact on patient outcomes.

One initial review focused on youth-serving organizations found 54 articles describing the implementation of TIC models (Lowenthal 2020). Researchers found high variability in the approaches to implementing TIC and in the quality of the research evidence; however, promising preliminary evidence is beginning to show that TIC implementation can reduce violent incidents and improve service provider knowledge, attitude, behavior, and practice. The review noted that successful TIC implementation required a comprehensive approach that includes commitment from senior leadership, ongoing support, and collaboration within and between service-providing organizations and systems.

A recent review covering youth and adult TIC interventions identified 15 studies that met inclusion criteria (Fernández et al. 2023). Researchers used many measures to assess the effectiveness of TIC implementation, with staff perceptions and safety management indicators being the most frequently used. The review found a positive trend in the effectiveness of the interventions included in the study, including improved functioning of beneficiaries, enhanced accessibility, and improved quality of services. However, the studies' low quality and high heterogeneity made it difficult to draw firm conclusions. They recommended that the primary endeavor in TIC research be to provide more solid evidence.

Very few studies in the general review articles focused on health services organizations; however, there is a growing interest in considering trauma in health services and some initial studies. For example, one study provided a conceptual framework (Raja et al. 2015) that grounds TIC in patient-centered communication and outlines changes to provider behavior and health system practice that can help establish trust with trauma survivors. A separate review article looked at outcomes of TIC educational interventions in emergency departments (ED) (Brown et al. 2022). All interventions suggested a positive impact from TIC on either clinicians or patients, but outcomes data were limited as the field is still early in implementing TIC interventions at the organizational, rather than patient-provider, level.

As with other areas of TIC research, the research needs more studies examining the impact of TIC in healthcare settings to understand the impact better and improve implementation.

3 Evaluation Methods Overview

While trauma-informed care (TIC) is relevant to a wide range of service delivery (e.g., social services, schools, criminal justice), this chapter focuses on implementing TIC in health services. Two different types of TIC implementation include:

- Trauma-informed healthcare/service delivery refers to using trauma-informed approaches and principles to improve patients' clinical and behavioral outcomes.
- Trauma-informed programs are organized efforts to implement trauma-informed health care/service delivery. Table 1 includes the various organizational changes to become a trauma-informed organization.

The following sections discuss evaluating *trauma-informed programs* in healthcare settings, including primary and specialty care and behavioral health. These are efforts to systematically bring trauma-informed principles into service delivery and make changes needed to embed and support TIC across all aspects of an organization (e.g., building leadership support, training and workforce development, and collaboration with partners). This chapter does not focus on evaluating trauma-informed health care/service delivery to determine whether it is efficacious as a care delivery approach.

To guide organizations seeking to implement TIC, SAMHSA identified six fundamental principles in designing their approach (referred to henceforth as "TI principles"), which are outlined in Table 2 (Huang et al. 2014).

We illustrate how to apply the principles of TIC to evaluating trauma-informed programs so that evaluation avoids inflicting additional trauma on evaluation participants and is more effective in supporting the overall effort of healthcare organizations to be more trauma-informed. Many of these concepts are also relevant more

Table 2 Trauma-informed principles

Principle	Description
Safety	The physical setting is safe and interpersonal interactions promote a sense of safety
Trustworthiness and transparency	Operations and decisions are conducted with transparency with the goal of building and maintaining trust
Peer support	Peers are a key vehicle for establishing safety and hope, building trust, enhancing collaboration, and promoting lived experience
Collaboration and mutuality	Importance on partnering and leveling power differences to demonstrate that healing happens in relationships and meaningfully sharing power and decision-making
Empowerment, voice, and choice	Individuals' strengths and experiences are recognized and built upon; there is a belief in the primacy of the people served; they are supported in shared decision-making, choice, and self-advocacy
Cultural, historical, gender issues	Cultural stereotypes and biases are actively moved past; historical trauma is recognized and addressed

generally to effectively evaluating programs that are not explicitly trauma-informed, but as TI principles are specifically applied with a lens of *recognizing*, *responding to*, and *resisting* trauma. Using the TI principles, rather than a general definition of, collaboration, for example, allows the evaluation to align with the healing approach of trauma-informed care. These ideas are also not exclusive to evaluation of trauma-informed programs and other evaluation approaches may use some of these concepts (e.g., participatory evaluation (Cousins and Earl 1992), community-based participatory research (Wallerstein and Duran 2017), participatory action research (Baum et al. 2006), and appreciative inquiry (Coghlan et al. 2003). However, as stated, the principles as defined in Table 2 are constructed specifically with healing in mind versus other objectives.

4 Evaluation Methods

This section contains evaluation phases based on the United States Centers for Disease Control and Prevention (CDC) framework (Milstein and Wetterhall 1999) for program evaluation in public health (we consolidated some phases for simplicity). While all TI principles likely need attention at each evaluation phase, we present the most salient ones based on our experience. The phases are presented linearly here but should be considered more of a feedback loop or continuous in practice. Table 3 at the end of this section summarizes the evaluation phases and TI principles presented.

We begin with a concept that is not a formal evaluation phase but touches each phase of the evaluation in substantial ways: *relationships*. A fundamental construct of being trauma-informed is that both trauma and healing happen in relationships. Therefore, the relationships developed among evaluators, program implementors, and program participants initially, and fostered throughout an evaluation of TIC programs, can potentially both harm and heal individuals and groups.

Table 3 Evaluation methods: summary

Evaluation phases[a]	Trauma-informed principles emphasized[b]	Implications for evaluation[c]	Example
Relationships[a]	• Safety • Cultural, historical, and gender issues	• Safety. The evaluation should have a learning orientation and not be used punitively or for judgment purposes • Historical. Evaluation should actively and intentionally resist its history of perpetuating trauma by operating top-down, extracting data that is used punitively, and failing to share results with participants	*Enact these principles through activities and approaches at every evaluation phase*
Design and decision making	• Trustworthiness and transparency • Collaboration and mutuality	• Trust. Make decisions about the evaluation with visibility between program implementors and evaluators • Collaboration. Program perspectives should take priority and influence evaluation design	• Collaboratively designed logic model • Program staff and grantees are engaged in reporting requirements. Metrics developed based on what is feasible and most beneficial to the program
Data collection	• Trustworthiness and transparency • Empowerment, voice, and choice	• Trust. Co-designing instruments with participants can help build trust • Empowerment. Participants should have authentic input into instruments and data collection methods to reduce the burden and increase the relevance of the information collected	• Annual capacity assessment developed with burden as a key consideration • Design the assessment to provide practical examples for teams to promote data validity and utility

(continued)

Table 3 (continued)

Evaluation phases[a]	Trauma-informed principles emphasized[b]	Implications for evaluation[c]	Example
Analysis and interpretation	• Trustworthiness and transparency • Collaboration and mutuality	• Trust. Evaluators should make clear the rationale for their methodology and approach and honestly and transparently communicate limitations in the data • Collaboration. See program implementors as valuable data interpretation partners and orient the data toward learning and improvement	• Building in processes to include program representatives in data analysis (as appropriate) • Interactive data dives to support reflection and data interpretation (e.g., data galleries), including implications for program and participant practice
Sharing findings	• Peer support • Collaboration and mutuality	• Collaboration. The primacy of external-facing, formal reporting should not be assumed; equal value should be placed on sharing findings with participants (to whom the data belong) and using informal sharing mechanisms if that is more useful to the program • Peer support. If multiple evaluators participate in the evaluation, they should be aligned in the types of sharing	Findings shared more frequently, in more digestible formats, and oriented toward a lay audience: • Presentation slides for more seamless repurposing by program implementors • Informal reports such as short, topic-specific learning briefs

[a] Evaluation phases. Based on the CDC framework for program evaluation in public health, we consolidate some phases for simplicity. For evaluating trauma-informed programs, an element that permeates all aspects is *relationships* among evaluators, program implementors, and program participants but is not a formal evaluation phase

[b] The trauma-informed principles are defined in Table 2 and are paraphrased from SAMHSA's Concept of Trauma and Guidance for a Trauma-Informed Approach, July 2014

[c] Implications for evaluation. Brief description of how evaluators may shape evaluation methods to apply trauma-informed principles to improve the quality and utility of the information gathered, synthesized, and shared

While evaluation of trauma-informed programs is primarily concerned with organizational implementation (versus individual service delivery), and therefore not typically interacting directly with patients experiencing trauma, evaluators should take care to avoid disrupting the relationships between program staff and participants. For example, evaluators should avoid asking staff to prioritize real-time data collection over time interacting with program participants.

Two important TI principles implicated in *relationships* are *safety* and *cultural, historical, and gender issues*. Evaluation practice has a history of, and a tendency toward, perpetuating trauma, e.g., by extracting data that is then used punitively. As Dean-Coffey (2018) describes this history in the USA, "The early forefathers of foundations… thought of evaluation as a tool for documenting outputs and costs as well as assessing efficiency and compliance." Evaluation should actively and intentionally resist this history and tendency, and there are a wide range of more recent evaluation approaches available to do so that account for context and culture. The evaluation should promote a sense of safety in interpersonal interactions by having a learning orientation and not be used to penalize participants, e.g., establishing a basis for withholding funds. Additionally, evaluators must prioritize relationship and rapport building with program implementors and participants, potentially affecting evaluation budgets, work plans, and timelines. Evaluators should work to manage participant burden and always consider how evaluation activities align with or complement program or participant priorities. These considerations are relevant to activities and approaches at every evaluation phase.

4.1 Design and Decision Making

Design is an essential phase for any evaluation, particularly for evaluations of TI programs. This phase lays the groundwork for evaluators and program implementors to use as a touchstone during subsequent evaluation phases. How evaluators make decisions at the outset sets the tone and is critical to build trust and a sense of mutual collaboration. An evaluation philosophy and approach aligned with TI principles helps cultivate empathy with program participants. It casts the evaluation as a partner in learning rather than an external judge or watchdog.

The TI principle of *trustworthiness and transparency* indicates that decisions about the evaluation should be made with visibility between program stakeholders and evaluators. Establishing a partnership approach to evaluation design fosters communication, promotes power sharing, emphasizes the collaborative nature of the process, and builds engagement and buy-in in the evaluation, in alignment with the *collaboration and mutuality* principle. A key example of how evaluators can operationalize this is through an iterative, responsive, and collaboratively designed logic model, which is also used in other evaluation approaches. Evaluators and program implementors have the complementary knowledge needed to create this foundational document. Program implementors have detailed knowledge about the inputs, intended outcomes, and intervention background. At the same time, evaluators provide both a process to articulate these elements and an outside viewpoint to clarify assumptions and potential logical leaps. Transparency about these roles and perspectives helps to create shared power and build collective agreement about a foundational evaluation framework.

Case Example: Collaboration and Mutuality in the *Design and Decision Making* Phase

Discussions with a program implementor revealed they were struggling with the logic model that the evaluation team had developed based on the existing program materials. Both implementors and evaluators acknowledged that they were new to the field of TIC and evaluating TIC programs and could benefit from more voices at the table. Program implementors connected evaluators to field experts who had influenced their program development and asked that the evaluation conduct interviews with these experts to inform the logic model. While this added time and expense to the evaluation design phase, it demonstrated that the evaluation could be influenced by and was ready to share power with program stakeholders.

The TI principle of *collaboration and mutuality* supports prioritizing program perspectives so that they meaningfully influence evaluation design. This prioritization signals that in addition to funders, the evaluation is also in service of program implementors and participants, who will ultimately use any learnings from the process. For example, engaging program staff and participants in deciding the reporting requirements and timing is one way to orient the evaluation toward the lived experiences of those engaged in the initiative. It also demonstrates the *empowerment, voice, and choice* TI principle. Metric development is another way to do this, deciding jointly which measures are feasible to collect given program participants' contexts and which measures provide the most helpful information to program partners.

In contrast, evaluations that seek to create firm separation between evaluators, program implementors, and participants reinforce a power hierarchy that can hamper evaluation implementation and buy-in. Program implementors may not agree with how the initiative is characterized in the logic model and resist reporting requirements, which undermines how useful or representative they perceive the evaluation to be and threatens the quality and utility of the overall evaluation. Without seeing organizational representatives' voices, experiences, and perspectives in the evaluation design and without being part of the decision-making process, the evaluation would be on shaky ground at the outset. Additionally, if evaluators are not present at the program outset or during implementation, the ability to influence program design and implementation in a supportive way is limited.

4.2 Data Collection

Trustworthiness and transparency are also crucial TI principles when developing data collection instruments. Instruments and their administration are the primary way program participants interact with the evaluation and are a mechanism for evaluators to build and maintain trust. Keeping *empowerment, voice, and choice* central is integral, creating flexibility for participants to engage with data collection in a way that aligns with their current context.

For example, if developing an assessment of an organization's capacity to deliver TIC, the burden on participants should be a key consideration, including the instrument's length and complexity and the number of administrations. Evaluators must also develop the assessment so that it is worthwhile for participants (i.e., respondents)—not just evaluators—especially at the first administration. Using grounded scales with descriptive elements can provide participants with transparent, practical examples of demonstrating TI practices while assessing their capacity to carry them out. Co-designing instruments with participants, when possible, can increase the relevance of information collected. Actively working to increase usefulness and reduce administration burden is one way to demonstrate respect for participants' time and energy.

Case Example: Empowerment, Voice, and Choice in the *Data Collection* Phase
During an evaluation of primary care health centers seeking to become more trauma-informed, care teams began sharing their feelings of overwhelm and burnout with program implementors during peaks in the COVID-19 pandemic. In response, rather than giving superficial accommodation, the program team and evaluation completely eliminated one quarterly data report and moved a deliverable due date by several months to lessen burden during the challenging time of year. Participants were able to submit relevant data in subsequent quarters, when their patient care responsibilities had returned to more typical levels.

Offering flexibility in when or how the participants complete the assessment and framing data collection asks as requests rather than requirements can also underscore that participants are in control of their level of engagement in the evaluation and that they have a choice in how they do so. This flexibility can affect data quality if some participants choose to forego data submission or complete the assessment in a limited way. However, our experience has been that this loss of data quality typically does not significantly impact evaluation results as it has not been widespread but rather isolated to only a few participants who may be experiencing extreme circumstances. Participants appreciate acknowledging the temporary factors preventing them from fully completing requests and maintaining the desired engagement with the evaluation.

In contrast, programs or evaluations that take an approach of "more data is better" can engender distrust by introducing the perception that some data are dilute or irrelevant because of the high number of assessment questions (i.e., not everything is essential) or high frequency of administration (i.e., expecting change that cannot reasonably be expected to occur within short periods). This is particularly relevant for evaluation of trauma-informed programs as reducing burden is of utmost importance. Also, inflexibility in how and when participants submit data diminishes participant voice and self-advocacy by ignoring their situation and the primacy of their experience and instead centers the needs of the evaluation.

4.3 Analysis and Interpretation

The TI principle of *trustworthiness and transparency* remains essential during data analysis and interpretation. *Collaboration and mutuality* are also important to support accurate and complete data sensemaking. This phase typically occurs with program implementors rather than program participants, so the following approaches for maintaining trust and leveling power differences are applicable in those relationships.

Case Example: Trustworthiness and Transparency in the *Analysis and Interpretation* Phase
In an evaluation of 15 health centers attempting to implement TIC, the evaluation conducted hour-long interviews with each one early in the initiative. The evaluation team qualitatively themed the interviews and produced an internal memo summarizing the themes. Along with the summary, the evaluation team also shared a detailed "under the hood" table that showed what each health center was working on, with the goal of providing tangible information to each heath center's program coach so they could provide better support. The evaluation proactively sharing detailed information about program participants (without violating confidentiality) underscores that the data are in service of the program, and not just for evaluators' use.

To maintain trust, evaluators should make clear the rationale for their analysis methodology and approach and honestly and transparently communicate limitations in the data. Doing this can underscore the message that data collected by the evaluation belongs to program partners, who have the right to know and understand what is happening with it. This practice does not mean evaluators should overwhelm program implementors in complex statistics or qualitative analysis theory. Instead, evaluators should use accessible language and share the reasoning for why they chose one approach over another. This information can also help mitigate power dynamics where evaluation may be perceived as opaque and trying to avoid questioning rather than scaffolding learning.

To this end, we should see program implementors as valuable partners in data interpretation, and we should position data with an orientation toward learning and improvement. This collaboration could look like building processes to include program implementors in data analysis (as appropriate) by involving key program staff in theming de-identified qualitative data. Another approach could be to use interactive data dives or data galleries to support reflection and data interpretation, including robust discussion of program and participant practice implications. Again, these approaches emphasize that the data belongs to program partners and that we conduct the evaluation for learning and practice improvement.

In contrast, evaluations that independently conduct data analysis and sensemaking absent engagement with program implementors reinforce power hierarchy and get in the way of their understanding of and usefulness of the data. In such structures, (1) program implementors may be hesitant or feel discouraged to share—and therefore evaluators are left in the dark about—program context relevant to the data, and (2) evaluators do not build the capacity of program implementors to interpret and identify practical implications of the evaluation's key findings. Without transparency and collaboration around data analysis and sensemaking, evaluation results may "sit on a shelf" because organizations do not know how to use them.

4.4 Sharing Findings

How evaluation results are shared and presented is heavily influenced by the TI principle of *collaboration and mutuality* among program participants, implementors, and evaluators. Too often, external-facing, peer-reviewed, or formal reporting at the end of the program is assumed to be the best and primary way evaluation results should be shared. This type of reporting typically preferences learning for stakeholders and the field outside the initiative rather than those within it. It also reinforces power differences by treating program participants and implementors as secondary audiences. Often, these external-facing outlets are behind paywalls that limit their accessibility. They also share findings in a way that privileges evaluators' professional reputations and visibility over relevance for program stakeholders and participants.

To promote a more TI approach, evaluators need to share findings at times that benefit program implementation, and they should place equal value on sharing findings with participants (to whom the data belong). Evaluators should also consider using informal sharing mechanisms if they are more valuable to the program. For example, in a program that includes periodic all-day, in-person convenings among participants, the evaluation can provide individualized assessment summaries or data placemats with whole-program preliminary insights to date for their use. Other examples of more informal, digestible formats to share evaluation findings include presentation slides that program implementors can more seamlessly repurpose for their own needs and short, topic-specific learning briefs oriented toward a lay audience instead of or in addition to traditional evaluation reports or peer-reviewed articles.

Also, multiple funding organizations can support trauma-informed program implementation and, therefore, include more than one evaluator with stakes in disseminating evaluation findings. In such cases, *peer support* among evaluators is an important TI principle to consider. If multiple evaluators participate in the evaluation, they should work to come to agreement in the types of sharing that will occur. When evaluators are working at cross purposes, not only does it break down collaboration among all parties—program participants, implementors, and evaluators—when conflicting messages are shared, but it undermines trust and confidence in the overall evaluation approach and findings. This breakdown could affect the uptake of evaluation findings and hinder learning and improvement, and consequently inhibit the effective implementation of TIC.

5 Discussion and Recommendations

Although there is limited empirical evidence supporting the benefits of a trauma-informed approach in evaluation, our experience suggests that taking this approach promotes collaboration and partnership among program stakeholders and participants, helps strengthen those relationships, ensures data quality and accurate interpretation, and improves evaluation results.

While this chapter explores applying TI principles to the evaluation of TIC programs expressly, the benefits of using trauma-informed approaches might warrant broader application to evaluation practice more generally, particularly given the historical context of evaluation (e.g., being a funder-imposed requirement, using extractive and punitive processes related to data collection). Many of the TI principles can also promote more equitable evaluation practice, which is increasingly a goal for both evaluators and funders. For example, equitable evaluation requires acknowledging and addressing cultural, historical, and gender issues. It also aims to mitigate oppressive power dynamics, an element of the collaboration and mutuality principle.

As discussed in previous sections, incorporating trauma-informed approaches in evaluation practice requires changes in how evaluators do their work, which may not align with partners' expectations or ways of working. Potential challenges include:

- Funder expectations. Evaluations are still primarily supported by philanthropy, who may expect to be the evaluation's primary decision maker and audience. What funders want to see might not be compatible with incorporating program implementor and participant input and feedback into the evaluation design. Incorporating these steps might mean adding to the evaluation's scope or choosing between what funders want to see and what is meaningful for program implementors and participants.
- Implications for budgets and timelines. The emphasis on relationships and being responsive to program participant context might require slowing down the evaluation timeline, investing more time in relationship building or participant engagement than is typical, or pivoting from the plan. This perspective requires flexibility that may not be typical for funders or evaluators.
- Training and habits of evaluation professionals. Evaluation training typically focuses on the technical aspects of evaluation practice, like data collection methodology and quantitative and qualitative analysis, with less emphasis on some of the relational or interpersonal aspects of the work that are critical for TI evaluation. Additionally, aligning with TI principles can require flexibility and adapta-

tion from the original plan in ways that evaluators may find unappealing because there are implications on methodology, rigor, and ability to understand and communicate (i.e., publish) on specific aspects of the evaluation. Generally, as described in the chapter, incorporating trauma-informed principles requires evaluators to step back and rethink how they do their work.

- Trauma-informed program implementation not aligning with TI principles. Adhering to trauma-informed evaluation principles is challenging when the program itself may be operating in direct conflict with those principles. For example, funders and programs sometimes center their perspectives on what data would be interesting without regard for feasibility and burden on participants. Adhering to the TI principles requires ongoing advocacy from evaluators, including potentially pushing back on what the program asks for from participants, including for the evaluation. Evaluators should continue operating according to TI principles even if those are not evident in the program and insist on sharing data and evaluation information with participants in tangible and accessible ways.
- Tension with other evaluators who are unfamiliar with or do not operate in alignment with TI principles. In projects with two professionals or firms partnering on the evaluation, values and approaches can be misaligned, resulting in peer conflict. This conflict detracts from a feeling of safety between evaluation professionals. It can breed animosity that threatens the well-being of evaluators as individuals and can potentially affect the evaluation itself.

Our experience shows that the benefits of using trauma-informed approaches outweigh the challenges encountered but require shifts in culture and expectations related to evaluation. Evaluators can leverage their positional power and push the field toward more trauma-informed practices and approaches. They can do this in various ways throughout every phase of the evaluation. Initially, evaluators should develop proposals and scopes of work that account for and incorporate relationship development and maintenance. They should include reporting deliverables and processes that provide information to program implementors and participants. Evaluators should also outline data collection plans informed by program activities and participant priorities that minimize participant burden. Throughout the project, evaluators can continue to position relationships as central to the evaluation process, build in and adhere to systems that provide transparency and allow participant voice and choice, and work to mitigate power dynamics within evaluation activities (e.g., data collection, analysis, and interpretation processes). Ultimately, evaluators must hold themselves accountable to these principles since program partners may not feel the need to meet the same requirements. Evaluators can be explicit with funders, program implementors, and participants that they incorporate TI principles into their evaluation practice to raise awareness, set expectations, and promote accountability.

References

Baum F, MacDougall C, Smith D (2006) Participatory action research. J Epidemiol Community Health 60:854

Bosk EA (2023) Creating a parallel process: a new methodological framework for conducting trauma-informed evaluation and research (TIER) in mental health settings. Eval Program Plann 97:102229

Brown T, Ashworth H, Bass M, Rittenberg E, Levy-Carrick N, Grossman S, Lewis-O'connor A, Stoklosa H (2022) Trauma-informed care interventions in emergency medicine: a systematic review. West J Emerg Med 23:334–344

Center for Substance Abuse treatment. SAMHSA/CSAT Treatment Improvement Protocols (2014) Trauma-informed care in behavioral health services. Substance Abuse and Mental Health Services Administration, Rockville

Coghlan AT, Preskill H, Tzavaras Catsambas T (2003) An overview of appreciative inquiry in evaluation. N Dir Eval 2003:5–22

Cousins JB, Earl LM (1992) The case for participatory evaluation. Educ Eval Policy Anal 14:397–418

Dean-Coffey J (2018) What's race got to do with it? Equity and philanthropic evaluation practice. Am J Eval 39:527–542

Fernández V, Gausereide-Corral M, Valiente C, Sánchez-Iglesias I (2023) Effectiveness of trauma-informed care interventions at the organizational level: a systematic review. Psychol Serv 20(4):849–862

Huang LN, Flatow R, Biggs T, Afayee S, Smith K, Clark T, Blake M (2014) SAMHSA'S concept of trauma and guidance for a trauma-informed approach. Substance Abuse and Mental Health Services Administration, Rockville

Lowenthal A (2020) Trauma-informed care implementation in the child-and youth-serving sectors: a scoping review. Int J Child Adoles Res 7:178–194

Mahon D (2022) Implementing trauma informed care in human services: an ecological scoping review. Behav Sci 12:431

Menschner C, Maul A (2016) Key ingredients for successful trauma-informed care implementation. Center for Health Care Strategies, Hamilton

Milstein B, Wetterhall SF (1999) Framework for program evaluation in public health. CDC, Atlanta

Raja S, Hasnain M, Hoersch M, Gove-Yin S, Rajagopalan C (2015) Trauma informed care in medicine: current knowledge and future research directions. Fam Community Health 38:216–226

Wallerstein N, Duran B (2017) The theoretical, historical and practice roots of CBPR. In: Community-based participatory research for health: advancing social and health equity. Wiley, Hoboken, pp 17–29

Evaluating Innovations in Health Services: A Team Competency Framework

Jackie Chandler, Andrew Sibley, Philippa Darnton, Amanda Lees, and Emmanuel Defever

Abstract

This chapter describes a team-based competency framework to undertake evaluations of innovations and new ways of working in health services. Six domains highlight competencies in communication, people management and relationship building to navigate real-world evaluation. The framework covers professional qualifications and experience, technical expertise and knowledge required. It addresses different forms of leadership and engagement with evaluation stakeholders as both participants and users of evaluation findings. The domains are structured to demonstrate competencies for simple and complex evaluations. This competency framework provides quality assurance of team skills needed to conduct evaluations to manage and ensure a credible evaluation with defendable findings.

Keywords

Evaluation · Competency · Health · Social · Innovation adoption

1 Introduction

This chapter presents a competency framework based on team level requirements to undertake evaluations of innovation adoption and new ways of working in health service settings. These competencies cover professional backgrounds and experience, technical expertise and knowledge, skills to project manage and quality assure a credible and impactful evaluation.

J. Chandler (✉) · A. Sibley · P. Darnton · A. Lees · E. Defever
Health Innovation Wessex, Southampton, UK
e-mail: jackie.chandler@hiwessex.net

A. Kaehne, J. Feather (eds.), *Handbook of Health Services Evaluation*,
https://doi.org/10.1007/978-3-031-87869-5_21

The work of an experienced team in the United Kingdom (UK) informs this framework. They evaluate a range of new medical devices, digital technologies, service transformations, and other solutions to facilitate the adoption of evidence-based innovation in the National Health Service (England). The National Health Service, a single payer service, has moved to an integrated care system that includes primary care, social and community care services, acute care, and emergency services.

The framework structures the competencies along a continuum from simple to complex evaluations of innovation in real-world settings. Defined and explained across six core domains involving 21 competency subdomains, it is the inter-play of these competencies across a team that facilitates successful evaluations of innovation. This novel competency framework provides a form of quality assurance for evaluations by describing skills for a team rather than an individual. For example, the framework describes different leadership functions in teams and that individuals should collectively engage in ethical, inclusive, and reflective practice. This framework acknowledges the identification, engagement, and activities involving evaluation commissioners and innovators as both participants in, and users of, evaluation findings.

1.1 Why Competencies for Evaluation Teams?

Health service evaluation teams need a broad set of skills to simultaneously run multiple and often complex evaluations typical within health service settings. Other evaluation frameworks focus on skills for individuals. To create an efficient health service requires timely evaluations (Smith et al. 2023) using multiple approaches that may include, for example, rapid appraisal techniques (Vindrola-Padros et al. 2021). This novel framework takes account of the need for adaptative decision-making by evaluation teams to address the complexity within health services, often creatively managing factors beyond their control. The team focus, based on the experience of a real evaluation team, allows breadth beyond an individual's skill and capacity and describes important influences on delivering health service evaluations. Commissioners of the evaluation either from within the health service or an innovator (commercial or non-commercial) or a sponsor or funder of the innovation, and other people including patients and patient representatives influence the success of an evaluation. Skilled evaluation teams evaluating innovations need to assess its stage of development and preparedness for its scale up and spread. Often the challenge for innovations in health service settings is that the "value proposition" does not match the needs of the health system and those it supports. A value proposition is a statement of the value an innovation can bring to the health and social care system. It usually includes information on what the innovation is intended to do; who it is for; how it works; and why patients, health, and care services might benefit from it.

1.2 The Health Service Evaluation Context

Health service evaluations are undertaken in highly pressurized settings involving healthcare professionals crossing multiple clinical disciplines across different hierarchical structures supported by different professional bodies. Health care is organized across primary (first point of care, family doctors), secondary (specialist care, local general hospital), and tertiary (highly specialist care, regional specialist hospital) care systems. Health systems around the world are designed differently to meet the needs of their populations. They may involve various arrangements of public and private funding, covering models offering universal healthcare (e.g., UK), private insurance systems, and systems that combine these elements.

1.2.1 The UK Context of Health Innovation Adoption

The UK provides a comprehensive universal healthcare system free at the point of use. All health systems need to develop efficient health care to maximize use of available resources. A key driver in the UK is to support its National Health Service to engage with technology and other innovations to maximize its healthcare resources. The Health Innovation Networks in England have a key role in scaling up and accelerating innovation to improve health and generate economic growth. Fifteen innovation networks provide support to innovators from innovation discovery to its development and subsequent deployment in the National Health Service. Innovations and in particular digital health technologies are becoming increasingly prevalent across all major health systems. One example in the UK context is an app for women and pregnant people to access information and advice based on their concerns and symptoms (Royal College of Midwives 2023). Similarly, in South Africa, another maternity app registers women who are pregnant and provides them with twice-weekly health information text messages as well as access to a help desk for queries and feedback throughout their pregnancy and postpartum period (Peter et al. 2018).

To support evaluation of health services implementing innovations (including new ways of working), an evaluation competency framework for evaluation teams describes team-based competencies. The following defines key terms used in this chapter.

- Innovation adoption: Innovation is not just about the originating idea but also the whole process of the successful development, implementation, and spread of that idea into widespread use (NHS Chief Executive Innovation 2011).
- Innovation (a): New approaches, practices, treatments, technologies, and services that aim to improve health care (Horton et al. 2018).
- Innovation (b): A novel, drug, device, app, model of care, set of behaviors or way of working that is directed at improving outcomes, efficiency, or experience (Albury et al. 2018).
- Innovator: An individual, team, or organization that developed the idea for the innovation (Horton et al. 2018).

- Implementation: Implementation is an actively planned and deliberately initiated effort with the intention to bring a given intervention into policy and practice within a particular setting (Pfadenhauer et al. 2017).

2 Summary of Existing Frameworks

Eleven evaluation competency frameworks were reviewed to provide the groundwork to develop a team focused competency framework. These were:

- UK Evaluation Society's framework of evaluation capabilities (UK Evaluation Society 2012)
- The NHS Knowledge and skills framework and the development review process (NHS 2004)
- UK Government analytical evaluation capabilities framework (UK Government 2011)
- The European Evaluation Society Evaluation Capabilities Framework (European Evaluation Society 2012)
- Australasian Evaluation Society Evaluators' Professional Learning Competency Framework (Australasian Evaluation Society 2013)
- American Evaluation Association competencies and self-assessment (Minnesota Evaluation Studies Institute 2018)
- United Nations Evaluation Group—Evaluation Competency Framework (United Nations 2016)
- International Development Evaluation Association—Competencies for Development Evaluation Evaluators, Managers, and Commissioners (International Development Evaluation Association 2012)
- German Evaluation Society—Standards for Evaluation (German Evaluation Society 2003)
- Canadian Evaluation Society—Competencies for Canadian Evaluation Practice (Canadian Evaluation Society 2018)
- Public Health England Skills for Health—NHS Health Check Competency Framework (Public Health England 2020)

Other work identified was quite specific to certain cultures (e.g., Aotearoa New Zealand Evaluation Association (Anzea) for the Professional Practice Development Evaluator Competency Project February 2010) and not relevant for the focus of the proposed team evaluation competency framework. Framework details were extracted into a structured template on the scope, focus, development as well as the basis for consensus of evaluation capabilities or competencies. Four frameworks did not fully describe the processes for consensus. Those that did seek consensus undertook various consultation methods including surveying membership, using modified Delphi approaches and expert validation. Core components or domains of components were extracted noting any useful or relevant components to provide a starting point for the new framework. This included noting the structure and organization of the individual frameworks. These frameworks assembled their core domains in different ways. In summary, the following were covered by these frameworks:

- Professional foundations
- Evaluation knowledge and theory, technical skills, and research methods
- Professional practice—behaviors, attitudes, and personal qualities
- Project management and interpersonal skills
- Management of stakeholders and the evaluation context
- Reflective practice and promotion of a culture of evaluation learning

The following section will describe how this background work informed the development of the new framework.

3 A Competency Framework for Evaluation Teams

The Evaluation Team Competency framework for Health Services (ETC-HS) V1 lists the competencies required for teams to run either simple or complex evaluations. In real-world settings, evaluations will cover a spectrum of features, such as:

- The range of skills required when evaluations are more complex—from delivery of an innovation into a single site, department or setting to multiple sites or hospital wide systems, increaseing complexity.
- The scale and scope of an evaluation needs to manage multiple levels of organization and interested stakeholders. For example, evaluation commissioners' and innovators' expectations and their capacity to support the evaluation.
- Authorizing timely access to data and study sites can present challenges in real world evaluation.

Successful evaluation teams need to respond to these challenges and complex evaluation scenarios and thus require a range of individual and organizational skills and support. Different forms of team leadership are set out in the framework. Team competencies need to include the ability to assess, cost, manage, and allocate team resources based on the achievability of the proposed evaluation framework. The following describes the development of the Evaluation Team Competency Framework for Health Services (ETC-HS V1 framework) and its core domains and related competencies. Accreditation for teams in hospitals provides similar expectations for team competencies to develop the right culture, good leadership, and staff engagement to support ongoing quality improvement (NHS Chief Executive Innovation 2011). Team-based competencies that support collaborative working will deliver optimal care within complex hospital settings (McLaney et al. 2022).

3.1 Framework Development

Members of the current evaluation team (chapter authors) collectively reviewed the 11 frameworks identified. Each appraised framework provided a checklist to guide inclusion of key competencies in the new framework. These competencies were viewed through the wider lens of competencies needed across a team. Through several rounds of internal review and consideration, a final set of core and subdomains were agreed. This incorporated the authors' own experience of managing a broad portfolio of health service evaluations. This included the wider context of situating the team in a wider organization for support, working with a variety of evaluation commissioners and the different forms of leadership required. Team-based approaches are required for large-scale and multi-site evaluations. Other evaluation frameworks describe competencies by seniority or staff role, and here they are described by type of evaluation. This does not refer to the type of evaluation framework, e.g., formative, summative, or process but the nature of the evaluation along a dimension continuum from simple to complex. Definitions and case examples are:

Simple evaluations will involve a well-defined innovation with low level of interdependency between its components. Elementary skills are only required by those delivering and those receiving the innovation. Only minor innovation tailoring or adaptation is necessary. There is a short direct pathway to the innovation recipient with a low level of dependency on contextual factors for delivery. These evaluations often involve small teams or individuals working on their own with basic evaluation skills and with some level of health service experience.

Case example: A tele-dermatology innovation evaluated in one hospital service cancer unit (Tele-dermatology is a field of dermatology that employs telemedicine techniques to allow clinicians to diagnose and treat patients remotely). This innovation provides special imaging devices attached to mobile phones for primary care practices to deliver high-resolution images of possible malignant skin conditions via a secure web platform to a consultant dermatologist for initial diagnosis. This triage care pathway reduces wait for diagnosis and averts a clinic appointment if not required. Routine data collection, interviews with general practice staff and consultant dermatologists, and a patient survey were the evaluation data collection activities. The evaluation required two team members with quantitative data analysis and qualitative data expertise. A single report, infographic, and conference abstract were dissemination output formats.

Complex evaluations will involve innovations with multiple components with substantial interaction or interdependency between components leading to anticipated synergistic[1] effects. Both those delivering and receiving the innovation may require skills and behavior change. The innovation may need to adapt or be tailored to different populations in different target contexts. Implementation of the innovation pathway is neither direct nor short, and the innovation is dependent on contextual factors and the implementation setting. Complex evaluations

[1] Synergist effects are a result of the combined effect of other elements to produce the desired end effect.

can be over multiple sites or a large single site (hospital wide rather than department), and may include a wide range of stakeholders and people with an interest in the evaluation outcomes. These evaluations require a larger skilled team with expertise and experience.

Case example: The management of ulcerated leg wounds is a significant problem in the UK. Leg ulcers occur because of either poor arterial or venous blood supply to the lower leg. These wounds need specific care to successfully heal, and patients can have these wounds for many years. A national wound care program produced recommendations for wound care and treatment, and care pathway redesign. This national program recruited eight sites to test and evaluate delivery of these national wound care recommendations across England. The real-world evaluation investigated the implementation of wound care recommendations and the impact on both clinical and nursing staff and patients. The evaluation used an implementation framework to capture data on staff training, staff experience of pathway change, and delivering complex care to promote wound healing. This care includes measuring arterial blood supply, taking accurate images of the wound, using dressings appropriately, and applying strong compression to the wound. Wound diagnosis and management and promotion of patient self-care present challenges. New quantitative metrics were required to ascertain improvements to patient caseloads. The evaluation conducted interviews with staff and patients, undertook an all staff clinical and business intelligence survey, and collected a wide range of data from all eight sites. Sites varied across their populations, size, and scale of their delivery plans, start times, and components of the recommendations they delivered. Multiple agencies were involved in supporting the delivery and conduct of the evaluation. The evaluation team provided up to six staff undertaking different roles from governance to data collection and analysis. This evaluation required multiple check-ins with different stakeholders. Key outputs are a program level report and eight individual site case reports.

A small-scale, single-site evaluation project may become a complex project if, for example, the implementation of the innovation causes an unintended disruptive effect. Likewise, a three-year long national-level transformational change evaluation involving multiple local stakeholders may seem like a complex evaluation, but if commissioned by an organization with well-established local networks committed to supporting the evaluation processes, the evaluation team may simply have oversight of the project.

3.2 Evaluation Team Competency Framework for Health Services V1

The Evaluation Team Competency Framework for Health Services (ETC-HS V1 framework) for teams of evaluation professionals seeks to demonstrate the breadth of skill required within a team and does not cover all individual competencies. The framework has six core domains and 21 individual competency subdomains (between three and four per core domain). Table 1 summarizes these six domains.

Table 1 ETC-HS: Six competency domains and areas of competency

Core domain	Definition	Areas of competency
1. Professional qualifications and experience	Evaluations of innovations in health services needs team members with a broad set of qualifications, experience, and skills	(1) Breadth of team skillsets (2) Evaluation knowledge (3) Evaluation field experience
2.Technical and methodological skillsets to conduct evaluations	Teams need skills to provide an evaluation service that enables multiple types of evaluations and their methods to evaluate different healthcare innovations	(1) Designing evaluations (2) Collecting data (3) Conducting data analysis, synthesis, and interpretation (4) Reporting an evaluation and its findings
3. Program management skills for teams	Evaluation context challenges need program and project management skills to work across multiple projects. This needs team cohesion and effective communication	(1) Allocating roles and responsibilities (2) Managing information governance and ethical practice (3) Project management (4) Portfolio management
4. Evaluation leadership for teams	Team leadership structure varies depending on team size and project portfolio and needs to ensure coordinated governance across the portfolio	(1) Strategic team leadership (2) Operational team leadership (3) Project leadership
5. People management skills for teams	People management skills are needed for both evaluation and team management to ensure cohesion and effective communication	(1) Collaborating with evaluation commissioners (2) Collaborating with innovators (3) Collaborating with patient representatives and groups (4) Collaborating with multiple different stakeholder groups
6. Communicating evaluation findings	The value of evaluation information and evidence to different audiences needs a structured plan to ensure findings achieve their anticipated impact	(1) Developing a dissemination plan and communication strategy (2) Using different outputs for different audiences (3) Offering feedback opportunities for the commissioning organization and target audience

3.2.1 Professional Qualifications and Experience

All evaluation frameworks reviewed outline expected educational and professional attainment of individuals undertaking evaluations. Teams are likely to vary in size, expertise, and experience. The demands on a team to deliver evaluations will need to take account of the professional qualifications and experience required. This domain looks at breadth of skills and defines evaluation knowledge requirements and field experience. To evaluate the program to implement care of ulcerated leg wounds benefitted from professional expertise (nursing), quantitative skills to analyze large datasets of newly collected data and define the quality limits for that data, rapid qualitative skills, and implementation expertise.

Small-scale, single-site evaluations require less specialist training or range of qualifications as well as less evaluation experience. This is because they are simpler in their requirements.

Complex large-scale, multi-site evaluations require a broader range of skillsets and larger teams, with team members assigned specific roles. These may include technical leads for quantitative or qualitative methods, program management, and team leadership based on the need to manage complex tasks, e.g., contracts and relationships with multiple stakeholders.

Subdomains are defined in Table 2, and further explanations for both basic and complex skills are provided.

Breadth of Team Skillsets

The minimum qualifications necessary are professional and degree or equivalent education level. Minimum experience may involve clinical and audit skills in healthcare systems. Individual evaluators can provide specific technical, or project program management qualifications required by the context of the specific evaluation.

Individuals may have research, clinical and academic and professional qualifications, project management qualifications, service evaluation and audit training, innovation adoption (e.g., digital technology) experience, applied implementation science, data analytics and business intelligence skills, and economics.

In addition, complex evaluations may require:

Table 2 Professional qualifications and experience domain

Core domain	Definition
1. Professional qualifications and experience for teams	Evaluations of innovations in health services needs team members with a broad set of qualifications, experience, and skills
(1) Breadth of team skillsets	Evaluation teams can include early career to expert individuals with a diverse range of qualifications and experience
(2) Evaluation knowledge	Evaluation knowledge includes context and history of evaluation, evaluation design, use of theory and methods, and their application for wide range of evaluation questions
(3) Evaluation field experience	To demonstrate the ability to conduct credible and valid evaluations by experience

1. Senior leadership qualifications that include master's level qualification or other post-graduate leadership courses or equivalent experience in a related area ("evaluator by experience").
2. Technical qualifications include master's level qualification, research experience (PhD level for some staff), and professional qualifications with 5 years' minimum experience.
3. Program management qualifications that can include formal training programs leading to a project management accredited certificate.

Evaluation Knowledge

At a minimum, for simple evaluations, team members will understand the objectives, processes, and procedures of conducting and reporting a limited evaluation of a simple innovation in a simple context. Team members will need to demonstrate a basic knowledge and use of quantitative and qualitative methods and their analysis.

For complex evaluations, the team should provide expert knowledge and skills in any of following:

- Quantitative data analysis and statistics
- Qualitative methods and analysis
- Mixed methods synthesis
- Economic analysis
- The application of theory and principles of applied implementation science

Evaluation Field Experience

Simple evaluations need both technical skills and project management skills and include:

- Basic computer literacy skills and use of software such as word, spreadsheet, databases, and simple formula
- Experience of managing information governance and applying data protection law
- Conduct of ethical practice
- Development of positive working relationships within the team and with all stakeholders

Complex evaluations need more advanced technical and project management skills which include:

- Advanced use of digital technologies and analytical skills for statistics, surveys, qualitative data management, spreadsheets, visualization, and graphics
- The ability to conduct multiple, multi-site, and large scale regional or national evaluations
- The ability to manage complex relationships across multiple agencies and conduct politically sensitive negotiations and complex information governance arrangements

3.2.2 Technical and Methodological Skills

The need for diverse technical and methodological skills provides flexibility to deliver high quality and highly valued evaluations. These skills are described at each key step of the evaluation process, from designing evaluations, collecting data, and conducting data analysis and synthesis to reporting findings. Specialist skills (e.g., economics or social media analysis) may not always be available, requiring the organization to identify and "buy in" this expertise to meet evaluation requirements. For example, cost benefit analysis skills are needed in evaluations to demonstrate innovation benefit either in monetary terms or impacts on services delivered. For the tele-dermatology project, an estimation of a 63% reduction in future outpatient appointments (Chandler et al. 2022) was able to demonstrate an important impact on consultant dermatologists and their time.

Simple evaluations need a basic knowledge and methodological competency in core concepts of evaluation design and methods, question formulation, quantitative and qualitative data collection, data analysis, report writing, and dissemination of findings. However, complex evaluations require experience and expertise in a range of technical and specialist skills across the team. This includes the ability to use a range of evaluation (or research) methods and combine them in a complex evaluation to address complex questions.

Subdomains are defined in Table 3, and further explanations for both basic and complex skills are provided.

Designing Evaluations

Basic evaluations need an understanding of the core elements to evaluate healthcare innovations in the real world to identify the evaluation framework need, formulate appropriate questions, utilize best methods, and conduct analysis and interpretation of findings. Also, the use of co-design or participatory techniques to ensure stakeholder patient and carer representatives involvement (Fetterman et al. 2018; Fetterman 2023).

Table 3 Technological and methodological skills domain

Core domain	Definition
2. Technical and methodlogical skillsets to conduct evaluations	Teams need skills to provide an evaluation service that enables multiple types of evaluations and their methods to evaluate different healthcare innovations
(1) Designing evaluations	Development of an evaluation framework or evaluation plan
(2) Collecting data	Development of data collections tools and the process of collecting data
(3) Conducting data analysis, synthesis, and interpretation	Skills in data analysis, data synthesis across datasets and the interpretation of the data
(4) Reporting an evaluation and its findings	Reporting evaluation findings should ensure transparency to the reader on the conduct of the evaluation and how its findings were derived. The use of research reporting standards is helpful

Complex evaluations need a wide range of knowledge and skills to design multimethod evaluations. Skillsets across teams need to provide a breadth of evaluation design skills, knowledge of methods, and advanced skills in applying theoretical and conceptual frameworks to support the development of complex questions and organization of complex data.

Collecting Data

Basic evaluations need:

1. The ability to link data required to answer an evaluation question.
2. The knowledge and experience to develop simple data collection tools, e.g., questionnaires and interview plans.
3. The ability to extract quantitative data from health service administrative systems for descriptive statistical analyses. Skills in data quality (consistency and accuracy) and data security are relevant for all types of evaluations.

Complex evaluations need:

1. For quantitative data, advanced data analysis techniques and the ability to manage data flows from multiple provider (administrative data) systems are more likely in complex evaluations.
2. For qualitative data, skills to create tailored and novel data collection tools (e.g., surveys, implementation data collection tools, outcome measures and adaption of other tools, e.g., visual analogue scales).
3. Project management skills are required to collect large scale or multi-site data, ensure data quality and accuracy, ethical practice, and timeliness of data retrieval.

Conducting Data Analysis, Synthesis, and Interpretation

From basic skills to collate data (qualitative or quantitative) include using appropriate software, the ability to develop simple data tabulations, graphs, and other tools to present data and understand the evaluation findings to advanced skills. These include the ability to synthesize multiple data sets and apply theory, where appropriate, as an explanatory framework to the findings.

Reporting an Evaluation and Its Findings

The team collectively should demonstrate effective written and visual communication skills. This includes technical skills: use of language, active voice, report format, style and use of charts, figures, and infographics, editing, and proofreading. Team members need to demonstrate transparency in reporting of evaluation limitations and their appropriate interpretation.

Larger evaluation reports of complex multi-site programs need greater scrutiny and organization of complex concepts, data, and conclusions. Useful experience and skills are those attained in data visualization and presentation of data. Advanced writing and editing skills along with report layout and design skills are necessary.

3.2.3 Program Management Skills

Program and project management skills are required to manage a portfolio of evaluations. Each evaluation requires project management. Depending on the size of the evaluation team, individual evaluators may be allocated to a variety of projects at any one time. Individual evaluators may need a certain level of skill to manage a portfolio of evaluation projects. Although the leg ulcer evaluation requires multiple team members to cover the demands of managing data collection for eight sites, each member will concurrently deliver a range of other projects varying in complexity, duration, and at different stages in the evaluation process. Subdomains are defined in Table 4, and further explanations for both basic and complex skills are provided.

Allocating Roles and Responsibilities

The team will need to match evaluation requirements to the skills and availability of a small evaluation team or individual in simpler evaluations. Complex, large-scale evaluations require the ability to allocate roles and responsibilities to a broader range of team members with various skills and expertise. Demand and capacity management skills are necessary, and use of external contractors can supplement in-house skills or support team capacity demands.

Managing Information Governance and Ethical Practice

Teams need a basic understanding of governance and ethical requirements for health service evaluation. This encompasses ethical conduct of evaluations (e.g., seeking informed consent, providing clear information about the right to opt-out), as well as

Table 4 Program management skills domain

Core domain	Definition
3. Program management skills for teams	Evaluation context challenges need program and project management skills to work across multiple projects. This needs team cohesion and effective communication
(1) Allocating roles and responsibilities	This requires the identification of individual skills and talents within a team and assignment to tasks based on their ability
(2) Managing information governance and ethical practice	Governance includes managing contractual arrangements, data protection, and sharing requirement. Ethical practice enshrined in law and good practice protects both evaluators and those evaluated
(3) Project management	Evaluations need project management. Consultancy principles help layout core tasks to organize work and manage expectations[a]
(4) Portfolio management	Teams manage multiple evaluations and require skills to ensure all evaluations are risk managed and meet their objectives. Portfolio management includes, contractual management, financial, and budgetary planning.

[a] Through a comprehensive specification of the evaluation and contract and building and maintaining professional relationships. This includes ensuring the safety of both healthcare professionals and patients

compliance with organizational processes to minimize the data protection risks of an evaluation (information governance).

The team will need to navigate information governance and ethics where required across multiple evaluation sites. It is important to appreciate the timescales involved in navigating these requirements, and the potential impact on data collection start dates. Both authoritative skills and persistence are necessary to manage these system challenges impacting on evaluation planning.

Project Management

Necessary project management skills include:

1. Set up: project specification (to establish aims, approach, outputs, roles, responsibilities, and timelines) and arrangements.
2. During the project: establishing regular communications between stakeholders, reporting progress, identifying, and mitigating risks.
3. Project close: reflecting on lessons learned, sharing, and wider dissemination of learning.

Larger scale and complex evaluations require more developed management skills to deal with complex evaluation designs, a greater range of stakeholders, longer project durations, multiple interdependencies, and the potential for multiple risks.

Portfolio Management

Accomplished team members should manage several projects simultaneously, responding to the interaction of tasks, risks, and deadlines. This requires skills of time management, multi-tasking, prioritization, and communication, as well as ensuring an appropriate balance of staffing, monitoring hours spent per project, and supporting project leads.

3.2.4 Team Leadership

The leadership structure within an evaluation team will vary depending on the team's size and nature of its project portfolio. Leadership at both project or program and team level is required to ensure coordinated governance across the portfolio. Senior team members are empowered to lead individual projects within a support structure. A team leader who sits within a larger organization needs to align evaluation team activity with that of the wider organization, ensuring strategic alignment and appropriate resourcing to the evaluation function. In addition to generic leadership competencies expected in any leadership role, we identify those competencies most important in leading the work of an evaluation team. The leg ulcer evaluation involved strategic leadership to identify the opportunity and tender for the evaluation as a strategic priority. Operational leadership supported the relationship with the commissioners, contractual, and other governance processes which required negotiating skills. The project lead supported evaluation design and its conduct and directly managed and supported other team members. This involved complex data

Table 5 Team leadership skills domain

Core domain	Definition
4. Evaluation leadership for teams	Team leadership structure varies depending on team size and project portfolio and needs to ensure coordinated governance across the portfolio
(1) Strategic team leadership	Strategic leadership sets the direction of the team and ensures team members are clear about the coherence and alignment of their work with the team's overarching strategy. Team members have clear roles and responsibilities and have the confidence and capabilities to self-organize
(2) Operational team leadership	Formal processes are essential to the smooth running and coordination of projects within a portfolio of evaluations
(3) Project leadership	The delivery of an end-to-end evaluation requires the identification of a project lead to provide oversight at the operational level

collection activities to understand the implementation challenges of the leg ulcer recommendations into health systems with competing demands on individual healthcare professional staff delivering changes at the point of care to the patient. Collecting data directly from these frontline staff is challenging and requires agility and adaptation to meet the evaluation requirements. Subdomains are defined in Table 5, and further explanations for both basic and complex skills are provided. Chapter 18 "Evaluating Leadership in Health Services" provides frameworks to evaluate leadership approaches in health services and discuss different leadership models with a focus on collaborative and shared forms of leadership. We adopt team leadership by role to support a team-based approach that empowers individual team members.

Strategic Team Leadership

Team members are empowered to lead individual projects within clear boundaries and within an enabling team structure. They will be clear about how their projects contribute to the performance objectives of the team. A "team with a plan" is equipped to manage the expectations of those who commission the services of the team.

Providing supportive leadership and team culture will facilitate a shared "burden" (frustrations and challenges), joint problem solving, and the space to continuously improve and innovate.

For both simple and complex evaluations, strategic awareness and influencing skills to optimize the impact of an evaluation output are key competencies. Teams undertaking complex evaluations will need to draw on strategic leadership for advice and oversight throughout the program. This includes:

- Making strategic decisions on which evaluations to undertake.
- Establishing and maintaining clear evaluation boundaries to avoid evaluation scope creep.

- Managing any escalation of conflicts and complaints.
- Navigating politically sensitive contexts and delivering sensitive evaluation findings.
- Navigating the "influencing landscape" (e.g., policy makers, commissioners) to optimize the impact of evaluation outputs. Positioning the team's contribution within the organization.

Operational Team Leadership

Simple evaluations require robust project management skills and access to leadership support if issues arise. Complex evaluations require robust operational leadership skills from experienced leaders to ensure evaluation delivery due to the substantial risk of complications, delays, and communication issues when multiple stakeholders are involved.

Project Leadership

Key competencies in project leadership of simple evaluations are technical knowledge in the evaluation methods required for this type of evaluation, and basic skills in collaboration, relationship management, and negotiation.

This individual may work alone (in small discrete projects, e.g., collecting and analyzing one type of data) or with other team members where they will need broader competencies in leading and supporting the work of others.

Complex evaluations often require project teams to be creative in the design of the evaluation. This requires agility and adaptability to actively identify innovative solutions.

3.2.5 People Management Skills

Individual evaluators may be involved in several simple and complex evaluation projects which will require good communication and coordination within the team to ensure a successful and supportive team approach. Commissioners of evaluations have an important role in evaluation success and the quality of evaluations. Evaluation commissioners need to engage with evaluators to provide necessary local intelligence and access to evaluation participants and data. Evaluators need skills to manage the commissioning relationship to negotiate scope and timeliness of project delivery including access and data collection to project closure. Important competencies to managing this relationship include demonstrating diplomacy and negotiation skills.

Innovators seek to engage health services to utilize their innovation and are heavily invested in its success. Working with innovators requires skills to manage this sensitive relationship that is simultaneously collaborative and supportive but also needs the evaluator to maintain the independence of the evaluation. Innovators are often operating in a competitive commercial environment such as the teledermatology solution. This becomes more challenging over a longer term, more complex evaluation, where there could be a risk of an evaluator becoming invested in the innovation. Reflexivity is required as well as the application of standard processes for upholding rigor and objectivity in evaluations. Subdomains are defined in Table 6, and further explanations for both basic and complex skills are provided.

Table 6 People management skills domain

Core domain	Definition
5. People management skills for teams	People management skills are needed for both evaluation and team management to ensure cohesion and effective communication
(1) Collaborating with evaluation commissioners	Commissioners require completion of the evaluation on time that meets their objectives
(2) Collaborating with innovators	Innovators seek to engage health services to use their innovation and so are invested in its success
(3) Collaborating with patient representatives and groups	Patient representatives are key stakeholders in health service evaluations and are important in contributing to and legitimizing evaluations
(4) Collaborating with multiple different stakeholder groups	Health services involve clinical professionals, management, innovators, and other organizations, e.g., public, private, and voluntary

Collaborating with Evaluation Commissioners

Relevant skills for working with evaluation commissioners involves building shared aims, objectives, and understanding of deliverables. Good project management and the establishment of regular check-ins facilitate this relationship. It is helpful to understand evaluation commissioners' contexts, pressures, and priorities as these may affect their levels of involvement and buy-in.

With more complex and larger scale evaluations, the number of stakeholders from the commissioning side increases, requiring more meetings and check-ins with greater effort to maintain communications and manage relationships. It is important to build these into project timelines.

Collaborating with Innovators

Working with innovators requires skills to manage this sensitive relationship that is simultaneously collaborative and supportive but also maintains distance, allowing for independent evaluation.

Maintaining a balanced relationship becomes more challenging over the longer term, especially in complex evaluations. The boundary between innovation implementation and its evaluation may overlap putting independence at risk. Reflexivity skills and the application of standard processes are important for upholding rigor and objectivity in evaluations.

Collaborating with Patient Representatives and Groups

It is important that team members are aware of good practice around how to engage with specific groups, including those typically underserved in health services and evaluations. Evaluators should be skilled at building relationships and establishing dialogue, learning what matters to people rather than imposing their own views. Teams should be able to employ principles of co-design and co-production where appropriate.

In complex designs, wider groups of patient representatives and community groups require a more sophisticated engagement plan. Public engagement expertise will support this important relationship carefully and appropriately through-out the course of the evaluation.

Collaborating with Multiple Different Stakeholder Groups

A team needs to understand the range of stakeholders, their roles, and points of involvement. Effective communication skills are required including the ability to adapt to stakeholder's preferred (or required) means of communication.

Complex evaluations require the same fundamental skills but with a greater array of stakeholders. This requires skilled influencing and engagement skills.

3.2.6 Communication of Evaluation Findings

It is important messages from evaluations are shared, and acted upon, by those in a position to do so. It is important to "close the loop" for evaluation participants by sharing findings with them in an appropriate format. In communicating their evaluation findings, teams should consider all potential audiences, and pathways to impact. The tele-dermatology case findings were presented at a recognized conference for dermatologists to ensure, although findings were derived from a single location, it was nevertheless important to contribute to other research or evaluations occurring in this important area of development. For the national leg ulcer evaluation, distributing the findings beyond the commissioners is vital to ensure the ongoing implementation of national recommendations in this area of care. Subdomains are defined in Table 7, and further explanations for both basic and complex skills are provided.

Table 7 Communication of evaluation findings skills domain

Core domain	Definition
6. Communicating evaluation findings	The value of evaluation information and evidence to different audiences needs a structured plan to ensure findings achieve their anticipated impact
(1) Developing a dissemination plan and communication strategy	Development of a dissemination plan and communication strategy ensures advance preparation to effectively plan evaluation findings reach their target audience in an appropriate format at the optimal time
(2) Using different outputs for different audiences	Evaluation outputs[a] tailored to target audiences ensures consideration of patients, innovators, healthcare professionals and health systems
(3) Offering feedback opportunities for the commissioning organization and target audience	Good practice for a learning organization follows good practice and provides a mechanism[b] for evaluation feedback from commissioners and other key stakeholders

[a] Format of evaluation output may include written (e.g. reports, articles, blogs), visual (e.g., infographics, video), audio (e.g., podcast), or interactive (e.g., workshops, seminars). The team needs to negotiate with the commissioning organizations around the format and delivery of evaluation outputs is also essential

[b] Feedback incorporated within the evaluation can occur as part of an interim update to the commissioning organization, at output phase (e.g., feedback on draft output), or after the completion of evaluation (e.g.. impact survey)

Developing a Dissemination Plan and Communication Strategy

A dissemination plan for a simple evaluation may require only an evaluation report submitted directly to a commissioning organization at the end of the evaluation project. They should expect to know the format of the output and the expected timeline. Complex evaluations require skills across a team to construct a well-considered dissemination plan and communication strategy. Team skills include clear identification of diverse audiences, versatility in delivering complex information in different digestible formats, and sophisticated use of multimedia platforms to maximize the exposure of the evaluation output. Communications expertise within the team may be a useful asset to coordinate the dissemination of complex evaluation findings.

Using Different Outputs for Different Audiences

Simple evaluations may require few formats tailored to the needs of intended audiences. Complex evaluation may challenge the team's resources in delivering multiple and different evaluation outputs to convey the findings effectively to different audiences at different delivery time points. Either a larger team with skills in output design and coordination of delivery is needed or outsourcing this expertise may be necessary.

Offering Feedback Opportunities for the Commissioning Organization and Target Audience

Teams should create a space to receive, review, and action feedback. A simple evaluation with a single commissioning organization or well-defined target audience may not require a structured feedback system due to opportunities through routine communication with the team.

A complex evaluation may require a team to establish a robust feedback mechanism, which allows regular feedback throughout the course of evaluations to enable ongoing learning as part of the evaluation process. The team's leadership should have knowledge and experience in managing and resolving potential complaints.

3.3 Health System Challenges for Evaluation Teams

ETC-HS V1 describes competencies based on experience in delivering real-world evaluations. This experience has also identified a range of challenges for evaluation teams.

The biggest challenge for teams delivering real-world evaluations stems from a lack of control in real-world contexts. The research environment permits the research team to have more control over data collection and analysis, to scientifically control variables, and to draw robust conclusions. Real-world evaluation is messier, co-designed, and co-produced with a range of stakeholders (e.g., innovators, commissioners, clinical teams, patients) with a range of vested interests in the findings. Throughout, evaluation practice in the real-world stresses the need for the "soft" skills of reflective practice, and interpersonal, effective communication and negotiation skills (Hutchinson 2019).

Other challenges are:

- Competing priorities, where evaluators are often confined by the availability of resource, time, and in competition with many other priorities and pressures faced by those working in health systems.
- Obtaining relevant data due to short evaluation timeframes because evaluation teams rely upon others within the health system to provide retrospective quantitative data, negotiate access, and gain buy-in for evaluation activities.
- Working with innovator and evaluation commissioner expectations might entail preconceived views of how the evaluation is conducted, and expectations on only reporting positive findings. They may not appreciate neither the independent nature nor the uncertainty of a real-world evaluation.

The need for skills to meet these challenges creatively and sympathetically to bring innovators and commissioners with them is often through a Joint Working Group. This seeks to ensure that both understand the technical aspects of an evaluation and its purpose.

This framework reflects the communication, people management, and relationship building competencies required to navigate this complex context, which for real-world evaluation are as important as—and at times take precedence to—the technical expertise that teams must also possess. So alongside professional qualifications (domain one), technical and methodological skill sets (domain two), and communicating for impact and evaluation findings (domain six), we have included program management skills for teams (domain three), evaluation leadership for teams (domain four), and people management skills (domain five). While required to a greater or lesser degree depending on the complexity of the evaluation, these "softer" skills are always crucial in health care evaluations and should be prioritized by those building evaluation teams.

4 Using the Framework

Based on the experience of a well-established evaluation team in the UK, to use this framework the following considerations are highlighted and will need adapting to different international contexts and settings.

4.1 Using the Framework to Review an Existing Team or to Set up an Evaluation Team

Team members need well developed interpersonal and people management skills including leadership and project management skills. Based on team size and numbers of individuals, different forms of leadership described may occur across different individuals or within one or two individuals. Different stakeholders will require a range of approaches to enable their inclusion. This needs both negotiation and technical skills to ensure their engagement.

Skilled management of data collection, ensuring data quality and data access to produce defendable findings requires negotiating with commissioners and others providing data to give authority for access and data release. Familiarity with the health service data environment is important knowledge for the team.

4.2 Using the Framework to Determine the Needs of Complex Evaluations

To understand expectations and ensure evaluations produce relevant and impactful findings requires early discussions with commissioners on the feasibility of their expectations and the evaluation questions they want answered.

Development of the evaluation framework and data collection tools affords an opportunity for co-production with stakeholders and those commissioning the evaluation. This enables management of complexity in evaluations, acknowledgment of risks, and mitigations negotiated.

Finally, the framework highlights the importance of disseminating evaluation findings which are often solely provided to those that commission the evaluation and not disseminated further. The Health Innovation Network evaluation team ensure that they make their evaluations publicly accessible and to optimise the potential impact of learning from evaluations. This affords an opportunity to build up an evidence base that is potentially accessible to agencies, such as the National Institute for Health and Care Excellence also part of the Guidelines International Network, which supports the use of real-world evidence as part of its evidence gathering for its guidelines.[2]

5 Conclusions

Real-world evaluations differ in size, complexity, resourcing, and timeframe. This team focused framework structures the competencies along a continuum from simple to complex evaluations. This approach supports mitigating challenges often experienced in complex evaluations. It is recommended that teams are resourced with multiple skill sets—beyond technical and methodological skills, to include program management, relational, and leadership skills.

Future work on the ETC-HS V1 framework would consider the importance of individual competencies within different contexts and explore skill development in working with innovators, evaluation commissioners, and other key stakeholders.

[2] Overview I NICE real-world evidence framework I Guidance I NICE.

References

Agenda for Change Project Team (2004) The NHS knowledge and skills framework and the development review process. NHS, London

Albury D, Beresford T, Dew S, Horton T, Illingworth J, Langford K (2018) Against the odds: successfully scaling innovation in the NHS. NHS, London

Australasian Evaluation Society Evaluators' Professional Learning Competency Framework (2013) Evaluators professional learning competency framework, 1st edn. Australian Evaluation Society, Fitzroy

Canadian Evaluation Society (2018) Competencies for Canadian evaluation practice. https://evaluationcanada.ca/

Chandler J, Barton S, Barker R, Woodhead P, Payne R (2022) The Dermicus tele-dermatology platform isle of wight primary care report. Health Innovation Wessex. https://healthinnovation-wessex.org.uk/

European Evaluation Society (2012) The European Evaluation Society evaluation capabilities framework. EES Secretariat, Prague

Fetterman DM (2023) Empowerment evaluation and social justice. Guilford, New York

Fetterman DM, Rodriguez-Campos L, Zukoski AP et al (2018) Collaborative, participatory, and empowerment evaluation: stakeholder involvement approaches. Guilford, New York

German Evaluation Society (2003) Standards 2003, standards for evaluation. www.degeval.de/standards

Horton T, Illingworth J, Warburton W (2018) The spread challenge: how to support the successful update of innovations and improvements in health care. The Health Foundation, London

Hutchinson K (2019) Evaluation failures: 22 tales of mistakes made and lessons learned. Sage Publications, Thousand Oaks

International Development Evaluation Association (2012) Competencies for development evaluation evaluators, managers, and commissioners

McLaney E, Morassaei S, Hughes L, Davies R, Campbell M, Di Prospero L (2022) A framework for interprofessional team collaboration in a hospital setting: advancing team competencies and behaviours. Healthc Manage Forum 35(2):112–117. https://doi.org/10.1177/08404704211063584

Minnesota Evaluation Studies Institute (2018) American Evaluation Association competencies and self-assessment

NHS Chief Executive Innovation (2011) Review call for evidence and ideas. 2011 Department of Health, Innovation Policy Branch

Peter J, Benjamin P, LeFevre AE et al (2018) Taking digital health innovation to scale in South Africa: ten lessons from MomConnect. BMJ Glob Health 3:e000592. https://doi.org/10.1136/bmjgh-2017-000592

Pfadenhauer LM, Gerhardus A, Mozygemba K et al (2017) Making sense of complexity in context and implementation: the context and implementation of complex interventions (CICI) framework. Implement Sci 12:21. https://doi.org/10.1186/s13012-017-0552-5

Public Health England Skills for Health (2020) NHS health check competency framework. PHE Publications, Mumbai

Royal College of Midwives (2023) Midwives from Southampton scoop national award for app that improves maternity safety. https://rcm.org.uk/

Smith J, Ellins J, Sherlaw-Johnson C, Vindrola-Padros C, Appleby J, Morris S et al (2023) Rapid evaluation of service innovations in health and social care: key considerations. Health Soc Care Deliv Res 11(11):5673. https://doi.org/10.3310/BTNU5673

The Magenta Book (2011) UK government analytical evaluation capabilities framework. The Magenta Book. www.gov.uk

UK Evaluation Society (2012) UK Evaluation Society's framework of evaluation capabilities. UK Evaluation Society, London

United Nations Evaluation Group (2016) Evaluation competency framework. UNEG, New York. www.unevaluation.org/2016-Evaluation-Competency-Framework.

Vindrola-Padros C, Brage E, Johnson GA (2021) Rapid, responsive, and relevant: a systematic review of rapid evaluations in health care. Am J Eval 42(1):13–27. https://doi.org/10.1177/1098214019886914

Artificial Intelligence, Healthcare, and Evaluation: Altering the Landscape

David Fetterman and David Fetterman II

Abstract

Artificial intelligence (AI) has altered the healthcare and evaluation landscapes, offering benefits from time efficiency to increased accuracy and productivity. AI-related healthcare improvements range from increased diagnostic accuracy to more face time with patients and insight into patients' medical needs. It has helped to build patient- and community-based healthcare evaluation capacity; helping individuals and communities become more self-determined concerning their health. Simultaneously, AI is transforming the field of evaluation, increasing evaluator's efficiency and precision. These synergistic changes are taking place in a rapidly evolving environment, making it imperative that AI healthcare products and services be continually evaluated. In addition, regulatory agencies need to be informed about AI-related developments in the healthcare and evaluation arena to help them appropriately guide and monitor these developments and innovations.

Keywords

Artificial intelligence · Healthcare · Evaluation · GPTs · Large language models · Bias

D. Fetterman (✉)
Fetterman and Associates and Claremont Graduate University, Claremont, CA, USA

D. Fetterman II
Northwestern University, Evanston, IL, USA
e-mail: davidfetterman2028@u.northwestern.edu

A. Kaehne, J. Feather (eds.), *Handbook of Health Services Evaluation*,
https://doi.org/10.1007/978-3-031-87869-5_22

1 Overview

In the first section of this chapter, we will clarify AI by defining terms and discussing the logic underlying AI focusing on mathematical probabilities. We will then present common AI chatbots, highlighting their capabilities and limitations. Finally, guidelines are also provided concerning prompts to harness AI's potential effectively.

Central to our discourse is the practical implementation of AI in healthcare and evaluation. Some of the most significant healthcare-related AI applications are in radiology, oncology, dermatology, and gastroenterology. AI applications in evaluation facilitate the development of logic models, theories of change, data analysis, and reporting. In addition, image creation and the construction of Generative Pre-trained Transformers (GPTs) are discussed to clarify how AI works. Unpacking GPTs helps to guide the assessment of AI-driven healthcare innovations.

AI-related healthcare products and services can, in large part, be evaluated using traditional and community and program-involvement-evaluation approaches. However, evaluating AI products and services also requires special considerations. This discussion addresses the need to adapt evaluation tools and techniques (including AI-guided evaluation approaches), develop and establish AI-related evaluation guidelines and standards, and establish AI evaluation-informed regulatory frameworks.

Finally, the chapter addresses common AI challenges and concerns. It also responds to the ethical considerations that emerge from integrating AI into healthcare and evaluation practices, underscoring the need for conscientious and informed use of this powerful technology.

2 Defining Terms

Artificial intelligence (AI) enables machines to emulate cognitive functions that humans associate with the human mind, such as learning and problem-solving. Within this field, machine learning (ML) allows computers to learn from data and improve at tasks through experience, without being explicitly programmed for every contingency. ML can categorize data as structured, which includes clearly defined data types such as numbers and dates, or unstructured, which encompasses more complex information like audio and video content.

Deep learning, a more intricate aspect of ML, harnesses neural networks with multiple layers to interpret data with a high level of abstraction. These networks can identify patterns and features within vast amounts of data to carry out complex operations.

Moving beyond analysis and into creation, generative AI (GenAI) is a progression of ML capabilities. While ML extracts patterns to predict outcomes, GenAI synthesizes entirely new content. This innovative AI generates novel outputs such as text, imagery, sounds, and video that mimic the quality of human-generated content. GenAI applications excel in streamlining processes, enhancing precision in data interpretation, and providing insights by identifying trends and motifs within datasets.

Among the various models underpinning GenAI, large language models (LLMs) stand out, especially in text-based applications. They understand and generate human-like text and can also support a myriad of tasks including translation, summarization, and content creation. Similar foundational models exist for audio and visual content, driving forward the capabilities of generative AI across multiple modalities. (See IBM Data and AI Team (2023) and Zewe (2023) for a more detailed explanation of AI terms.)

3 Understanding the Logic of AI

At the core of AI, particularly Large Language Models (LLMs), is the capacity to process and learn from extensive datasets. These models generate predictions by assessing mathematical probabilities derived from the data they have been trained on. For instance, in the phrase "United States of...," the model predicts that the word "America" will follow based on the likelihood of this sequence in its training data—not less probable continuations like "pizza."

This predictive capability extends to more complex patterns. Consider an LLM prompted with "My favorite drink." It logically infers the subsequent word to be "is," given the common structure of such a statement in English. As the sentence progresses, the LLM continues to anticipate the next most probable word: "Earl" might follow "My favorite drink is," and "Grey" after "My favorite drink is Earl." Ultimately, the model completes the sentence with "My favorite drink is Earl Grey tea," a pattern it recognizes as commonly occurring in its training data.

While LLMs are proficient in pattern recognition and prediction, their reliability is not guaranteed. These models necessitate ongoing training, corrective feedback, and reinforcement to refine their accuracy. An LLM's strength lies in its ability to learn and improve over time, which is why iterative training is a crucial aspect of enhancing its performance and precision in AI evaluations. [See IBM (2024) for a description of large language models.]

4 AI Accessibility: Chatbots and Image Generators

Generative Pre-trained Transformers (GPT) are neural network models that use AI to create human-like content. They are trained on large amounts of unlabeled text data. GPT models can respond to questions conversationally. They are also used to produce images and music.

AI chatbots and image generators come in various forms, often featuring both free and premium versions. A variety of chatbots are listed in Box 1.

Box 1 Types of Chatbots

- ChatGPT 3.5: This version is accessible without charge, but its knowledge is static and limited to information up until January 2022.
- ChatGPT 4 and 4o: For a monthly fee of $20, users gain access to the latest updates and a suite of advanced tools, including templates for generating custom GPT responses. [Team is $25].
- Claude: Known for handling extensive texts and supporting document attachments.
- Gemini: Offers a standard free version and an advanced "Ultra" subscription at $20 per month.
- Microsoft Copilot AI: Bundles features from ChatGPT 4 and the image creator DALL-E 3.

Challenges related to chatbots include the quality of the database used. The internet, for example, consists of widely variable quality. Similarly, how a chatbot is trained is rarely disclosed. The training may be systematically skewed or biased resulting in poor quality outputs or responses. The quality of chatbot prompts also determines the quality of the output (discussed later). In addition, chatbots are dependent on the quality of the algorithms employed.

Constructing a personalized GPT is not difficult and provides an additional measure of trust or security in the validity of the data and corresponding outputs. For example, GPT Creator or GPS Builder are free software tools to create a GPT. GPT Creator was used to create my "EmpowerEval Assistant," an AI tool used to guide communities in self-evaluations of healthcare-related programs for continuous improvement. The software provides self-guided instructions including how to create a GPT, recommended GPT names, images for a GPT profile, and most importantly uploading relevant and vetted files (GPT knowledge content). The benefit of creating a GPT is that it provides insight into how GPTs are built, making them easier to evaluate and modify to ensure quality results. The drawback of personalized GPTs is that they require large volumes of data and are time-consuming to maintain.

AI-driven image creation can significantly enhance the impact of evaluation findings. They can be used in evaluation reports, articles, blogs, and social media to punctuate a finding or illuminate a point. (See Box 2 below concerning types of image creators.)

Box 2 Types of AI-Driven Image Creators

- DALL-E 3: A standout in the field, it generates images from detailed prompts. Users may need to request multiple iterations for precise results. Its outputs are characterized by their artistic and stylized nature.
- KREA: Similar to DALL-E 3, but tends to produce more lifelike and realistic images, such as portraits.
- Midjourney: Another popular choice for generating images, noted for its distinct style and capabilities.

While these AI tools offer impressive features, they are not without limitations. For instance, image creators may sometimes render anatomical elements, like hands, with inaccuracies. Pictures of ethnic and racial group members' faces may be systematically distorted (Small 2023).

The ongoing debate questions whether AI-generated images sufficiently acknowledge and credit the original artists they reference. Additionally, there are concerns that AI may supplant human graphic designers. While AI can produce impressive results, it still needs human oversight and adjustments to reach the subtle expertise of professional designers. Despite these challenges, AI image generators are celebrated for their ability to deliver quality visuals quickly and at a lower cost compared to traditional methods.

In summary, the selection of an AI chatbot or image generator depends on specific requirements and preferences. These technologies are evolving rapidly, with new iterations entering the market as competition intensifies and user needs develop.

5 Prompts

Crafting effective prompts is essential for leveraging AI's capabilities, whether for text generation or image creation. A well-constructed prompt should be direct and specific and include any required style, such as academic or creative. It can also request adherence to a specific school of thought. If necessary, it should also ask for a specific format and sources to be cited.

The process often involves a series of iterative refinements. Take, for instance, the quest for an appropriate image to accompany a tuberculosis prevention evaluation report. The initial prompt—"a picture of a hypodermic needle eliminating tuberculosis"—may yield an image that is metaphorically correct but contextually inappropriate, perhaps showing a needle in an alarming scenario. A revised prompt aiming for sensitivity might be, "show a hypodermic needle used for lung disease prevention in rural India," but this too might return an image that, while closer to the goal, still misses the mark by portraying an unsettling scene.

Finally, a prompt that specifies the context and the action, such as "an illustration of a vaccine being administered in a rural Indian setting for lung disease prevention," is more likely to result in a suitable and effective image. It may depict a person receiving a vaccination with a visual cue indicating lung health, aligning with the report's communicative intent (see Fig. 1: iterative prompts and generated pictures).

This iterative process underscores the importance of precise and evolving prompts to guide AI toward producing the most relevant and effective outcomes.

6 Practical Applications of AI

Artificial intelligence (AI) boasts a wide range of practical uses across various industries. It streamlines tasks by generating outlines, summarizing documents, creating images, and composing various types of written content,

Iterative Prompts	Generated Pictures
First Prompt: "A picture of a hypodermic needle eliminating tuberculosis."	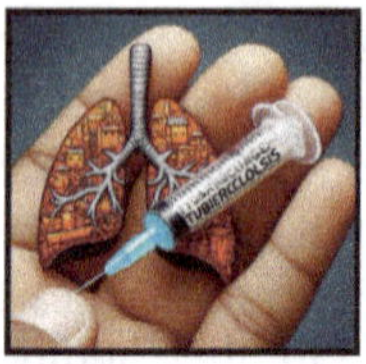
Second Prompt: "A hypodermic needle eliminating lung disease in rural India."	
Third Prompt: "A hypodermic needle in a person's arm to eliminate lunch disease in rural India."	

Fig. 1 Iterative prompts (generated using DALL-E 3)

including letters, blog entries, social media updates, and comprehensive reports. AI's analytical prowess extends to parsing large databases and writing programming code.

Deep Learning, a form of pattern recognition, harnesses neural networks to teach a computer how to recognize certain symptoms or radiological images. One of the classic examples is Google's project to recognize cats based on ten million YouTube videos with a 75% accuracy rate (Clark 2019).

7 AI in Medicine

AI is already embedded in medicine. The virtual representation of AI in medicine includes online scheduling of appointments, online check-ins, digitized medical records, listening, transcribing, and writing progress notes services (i.e., AI Notetaker, NextGen Ambient Assist, Scribe, and TheraPro), telemedicine platforms, responses to patient inquiries (see Small 2023), as well as neural network-based guidance to facilitate differential diagnoses. The physical stream of AI in medicine includes robotic-assisted surgery and intelligent prostheses (Hamlet and Tremblay 2017). Great strides are being made in the mainstream medical specialties.

Ophthalmologists leverage AI to examine hundreds of thousands of retinal scans, enhancing the precision of diagnoses related to conditions like diabetes, hypertension, kidney disease, and neurological disorders, such as Parkinson's disease and Alzheimer's (Cao et al. 2022; Sayres et al. 2018; Gulshan et al. 2016).

Similarly, gastroenterologists employ AI to sift through vast numbers of colonoscopy images, improving the detection of polyps (Wallace et al. 2022; Zhao et al. 2022). AI systems have also been able to outperform dermatologists in correctly classifying suspicious skin lesions (Esteva et al. 2017).

One of AI's most notable contributions is in radiology. AI provides faster diagnoses (Esteva et al. 2017; Teare et al. 2017; Bar et al. 2017; Makeeva, 2022), improved visualizations (Gulshan et al. 2016; Laukamp et al. 2018; Bejnordi et al. 2017; Li et al. 2012, 2014), and faster identification of alert situations (Prevedello et al. 2017; United States Food and Drug Administration 2018; Barreira et al. 2018), and is responsive to the shortage of experienced radiologists (Rosenkrantz et al. 2016; Nakajima et al. 2008).

In addition, it has been known to outperform experienced radiologists in diagnosing from medical images (Allen et al. 2021; Stiepan 2022; Somashekhar et al. 2018). The technology's edge lies in its ability to review far more images than human professionals can, operating continuously without fatigue and maintaining consistent performance. [See Eric Topol's TED Talk (2023) Can AI Catch What Doctors Miss?; see also Mayo and Leung, 2018 concerning the use of computer-assisted diagnosis.] A list of AI tools used in medicine is provided in Box 3.

Box 3 AI Tools in Medicine

AI Notetaker: listens, transcribes, and writes automated progress notes.

AI Therapy: online course for people with social anxiety using Cognitive Behavioral Therapy.

Einstein Copilot: Health Actions: use conversational AI to enable qualified healthcare professionals to trigger workflows, including capturing and summarizing patient details from different sources, sending referrals, booking appointments, and revising care plans.

eMed: telemedicine platform where patients can meet doctors through mobile apps and chat.

NextGen Ambient Assist: transforms patient-provider conversations on mobile devices into temporary transcripts, generating structured SOAP notes (allows physicians to spend more time observing body language instead of typing while listening to the patient).

NYU Langone's Electronic Health Record GPT-4: AI chatbot that responds to patient email inquiries to physicians, providing an empathetic response similar in quality to human providers (see Small et al. 2024).

Scribe: collects symptoms from patients online, assists with potential diagnosis of symptoms (in real-time), helps create a plan for the case, and turns conversations into medical notes.

TheraPro: creates therapy session summaries, enabling therapists to focus on their patients instead of taking notes.

Youper: mental health chatbot app that uses cognitive behavioral therapy and positive psychology techniques to help users deal with anxiety and depression (clinically effective).

8 Patient Use of AI

The online application eMed is used by patients to consult with their physician, inquire about symptoms, monitor health, and order tests. AI-driven therapy services range from online courses to consultations designed to help patients use cognitive behavior therapy and positive psychology to treat social anxiety (McCall et al. 2018).

Fitbit, Apple, and Qardio are health trackers. They monitor heart rate, sleep levels, steps, environmental sound levels, blood oxygen, blood pressure, cardio fitness, and sexual activity.

9 AI Applications in Evaluation

AI helps make evaluation more efficient and effective. It is used to organize thinking, streamline tasks, improve writing quality, analyze data, and build capacity. A few examples drawn from community health evaluations are provided below, such as a logic model, theory of change, and interview questions.

10 Logic Model

A logic model is a visual tool that shows how a program works. It breaks down the program into different parts:

1. Inputs: The things needed to make the program happen, like money, people, and materials.
2. Activities: The things the program does, like workshops or events.
3. Outputs: The results of these activities, like reports or numbers of people reached.
4. Outcomes: The changes or benefits the program aims to achieve, both short-term and long-term.
5. Impact: The bigger, long-lasting changes the program hopes to make in society.

Overall, a logic model helps us understand how a program is supposed to work and what it aims to achieve. It's like a roadmap for planning, running, and evaluating programs. The example below shows how a logic model for a program was created.

The AI prompt requested a logic model for a tobacco prevention program, and it provided all the necessary components, including inputs, activities, outputs, outcomes, and impacts. Additionally, it included relevant details specific to the program's logic model. The AI response generated is presented below.

Inputs
- Funding and resources
- Trained staff and volunteers
- Partnerships with schools, community organizations, and healthcare providers

Activities
1. Research and planning
2. Community outreach
3. Education and awareness
4. Policy advocacy
5. Access to resources

Outputs
- Number of workshops conducted
- Number of presentations delivered
- Number of educational materials distributed
- Number of media campaigns launched
- Number of community partnerships established

Outcomes
- Increased knowledge and awareness of tobacco-related risks and consequences.
- Improved attitudes and perceptions toward tobacco use
- Increased adoption of tobacco-free policies in schools and public spaces
- Increased utilization of cessation resources and support services

Impact
- Decreased tobacco use among the target population
- Improved overall health and well-being of the community
- Reduced tobacco-related illnesses and associated healthcare costs

This logic model outlines the key components of a tobacco prevention program, starting with inputs like funding, staff, and partnerships. These inputs fuel activities such as research, outreach, education, advocacy, and resource provision. The program then generates outputs like workshops, presentations, and materials, which contribute to outcomes such as increased knowledge, changed attitudes, policy adoption, and resource utilization. Ultimately, the impact is seen in reduced tobacco use, improved community health, and lower healthcare costs. The model emphasizes the importance of setting clear goals, understanding the target population, and utilizing available resources effectively. AI can be used in a similar way to generate theories of change, which help identify causal connections between program interventions and program outcomes.

11 Theory of Change

Weiss (1995), a leading figure in evaluation research, stated, there is "nothing as practical as a good theory". This statement underscores the significance of theory in informing practical decision-making and actions across different domains, such as program evaluation and policy analysis. It implies that robust theoretical frameworks offer valuable insights and tools for comprehending intricate phenomena and crafting successful interventions.

A theory of change is an explanation of how and why a desired transformation is anticipated to unfold within a specific context. It lays out the fundamental assumptions, causal pathways, and mechanisms through which interventions or activities are expected to generate particular outcomes or impacts.

By explaining the reasoning behind how interventions will cause change, a theory of change acts as a guiding framework for designing, implementing, and evaluating healthcare programs or initiatives. It facilitates stakeholders' understanding of the cause-and-effect relationships, thereby empowering them to make informed decisions and adaptations throughout the intervention process.

A *theory of change* for a tobacco prevention program outlines the causal pathway from program activities to desired outcomes. In this specific case, AI produced the following result:

1. Resource mobilization:
   (a) Funding: Secure financial resources to sustain program activities.
   (b) Human capital: Recruit and train skilled staff, educators, and counselors.
   (c) Partnerships: Collaborate with schools, healthcare providers, NGOs, and community leaders.
2. Awareness and advocacy:
   (a) Education campaigns: Conduct targeted campaigns in schools, workplaces, and public spaces.
   (b) Policy advocacy: Engage policymakers to enforce smoke-free laws and regulations.
   (c) Media outreach: Utilize TV, radio, and social media to disseminate anti-tobacco messages.

3. Empowerment and skill-building:
   (a) Youth programs: Develop age-appropriate curricula on tobacco risks.
   (b) Life skills training: Equip youth with refusal skills, stress management, and coping mechanisms.
   (c) Counseling services: Offer personalized support for smokers aiming to quit.
4. Behavioral change:
   (a) Preventing initiation: Educate youth about the dangers of tobacco use.
   (b) Promoting compliance: Encourage adherence to smoke-free policies.
   (c) Facilitating cessation: Provide evidence-based interventions for smokers.
5. Intermediate outcomes:
   (a) Shift in attitudes: Reduced social acceptance of smoking.
   (b) Increased knowledge: Improved understanding of health risks.
   (c) Behavioral shift: Decreased experimentation and initiation among youth.
6. Long-term impact:
   (a) Health improvements: Reduced tobacco-related diseases (cancer, respiratory issues).
   (b) Economic benefits: Lower healthcare costs and increased productivity.
   (c) Social norms transformation: Tobacco use becomes less normalized.

The theory represents a useful starting point to ensure the major steps are included. It can be refined with more detail about the specific tobacco prevention and cessation program.

12 Interview Questions and Surveys

Another useful application of AI in evaluations is in designing data collection instruments. Interview questions and surveys are essential in evaluations. AI can generate various types of questions, including informal, formal, structured, and semi-structured ones. These questions are logically organized and avoid compound or leading formats. Additionally, AI can create targeted professional surveys and questionnaires.

AI can be useful for specific community-based healthcare evaluation approaches, such as empowerment evaluations,[1] in which community and program members are responsible for the assessment process (Fetterman et al. 2010, 2015; Fetterman 2023a, b). AI enables community members to generate guides and steps needed when they lack the funds to employ experienced evaluation teams. Recommended empowerment evaluation steps based on an AI inquiry include a three-step and ten-step approach. AI can also generate a list of interview questions for this purpose, and The Empowerment Evaluation Interview Questions below are an example of an AI generated qualitative data collection instrument.

[1] See Fetterman et al. (2010), in which empowerment evaluation was used to transform the curriculum and prepare for and pass an accreditation review at Stanford University's School of Medicine.

Empowerment Evaluation Interview Questions and Guidelines

Understanding Needs and Perceptions

- What were your initial hopes and goals for this program/initiative?
- How has this program/initiative impacted your ability to address those goals?
- What aspects of your daily work or life do you feel most empowered by?
- Conversely, what aspects leave you feeling powerless or limited?

Assessing Capacity Building

- Have you gained any new skills or knowledge through your involvement?
- How comfortable do you feel using these skills to advocate for yourselves or others?
- Does this program/initiative provide opportunities for you to share your knowledge with others?

Gauging Participation and Ownership

- How involved have you been in shaping the direction of this program/initiative?
- Do you feel your voice is heard and valued in decision-making processes?
- What suggestions do you have for increasing community and program staff, and participant member participation in the future?

Identifying Strengths and Weaknesses

- What are the biggest strengths of this program/initiative from your perspective?
- Conversely, what are some areas where you see room for improvement?
- How can we better address any challenges or barriers you've encountered?

Promoting Reflection and Learning

- What have you learned the most from your participation in this program/initiative?
- How can we use this evaluation process to improve our work moving forward?
- What are your hopes for the future of this program/initiative?

Remember

- Empowerment evaluation emphasizes open-ended questions that encourage community and program staff members to share their experiences and perspectives.
- Wording should be clear and easy to understand, avoiding jargon or overly technical terms.
- Actively listen and acknowledge the responses of interviewees.
- The goal is to create a collaborative space for learning and improvement.

TRENDS: SALARIES - MACHINE LEARNING AND AI

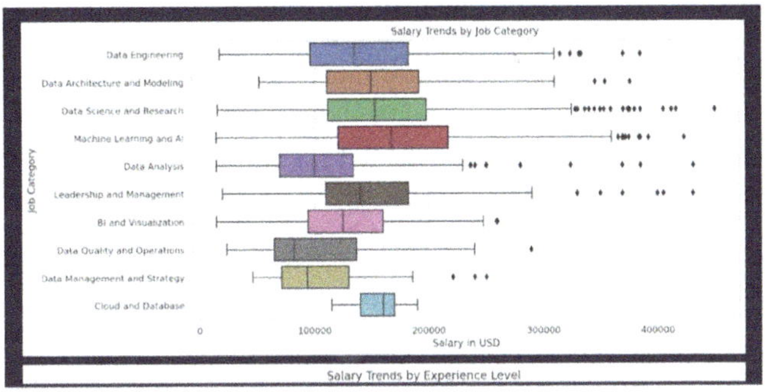

1. Salary Trends by Job Category – boxplots show a wide range of salaries across different job categories
2. Salary Trends by Experience Level – clear trend showing higher salaries for more experienced levels
3. Salary Distribution by Employment Type – plot indicates the salary distribution across different types
4. Number of Jobs by Company Size – bar graph shows the distribution of job types across companies with different sizes

Fig. 2 Using AI to analyze data sets (generated using ChatGPT 4o)

13 Data Analysis

Data analysis is a critical step after data collection in most evaluations. It typically involves triangulation, identification of patterns, content analysis, and statistics (Fetterman 2020). AI can streamline much of this process, saving time and providing rapid results. AI chatbots can interpret, clean, and analyze data efficiently.

For instance, an analysis of salary trends in computing by job category is useful when hiring a team in a healthcare system, e.g., management, data engineering, cloud and database management, and machine learning and AI. To determine the appropriate compensation when hiring a computing staff, consider a publicly available dataset on salary trends in computing from Kaggle (free, public data collections for research and training). The initial prompt asked AI to interpret the data, and it promptly provided insights on salary trends by job category, experience level, employment type, and company size. Next, AI cleaned the data by removing duplicate rows, ensuring better accuracy. Typically, manual data cleaning takes days, but AI accomplishes it in seconds. Finally, when asked about trends, AI swiftly generated salary trend visualizations. [See Fig. 2. Using AI to Analyze Data Sets.]. The same approach applies to any healthcare database.

14 Reporting and Images

Disseminating findings is as important as producing evaluation results. AI can assist in organizing and presenting these findings logically, persuasively, and with visual impact. It can summarize extensive documents and revise draft reports, eliminating typos and unnecessary jargon for better readability. Styles can vary from professional and balanced to marketing-oriented or even poetic. AI also aids in creating social media posts, presentation materials, and scholarly journal manuscripts. While the evaluator remains responsible for data and manuscript drafts, AI significantly enhances the quality of text and the impact of presentations.

For instance, AI-generated images effectively conveyed the global impact of smoking on public health. By requesting an image of a hand holding a globe with a cigarette (using DALL-E 3), the message was powerfully communicated: cigarette smoking is a worldwide health issue. These visuals captured the attention of policymakers and community members, drawing them to the evaluation findings and recommendations.

15 Evaluating AI

Much of AI can be evaluated using traditional evaluation approaches. Traditional evaluation tools include both qualitative and quantitative approaches, such as interviews, observations, online surveys, and statistical analysis (Davidson 2004; Fetterman 1988, 2020; Patton and Campbell-Patton 2021). However, evaluating AI products and services also requires special considerations, including adapting evaluation tools and techniques (including using AI-guided evaluation approaches), developing and establishing AI-related evaluation guidelines and standards, and establishing AI evaluation-informed regulatory frameworks. An outline of recommended steps is presented below:

16 Apply Traditional Evaluation Tools and Techniques

The majority of the existing evaluation theories, concepts, techniques, and tools apply to evaluating AI. This includes systematically applying existing evaluation approaches, methods, tools, and techniques. It also extends to stakeholder involvement approaches to ensure involvement and participation in the evaluation of community healthcare initiatives, e.g., collaborative, participatory, and empowerment evaluation approaches (Fetterman et al. 2018). In addition, evaluation standards, e.g., utility, feasibility, propriety, accuracy, usability, and accountability, are applicable to AI in medicine or health care services.

And while ethical and legal requirements, e.g., informed consent, transparency, and confidentiality, are certainly relevant, the nature and quality of AI supported activities in health services require careful calibration and discussion of AI's impact on them. This remains a topic of heated debate, which is likely to continue as AI is being increasingly incorporated into medical and health care processes. We set out below how current evaluation approaches may be adapted in this newly emerging context.

17 Adapt Existing Evaluation Tools and Techniques

Although most evaluation approaches, tools, and techniques apply to evaluating AI, new rapid formative evaluation approaches and methods are needed. Evaluation and evaluators need to evolve and adapt to the "moving targets" nature of the development of AI products and services, e.g., changes in the community, market, and AI product or service. In particular, the rapid timeline associated with the development and deployment of AI-driven products and services, e.g. "fail quickly" mindset; "beta" quality testing; market, company, patient or client, and stockholder timeline considerations are of significant importance. In addition, there is a variability concerning the quality and efficacy of AI products, services, and solutions, which requires close scrutiny by evaluators using AI tools. It remains critical to be aware of the difficulties in interpreting and validating the outputs of AI systems in complex healthcare settings and the need to cross-validate evaluation findings. Last but not least, the field needs to develop, test, and refine the use of AI-guided evaluation approaches.

18 Develop and Establish AI-related Evaluation Guidelines and Standards

Evaluators need to develop and establish quality, defensible, and realistic guidelines and standards concerning AI-related development, performance, and evaluation. Important considerations include time and resource constraints, an understanding of the dimension and urgency of the problem, the impact of the dimensions of fairness, interpretability, and bias of AI algorithms as well as at what stage a specific AI product or service development is, e.g., its conceptualization, product development, and/or implementation. Moreover, evaluators should be aware of the security, validity, and cost-effectiveness of AI tools and develop multiple "gold standards" depending on the task and application with a focus on end-user of technology to help determine effectiveness of AI tools. Arguably, this requires the inclusion of a wide spectrum of AI developers and relevant healthcare stakeholders (including healthcare providers and patients) in the development of AI evaluation guidelines and standards as well as open data repositories to save time and expense and foster collaboration.

Checklists are useful tools to remind evaluators to adhere to existing and newly developed guidelines and standards. An abbreviated example is provided below concerning a tuberculosis "cough" sound-based AI early detection tool evaluation, which was part of a USAID and Tuberculosis Implementation Framework Agreement (TIFA) funded project in India.

Tuberculosis "Cough" Sound-Based AI Early Detection Tool Evaluation Evaluation Checklist

This is an abbreviated evaluation checklist designed to guide the evaluation of an AI-driven tuberculosis "cough" app in India. People cough into the speaker of a phone and the app uses the sound of the cough to help determine if the person has tuberculosis and needs to come to the clinic for testing. The checklist highlights how evaluation is applied to the task and how, in some cases, it needs to adapt to properly evaluate AI-related healthcare products and services.

1. Does this app respond to a societal need?
   Answer: Yes. TB is among the top ten causes of death globally and India has 27% of the total TB burden.
2. Does the app do what it claims to do? If so, how well?
   Answer: Yes, it is an early detection tool. The effects vary as per context and feasibility of confirmatory tests. It has shown exclusive results in identifying TB at very early stages during deployments.
   Degree of difficulty factor: The app is designed to reach people living on the street who are difficult to reach with conventional healthcare approaches after appropriate regulatory approvals.
   Recommendations: More resources will benefit to adjust algorithms and sound sensitivity and test on a larger population
3. Are there any ethical considerations associated with the use of the app?
   Answer: Yes. The healthcare provider may get infected if they hold the phone in front of the prospective patient as they cough.

Solutions:
1. The healthcare provider can stand behind the prospective patient as they cough into the phone.
2. The healthcare provider can use a selfie stick to hold the phone away from themselves.
3. The prospective patient can hold the phone.
4. The health care worker and patient, both, wears the mask (this is the current practice).

Source: Fetterman et al. (2015). Evaluation Checklist Based on Learning Meeting on Cough Sound-Based AI Tools for Improved TB Care.

19 Establish AI-Related Evaluation Regulatory Frameworks

Authorizing, governing, and regulatory bodies need assistance evaluating AI applications and solutions in healthcare settings. They need guidance to inform the development of regulations, regulatory decision-making, and enforcement. Their work should be guided by a variety of considerations, including accessibility, accuracy, cost, ethics, inclusiveness, quality, responsibility, responsiveness, safety, and sustainability.

Specifically, they need to be aware of relevant criteria to evaluate AI solutions, specific criteria to determine if AI solutions align with social values and the need to update regulations to adapt to advancements in AI technology. This also requires updating and incorporating ethical and legal considerations ranging from handling sensitive patient information to copyright protection and IP concerns. Ideally this should result in streamlined evaluation processes and recognized approval frameworks based on credible assessments.

20 Common Challenges and Concerns Using Artificial Intelligence

Artificial intelligence (AI) is a powerful tool with substantial potential, but it is not infallible. Much like a developing child, AI requires ongoing nurturing in the form of continuous training and feedback to enhance its accuracy. Several common issues can arise if AI systems are not carefully managed and updated.

One such issue is the handling of sources and references. AI does not inherently know to cite sources unless this practice is built into its design, or it is specifically prompted to do so. Microsoft Copilot AI, by design, is an example in which AI automatically includes links to references to facilitate additional inquiry concerning the topic and make it easier to assess the authenticity and validity of the citation. However, at this stage of AI development, users must continue to be diligent in verifying the information AI provides.

Bias within AI systems is a critical issue that can skew results, reinforcing and amplifying social inequalities. Known as an "alignment problem," it arises when AI's outputs are not aligned with intended goals and societal norms (Watkins 2024). For instance, AI can inadvertently uphold stereotypes by unfairly correlating certain races or genders with particular professional roles (UNESCO 2024; Ahn and Costigan 2019; Mwangi and Kimani 2023). Such biases can adversely affect decisions in employment, healthcare, and law enforcement (Banaji et al. 2021; Swarns 2023). For example, predictive policing algorithms have produced racist results, including unjust incarceration (see ShotSpotter example: Burke et al. 2022; Heaven 2020). Addressing AI bias requires expertise specific to the affected domains, such as deep understanding and experience with minority communities, to lessen or prevent harmful social impacts.

Confidentiality presents a significant challenge as well. When AI systems are trained on proprietary (or private) data, there's a risk that sensitive information could inadvertently be disseminated. To address this, some organizations opt for private AI models or enterprise solutions that can be customized and controlled to safeguard proprietary information.

One of the most commonly reported issues with AI is the occurrence of "hallucinations," or the generation of factually incorrect information. This is not a result of deliberate deceit but rather a limitation of the AI's understanding. For example, if AI is asked to produce images of the far side of the moon, a side that is largely unphotographed by humans, it may generate plausible but not factual images based on available data. It is not an act of deception but an attempt to fulfill the request with the available information, often drawing on what it has learned about similar subjects. This problem persists; however, it is much less frequent because LLMs are learning on larger data systems.

All of these issues are escalated in healthcare contexts because the risks are higher when human lives and the quality of care are at stake in a litigious environment. Understanding these limitations is crucial in managing expectations of AI's capabilities. It's important to recognize that AI operates within the scope of its programming and training, always aiming to provide the most informative response possible. [See Villasenor 2019 for an additional discussion about artificial intelligence and bias.]

21 Conclusion

AI has significantly enhanced healthcare and healthcare evaluation practices. It efficiently analyzes large datasets and produces compelling, accurate texts and visual presentations. In medicine, AI is already embedded in the healthcare system, including notation and scheduling programs. It is also helping to improve patient care ranging from early detection and diagnosis to reducing morbidity and mortality. AI is even responding to workforce issues by providing prompt and accurate diagnostic responses to radiological inquiries, despite a reduced labor force of radiologists.

However, it is not flawless. AI makes errors. Moreover, it can perpetuate existing biases found in the data it is trained on, potentially amplifying historical biases on a large scale automatically and rapidly. The problem of AI misalignment with our social values is of paramount significance. It is fundamental to our vision of a fair, equitable, and democratic society. The best approach to improvement is to include stakeholders with domain-specific expertise in AI development decision-making.

Oversight and regulations are also needed to monitor the development and use of AI healthcare products and innovations. Human subjects issues that need to be taken into consideration range from data sharing and data security to patient confidentiality. The safety and security of AI-informed medical devices also require review. Do they provide accurate diagnostic information about health (as claimed)? Are the devices calibrated? Are they monitored continually as they continue to develop and improve (Dennis 2022)?

AI will continue to expand its boundaries in medicine and evaluation. The best way to monitor and improve it is to use it. AI requires consistent usage, continuous feedback, and ongoing learning to make it a surgically precise tool aligned with our social values and a commitment to democratic ideals. With sufficient care and oversight, AI can continue to enhance healthcare and healthcare evaluation practices.

References

Ahn S, Costigan A (2019) How AI reinforces gender stereotypes (trend brief). https://www.catalyst.org/research/ai-gender-stereotypes/

Allen B, Agarwal S, Coombs L, Wald C, Dreyer K (2021) 2020 ACR data science institute artificial intelligence survey. J Am Coll Radiol 18(8):1153–1159

Banaji MR, Fiske ST, Massey DS (2021) Systemic racism: individuals and interactions, institutions and society. Cogn Res 6:82. https://doi.org/10.1186/s41235-021-00349-3

Bar A, Wolf L, Amitai O et al (2017) Compression fractures detection on CT. Med Imaging 2017:10134

Barreira CMA, Bouslama M, Lim J et al (2018) ALADIN study: automated large artery occlusion detection in stroke imaging study- a multi-center experience. Eur Stroke J 3:75

Bejnordi BE, Veta M, van Diest PJ et al (2017) Diagnostic assessment of deep learning algorithms for detection of lymph node metastasis in women with breast cancer. JAMA 318:2199–2210

Burke G, Mendoza M, Linderman J, Tarm M (2022) How AI-powered tech landed man in jail with scant evidence. https://apnews.com/article/artificial-intelligence-algorithm-technology-police-crime-7e3345485aa668c97606d4b54f9b6220

Cao J, Chang-Kit B, Katsnelson G et al (2022) Protocol for a systematic review and meta-analysis of the diagnostic accuracy of artificial intelligence for grading of ophthalmology imaging modalities. Diagn Progn Res 6:15. https://doi.org/10.1186/s41512-022-00127-9

Clark L (2019) Google's artificial brain learns to find cat videos. Wired UK Science. http://www.wired.com/2012/06/google-xneural-network

Davidson J (2004) Evaluation methodology basics: the nuts and bolts of sound evaluation. Sage, Thousand Oaks

Dennis A (2022) Defining artificial intelligence (AI) and why it matters for medical device regulation. Digital Health. Taylor and Wessing. https://www.taylorwessing.com/en/insights-and-events/insights/2022/06/defining-artificial-intelligence-and-why-it-matters-for-medical-device-regulation

Esteva A, Kuprel B, Novoa RA, Ko J, Swetter SM, Blau HM et al (2017) Dermatologist-level classification of skin cancer with deep neural networks. Nature 542:115–118

Fetterman DM (1988) Qualitative approaches to evaluation in education: the silent scientific revolution. Praeger, New York

Fetterman DM (2020) Ethnography: step by step. Sage, Thousand Oaks

Fetterman DM (2023a) Empowerment evaluation and social justice: confronting the culture of silence. Guilford Press, New York

Fetterman DM (2023b) Searching for self-determination and results. YouTube. https://www.youtube.com/watch?v=lsY1APZVUwI

Fetterman DM, Deitz J, Gesundheit N (2010) Empowerment evaluation: a collaborative approach to evaluating and transforming a medical school curriculum. Acad Med 85(5):813–820

Fetterman DM, Kaftarian S, Wandersman A (2015) Empowerment evaluation: knowledge and tools for self-assessment, evaluation capacity building, and accountability. Sage, Thousand Oaks

Fetterman, D.M., Rodriquez-Campos, L. Zukoski, A.P., and Contributors, (2018). Collaborative, Participatory, and Empowerment Evaluation: Stakeholders Involvement Approaches. New York: Guilford Press.

Gulshan V, Peng L, Voram M et al (2016) Development and validation of a deep learning algorithm for detection of diabetic retinopathy in retinal fundus photographs. JAMA 16:2402–2410

Hamlet P, Tremblay J (2017) Artificial intelligence in medicine. Metabolism 69:36–40

Heaven W (2020) Artificial intelligence: predictive policing algorithms are racist. They need to be dismantled. MIT Technology Review, Cambridge. https://www.technologyreview.com/2020/07/17/1005396/predictive-policing-algorithms-racist-dismantled-machine-learning-bias-criminal-justice/

IBM (2024) What are large language models (LLMs)? https://www.ibm.com/topics/large-language-models

IBM Data and AI Team (2023) AI vs. machine learning vs. deep learning vs. neural networks: what's the difference. https://www.ibm.com/blog/ai-vs-machine-learning-vs-deep-learning-vs-neural-networks/

Laukamp KR, Thiele F, Shakirin G et al (2018) Fully automated detection and segmentation of meningiomas using deep learning on routine multiparametric MRI. Eur Radiol 29:124–132

Li YH, Zhang L, Hu QM et al (2012) Automatic sub-arachnoid space segmentation and hemorrhage detection in clinical head CT scans. Int J CARS 7:507–516

Li R, Zhang W, Suk HI et al (2014) Deep learning based imaging data completion for improved brain disease diagnosis. Med Image Comput Assist Interv 17:305–312

Makeeva A (2022) An essential roadmap for AI in radiology. ACR Bulletin https://www.acr.org/Practice-Management-Quality-Informatics/ACR-Bulletin/Articles/September-2022/An-Essential-Roadmap-for-AI-in-Radiology

Mayo RC, Leung J (2018) Artificial intelligence and deep learning-radiology's next frontier? Clin Imaging 49:87–88

McCall HC, Richardson CG, Helgadottir FD, Chen FS (2018) Evaluating a web-based social anxiety intervention: a randomized controlled trial among university students? J Med Internet Res 20:e91. https://doi.org/10.2196/jmir.8630

Mwangi L, Kimani E (2023) The hidden burden: gender bias and stereotyping as a barrier to women's leadership. IDInsight https://www.idinsight.org/article/the-hidden-burden-gender-bias-and-stereotypes-as-a-barrier-to-womens-leadership/

Nakajima, Y., Yamada, K., Imamura, K., Kobayashi, K. (2008). Radiologist supply and workload: international comparison—Working Group of Japanese College of Radiology. Radiat Med (2008) 26:455–465. https://doi.org/10.1007/s11604-008-0259-2

Patton MQ, Campbell-Patton C (2021) Utilization-focused evaluation, 5th edn. Sage, Thousand Oaks

Prevedello LM, Erdal B, Ryu JL et al (2017) Automated critical test findings identification and online notification system using artificial intelligence. Radiology 285:923–931

Rosenkrantz AB, Hughes DR, Duszak R Jr. The U.S. Radiologist Workforce: An Analysis of Temporal and Geographic Variation by Using Large National Datasets. Radiology. 2016 Apr;279(1):175-84. https://doi.org/10.1148/radiol.2015150921. Epub 2015 Oct 28. PMID: 26509294.

Sayres R, Taly A, Rahimy E, Blumer K, Coz D, Hammel N, Krause J, Narayanaswamy A, Rastegar Z, Wu D, Xu S, Barb S, Joseph A, Shumski M, Smith SA, Corrado G, Peng L, Webster D (2018) Using a deep learning algorithm and integrated gradients explanation to assist grading for diabetic retinopathy. Am Acad Ophthalmol 126:552–564. https://doi.org/10.1016/j.ophtha.2018.11.016

Small Z (2023) Black artists see clear bias in A.I. New York times (New York edition), July 5, section C, page 1

Small WR, Wiesenfeld B, Brandfield-Harvey B et al (2024) Large language model–based responses to patients' in-basket messages. JAMA Netw Open 7(7):e2422399. https://doi.org/10.1001/jamanetworkopen.2024.22399

Somashekhar SP, Sepulveda MJ, Puglielli S et al (2018) Watson for oncology and breast cancer treatment recommendations: agreement with an expert multidisciplinary tumor board. Ann Oncol 29:1–6

Stiepan D (2022) Using AI in radiology clinical practice. Mayo Clinic, September 14, 2022

Swarns C (2023) When artificial intelligence gets it wrong. Innocence Project. https://innocenceproject.org/when-artificial-intelligence-gets-it-wrong/

Teare PFM, Benzaquen O, Toledano E, Elnekave E (2017) Malignancy detection on mammography using dual deep convolutional neural networks and genetically discovered false color input enhancement. J Digit Imaging 30:499–505

Topol E (2023) Can AI catch what doctors miss? TED Talk. YouTube. https://www.youtube.com/watch?v=lI5LY7wI_Xc&t=306s

UNESCO (2024) Challenging systematic prejudices: an investigation into bias against women and girls in large language models. https://unesdoc.unesco.org/ark:/48223/pf0000388971

United States Food and Drug Administration (2018) FDA permits marketing of clinical decision support software for alerting providers of a potential stroke in patients

Villasenor J (2019) Artificial intelligence and bias: four key challengers. Brookings. https://www.brookings.edu/articles/artificial-intelligence-and-bias-four-key-challenges/

Wallace M et al (2022) Impact of artificial intelligence on miss rate of colorectal neoplasia. Gastroenterology 163:295

Watkins SC (2024) Dr. S. Craig Watkins on why AI's potential to combat or scale systemic injustice still comes down to humans. https://chartable.com/podcasts/unlocking-us-with-brene-brown/episodes/165526994-dr-s-craig-watkins-on-why-ais-potential-to-combat-or-scale-systemic-injustice-still-comes-down-to-humans

Weiss CH (1995) Nothing as practical as good theory. Aspen Institute, Washington

Zewe A (2023) Explained: generative AI. How do powerful generative AI systems like ChatGPT work, and what makes them different from other types of artificial intelligence? MIT News. https://news.mit.edu/2023/explained-generative-ai-1109

Zhao Q, Jia Q, Chi T (2022) Deep learning as a novel method for endoscopic diagnosis of chronic atrophic gastritis: a prospective nested case–control study. BMC Gastroenterol 22:352. https://doi.org/10.1186/s12876-022-02427-2

Evaluating the Performance of Integrated Care Services

Oliver Groene and Nicolas Larrain

Abstract

Countries enact healthcare reforms for integrated care services. Evaluating their impact and setting performance indicators is crucial yet challenging. This chapter outlines principles for evaluation. Designs must define goals, identify value-creating mechanisms, select indicators, and aid improvement plans. Integrated services aim for the "triple aim": better population health, patient/carer experience, and cost reduction. Evaluators must also consider structural factors like political support, governance, and value creation mechanisms, such as health intelligence and system coordination. Contextual factors like population size and initiative scale matter too. Various data sources are needed, but challenges include complexity and limited trial designs. Drawing from experience, this chapter offers insights for assessing integrated care system performance, aiding healthcare stakeholders.

Keywords

Health services · Integrated care · Performance assessment · Indictors · Logic model

O. Groene (✉)
OptiMedis and University of Witten/Herdecke,
Witten, Germany
e-mail: o.groene@optimedis.de

N. Larrain
OptiMedis and Hamburg Center for Health Economics, University of Hamburg, Hamburg, Germany
e-mail: n.larrain@optimedis.de

A. Kaehne, J. Feather (eds.), *Handbook of Health Services Evaluation*,
https://doi.org/10.1007/978-3-031-87869-5_23

1 Introduction

Healthcare systems are currently grappling with unprecedented challenges. It is estimated that around 50 million people in the European Union are living with multiple chronic diseases, and this number is rapidly increasing due to the aging population (Organisation for Economic Co-operation and Development, Europeiska Unionen 2020; Souza et al. 2021; Wang et al. 2022). Many healthcare systems are struggling to cope with these challenges as they were originally designed to be supply-led and focused on care delivery processes within healthcare organizations, resulting in fragmented care. This fragmentation is exacerbated by systems that prioritize reimbursement based on the provision of healthcare services (volume) rather than focusing on health outcomes and patient responsiveness (value) (Porter 2014). As of today, numerous health systems still maintain an artificial separation of different levels of care and emphasize reactive healthcare delivery, failing to systematically incentivize prevention, patient-centered care, and disease management. To address these pressing policy challenges, a more proactive approach is necessary, focusing on person-centered service delivery, health promotion, and anticipating health needs. This shift is essential for achieving high-quality, high-value care and reducing healthcare costs associated with system fragmentation (WHO 2021; McClellan et al. 2013).

Integrated healthcare services (IHS) offer benefits such as providing patient-centered and holistic care across different settings, improving care continuity, coordination, and communication, and reducing duplication, fragmentation, and service gaps. Integrated care has been defined as "a concept bringing together inputs, delivery, management and organization of services related to diagnosis, treatment, care, rehabilitation and health promotion. Integration is a means to improve the services in relation to access, quality, user satisfaction and efficiency" (Grone and Garcia-Barbero 2001). IHS services are characterized by their focus on value-based principles (where reimbursement of the service is based on its value, rather its volume), aiming to transition from a supply-led to an outcomes-led approach (Amelung et al. 2021). This outcomes-led approach is centered on achieving the "Triple Aim" at the population level, seeking to improve the patient experience, enhance population health, and reduce per capita healthcare costs (Berwick et al. 2008). In practical terms, integrated care involves linking and coordinating providers' services along the continuum of care to address care fragmentation. IHS are well-positioned to address the comprehensive needs of individuals with chronic illnesses, personalize patient care, and effectively manage budget constraints by prioritizing the overall health of the population. IHS offer a collaborative approach to patient care that combines the physical, mental, behavioral, and financial aspects of healthcare. They aim to provide holistic treatment and prevention for a wide array of chronic conditions and collective responsibility for planning services, improving health, and reducing inequalities across geographical areas.

Assessing performance is essential to guide service improvement (Smith 2009). However, the availability of specific tools, frameworks, and guidance on the performance assessment of IHS services is limited (European Commission 2018; Larrain and Groene 2021). This chapter provides insights and guidance for assessing integrated care performance, addressing the complexities and challenges faced by healthcare stakeholders. It provides awareness on specific measurement approaches, objectives of integrated care services and an understanding of causal assumptions, thus enabling a thorough and practically focused approach to evaluation.

2 Conceptualizing Integrated Care Systems

Conceptualizing integrated care services requires a broad understanding of health systems as well as the factors that contribute to health outcomes. Several classic works in the health services/health system field have addressed the relationship between health service structures and outcomes. Firstly, Evan's et al. work on "Why are some people healthy and others not" is a milestone in conceptualizing previous studies in a comprehensive framework of health determinants, linking individuals to population health outcomes and addressing the role of the health system. Their framework focuses on health and function, not just disease, and emphasizes the individual response to health, affected by various factors such as the social environment, physical environment, and genetic endowment (Evans et al. 1994). Secondly, the Chronic Care Model (Wagner 1998) focused on the care delivery design and posits that outcomes are the result of informed and activated patients and prepared, proactive practice teams. The model emphasizes the need for reorienting delivery systems, providing decision support to health professionals, aligning community resources with the health system, and ensuring patient self-management potentials are used where possible (Wagner 1998). Thirdly, aligned with the Chronic Care Model, the Triple Aim model seeks to improve the patient's experience of care, the health of the population, and reduce the per capita cost of healthcare. It emphasizes the need to balance these dimensions for sustainable achievements at the health system level (Berwick et al. 2008). Common to all these conceptualizations is the need to go beyond the remit of traditional curative health care and an emphasis on preventative care, resulting in healthier outcomes for patients and long-term cost savings for health care systems. It also helps employers attract and retain top talent by highlighting the importance of employee health to the organization.

A solid understanding of population health needs and the health outcomes that the IHS aims to achieve is central to have a robust assessment of its performance, in particular if the purpose of the assessment is to guide further performance improvements. Causal models, such as logic models consider resources, activities, outputs, outcomes, and short- to long-term goals. By following a logical sequence, one can better understand how the individual components and activities may lead to the desired program goals. For the evaluator, a logic model serves as a blueprint of what the integrated care system intends to achieve, and which mechanisms are employed to achieve those aims. Logic models can help to (a) understand the baseline and contextual factors of integrated care systems; (b) elicit the value creation mechanisms which are required to establish the causal relationship between activities and outcomes; and, finally, (c) measure the outputs and outcomes (Wang and Groene

2022). Causal models can be understood as an extension of the Donabedian approach to quality assessment which is defined according to: Structure, Process, and Outcomes with the premise that "good structure increases the likelihood of good process, and good process increases the likelihood of good outcome" (Donabedian 1988). An understanding of the conceptual models underpinning integrated care and the logical (causal) framework about the relationships between inputs and outcomes is critical for the performance assessment of integrated care services.

3 Performance Assessment of Integrated Care Services

Existing evaluations of integrated care systems sometimes focus on these system goals only and employ advanced statistical techniques to create a counterfactual to the implementation of the integrated care systems: What would be the outcomes that had been achieved in the absence of the integrated care efforts? While such evaluations are applaudable, they may fail to evaluate the mechanisms that contribute to the system goals or outcomes and thus reduce the potential of the evaluation to drive improvement efforts. Evaluators of integrated care systems needs to answer both questions: did the system achieve the aims it intended to achieve and, which mechanisms contributed to this. The latter question is of great relevance given that integrated care evaluations are rarely conducted in controlled environments but in real-life situations; therefore, to gain an understanding of the scalability of the effort, the value creation mechanisms need to be explored.

The starting point for a performance assessment of integrated healthcare systems is to define the main goal or goals the system seeks to achieve. At the high level, IHS strive toward three main goals (the 'Triple aim') (Berwick et al. 2008): Improving population health, improving the patient experience of care, and reducing health cost growth. Later, "improving career experience of care" has been added, creating the "Quadruple aim," or the "Quintuple aim," which includes the equity dimension (Bodenheimer and Sinsky 2014; Nundy et al. 2022).

3.1 Value Creation Mechanisms of Integrated Care Systems at the Structural Level

Understanding the value-creating mechanisms of integrated healthcare systems helps to define what to measure when assessing performance at the structure and process levels (Levesque and Sutherland 2020). Integrated systems' value-creating mechanisms are the contexts, preconditions, interventions, focus areas, and activities that systems pursue to work towards the triple aim. Once the value-creating mechanisms of integrated systems are known, their implementation can be assessed (type, number, range, scope) and evaluated to what extent they contribute to achieving the overall aims. Value-creating mechanisms can be addressed at the structural and the process level, both will be explained in the following.

Value-creating mechanisms at the *structure level* provide five essential elements for the proper functioning of integrated care systems. First, the complex transition to integrated care needs political support, including the willingness to change the organizational and structural face of the healthcare system. Second, well-defined and robust governance mechanisms are essential to determine accountability and facilitate connections between stakeholders; ideally, this value creating-mechanism is reflected in a facilitator for integrated care, also called a "regional integrator" (Berwick et al. 2008). Third, stakeholder engagement is essential for creating an integrated and accountable health system to promote cooperation, coordination, collaboration, and trust, all critical values in integrated care. Fourth, population characteristics determine baseline performance and advancement towards systems goals. Finally, system-wide shared goals and incentives schemes need to be established, as all the elements of the integrated system must be pushing towards the same objectives (Nuño Solinís and Stein 2016). Additionally, there is also a need for IT infrastructure, capacity, and intelligence, as well as data integration, when implementing a performance assessment. Data should ideally be based on Electronic Health Records and can include health, healthcare utilization, behavioral, physiological, socio-economic, and costing data (Moll et al. 2023). Moreover, when building performance assessment, there is a need for a continuous and effective monitoring system that can detect, correct, and improve system processes and performance. Finally, an adequate capable, and continuously learning health system workforce is a requirement at the structural level.

3.2 Value Creation Mechanisms of Integrated Care Systems at the Process Level

In contrast to value creation mechanisms at the structural components of IHS, which are more inward oriented to set up the service to function, value-creation mechanisms at the process level refer to the actions of the IHS directed at people and patients. Depending on the level of integration of the system, which can be either horizontal (at the same level of care) or vertical (across levels of care) and the level at which the system operates: micro (patient-level), meso (organizational context), and/or macro (financing and policy context), different value creation mechanisms apply (Baxter et al. 2018; Zonneveld et al. 2018; Bautista et al. 2016). Common mechanisms that we have identified in previous research are the following six:

1. Health intelligence: including risk stratification, needs assessment, impact evaluation, process evaluation, feedback and auditing, decision support tools, per-patient costing, and healthcare utilization analyses.
2. Data strategy: considering vital elements such as data infrastructure, data governance, data collection, data access and distribution, data regulation.
3. Disease management: case management, self-management interventions, shared decision-making interventions, patient focus/empowerment/patient centeredness.

4. Health promotion: as public health campaigns and health promotion interventions (health promotion discounts).
5. System coordination, collaboration, and cooperation: stakeholders' involvement, care pathway design, alignment of incentives, protocols and guidelines, promotion of provider network teamwork, constant revision, and promotion of best practices.
6. Communication, dissemination, and exploitation: emphasizing health and economic results, benchmarking, market access, and knowledge transfer with top-performing health systems.

3.3 Guiding the Performance Evaluation with a Logic Model

The performance of an integrated healthcare system will depend on the structural characteristics and the deployment of value creation mechanisms at the process level.

Evaluators may assess the extent of healthcare delivery system integration as an intermediate goal of integrated care initiatives, for which multiple measures have been developed and validated, to some extent, with more emphasis than working toward consensus on the measurement of the final goals of the integrated care system (Bautista et al. 2016; Strandberg-Larsen and Krasnik 2009). Mapping structures (inputs), value creation mechanisms (processes), and short-, medium-, and long-term results (outcomes) in a logic model guides the evaluator and helps answering questions such as: how did the system achieve its results, or: how can these results be replicated. An example of a logic model is given in Table 1.

3.4 Indicators for Performance Assessment of Integrated Care Systems

There is substantial literature gathering and proposing indicators to measure the performance of integrated systems, but not all validated indicators are actually of use to track progress over time or to compare systems (McDonald et al. 2014; Dates et al. 2018; Pinter et al. 2021; Raleigh et al. 2014). For the purpose of this paper, we have compiled the list of indicators and classified them by source, construct, data source, the burden in data collection, time frame to assess impact, the ability to be influenced by integrated care, and the type by the Donabedian approach to performance assessment. At the outcome level, population health is measured with indicators in the constructs of health outcomes (mortality, health status), disease burden (at-risk population, incidence/prevalence), and behavioral and physiological factors (risky behaviors). Patient/carer experience is measured mainly directly as patient/carer experience, plus sub-constructs related to safe, effective, timely, patient-centered, equitable, and efficient care experience. Healthcare costs are measured directly as healthcare costs, highlighting the indicator "per capita cost of care," and healthcare utilization. At the process level, the constructs relate to the value-creating mechanisms explained above. At the structural level, population characteristics and

Table 1 Example of a high-level Logic Model to guide the implementation and evaluation of an integrated care system

Inputs	Activities	Results		
		Short-term (1–3 years)	Medium term (3–5 years)	Long-term (>10 years)
• Support from regional healthcare administration • Establishment of the regional integrator unit • Stakeholder engagement • System boundaries (for which the integrated system is accountable) • Incentives schemes • Upfront investment • IT infrastructure • Healthcare workforce	• Health intelligence • Data Strategy and governance • Disease Management and care programs • Health promotion and campaigns • System coordination efforts • Communication	• Successful implementation the regional integrator • Activated patients • Reaching vulnerable target groups • Provider compliance with health promotion/ integrated care standards • Adequate utilization and transfer behavior • Health as a core element of community identity • Attractive working conditions and collaboration opportunities for service providers	Achieving the quadruple Aims: • Reduction of per capita health expenditure • Improving patient satisfaction/ experience • Improving population health • Improving the working conditions of service providers	Reduced disease burden: incidence and/or prevalence of major chronic conditions or delayed onset of disease Delayed nursing need amongst the elderly (compression of morbidity) Strengthening resilience and sustainability of a healthcare system geared to patient needs and expectations
Assumptions: • Start-up invest for the integrated care system • Broad support from the relevant stakeholders • Patients enrolled in the integrated initiative at a high rate		External factors affecting implementation: • Stable health policy conditions • Acceptance of regional integrator function • Development of payment and incentive schemes that reward prevention efforts		

contextual factors determine both processes and outcomes. For all indicators, quality criteria should be met with an emphasis on the indicators' act *actionability*.

We present a comprehensive and manageable list of key indicators that serve as a basic set for assessing performance of an integrated healthcare system (Fig. 1). Performance assessment does not end when the performance measures are constructed. A plan to contextualize results and trigger the appropriate actions for improving performance is needed. Even though a challenge, laying out the interdependencies of stakeholders and their relation to system performance will guide the transformation of data into action.

System goals, Triple aim	Value-creating mechanisms	Short-term indicators (<2 years)	Medium-term indicators (2-3 years)	Long-term indicators (5+ years)
			Results can be observed	
Population Health				**Mortality outcomes: Mean age at the time of death; years of potential life lost or gained; premature death; mortality and survival time.**
		Increase in patient activation		**Mean age at the onset of long-term nursing need**
	Health Promotion	% Provider compliance with health promotion/integrated care standards	**Vaccination coverage** *Changes towards healthy lifestyles*	**Disease Burden: Incidence (yearly rate of onset, avg. age of onset) and/or prevalence of major chronic conditions**
	System coordination	*Quality of multi-professional teams as assessed by surveys*	**Reducing ambulatory care sensitive hospital admissions** **Waiting times for urgent treatment (esp. cancer, severe mental health access, elective treatment)**	**Mortality or all-cause readmission within 30 and 365 days after discharge**
Patient/Carer experience	Disease Management	**Medication adherence after heart failure**	*Patient overall experience with care, - involvement in decision-making, -care transitions, / Patient-reported outcomes pre/post treatment, -in the community*	**Mortality or disease-specific readmission within 30 and 365 days after discharge**
		Percentage of patients that have received help to stop smoking after an AMI		
	Health intelligence		*Providers reporting useful feedback & decision support*	
	Data strategy	*Information integration as evaluated by providers*		
	Communication & Dissemination		*Recognition, acceptability and impact of health communication efforts in the community*	
			Academic/business recognition reflected on publications, certifications	
Financial performance			**Patient-level cost savings over the whole continuum of care relative to the costs normally expected**	

Legend

Coding	Donabedian levels	N°
(blue)	Structure	2
(yellow)	Process	10
(green)	Outcome	8

Coding	Type of data	N°
Italic	Surveys	7
Bold	Claims/Administrative	13

Fig. 1 Key set of performance indicators for evaluating IHS

3.5 Data Sources for Performance Assessment and Evaluation

Data is necessary to construct the measures that will assess system performance. At the same time, it is essential to measure the performance of the system regarding its data strategy. A data strategy is the structured set of choices an organization takes regarding how data is identified, stored, provided, processed, and governed (Larrain et al. 2022). Integrated systems seek to construct a primary data unit containing a patient-level characterization of clinical records, healthcare utilization, healthcare cost, behavioral factors, physiological information, and socio-demo-economic information (Pimperl et al. 2017). Likewise, periodic data to construct time series and panels are a core element of successful data strategies. Without an effective data strategy, integrated care systems will not be able to monitor their progress toward the established goals, nor are evaluators likely to encounter access to data required to conduct the evaluation.

Given the wide range of goals and value-creating mechanisms in integrated systems, there is a need for several types of data. Health service administrative data, clinical data, population health data (including health status and behavioral and physiological factors), experience data, socio-demo-economic data, and claims or costing data are identified in the reviewed literature. Health services administrative data, derived from claims data, is mainly used to construct information about healthcare utilization but can be used to construct various relevant outcome measures (e.g., mortality rates), too. Clinical data comes from electronic health records, which provide an immense advantage for a successful data strategy. Population health data is constructed from different sources. Health status data comes from patient records and patient recorded outcomes (PROMs). Behavioral factors data will typically come from specific surveys or questionnaires. Patient recorded experiences (PREMs) are the primary source for experience data. Public records and specific questionnaires provide socio-demo-economic data. Finally, claims or costing data comes from the health system payors (national health funds, health insurance companies) and care provider administration and provides insight into the reimbursable price of the system's efforts and in few cases insight into the actual costs of care delivery.

4 Methodological and Design Approaches in Evaluating Integrated Care Systems Performance

Fundamental to the quality of the evaluation is the evaluation design applied and the extent to which it allows causal inference (White and Sabarwal 2014). Simple before-after designs are often applied but their validity is limited. More frequently in robust evaluations of integrated care, time series data is leveraged, or system performance is compared to benchmarks and/or control groups (Optimity 2018; Bevan et al. 2019). Typically, experiments, quasi-experiments, and comparisons of standardized assessments are used for this purpose. Standardized assessments are very useful to contextualize results, but they are often conducted as observational studies and can't determine causality over the outcomes with certainty. At the same time, both from an ethical and a pragmatic perspective, it is virtually impossible to conduct RCTs (Black 1996).

Quasi-experimental designs combine rigor and flexibility adequate for evaluating impact of integrated systems, and researchers have employed these for this purpose. Table 2 presents a high-level overview of the most common quasi-experimental methods in integrated care evaluation (Pischke 2018; Petticrew et al. 2019; Brookhart et al. 2010; Heckman 1979; Stuart 2010; Taiwo 2022; Hainmueller 2012). These

Table 2 Overview of common quasi-experimental designs

Method	Overview
Regression discontinuity	The design is defined by identifying a mechanism that defines the assignment of the treatment. Once we control by the mechanism (assuming its level is uncontrollable by participants), the assignment of intervention is nearly as good as randomization for the participants immediately above or below the threshold, as the only difference between them is the intervention. The method requires the intervention to be assigned by a clear qualitative threshold on a (running) variable, such as cut-off scores for university selection
Natural experiments	The method requires a natural treatment assignment exogenous to the variable of interest or its determinants. As such, it can be thought of as a random assignment. A random treatment assignment will secure that the treated and untreated portions of the sample (if big enough) will have, on average, comparable characteristics and, hence, their difference in the variable of interest can be attributed to the treatment
Instrumental variables/sample selection (Heckman) models	These methods are regression based and take care of selection bias by introducing a statistical correction to the non-random treatment assignment. The correction in instrumental variables is related to finding a different variable (instrument) that is related to the conflicting variable but not to the outcome of interest. In Heckman models, the probability of receiving treatment is modelled for each observation and included in the estimation as a corrector in the treatment regressor
Matching	Matching methods rely on observed characteristics to find statistical twins (matches) to the treated units among untreated units and, by doing so, constructing a comparable control group
• Exact	Exact matching refers to finding matches to each of the units in the treated sample so that they have the same value in the observed covariates
• Propensity score matching	With this method, treated units are not matched on observable characteristics but on the likelihood that the individual will be assigned to treatment (propensity score), in time determined by observable characteristics
• Mahalanobis metric matching	A common alternative to propensity score matching when there are few covariates (<8), the method matches treated units by comparing the Mahalanobis metric. This metric is a multi-dimensional generalization of the idea of measuring how many standard deviations away an observed covariate value is from the mean of the distribution of said covariate
• Genetic matching	Using an evolutionary algorithm, the method generalizes previously seen matching approaches to find the control group that optimizes the post-matching observed covariate balance

(continued)

Table 2 (continued)

Method	Overview
Entropy balancing	It is a multivariate reweighting method to produce balanced samples. In a pre-processing procedure, the methodology calculates control unit weights so that the reweighted control group satisfies a pre-set of balance conditions that are imposed on the sample moments of the observed covariate distributions. The optimization problem will search for the set of weights that satisfies the balance constraints and create comparable samples where, on average, the only difference between them is the treatment in question
Synthetic control groups	Mostly used when there is one or few treated units and many untreated units observed through time. The method consists of creating a control group for the treated unit out of a weighted combination of the untreated units

designs use statistical methods to create a counterfactual that captures what would have been the outcomes if the program/policy had not been implemented. Depending on the data at hand, the estimation methods can be ex-post single difference or double difference (also known as difference-in-differences or DID). The difference between the approaches is related to the method used for minimizing the counterfactual's risk of bias, or in other words, to be as certain as possible that the only difference between groups is the effect of the intervention being evaluated.

Quasi-experiments, the evaluation design better equipped to evaluate IHS, have the challenge of identifying an appropriate counterfactual. Separating the evaluation according to the types of effect and sub-sampling population that fits partitioned evaluations can facilitate this task and generate more accurate assessments. However, common methods for the creation of control groups using statistical analysis (matching methods) have a shortcoming that is particularly detrimental to IHS. Cases of high leverage or low prevalence (particularly in small to medium-size systems) will typically be excluded from the analysis. This practice is called "Winsorization," and it is harmless when the effect of an intervention is constant for the affected population. However, the population approach of integrated systems and their accountability for the full spectrum of care push the system to have differentiated interventions for all its patients. In this context, we recommend to utilize methods that don't exclude participants, such as the entropy balancing method (Larrain and Groene 2023). Innovative assessment methods can be used to assess integrated care value creating mechanisms that are difficult to measure. IT-based measures, EHR-based measures, and social network analysis are examples of these methods.

The unique nature of IHS presents challenges for performance assessment. While enhancing the interconnections of the system's stakeholders at various levels, integrated care increases the complexity of an already complex system (Edgren and Barnard 2012). Under these circumstances, understanding the causal effects between the system actions and the observed results becomes more challenging. The solution is to complement the monitoring of performance indicators with models capable of integrating complexity when assessing performance. Simulation models are an excellent example of such complements (Larrain and Groene 2021).

5 Conclusions and Recommendations for the Performance Assessment of Integrated Care Systems

Designing a robust performance assessment plan is essential for evaluating the effectiveness of interventions within the complexity of services delivery. The use of logic models as a conceptual foundation provides a structured approach to delineating causal links between inputs, activities, outputs, and short-, mid-, and long-term objectives. This systematic approach ensures clarity in understanding the overall performance assessment framework. Furthermore, assessing performance at multiple levels, including structure, process, and outcome, is crucial. The triple aim serves as a valuable framework for evaluating primary constructs at the outcome level. Understanding the system's value-creating mechanisms is imperative for measuring performance at the process and structure levels, offering insights into the underlying dynamics of the system. Careful selection of indicators is pivotal, considering factors such as importance, scientific acceptability, usability, and feasibility. Additionally, emphasis on indicators' actionability, time frame for signaling effects, and their relation to economic outputs enhances the overall effectiveness of the assessment plan. Benchmarking, impact evaluation, and understanding performance evolution are integral components for contextualizing assessment results and guiding system improvement. In the evaluation of integrated care, the gold standard involves a patient-level characterization of various performance dimensions, including data on healthcare utilization, costs, behavioral factors, physiological information, and socio-demo-economic information. Periodical data updates and a clear plan to transform data into actionable insights are imperative to guide continuous system improvement.

To summarize, in the evaluation of integrated care, it is critical to put as much emphasis on assessing the system outcomes as to understand the contribution of different value creation mechanisms in driving these outcomes. In the absence of randomized controlled experiments, this will enhance validity, comprehension of the causal chain, as well as guiding system improvements and policy learning.

References

Amelung V, Stein V, Suter E, Goodwin N, Nolte E, Balicer R (2021) Handbook integrated care. Springer, Cham

Bautista MAC, Nurjono M, Lim YW, Dessers E, Vrijhoef HJ (2016) Instruments measuring integrated care: a systematic review of measurement properties: instruments measuring integrated care. Milbank Q 94(4):862–917. https://doi.org/10.1111/1468-0009.12233

Baxter S, Johnson M, Chambers D, Sutton A, Goyder E, Booth A (2018) The effects of integrated care: a systematic review of UK and international evidence. BMC Health Serv Res 18(1):350. https://doi.org/10.1186/s12913-018-3161-3

Berwick DM, Nolan TW, Whittington J (2008) The triple aim: care, health, and cost. Health Aff 27(3):759–769. https://doi.org/10.1377/hlthaff.27.3.759

Bevan G, Evans A, Nuti S (2019) Reputations count: why benchmarking performance is improving health care across the world. HEPL 14(2):141–161. https://www.cambridge.org/core/product/identifier/S1744133117000561/type/journal_article

Black N (1996) Why we need observational studies to evaluate the effectiveness of health care. BMJ 312(7040):1215–1218. https://doi.org/10.1136/bmj.312.7040.1215

Bodenheimer T, Sinsky C (2014) From triple to quadruple aim: care of the patient requires care of the provider. Ann Fam Med 12(6):573–576. https://doi.org/10.1370/afm.1713

Brookhart MA, Rassen JA, Schneeweiss S (2010) Instrumental variable methods in comparative safety and effectiveness research. Pharmacoepidem Drug Safe 19(6):537–554. https://doi.org/10.1002/pds.1908

Dates M, Lennox-Chugani N, Pereira HS, Tedeschi M (2018) Health system performance assessment—integrated care assessment (20157303 HSPA). Public Health - European Commission, Brussels

Donabedian A (1988) The quality of care. How can it be assessed? JAMA 260(12):1743–1748

Edgren L, Barnard K (2012) Complex adaptive systems for management of integrated care. Leadersh Health Serv 25(1):39–51. https://www.emerald.com/insight/content/doi/10.1108/17511871211198061/full/html

European Commission (2018) Directorate general for health and food safety. Tools and methodologies to assess integrated care in Europe: report by the Expert Group on Health Systems Performance Assessment. https://data.europa.eu/doi/10.2875/017891

Evans R, Barer M, Marmor T (1994) Why are some people healthy and others not? In: The determinants of health of populations. Aldine de Gruyter, New York

Grone O, Garcia-Barbero M (2001) Integrated care: a position paper by the WHO European Office of Integrated Health Care Services. Int J Integr Care 1:e21

Hainmueller J (2012) Entropy balancing for causal effects: a multivariate reweighting method to produce balanced samples in observational studies. Polit Anal 20(1):25–46. https://www.cambridge.org/core/product/identifier/S1047198700012997/type/journal_article

Heckman JJ (1979) Sample selection bias as a specification error. Econometrica 47(1):153. https://www.jstor.org/stable/1912352?origin=crossref

Larrain N, Groene O (2021) Simulation modeling to assess performance of integrated healthcare systems: literature review to characterize the field and visual aid to guide model selection. PLoS One 16(7):e0254334

Larrain N, Groene O (2023) Improving the evaluation of an integrated healthcare system using entropy balancing: population health improvements in Gesundes Kinzigtal. SSM Popul Health 22:101371. https://doi.org/10.1016/j.ssmph.2023.101371

Larrain N, Morando V, Groene O (2022) Data strategy for population health management: review of leading accountable care organizations. Working Paper

Levesque J-F, Sutherland K (2020) Combining patient, clinical and system perspectives in assessing performance in healthcare: an integrated measurement framework. BMC Health Serv Res 20(1):23

McClellan M, Kent J, Stephen B, MacDonnell M, Thoumi A, Shuttleworth B, et al (2013) Accountable care: focusing accountability on the outcomes: report of the accountable care working group 2013 (internet). World innovation summit for health (WISH), Qatar Foundation. https://www.wish.org.qa/wp-content/uploads/2018/01/27425_WISH_Accountable_care_Report_AW-Web.pdf

McDonald K, Schultz E, Albin L, Pineda N, Lonhart J, Sundaram V et al (2014) Care coordination measures atlas (internet). Agency for Healthcare Research and Quality, Rockville. https://www.ahrq.gov/ncepcr/care/coordination/atlas.html

Moll C, Arndt F, Arvanitis TN, Gonzàlez N, Groene O, Ortega-Gil A, Verdoy D, Bloemeke J (2023) It depends on the people! A qualitative analysis of contextual factors, prior to the implementation of digital health innovations for chronic condition management, in a German integrated care network. Digit Health 9:20552076231222100. https://doi.org/10.1177/20552076231222100

Nundy S, Cooper LA, Mate KS (2022) The quintuple aim for health care improvement: a new imperative to advance health equity. JAMA 327(6):521–522. https://doi.org/10.1001/jama.2021.25181

Nuño Solinís R, Stein KV (2016) Measuring integrated care—the quest for disentangling a gordian knot. Int J Integr Care 16(3):18. https://doi.org/10.5334/ijic.2525/

Optimity (2018) Performance assessment framework (Internet). EU Third Health Programme (2014–2020). https://ec.europa.eu/chafea/health/archives/documents/health/icic-18-santanapereira_en.pdf

Organisation for Economic Co-operation and Development, Europeiska Unionen (2020) Health at a glance: Europe 2020: state of health in the EU cycle

Petticrew M, Knai C, Thomas J, Rehfuess EA, Noyes J, Gerhardus A et al (2019) Implications of a complexity perspective for systematic reviews and guideline development in health decision making. BMJ Glob Health 4(1):e000899. https://doi.org/10.1136/bmjgh-2018-000899

Pimperl A, Schulte T, Mühlbacher A, Rosenmöller M, Busse R, Groene O et al (2017) Evaluating the impact of an accountable care organization on population health: the quasi-experimental design of the German Gesundes Kinzigtal. Popul Health Manag 20(3):239–248. https://doi.org/10.1089/pop.2016.0036

Pinter KA, Zhang H, Liu C, Tran B, Chokshi M, Lucerno-Prisno DE et al (2021) Elements and performance indicators of integrated healthcare programmes on chronic diseases in six countries in the Asia-Pacific region: a scoping review. Int J Integr Care 21(1):3. https://doi.org/10.5334/ijic.5439/

Pischke J-S (2018) Regression discontinuity design (internet). London School of Economics, London. https://econ.lse.ac.uk/staff/spischke/ec533/RD.pdf

Porter M (2014) Redefining German health care. In: Moving towards a value-based system. Springer, Cham

Raleigh V, Bardsley M, Wistow G, Wittenberg R, Erens B, Mays N (2014) Integrated care and support pioneers: indicators for measuring the quality of integrated care. Policy Innovation Research Unit, London School of Hygiene & Tropical Medicine, London

Smith P (ed) (2009) Performance measurement for health system improvement: experiences, challenges and prospects. Cambridge University Press, Cambridge, p 726

Souza DL, Oliveras-Fabregas A, Minobes-Molina E, de Camargo CM, Galbany-Estragués P, Jerez-Roig J (2021) Trends of multimorbidity in 15 European countries: a population-based study in community-dwelling adults aged 50 and over. BMC Public Health 21(1):76. https://doi.org/10.1186/s12889-020-10084-x

Strandberg-Larsen M, Krasnik A (2009) Measurement of integrated healthcare delivery: a systematic review of methods and future research directions. Int J Integr Care 9(1):305. https://doi.org/10.5334/ijic.305/

Stuart EA (2010) Matching methods for causal inference: a review and a look forward. Stat Sci 25(1):1–21. https://doi.org/10.1214/09-STS313.full

Taiwo AA (2022) Quasi-experimental design: genetic matching https://taiwoahmed.com/2020/11/27/genetic-matching-for-causal-inference-in-experimental-and-observational-studies/

Wagner EH (1998) Chronic disease management: what will it take to improve care for chronic illness? Eff Clin Pract 1:2–4

Wang S, Groene O (2022) Using logic models to support integrated care implementation - lessons from implementation in 9 European integrated care regions. Int J Integr Care 22:93. https://doi.org/10.5334/ijic.ICIC21217

Wang SY, Seghieri C, Vainieri M, Groene O (2022) Changes in acute myocardial infarction, stroke, and heart failure hospitalizations during COVID-19 pandemic in Tuscany-an interrupted time series study. Int J Public Health 67:1604319. https://doi.org/10.3389/ijph.2022.1604319

White H, Sabarwal S (2014) Quasi-experimental design and methods: methodological briefs - impact evaluation no. 8. (methodological Briefs no. 8)

WHO (2021) Spending on health in Europe: entering a new era. WHO, Copenhagen

Zonneveld N, Driessen N, Stüssgen RA, Minkman MM (2018) Values of integrated care: a systematic review. Int J Integr Care 18(4):9. https://doi.org/10.5334/ijic.4172

Person and Community Centered Evaluation Approaches

Participatory Methods in Health Service Evaluations

Elizabeth McGee

Abstract

This chapter provides an overview of community engagement, why it's important, and its criticality to evaluative processes. The history of the interaction of community engagement in evaluation and research practices will be discussed, including participatory evaluation, empowerment evaluation, and culturally Responsive Evaluation that centers on community, diversity, equity, inclusion, and social justice pursuits. We will also explore how to improve health-service evaluation practices using strategies like relationship-building, reflexivity, and adaptability. We also inquire how current trends in health-based interventions, such as capacity building and cultural humility, should be reflected in the evaluative process, and what this looks like practically for evaluative methodologies. The chapter further connects these concepts to the health field through case studies.

Keywords

Community engagement · Participatory evaluation · Culturally responsive evaluation · Cultural humility

---

E. McGee (✉)
LEAP Consulting, New Haven, CT, USA
e-mail: elizabeth@leapevalconsulting.com

A. Kaehne, J. Feather (eds.), *Handbook of Health Services Evaluation*,
https://doi.org/10.1007/978-3-031-87869-5_24

1 Introduction: Why Should You Care About Community Engagement in the Context of Health-Service Evaluations?

Community engagement (CE) plays a pivotal role in the context of health-service evaluations, offering a myriad of benefits that contribute to the effectiveness and sustainability of health interventions. Broadly, CE-driven evaluations can inform the design and implementation of targeted interventions that are culturally relevant and locally accepted. Leveraging CE in evaluations enhances the data quality of evaluations, as it ensures the development of culturally appropriate data collection tools and fosters an environment that is comfortable, helping to facilitate authentic information sharing. Further, involving communities in the evaluation process ensures the incorporation of community insights into health vitalities, challenges, and cultural practices around specific health issues, which supports a holistic understanding necessary for the development of comprehensive health strategies. CE-drive evaluations support a stronger understanding of the diverse beliefs and practices that influence specific health behaviors, helping to cognize the significance of local knowledge and expertise. This in turn fosters both community empowerment and cultural responsiveness in health programming and interventions.

2 Background on Community Engagement

The discourse on the importance of inclusive CE has experienced a significant surge over the past two decades. CE is referred to by various names, such as *civic engagement*, *political participation*, *public engagement*, *citizen involvement*, and *consumer participation* (Bracht and Tsouro 1990). One definition of CE includes "having people work collaboratively, through action and learning, to realize and create a common future" (Tamarack Institute for Community Engagement 2007, p. 8). Similarly, the Active Citizen Centre in London, England, defines CE as "the opportunity, capacity, and willingness of individuals to work collectively to shape public life" (Rogers and Robinson 2004, p. 434, as cited in Seyfang 2006). While there are many definitions of CE, common threads across most include recognition and attention to public concerns, collaboration, learning, capacity-building, and the generation of action to forge a shared future. CE can manifest in both formal and informal settings, within various societal structures (e.g., local neighborhoods, public interest groups, municipalities), and can take individualistic forms (e.g., volunteerism) as well as collective forms (e.g., organizational involvement and electoral participation).

Arnstein (1969) was one of the first theorists to create a conceptual representation for community engagement. Arnstein explores CE in terms of citizen power orientations, with the core belief of this model being the use of participation to enhance citizen power. Arnstein's Ladder of Citizen Participation illustrates levels of citizen involvement in planning processes and the degree of control a community citizen has over a particular initiative. Participation levels on the ladder are represented by "rungs." Arnstein identifies the first two rungs as manipulation and therapy, which are described as non-participatory in nature. The third, fourth, and fifth rungs of participation are informing, consultation, and placation, which have the possibility of eliciting community tokenism. The last three rungs: partnership, delegated power, and citizen control, offer higher degrees of citizen power (Arnstein 1969).

CE conceptual frameworks are used to theoretically illustrate differentiating levels of participation, power, and/or influence. Such frameworks are often represented by a continuum or spectrum, and can be used to provide a greater understanding of CE practices, facilitate greater consistency within the implementation of CE practices, as well as make power dynamics more explicit. Other significant CE conceptual frameworks that have emerged since Arnstein (1969) work, including, The New Ladder of Citizen Participation (Connor 1988), Ladder of Children's Participation (Hart 1992), The Public Participation Ladder (Widemann and Femers 1993), Typology of Participation (White 1996), Ladder of Empowerment (Rocha 1997), Ladder of Volunteer Participation (Fletcher 2003), and Spectrum for Public Participation (International Association for Public Participation 2007), among others.

2.1 Importance of Community Engagement

In complex community and socio-political environments, cynicism, and division are prevalent (Traynor and Anxdors 2005). In response to this complexity, CE stands out as a promising tool for supporting citizen participation and community well-being. If done effectively, CE is a catalyst for inclusivity, engaging members of the community most marginalized, as well as equipping them with the skills and networks necessary to confront social exclusion (Kagan 2008). Nowhere is the impact of CE more pivotal than in the realm of community health settings, where active collaboration with community members becomes instrumental in addressing health challenges, disparities, and enhancing overall well-being (Schiavo 2021).

The absence of CE in health-service settings can result in detrimental consequences for both health programs and the well-being of the community. A lack of active community involvement in health programs may lead to an insufficient understanding of specific health needs, contributing to poorly targeted interventions (Cyril et al. 2015). Additionally, a diminished cultural relevance in health programs can decrease community interest and participation, impeding the acceptance of health information and services (Weger et al. 2018). The consequences of such disengagement include the perpetuation of existing health disparities, as interventions may not adequately address the unique challenges faced by different demographic groups. Without community buy-in, community apathy may be high, resulting in the low utilization of available healthcare services, and opportunities for preventive health measures might be overlooked, potentially leading to increased healthcare costs in the long run. In health settings, CE should be a dynamic and continuous process requiring a commitment to collaboration, cultural competence, and responsiveness to evolving community needs. This involves building partnerships, empowering community members, and addressing health issues through accessible and culturally responsive programs. CE can result in improved health-programming, enhanced accountability on the part of health programming implementers, and even health-specific policy change. Ultimately, the effectiveness and sustainability of health programs is compromised when they lack the essential support and input from the communities they aim to serve.

3 The Intersection of Community Engagement and Evaluation: Participatory Evaluation

CE is a critical element in the evaluation process, playing a pivotal role in ensuring the relevance, effectiveness, and sustainability of programs and initiatives. It fosters transparency, trust, and collaboration between evaluators and those being evaluated, bringing diverse perspectives, local insights, and firsthand experiences to the table (Lasker and Weiss 2003). In health-service evaluations, CE is particularly vital as it enhances the validity and relevance of assessments while contributing to the development of more equitable, community-responsive interventions and policies. Beyond being an ethical imperative, CE serves as a strategic approach that enriches evaluations, making them more impactful, inclusive, and attuned to the needs of the communities being served. Empowering communities through active engagement and involvement in decision-making fosters ownership of health programs and a sense of individual responsibility for health outcomes. To achieve effective CE, health professionals and evaluators must build trust and credibility with communities, demonstrating a commitment to collaboration and transparency throughout the evaluation process.

3.1 What Is Participatory Evaluation?

Traditional evaluation frameworks may not always align with community needs, values, or priorities. Utilizing evaluation methods that have the ability to become better suited to community needs and perspectives is an ongoing challenge. Although the idea of stakeholder participation in evaluation is now widely accepted within the evaluation community (White 1996), when and how to best perform CE in the context of evaluation is still not widely agreed upon.

Participatory evaluation methods have made significant headway in the past 30 years and offer guidance in how to integrate CE into evaluation. Participatory evaluation can be defined as "an evaluation in which trained evaluators work in partnership with [program] stakeholders to produce evaluative knowledge" (Cornish et al. 2023; Cousins and Earl 1992; Cousins and Whitmore 1998). More concretely, CE in evaluation involves the active involvement of stakeholders, including community members, beneficiaries, and other relevant parties, in the evaluation process (Garaway 2004). Participatory evaluation has expanded on the conventional community involvement models, by advocating for joint ownership and control of technical evaluation decision making (Cornish et al. 2023; Earl 1995).

3.2 Benefits of Participatory Methods

By involving the community throughout the evaluation journey, from evaluation design to data dissemination, evaluations become more inclusive, reflective of community needs, and better positioned to drive positive program or social change. In the context of health-service participatory evaluations, communities offer valuable insights into the social determinants of health, crucial for understanding the broader context influencing health outcomes. As such, participatory methodologies in health-service evaluations are essential for creating inclusive, patient-centered, and contextually relevant healthcare strategies. CE helps identify barriers to healthcare access, address disparities, and generate more accurate and culturally sensitive data, contributing to the development of targeted and responsive health interventions (Lasker and Weiss 2003). Additionally, engaging communities in the evaluation of health programs fosters a sense of partnership and collaboration, enhancing the likelihood of successful implementation and sustainable health improvements (Weger et al. 2018). Below, some key reasons are summarized why participatory methods are considered important in evaluation:

3.2.1 Capacity Building and Empowerment

Participatory evaluation methods can contribute to building the capacity of local communities and organizations. By actively involving them in the evaluation process, participants can gain valuable skills, knowledge, and a better understanding of evaluation methodologies. Further, by involving a diverse range of participants, including those directly affected by a program or intervention, evaluators can gather a broader range of perspectives. This inclusion promotes a sense of empowerment and ownership among the participants. It also enhances the quality, relevance, and credibility of the evaluation process by actively involving those with a stake in the program or project (Lennie 2006; Israel et al. 2010).

3.2.2 Contextual Understanding

Participants often have unique insights into the local context, cultural nuances, and specific challenges that may not be fully understood by external evaluators. Participatory evaluation methods enable a deeper exploration of the contextual factors influencing the outcomes of a program. Through participation, stakeholders can contribute to the identification of problems, the development of evaluation criteria, and the formulation of recommendations. This helps in creating more tailored and context-specific solutions that are more likely to be effective and sustainable (Garaway 2004).

3.2.3 Transparency and Accountability

Participatory evaluative methods align with ethical principles by respecting the rights, voices, and perspectives of the individuals and communities being evaluated (Amauchi et al. 2021). This contributes to a more culturally responsive and ethical and respectful evaluation process. Relatedly, the participatory approach fosters transparency in the evaluation process. When stakeholders are involved, there is increased accountability, and the evaluation findings are more likely to be accepted and acted upon by those involved in the program.

3.3 Types of Participatory Methods

3.3.1 Practical Participatory Evaluation (P-PE) and Transformative Participatory Evaluation (T-PE)

Within the participatory evaluation field, Cousins and Whitmore (1998) have identified two broad types of participatory evaluation that have been identified. Practical Participatory Evaluation (P-PE) and Transformative Participatory Evaluation (T-PE). There is some overlap between the two types, primarily their focus on community participation, development of valid local community knowledge, and joint collaboration around the development of meaning (Cousins and Whitmore 1998). With that said, there are also important distinctions; these distinctions are important to consider when deciding what type of participatory process you wish to engage in with your evaluation.

P-PE is understood as fostering evaluation use with the implicit assumption that the evaluation is geared toward program, policy, or organizational decision-making. P-PE also assumes that community participation in evaluation will enhance evaluation relevance, ownership, and thus utilization (Cousins and Whitmore 1998). T-PE has roots in participatory research and participatory action research and is considered more radical than P-PE, especially in regards to its exploration of the connections amongst knowledge, power and control (Fals-Borda and Anisur-Rahman 1991). T-PE involves "participatory principles and actions in order to democratize social change" (Cousins and Whitmore 1998). More simply, the goal of T-PE is to elicit social change by empowering disempowered communities. Table 1 further illuminates both the similarities and differences between the two major types of participatory evaluation.

3.3.2 Culturally Responsive Evaluations

Definition of Culturally Responsive Evaluations

Culturally Responsive Evaluations (CRE) has emerged as a response to the recognition that traditional evaluation methods may not adequately capture the diversity and complexity of different cultural contexts. CRE can be applied whether conducting a (P-PE) or (T-PE) evaluations. Culturally Responsive Evaluation (CRE) is an approach that integrates cultural contexts and perspectives throughout the design, implementation, and interpretation of evaluation processes. CRE emphasizes the

Table 1 Participatory evaluation (modified from Cousins and Whitmore 1998)

Label	Primary goal	Control of decision-making	Selection for participation	Depth of participation
Practical participatory evaluation	Practical: Support for program decision making and problem solving; evaluation utilization	Balanced evaluator and participatory in partnership	Primary users: Program sponsors, managers, development, implementers, etc.	Extensive participation in all phases of the evaluation
Transformative participatory evaluation	Political: Empowerment, emancipation, social justice	Balanced partnership, but ultimately decision making control by participants	All legitimate groups: Especially program and project beneficiaries	Extensive: Participation in all phases of the evaluation

importance of recognizing the cultural dimensions of both the programs being evaluated and the communities involved. This approach not only respects cultural diversity but also ensures that evaluations are more relevant, equitable, and effective by engaging stakeholders meaningfully and reflecting their lived experiences and priorities (Hood et al. 2015). Some CRE incorporates principles such as social justice and power-sharing, positioning communities as co-creators in the evaluation process to enhance program outcomes and sustainability. By centering cultural knowledge, CRE strengthens trust and collaboration between evaluators and community members, ensuring that results are both actionable and reflective of the community's needs and values (Frierson et al. 2010).

Goal of Culturally Responsive Evaluations

The goal of CRE is to ensure that evaluation methods and findings are relevant, valid, and useful for diverse cultural groups. It is particularly relevant in the evaluation of programs or interventions that target specific cultural groups or communities. Cultural competence is crucial for evaluators, necessitating an understanding of the cultural nuances and contexts of the communities involved, encompassing awareness of norms, values, and communication styles. CRE frameworks emphasize the significance of incorporating diverse voices and perspectives in evaluations, actively engaging stakeholders from various cultural backgrounds for a comprehensive understanding. CRE also underscores the importance of cultural validity and appropriateness in evaluation methods, advocating for tools aligned with the cultural context of the community studied. Furthermore, CRE promotes cultural responsiveness in data collection, calling for the use of culturally appropriate methods. Ethical considerations are paramount in CRE, focusing on respecting cultural values, obtaining informed consent, ensuring confidentiality, and adhering to cultural protocols. Linked to broader goals of equity and social justice, CRE evaluators strive to identify and address issues of inequality and injustice within the programs or interventions they assess. By incorporating these principles, CRE aims to produce evaluations that are more accurate, relevant, and actionable for diverse cultural communities.

Benefits of Culturally Responsive Evaluations

Culturally responsive methodologies enhance evaluations by fostering clear communication, inclusivity, and equity. These approaches improve communication by addressing linguistic nuances and cultural differences, building trust, and encouraging open community engagement (Frierson et al. 2010). They promote inclusivity by incorporating diverse perspectives and involving communities directly in evaluations, ensuring that findings reflect cultural nuances and align with community priorities (Baker and Collier 2003; Smith 2021). Additionally, these methods enhance the validity and reliability of evaluations by customizing approaches to fit the unique context of each community, leading to more accurate and meaningful results (Hood et al. 2015). Finally, they promote equity and social justice by addressing biases, rectifying disparities, and empowering communities to advocate for sustainable, culturally aligned changes (Hood et al. 2015; Johnson 2014; Chen 2015).

4 Implementing Participatory Methodologies

The process and goals of evaluation should simultaneously improve the community, distribute power, and subvert harmful norms (Greenhalgh et al. 2016). To do this, we need to meaningfully place the voices of marginalized people and communities at the forefront of our health evaluation work, while concurrently challenging the systems founded on white supremacist ideologies that are responsible for continued marginalization and social injustice. A community authentically engaged in evaluation builds power. Providing a process for community members to reflect on how they are engaged in a project and what changes they want in their community sends a different message than asking people to give feedback about the health organization's success. Instead of thinking about how to include participants in the evaluation that the organization conducts, practitioners must consider how the organization can support the community in evaluating itself and its work (Building the Field of Community Engagement 2015).

As such, it is essential to emphasize that community engagement in health-service evaluations transcends a mere checklist or a one-size-fits-all approach. Instead, it is a value-driven endeavor that prioritizes culturally centered and context-specific methodologies. Recognizing the unique aspects of each community, this approach seeks to move beyond generic frameworks, acknowledging that health interventions must be tailored to the specific cultural, social, and economic contexts of the communities being served. It values the importance of local nuances, traditions, and community dynamics, striving to create evaluation processes that are not only methodologically robust but also deeply respectful of the communities involved. This commitment to cultural responsiveness and context specificity underscores a dedication to meaningful collaboration, ensuring that the resulting health interventions are not only effective but also resonate with the diverse identities and needs of the communities at the heart of the evaluation process.

4.1 Implementing Participatory Methods

Thus far, we've talked about the importance of Participatory Evaluation (PE) and the use of CRE in doing health community-engaged evaluative work. Below is a step-by-step outline of practical actions for applying Participatory Evaluation (PE) and Culturally Responsive Evaluation (CRE) within health-related community evaluations:

1. Identifying the issue
   (a) Identify a relevant health issue or problem within the community.
   (b) Engage community members in the process, particularly those accessing or in need of health programs or services.
2. Building partnerships
   (a) Establish collaborative partnerships with community members and stakeholders.
   (b) Include staff from local health services or programs to ensure diverse perspectives are represented.
3. Defining evaluation questions
   (a) Work together as a team to develop evaluation questions that address the identified health issue.
   (b) Ensure the questions reflect the concerns and priorities of the community.
4. Planning and design
   (a) Collaboratively plan the evaluation design and methodology.
   (b) Decide on data collection methods (e.g., interviews, surveys, focus groups), define participant selection criteria, and plan data analysis approaches.
5. Data collection
   (a) Actively engage community members in collecting data through agreed-upon methods.
   (b) Gather insights that provide a comprehensive understanding of the issue under investigation.
6. Analysis and reflection
   (a) Analyze the collected data through collaborative reflection and discussion.
   (b) Use an iterative process to refine the analysis, ensuring the findings are grounded in the community's experiences.
7. Sharing findings
   (a) Present the findings to the community through meetings, presentations, or other accessible formats.
   (b) Seek feedback from the community to validate and refine the findings.
8. Action planning
   (a) Develop action plans collaboratively based on the evaluation findings.

   (b) Ensure community members play an active role in deciding which actions to take.
9. Implementation of actions
   (a) Put the action plans into practice with community members actively involved.
   (b) Support these actions through healthcare advocacy, policy change, or community-led initiatives.
10. Monitoring and evaluation
    (a) Monitor the implementation process and evaluate its impact.
    (b) Identify areas for improvement through ongoing evaluation.
11. Reflection and iteration
    (c) Maintain an iterative process with cycles of action, reflection, and adjustment.
    (d) Ensure continuous learning, adaptation, and improvement throughout the evaluation.

4.2 Other Considerations in the Implementation of Participatory Evaluations

4.2.1 Evaluator Reflexivity and Methodological Adaptivity

Evaluator reflexivity involves critically examining and acknowledging how personal experiences, beliefs, and assumptions influence the evaluation process (Olmos-Vega et al. 2023). Evaluator reflexivity requires evaluators to recognize how personal experiences, beliefs, and assumptions shape the evaluation process (Olmos-Vega et al. 2023). Reflexivity promotes transparency by encouraging evaluators to examine their positionality, ensuring that their perspectives do not unduly influence outcomes (Holmes 2020). Reflexive practices, such as journaling, allow evaluators to document thoughts and decisions throughout the study, enhancing credibility and minimizing bias (Ortlipp 2008). This ongoing self-awareness helps evaluators foster trust and transparency, leading to more reliable and meaningful results (Finlay 2002).

Methodological adaptivity complements reflexivity by enabling evaluators to tailor approaches to meet the diverse needs of communities. Adaptive methods include data triangulation, which enhances reliability by incorporating multiple data sources and perspectives to balance power dynamics and address uncertainties (Patton 1999). This iterative process ensures that findings remain relevant and ethical by contextualizing data within the community's social, economic, and cultural realities. Developmental evaluation further supports health-related evaluations by promoting continuous learning and adaptation in dynamic environments (Patton 2011). Through collaboration with stakeholders and real-time feedback, developmental evaluation fosters innovative, responsive interventions that evolve with the community's changing needs. Together, reflexivity and adaptivity ensure evaluations are not only rigorous but also culturally sensitive, participatory, and sustainable.

4.2.2 Community Relationship-Building and Collaboration

Building relationships is central to collaborative community partnerships and successful engagement efforts (Bracht and Tsouros 1990; Russell et al. 2008). Effective partnerships rely on including diverse stakeholders to prevent bias and ensure all community voices are represented (Woolcock and Brown 2005). Establishing trust through frequent interactions and mutual benefit strengthens these partnerships, fostering problem-solving and promoting long-term collaboration (Mertens 1999). Trust and reciprocity also reduce barriers to social exchange, facilitate sharing of information, and improve access to resources (Hawe and Shiell 2000).

Transparency and accountability are essential in building trust, ensuring open communication, and empowering communities to engage actively in decisions (National Centre for Involvement 2008). Transparency involves clearly explaining how priorities are determined and decisions made, while accountability ensures that organizations assume responsibility for their actions (Schwandt 1998). Participatory decision-making—such as town hall meetings and community forums—further promotes engagement by involving community members directly in the process. In health-service evaluations, collaboration can involve partnerships with community groups, leveraging local networks and champions to facilitate communication and problem-solving. Community champions act as bridges between residents and authorities, enhancing trust and participation (Public Health England 2021). Additionally, member checking ensures the validity of findings by involving participants in verifying interpretations, balancing input with analytical integrity (Lincoln and Guba 1986).

4.2.3 Capacity Building

Building capacity within communities is essential for sustainable health evaluations, empowering community members with the skills, knowledge, and resources to actively engage in and contribute to the evaluation process. This participatory approach fosters ownership, promotes collaboration, and ensures that evaluations are culturally relevant and aligned with community needs (Organisation for Economic Cooperation and Development [OECD] 2009a). Training programs play a critical role by equipping individuals with leadership, communication, project management, and conflict resolution skills, allowing communities to monitor and evaluate their own initiatives and maintain local control. These efforts enhance resilience and ensure that evaluations have a lasting impact by fostering problem-solving capabilities within the community.

Recognizing and celebrating community achievements are also crucial for sustaining engagement. Public recognition events, such as award ceremonies, inspire participation, establish role models, and create opportunities for feedback and continuous improvement (Mitchell et al. 2021; Delgado 2016). Acknowledgment practices tailored to individual preferences reinforce the importance of leadership efforts, helping to cultivate a thriving community and ensuring long-term commitment to health initiatives. Together, capacity-building efforts and recognition strategies empower communities to take ownership of their health outcomes and foster sustainable development.

4.2.4 Co-creation and Empowerment

Empowerment is a central concept in engagement frameworks, emphasizing community control, citizen participation, and deliberative democracy (Maslach and Jackson 1981). It aligns with asset-based community development, which focuses on leveraging existing strengths rather than fostering dependency (Kretzmann and McKnight 1993). Co-creation fosters mutual learning, where community members, organizations, and experts collaborate in designing and implementing projects that impact the community (Greenhalgh et al. 2016). This inclusive approach ensures contextually relevant health solutions while building a sense of ownership among stakeholders, encouraging long-term engagement and meaningful outcomes (Akoglu and Dankl 2021).

Community Advisory Boards (CABs) play a crucial role by representing diverse voices, providing input on programs and policies, and serving as communication bridges between organizations and communities (Strauss et al. 2001). Although CABs lack decision-making authority, they contribute to inclusive decision-making by promoting cultural competence and fostering shared responsibility (Chené et al. 2005). Additionally, community participation can also extend beyond the evaluation process, with members involved in disseminating findings through accessible formats such as visual aids and storytelling. This iterative approach empowers communities to advocate for change, refine initiatives, and sustain long-term impact by ensuring that ongoing efforts respond to evolving needs and feedback (Building the Field of Community Engagement 2015).

What Does Community-Centered Work Look Like in a Health-Service Evaluation Context?

Highlight: Case Study of Bronx

The Bronx has an extensive, complex history with its residents facing medical and socio-economic challenges, and it is thus one of the most studied regions in the vicinity. It has attracted much attention from academic researchers, and unfortunately, residents have experienced the negative impacts of unethical research practices like lying about the danger of studies and human rights violations. So a group of concerned community members came together to create the Bronx Community Research Review Board (BxCRRB).

BxCRRB is a non-profit, volunteer organization focused on ensuring the proper representation of Bronx residents during community research projects, regardless of social status or economic standing. Broadly, the organization aims to eliminate health inequities present in marginalized communities in the Bronx. They aim to transform health research culture from "top-down to bottom-up" by growing the power of the people being researched. They are also working to protect the health of residents through community engagement, a radical review process, and ensuring that research findings come back to individuals and groups impacted.

BxCRRB is resolute on shared control over research gains and products. They also provide healing-focused education to both patients and researchers through their Community Engaged Research Academy (CERA). The work of BxCRRB exemplifies the principles of research co-creation, empowerment, and community-led results dissemination and is ground-breaking in how it enacts community-centered, health service research-related work. Through the self-determination of residents, rigorous community engagement, meaningful collaboration, a strength-based approach to research, and centering the lived experiences of marginalized residents, BxCRRB is creating a healthier Bronx. It is an exemplary case of a Community Advisory Board (CAB) that could be used to model such boards in other communities.

4.2.5 Strategization for Sustainability After Evaluation

Long-term sustainability in health-service evaluations requires a community-centered approach that addresses future needs beyond the immediate evaluation (Centers for Disease Control and Prevention 2011). Economic sustainability focuses on assessing financial viability, job creation, and income generation, involving local businesses and workers to ensure economic considerations are integrated into future planning (Love et al. 2021). Evaluators play a critical role in helping communities build resilience to external shocks through strategic long-term planning. Social sustainability entails evaluating the long-term impact of programs on social cohesion and inclusivity, ensuring that community members' perspectives shape socially sustainable initiatives (Spangenberg and Omann 2007).

Facilitating access to funding involves a multifaceted approach to empower communities in securing financial support for health-related projects. This includes identifying diverse funding sources and building networks with relevant stakeholders. Evaluators assist with grant preparation, provide training on grant writing and financial management, and tailor funding strategies—whether through grants, loans, or a combination—based on the specific needs of each project. Strong financial planning ensures alignment with funding requirements, while community involvement fosters a sense of ownership in decision-making. The aim is to create a supportive ecosystem, enabling communities to access external funding and sustain local projects across sectors like healthcare, education, and infrastructure.

5 Challenges in Implementing Participatory Evaluations in a Health-Service Context

Navigating the terrain of health-related community engagement within the realm of evaluation can present a myriad of challenges. As evaluators seek to implement evaluation processes that involve and resonate with communities, they may find themselves confronted by a complex interplay of factors that can significantly impact the effectiveness of such initiatives. This journey toward meaningful community engagement demands a nuanced understanding of the obstacles that may arise, emphasizing the need for thoughtful strategies and approaches to ensure the success of evaluation endeavors. In this exploration of challenges in implementation, we delve into the intricacies of engaging with communities within the context of health evaluation, shedding light on the hurdles that practitioners and stakeholders must navigate to foster genuine and impactful connections.

5.1 Challenges to Evaluation Implementation

5.1.1 Resource and Time Constraints

Limited time and funding pose significant challenges to sustaining long-term community engagement in health services. Adequate resources are essential to build trust and meaningful relationships. In evaluations, "time constraints" affect both evaluators and community members, limiting the depth and quality of engagement. Evaluators may face fixed timeframes to assess projects, compromising the thoroughness and fairness of their reviews. Swift decisions can limit opportunities for careful analysis and consultation. Similarly, community members often struggle to participate fully due to busy schedules, hindering their ability to contribute meaningfully. Building trust, a critical element of engagement, is impeded by rushed interactions, reducing transparency and open communication. Additionally, limited time restricts opportunities for deep conversations, feedback loops, and listening sessions, increasing the risk of overlooking important community perspectives and nuances.

5.1.2 Presence of Harm

Recognizing the presence of harm that can exist within evaluative practices is essential when conducting health-based evaluations, especially those that are participatory in nature. It is important to recognize that even systems that are in place to protect against harm within research and evaluative settings are insufficient. For example, Institutional Review Boards (IRBs) are designed to protect participants' rights from harm; however, their historical rooting in the medical model results in a medically-focused exploration of harm. Because of this, the IRB model often fails to address the harm that can persist within evaluative practices in community-based settings, such as: funders dictating initiative focuses, top-down evaluative approach, evaluator bias, and a lack of compensation to community members for participation, among others. Further, the lack of models that explore the harm inherent in the evaluation process leaves evaluators unprepared to recognize or mitigate harm effectively. As a result, harm and exploitation can persist, even with good intentions.

In order to describe the phenomena of harm within research and evaluative processes, we introduce the concept of *data violence*. This term is defined as, any harm done to individuals, community, or systems we intend to benefit, through research and evaluation practices. Addressing the harm embedded in participatory requires a transformation of both personal and professional approaches to ensure both ethical engagement and healing within communities.

5.1.3 Community Diversity and Cultural Nuance

Cultural differences between evaluators and community members can lead to misunderstandings in health-related evaluations, making cultural sensitivity essential for effective engagement. Diverse communities require inclusive approaches that represent all voices, though this can be challenging due to varying needs and perspectives. Trust-building is critical but often takes time, especially where historical mistrust exists. Power imbalances must be acknowledged and mitigated to ensure equitable decision-making. Communication barriers, including language differences, can hinder collaboration, while limited resources constrain relationship-building efforts. Capacity-building through education and training empowers communities to participate meaningfully in evaluations. Navigating ethical considerations, data ownership, and equitable technology access are also vital, particularly when working with vulnerable populations. Creating sustainable engagement models requires a long-term commitment, continuous communication, and flexibility to adapt to evolving needs.

What Roles Does Medical Mistrust Play in Participatory Evaluations in Health Contexts?

Highlight: Medical Mistrust

A key factor to consider when attempting to engage in health-related evaluations in a culturally sensitive way is to consider how medical mistrust may be at play in a given community. Medical mistrust refers to a lack of confidence or trust in the healthcare system, healthcare providers, or medical research (Benkert et al. 2019). Addressing medical mistrust requires efforts to build trust through transparency, effective communication, and culturally sensitive care. Healthcare providers and institutions must acknowledge historical injustices, work towards eliminating biases, and engage in open and honest communication to foster trust and collaboration with patients. Building trust is essential for promoting health equity and ensuring that individuals receive the care they need. In the context of community-based evaluations, medical mistrust can manifest in various ways that impact the effectiveness and validity of the evaluation process.

Medical mistrust can manifest as skepticism, suspicion, or reluctance to engage with medical professionals or follow their recommendations. Medical mistrust can be rooted in various factors, including historical injustices, systemic biases, cultural differences, and personal experiences. Historical events, such as unethical medical experiments or discriminatory practices, have contributed to the mistrust of healthcare systems, particularly among marginalized communities. For example, the Tuskegee Syphilis Study in the United States, where 400 African American men between 1932 and 1972 were deliberately left untreated for syphilis without their informed consent, is a notorious example that has fueled mistrust in medical research (Jones 2008). Contemporary issues, such as disparities in healthcare access and treatment outcomes, can also contribute to medical mistrust. Discrimination, stereotypes, and unequal treatment experienced by individuals based on factors like race, ethnicity, gender, or socioeconomic status can erode trust in the healthcare system.

5.1.4 Environmental Challenges

Sustaining community engagement throughout an evaluation is intricately linked to navigating environmental changes that may impact the community. External factors, such as economic shifts or political developments, can divert attention and resources away from ongoing health engagement efforts, particularly in the context of the evaluation. Moreover, these changes can contribute to a sense of uncertainty within the community regarding the evaluation process. The challenge lies in maintaining community interest and commitment amid external influences that may cause skepticism or hesitation among community members. This challenge is further compounded by the dynamic nature of communities, as their needs, priorities, and demographics may shift during the evaluation period. Additionally, resource constraints, including limited funds and technology access, pose ongoing challenges to sustaining engagement throughout the evaluation process.

6 Conclusion

Community engagement (CE) is indispensable in health-service evaluations, serving as a bridge between evidence-based research and culturally meaningful health interventions. The participatory nature of CE ensures that evaluations transcend traditional methodologies by placing the community's lived experiences, cultural values, and local knowledge at the core of health programming. This approach fosters mutual trust, transparency, and inclusiveness, ultimately empowering communities to shape health services that reflect their unique needs and aspirations. Through participatory evaluation, stakeholders are not just passive subjects but active collaborators—co-creators of knowledge and change. This dynamic partnership enhances the relevance and impact of health interventions, ensuring that programs are not only responsive but also sustainable. Participatory methodologies build community capacity, foster social change, and generate culturally relevant insights that are critical in addressing disparities and advancing health equity. Further, culturally responsive evaluations add depth by integrating nuanced community perspectives, promoting empowerment, and aligning health interventions with social justice principles. These evaluations challenge power dynamics, enabling marginalized communities to reclaim control over the narrative of their health needs and outcomes. Ultimately, the strength of health-service evaluations lies in their ability to adapt to local contexts, respect cultural diversity, and maintain an ongoing dialogue with communities. By embedding participatory and culturally responsive principles at every stage, evaluators ensure that programs are not only effective but also meaningful to the people they serve. The future of health-service evaluations depends on our collective ability to listen, learn, and act in partnership with communities—transforming evaluations into powerful tools for advocacy, empowerment, and lasting impact.

References

Akoglu C, Dankl K (2021) Co-creation for empathy and mutual learning: a framework for design in health and social care. CoDesign 17(3):296–312. https://doi.org/10.1080/15710882.2019.1633358

Amauchi JFF, Gauthier M, Ghezeljeh A, Giatti LL, Keats K, Sholanke D, Zachari D, Gutberlet J (2021) The power of community-based participatory research: ethical and effective ways of researching. Commun Dev J 53(1):1936102. https://doi.org/10.1080/15575330.2021.1936102

Arnstein S (1969) A ladder of citizen participation. J Am Inst Plann 35(4)

Baker QE, Collier AK (2003) Commentary: inclusive community engagement: a grounding principle for collaborative problem solving. J Urban Health 80:48–49. https://doi.org/10.1007/2FBF02417841

Benkert R, Cuevas A, Thompson HS, Dove-Meadows E, Knuckles D (2019) Ubiquitous yet unclear: a systematic review of medical mistrust. Behav Med 45(2):86–101. https://doi.org/10.1080/08964289.2019.1588220

Bracht N, Tsouro A (1990) Principles and strategies of effective community participation. Health Promot Int 5(3):199–208. https://doi.org/10.1093/heapro/5.3.199

Building the Field of Community Engagement (2015) Evaluation and community engagement: everyone is an evaluator. https://www.nexuscp.org/evaluation-community-engagement-everyone-is-an-evaluator-written-by-building-the-field-of-community-engagement-partners-and-tracy-babler/

Centers for Disease Control and Prevention (2011) Developing an effective evaluation plan: setting the course for effective program evaluation. Centers for Disease Control and Prevention, Atlanta. https://www.cdc.gov/evaluation/tools/developmenttools/

Chen HT (2015) The experimentation evaluation approach to outcome evaluation. In: Practical program evaluation: theory-driven evaluation and the integrated evaluation perspective, 2nd edn. SAGE, Thousand Oaks

Chené R, García L, Goldstrom M, Pino M, Roach DP, Thunderchief W, Waitzkin H (2005) Mental health research in primary care: mandates from a community advisory board. Ann Fam Med 3(1):70–72. https://doi.org/10.1370/2Fafm.260

Connor DM (1988) A new ladder of citizen participation. Natl Civ Rev 77:249–257. https://doi.org/10.1002/ncr.4100770309

Cornish F, Breton N, Moreno-Tabarez U, Delgado J, Rua M, Aikins AD, Hodgetts D (2023) Participatory action research. Nat Rev Methods Primers 3:34. https://doi.org/10.1038/s43586-023-00214-1

Cousins JB, Earl LM (1992) The case for participatory evaluation. Educ Eval Policy Anal 14(4):397–418

Cousins JB, Whitmore E (1998) Framing participatory evaluation. N Dir Eval 80:5–23. https://doi.org/10.1002/ev.1114

Cyril S, Smith BJ, Possamai-Inesedy A, Renzaho AMN (2015) Exploring the role of community engagement in improving the health of disadvantaged populations: a systematic review. Glob Health Action 8(1):29842. https://doi.org/10.3402/gha.v8.29842

Delgado M (2016) An overview of urban community practice. In: Celebrating urban community life: fairs, festivals, parades, and community practice. University of Toronto Press, Toronto

Fals-Borda O, Anisur Rahman M (1991) Action and knowledge breaking the monopoly with participatory action research. Practical Action Publishing

Finlay L (2002) "Outing" the researcher: the provenance, process, and practice of reflexivity. Qual Health Res 12(4):531–545. https://doi.org/10.1177/104973202129120052

Fletcher A (2003) Purpose, empowerment and the experience of volunteerism in community. Freechild project. https://participationpool.eu/resource/purpose-empowerment-and-the-experience-of-volunteerism-in-community/

Frierson HT, Hood S, Hughes GB (2010) A guide to conducting culturally-responsive evaluations. In: Frechtling J (ed) The 2010 user-friendly handbook for project evaluation. National Science Foundation, Alexandria

Garaway G (2004) Participatory evaluation. In: de Marrais K, Lapan SD (eds) Foundations for research: methods of inquiry in education and the social sciences. Lawrence Erlabaum Associates, Mahwah. https://doi.org/10.1016/0191-491X(95)00007-H

Greenhalgh T, Jackson C, Shaw S, Janamian T (2016) Achieving research impact through co-creation in community-based health services: literature review and case study. Milbank Q 94(2):392–429. https://doi.org/10.1111/1468-0009.12197

Hart RA (1992) Children's participation. From tokenism to citizenship. Innocenti essays, no. 4. UNICEF, United Nations Children's Fund, Florence

Hawe P, Shiell A (2000) Social capital and health promotion: a review. Soc Sci Med 51:871–885

Holmes AGD (2020) Researcher positionality - a consideration of its influence and place in qualitative research - a new researcher guide. Shanlax Int J Educ 8(4):1–10. https://doi.org/10.34293/education.v8i4.3232

Hood S, Hopson RK, Kirkhart KE (2015) Culturally responsive evaluation. In: Newcomer KE, Harry HP, Wholly JS (eds) Handbook of practical program evaluation, 4th edn. Wiley, Hoboken. https://doi.org/10.1002/9781119171386.ch12

International Association for Public Participation (2007) Spectrum for public participation. http://iap2.org/

Israel BA, Coombe CM, Cheezum RR, Schulz AJ, McGranaghan RJ, Lichtenstein R, Reyes AG, Clement J, Burris A (2010) Community-based participatory research: a capacity-building approach for policy advocacy aimed at eliminating health disparities. Am J Public Health 100(11):2094–2102. https://doi.org/10.2105/AJPH.2009.170506

Johnson L (2014) Cultural responsive leadership for community empowerment. Multicult Educ Rev 6(2):145–170

Jones JH (2008) The Tuskegee syphilis experiment. In: The Oxford textbook of clinical research ethics. Oxford University Press, Oxford

Kagan J (2008) In defense of qualitative changes in development. Child Dev 79(6):1606–1624

Kretzmann JP, McKnight J (1993) Building communities from the inside out: a path toward finding and mobilizing a community's assets. Asset-based Community Development Institute

Lasker RD, Weiss ES (2003) Broadening participation in community problem solving: a multidisciplinary model to support collaborative practice and research. J Urban Health 80(1):14–60. https://doi.org/10.1093/jurban/jtg014

Lennie J (2006) Increasing the rigour and trustworthiness of participatory evaluations: learnings from the field. Eval J Austr 6(1):27–35. https://doi.org/10.1177/1035719X0600600105

Lincoln YS, Guba EG (1986) But is it rigorous? Trustworthiness and authenticity in naturalistic evaluation. New Direct Progr Eval 30:73–84. https://doi.org/10.1002/ev.1427

Love H, Vey JS, Taft W, Demetriou E (2021) Community-centered economic inclusion: a strategic action playbook. Brookings metropolitan policy program https://www.brookings.edu/wp-content/uploads/2021/10/Brookings-Playbook.pdf

Maslach C, Jackson SE (1981) The measurement of experienced burnout. J Organ Behav 2(2):99–113

Mertens DM (1999) Inclusive evaluation: implications of transformative theory for evaluation. Am J Eval 20(1):1–14

Mitchell C, O'Flaherty S, Jones L, Sanders M, Whillans A (2021) Happier, healthier professionals: small scale interventions to improve social worker Well-being. What works for children's social care. https://whatworks-csc.org.uk/research-report/happier-healthier-professionals-small-scale-interventions-to-improve-social-worker-well-being/

Olmos-Vega FM, Stalmeijer RE, Varpio L, Kahlke R (2023) A practical guide to reflexivity in qualitative research: AMEE guide no. 149. Med Teach 45(3):241–251. https://doi.org/10.1080/0142159X.2022.2057287

Organisation for Economic Cooperation and Development [OECD] (2009a) Community capacity building and social policy: health, housing and community regeneration. OECD Publishing, Paris

Ortlipp M (2008) Keeping and using reflective journals in the qualitative research process. Qual Rep 13(4):695–705. https://doi.org/10.46743/2160-3715/2008.1579

Patton MQ (1999) Enhancing the quality and credibility of qualitative analysis. Health Serv Res 34(5):1189–1208

Patton MQ (2011) Developmental evaluation: applying complexity concepts to enhance innovation and use. Guilford Press, New York

Public Health England (2021) Community champions: a rapid scoping review of community champion approaches for the pandemic response and recovery. UK Department of Health and Social Care. https://www.gov.uk/government/publications/community-champion-approaches-rapid-scoping-review-of-evidence

Rocha MA (1997) A ladder of empowerment. J Plan Educ Res 17(1):4. https://doi.org/10.1177/0739456X9701700104

Rogers BM, Robinson E (2004) The benefits of community engagement: a review of the evidence. Active Citizenship Centre

Russell R, Guimarães PR, Aloy P (2008) Structural bioinformatics and network biology: new tools for predicting function and drug targets. FEBS Lett 582(8):1235–1242

Schiavo R (2021) What is true community engagement and why it matters (now more than ever). J Commun Healthc 14(2):91–92. https://doi.org/10.1080/17538068.2021.1935569

Schwandt TA (1998) Editor's notes. New directions for. Evaluation 77:1–4. https://doi.org/10.1002/ev.1091

Seyfang G (2006) Sustainable consumption the new economics and community currencies: developing new institutions for environmental governance. Reg Stud 40(7):781–791. https://doi.org/10.1080/00343400600959173

Smith LT (2021) Responding to the imperatives of an indigenous agenda: a case study of Maori. In: Decolonizing methodologies: research and indigenous peoples. Bloomsbury Publishing, London

Spangenberg JH, Omann I (2007) Assessing social sustainability: social sustainability and its multicriteria assessment in a sustainability scenario for Germany. Int J Innov Sustainable Dev 1(4):318–348. https://doi.org/10.1504/IJISD.2006.013734

Strauss RP, Sengupta S, Quinn SC, Goeppinger J, Spaulding C, Kegeles SM, Millett G (2001) The role of community advisory boards: involving communities in the informed consent process. Am Publ Health Assoc 91(12):1938–1943. https://doi.org/10.2105/2Fajph.91.12.1938

Tamarack Institute (2007) Our growing understanding of community engagement. Tamarack Institute for Community Engagement

Weger ED, Vooren NV, Luijkx KG, Baan CA, Drewes HW (2018) Achieving successful community engagement: a rapid realist review. BMC Health Serv Res 18:265. https://doi.org/10.1186/s12913-018-3090-1

White S (1996) Depoliticising development: the uses and abuses of participation. Dev Pract 6:6–15. https://doi.org/10.1080/0961452961000157564

Widemann PM, Femers S (1993) The public participation in waste management decision making: analysis and management of conflicts. J Hazard Mater 33(3):355–368. https://doi.org/10.1016/0304-3894(93)85085-S

Woolcock G, Brown V (2005) Principles of community engagement: from the literature on natural resource management, local community development, human services and sustainability

Human-Centered Healthcare Evaluation Using Personas and Journey Mapping Techniques

Amanda L. Joseph

Abstract

This chapter presents a roadmap and a series of applied scenarios in which a persona used in conjunction with five diverse journey mapping techniques can be positioned as effective human-centered tools for health service evaluation. When used together, personas and journey maps can provide unique lenses to empathize with patient experiences and organizational perspectives. Further, they visualize the intersections and pain points of complex health systems and health service navigation, illustrating operational synergies and relationships. A persona is presented and applied to a simplified healthcare scenario, and the Journey Map Evaluation Guide and Decision Support Tool are used to select the appropriate technique for each perspective. The study demonstrates how personas and journey mapping can be valuable knowledge translation tools to effectively evaluate and inform healthcare services.

Keywords

Patient journey map · Persona · Healthcare service evaluation · Service delivery · Human-centered design · Health informatics

A. L. Joseph (✉)
School of Health Information Science, University of Victoria, Victoria, British Columbia, Canada

Majestic Global Consulting Inc., Vancouver, British Columbia, Canada
e-mail: amandalynnjoseph@uvic.ca

A. Kaehne, J. Feather (eds.), *Handbook of Health Services Evaluation*,
https://doi.org/10.1007/978-3-031-87869-5_25

1 Human-Centered Perspective

It is important to design and deliver healthcare services from the perspective of their principal end-users (i.e., humans, patients, physicians, caregivers, nurses) who work in healthcare environments and use technologies (i.e., clinical, nonclinical) or are recipients of care and are therefore impacted by them. Additionally, with the advent of emerging diseases and pandemics such as COVID-19, there has been an increasing uptake in technological adoption in the healthcare sector (Joseph et al. 2022b; Liu and Miguel-Cruz 2022). Global digitalization introduces many diverse health information technologies (HIT) and health information systems (HIS) into healthcare settings (Borges do Nascimento et al. 2023; Joseph et al. 2022a; Junaid et al. 2022). The deployment and implementation of HIT and HIS present a multitude of ways in which operational processes, business practices, and patient safety can be ameliorated (Joseph et al. 2020, 2021, 2022a; Borges do Nascimento et al. 2023). Yet prior to procurement, deployment, and implementation, technologies such as personal health records (PHRs), computerized physician order entry (CPOE) systems, electronic health records (EHRs), clinical decision support systems (CDSS), and artificial intelligence (AI) are rarely evaluated for their safety, efficacy, or organizational fit (Joseph et al. 2020, 2022c, 2021; Labkoff et al. 2024; Rozenblit et al. 2025)

Thus end-users aren't always sufficiently engaged or educated on the context and intended use of these technologies, nor are their unique needs or preferences always understood (Joseph and Monkman 2025; Watkinson et al. 2021). Providing comprehensive training resources can improve end-user confidence in using HIT and HIS, by increasing awareness of the proposed value that the technologies can provide (Watkinson et al. 2021). Strategic organizational communication campaigns can foster environments where end-users feel supported to share feedback (i.e., system use, performance, identify training gaps), which can enhance adoption and workflow integration and create better training outcomes (Koppel and Kuziemsky 2019; Watkinson et al. 2021). In order to safeguard the sustainability and effectiveness of technological advancement, health systems must prioritize and evaluate the following factors: organizational culture, change management processes, human and financial resources, logistics and supply chain constraints, institutional capacity, political economy and legal frameworks of healthcare governance, healthcare workforce shortages, and the mental health of patients and healthcare workers (Cutler 2023; Joseph and Monkman 2025; Figueroa et al. 2019; Zhang et al. 2020).

The complexities of healthcare organizations, healthcare worker staffing composition, and diverse patient needs are also reflected in the heterogeneity of evaluation frameworks and models currently used to assess and evaluate various facets of healthcare practice (Davis and Granić 2024; Erlirianto et al. 2015; El Burai Felix et al. 2024; Honekamp and Ostermann 2011; Joseph et al. 2022a; Longworth et al. 2023; Skivington et al. 2021). There is an urgency for the creation of scalable frameworks to evaluate healthcare service delivery, technologies, and patient needs from stratified human-centered perspectives (Joseph et al. 2022a, 2022e; Zhang et al. 2020). Cost-effective, outcome-focused, and value-based care requires provider and patient-centric approaches to the institutional planning of healthcare organizations and services (Joseph et al. 2023b, p. 52; Sullivan 2023; Teisberg et al. 2020). Design thinking perspectives and techniques can serve as a conduit to circumvent ineffective transactional and siloed paradigms devoid of humanity and stakeholder (i.e., patient, healthcare providers, operational personnel) understanding. Specifically human-centered design (HCD) provides a design philosophy (Norman 2007, 2023) with promise to guide the humanization of: service design and delivery, procurement, technology deployment and implementation, and organizational governance. Adopting HCD practices can ensure that systems are designed and evaluated with 'human in the loop' (Labkoff et al. 2024; Nunes et al. 2015) perspectives; where collaboration between humans and technology is symbiotic (Chandler et al. 2022) and part of organizational culture. Furthermore, there is increasing demand for tailored, personalized healthcare services that adopt biopsychosocial (i.e., biological, psychological, social) approaches to service delivery and evaluation (Bartels et al. 2023; Stefanicka-Wojtas and Kurpas 2023; Vögele 2015). As such in addition to traditional biological ailments, psychological (i.e., behaviors, emotions, thoughts), and social (i.e., culture, socioeconomic) factors should be evaluated as they can contribute to disease and health outcomes (Bartels et al. 2023; Joseph and Monkman 2025; Joseph et al 2023b; Vögele 2015). Evaluators can leverage design thinking techniques (i.e., personas, journey maps) to evaluate human experiences as patients navigate continuums of care along their health journeys (Bate and Robert 2007). Such perspectives and human experience data could be evaluated to inform and plan the design of strategic and more effective healthcare services.

2 Persona Perspective

Personas are exemplary and often fictional character profiles comprised of contextualized scenarios that represent prospective end-users of products or services (Bartels et al. 2023). Their detailed narrative is fictional; however, the methodology in which they are created can be based on scientific literature, data, observation, or the intrinsic knowledge of the designer (Bartels et al. 2023). Therefore, a persona can be conceptualized as a design tool illustration comprised of visuals with complementary text that provides a framework of character for individuals or a group of individuals at a point in time. They are based on real-life typologies of people and can be used to create characters or communicate important health information through relatable narrative storylines (Bartels et al. 2023; Massey et al. 2021). Thus, they can represent and provide an empathetic context of defined end-user (i.e., healthcare consumer) groups and detail their characteristics: photo, name, individual preferences, and life circumstances (Bartels et al. 2023; Massey et al. 2021). As personas can represent human archetypes, they are helpful to assist product and service designers to personify the prospective end-users' (i.e., humans) wants and needs (Nielsen 2013, 2018; Pruitt and Grudin 2003). The persona method has evolved from being a method for information technology (IT) system development to being adopted by other industries and now used in a multitude of contexts including but not limited to: agile systems development, marketing, communications, user experience (UX), product development, service design, and innovation and ideation of IT products (Nielsen 2013, 2018).

3 Journey Map Perspective

Journey maps are design tools which provide a framework to visualize complex scenarios and intersections of human experiences at points in time along a continuum. The outputs of journey mapping activities can facilitate the visualization of complex scenarios, human experience intersections, cognitive thoughts, and spatial relationships. Likened to personas, journey maps can be used as varied instruments of design thinking; they are not only a design method but are visualization techniques that can facilitate the diagrammatic representation of stakeholder groups by interest or function for comparative visual analysis (Joseph et al. 2020, 2022d, 2023a, b, c, d; Kalbach 2016). Their ability to effectively detail intersections and relationships between organizations and consumers using products or services (Joseph et al. 2020, 2022e, 2023c; Stickdorn and Schneider 2010) is striking. In essence, journey mapping activities synthesize the data sourced from human experiences and interactions to create novel and unique visual diagrams (i.e., journey maps). Moreover, they can illustratively display and identify issues in service delivery, process bottlenecks, and workflow disruptions, highlight opportunities for improvement in various settings and contexts, and identify geographic and spatial relationships (Joseph et al. 2023c). Thus, the visual findings of journey mapping activities can assist healthcare stakeholders in not only designing but evaluating business continuity efforts, establishing operational risk, and diversifying service offerings (Joseph et al. 2023c, 2023d).

4 Five Different Perspectives of the Journey

Historically, journey maps have lacked nomenclative consistency, which broadly has stifled their adoption in healthcare settings (Joseph et al. 2020, 2022e), 2023c). As depicted by Fig. 1 there are five different journey mapping techniques: (1) Mental (Cognitive) Model Map, (2) Customer Journey Map, (3) Experience Map, (4) Service Blueprint Map, and (5) Spatial Map.

Each journey map technique evaluates a scenario from a different perspective and presents a unique opportunity to understand varied contextual lenses. The techniques can also be applied and used in various ways to assist in product development, usability testing, service design, and evaluation (Joseph et al. 2020, 2022e, 2022d, 2023c). Albeit that methodological commonalities exist, each technique produces a unique artifact (i.e., diagrammatical output) which depicts differences in perspectives, perceptions, activities, experiences, and relationships (Joseph et al. 2020, 2023c, 2022d). The roadmap (Fig. 1) displays, the sequence of use and ideal execution for each journey mapping technique if used in combination to holistically

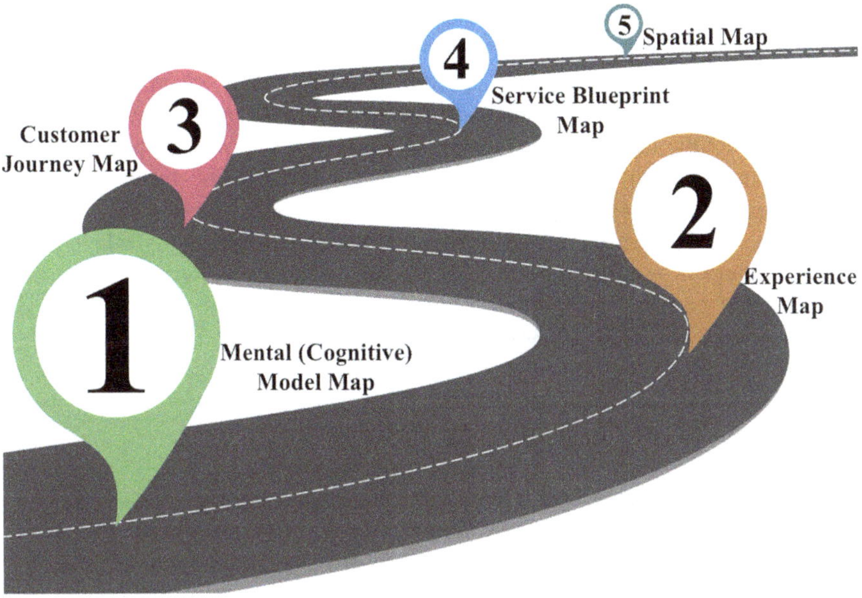

Fig. 1 Roadmap of the Five Journey Map Techniques (used with permission from ISO Joseph et al. 2022e)

evaluate a healthcare service or technology from an end-users' perspective. Thus, the Mental (Cognitive) Map activities should be conducted first, to gain a thorough understanding of the individual's thoughts, feelings, and perception of the service or product (Joseph et al. 2020, 2022e, 2023c). Following this, the Experience Map activities should be done to gain awareness of the human behavioral patterns, activities, emotions, and the individuals' experience across products, services, and organizations (Joseph et al. 2020, 2022e, 2023c).

Next, the Customer Journey Map activities should be executed to comprehend an individual's experiences and interactions with a single product, service, or organization from a consumer perspective (Joseph et al. 2022d, 2022e, 2023c) and then the Service Blueprint Map activities to provide a holistic view of the process intricacies, dependencies, and intersections of varied organizational workflows (Joseph et al. 2020, 2022e, 2023c). Further, the Service Blueprint Map technique can also be conducted iteratively to remediate the service pain points, gleaned from the Customer Journey Map technique mapping activities (Joseph et al. 2020, 2022e, 2023c). Thus, the Customer Journey Map technique produces customer experience data from end-users using a product or service, which can inform the design of the Service Blueprint Map (Joseph et al. 2020, 2022e, 2023c). Lastly, the Spatial Map technique can be carried out to establish high-level interrelationships and patterns (Joseph et al. 2020, 2022e, 2023c). Between end-user groups, and geographies.

Each of the five journey map techniques evaluates a different situational narrative and can produce diverse targeted perspectives. As such the selection of each technique is contingent on scenario specifics and the desired organization assessment. Ideally to gain a truly holistic evaluation of healthcare services evaluators should conduct the five journey mapping techniques in sequence (Fig. 1), as each perspective provides diverse human experience data which can be measured against organizational service delivery design and healthcare outcomes. However, the five techniques can also be used independently or in parallel, depending on which interpretive framework (i.e., journey map technique) would better serve the intended organizational outcome and provide the necessary data for its evaluative needs (Joseph et al. 2020, 2022e, 2023c).

5 The Persona and Journey Map Perspective

The opportunity to illustrate and contextualize the human experience via the utilization of personas and journey map techniques holds promise to evaluate gaps in healthcare service design, implementation, and delivery. By integrating these two complementary yet stratified perspectives, a holistic evaluation of end-to-end service design, utilization, and identification of the barriers and facilitators of effective health service offerings is possible. In order to demonstrate how these two tools (i.e., persona, journey map techniques) can be used in an evaluation context a persona, named Emma, was created and applied to a simplified healthcare scenario using the five different journey map techniques (Fig. 1). The five techniques evaluate Emma's patient journey differently; each scenario provides a distinct set of human experience data points, outcomes, and perspectives (i.e., unique service delivery experience, spatial relationships). The study design demonstrates how the persona and journey mapping techniques can be valuable knowledge translation tools, providing rich experience data for organizations to evaluate healthcare services. Thus, when used in conjunction, personas and journey maps hold promise to be valuable design and evaluative tools in the assessment of simple and complex healthcare scenarios.

6 Introducing Emma

The Emma persona (Fig. 2) was created inspired by the iron deficiency research of Hanif and Anwer (2023) along with Tang and Sholzberg (2024) and data from the World Health Organization (WHO) (World Health Organisation 2021). The authors detail that iron deficiency is the most common and widespread nutritional deficiency in the world, and state it can be challenging to diagnose, as the symptoms can be vague and easily missed (Hanif and Anwer 2023; Tang and Sholzberg 2024). In females, the risk of iron deficiency and related anemia can increase during reproductive years (Tang and Sholzberg 2024), therefore this persona (Fig. 2) was created with these factors in mind, using a combination of software (i.e., UXPressia®;

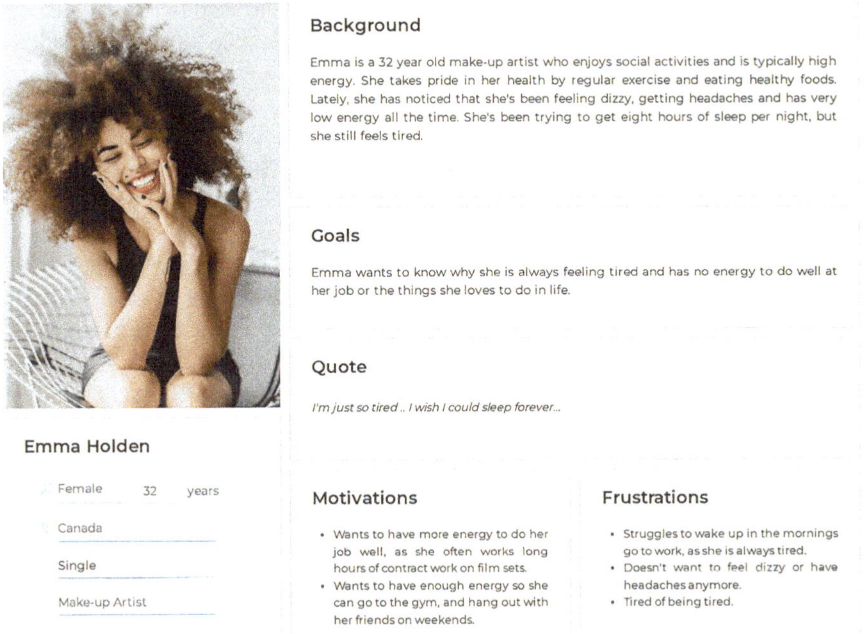

Fig. 2 Application of the Emma Persona Evaluation Approach

Microsoft PowerPoint®). The persona provides context into a unique enduser (i.e., patient) perspective while seeking healthcare services and interfacing with the health system to treat a medical concern. Emma is a 32-year-old Canadian female and a make-up artist by trade. She enjoys the social components of her job, and the long hours don't typically bother her, as she is excited by the work she does while working in the film industry. Emma is a high-energy person by nature, in good physical shape; she eats a well-balanced diet and tries to get eight hours of sleep each night. Recently, she has been experiencing extreme fatigue, dizziness, and headaches but doesn't know why. Lately, she has been finding even getting out of bed a challenge and has not had the energy to do the long hours that her work entails. She overheard one of her clients describe their vitamin deficiency and is worried that she may have something wrong as well. She doesn't want to go to the doctor, but instinctually feels she should.

Henceforth the Emma persona (Fig. 2) will be applied to the five journey mapping techniques to illustrate how her personal experiences (i.e., experience data) can be utilized as rich data sources for service design and evaluation. The application of the Emma persona used in conjunction with the five different journey map perspectives aligns with the multifactorial approach necessary to adequately evaluate healthcare services in real-world settings. A thorough analysis of healthcare services requires stratified evaluation and perspectives. Scenarios should be dissected from various vantage points to understand the human experience of the patients and providers as they interact with health systems. Such data can inform operational planning and assess service efficiency and utilization, and resource (i.e., human, financial, technological) allocation. As such stratified examples of Emma's patient experience are provided in context.

7 Mental (Cognitive) Model Map Evaluative Technique

The Mental (cognitive) Model Map details the cognitive experiences of a person and what the internal thoughts and feelings are in the desired scenario to be evaluated. This technique displays the end-to-end cognitive experience of an individual, presents a sequenced hierarchical visualization, and views a patient's perception of an organization or service (Joseph et al. 2020, 2022e, 2023c). Essentially, this technique garners data from the contents of internal dialogue and can be a valuable tool for understanding human behavior in relation to systems, beliefs, knowledge, and theories (Payne 2012). In this scenario the cognitive thoughts and mental states of the Emma persona are illustrated diagrammatically (Fig. 3) as she contemplates and evaluates the benefits and consequences to remedy her Problem Statement (i.e.,Why am I so tired all the time?) and each action that she can take: (1) Research Symptoms Online, (2) Consult with Mom, (3) Consult with a Medical Doctor (MD), (4) Self-manage her Condition, and (5) Sleep more.

The Mental (Cognitive) Model Map is a complicated journey mapping technique, that provides simplified, and high -level insights into the complexities of decision making and the human mind. This journey map illustrates an example of

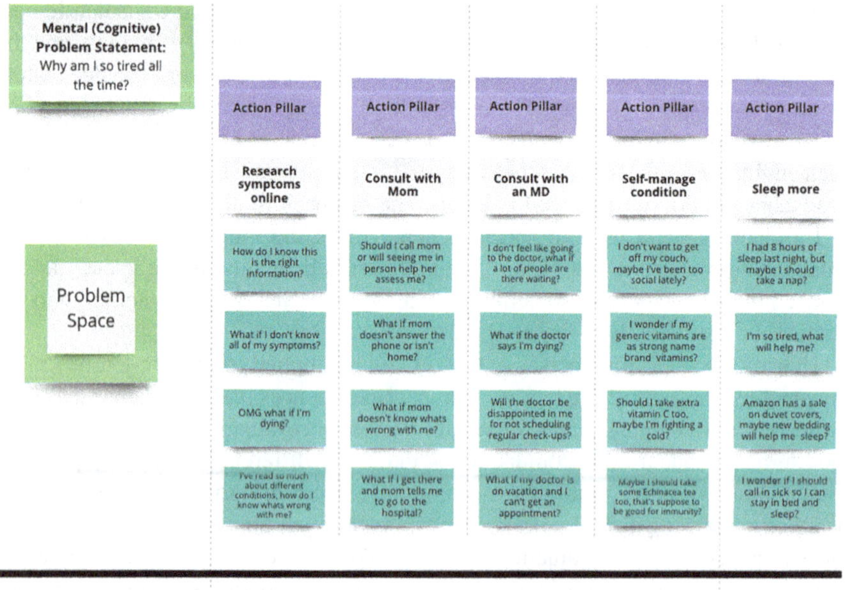

Fig. 3 Application of a Mental (Cognitive) Model Map Evaluation Technique

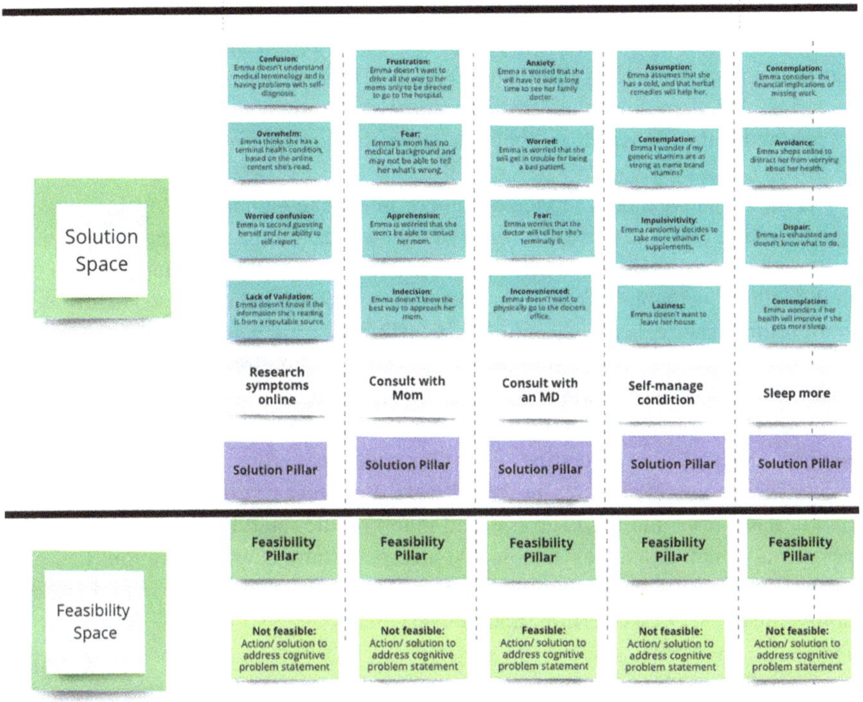

Fig. 3 (continued)

an individual's cognitive processes, mental states, and perceptions of a service, activity, or organization (Kalbach 2016; Joseph et al. 2020, 2022e, 2023c; Young 2008). This technique (Fig. 3) adopted from Kalbach (2016), Young (2008), and Joseph (2020, 2022e, 2023c) was created leveraging a combination of software (i.e., Microsoft PowerPoint®; Miro©).The figure is guided by the Problem Statement and is comprised of three cognitive analysis segments: (1) Problem Space, (2) Solution Space, and (3) Feasibility Space. The Problem Statement 'Why am I so tired all the time?' establishes the context for the evaluation, and the Problem Space details the potential actions (i.e., Action pillars) Emma could take to remediate her tiredness: (1) Research Symptoms Online, (2) Consult with Mom, (3) Consult with an MD, (4) Self-manage Condition, and (5) Sleep more. Each Action Pillar displays the sequenced categories of thought associated with each of the five potential actions. The Solution Space, the second segment details the potential solutions and outcomes (i.e., Solution Pillars) that correspond with each Action Pillar option. The Solution Space provides context into the potential outcome of each thought choice. Lastly the Feasibility Space is the thought synthesis segment for decisive action and choice. The Feasibility Pillars assesses and compare each Action Pillar with its corresponding Solution Pillar to establish the most effective path forward to remediate the Problem Statement (i.e., Problem Space). The thought synthesis findings are then established (i.e., feasible, not feasible). For effective interpretative consistency of the Mental (Cognitive) Map, analysis should commence at the points of intersection of the bilaterally divided Problem Space and Solution Space, and it should be read bottom up from the centre line (Young 2008). In other words the top segment (i.e., Problem Space) is the inverse of the middle segment (i.e., Solution Space), with the Feasibility Space a seperate but interrelated segment read top down.).

The findings reveal how service designers are able to gain insight by understanding the motivations and drivers of the end-user's (i.e., Emma's patient perspective) illustrated internal dialogue. Thus, they are able to understand the language of the mind. Gaining valuable information on Emma's thought patterns specifically with regard to how she feels about going to the MD, receiving a service, and managing her own health (i.e., Actions, Solutions, Feasibility). Therefore, as depicted (Fig. 1) service design and evaluation should commence with the Mental (Cognitive) Map technique to gain insight into the end-users' (i.e., patients, providers, citizens) perspectives, values, and intention of using and delivering healthcare services. Understanding and evaluating the key drivers of patient healthcare service utilization via interviews and focus groups and mapping the interview data will assist in operational planning and sustainable resource procurement and allocation (i.e., hiring staff, purchasing technology). This visual data can also inform health system improvements, service offerings, and delivery methods.

8 Experience Map Evaluative Technique

The Experience Map details the human experiences of an individual's activity which is not specific to a single product, service, or organization (i.e., can include experiences with multiple organizations or services) in the desired scenario to be evaluated (Joseph et al. 2020, 2022e, 2023c). This technique displays the end-to-end human experience of an individual, presents a sequenced chronological visualization, and views an end-users' (i.e., human) perception of an organization or service and is typically comprised of multiple columns and rows (Joseph et al. 2020, 2022e, 2023c). Thus, the value of the Experience Map (Fig. 4) lies in its ability to detail the end-to-end human experience (Joseph et al. 2020, 2022e, 2023c). In this scenario we see Emma go through four phases as she becomes aware of her condition and contemplates going to the MD: (1) Awareness - Health Considerations, (2) Initial Consultation - Doctors Office, (3) Blood Work - Laboratory (lab), and (4) Follow Up Consult - Diagnosis.

The evaluative findings reveal Emma's activities, internal dialogue, and her experience interacting with her MD during the consultation. It describes how she felt during the consult when her MD was distracted by technology (i.e., the computer), her experience at the lab, and then finally her diagnosis. Such insights are beneficial to not only the healthcare organization that provided the siloed healthcare services but the MDs and lab personnel as well. Workflow improvements would lead to a better experience for Emma, and the scenario also provides insight into her motivations, triggers, and how improvements to the overall service delivery could

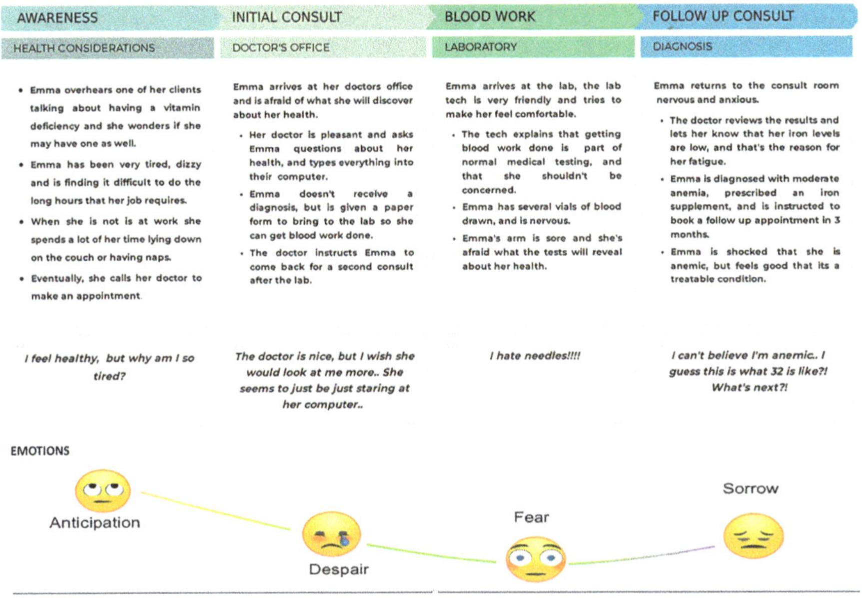

Fig. 4 Application of an Experience Map Evaluation Technique

be made. The simplified illustration designed using varied software (i.e., Microsoft PowerPoint®; UXPressia®) also details the categorization of Emma's emotions (i.e., the emotive layer) within each column, during each phase of her journey. Such a scenario could be executed in real-world settings via interviewing patients and MDs after their consults, and then tabulating their interview data in aggregate into Experience Journey Map diagrams for evaluation and analysis (Joseph et al. 2020, 2022e, 2023c).

9 Customer Journey Map Evaluative Technique

The Customer Journey Map details the consumer experiences of an individual's activity which is specific to a single product, service, or organization (i.e., can only include experiences with a single organization, product, or service) in the desired scenario to be evaluated (Joseph et al. 2020, 2022e, 2023c). Although perceivably similar to the Experience Journey Map and software origins (i.e., Microsoft PowerPoint®; UXPressia®), this technique differs in that an individual is interfacing with a specific product or service only, whereas the latter can involve multiple organizations or diverse services within an organization or several organizations (i.e., seeking treatment various hospitals or clinics). This technique displays the end-to-end consumer experience in sequenced chronological order, views end-users (i.e., people) as consumers of a specific product or organization, and displays information in multiple columns and rows. In this scenario (Fig. 5) we see Emma go through

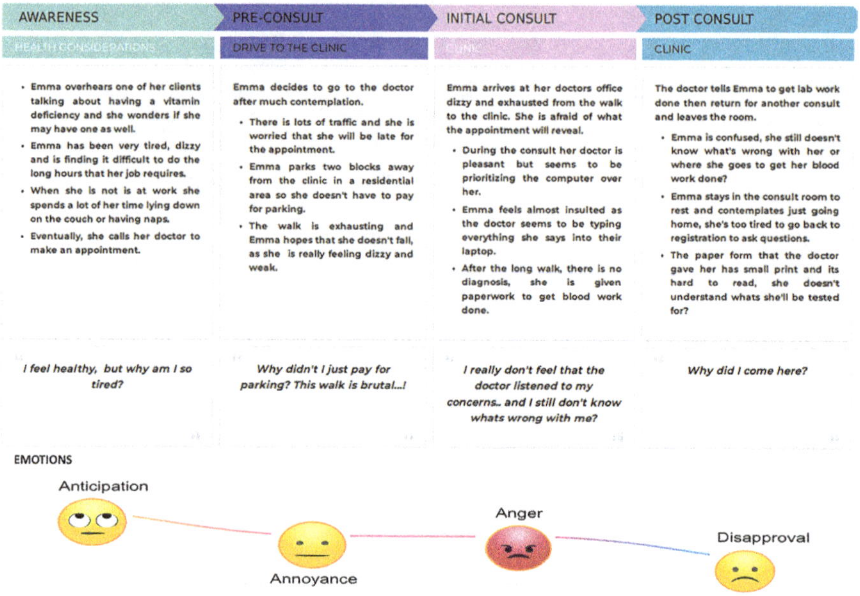

Fig. 5 Application of a Customer Journey Map Evaluation Technique

four phases as she seeks medical care for her condition by going to the MD: (1) Awareness - Health Considerations, (2) Pre Consult - Drive to the Clinic, (3) Initial Consult - Clinic, and (4) Post Consult - Clinic.

Emma's activities, experiences, and internal dialogue in the Awareness phase are illustrated (Fig. 5) as she contemplates going to the MD. Next, we see how she felt during the Pre Consult phase getting to the appointment, avoiding paying for parking and having to walk when feeling unwell. Emma's frustrations and anger are illustrated by the emotive layer of the journey map—she is confused by the inconsistent communication from her time-pressed MD. Lastly, Emma's disapproval of her overall experience as a consumer of a healthcare service is realized via the last column of the journey map (i.e., Post Consult phase). This evaluation is helpful, as it could lend perspective to the clinic in assessing its overall capacity and effectiveness in providing healthcare services. The evaluation of Emma's experience also highlights the importance of the MD–patient relationship, and how inadequate communication can create barriers to care, frustration, and potentially lead to poor healthcare outcomes. The scenario also depicts that technology was a barrier to effective and human-centered care. It is unclear if the MD was learning to use a new clinical system on their computer, didn't receive sufficient training, or if the root cause of their distraction was workload related. This example also illustrates tangible benefits to health service evaluators when using this combined approach in real-world settings (e.g., via multi-stakeholder interviews, observations, focus group activities).

10 Service Blueprint Map Technique

The Service Blueprint Map (Fig. 6) provides an overview of the overall service delivery experience provided by the organization. It displays how services are delivered to consumers across all facets of the service experience. Although each journey mapping technique provides a human-centered lens and context into the organizational sphere, the Service Blueprint Map is frequently used to evaluate services, as each actor and every business unit touch point is detailed in the diagrammatic representation. This technique illustrates the end-to-end service experience in sequenced chronological order and provides a view of relationships between people, processes, and service delivery using columns and multiple rows (Joseph et al. 2020, 2022e, 2023c). In this scenario each of Emma's patient actions (i.e., activities, interactions) are identified as well as her trajectory across business units in chronological order: (1) Call clinic to make appointment, (2) Arrive at clinic, (3) Provide identification and Explain health issues, (4) Initial consult and receives blood requisition for lab testing, (5) Visits lab, (6) Second consultation, (7) Visit pharmacy to pick up prescription, and (8) Leave clinic.

The visual evaluation (Fig. 6) was created using software (i.e., Lucidchart©; Microsoft PowerPoint®) and clearly details Emma's end-to-end service experience and demonstrates each activity and actor (i.e., healthcare stakeholder) that she engaged with through her interactions with the health system: (1) Physical evidence, (2) Patient actions, (3) Onstage actions, (4) Backstage actions, (5) Other support processes. Thus, ineffective processes, organizational gaps, and process bottlenecks displayed (Fig. 6) were quickly identifiable through the Service Blueprint evaluation; demonstrating the potential for further analysis and remediation. Therefore, the operational data can be viewed, collected, and evaluated to support knowledge translation of root cause issues in service delivery that impacted Emma's holistic experience in seeking care. This technique, when applied in real-world settings, can facilitate quick insights into organizational problem areas and identify opportunities

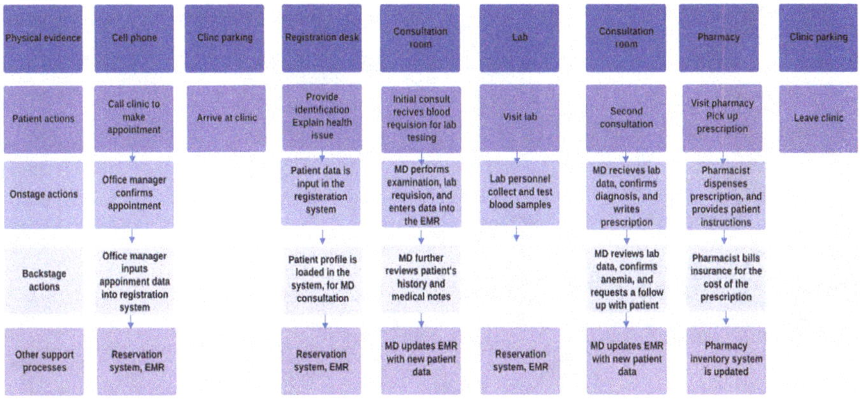

Fig. 6 Application of a Service Blueprint Map Evaluation Technique

to improve internal processes and procedures. To effectively employ the Service Blueprint Mapping technnique, evaluations should span broad business units at a macro organizational level where shared services, and cross-functional activity are intrinsic to operations.

11 Spatial Map Evaluative Technique

Lastly, Spatial Maps are excellent tools to display disparate data or geographic patterns, and trends. They can have a range from heat map types, to elaborate scatter points visualizations designed from elaborate graphical interfaces. In this scenario a simple scatter point graph was created (i.e., Microsoft Excel®; Microsoft PowerPoint®) and applied to the Emma persona (Fig. 2) with data obtained from the WHO's Global Health Observatory (World Health Organisation 2021). This dataset was selected as it enabled a simplified high-level spatial comparison. Specifically, the data showcased the percentage of women between the ages 15 and 49 who have moderate anemia and positioned Emma among her global peers for comparative spatial analysis (World Health Organization 2021). This journey map technique is currently in flux and will continue to evolve as the utilization of big datasets, and visualization software solutions continue to emerge across the global marketplace. The Spatial Map technique (Fig. 7) displays broad relationships and interactions in an unsequenced and spatially distributed fashion. The benefit of this technique lies in its ability to effectively identify and illustrate relational patterns across geographic locations (Joseph et al. 2020, 2022e, 2023c; Kalbach 2016). Thus, the Spatial Map technique was applied to the Emma persona, to simplistically demonstrate how spatially disperate data could be displayed across four different geographies: Canada, the United States (USA), Brazil, and Mexico.

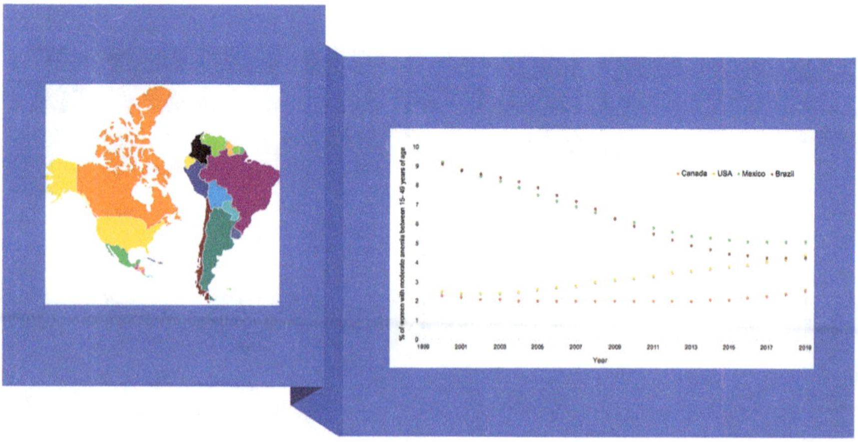

Fig. 7 Application of a Spatial Map Evaluation Technique

The intent of this evaluation scenario was to demonstrate how the Emma persona, a 32-year-old Canadian female with moderate anemia, fared in her country and when compared to women in her age range globally. The visualization details trends and relationships over time between the years of 2000–2019 of women with moderate anemia across Canada, the USA, Brazil, and Mexico. As Emma's diagnosis was moderate anemia; the evaluative findings provide comparative clarity into the prevalence of moderate anemia for women in Emma's age range (i.e., 15–49 years old), with data being derived from the WHO's Global Health Observatory (World Health Organisation 2021). Additionally, a complementary geographic visualization was embedded in the Spatial Map visualization to provide further geographic context into the spatially distributed regions of the WHO's study's participants. Although both spatial visualizations are different, they are complementary in expressing relationships and patterns of regionally dispersed data.

Information visualization can improve the overall decision-making process and decision capabilities of business leaders and improve the interpretation of data (Eberhard 2023; Joseph et al. 2023b; Shneiderman 1996). Thus, in lieu of demonstrating the numeric data set (World Health Organization 2021), this journey mapping technique complements intrinsic human perceptual and information processing abilities such as image recall and the capability to detect nuanced changes in colour, size, and shape (Joseph et al. 2021, 2023b; Shneiderman and Plaisant 2010). The benefit of conducting Spatial Mapping evaluation can be multifaceted and span many industries and organizational needs. The Spatial Map can also provide valuable insights to help organizations, industries, countries understand complex relationships and patterns across geographies (Shneiderman and Plaisant, 2015). In a healthcare context it can serve as a tool to establish patient outcomes and disease trends, from geographical contexts. Such approaches were commonly used to manage COVID-19, as the disease trends across global health systems and were closely monitored, and evaluated (Joseph et al. 2022b; Praharaj et al. 2023; Vahedi et al. 2022a, 2022b). The insights gleaned from the visualized data synthesis (i.e., Spatial Map creation) can inform holistic and strategic organizational decisions, and improve service delivery practices (Joseph et al. 2023d; Shneiderman and Plaisant, 2015). The Spatial Map is well positioned to be an effective high-level solution to complex data analysis. It holds promise to alleviate some of the challenges associated with processing, interpreting, and displaying large volumes and varieties of available data, by providing an effective high-level solution to complex data analysis (Joseph et al. 2023d; Shneiderman and Plaisant, 2015).

12 Knowledge Translation of the Five Journey Map Evaluative Techniques

Albeit a simplified healthcare scenario was used to display the five diversified diagrammatical representations contextualized by the Emma persona; Figs. 3, 4, 5, 6, and 7 demonstrated that there are differences and similarities between each technique. The intention here is to provide an application of the Emma persona (Fig. 2) utilizing the various lenses of each journey map technique. The varied applications reveal the powerful knowledge translation potential and interpretive ease in which each diverse visualized scenario presents. Conceptually speaking, Emma's human story was stratified into five different frames (i.e., five journey mapping techniques), and analyzed simultaneously from various perspectives.

Moreover, each journey mapping technique provides a rich set of data which can foster continuous improvements in the healthcare landscape, if adopted at scale and conducted iteratively in organizations. It is important to note that the illustrations of the five fictional scenarios and techniques were created with the intent to make them simple high-level scenarios, which could be succinctly diagrammatically represented, and easily visualized for the context of the chapter. Thus, the actual complexities of healthcare services, organizations, and patient and healthcare provider perspectives are not truly represented by the narratives (Figs. 3, 4, 5, 6, and 7). When applied in real-world settings the five journey mapping techniques will produce more elaborate and complex journey maps; they will present a multitude of service delivery intersections, and operational pain points depending on the chosen evaluative need.

13 Journey Map Evaluation Guide

13.1 Purpose: Facilitate Appropriate Journey Map Technique Selection and Application

The Journey Map Evaluation Guide can help healthcare service providers and stakeholders to assess which journey map technique is most applicable for their given business scenario and evaluative need. As demonstrated in Figs. 3, 4, 5, 6, and 7 the technique must be complementary to the desired organizational outcomes assessment and must serve the need of the evaluation strategy to be an effective evaluative practice. Thus, with proper organizational alignment, the data outputs of the mapping activities can provide valuable information which can be translated to action items for service improvements.

The illustrative scenarios depicted by each technique (Figs. 3, 4, 5, 6, and 7) provided unique contexts and data points, which could be collected in aggregate and assessed organizationally. The opportunities to use such rich data are endless and could catalyze targeted initiatives such as change management, procurement, service evaluations, HIT and HIS implementations, and resource management evaluation activities (Joseph and Monkman 2025; Joseph et al. 2022a, 2023b; Fu et al. 2020; Stefanicka-Wojtas and Kurpas 2023). Moreover, the Journey Map Evaluation Guide (Fig. 8) can be used to select the most effective journey map technique to satisfy a specific health service evaluation or organizational inquiry and application (Joseph et al. 2020, 2022e, 2023c).

Although the Journey Map Evaluation Guide is presented in a healthcare context in this chapter, it should not be restricted by industry, and can be applied to the evaluative needs across sectors (Joseph et al. 2022e). The Journey Map Evaluation

Map	Mental (Cognitive) Model Map	Experience Map	Customer Journey Map	Service Blueprint Map	Spatial Map
Focus	End-to-end **cognitive** experience	End-to-end **human** experience	End-to-end **consumer** experience	End-to-end **service** experience	Broad relationships and **interactions**
Flow	Sequenced hierarchical visualization	Sequenced chronological visualization	Sequenced chronological visualization	Sequenced chronological visualization	Unsequenced spatially distributed visualization
Intent	View of user perception of a service, activity or organization	View of user activity which are not specific to a product, service or organization (i.e., can involve multiple)	Views users as consumers of a specific product, service or organization	View of relationships between people, processes and service delivery	View of relationships between locations, patterns and interactions of spatially arranged data
Form	Bilaterally divided	Multiple columns or rows (e.g., swim lanes)			Spatially arranged information

Fig. 8 The Journey Map Evaluation Guide (used with permission from ISO (Joseph et al. 2022e)

Guide (Fig. 8) provides an efficient comparison of the different types of journey mapping techniques: (1) Mental (Cognitive) Model Map, (2) Experience Map, (3) Customer Journey Map, (4) Service Blueprint Map, and (5) Spatial Map. It enables service designers and applicable stakeholders to understand the differences of each technique across four categories: (1) Focus, (2) Flow, (3) Intent, and (4) Form (Joseph et al. 2020, 2022e, 2023c). The Focus category highlights the type of experience each journey map technique evaluates including: end-to-end cognitive experience; end-to-end human experience; end-to-end consumer experience; end-to-end service experience; and broad relationships (Joseph et al. 2020, 2022e, 2023c). The Flow category describes the visualization styles: sequenced hiearachical visualization; sequence chronological visualization; and unsequenced spatially distributed visualization (Joseph et al. 2020, 2022e, 2023c). The Intent category explains the perspective and context that each journey map technique evaluates: user perception of a service, activity or organization; user activities not specific to a product, service or organization; users as consumers of a specific product, service or organization; holistic relationships between people, processes and service delivery; spatial relationships between locations, patterns and interactions (Joseph et al. 2020, 2022e, 2023c). Lastly, the Form category details the structural layout of the journey map techniques with range from bilaterally divided, multiple columns or rows, or spatially arranged information (Joseph et al. 2020, 2022e, 2023c).

14 Journey Map Decision Support Tool

14.1 Purpose: Streamline Technique Selection

To further streamline the journey map classification process, and cater to varied human perceptual preferences, the Journey Map Decision Support Tool Fig. 9 is

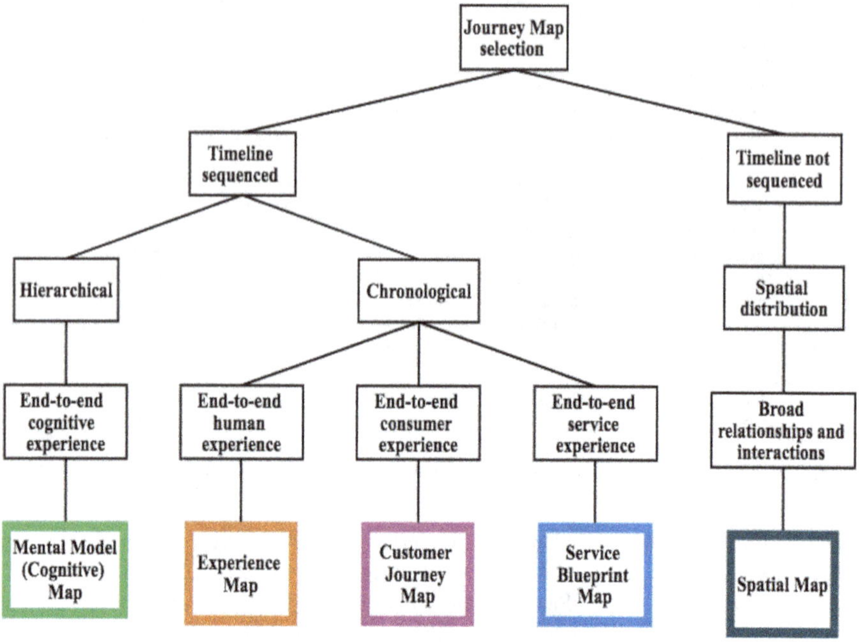

Fig. 9 The Journey Map Decision Support Tool (used with permission from ISO (Joseph et al. 2022e)

a complementary resource that can be used alongside the Fig. 8 Evaluation Guide (Joseph et al. 2022e). This tool can assist time pressed healthcare and organizational stakeholders (i.e., healthcare administrator, MD, patient, citizen) quickly classify the most effective technique for their desired evaluative outcome. Albeit the visual interpretation of the Fig. 9 image is intuitive and easy to interpret, its textual description is not. The Journey Map Decision Support Tool can be conceptualized as a flowchart-like decision tree, to assist with journey map technique selection. The selection process begins with "Journey Map selection," as the decision starting point (i.e., initial decision node), which then branches into two secondary decision nodes: (1) "Timeline sequenced," and (2)"Timeline not sequenced." Next the "Timeline sequenced," decision node category is then further branched and divided into the "Hierarchical" and "Chronological" decision node categories that each have their own subcomponents. The "Hierarchical" decision pathway leads to "End-to-end cognitive experience," followed by the "Mental Model (Cognitive) Map" decision end node. Whereas the "Chronological" decision pathway is further divided into a set of three decision node branch categories: (a) "End-to-end human experience" leading to the "Experience Map decision end node," (b) "End-to-end consumer experience" leading to the "Customer Journey Map "decision end node, and (c) "End-to-end service experience" leading to the "Service Blueprint Map" decision end node. Contrary to the "Timeline sequenced" secondary decision node, the "Timeline not sequenced" decision pathway is much less complex. This pathway connects to "Spatial distribution" and "Broad relationships and interactions," and results in the "Spatial Map" decision end node.

15 Journey Map Evaluation Guide + Journey Map Decision Support Tool

Using the Journey Map Evaluation Guide in conjunction with the Journey Map Decision Support Tool (Figs. 8 and 9) can enable healthcare stakeholders to effectively select the most appropriate technique for their operational needs and desired observational outcomes (Joseph et al. 2022e). Adherence to both tools (Figs. 8 and 9) will enable standardization of the journey map concept and techniques (Joseph et al. 2022e). Standardization of the mapping activities, data categorization, and nomenclature will ensure that comparable and useful data is collected and visually represented (Joseph et al. 2022e). "There is value in understanding the journey of others to help understand your own" (Chopra 2015), and innovative, empathetic and sympathetic approaches are required to improve the state of healthcare services (Joseph and Monkman 2025). Thus, adequately and systematically collecting the human experience data associated with organizational processes, products, or services can facilitate human-centered practices, leading to the adoption of an HCD organizational philosophy. An organizational culture rooted in HCD principles places humans at the heart of health systems (Norman 2023). Further, standardization of the journey mapping techniques could also facilitate the expedient exposure of pain points via the stratified visualizations, which could result in cost savings, efficiency gains, and effective resource allocation for health systems (Joseph et al. 2020, 2022e, 2023c).

Thus, the five journey mapping techniques, the Journey Map Evaluation Guide and the Journey Map Decision Support Tool provide a structured and multi-level data collection and classification framework which can catalyze standardization (Joseph et al. 2022e). Standardization enables scalability and provides a conduit for wide adoption, application, implementation, and evaluation of these tools in healthcare settings and practice. Such strategies could provide structure and generalizability to health service evaluation such as business process planning, project management, HIT and HIT procurement and implementations, and guide legislative policies. Standardized evaluative metrics could provide consistency and contribute to a safer, more efficient, and cost-effective healthcare systems. The continuous data points from each diagrammatic scenario could also provide rich data to inform learning health systems (LHS) globally (Joseph et al. 2020, 2023a, 2023b, 2023c; Payne et al. 2022).

16 Future Directions

The concept of journey mapping can lead to innovative evaluative practices such as the Visualized Combined Experience Diagram (VCE) presented by Joseph et al. (2023b) which demonstrated a novel diagram which combines three visualization techniques a persona, an Experience Map, and Sankey diagram to illustrate a patient experience in the context of social determinants of health, and mortality from COVID-19. Further cross-disciplinary approaches to evaluate healthcare services and remediate complex healthcare service delivery issues may also have merit (Joseph et al. 2023d). The potential benefits of applying service design and evaluative research concepts in healthcare are endless; a study demonstrated the feasibility of how a Customer Journey Map and a Logic Model could be used in unison to identify barriers to care and remedy service delivery gaps in healthcare settings (Joseph et al. 2023d). Another application of the Customer Journey Mapping technique was illustrated in a qualitative study that demonstrated the complexity of interpreting and accessing online lab results for Canadian citizens (Joseph et al. 2022d). The mapping activity succinctly revealed opportunities for functionality enhancement for the lab portal, and illustrated a combination of problematic factors faced by the participant including: eHealth literacy, limited access to providers, and difficulty interpreting results (Joseph et al. 2022d). Innovation and transformation in healthcare are urgently required to make it safer, more effective, and conducive to patient and healthcare provider care (Joseph and Monkman 2025). Thus, the structured and proposed multi-level data collection methodology can not only inform LHSs, but provide a set of best practices so that human experience and quality improvement data can serve as computable data streams to catalyze continuous learnings and knowledge generation (Embi et al. 2021; Guise et al. 2018; Joseph et al. 2020, 2022e, 2023c).

17 Conclusion

This chapter introduced varied components of design thinking, the persona, and five journey mapping techniques (Hanif and Anwer 2023; Bartels et al. 2023; Tang and Sholzberg 2024; Joseph et al. 2020, 2022e, 2023c). Additionally, there was an application of the five diagrammatically diverse journey map techniques in which similar, yet contextually diverse scenarios were applied to the Emma Persona. The Journey Map Evaluation Guide and Decision Support Tool (Joseph et al. 2022e) streamlined journey map technique selection, and revealed the importance of standardized evaluation practices to safeguard data quality, and facilitate adoption across sectors. The power of the journey map lies within their data source, which stems from the shared, emotional and often relatable human experiences. Specifically, the visualizations illustrate narratives of human stories and experiences which resonate with the human collective (Norman 2007). Visualized stories are powerful tools as they can evoke emotion and catalyze human connection, empathy, and relatedness. Allowing the evaluator to envision themselves as the end- user (i.e., patient, healthcare providers) in a similar situation enables them to recognize their own humanity by reflecting on their own feelings and experiences (Joseph and Monkman 2025).

Thus, when used in conjunction, personas and journey map techniques have the potential to be engaging empathetic and situational tools. In this study, the Emma persona was anthropomorphized, she had a story, and her various journeys in seeking care were illustrated visually from five different stratified lenses (Joseph et al. 2020, 2022e, 2023c). By providing an emotional connection to an individual's healthcare journey, the transactional and (often callous) perspectives associated with healthcare services and delivery can move towards human-centered care modalities.

Understanding how the human fits into healthcare in a service delivery capacity is vital to understanding the holistic circle of care and is intrinsic to strategic health service evaluation and utilization. Many operational shortcomings or failed HIS and IT projects stem from not engaging with the right people at the right time (Hudson 2009). Therefore, empowering patients, healthcare providers, and stakeholders by including them as collaborators in the design and evaluation of healthcare services could ameliorate the quality, efficacy, and safety of services (Joseph and Monkman 2025; Quintana and Safran 2015). "With the passage of time, the psychology of people stays the same, but the tools and objects in the world change," (Norman 2007) thus governments, industry, and designers must broaden their services, and incorporate human-centered evaluation strategies to support the true holistic circle of care (Norman 2023).

References

Bartels SL et al (2023) Using personas in the development of eHealth interventions for chronic pain: a scoping review and narrative synthesis. Internet Interv 32:100619

Bate P, Robert G (2007) Bringing user experience to healthcare improvement: the concepts, methods and practices of experience-based design. CRC Press, Boca Raton

Borges do Nascimento IJ, Abdulazeem H, Vasanthan LT, Martinez EZ, Zucoloto ML, Østengaard L, Azzopardi-Muscat N, Zapata T, Novillo-Ortiz D (2023) Barriers and facilitators to utilizing digital health technologies by healthcare professionals. NPJ Dig Med 61:28

Chandler C, Foltz PW, Elvevåg B (2022) Improving the applicability of AI for psychiatric applications through human-in-the-loop methodologies. Schizophr Bull 48:949–957

Chopra G (2015) Kobe Bryant's Muse [Film]. Showtime Sports

Cutler DM (2023) Health system change in the wake of COVID-19. JAMA Health Forum 4:e234355

Davis FD, Granić A (2024) Evolution of TAM. In: The technology acceptance model. Human–computer interaction series. Springer, Cham, pp 19–57

Eberhard K (2023) The effects of visualization on judgment and decision-making: a systematic literature review. Manage Rev Q 73:167–214

El Burai Felix S, Yusuf H, Ritchey M, Romano S, Namulanda G, Wilkins N, Boehmer TK (2024) A standard framework for evaluating large health care data and related resources. MMWR Suppl 73:1–13

Embi PJ, Payne PRO, Friedman CP (2021) Learning from data: a recurring feature on the science and practice of data-driven learning health systems. Learn Health Syst 6(1):e10302

Erlirianto LM, Ali AHN, Herdiyanti A (2015) The implementation of the human, organization, and technology–fit (HOT–fit) framework to evaluate the electronic medical record (EMR) system in a hospital. Proc Comp Sci 72:580–587

Figueroa CA, Harrison R, Chauhan A, Meyer L (2019) Priorities and challenges for health leadership and workforce management globally: a rapid review. BMC Health Serv Res 19:1–11

Fu MR, Kurnat-Thoma E, Starkweather A, Henderson WA, Cashion AK, Williams JK, Katapodi MC, Reuter-Rice K, Hickey KT, Barcelona de Mendoza V, Calzone K, Conley YP, Anderson CM, Lyon DE, Weaver MT, Shiao PK, Constantino RE, Wung S-F, Hammer MJ, Voss JG (2020) Precision health: a nursing perspective. Int J Nurs Sci 7:5–12

Guise JM, Savitz LA, Friedman CP (2018) Mind the gap: putting evidence into practice in the era of learning health systems. J Gen Intern Med 33(12):2237–2239

Hanif N, Anwer F (2023) Chronic iron deficiency. In: StatPearls. StatPearls Publishing, Treasure Island

Honekamp W, Ostermann H (2011) Evaluation of a prototype health information system using the FITT framework. J Innov Health Inf 19:47–49

Hudson W (2009) The challenges of user-centred design. In: Computer aided-design of user interfaces VI. Springer, London, pp 1–8

Joseph AL, Kushniruk AW, Borycki EM (2020) Patient journey mapping: current practices, challenges and future opportunities in healthcare. Knowl Manage E-Learning 12:387–404

Joseph AL, Borycki EM, Kushniruk AW (2021) Alert fatigue and errors caused by technology: a scoping review and introduction to the flow of cognitive processing model. Knowl Manage E-Learning 13:500–521

Joseph AL, Stringer E, Borycki EM, Kushniruk AW (2022a) Evaluative frameworks and models for health information systems (HIS) and health information technologies (HIT). Stud Health Technol Inform 289:280–285

Joseph AL, Monkman H, Kushniruk A, Borycki EM (2022b) The utilization of health informatics interventions in the COVID-19 pandemic: a scoping review. Stud Health Technol Inform 295:163–166

Joseph AL, Monkman H, Kushniruk A, Borycki EM (2022c) Are personal health records (PHRs) facilitating patient safety? A scoping review. Stud Health Technol Inform 294:535–539

Joseph AL, Monkman H, MacDonald L, Kushniruk AW (2022d) Contextualizing online laboratory (lab) results and mapping the patient journey. Stud Health Technol Inform 295:175–178

Joseph AL, Monkman H, Kushniruk AW (2022e) An evaluation guide and decision support tool for journey maps in healthcare and beyond. Stud Health Technol Inform 295:171–174

Joseph AL, Shah LM, Kushniruk A, Quintana Y (2023a) A human-centered physician journey. Stud Health Technol Inform 304:76–77

Joseph AL, Monkman H, Minshall SR, Quintana Y (2023b) Humanizing big data and detailing social determinants of health via information visualizations. Stud Health Technol Inform 304:112–116

Joseph AL, Monkman H, Kushniruk A, Quintana Y (2023c) Exploring patient journey mapping and the learning health system: scoping review. JMIR Hum Factors 10:e43966

Joseph AL, Costello J, Monkman H, Quintana Y (2023d) Applying logic to the healthcare journey. Stud Health Technol Inform 30:474–475

Joseph AL, Monkman H (2025) The Kübler-Ross five stages of grief model: a framework for human-centered health informatics. Stud Health Technol Inform 326:70–74

Junaid SB, Imam AA, Balogun AO, De Silva LC, Surakat YA, Kumar G, Abdulkarim M, Shuaibu AN, Garba A, Sahalu Y, Mohammed A, Mohammed TY, Abdulkadir BA, Abba AA, Kakumi NAI, Mahamad S (2022) Recent advancements in emerging technologies for healthcare management systems: a survey. Healthcare 10:1–45

Kalbach J (2016) Mapping experiences: a guide to creating value through journeys, blueprints and diagrams, 1st edn. O'Reilly, Beijing

Koppel R, Kuziemsky C (2019) Usability across health information technology systems: searching for commonalities and consistency. Stud Health Technol Inform 264:649–653

Labkoff S, Oladimeji B, Kannry J, Solomonides A, Leftwich R, Koski E, Joseph AL, Lopez-Gonzalez M, Fleisher LA, Nolen K, Dutta S, Levy DR, Price A, Barr PJ, Hron JD, Lin B, Srivastava G, Pastor N, Luque US, Thi T (2024) Toward a responsible future: recommendations for AI-enabled clinical decision support. J Am Med Inform Assoc 31:2730–2739

Liu L, Miguel-Cruz A (2022) Technology adoption and diffusion in healthcare at onset of COVID-19 and beyond. Healthc Manage Forum 35:161–167

Longworth GR, Goh K, Agnello DM, Messiha K, Beeckman M, Zapata-Restrepo JR, Cardon G, Chastin S, Giné-Garriga M (2023) A review of implementation and evaluation frameworks for public health to inform co-creation. Eur J Pub Health 22:39

Massey PM, Chiang SC, Rose M, Murray RM, Rockett M, Togo E, Klassen AC, Manganello JA, Leader AE (2021) Development of personas to communicate narrative-based information about the HPV vaccine on twitter. Front Dig Health 3:682639

Nielsen L (2013) Personas - user focused design. Springer, London

Nielsen L (2018) Design personas - new ways, new contexts. Persona Stud 4:1

Norman DA (2007) Emotional design: why we love (or hate) everyday things, 1st edn. Basic Books, New York

Norman DA (2023) Design for a better world: meaningful, sustainable, humanity centered. The MIT Press, Cambridge

Nunes DS, Zhang P, Sá Silva J (2015) A survey on human-in-the-loop applications towards an internet of all. IEEE Commun Surv Tutorials 17:944–965

Payne SJ (2012) Mental models in human–computer interaction. In: Human computer interaction handbook, 3rd edn. Routledge, London

Payne PRO, Wilcox AB, Embi PJ, Longhurst CA (2022) Better together: integrating biomedical informatics and healthcare IT operations to create a learning health system during the COVID-19 pandemic. Learn Health Syst 6:e10309

Praharaj S, Solis P, Wentz EA (2023) Deploying geospatial visualization dashboards to combat the socioeconomic impacts of COVID-19. Environ Plan B Urban Anal City Sci 50:1262–1279

Pruitt J, Grudin J (2003) Personas: practice and theory. In: Designing for user experiences. ACM, New York, pp 1–15

Quintana Y, Safran C (2015) Global challenges in people-centered E-health. Stud Health Technol Inform 216:977

Rozenblit L, Price A, Solomonides A, Joseph AL, Srivastava G, Labkoff S, deBronkart D, Singh R, Dattani K, Lopez-Gonzalez M, Barr PJ, Koski E, Lin B, Cheung E, Weiner MG, Williams T, Bui T, Quintana Y (2025) Towards a Multi-Stakeholder process for developing responsible ai governance in consumer health. Int J Med Inform 195(9):105713

Shneiderman B (1996) The eyes have it: a task by data type taxonomy for information visualizations. In: Proceedings 1996 IEEE symposium on visual languages. IEEE, Piscataway, pp 336–343

Shneiderman B, Plaisant C (2010) Designing the user interface: strategies for effective human-computer interaction. Pearson Education India

Shneiderman B, Plaisant C (2015) Sharpening analytic focus to cope with big data volume and variety. IEEE Comput Graph Appl 35(3) 10–14

Skivington K, Matthews L, Simpson SA, Craig P, Baird J, Blazeby JM, Boyd KA, Craig N, French DP, McIntosh E, Petticrew M, Rycroft-Malone J, White M, Moore L (2021) A new framework for developing and evaluating complex interventions: update of medical research council guidance. BMJ 374:2061

Stefanicka-Wojtas D, Kurpas D (2023) Personalised medicine-implementation to the healthcare system in Europe (focus group discussions). J Personal Med 13:380

Stickdorn M, Schneider J (2010) This is service design thinking: basics-tools-cases. BIS Publishers, Amsterdam

Sullivan RJ (2023) Outcomes-based standardization: a new approach to an old problem. Nurse Lead 21:569–574

Tang GH, Sholzberg M (2024) Iron deficiency anemia among women: an issue of health equity. Blood Rev 64:101159

Teisberg E, Wallace S, O'Hara S (2020) Defining and implementing value-based health care. Acad Med 95:682–685

Vahedi A, Moghaddasi H, Asadi F, Hosseini AS, Nazemi E (2022a) Applications, features and key indicators for the development of Covid-19 dashboards: a systematic review study. Inf Med 30:100910

Vahedi A et al (2022b) Applications, features and key indicators for the development of Covid-19 dashboards: a systematic review study. Inf Med 30:100910

Vögele C (2015) Behavioral medicine. In: International encyclopedia of the social & behavioral sciences, 2nd edn. Elsevier, Amsterdam, pp 463–469

Watkinson F, Dharmayat KI, Mastellos N (2021) A mixed-method service evaluation of health information exchange in England: technology acceptance and barriers and facilitators to adoption. BMC Health Serv Res 211:737

World Health Organisation (2021) Prevalence of anaemia in women of reproductive age (%). World Health Organisation, Geneva. Available https://www.who.int/data/gho/data/indicators/indicator-details/GHO/prevalence-of-anaemia-in-women-of-reproductive-age-(-)

Young I (2008) Mental models: aligning design strategy with human behavior. In: Ubiquity - association for computing machinery. Rosenfeld Media, Brooklyn

Zhang X, Lin D, Pforsich H, Lin VW (2020) Physician workforce in The United States of America: forecasting nationwide shortages. Hum Resour Health 188:8

Co-production in Health Services Evaluation

Adrienne M. Young, Anja Christoffersen, Dale Trevor, and Kelsey Pateman

Abstract

End-users of health services can and should play a key role in health services evaluation. This chapter describes how people evaluating health services can use co-production to partner with patients, caregivers, and community members in their evaluation. Guidance will be provided to support evaluators to decide what to evaluate, when and how to measure it, and importantly what the data means and what health services should do with it to drive improvement. The "principles

A. M. Young (✉)
Centre for Health Services Research, The University of Queensland, Brisbane, QLD, Australia

Dietetics and Food Services, Royal Brisbane and Women's Hospital, Brisbane, QLD, Australia
e-mail: a.m.young@uq.edu.au

A. Christoffersen
Centre for Health Services Research, The University of Queensland, Brisbane, QLD, Australia

Champion Health Agency, Fortitude Valley, QLD, Australia
e-mail: anja@championhealthagency.com

D. Trevor
Champion Health Agency, Fortitude Valley, QLD, Australia

Consumer Representative, Metro North Health and University Partners, Herston, QLD, Australia

K. Pateman
Centre for Allied Health Research, Royal Brisbane and Women's Hospital, Brisbane, QLD, Australia
e-mail: Kelsey.Pateman@health.qld.gov.au

A. Kaehne, J. Feather (eds.), *Handbook of Health Services Evaluation*,
https://doi.org/10.1007/978-3-031-87869-5_26

of co-production" are explained, and case examples are used to demonstrate how evaluators can move from a mindset of consultation, towards genuine "co-evaluation" where decisions are made together with patients, caregivers, and community members at every stage of the evaluation.

Keywords
Co-production · Co-design · Consumer engagement · Patient and public involvement

1 Introduction

Evaluation of health services ultimately aims to improve efficiency, value, and the service's ability to provide high quality health care for its patients, clients, and the broader community. To determine whether these outcomes are achieved, it stands to reason that the end-users of the health system (i.e., the patients, clients, and community) need to be involved in the evaluation process. Co-production is a way of working, thinking, and approaching each step of your health services evaluation in partnership with end-users (herein referred to as "consumers").

In this chapter, we introduce the concept of co-production in health service evaluation (herein referred to as "co-evaluation") and provide an overview about how to co-evaluate health services with consumers. This chapter is co-authored with two health consumers, who have contributed to the ideas within the main body and case example, as well as providing their "consumer perspective" in designated boxes throughout the chapter.

2 What Is Co-production?

Co-production in healthcare is increasingly recognized as "the right thing to do" from a moral and political perspective, and an aspirational goal to improve the quality and person-centeredness of health services (Lowe et al. 2021). The benefits of co-production include improving person-centeredness of health services and health service design and delivery, deepening relationships and trust between community and health services, building skills, and empowering individuals involved (Gagliardi et al. 2008; Merner et al. 2023; Näslund et al. 2023; Wright et al. 2021). Whilst there is limited research on the benefits of co-evaluation, this should not be interpreted as a lack of value (Lowe et al. 2021), with partnerships with consumers shown to ensure that evaluation data is collected in a way that is relevant and credible, represents the diverse population accessing health services, measures what is important to the community, and builds community pressure to act on this data in a meaningful way (Wright et al. 2021; Gagliardi et al. 2008).

Despite increasing interest in co-production, there is a lack of a universally accepted definition, with "co" approaches such as "co-production," "co-design," and "co-creation" often being used interchangeably (Masterson et al. 2022). In this chapter, we use the term "co-evaluation" to describe the co-production of health services evaluation, which we define as the process of people with professional and lived experience partnering as equals to evaluate and improve health services by listening, learning, and making decisions together at every stage. This definition is based on our own co-production experience (informed by the perspectives of >120 health professionals, health service managers, researchers, and consumers in our health service) and shares commonalities with other definitions related to power sharing and partnership from the start to the end of a project (Involve 2021; Masterson et al. 2022). In this chapter, we use the term "consumers" to describe the "past, current, or future users of the health service" involved in co-evaluation (NSW Health 2023), noting that other terms may be used in other countries or settings (e.g., "patient and public involvement," "citizen involvement," "community engagement," or "engaging with lived experience"). We use the term "consumer" broadly to capture a range of roles, including both designated representatives (who are elected or nominated to contribute on behalf of a group of consumers) and individual consumers (who contribute based on their own health care experience and informal interactions with others).

A key difference between co-evaluation and traditional evaluation approaches is the role and level of influence of consumers in the process. The International Association of Public Participation Spectrum of Public Participation (Fig. 1) has

IAP2 Spectrum of Public Participation

iap2 international association for public participation

IAP2's Spectrum of Public Participation was designed to assist with the selection of the level of participation that defines the public's role in any public participation process. The Spectrum is used internationally, and it is found in public participation plans around the world.

INCREASING IMPACT ON THE DECISION →

	INFORM	CONSULT	INVOLVE	COLLABORATE	EMPOWER
PUBLIC PARTICIPATION GOAL	To provide the public with balanced and objective information to assist them in understanding the problem, alternatives, opportunities and/or solutions.	To obtain public feedback on analysis, alternatives and/or decisions.	To work directly with the public throughout the process to ensure that public concerns and aspirations are consistently understood and considered.	To partner with the public in each aspect of the decision including the development of alternatives and the identification of the preferred solution.	To place final decision making in the hands of the public.
PROMISE TO THE PUBLIC	We will keep you informed.	We will keep you informed, listen to and acknowledge concerns and aspirations, and provide feedback on how public input influenced the decision.	We will work with you to ensure that your concerns and aspirations are directly reflected in the alternatives developed and provide feedback on how public input influenced the decision.	We will look to you for advice and innovation in formulating solutions and incorporate your advice and recommendations into the decisions to the maximum extent possible.	We will implement what you decide.

Fig. 1 International Association of Public Participation (IAP2) Spectrum of Public Participation © International Association of Public Participation 2019 www.iap2.org

been a standard of practice for more than 30 years and builds on previous participation models such as Arnstein's Ladder (Arnstein 1969). The IAP2 spectrum outlines five levels of influence that consumers may have in health service improvement or evaluation. Traditional evaluation approaches may use more passive levels of consumer engagement, where consumers are only consulted (e.g., a survey asking for their feedback or ideas) or involved on a committee but decisions are still ultimately made by the health service or evaluators. In contrast, co-evaluation promises to partner with consumers in each aspect of the decision making and formulating solutions, and "incorporate your advice and recommendations into the decisions to the maximum extent possible" (collaborate) (International Association for Public Participation 2023). Co-evaluation also engages consumers at other levels, for example, to "inform" (to close the feedback loop) and "consult" (to bring a wide range of perspectives into the evaluation), but consumers are partners in decision making about how this is done and what is done with the data collected (Fig. 1).

A Consumer Perspective on the Term "Co-production"

"The more that projects are called co-production (or other 'co' words) when they are not, the more the value and true meaning of the word is lost. Evaluators and project leaders think they are doing 'co-production' but it can't truly be co-production if consumers are not included in the original question or the findings and dissemination."

Dale Trevor, Health consumer

3 The Principles of Co-production

For successful and authentic co-production, there must be conscious commitment and prioritization of the eight principles of co-production: elevating lived experience, co-govern, equity centric, diversity, inclusion, skill building, co-decide, and safety. These principles primarily focus on addressing the power imbalance inherent in health services, and therefore in health service evaluation. Therefore, it stands that co-evaluation needs to adhere to these same principles. Otherwise, consumers are unlikely to feel as though they can have their say and may not challenge professionals when they have misunderstood or disregarded lived experience, ultimately limiting their ability to effect change. Table 1 outlines a few ways that evaluators can practise the principles of co-production to address power imbalance.

In co-production, power refers to the ability to bring about change (McKercher 2020) and is particularly important for evaluators and other professionals to build an awareness of and to challenge, rather than reproduce structural inequalities (Costanza-Chock 2020). As part of building power literacy, it is helpful for

Table 1 Co-production principles and their application to co-evaluation (based on checklist by Meloncelli et al. 2023)

Principles	Definition	Examples of practicing these principles
Elevate lived experience	Perceiving and acknowledging lived experience as legitimate expertise. Consumers are supported to have their voices heard, and their contributions are listened to	Consumer experiences and views are not disregarded because they are in conflict with published research or local data. Instead, the team works together to understand why (e.g., research did not involve consumers, local data did not measure the right thing)
Co-govern	Responsibilities and roles are shared between people with professional and lived experience	Team meetings are co-chaired by a consumer who has the same access and authority as the professional co-chair. Each team member has a specific role and accountability
Equity-centric	Engagement activities and recruitment strategies are intentionally and collaboratively designed and put in place to address imbalances in power	Aim for half of the evaluation team identifying as part of the consumer community. Additional evaluation efforts are focused on understanding health service outcomes and experience for indigenous communities
Diversity and inclusion	Intentional efforts are made to enable participation of diverse groups to ensure the evaluation reflects the diversity of the community. This includes when, how, and where you engage consumers	The evaluation team includes people with diverse gender identity, health status/ ability, cultural and socioeconomic backgrounds, age, etc. community leaders help to plan engagement activities outside the health service environment. People are asked how they want to participate and what they need to allow them to do this. Payment is offered, and out-of-pocket expenses are covered
Skill building	The team creates conditions to promote team members to unlearn, learn, and re-learn together, recognizing that everyone has something to teach and something to learn	Training and mentoring are offered to consumer team members to develop their evaluation skills; consumers contribute diverse knowledge and skills (e.g., from their professional background) to enrich the broader capacity of the group
Co-decide	Major decisions on what to evaluate and how to measure are made collectively	Flattened hierarchy and shared decision making at team meetings that allow the different perspectives "at the table" to be heard and contribute equally to the decision
Safety	The physical, emotional, and psychosocial safety of the team and community are prioritized, and the evaluation process is grounded in a trauma-informed approach	Team members know how to escalate concerns and access support. Consumers have opportunities to debrief with people external to the evaluation team. Meetings are in a neutral space where all have access, feel safe, comfortable, and welcomed

evaluators and other professionals to critically reflect on their own privilege, and how this may influence relationships, biases, and assumptions about working with communities. Privilege has been described as a "special right or advantage granted or available to only a particular person or group" (Noel 2019). This relates to social inequality, especially in regard to race, ethnicity, age, disability, religion, sexuality, and social class. Community-led health service design and evaluations carry a social justice imperative to elevate (rather than ignore) the perspectives of marginalized communities and groups.

It can be challenging for evaluators and other professionals to critically reflect on their own privilege and identify power imbalances in evaluation, as this is often felt most by those who have little power (especially those who are intersectionality disadvantaged by class, race, sexual orientation, age, disability, and gender). Intersectionality refers to amplified disadvantage and overlapping marginalization and discrimination due to multiple aspects of a person's identity (Noel 2019). For example, a person who is from a culturally and linguistically diverse background and has a disability may face racism and ableism at the same time. Power can be inherited (e.g., being born white, being born into a wealthy family), gained and developed (e.g., education, networks, experience, and reputation), and positional (e.g., member of a majority group, decision making authority) (McKercher 2020). In traditional evaluation models, people often charged with evaluating health services are in a position of significant power, whilst consumers (e.g., patients of a health service) have low power amplified by their dependence on the health service itself.

Prompts to Think More Deeply About Power (Noel 2019):

- What forms of power do you hold?
- Have you acknowledged your privilege? How might this impact on the co-evaluation and the consumers that you are collaborating with?
- What are the multiple forms of oppression that affect the consumers in your health service and those involved in your evaluation?
- How might this affect their ability to have their say, challenge people with power and affect change?

It is important to note at this point that being able to truly commit to these principles of co-production requires not only the "right mindset" of those involved but also the building of relationships between individuals within the team where there is trust and mutual respect for diverse skills and perspectives. This takes time. Perhaps more importantly, though, is the need for "engagement-capable environments" (Baker et al. 2016); that is, a supportive context and culture within the health service where lived experience is valued, funding and time are allocated to co-production, and grass-roots innovation and change are embraced. There are co-production self-assessment tools available from various groups internationally (New Economics Foundation 2009; Harpur and Garvey 2021) that might be useful to assess your health service's readiness to support co-production and identify where preparatory work may be needed before true co-production can begin.

As co-production and "co" approaches gain popularity, there are risks of tokenism and harm for consumers (Ocloo and Matthews 2016). For consumers and community, co-production comes with an expectation: to be an equal partner who is valued, heard, and respected. Mislabeling processes as co-production perpetuates distrust and poor experiences with health services, the irony being that rectifying what went "wrong" in their past care experiences is a driving factor for many consumers to be involved in healthcare improvement and evaluation.

A Consumer Perspective on Tokenism and Potential Harm from Poor Co-production:

*"Tokenistic co-production can lead to re-traumatisation due to the parallels between poor consumer engagement practices and previous poor healthcare experiences. Healthcare workers and people involved in co-evaluation have a shared responsibility to provide patients and consumers with choice, information, respect, listen to them and take a shared decision-making approach. When this is promised, and not delivered, feelings from the consequences of a healthcare interaction (*e.g. *threat to wellbeing, death), despite misplaced, can be felt in the context of the co-production process. In fact, it can even be worse in the co-production context, where consumers feel a responsibility for the wellbeing of their community. This can be further amplified when the co-production is happening in the same environment as people receive healthcare, rather than a neutral space. This reinforces the need for co-evaluation to be approached with care and clear expectations, incorporating the principles of co-production to prioritise genuine and meaningful engagement."*

Anja Christoffersen, Health Consumer

4 Co-evaluation: Co-production Across the Evaluation Cycle

In this section, we will demonstrate how co-production can be applied across the evaluation cycle, and how stakeholders can share decision making power and responsibility for the evaluation process. In doing this, we have drawn from process frameworks for co-production (Metro North Health 2022a) and evaluation (Better Evaluation 2022) to present how the two approaches can be integrated. A case example is presented at the end of this section to demonstrate the application of the principles of co-production across the evaluation process (Fig. 2).

Deciding on co-production as your evaluation approach requires a commitment to practicing the principles of co-production of co-deciding and elevating lived experience. Co-evaluation should begin with a shared need and curiosity. Consumers should be involved from the beginning when the decisions are made about what to evaluate, when and how to measure it, and importantly what the data means and

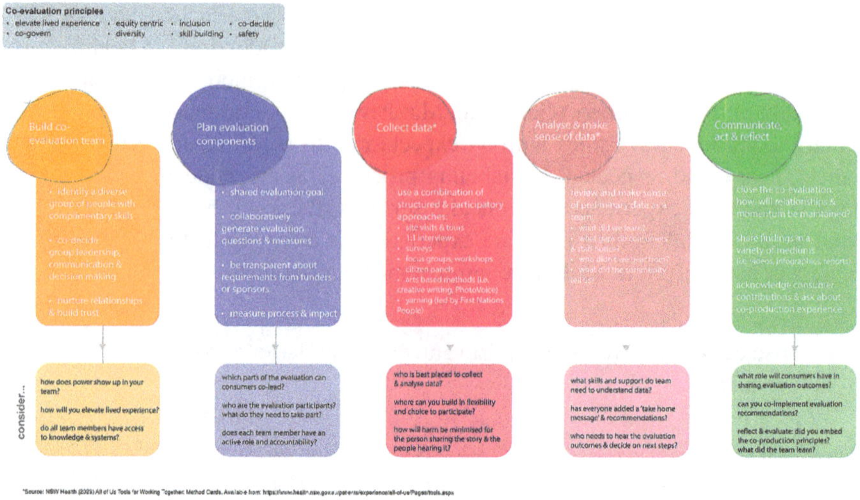

Fig. 2 Overview of the co-evaluation process. Source NSW Health (2023)

what health services should do with it to drive improvement. There are a few key questions to ask yourself and your evaluation team before you start to ensure that you are planning to truly co-produce your evaluation, and to avoid calling something co-production when it is not.

Box 1 Questions to Ask Before You Start Co-evaluation (Adapted from Metro North Health 2022a)

- Has a decision already been made about what will be evaluated, and how this will be done? (if yes, consider if another engagement method is better suited, e.g., consultation or involvement; or identify whether aspects of the evaluation can be co-evaluated).
- Do consumers/community see the evaluation topic as a priority? (if not, reconsider your topic. If you aren't sure, engage with community/consumers to understand further).
- Can you secure the resources (e.g., funding) and commitment from key decision makers to conduct your evaluation (and following through on actions identified from the evaluation)? (if not, consider the potential damage to relationships by not being able to fulfil your commitment to co-production).
- If funds are already committed, is there a budget for consumer/community engagement? (you will need to have budget to fund consumer involvement adequately).

It is important to note that a co-production approach is not an all or nothing approach. Individual steps within the evaluation process can be co-produced, as long as there is a commitment to the co-production principles by the team.

4.1 Step 1: Build a Co-evaluation Team

Identify a small team of 5–7 people with cross-cutting skills, diverse viewpoints, and roles to plan and implement the evaluation.

Building the team sets the foundation for the entire co-evaluation process and to ensure that the principles of "equity centric," "diversity and inclusion," "elevate lived experience," and "co-govern" are upheld. Consideration needs to be given to both the team composition and roles and group dynamics and how the group will work together.

4.1.1 Team Composition and Roles

Co-evaluation involves multiple consumer team members with active roles on the evaluation team. It is important that the team has balanced representation from consumer representatives, health service representatives, and people with expertise in evaluation design. Multiple consumer team members (ideally making up equal numbers to professionals, e.g., evaluators, health service managers, clinicians) will balance power and bring diverse perspectives to the team. Aim for a small group of 5–7 individuals with cross-cutting skills and diverse viewpoints, as diversity in group composition will lead to greater appreciation of the complexity of the issue being evaluated, improved problem solving, and better group decision making.

When forming your team, consider the collective skills and perspectives that are needed for your evaluation, and then identify the individuals that can bring these skills.

Think laterally about the important relational, leadership, and facilitatory skills that will be essential to the success of the evaluation, team dynamics, and rapport with the community. Evaluation is a process that can be fraught with friction, due to competing interests and expectations (Brewster et al. 2015); these may be amplified during co-production with inherent power imbalance between patients and providers. Including a person in your team who is external to the service offers an opportunity to bring a fresh and neutral perspective or to incorporate a "provocateur" role (McKercher 2020). This role can identify blind spots and assumptions, by asking questions that may gently illuminate inherent power balances between patients and providers.

A Consumer Perspective on "Diversity and Inclusion":

"Having diverse stakeholders with lived and professional experience in the process is vital so it captures enthusiasm of consumers, carers and families, administration staff, clinicians and others. Encouraging their perspectives and truly listening to them is part of seeing the problem from a different position. Building knowledge together on the issue being evaluated helps to frame the problem together and begin to look at how best to collect data on the issue. Going forwards together has the power of uniting multiple perspectives and generating solutions that come from angles that might not have been thought about before."

Dale Trevor, Health Consumer

In line with the principle of "elevate lived experience," the evaluation team must acknowledge that, while community members may not bring expertise in evaluation methods, their lived experience in understanding the impact of what is being evaluated is invaluable. Consumer members bring diverse skills beyond their lived experience (e.g., professional skills, cultural knowledge) that will enrich the evaluation, if you invite the "whole person" to participate, rather than only looking at their lived experience. However, there should not be an expectation that consumers must bring skills beyond their lived experience when selecting who is best for the evaluation team—view additional skills as a "bonus."

In the planning phases, allow time to get to know individual strengths of each team member and consider who is best matched to evaluation roles and accountabilities. It can be helpful to think outside any initial assumptions about the roles of "health service professional" and "consumer" here and instead focus on the tasks required to plan and complete the evaluation, and who might be best placed to take on each role. Also, in line with the principle of "skill building," consider and discuss where there are opportunities to build skills and experience for consumer partners, and how this will be supported by other members of the evaluation team (e.g., taking an active role in evaluation data collection and/or analysis). Ensuring each team member has a critical role, accountability, and can see the value of their contribution creates shared responsibility and can be one way to reduce power imbalance.

4.1.2 Building a Supportive Group Dynamic

Spending time at the project outset to develop the team relationships and establish a model of collective decision making will ensure all team members are clear on their roles and responsibilities, how the group will function, and what to do in cases of uncertainty or when problems arise. Group dynamics are purposefully built and are supported by a shared vision, trust, transparency, respect, and facilitative leadership. Dynamics are negatively impacted by unmitigated power differentials, expert mindsets, time pressures, high levels of uncertainty, and unaddressed conflict.

A Consumer Perspective on Supporting Consumer Contributions:

"It is important to understand that consumers are often coming 'to the table' from a personal rather than a professional perspective, as their lived experience is a deeply personal experience. The expectation for some team members to disclose personal perspectives, while others are 'protected' behind professional roles, creates power imbalances and is not conducive with genuine relationship building. This can be mitigated through having conversations and building relationships without an agenda, and beyond the scope of the project (e.g. over a shared meal). Consider what personal information you are comfortable sharing—what motivated you to begin your career? What do you enjoy doing on the weekend? What are you looking forward to most? What are your upcoming holiday plans? Treat the other people in your team as human beings, rather than stakeholders in a project. This method of relationship building will create a more authentic and enjoyable co-production process."

Anja Christoffersen, Health consumer

4.1.3 Group Leadership and Decision Making

In line with the principles of "co-deciding" and "co-governing," decide together how the team will work together and make decisions. Successful leadership is collaborative and facilitative, and the best leader may not be the most senior person in the room. Consider creating co-leadership roles, jointly held by both consumers and health service representatives, who can together ensure that decisions made by the group consider both lived and professional expertise.

It is essential to clearly name and discuss how decision making will work in the group. For instance, will the group aim to use democratic, consensus, or consultative decision making? It is likely that a combination of these and other approaches will be needed at different points. Will decisions be made within or outside of meetings? Those who may be unable to attend (e.g., due to other commitments or ill health) may require more time to process information and can feel more pressure to conform to group expectations. It is important to consider how all people can contribute effectively. These are important conversations to ensure all team members feel heard, respected, and their contributions valued. Agree on the preferred channels and frequency of communication. Check about preferences and access: do all team members have the same access to email or key computer programs? For example, cloud-based shared documents will facilitate collaborative note taking during meetings and project documents with greater accessibility, but only if all members have the same access.

Working in diverse groups and teams inevitably raises conflicting ideas and disagreements. If left unaddressed, this can lead to division and resentment within a group. Group leaders who manage disagreements using cooperative resolution strategies (i.e., balancing contributions and not trying to force consensus) can skillfully enable the team to work through critical decisions and produce stronger evaluations (Berditchevskaia and Bertoncin 2021).

4.1.4 Roadblocks to Building a Team

Building an effective co-evaluation team can be hindered by expert mindsets, time pressures, uncertainty, and lack of resourcing. Expert mindsets can quickly erode mutual respect among the team. An expert mindset is the belief that someone (often staff members, researchers, and professional evaluators) has the knowledge and/or experience to be the only expert on the "way things should be done." In evaluations, this can manifest as experts in *how* something should be evaluated (e.g., process, data collection, and analysis) or *what* is being evaluated. In co-production, everyone and no one is an expert.

A Consumer Perspective on "Expert Mindsets":

"Until experts have seen the value of true innovative suggestions from within the team, they won't relinquish power over the process. True science either tests out what is known or chooses an unbuilt road that we research as we build, using principles of test and measure, posing problems and finding solutions together. Those experts with good attitudes towards the team and true 'expert humility' will reap the rewards of working with a variety of stakeholders by making sure they are part of true decision making. The implicit knowledge that all are valuable and respected in the process makes them true experts."

Dale Trevor, Health Consumer

Time pressures, uncertainty, and lack of resourcing are common in health service evaluation, but pose significant challenges in co-evaluation. Co-produced evaluations can take a little longer to plan and deliver than professional-led evaluations due to the emphasis on team building, seeking and supporting diverse perspectives, and collaborative decision making. However, it is our position that co-produced evaluation yields more value as it ensures the evaluation team is "measuring what matters," asking the right evaluation questions and measuring outcomes in the right way, thereby reducing wasted time and efforts.

Funding to pay consumer team members fairly for their time and the value they bring is important, to balance power and promote inclusion (National Institute for Health and Care Research 2023). Paying consumers means that everyone in the evaluation team is being paid to be there, and offering payment can widen the pool of consumers who can be involved (rather than limiting to those in the financial position to volunteer and engage in unpaid work). Refer to local organizational policies and best practice guidelines for payment rates, and where possible ask the consumers what rate they wish to be paid, noting that these guidelines are often not designed for highly skilled project-based work. Wherever possible, offer flexibility in payment methods to allow people to choose how to receive money in a way that best suits them (rather than only offering a gift card when they need money to pay bills) or that does not disadvantage them (for example, receiving cash payments may reduce benefit payments or preference to invoice rather than submitting claim forms).

Key Questions to Ask as You Build Your Team

- What skills and perspectives do you need in your team?
- Is there representation of consumers, health professionals, and evaluators?
- How will you ensure that all team members are involved and have influence in decision making about the vision and process for the evaluation?
- What roles do consumers want in the project? How can consumers take on leadership roles within the project? How will you support them in this?
- Can all members of your team access all of the necessary information, systems, documents, and resources to effectively contribute?

4.2 Step 2: Plan Evaluation Components

Collaboratively discuss and plan the evaluation purpose, methodology, and how findings will be used with the co-production team.

4.2.1 Establish a Shared Vision and Evaluation Purpose

Co-evaluation relies on collective decision making and teamwork, requiring a shared vision among all team members. Dedicate time at the start of evaluation planning to establish shared goals and purpose of the evaluation. This open and collaborative activity is facilitated by the group leaders, where each team member is offered an opportunity to consider the purpose and goals of the evaluation, as well as understanding any pre-existing evaluation requirements (e.g., must include an economic evaluation), and who the key decision makers and target audience are (e.g., a program funder or sponsor). Resist asking team members to "brainstorm" straight away (Berditchevskaia and Bertoncin 2021), as this can preference existing hierarchies and group think. Instead, ask each team member to note down a goal or question they have before discussing all ideas as a group. Group leaders then facilitate a collective discussion, where the team may group similar questions and categorize based on feasibility and priority.

A Consumer Perspective on Developing a Shared Vision:
"Take note of evaluation questions prioritised by the community and consumer representatives. These questions can reveal gaps in consumer knowledge and understanding that need to be filled, what their immediate solution may look like, and whether the focus of the evaluation should shift to address the "cause", and not the "symptoms", of the problem. Not all evaluation questions may be within the scope of the project, however think flexibly about how the evaluation can build in important community measures and metrics to balance those important to program funders and other stakeholders."
Dale Trevor, Health Consumer

Both processes and impacts of the program should be considered when establishing the evaluation purpose and questions. Mapping these as a group can help identify gaps (i.e., is there too much focus on measuring one type of program outcome over another, without understanding how these changes may have occurred?). Information from this stage will serve as initial ideas to develop technical evaluation components such as monitoring and evaluation frameworks and program logic models. Keep a record of what was discussed and decided, and share them with the team so that each group member has the same opportunity to access, reflect, and add additional thoughts. There are many online tools and whiteboards to facilitate collaborative planning (for example, Google Docs, Miro); however, this can also be as simple as an email summary with key decisions made. Multiple team meetings or workshops are often needed to plan the evaluation, requiring strategies to ensure that all members have an opportunity to refresh and review what was done at the previous meeting and decided on.

4.2.2 Develop Evaluation Methods

Designing the evaluation methods requires the team to decide what data needs to be collected, how and by whom, and making these decisions together with consumers can provide a different perspective on this. When collecting data directly from patients or clients of the service (e.g., via surveys), the consumers' lived experience will offer perspective into what support might be needed to participate and the best way to ask the questions in a way that they are understood and that patients feel comfortable to answer honestly. Consumers can contribute to planning and implementing strategies to reduce inequity and power differentials in evaluation methods and data collection processes, by highlighting the people whose voices need to be amplified (e.g., people who are often left out of routine data collection due to language barriers and cognitive or communication impairments), identifying where alternative methods are needed (e.g., offering a range of options to participate) and when you need to consider inclusivity and access requirements (e.g., online options, access to interpreters and support people). Informed by their lived experience, consumers may identify and help to mitigate potential harm for patients/clients that may come from participating in your evaluation.

4.2.3 Understand Stakeholder Needs and Expectations

During planning, map out a stakeholder matrix and identify key audiences for evaluation findings, and their level of interest and influence over understanding the evaluation outcomes and deciding next steps. Consider:

- What are the expectations and involvement of consumers, community members, and evaluation participants in knowing the results and influencing decision making about next steps?
- What are program funders, decision makers, and staff involved in delivering a program or initiative expecting to see from the evaluation findings? What is their involvement in decision making?

This reflective activity may identify initial stakeholders who the evaluation team needs to engage with during the planning stage. Involving consumers in this process may identify new audiences for the evaluation findings (e.g., community organizations, consumer advocacy groups and the general public) and methods of approaching or engaging with stakeholders (e.g., peer-to-peer engagement in culturally diverse communities). At this early stage, it is important to co-plan how evaluation findings will be communicated and to which audiences. This is covered in more detail later in this section.

Key Questions to Support Evaluation Planning (from NSW Health 2023):

- How can we ensure that all team members contribute to defining the evaluation goals and purpose?
- Who is best to lead the data collection and analysis? Does this need to be staff, or could we involve consumers? How do we support this?
- Who are the evaluation participants and what do they need to take part?
- Who is the audience for our evaluation and what do they need and want to know?

4.3 Step 3: Collect Data

Move from planning and working within the co-production team to wider involvement with consumers, caregivers, community members, and staff as evaluation participants.

Often data collection methods in co-evaluation are similar to those used in other evaluation approaches. What is different in co-production is that consumer team members have been involved in deciding what and how data will be collected. This often results in participatory community-based methods being combined with the more structured evaluation measures (i.e., service metrics, interviews, surveys) to add insight and context to the data. Participatory methods help expand an evaluation's frame of reference and center the experience of program users or recipients, giving them power over how their experiences and stories are told. Table 2 outlines several participatory data collection methods. Using qualitative participatory

Table 2 Participatory data collection methods and considerations for their use

Method	Suited to	Resources required	Considerations
Arts-based methods e.g., PhotoVoice Learn about people's experiences through creative writing, art, performances, or visuals/photos	Emotive evaluation topics, to capture expression of individual experience	Low-moderate: Vary by method used, consider providing materials to participants to support engagement	Must seek consent and permission from participants to use any materials in final evaluations and presentations
Tours Allow community to see a space or site for themselves to inform opinions/ feedback	Place-based evaluations Engagement prior to workshops	Moderate: Can be virtual or in person. Physical tours must ensure accessibility, hospitality, and occupational health and safety	Involve consumers in planning and ensure understanding of accessibility requirements
Citizens panel Representative group of community members who serve on a standing panel to collect and provide input into decision making	Projects with ongoing engagement and community decision making. Surveys are distributed to understand community attitudes, feedback, and behavior	High: May meet over multiple days and require experienced facilitation	Facilitated method. All materials to be provided to the group, including preparation materials ahead of time
Yarning Deep listening circle that is culturally significant to Australian Aboriginal and Torres Strait Islander peoples	Community-led evaluations and ensuring culturally safe methods	Low: Small scale	Must always be led or co-led by First Nations peoples

References: NSW Health (2023), International Association for Public Participation (2023)

methods will also encourage service users or program recipients to share what they think is important, which adds important incidental findings to what the evaluation team determines important to measure. This reduces bias in the evaluation methodology and helps to test assumptions held by the evaluation team. For more examples of participatory-based methods, we suggest reviewing resources such as the NSW Health All of Us Guide and IAP2 Engagement Planner and considering which method will suit your project scope, timeframes, resources, and community.

Another difference in co-production is the opportunity for consumer partners to be involved in the data collection. This may be through roles as peer evaluators (e.g., undertaking a consumer assessment of a service), research assistant collecting data from participants (e.g., administering surveys with patients in the waiting room), or coaches/mentors for other consumers in the community involved in the evaluation (e.g., support person during an interview). In line with the principles of "skill building," consider how you might build skills and share technical evaluation knowledge to allow consumers to take on these roles. It is important to always ensure the physical, emotional, cultural, and psychological safety of both the consumers and participants during the data collection process. Ethical frameworks should be adhered to in order to ensure confidentiality, data security and minimization of physical and psychological harm, and responsibility for consumers to be informed and capable of acting within ethical frameworks rests with those with research and evaluation skills. Involving and listening to consumers when planning data collection processes should assist the evaluation team in identifying and mitigating safety concerns.

Key Questions to Support Participatory Data Collection from (NSW Health 2023):

- Where are the opportunities to use participatory, community-based methods to answer consumer-prioritized evaluation questions?
- Who are the evaluation participants and what do they need to take part?
- Are you expecting one method (e.g., surveys) to work for everyone and tell you everything?
- Where can you build in flexibility and choice to participate?
- What active roles can consumers play in gathering data?
- How are you considering physical, emotional, psychological, and cultural safety?
- How will you minimize harm for the person sharing the story and the people hearing it?

4.4 Step 4: Analyze and Make Sense of Data

Reconvene the co-evaluation team to review and make sense of the findings.

The purpose of this step is for the team to review and align on what the evaluation findings mean in a broader context. All stakeholders, including consumers, should be invited and supported to participate in the data analysis process. For quantitative data, this might involve reviewing preliminary data outputs and summary statistics to identify different ways to analyze or interpret the data (e.g., exploration of specific sub-groups, re-categorizing variables). For qualitative data, consumers could review interview transcripts, contribute to the development of coding frameworks, co-code data, develop, or review thematic summaries, and/or select exemplar quotes for inclusion in reports and presentations.

To support this process, a facilitative approach should be used to ask broad questions that enable diverse understandings to arise from the group, rather than a directive approach. Give each team member the opportunity to contribute their interpretation of the data. Questions should prompt the group to discuss and debate what they are seeing in the data and what perspectives are missing, with consideration of the need to collect additional data or seek further perspectives to complete the evaluation. When meeting to discuss data analysis, understanding the learning styles and preferences of the group will help inform what format the meeting should take and how best to share the results. Ask team members how they would like to visualize and discuss the data, and what is needed to support their understanding.

Key Questions to Support Participatory Data Analysis:

- How do team members want to be involved in data analysis? Do they want to contribute across the whole process, or do they want to come in at the end to review and discuss preliminary data summaries?
- What skills and support do people need to understand the data? How can we build these skills?
- Where and how should the team come together to discuss the data? Is this best done in a longer workshop-style meeting, or by working through data over a series of meetings? How can people be supported to prepare to participate in these meetings?
- Has everyone had the chance to put forward their "take home messages" and recommendations from the data?

During meetings, these questions will enable a facilitative approach to interpreting the data:

- What did we learn? What gaps do consumers and staff notice?
- When reflecting on the quality of evaluation data—what is missing? Who didn't we hear from?
- What were the results of community-based consultation or engagement?
- Based on the evaluation findings, what are our next steps/recommendations?
- What is the best way to communicate the findings/information with preliminary data analysis shared ahead of time?.

4.5 Step 5: Communicate and Plan for Action

Decide how to communicate findings to diverse stakeholders and plan for "next steps."

After achieving a shared understanding of the evaluation findings, the team should decide how to communicate these to various audiences and stakeholders. This includes those who commissioned and/or initiated the evaluation, but this especially needs to include the community and those who participated in the evaluation. Consider where different audiences currently seek out information and distribute your evaluation findings there, rather than having the expectation that evaluation findings will be sought out.

The co-production of a communications plan should identify diverse stakeholders and inform tailored communication methods and messages to enhance awareness and understanding of the evaluation findings. It is important that consumers are supported to lead dissemination and communication activities. Consumers may identify innovative methods to amplify your message and ensure that it reaches all relevant groups. They may have networks across communities and sectors that professionals do not have access to. Their input into the project needs to be recognized (e.g., co-authors on reports, co-presenters at forums and meetings, co-owners of outputs) as often the contribution of consumers is invisible. Consider holding a community event or forum where recommendations and findings can be shared widely and contributors can be openly recognized and celebrated. Invitations to community events should be open and broader than just those involved in the evaluation.

A Consumer's Perspective on "Closing the Loop" and Recognition:
"When the paper is written and solutions and conclusions disseminated, it is time to remember all those that had input. Let's not leave anybody out of this vital stage. Leaving consumer partners out of this stage disconnects people from the engagement experience and future work. It is disheartening to see the awards and accolades given to few when your own input is etched into their information."

Dale Trevor, Health Consumer

Finally, an evaluation of health services usually concludes with a series of recommendations based on the findings. These should be co-produced with all members of the team and be directly informed by the collective team insights. It is at this stage that co-production processes are traditionally "handed over" to the health service to lead the implementation of recommendations. Consider whether there is opportunity for co-implementation, supported by emerging fields such as integrated knowledge translation (Kothari et al. 2017). Ideally, the co-production process does not end here, and team members have built relationships and a shared vision for future improvement and ongoing monitoring and evaluation, particularly if they have had a positive experience. This is how co-production shifts from tokenism to a movement.

Key Questions to Support Co-dissemination of Findings and Next Steps:

- Who needs to know about our evaluation findings to ensure that action is taken?
- How do different audiences or stakeholders receive and process information? Who do they listen to?
- Who will present the findings? Can we co-present the findings?
- How will we keep momentum going after the project finishes? Can we co-produce and co-implement the next steps?
- Have all team members been acknowledged in the way in which they wish to be acknowledged?
- How do we continue to nurture the relationships we have built after the evaluation ends?

Case Example: Evaluating Patient Reported Experience Measures

Patient reported experience measures (PREMs) are routinely collected to evaluate health services and drive quality improvement. The survey used in our health service includes 37 items, including 2 qualitative questions. There was no method or process to analyze and use this data to gain deeper insights into patient experience. The hospital safety and quality committee (inclusive of consumers) identified a need for a user-friendly tool to analyze qualitative PREMs data in a meaningful way to evaluate patient experience.

Step 1: Build a co-evaluation team. A multidisciplinary team of consumers ($n = 2$), health service managers ($n = 3$), safety and quality leads ($n = 3$), and researchers ($n = 2$) came together and co-decided that person-centered care was a shared priority of consumers and the organization and was applicable to PREMs data. A project lead was identified, who partnered with a consumer representative to deliver the project as co-leads.

Step 2: Plan evaluation components. The team decided together through a series of meetings that measurement should use a person-centered framework with co-designed definitions. The group had discussions with the stakeholder groups they represented to decide together that the coding tool should be an excel spreadsheet to ensure accessibility to all users.

Step 3: Collect data. PREMs were routinely collected from inpatients 2 days after discharge via an online questionnaire that included two qualitative questions. Qualitative data were exported monthly into an excel database for analysis by each service line (~1800 qualitative responses per month). The multidisciplinary team chose two service lines (women's and newborn services; surgical and perioperative services) to pilot the tool with a sample of their data.

Step 4: Analyze and make sense of data. Safety and quality leads and consumer representatives of the health services were involved in coding, with collaborative learning and reflective meetings. These meetings were facilitated by a team member external to the service lines where data was being analyzed. Review of the data revealed that consumer perceptions of data were different to staff perceptions, and adjustments were made to the framework to include first-person definitions of coding domains and keywords to improve consistency and reduce bias. Having consumer partners interpret what the data meant, and provide their perspectives allowed the framework for patient experience evaluation to be more true to the patient voice and priority areas.

Step 5: Communicate and plan for action. The coded data was used to drive improvements and has resulted in numerous changes within the health service including changing the timing of meals, extended visiting hours, improving discharge processes, and increasing access for support people at crucial times for patients. The results were co-presented at academic conferences and health service forums by a researcher and consumer. The team co-authored an academic manuscript reporting on this work (Pateman et al. 2023) and were named on awards for the work.

5 Reflecting on and Evaluating the Co-production Process

Co-production is being increasingly used across health service evaluation, improvement, and research; however, it is rarely evaluated, with research to date largely limited to narrative case studies (Marsilio et al. 2021). This makes it challenging to provide empirical evidence of the benefits of co-production or know what is needed to support the process (e.g., skills, funding, time). Evaluating the co-evaluation of health services would be a novel and valuable addition to the literature on "co" approaches, and should be considered by evaluation teams. Most importantly, the evaluation process provides the opportunity for people to individually and collectively reflect on the co-production process: what was done, what was learned, and how it could be improved in future.

The team should plan how they will evaluate the co-evaluation process from the beginning, and decide together what should be evaluated, when, and how. Ultimately, this evaluation serves to answer the question: "did we use a collaborative process to co-produce this evaluation?" The principles of co-production from Sect. 2 could be used to underpin this evaluation, as outlined in Table 3. Ideally, this evaluation would be performed at predetermined intervals throughout the process (e.g., at the end of each major phase/milestone/activity) as well as at its conclusion. This could be a formal evaluation process or it may be a more informal process of de-briefing or reflecting. Either way, undertaking this formative evaluation at intervals during the process would help to identify whether strategies and team processes are supporting co-production, or if the team needs to find a new way of working together.

Anonymous surveys or interviews undertaken by an external party could be used to evaluate the experiences of all team members, including both consumer and

Table 3 Example questions to evaluate the experience of participating in the co-production process

Co-production principles	What could be measured?
Elevate lived experience	Did all people involved feel heard, respected, engaged, empowered, and equal? Did those involved feel their unique knowledge and skills were recognized, acknowledged, and valued?
Co-govern	Did people feel that there were processes and supports in place to allow all team members to take on key roles in the project?
Equity centric	How many people were involved, and how many were primarily representing their lived experience/consumer perspective?
Diversity	Who is involved in the co-design process? Was there inclusion of diverse consumer perspectives, including marginalized groups and intersectionality?
Inclusion	Did people feel that they could contribute in the way that they wanted? Did people feel adequately prepared and supported to contribute? Were there any accessibility practices included?
Skill building	Did all people feel that they were supported to learn something new? Did all people feel that they were able to share their knowledge and teach others? Did those involved feel that they now have increased skills and confidence to undertake co-production in future?
Co-decide	Did all people feel that they were able to influence and take part in the decisions being made? Did those involved feel like they had an impact on the outcome?
Safety	Did all people feel that their well-being was supported? Did all people feel that they could trust the other people in the evaluation team?
Describing co-production	What did the co-production process involve? (e.g., type and number of meetings/engagement activities) What strategies were put in place to support each principle of co-production? What costs/resources were involved? What participatory data collection methods were used?

health service representatives. A "peer performance review" may be another way to check how the process is tracking and to hold one's self and others accountable to the principles of co-production (Metro North Health 2022b). Care should be taken during the evaluation process to uphold the principle of "safety" to ensure that people trust in the process and are able to share their experiences with the goal of improving relationships and teamwork.

6 Conclusion

Co-production enriches health service evaluation through the inclusion of diverse lived experience perspectives and measuring what matters to those who use health services. It requires evaluators to invest time early in the process to plan and develop a shared vision to balance the evaluation needs of those accessing health services and those delivering health services. Co-evaluation is highly relational. The time invested in building and maintaining relationships and group dynamics builds trust and sets the foundations for future co-evaluation, co-implementation, and health service improvement. Deliberate and tailored strategies are needed to uphold the principles of co-production in order to balance power imbalance, elevate lived experience, and ensure safety of all participants. Co-evaluation needs evaluation of its process to understand the extent to which these strategies are working and to continuously improve the co-production process. With global movements to value-based care and person-centered models of care, it is essential that health services are both designed and evaluated based on what matters most to the end-user, the patient, their family, and the broader community. Co-evaluation offers an approach for health service evaluators to position their evaluation in line with these trends and to ultimately improve health service delivery and outcomes.

References

Arnstein SR (1969) A ladder of citizen participation. J Am Inst Plann 35:216–224

Baker G, Judd M, Fancott C, Maika C (2016) Creating “engagement-capable environments” in healthcare. In: Baker GR, Judd M, Maika C (eds) Patient engagement—catalyzing improvement and innovation in healthcare. Longwoods, Toronto

Berditchevskaia A, Bertoncin C (2021) How to make good group decisions. Nesta https://media.nesta.org.uk/documents/Collective-Intelligence-Good-Decision-Making.pdf. Accessed 8 December 2023

Better Evaluation (2022) Rainbow framework. https://www.betterevaluation.org/frameworks-guides/rainbow-framework

Brewster L, Aveling E-L, Martin G, Tarrant C, Dixon-Woods M (2015) What to expect when you’re evaluating healthcare improvement: a concordat approach to managing collaboration and uncomfortable realities. BMJ Qual Saf 24:318–324

Costanza-Chock S (2020) Design justice: community-led practices to build the worlds we need. https://designjustice.mitpress.mit.edu/. Accessed 8 December 2023

Gagliardi AR, Lemieux-Charles L, Brown AD, Sullivan T, Goel V (2008) Barriers to patient involvement in health service planning and evaluation: an exploratory study. Patient Educ Couns 70:234–241

Harpur S, Garvey K (2021) Co-production for health research: a self-assessment framework tool for research team members to complete and review together. Public Health Services Tasmania. Accessed 8 December 2023

International Association for Public Participation (2023) IAP2 engagement methods tool. https://emt.iap2.org.au/about/. Accessed 8 December 2023

Involve (2021) Guidance on co-producing a research project. National Institute for Health and care Research https://www.learningforinvolvement.org.uk/wp-content/uploads/2021/04/NIHR-Guidance-on-co-producing-a-research-project-April-2021.pdf. Accessed 8 December 2023

Kothari A, McCutcheon C, Graham ID (2017) Defining integrated knowledge translation and moving forward: a response to recent commentaries. Int J Health Policy Manage 6:299–300

Lowe D, Ryan R, Schonfeld L, Merner B, Walsh L, Graham-Wisener L, Hill S (2021) Effects of consumers and health providers working in partnership on health services planning, delivery and evaluation. Cochrane Database Syst Rev 9(9):CD013373

Marsilio M, Fusco F, Gheduzzi E, Guglielmetti C (2021) Co-production performance evaluation in healthcare. A systematic review of methods, tools and metrics. Int J Environ Res Public Health 18:3336

Masterson D, Areskoug Josefsson K, Robert G, Nylander E, Kjellström S (2022) Mapping definitions of co-production and co-design in health and social care: a systematic scoping review providing lessons for the future. Health Expect 25:902–913

McKercher KA (2020) Beyond sticky notes. In: Doing co-design for real: mindsets, methods, and movements. Beyond Sticky Notes, Sydney

Meloncelli N, Young A, Christoffersen A, Rushton A, Zhelnov P, Wilkinson SA, Scott AM, de Jersey S (2023) Co-designing nutrition interventions with consumers: a scoping review. J Hum Nutr Diet 36:1045–1067

Merner B, Schonfeld L, Virgona A, Lowe D, Walsh L, Wardrope C, Graham-Wisener L, Xafis V, Colombo C, Refahi N et al (2023) Consumers' and health providers' views and perceptions of partnering to improve health services design, delivery and evaluation: a co-produced qualitative evidence synthesis. Cochrane Database Syst Rev 3(3):CD013274

Metro North Health (2022a) Metro North co-design framework. https://metronorth.health.qld.gov.au/get-involved/co-design. Accessed 8 December 2023

Metro North Health (2022b) Peer performance review. https://metronorth.health.qld.gov.au/get-involved/co-design/team/peer-performance-review. Accessed 8 December 2023

Näslund H, Grim K, Markström U (2023) User-led mental health service evaluation: the contribution of user-focused monitoring to recovery-oriented quality development. J Psychosoc Rehabil Mental Health 10:189–202

National Institute for Health and Care Research (2023) Payment guidance for researchers and professionals

New Economics Foundation (2009) Co-production self-assessment framework. https://www.seemescotland.org/media/7287/co-production-self-assessment-framework.pdf

Noel L-A (2019) The designer's critical alphabet

NSW Health (2023) All of us tools for working together: method cards. https://www.health.nsw.gov.au/patients/experience/all-of-us/Pages/tools.aspx. Accessed 8 December 2023

Ocloo J, Matthews R (2016) From tokenism to empowerment: progressing patient and public involvement in healthcare improvement. BMJ Qual Saf 25:626

Pateman KA, Christoffersen A, Hanly-Platz A, Williams C, Heffernan D, Alexander A, Ryan E, Petrie C, Banks M, Young A (2023) Partnering with consumers to co-design a person-centred coding framework for qualitative patient experience data. Patient Educ Couns 116:107938

Wright M, Getta AD, Green AO, Kickett UC, Kickett AH, McNamara AI, McNamara UA, Newman AM, Pell AC, Penny AM, Wilkes UP, Wilkes AS, Culbong T, Taylor K, Brown A, Dudgeon P, Pearson G, Allsop S, Lin A, Smith G, Farrant B, Mirabella L, O'Connell M (2021) Co-designing health service evaluation tools that foreground first nation worldviews for better mental health and wellbeing outcomes. Int J Environ Res Public Health 18:8555

Community-Led Evaluation of Health Services

Solange L. Baptiste and Krista Lauer

Abstract

This chapter explores the concept, programmatic elements, and impact of community-led monitoring (CLM). It begins with a brief overview of what CLM is and how CLM improves the evaluation of health services. The chapter then delves into a four-step CLM model pioneered by an HIV treatment organization. Step 1 details *Community Science Education*, which builds community knowledge on the science of relevant transmissible diseases and health policies. Step 2 focuses on *Evidence* and how CLM utilizes strategic data collection and analysis. Step 3 unpacks *Engagement*, when data is shared with other parties to improve health services. Step 4 explains *Advocacy*, when communities create evidence-based strategies to effect change. The chapter concludes with a discussion on the different strengths, limitations, and future possibilities for CLM.

Keywords

Community-led · Monitoring · Accountability · Evaluation · Communities · Leadership

1 What Is Community-Led Monitoring (CLM)?

The International Treatment Preparedness Coalition (ITPC), a global network of people living with Human Immunodeficiency Virus (HIV) and community activists, defines CLM as a science-based accountability innovation that puts communities first. CLM does this through placing recipients-of-care squarely in charge of

S. L. Baptiste (✉) · K. Lauer
The International Treatment Preparedness Coalition (ITPC Global), Johannesburg, South Africa
e-mail: sbaptiste@itpcglobal.org; klauer@itpcglobal.org

A. Kaehne, J. Feather (eds.), *Handbook of Health Services Evaluation*,
https://doi.org/10.1007/978-3-031-87869-5_27

defining which factors matter most in the evaluation of health services. These concerns may differ from the priorities of healthcare providers, health administrators, health facility managers, policymakers, donors, and governments.

While initially applied in HIV and transmissible disease contexts, CLM's principles can be adapted across diverse health challenges, from noncommunicable diseases to maternal and child health, allowing for tailored, community-centered approaches in any health evaluation.

When it comes to the evaluation of health services, who decides what we evaluate? The power to select what matters sets the direction of the entire evaluation effort. For example, at a bakery, who defines how to evaluate "success"? The people who eat the cookies? (Priority: taste). The baker who makes the cookies? (Priority: ease of production). The business owner who analyzes the costs? (Priority: profit). All three stakeholders have a legitimate role in the system, but their metrics of success vary significantly. When it comes to the evaluation of health services, approaches that center the perspectives and priorities of recipients of care can identify barriers to services and implement solutions in a timely manner.

While specific implementation methodologies of CLM differ, shared principles have been developed by three consortia operating in the global health space (CD4C, CLAW, EANNASO-APCASO-ATAC, 2022). Common across all CLM models are the following tenets: service users (or affected communities) decide which issues should be tracked; communities lead a systematic data collection effort; and data are analyzed and used to support advocacy with the overall aim of improving the quality of healthcare services.

While there are different initiatives that involve affected communities in the monitoring and evaluation (M&E) of health services, not all of these qualify as CLM, particularly if they are not community-led or part of a recurring cycle. See Fig. 1 for a checklist of what is and what is not CLM.

It is important to note the specific principles of CLM, as the efficiency of the model depends on their careful implementation, as we explore in the next section.

2 How CLM Improves the Evaluation of Health Services

A CLM intervention enhances traditional methods of health services evaluation by enabling recipients of care to rigorously collect granular data. This data can then identify and address gaps and barriers to services, ultimately resulting in improved programs. Who asks the question matters—and when the end-users of a health service are given the opportunity to lead the inquiry, the resulting information is directly relevant to addressing their needs.

CLM interventions begin by interrogating gaps, barriers, and pain points experienced by groups of people attempting to access health services. Instead of casting a wide net and monitoring a broad swath of indicators, CLM narrows the focus of the inquiry, creating tailored indicators to document the nature and scope of specific problems. The adaptability of CLM also makes it a valuable tool across health service areas, providing tailored evaluation methods for a variety of disease contexts and enabling responses suited to each community's unique health priorities.

CLM Is NOT	CLM IS
✗ Community-BASED	✓ Community-**LED**
✗ Indicators are set by outside entities (governments, donors); data collected corresponds to established M&E systems and frameworks	✓ Indicators are determined by communities and correspond to their own priorities; provide a valuable piece of the **whole data story**
✗ One-time evaluation (a "snapshot")	✓ Routine, **recurring data collection** over time (usually monthly or quarterly)
✗ Data is owned by entities outside of the community (governments, healthcare facilities)	✓ Data is owned by communities
✗ Fault-finding	✓ Fact-finding
✗ The end goal of the data is to understand the trends and issues	✓ The end goal is to **improve a particular issue** that has been identified as important by communities

Fig. 1 What is, and what is not, CLM. Source: PowerPoint presentation Community-Led Monitoring SSLN Learning, ITPC November, 2023

As a result, CLM interventions quickly generate detailed information about bottlenecks, often down to specific facilities. By using a combination of qualitative and quantitative indicators, CLM generates rich data that not only describes the scope of a problem (i.e., that clinic wait times were too long at a district's major health facilities in the last quarter) but unpacks the driving factors behind the issue (i.e., interviews with healthcare providers indicate that salaries were not paid for 3 weeks and as a result some providers did not come to work).

CLM data collection occurs on a regular basis—such as monthly or quarterly—and by collecting data on the same indicators recurrently, CLM data quickly identifies trends. This includes gaps that are increasing, improving, or staying the same, such as whether members of a specific group receive a service. This cycle of data collection leads to ongoing relationships between the data collectors and healthcare workers, and recent operational research indicates that this collaborative relationship results in increased opportunities for advocacy (UNAIDS 2023).

CLM interventions also establish governance mechanisms from the beginning. This ensures that a group of decision-makers and powerful actors have regular briefings on the data collected through CLM. Governance mechanisms have a mandate to co-create solutions: data is not collected for data's sake but to concretely improve the lives of health users.

3 Inside a CLM Implementation Model

CLM is an emerging discipline, though implementation efforts are growing around the world, fueled in part by major bilateral and multilateral funders in the global health space. The Global Fund to Fight Acquired Immunodeficiency Syndrome (AIDS), Tuberculosis (TB), and Malaria, the US President's Emergency Plan for AIDS Relief (PEPFAR), and the French 5% Initiative annually commit to support

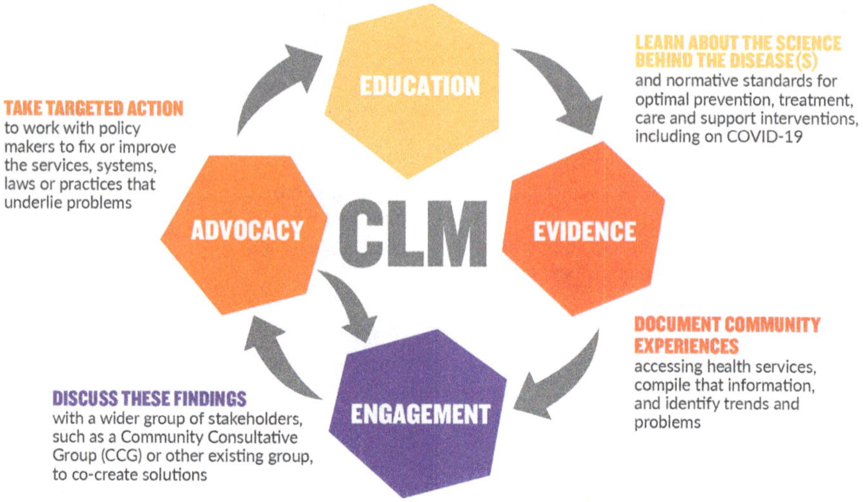

Fig. 2 ITPC's CLM Implementation Model. Source: Community-Led Monitoring of HIV Services, PowerPoint presentation at HIV Learning Network; ITPC 2022

CLM in a variety of contexts. CLM also appears in international and national strategies to address diseases like HIV, TB, malaria, and some noncommunicable diseases. In this section, we describe the practice of CLM implementation using references to published literature and research where possible but focus primarily on the model pioneered by ITPC.

ITPC's model is of a four-step CLM cycle consisting of: education, evidence, engagement, and advocacy (Fig. 2). Other CLM models may follow a slightly different set of steps, but most incorporate the use of quantitative data collection to fuel advocacy efforts. (For further description of ITPC's model, see the How to Implement Community-led Monitoring: A Community Toolkit.)

4 Step 1: Community Science Education

CLM implementation begins with building community knowledge about the science of relevant transmissible diseases that will be monitored, including HIV, TB, COVID-19, and malaria. Community science education incorporates information on the standards of prevention, testing, and care set by the World Health Organization (WHO), and any relevant national guidelines or associated policy commitments established by national governments.

This step is important for two main reasons. The first is that it equips communities to understand and confidently demand the quality of services they deserve, not as a favor, but as a right. The second is that it makes for more effective monitoring. For example, if a community wants to monitor HIV treatment, and they learn that interruptions can cause drug resistance and treatment failures, they are more incentivized to closely monitor drug stockouts and rapidly rally decision-makers to address them. Knowledge about key strategic commitments later helps communities to craft their monitoring priorities and to link CLM data to advocacy. For example, when monitoring HIV testing rates among adolescent girls and young women, CLM initiatives can compare existing testing rates against national targets to illustrate the extent of the gap and to push for improvements.

CLM builds on a rich history of community health education that informs the community science methodology. In the context of HIV, multiple community education efforts developed from the global civil society response to AIDS. One example is treatment literacy, when people living with and affected by HIV sought to educate themselves and their peers about the virus in an evidence-based and accessible manner. Key elements of treatment literacy programs include elimination of jargon and inaccessibly complex technical terminology, which puts knowledge about science and one's own body into the hands of affected individuals. As an example, the infographic below was developed by ITPC as part of a series of treatment education resources (ITPC 2022c) and explains the importance of viral load monitoring for people living with HIV, as well as what actions should occur depending on the results received (Fig. 3). It relies on clear and simple language to walk a reader through viral load monitoring and is an example of how to create accessible community education materials.

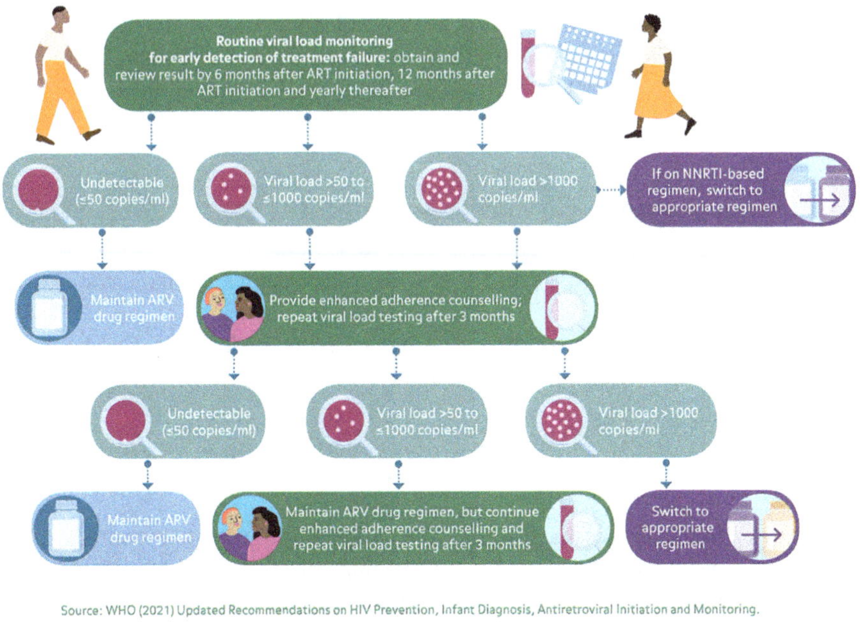

Fig. 3 Viral Load Monitoring Guide. A Guide to HIV for Community Education and Advocacy; ITPC, 2022. Original Source: Updated Recommendations; WHO 2021

Recommendations on HIV Prevention, Infant Diagnosis, Antiretroviral Initiation and Monitoring, 2021. Infographic developed by ITPC (2022a).

Another example of how community health education informs the first building block of CLM occurred more recently. The advent of the COVID-19 pandemic in 2020 served as a worldwide case study about the importance and necessity of providing clear and credible scientific information about the virus to the public. In response to the pandemic, communities led the way in disseminating information about prevention, treatment, vaccination, and the right to health services that individuals could and should demand of their leaders.

While educating communities is critical, broader education about CLM principles, processes, and methodology extends to all actors. CLM develops a framework for shared responsibility among a network of interconnected actors (including the state, service providers, and communities). Each party must consistently understand the CLM process in order to later respond to the emerging data. Skepticism about the purpose of monitoring or the quality of the process (and the resultant data) dooms a CLM intervention from the start. Educational workshops and trainings bring together diverse stakeholders and create momentum for CLM.

After educating communities and stakeholders about the concept and benefits of CLM, it is important to conduct a desk review, analyze community needs, and consult with partners.

After completing the analysis, conducting a stakeholder mapping helps map the important players. The mapping identifies stakeholders at a community level; within healthcare supervisory structures; at a healthcare service provision level; and at a government level (often ministries of health and ministries of finance, or their regional- or district-level equivalents). The mapping should be as comprehensive as possible because leaving out any groups that have a role to play in the co-creation of solutions leads to difficulties down the line.

5 Step 2: Evidence

The evidence quadrant of the CLM cycle involves creating the indicators to be monitored.

Figure 4 outlines a roadmap for generating and using evidence for CLM, which we will explore in more detail in sub-sections A–E.

5.1 Define Strategic Priorities for CLM

The first step in this process is to define what communities need to monitor. Often, this begins by asking the question: What is the immediate problem we are trying to solve? Typically, CLM implementers begin by facilitating a consultation with community stakeholders to identify and define indicators. This is a guided group discussion to pinpoint the primary challenges, barriers, and pain points that recipients of care (RoCs) experience when seeking healthcare.

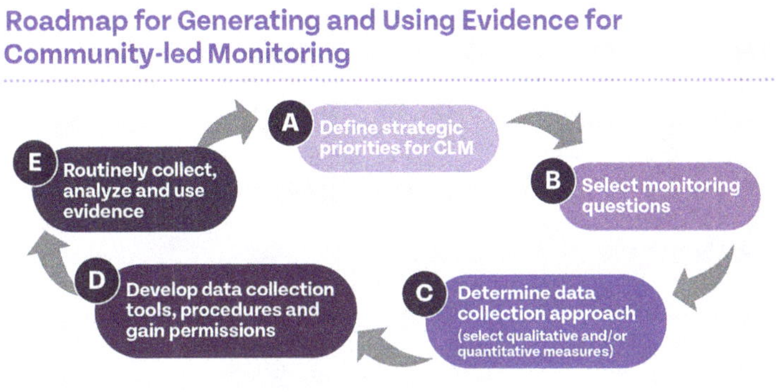

Fig. 4 Roadmap for Generating and Using Evidence for Community-led monitoring. Source: From Insights to Evidence; ITPC 2022

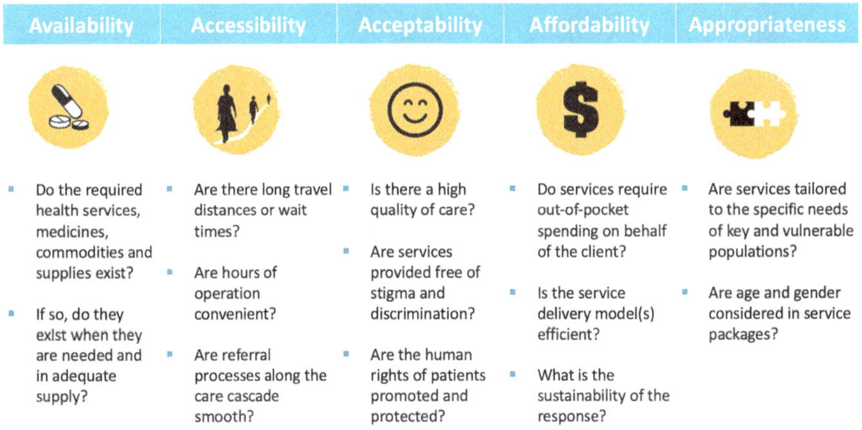

Fig. 5 The AAAAA framework. Source: Watch What Matters: Understanding Gaps in the HIV Treatment Cascade in 11 West African Countries; ITPC 2019

To help give structure to these discussions, ITPC recommends using the AAAAA framework to group questions into key themes (refer to Fig. 5). This framework builds upon the work by Levesque et al. (2013). Discussing issues of availability, accessibility, acceptability, affordability, and appropriateness of healthcare and services can pinpoint which types of CLM data would be strategic to collect to reveal the scope of the problem. We also recommend a sixth discussion area on quality of healthcare. Growing scholarship on health services improvements indicates that improving *access* to health care is not enough; rather, *quality* of care is most needed to improve outcomes (Kruk et al. 2018). The AAAAA(Q) framework can be applied beyond HIV to various contexts and disease focus areas.

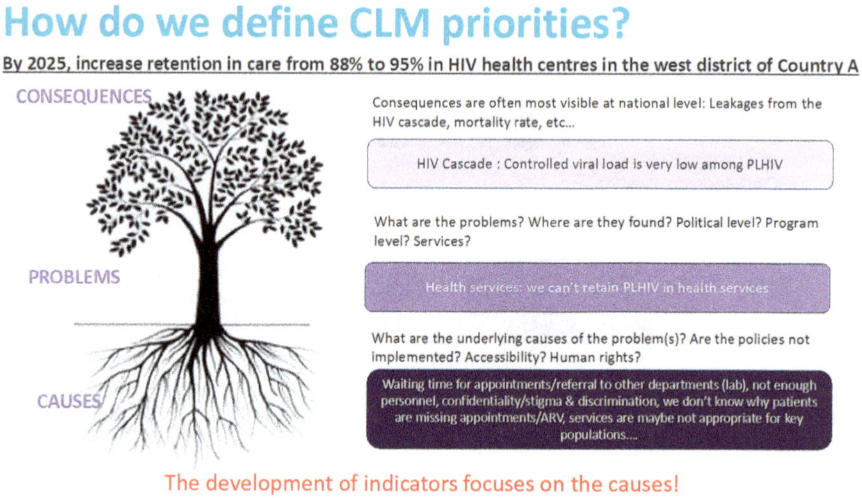

Fig. 6 Defining Priority Issues to Monitor in CLM. Source: Development of the CLM framework - Indicators and data collection, Francophone CLM Academy; ITPC 2023

5.2 Select Monitoring Questions

The selection of monitoring questions is informed by the pain points uncovered in facilitated discussions with communities. When selecting monitoring questions, it is important that these questions can guide us to the root causes of a problem, as outlined in Fig. 6. This figure takes a hypothetical scenario—the desire of a country to increase patient retention in care from 88% to 95% in one district—and assesses which factors contribute to patients dropping out of care. This approach of working backwards from the current problem to the possible cause shapes effective monitoring questions.

5.3 Determine Data Collection Approach

CLM indicators collect both quantitative and qualitative data. To have a credible understanding of the problem, and suitable insights for the necessary solutions, communities need to gather evidence about both (a) the magnitude of these problems and (b) the underlying factors that drive them. For example, if communities indicate that there are long wait times for healthcare services, information is needed to establish both (a) the length of the wait (i.e., on average, a four-hour wait at eight facilities over the last quarter) and (b) the factors underpinning the wait time (i.e., health facility staff indicate their wages have not been paid consistently, leading to attrition and a depleted healthcare workforce to meet the demand of recipients of care).

Leveraging digital tools such as mobile data collection apps and cloud-based analysis platforms can streamline data gathering, allowing for faster and more accurate data aggregation and insights. These tools also facilitate real-time feedback loops, enabling communities to monitor and adjust approaches rapidly. However, successful implementation depends on addressing challenges in data security, connectivity, and the technical capacity of community members. CLM programs must therefore balance digital integration with training and secure protocols to protect sensitive community data.

When developing CLM indicators, keep in mind that fewer, targeted indicators are better than many indicators. In general, 20–25 indicators should be the maximum number. The more indicators, the more time-consuming—and expensive—the data analysis process later becomes. Further technical documents describe CLM indicator development in more detail (ITPC 2022e), but some key factors to keep in mind include whether you have the resources to collect the amount of data at the chosen frequency; what qualitative data will contribute context to the quantitative data; and whether the data you need is available, i.e., disaggregated. (If data is not disaggregated, you can consider advocacy efforts to push for disaggregation.)

The development of CLM indicators is an iterative process; typically, multiple drafts are written and circulated to community leaders for comments and adjustments. It is important to also hold a consultation with government stakeholders to discuss the selection of data collection sites; this can avoid duplication of efforts or the overlap of concurrent CLM initiatives at the same facilities.

5.4 Develop Data Collection Tools, Procedures, and Gain Permissions

Once you finalize the indicators, develop data collection methods and tools for use by data collectors. Depending on the context, data collection methods include individual interviews with key informants, surveys, and focus group discussions or semi-structured interviews (further guidance describes this in detail in ITPC 2022b). Data collection tools include paper forms or digital forms using devices such as a tablet or phone; most programs will use both.

This is also the time to determine which sites to monitor, the monitoring schedule, and to secure all necessary permissions for the selected sites. Data collectors are then recruited from the affected community; for example, people living with TB should be data collectors for a CLM program monitoring TB services. The role of data collectors is pivotal: they should be selected through an open call, adequately renumerated and receive at least 2–3 days of training prior to beginning work. The trainings typically include ethics of data collection, testing data collection tools, and troubleshooting potential issues. Depending on the context, conduct a risk analysis and develop a subsequent safety plan to ensure data collectors stay safe.

After the data collectors are selected and trained, organize consensus-building workshops on the role of CLM with various strategic partners (civil society organizations; government actors; technical and financial partners); prepare to set up the partners' consultation framework, including drafting the terms of reference of the Community Consultative Group or other instrument that will serve as the body that reacts to CLM data and is charged with co-creation of solutions; and convene a consultation with the various stakeholder groups to identify and appoint their representatives to the consultation framework (CCG or other). Finally, create and share a participatory CLM implementation work plan.

Careful preparatory work leads to a better understanding of CLM among stakeholders, shared ownership of the CLM intervention, and mutual understanding of each stakeholders' expectations. These steps strengthen collaboration between all players from the outset of the process.

5.5 Routinely Collect, Analyze, and Use Evidence

Recurring data collection of the same indicators allows communities to identify trends over time. Data are collected on a routine basis, usually every month or every quarter. After collecting data, data analysts identify the scope and scale of a problem. They determine when programmatic or policy changes make a positive or negative difference (or if there are no changes at all).

Monthly checks build accountability and allow for constructive relationships to develop between data collectors and institutional staff. Operational research conducted by ITPC indicates that the recurring presence of data collectors at monitored health facilities is one of the most important avenues for sharing CLM-derived feedback with healthcare providers.

A CLM program's credibility rests on the quality and integrity of the data collection process. This includes managing data security, data verification, and conducting quality checks. To ensure high-quality data, many CLM programs also now employ software-driven data verification and analysis processes that reduce human error and increase efficiency. Integrating these tools requires community training and a focus on digital literacy to empower data collectors with the skills needed to navigate new technologies. Additionally, safeguarding data security in digital systems is critical, as CLM data often contains sensitive information.

Figure 7 provides an operational roadmap of a CLM intervention called a Community Treatment Observatory, which collects data for monitoring trends along the HIV care cascade. In Fig. 7, you can see how data from each individual data collector feeds into the larger process, from analysis to advocacy, and the various safeguards to ensure data quality along the way. Other publications further describe data collection best practices and provide further guidance on implementation (ITPC 2023).

ITPC advocates for a mixed methods approach to CLM data analysis and has written technical guidance on this subject (ITPC 2023). In short, qualitative and quantitative data can inform each other—rather than completing analyses of quantitative and qualitative data in isolation from each other.

Not all community networks are familiar with data analysis methods, and ITPC encourages partnerships between Non-governmental organizations (NGOs) and

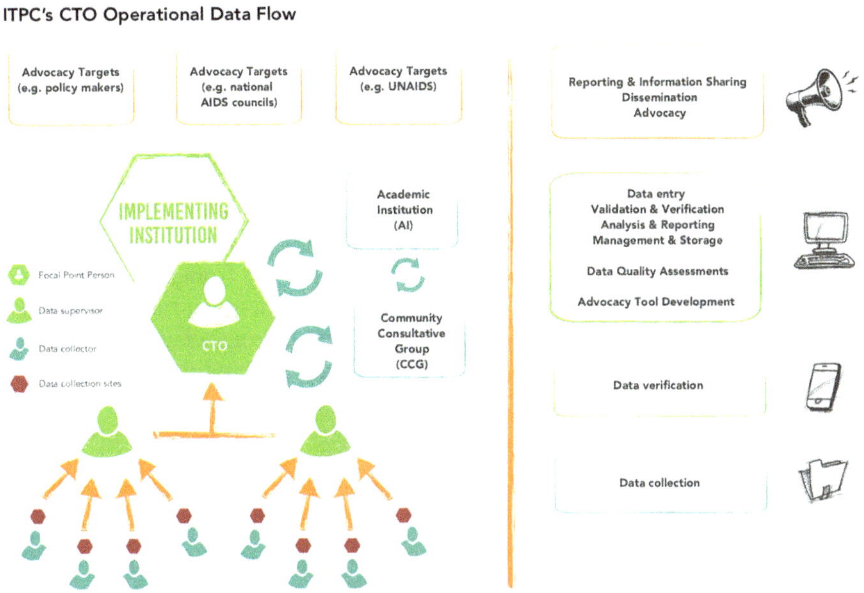

Fig. 7 Operational Data Flow of a Community Treatment Observatory. Source: The CTO Model Explained; ITPC 2019

local academic institutions, or with expert consultants who have the technical skills to assist with this process. However, in all cases, technical support should take the form of mentorship, with the aim of building the skills of community groups to increasingly take on this role themselves. If data analysis is entirely outsourced to another entity, community groups lose the opportunity to delve into and interpret their own data and its alignment with their lived experiences. Communities that work closely with CLM-collected data gain confidence and are empowered to speak about their data and results with authority.

Recurrent data collection and analysis is a large job not only for data collectors but for the analysts. One program indicated that for each month of data collected, it took their small monitoring and evaluation (M&E) team up to 4 months to fully process the data. Earlier, we mentioned that maintaining an overly ambitious set of indicators was not sustainable. If any indicators do not show changes over several months, we suggest dropping the indicator and selecting a more relevant one.

6 Step 3: Engagement

A core advantage of the CLM methodology is that sharing and discussing CLM data with other stakeholders are integrated into the process on a recurrent basis. As we detailed at the outset of CLM initiation, part of the work entails identifying the correct individuals who have the roles, responsibilities, and power needed to co-create solutions when CLM data reveals issues.

After communities collect, analyze, and organize their data, they present the findings to this larger group of stakeholders.

We advise that implementors create a plan for recurrent engagement with these actors, often via a Community Consultative Group (CCG). A CCG is a multistakeholder technical advisory board that meets on a monthly or quarterly basis to review CLM data analysis and to prioritize advocacy issues. The CCG typically has 10–15 members, including a chair, a vice-chair, and representatives from normative agencies (UNAIDS, PEPFAR, WHO, Global Fund); government organizations (national AIDS and/or TB, malaria programs; Ministry of Health); civil society organizations and partners (networks of key populations and affected communities); and research institutes or independent experts.

While it can be tempting to present data from every indicator, effective presentation of analyzed data emphasizes trends over time and pinpoints the most urgent issues for action. Communities may benefit from training and mentorship in effective data visualization and communication skills, but perhaps most of all, from recurring opportunities to try, fall short/fail, and improve their engagement efforts. There are a wide variety of techniques that can support engagement efforts—use of handouts; charts; PowerPoint presentations; written reports; and community testimonials—but ultimately the best form of engagement is context-specific to the location, culture, and group of decision-makers.

Partnerships and mentorship are key in supporting communities through the engagement process. Often the best mentors are other CLM implementers, who can share their experiences in other contexts and countries. Communities of practice and country-to-country learning opportunities can also assist with this step.

The end goal of any effort by communities to engage with others and share CLM data is concrete change that improves the quality of healthcare services for recipients of care. In CLM, reporting alone is insufficient. Action to improve the conditions identified is vital. Figure 8 illustrates the CLM data journey for change.

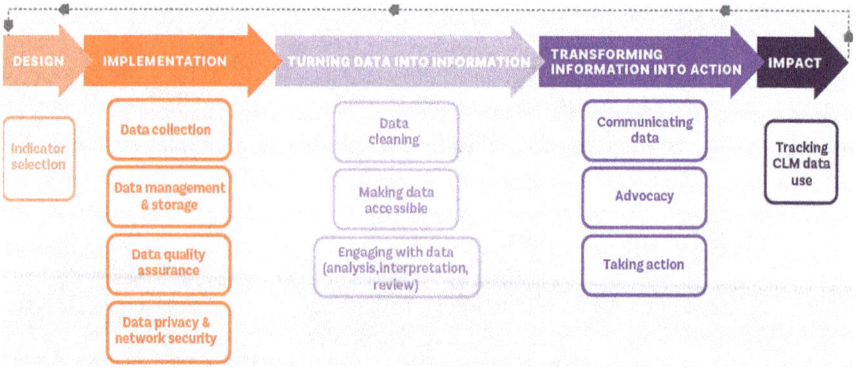

Fig. 8 CLM Data Journey for Change. Source: Community-led Monitoring Guide to Support CLM Data Use in Decision-Making; ITPC 2023

If engagement via the CCG or other direct mechanisms is not effective, community groups can escalate to advocacy.

7 Step 4: Advocacy

When problems identified via CLM aren't addressed via the regular reporting process to the satisfaction of recipients of care, communities escalate to advocacy. CLM data is compelling, but most often, the data alone is not enough to ensure the necessary changes. To be successful, CLM implementers must conduct advocacy efforts. This starts with identifying who has the power to affect change and then crafting evidence-based arguments to persuade those bodies to act.

Advocacy tactics must be context-specific to be successful. Determining which mix of data, storytelling, diplomacy, and demanding accountability from duty-bearers yields action is precisely why CLM is both an art and a science. It often takes many attempts and months or years of effort to produce results.

Governments are key to improving health services, and in first-time or nascent CLM programs, there can be skepticism about the advocacy step of the process. The question inherent in this reticence is often: Will this effort culminate in civil society action to embarrass or shame elected officials? An important balance is required. Advocacy is not only protests and placards in the streets—it can take many forms, including cups of tea with stakeholders; dialogues around a boardroom table; citizen journalism; and presentations to elected officials or funders. It is impossible to be prescriptive about what kind of advocacy "works," as contexts, vary enormously. In our experience, advocacy requires patience and persistence—in some cases, progress is slow, and then suddenly the right constellation of actors with a shared interest in the work comes together and progress moves forward significantly. In the next section, we will explore how this plays out in several real-world contexts.

Figure 9 outlines a general framework for thinking through advocacy efforts.

Audiences	Who are the audience(s)? What is their level of knowledge about the topic? What are their information needs? What level of detail and complexity should be included?
Messaging	What are the main message(s) that we want to convey? How can we communicate it in a clear, precise and concise manner? Must be in line with scope and size of data.
Context	Can we add narrative or place the data in context, to facilitate user understanding?
Human interest	Are we telling the stories of people and communities with their informed consent, and due respect to protecting their privacy, confidentiality and security?
Visualizations	What is the best way to represent the data such that the message is conveyed? (tables, charts, maps, infographics are all options- and graphics are very effective tools)
Dissemination	What is the best channel through which to share the message(s)? (reports, briefings, slide decks, media articles, case studies, listservs, social media). How can we feed the data back to the community? What role do communities play in dissemination and subsequent advocacy?

Fig. 9 Framework for Planning Advocacy Efforts. Source: Community-led Monitoring Guide to Support CLM Data Use in Decision-Making; ITPC 2023

8 Case Studies

The following case studies document different CLM programs in four African countries where communities sought to monitor HIV services, including in one context service disruptions due to the COVID-19 pandemic. Among the literature, there are numerous case studies about *process improvements* because of CLM, but here we try to focus on what evidence there is of CLM's *impact* on health services amelioration.

9 Elimination of User Fees in Cote D'Ivoire

From January 2018 to June 2019, ITPC in partnership with the Réseau Ivoirien des Organisations de Personnes Vivant avec le VIH/SIDA (RIP+) implemented a CLM project at 27 health facilities across Cote d'Ivoire. Over this period, field researchers conducted a total of 600 interviews and 34 focus group discussions with recipients of care to assess barriers to HIV services along the treatment cascade. Seventeen percent of the recipients of care identified payment or considerable out-of-pocket expenditure as a reason for not accessing antiretroviral therapy (ART). Even at facilities where ART was free, fees for diagnostic tests, consultations with health-care providers, and medicines for opportunistic infections represented additional cost barriers. These findings on barriers to access were presented by the Cote D'Ivoire Community Treatment Observatory (CTO) team at the annual meeting negotiating the following year's investment in US Foreign Assistance for the global HIV response (the PEPFAR COP19 meeting).

The Ministry of Health of Cote D'Ivoire, the US Global AIDS Ambassador, and the PEPFAR team were present. Anecdotally, CTO team members indicated that the PEPFAR team was initially skeptical of the credibility of the community data, and quickly conducted their own investigation—which proved to be concurrent with the findings from CLM. This established trust in the community process and opened doors for a more constructive problem-solving relationship. In April 2019, a circular was issued by the Ministry of Health which signaled its commitment to stop charging people for accessing HIV testing and treatment services, declaring that it would strictly monitor previously announced decisions to prevent people living with HIV from being asked to pay user fees (UNAIDS 2023).

10 Increasing Uptake of PrEP Among Young Women in South Africa

In 2022, a CLM intervention in South Africa's West Rand monitored 19 health facilities, where data revealed that 20–24-year-olds had the lowest pre-exposure prophylaxis (PrEP) uptake among women despite having the highest HIV incidence rate. From January to October 2022, just 333 women aged 20–24 years initiated PrEP at the monitored sites, compared with 527 15–19-year-olds and 849 women aged

25 years and above. Data analysis indicated that young women had limited to no understanding of PrEP, and most had never been offered the service.

To address this, the CLM team convened meetings with health facility managers; organized PrEP refresher courses among healthcare workers; conducted health education sessions among young women to generate demand for PrEP services; and collaborated with the Department of Health to distribute approved PrEP information, education, and communication materials in two areas. Crucially, an advocacy meeting was also held with government disease officials, including district health officials, to discuss the PrEP gap. Directly following this meeting, the government created new PrEP targets for health facilities.

As CLM implementation continued, the total number of people remaining on PrEP grew steadily at the monitored sites, from 3527 in January 2023 to 5266 in December 2023, with a total of 2520 new PrEP initiations in 2023. Of these, 368 were among young women aged 20–24 years, up from 333 in 2022. In 2023, people who visited the CLM-monitored sites were 32% more likely to initiate PrEP following an HIV test compared with other West Rand facilities (ITPC 2024).

11 Alleviating TB Medicine Stockouts in South Africa

In 2022, a CLM intervention in South Africa at two sites identified stockouts of four TB medicines for a cumulative 210 days. Stockouts continued into 2023 and included 17 different TB medicines at these two locations. At the site where the stockouts were most severe, the TB treatment initiation rate was only 50% in February 2023 as compared to 88.4% at the other monitored sites. Qualitative data notes reported that these two facilities only reacted once the medicines were already missing—rather than taking a proactive approach to prevent stockouts.

As a result of this data, the CLM team alerted the facility managers and district health office. They then worked with the facility pharmacist to develop stock monitoring and forecasting protocols. In the last quarter of 2023, there were only six days of stockouts, and the treatment initiation rate had improved above the national average (ITPC 2024)

12 CLM Insulates Health Facilities in Malawi from Severe Service Disruptions from COVID-19 and Promotes Swift Recovery

CLM data collected in Malawi over a period during the COVID-19 pandemic sought to monitor the impact of COVID-19 on the disruption of HIV services. Data collected by the Malawi Network of Religious Leaders Living with or Personally Affected by HIV and AIDS (MANERELA+) indicated that HIV service access was of higher quality at health facilities that were undergoing community monitoring efforts than at nonmonitored sites. At 15 monitored health facilities in Dedza and Kasungu where data collectors routinely collected data and discussed trends with healthcare workers, HIV testing services fell by a less severe degree (25.5%) during COVID-19 as compared to falling by 39.0% at eight other health facilities in Lilongwe where no CLM mechanism was in place. This study was not a randomized controlled trial, and while CLM was not the only factor at play, the comparison of these two groups of facilities nonetheless suggests that CLM had a mitigating effect on the rate of HIV testing services during COVID-19 (ITPC 2024).

13 Strengths, Limitations, and the Way Forward

What can Community-Led Monitoring (CLM) bring to health services evaluation that is above and beyond other practices?

The community-led nature of CLM creates maximum efficiency: rather than casting a wide net and collecting information on hundreds of indicators about program quality, as is the case with traditional evaluation methods, communities begin by pinpointing their primary pain points, enabling the inquiry to begin from a targeted place. As we demonstrated in the Case Study section, CLM data rapidly identifies gaps between normative guidance and the actual standard of care, applying these insights quickly and nimbly toward improved service delivery. CLM-derived insights have led to fewer drug and supply stockouts, the elimination of user fees, and a more resilient bounce-back in the face of health system disruptions. CLM-driven results occur faster than many other health evaluation approaches, which often wait until research concludes to share the results with decision-makers.

Facility or healthcare provider-led evaluation methods that ask recipients of care to share their feedback also remain limited by an inherent power dynamic. It is difficult to share honest (and sometimes critical) feedback with the exact person or entity that you rely on to provide you with care. CLM alleviates this power dynamic through a peer-to-peer process in which members of a community seek the perspectives and experiences of other community members on health services. ITPC's operational research has found that many data collectors take this responsibility to their communities very seriously and have carried out roles beyond their CLM data collector job description. This includes providing treatment education, broader community updates about the trends identified via CLM, and information about subsequent changes to protocols, policies, and programs at their local health facilities.

At the same time as CLM incentivizes positive relationships among communities, it also elevates community expertise in the broader health field. CLM sets up a structure in which community networks have an equal seat at the decision-making table. This extends from local and national level processes and spaces of learning to international ones. Too often, "expert panels" at global health conferences are populated with academics, government leaders, and donors, with a short time slot for a community testimonial at the end. It is shortsighted that the individuals with the most lived experience navigating broken or challenging health services are sprinkled in as an afterthought to share their "story," but not necessarily to come forward with their own data, analysis, and ideas about solutions. CLM subverts this dynamic through the creation of community-owned data and community-led solutions.

A common criticism of CLM is that the data is too locally specific and that any findings are only applicable to the specific health facilities and catchment areas where the information was collected. In our experience though, this is not the case. In September 2020, ITPC and our partners started collecting data on multi-month dispensing of anti-retroviral treatment in Malawi and South Africa—driven to do so because communities indicated how important it was to the health of people living with HIV in the context of COVID-19. The specificity and relevance of the indicator soon resonated beyond our project; UNAIDS added multi-month dispensing of ART as a brand-new indicator in the Global AIDS Monitoring framework in February 2022 (Lauer 2022).

As the case studies in this chapter illustrate, CLM is a long-term process that does not achieve results overnight. However, as CLM has become a buzzword and gained attention from major donors in the global health space, there are high expectations for concrete results without appropriate long-term investment toward achieving program maturity. We have found from our partners on the ground that there is enormous pressure to initiate CLM programs, report data, and achieve major changes in very short timelines—sometimes as little as 6 months. This is not only unrealistic but also places an undue burden on communities to strive for impossible targets. To be successful and sustainable, CLM requires multi-year investments and a generous enough timeline to allow communities to find their footing by establishing indicator frameworks, initiating data collection, carrying out analysis, and honing their experience stepping into decision-making spaces. CLM entails ongoing collaborative work that requires trust and will not succeed if critical steps are missed or rushed.

As CLM is still a nascent field, while there are shared principles, there is no single established implementation methodology. Given the combination of funder interest and pressure to deliver results quickly, there has been a rush of new players entering the field, sometimes with limited time, little implementation training, and insufficient budgets. In this context, there is risk of cutting corners such that programs do not uphold the fidelity and rigor of the CLM model. The resulting "partial CLM" or other forms of monitoring or community data collection may discredit the credibility of more robust CLM interventions.

There are also areas of CLM that need further research. Quantifying the specific impact of CLM is challenging; the structure of most CLM programs does not allow for direct comparison with "control groups," making it difficult to isolate CLM's specific effects. In addition, few CLM programs receive long-term investments that would offer the opportunity to measure the long-term effects of mature CLM programs. We are not aware to date of any studies that have revisited previous CLM programs to determine whether there have been ongoing or long-term continuation of improvements after the cessation of CLM efforts.

Numerous outstanding questions remain for the field of CLM, including: How "much" CLM is needed to reach a critical tipping point for action? When should monitored facilities "graduate" from CLM? Would a limited set of indicators (perhaps five?) applied to all CLM programs in a country enable more powerful, national-level analysis than small-scale or district-level CLM efforts? These questions should not be considered limitations, but rather as an invitation to further hone the methodology and to apply CLM with even more rigor and scale.

14 Conclusion

Community-led monitoring is a promising innovation that may finally unlock a pathway for community leadership to play a credible and powerful role in shaping health programs and policies. As a bottom-up, data-driven form of health system evaluation, CLM puts equity into action and in so doing, brings insights to bear that are not captured via other evaluation methodologies. CLM ultimately offers us an opportunity to shift the way we conduct science and programming in global public health, integrating meaningful community leadership within research, program science institutions, and academia.

Moving forward, the sustainability of CLM hinges on bringing more actors into the "big tent," in which there is a shared perspective that CLM is a win-win investment. We should give governments the opportunity to learn more about the powerful outcomes that CLM can achieve for health services, alleviating their fears of potential criticism. We can highlight that CLM goes beyond an investment in data and programs and strengthens community services—one of the most critical structures for ensuring health services remain resilient in the face of new pandemics, as COVID-19 so aptly illustrated. However, while CLM is a technically sound mechanism, its success also requires political feasibility to ensure effective implementation. CLM demonstrates that communities are capable of nuanced, credible, and timely analyses that offer a pathway to improving the health of their societies and countries.

References

Community Data for Change Consortium (CD4C), Community-led Accountability Working Group (CLAW), and EANNASOAPCASO-ATAC Consortium (2022) Community-led monitoring: best practices for strengthening the model. https://clm.itpcglobal.org/download/cd4c-claw-eannaso-atac-apcaso-community-led-monitoring-best-practices-for-strengthningthe-model.pdf. Accessed 15 September 2023

ITPC (2022a) A guide to HIV for community education and advocacy. https://itpcglobal.org/resource/a-guide-to-hiv-community-education-and-advocacy/. Accessed 20 September 2023

ITPC (2022b) Data management tools: consideration for choosing tools for data collection, analysis, and presentation for community-led monitoring. https://itpcglobal.org/resource/data-management-tools-for-community-led-monitoring-clm/. Accessed 25 August 2023

ITPC (2022c) Treatment education for people living with HIV: a community guide. https://itpcglobal.org/wp-content/uploads/2022/04/ITPC-TX%20education-full-web.pdf. Accessed 2 October 2024

ITPC (2022d) From insights to evidence: a guide for translating program and policy priorities into qualitative and quantitative measures for community-led monitoring. https://itpcglobal.

org/resource/from-insights-to-evidence-a-guide-for-translating-priorities-into-qualitative-quantitative-measures-for-community-led-monitoring/. Accessed 7 September 2023

ITPC (2022e) Precision in a pandemic: a data quality assurance guide for community-led monitoring during COVID-19. https://itpcglobal.org/resource/precision-in-a-pandemic/. Accessed 17 September 2023

ITPC (2023) A guide to data analysis methods in community-led monitoring. https://itpcglobal.org/resource/a-guide-to-data-analysis-methods-in-community-led-monitoring/. Accessed 21 August 2023

ITPC (2024) Insight, influence & impact. 10 big change stories from the citizen science community-led monitoring project in 2023. https://bit.ly/CLM-Data-Report-2023. Accessed 23 May 2024

Jallow W et al (2021) How to implement community-led monitoring: a community toolkit. ITPC, Chennai. https://itpcglobal.org/blog/resource/how-to-implement-community-led-monitoring-toolkit/. Accessed 20 August 2023

Kruk ME, Gage AD, Arsenault C, Jordan K, Leslie HH, Roder-DeWan S et al (2018) High-quality health systems in the sustainable development goals era: time for a revolution. Lancet Glob Health 6(11):e1196–e1252. https://doi.org/10.1016/S2214-109X(18)30386-3

Lauer K (2022) Community-led monitoring: advancing public health equity and accountability. https://cquin.icap.columbia.edu/wp-content/uploads/2022/12/Lauer_CLM-Keynote_FINAL.pdf. Accessed 18 September 2023

Levesque JF, Harris MF, Russell G (2013) Patient-centred access to health care: conceptualising access at the interface of health systems and populations. Int J Equity Health 12:18. https://doi.org/10.1186/1475-9276-12-18

UNAIDS (2023) Community-led monitoring in action. https://www.unaids.org/sites/default/files/media_asset/JC3085E_community-led-monitoring-in-action_en.pdf. Accessed 18 October 2023

Culturally Responsive Evaluation: The Added Value of Cultural Humility

Elvire Toure-Pegnougo, Emilie Gélinas, Naïma Bentayeb, and Lara Gautier

Abstract

The diversity of the contexts and the population benefiting from social, health, education and community services requires evaluators to develop new skills to (re)consider culture in their evaluation approaches. In this chapter, we illustrate through empirical case studies the value of approaches aimed at reinforcing culturally responsive evaluation (CRE) with the added value of the evaluator's cultural humility. The cases present international situations involving different communities, various fields of intervention, and various cultural contexts. We demonstrate the importance of equipping evaluators with cultural humility, to produce credible results adapted to the context of the evaluation. In the cases reviewed in this chapter, this approach not only serves to illustrate its positive added value in the evaluation process but also emphasizes its significance for all evaluation stakeholders and beyond.

Keywords

Responsive evaluation · Culture · Health and social services · Cultural humility

E. Toure-Pegnougo · E. Gélinas
School of Public Health, University of Montréal, Montreal, QC, Canada
e-mail: emilie.gelinas@umontreal.ca

N. Bentayeb
McGill University, SHERPA University Institute, Montreal, QC, Canada
e-mail: naima.bentayeb.ccomtl@ssss.gouv.qc.ca

L. Gautier (✉)
SHERPA University Institute, Montreal, QC, Canada
e-mail: lara.gautier@umontreal.ca

A. Kaehne, J. Feather (eds.), *Handbook of Health Services Evaluation*, https://doi.org/10.1007/978-3-031-87869-5_28

1 Introduction

In this chapter, we argue that, as we evaluate health care and social services, it is important to consider the diverse range of cultural contexts and cultural backgrounds of populations benefiting from these services. Culture "… is that complex whole which includes knowledge, belief, art, morals, law, custom, and any other capabilities and habits acquired by man as a member of society" (Tylor 1920, p. 1). Culture is shared, transmitted, dynamic, and evolves according to the social, economic, and political context. Many authors agree on the importance of cultural elements in the practice, research, and evaluation of health care and social services as they influence the beliefs, knowledge, and behaviors of individuals identifying with a respective group (Cleaver et al. 2016; Tervalon and Murray-García 1998). Evaluations that do not sufficiently consider the influence of dominant social and cultural norms are being challenged regarding their relevance, methodology, and validity. These evaluations also raise issues related to the persistence of power imbalances, colonial practices, and the lack of community involvement. Faced with such observations, several approaches, including culturally responsive evaluation, have emerged to enable the integration of culture into evaluations (Foronda et al. 2016; Kushnier et al. 2023; SenGupta et al. 2004).

Culturally responsive evaluation (CRE) is defined as an approach that places culture at the center of the evaluation process: a system of strategies and practical frameworks that allow all cultural elements of a target population to be taken into account (Frierson et al. 2002; Hopson 2009; Hood et al. 2015). CRE also invites evaluators to recognize that reality is intersubjective, to understand how it is perceived by others and that it is necessary to legitimize the knowledge of the targeted populations (Botcheva et al. 2009). Above all, it requires adopting "a cultural perspective different than one's own" (Dunaway et al. 2012, p. 497). CRE, therefore, requires the participation of the communities concerned in all phases of the evaluation to integrate their perspectives and values into the design of the project and to adapt the implementation in the event of concerns or discomfort (Acree and Chouinard 2020; Askew et al. 2012; Botcheva et al. 2009; Dinh et al. 2019).

In health and social services, CRE often involves acquiring cultural skills. Therefore, cultural competence as a common approach for acknowledging and respecting culture is defined as the ability of professionals or systems to provide care and services in line with the social, cultural, and linguistic realities of the target populations. It involves considering the social, economic, historical, and political dimensions of potential project participants (Anderson et al. 2022; Brottman et al. 2020). However, cultural competence in CRE has limitations as it does not reflect the dynamic and reflective nature of the culture; cultural humility does. In this sense, engaging in a cultural humility approach has been proposed by several authors as the guiding principle for CRE to position evaluator's actions in a dynamic process, and a continuous commitment to learning from others to provide authentic results in evaluation (Gautier 2022).

Cultural humility, long addressed in the field of healthcare and social services to promote better care for users (representing diverse communities), is relevant in all areas where interactions between individuals occur within the context of culturally responsible evaluation (Brottman et al. 2020; Fang et al. 2021; Hughes et al. 2020; Tervalon and Murray-García 1998). Cultural humility refers to evaluators' awareness of the importance of dynamic culture in the dynamics of the evaluation process and that at various levels including intrapersonal (e.g., self-criticism, reflexivity, recognition of one's own biases and preconceived ideas), interpersonal (e.g., active and attentive listening to the subject of the evaluation, understanding the beliefs and practices of the communities), and organizational/systemic levels (e.g., providing a framework for discussion and a safe space for community members so that they can give their opinions, promote cultural humility in evaluation practices) (Gautier 2022; Hughes et al. 2020). These three levels translate into analytical components, such as those designed by Tervalon and Murray-García (1998). The authors suggest three characteristic elements of cultural humility: (1) a permanent commitment to self-evaluation and self-criticism (intrapersonal level); (2) a desire to redress power imbalances in relationships (interpersonal and systemic levels); and (3) the development of mutually beneficial and non-paternalistic partnerships (interpersonal and systemic levels) (Tervalon and Murray-García 1998).

In this chapter, we aim to illustrate through empirical case studies the value of cultural humility in CRE practices. Our analysis of each case is based on the application of the three aforementioned characteristic components of cultural humility developed by Tervalon and Murray-Garcia: (1) a permanent commitment to self-evaluation and self-criticism; (2) a desire to redress power imbalances in relationships; and (3) the development of mutually beneficial and non-paternalistic partnerships. These case studies were selected based on the authors' evaluation experiences (cases 1 and 2) and a literature review (case 3). The first case describes an evaluation of a program related to both social services and health services in Indonesia. This case was chosen because it brought out the characteristics of cultural humility in a collaboration where the teams working on the evaluation come from different countries and research cultures. The second case presents the evaluation of a restorative justice project in Québec, Canada, which is linked to social services considering the impact of interactions with the Québec justice system on the state of health of people. The third case depicts a research project in the United States of America (USA) where an evaluation dimension was integrated to ensure cultural relevance and safety. Although we discerned nuances between research and evaluation, particularly regarding financial and time resources, the lessons from this experience resonate in the evaluation field.

The presented cases illustrate diverse international experiences involving different communities, in varied cultural contexts and highlight the efforts made by evaluators to adapt to the values and social norms of communities and to highlight their cultural knowledge.

2 Families First with Home Visitation Program (FFHVP) in West Java, Indonesia

Physical punishment of children is common in low- or middle-income countries (Lansford and Deater-Deckard 2012). In several Indonesian provinces, available data show that children who were subject to at least one form of physical or psychological punishment by their caregiver or another member of their household experienced child maltreatment (UNICEF 2012). According to WHO (World Health Organization), child maltreatment is "the abuse and neglect that occurs to children under 18 years of age. It includes all types of physical and/or emotional ill-treatment, sexual abuse, neglect, negligence, and commercial or other exploitation, which results in actual or potential harm to the child's health, survival, development, or dignity in the context of a relationship of responsibility, trust, or power" (WHO 2022). Considering the impact of child maltreatment on the health of these children and on society at large, WHO has proposed seven strategies which represent areas of action to combat child maltreatment: implementation and enforcement of laws, standards, and values, environmental safety, support for parents and caregivers, income and economic strengthening, response and support services, education, and practical know-how (WHO 2022). So to improve parenting skills and replace physical or psychological punishment with positive discipline, the Families First with Home Visitation Program (FFHVP) which is a local adaptation of the Positive Discipline in Everyday Parenting (PDEP) program to the West Java context was implemented (Durrant 2007, 2013). Positive discipline refers to techniques of guidance in children's education that combine child rights principles and research results on effective parenting and healthy child development (Durrant 2016).

The FFHVP was delivered between May and August 2017 by locally recruited and trained community facilitators and supervised on a weekly basis by mentors (Irwanto 2014; UNICEF 2012). It consisted of 10 group sessions with child caregivers and four home visits. An evaluation was designed and conducted by McGill University (Canada) in collaboration with the SMERU Research Institute (Indonesia) to assess the effectiveness of the FFHVP and its implementation in selected locations in Cianjur District, West Java. The team measured the efficacy of the FFHVP through a clustered randomized controlled trial and documented program implementation through a process evaluation. Qualitative interviews were conducted with 134 participants, including caregivers (mainly women), facilitators, mentors, Save the Children staff at national and local levels, and a few local authorities. Participants were offered symbolic compensation (i.e., an umbrella, a tote bag, etc.), and transportation costs were reimbursed for group interviews. Ethical approval and all the relevant permits were obtained in Montréal, Canada, and in Indonesia. A detailed description of the protocol is freely accessible online (Ruiz-Casares et al. 2019). This case study only presents findings from the process evaluation.

A culturally responsive evaluation approach considering characteristics of cultural humility was chosen. First, to develop a mutually beneficial and non-paternalistic partnership, an independent advisory committee (composed of academics and specialists with expertise in child protection in Indonesia from government and nongovernmental, academic, and donor agencies) participated in the continuous monitoring of the evaluation process, proposing methodological adjustments when and where ethically needed, and advising on the dissemination of information at the end of the evaluation. The expertise of the committee members strengthened the relevance and quality of the evaluation and helped reduce power imbalances. Close and continued supervision of interviewers during data collection was ensured using instant messaging (WhatsApp and email) to adapt to local preferences in terms of communication means. Such monitoring enabled early correction of any misinterpretations and allowed for a safe space for the community and evaluators to communicate. In addition, all mentors overseeing community facilitators were supported throughout the program by representatives from the University of Manitoba, Save the Children Indonesia, and the University of Padjadjaran (Indonesia).

Second, the evaluation team used a collaborative approach to community engagement to minimize power differentials and allow participants to get and understand information about the project. On the one hand, the evaluator and academic staff at McGill University provided scientific leadership and oversight to the evaluation, carried out all analyses, and coordinated all aspects of the trial. On the other hand, the research staff at the SMERU Research Institute in Jakarta conducted the data collection and coordinated the research locally. Entrusting data collection to a local team (SMERU Research Institute) demonstrated the evaluation team in Canada's desire to ensure that participants were completely comfortable sharing their perceptions and feelings regarding the program. This decision minimized unconscious bias or the consequences on the data understanding due to a lack of knowledge of local realities and customs. Training sessions prepared by Save the Children and the University of Manitoba were given to the selected interviewers, mentors, and community facilitators before the data collection activities. Teaching materials and questionnaires were adapted and translated from English to Sudanese and Bahasa by Durrant and colleagues in collaboration with Save the Children-UK and Sayagi Tunas Cilik/Save the Children-Indonesia.

Third, the evaluation team in Canada analyzed and interpreted data they did not directly collect, and in a language, they did not speak and understand. Although all the data were translated into English by professional translators and verified by the SMERU team, it was a challenge for the evaluation team in Canada, who needed a cultural lens to read the data and to understand the context and the cultural considerations underlying some results. For the evaluation team in Canada, it led to a permanent commitment to self-evaluation and self-criticism during the analysis and interpretation of the collected data. To limit the impact of the team biases and preconceived ideas, many conversations in feedback loops took place to ensure that the data interpretation considered all the relevant context factors. The team collaborated with the SMERU team and the advisory committee to culturally contextualize the data. For instance, fathers mostly did not attend the sessions and/or were absent during the home visits.

That absence could be interpreted as a lack of interest or engagement of fathers concerning the education of their children. However, the advisory committee members emphasized the importance of religion and cultural factors to interpret these data. In fact, religion and culture were determinant factors in program understanding and participation. Culturally, mothers are responsible for the education of children, and fathers are responsible for the financial survival of the family. For husbands, not being at home during the home visits is a sign of respect for the intimacy of women discussing a subject (children's education) that is mainly their first concern. The evaluation team considered this factor when reporting results to ensure the actors' voices were represented. Adopting this perspective allowed the team to highlight the importance of preparing husbands for program implementation about the role they can and have to play in their children's education.

The collaboration between the SMERU team, the advisory committee, and the evaluation team in Canada allowed for the creation of a safe space for continued dialogue throughout the evaluation process, giving equal weight to all expressed perspectives and not only to those that comforted the evaluation team's worldview. Behind those good practices of attentiveness to local culture and norms, and efforts to balance power dynamics, the Canadian evaluation team's work was marked with cultural humility during the evaluation process as well as during the data interpretation. Openness to understand communities' cultural beliefs and practices was a key practice to enhance the use of evaluation results.

3 *Justice Hoodistique* for Black Youth in Montréal, Canada

In Canada, since 1996, the federal legislator has concluded that certain offenses can be the subject of nonjudicial treatment if the accused recognizes, among other conditions, responsibility and is ready to follow an alternative measures program (AMP) (Rossi et al. 2020). Sections 716 to 717.4 of the Criminal Code of Canada (CCC) specifically deal with alternative measures by defining them as measures taken against a person aged 18 and over to whom an offense is attributed rather than the recourse to the legal proceedings provided for by this Act (Ministère de la justice du Canada 2023). In Québec, a diversion system for offenders under the age of 18 has been established through alternative measure programs, and nearly 75% of adolescent offenders in Québec today benefit from these programs (AMP; section 119 of the Youth Criminal Justice Act (YCJA)) (Rossi et al. 2020). In Montréal (the largest city of the Québec province), as of 2016, Black communities represent 9.5% of the total population but account for 27% of people arrested, 13% of people who received reports for violations of municipal by-laws, and 20% of people accused or arrested (Armony et al. 2019). Systemic racism, racial profiling by a person in authority that contributes to up to 58% of Black people overjudicialization, the lack of referral of Black people for AMP, and their impact on mental health led Hoodstock (a community organization in the Montréal-Nord neighborhood, in Montréal) to develop and implement *Justice Hoodistique* project which is funded by Canada Public Health Agency (Eid et al. 2011; Gignac et al. 2023). *Justice Hoodistique* is intended to be a restorative justice project conceptualized by a group of specialists from various backgrounds (clinical, university, community, etc.) and developed by

Black people, for accused Black people aged 18–64. It's a pilot project that places great importance on the participation of all actors affected by the conflict and aiming diversion of justice and healing of the accused Afro-descendant person. Participants engage in group workshops during urban or rural weekend retreats; in individual follow-ups with speakers; and at the end of the participation in the project, in a hoodistic circle (made up of people chosen by the participants), which will determine the applicable measure or sanction.

Being a pilot project and being tested for the first time, a developmental evaluation supported the implementation of the project (Patton 2011). The evaluation team opted for a (1) flexible design (Robson 2002), allowing the evaluation team to be proactive and adapt to the evolving context of the project, and (2) a combination of quantitative and qualitative methods to study a phenomenon in a complementary way (Pluye 2012). The objective was to document the context, processes, difficulties, and issues, as well as participants' perceptions of the success of the *Justice Hoodistique* project (Sta-Ali et al. 2024). Stakeholders and beneficiaries of the project were involved in this process as participants. For this evaluation, a combination of various data collection techniques was used: (1) nonparticipant observation of retreats; (2) evaluative talk spaces (at the end of the second retreat for each group of participants); (3) individual interviews with participants; (4) logbooks for workshop facilitators during retreats; (5) focus groups with project professionals, workshop facilitators, and partners; (6) participant satisfaction questionnaire; (7) participant profile questionnaire (at three times during participation); (8) goal attainment scale by participant (at three times during participation); and (9) project documentation from Hoodstock.

Participation was voluntary and participants could withdraw from the evaluation at any time without any consequences regarding their participation in the project itself. Moreover, participants could choose to only participate in select evaluation activities. The information and consent form listed the different activities and participants had the choice of "yes or no" for each activity. Likewise, they could decide whether the evaluation team would have access to some of their data collected by the project team. No participant was excluded from the evaluation based on the linguistic criterion. The evaluation team provided a trained interpreter so participants of any language could participate in the evaluation activities. To ensure that the evaluation process did not constitute overly demanding activities and that the privacy of participants was always preserved, the evaluation team proposed that data collection be a shared responsibility with the project team. Given the realities of the people served and the importance of considering their experiences and stories, a culturally responsive approach with cultural humility was necessary to maximize the use and the utility of this evaluation.

Aligning CRE approach with cultural humility, the evaluation team decided to develop a mutually beneficial partnership with the project team by developing the *Justice Hoodistique* team's capacity to do and use evaluation. Data collection was carried out jointly by the evaluation team and the project team. The questionnaire on the profile of the participants and the goal attainment scale were co-developed with the project team, and the project professionals were responsible of administering the questionnaire and completing the scale with the participants. This type of collaboration made it possible to establish not only a non-paternalistic relationship between the evaluation team and the project team but also to achieve a double objective. The first was to equip the project team and allow them to enhance their capacity to monitor and evaluate their project using the developed tools, after the evaluation team finished their evaluation mandate. The second was to allow the project professional—who has developed over time a bond of trust with the participant—to choose the best time for collecting this data. According to *Justice Hoodistique* professionals, this process made it possible for participants to be at ease and to benefit from a safe space shared with people from the Black communities. This reflects a characteristic element of cultural humility at a systemic level.

The evaluation team showed cultural humility during the evaluation process at an interpersonal level by listening and understanding the beliefs and practices of the Black communities. For instance, while the individual interviews, evaluative talk spaces, logbooks, and focus groups—which are the responsibility of the evaluation team—went smoothly, the nonparticipant observation became a challenge. From the first retreat, the evaluation team noticed a reluctance regarding the presence of an evaluation team member, a person external to the Black community, to observe the actions of the members of this community (speakers, facilitators, beneficiaries, etc.). Moreover, a facilitator raised the fear of "reproducing colonial protocols because of the non-participating observer." Following a discussion with project team members and retreat facilitators, the evaluation team, engaged in permanent reflexivity and self-criticism, decided to abandon this method of data collection to prioritize the well-being of the participants and to avoid any bias relating to the presence of the evaluation team during the weekend retreat. Thus, to ensure and maintain access to the participants' experiences during the retreat, it was decided to proceed with a review meeting after the retreat. During these recorded meetings, the evaluation team, the workshop facilitators, and the project team members discussed the progress of the retreat: what went smoothly, what went less smoothly, the feedback from the participants, the retreat environment, etc. These meetings constituted privileged moments where facilitators and professionals took a reflective look and critical self-evaluation on the progress of the workshops they led, the different biases they had, or even their perception of participant satisfaction and participation.

The data from these meetings, triangulated with those from the logbooks, offered a rich understanding of the progress of the retreats without there being an "intrusion" into the private lives of the participants. To ensure that the participants' perspective was represented, the evaluation team traveled during the retreats (the second and final retreat for each group of participants) to an in-person evaluation space where the participants—without the presence of facilitators and professionals—had the opportunity to share their opinions with the evaluation team regarding the workshops, the location of the retreat, the facilitators, etc. These evaluative spaces made it possible to leave an important place for a form of collective reflexivity for the participants on their own participation in the retreat as well as on the role they played. Another methodological change concerned satisfaction questionnaires.

To limit requests, the questionnaires were included at the end of the individual interview with the participants. This inclusion was greatly appreciated by all those involved.

Despite the cultural humility approaches adopted by the evaluation team and the fact that the evaluation design was co-developed with the project team (all from the Black community), the issue experienced at the level of nonparticipant observation was not predictable either by the project team nor by the evaluation team. This lack of predictability highlighted the necessity of permanent self-evaluation and the particularity of evaluations carried out in partnership with communities who have suffered from different forms of oppression and discrimination in various fields including healthcare and social services. In this, a challenge consists of creating and maintaining a relationship of trust with the communities under study by ensuring them a certain level of comfort so they can freely express themselves and debate and present their points of view. The evaluation team offered a safe space which allowed the retreat facilitators to name this discomfort and, above all, to collectively find alternatives.

This case study clearly demonstrated the importance of cultural humility during a CRE process and showed us that cultural humility in CRE is not acquired. It is important that evaluation teams devote the space and time necessary throughout an evaluation process. This posture allows the evaluation team to listen to those involved in the evaluation and to react to any situation requiring adaptation of the evaluation process, which was possible in this evaluation offering a flexible design.

4 Hearing the Deaf when evaluating a program in the United States

There are considerable inequalities between deaf people and the general population concerning health care and social services (Emond et al. 2015; Fellinger et al. 2012). For example, higher rates of obesity, domestic violence, and suicide are observed among this population in the United States (Barnett et al. 2011). Having access to health data allows us to better understand the needs of populations and guide actions aimed at improving the prevention, diagnosis, and treatment of diseases (Gouvernement du Canada 2023). However, deaf people are often understudied and poorly represented in the data collected within populations (Canadian Association of the Deaf 2015). This reality is explained by the barriers to accessing research and data collected in the context of public health surveillance that these people face. These include language-related exclusion criteria, recruitment strategies using written and scientific language, inappropriate data collection methods (e.g., random phone survey), as well as the absence of a sign language interpreter or other communicative accommodations (Canadian Association of the Deaf 2015; Livermore et al. 2011; McKee et al. 2013). The deaf community belongs to a culturally minority community defined as "any group of persons which constitutes less than half of the population in the entire territory of a State whose members share common characteristics of culture, religion or language, or a combination of any of these"

(Haut-Commissariat des droits de l'homme, Nations Unies 2023, paragraph 5). Also, many deaf people share a negative view of biomedical research due to the different forms of oppression and discrimination that this community has suffered historically (McKee et al. 2013). These include the dichotomous vision of deafness between researchers and deaf people, which, on the one hand, is seen as a deficiency to be repaired, while on the other, represents a cultural and linguistic specificity (Lane 2005; McKee et al. 2013). This difference may increase deaf people's feelings of mistrust in interacting with hearing people in the context of research.

To understand and overcome these barriers, researchers affiliated with the University of Massachusetts Medical School implemented the Deaf ACCESS study. This study, based on a participatory action research model, consisted of three phases: (1) holding community forums, (2) conducting focus groups, and (3) developing an intervention and its evaluation. The ultimate goal of the Deaf ACCESS study was to develop an intervention model aimed at training research staff to competently and sensitively interact with deaf people during the research consent process (Anderson et al. 2020).

This study was innovative in the way researchers involved deaf people in the research process to create mutually beneficial and non-paternalistic partnerships. The principal investigator was a hearing woman who had experience conducting research with deaf people (Anderson et al. 2018). Despite her knowledge of the context, she recognized the uniqueness of the culture and history of deaf people and the need to make methodological choices aimed at avoiding the replication of the paternalistic relationships sometimes present in research. The first choice was to establish a research committee mostly composed of deaf people and people with a strong command of American Sign Language (ASL) and create an administrative support and methodological rigor consultant role (Anderson et al. 2018). By engaging in self-criticism and acknowledging her own limits in understanding the experiences of deaf people, the researcher demonstrated cultural humility and favored the design and implementation of a culturally relevant and safe study for deaf people. The efforts that have been made to make data collection and analysis methods more sensitive to deaf culture and language bear witness to this progress. It included the use of ASL during data collection, the use of qualitative analysis software enabling video import and coding (ATLAS.ti), and data analysis in ASL in collaboration with the research committee (Anderson et al. 2018). Subsequently, the preliminary results were filmed in ASL and then posted on the research team's Facebook page and website in order to inform deaf people about the study's progress. Furthermore, deaf members on the research committee guided the translation of sign language data into written form for scientific articles (Anderson et al. 2018).

Other actions were also carried out to better understand the reality of deaf people and their research experience. These included conducting community forums and focus groups in ASL (Anderson et al. 2022). While these actions had practical implications for the development of training on free and informed consent for research, they also allowed members of the deaf community to meet the research team and express their concerns and needs regarding research engagement (Anderson et al. 2023). Providing members of a culturally minority community with the opportunity to have authentic discussions about their history, culture, knowledge, and needs in a culturally safe space has the potential to not only foster culturally competent research practice but also establish a trustful connection between researchers and community members and therefore redress power imbalances in relationships. The researchers in this study also took this opportunity to apologize for the mistreatment that the deaf community has suffered historically (Anderson et al. 2020). To do this, the four principles of the Truth and Reconciliation model have structured these community forums: (1) truth-telling, (2) acknowledging, (3) restoring, and (4) collaborating (Anderson et al. 2018).

The participatory action research design used in this study created a flexible environment allowing the research team to adapt to the preferences of the deaf community. For example, the fourth community forum initially planned was replaced by a focus group following the discomfort expressed by several deaf people during community forums (Anderson et al. 2018). By making these adaptations, the researchers showed their sensitivity to the discomfort and demonstrated cultural humility.

Our analysis of the Deaf ACCESS study from a CRE perspective showed how the study was able to achieve the three defining components of cultural humility. Cultural humility first had an impact on the evaluators themselves, who showed humility in their acknowledgment of a limited cognizance of the culture of the studied communities and in confronting their preconceived ideas. This awareness resulting from a process of self-criticism reflected a strong intrapersonal commitment for each evaluator. This approach translated into efforts to understand the beliefs and practices of the communities, as well as active listening of evaluation participants. For example, considerable efforts were made by the research team to promote the implementation of an approach sensitive to the specific issues of deaf people throughout the research process, including improving the informed consent procedures for deaf participants. At the interpersonal level, providing a framework for discussion and a safe space for community members to express their opinions was found to be important. Such strategies subsequently allowed for the adaptation of the evaluation process in order to respect the social and cultural norms of the communities, in an explicit move to redress power imbalances in relationships with deaf community members who participated in the study.

The cultural humility demonstrated throughout various stages of the evaluative research made it possible to obtain authentic results. These included the design of various tools promoting and facilitating the inclusion of deaf community members in research and evaluation. For example, the development of the "Sign Here: How to Conduct Informed Consent with Deaf Research Participants" training program aimed at ensuring informed consent that is culturally and linguistically appropriate for deaf participants (Anderson et al. 2020). This involved choosing to opt for a video format involving deaf people and using ASL for consent (Anderson et al. 2020). Various auditory and visual learning strategies, as well as entertainment elements, were also integrated into the training based on the recommendations of deaf people (Anderson et al. 2020). System-wide impacts are considerable—these tools could enable researchers to conduct more research within these communities and, therefore, accumulate data to improve the healthcare and social services. Other benefits have also been identified such as strengthening the capacities of local partners and establishing or reestablishing a bond of trust and respect both among community members and between them and the evaluation teams.

5 Conclusion

The cases presented in this chapter highlighted the benefits of cultural humility in evaluations and research through intrapersonal, interpersonal, and systemic approaches (Gautier 2022; Hughes et al. 2020). These evaluations were carried out in partnership with the targeted communities. They demonstrated that mutually beneficial and respectful collaboration between teams working on an evaluation allows the evaluation team to get not only translated data (from one language to another) but also interpreted data through the lens of participants' culture. The evaluation teams were attentive during the evaluation process to ensure and maintain a certain comfort so participants could express themselves freely.

However, certain limitations have led to challenges. First, in the three cases, the evaluators were not part of the communities targeted by the evaluation and had to establish a partnership with members of these communities in order to understand their beliefs and practices. Second, there were challenges in adapting the evaluation methodology to the preferences of the communities while ensuring respect for scientific rigor. Third, analyzing data in a language other than the one used during data collection could result in translation bias. Furthermore, the translation of tools, data, and results is a long, expensive, and complex process for evaluators who have to find adapted and appropriate solutions to the context and feasible to carry out the projects within the allotted deadlines and resources.

Finally, approaches to include cultural humility in CRE promote the establishment of mutually beneficial partnerships for communities and evaluators. The dynamic and adaptive characteristics of culture require evaluators to continually work on reflection and self-criticism. It is in this sense that cultural humility can become an asset to CRE. More studies should be conducted on cultural humility with CRE not only by analyzing the processes between evaluators and participants but by analyzing the relationships between evaluators from different backgrounds or countries when working on the same project.

Acknowledgments With regards to the first case study, we want to thank collaborators at Save the Children UK and Indonesia, all the team in Jakarta and in Canada as well as the funding organization. "Funding was provided by Save the Children Fund (no grant number) and the Children and Violence Evaluation Challenge Fund (grant number 058), a joint initiative funded by the Bernard van Leer Foundation, Oak Foundation, UBS Optimus Foundation, and an anonymous donor and hosted by the Network of European Foundations. The sole responsibility for the content lies with the authors and the content may not necessarily reflect the positions of NEF/Children and Violence Evaluation Challenge Fund or the sponsoring Foundations."

In relation to the second case study, we thank the funding organization, Health Canada, and the implementers of *Justice Hoodistique*, Hoodstock, and all the actors who contributed to this evaluation as part of the team or as participants.

Lastly, we are grateful to the authors of the Deaf ACCESS study, and Melissa L. Anderson and her team for allowing us to use their Deaf ACCESS project as a case study.

References

Acree J, Chouinard JA (2020) Exploring use and influence in culturally responsive approaches to evaluation: a review of the empirical literature. Am J Eval 41(2):201–215. https://doi.org/10.1177/1098214019879505

Anderson ML et al (2018) Deaf qualitative health research: leveraging technology to conduct linguistically and sociopolitically appropriate methods of inquiry. Qual Health Res 28(11):1813–1824. https://doi.org/10.1177/1049732318779050

Anderson ML et al (2020) Deaf ACCESS: adapting consent through community engagement and state-of-the-art simulation. J Deaf Stud Deaf Educ 25(1):115–125. https://doi.org/10.1093/deafed/enz035

Anderson KC et al (2022) A culturally responsive evaluation framework and its application in environmental education. Eval Program Plann 92:10. https://doi.org/10.1016/j.evalprogplan.2022.102073

Anderson ML, Riker T, Wilkins AM (2023) Application of the truth and reconciliation model to meaningfully engage deaf sign language users in the research process. Cultur Divers Ethnic Minor Psychol 29(1):15–23. https://doi.org/10.1037/cdp0000445

Armony V, Hassaoui M, Mulone M (2019) Les interpellations policières à la lumière des identités racisées des personnes interpellées: analyse des données du Service de Police de la Ville de Montréal (SPVM) et élaboration d'indicateurs de suivi en matière de profilage racial, Canada, p 134. Available https://spvm.qc.ca/upload/Rapport_Armony-Hassaoui-Mulone.pdf. Accessed 21 September 2023

Askew K, Beverly MG, Jay ML (2012) Aligning collaborative and culturally responsive evaluation approaches. Eval Program Plann 35(4):552–557. https://doi.org/10.1016/j.evalprogplan.2011.12.011

Barnett S et al (2011) Community participatory research with deaf sign language users to identify health inequities. Am J Public Health 101(12):2235–2238. https://doi.org/10.2105/AJPH.2011.300247

Botcheva L, Shih J, Huffman L (2009) Emphasizing cultural competence in evaluation: a process-oriented approach. Am J Eval 30(2):176–188. https://doi.org/10.1177/1098214009334363

Brottman MR et al (2020) Toward cultural competency in health care: a scoping review of the diversity and inclusion education literature. Acad Med 95(5):803–813. https://doi.org/10.1097/ACM.0000000000002995

Canadian Association of the Deaf (2015) Statistics on Deaf Canadians, Canadian Association of the Deaf - Association des Sourds du Canada. Available https://cad-asc.ca/issues-positions/statistics-on-deaf-canadians/. Accessed 22 September 2023

Cleaver SR, Carvajal JK, Sheppard PS (2016) Cultural humility: A way of thinking to inform practice globally. Physiotherapy Canada, 68(1):1–2.

Dinh K et al (2019) Confucian evaluation: reframing contribution analysis using a Confucian lens. Am J Eval 40:109821401881300. https://doi.org/10.1177/1098214018813008

Dunaway KE, Morrow JA, Porter BE (2012) Development and validation of the cultural competence of program evaluators (CCPE) self-report scale. Am J Eval 33(4):496–514. https://doi.org/10.1177/1098214012445280

Durrant JE (2007) Positive discipline: what it is and how to do it. Save the Children Sweden, Southeast Asia and Pacific Region, Bangkok

Durrant JE (2013) Positive discipline in everyday parenting, 3rd edn. Save the Children, Stockholm

Durrant JE (2016) Positive discipline in everyday parenting. Save the Children, Stockholm

Eid P, Magloire J, Turenne M (2011) Profilage racial et discrimination systémique des jeunes racisés: rapport de la consultation sur le profilage racial et ses conséquences. Commission des droits de la personne et des droits de la jeunesse du Québec, Montreal, p 126. Available https://www.cdpdj.qc.ca/storage/app/media/publications/Profilage_rapport_FR.pdf. Accessed 21 September 2023

Emond A et al (2015) The current health of the signing deaf community in the UK compared with the general population: a cross-sectional study. BMJ Open 5(1):7. https://doi.org/10.1136/bmjopen-2014-006668

Fang Q, Fisher KR, Li B (2021) How can coproduction help to deliver culturally responsive disability support? A case study from Australia. Health Soc Care Community 29(6):e396–e404. https://doi.org/10.1111/hsc.13364

Fellinger J, Holzinger D, Pollard R (2012) Mental health of deaf people. Lancet 379(9820):1037–1044. https://doi.org/10.1016/S0140-6736(11)61143-4

Foronda C et al (2016) Cultural humility. J Transcult Nurs 27(3):8. https://doi.org/10.1177/1043659615592677

Frierson HT, Hood S, Hughes GB (2002) Strategies that address culturally responsive evaluation: a guide to conducting culturally responsive evaluations. In: The 2002 user-friendly handbook for project evaluation. NSF, Arlington, pp 63–76

Gautier L (2022) Towards CR evaluation: culturally-reflexive and -responsive evaluation in crises times and beyond. Int J Health Plan Manage 37(Suppl 1):32–36. https://doi.org/10.1002/hpm.3579

Gignac C, Bernier D, Zagbayou N (2023) Justice Hoodistique: à l'intersection de la justice réparatrice et transformative par et pour les communautés noires. rapport de recherche Aout 2023. Québec, Canada, p. 54. https://www.hoodstock.ca/wp-content/uploads/Rapport_Hoodstock_-_8_septembre_-_FN_-_PRINT_2.pdf. Accessed 2 May 2024

Gouvernement du Canada (2023) Raisons pour lesquelles les données de santé publique sont utilisées et façons dont elles le sont. https://www.canada.ca/fr/sante-publique/services/donnee/en-utilisant-les-donnees.html. Accessed 22 September 2023

Haut-Commissariat des droits de l'homme, Nations Unies (2023) La notion de minorité: définition utilisée dans le cadre du mandat, OHCHR. https://www.ohchr.org/fr/special-procedures/sr-minority-issues/concept-minority-mandate-definition. Accessed 2 October 2023

Hood S, Hopson R, Kirkhart K (2015) Culturally responsive evaluation: theory, practice and future implications. In: Handbook of practical program evaluation, 4th edn. Wiley, Hoboken, pp 281–317. https://doi.org/10.1002/9781119171386.ch12

Hopson RK (2009) Reclaiming knowledge at the margins: culturally responsive evaluation in the current evaluation moment. In: Ryan KE, Cousins JB (eds) The SAGE international handbook of educational evaluation. SAGE Publishing, Thousand Oaks, pp 429–446. https://doi.org/10.4135/9781452226606.n24

Hughes V et al (2020) Not missing the opportunity: strategies to promote cultural humility among future nursing faculty. J Prof Nurs 36(1):28–33. https://doi.org/10.1016/j.profnurs.2019.06.005

Irwanto K (2014) Understanding vulnerability: a study on situations that affect family separation and the lives of children in and out of family care. In: Research in DKI Jakarta, Central Java and South Sulawesi. Center on Child Protection, Jakarta

Kushnier L et al (2023) Culturally responsive evaluation: a scoping review of the evaluation literature. Eval Program Plann 100:14

Lane H (2005) Ethnicity, ethics, and the deaf-world. J Deaf Stud Deaf Educ 10(3):20. https://doi.org/10.1093/deafed/eni030

Lansford JE, Deater-Deckard K (2012) Childrearing discipline and violence in developing countries. Child Dev 83(1):62–75. https://doi.org/10.1111/j.1467-8624.2011.01676.x

Livermore G et al (2011) Disability data in national surveys. U.S. Department of Health and Human Services, Washington, p 208

McKee M, Schlehofer D, Thew D (2013) Ethical issues in conducting research with deaf populations. Am J Public Health 103(12):2174–2178. https://doi.org/10.2105/AJPH.2013.301343

Ministère de la justice du Canada (2023) Code criminel du Canada. https://laws-lois.justice.gc.ca/PDF/C-46.pdf. Accessed 2 October 2023

Patton MQ (2011) Developmental evaluation: applying complexity concepts to enhance innovation and use. Guilford Press, New York. https://www.guilford.com/books/Developmental-Evaluation/Michael-Quinn-Patton/9781606238721. Accessed 21 September 2023

Pluye P (2012) Les méthodes mixtes. In: Ridde & Dagenais, Approches et pratiques en évaluation de programme. Université de Montréal, Montreal, pp 125–143

Robson C (2002) Real world research. A resource for social scientists and practitioner researchers. Blackwell, Oxford. https://qualitativeresearcherme.files.wordpress.com/2018/04/robson-2005.pdf. Accessed 21 September 2023

Rossi C et al (2020) Le programme de mesures de rechange général pour adultes 2017–2019 au québec: portrait, analyse et enjeux. In: Rapport de recherche soumis au ministère de la Justice du Québec. Université Laval, Montreal, p 54

Ruiz-Casares M et al (2019) Protocol for a cluster randomised controlled trial evaluating a parenting with home visitation programme to prevent physical and emotional abuse of children in Indonesia: the families first Programme. BMJ Open 9(1):e021751. https://doi.org/10.1136/bmjopen-2018-021751

SenGupta S, Hopson R, Thompson-Robinson M (2004) Cultural competence in evaluation: an overview. N Dir Eval 102:5–19. https://doi.org/10.1002/ev.112

Sta-Ali, Iman, Ben Zerrouk, Ghizlaine et Naïma Bentayeb (2024). Mise en oeuvre et retombées du projet Justice hoodistique, rapport d'évaluation. Institut universitaire SHERPA, CIUSSS du Centre-Ouest-de-L'Île-de-Montréal. [On ligne]

Tervalon M, Murray-García J (1998) Cultural humility versus cultural competence: a critical distinction in defining physician training outcomes in multicultural education. J Health Care Poor Underserved 9(2):117–125. https://doi.org/10.1353/hpu.2010.0233

Tylor EB (1920) Primitive culture: researches into the development of mythology, philosophy, religion, language, art, and custom, 6th edn. John Murray, London, p 1. http://archive.org/details/primitiveculture01tylouoft. Accessed 30 April 2024

UNICEF (2012) Child maltreatment: prevalence, incidence and consequences in the East Asia and Pacific region: a systematic review of research. UNICEF East Asia and Pacific Regional Office, Bangkok. https://www.unicef.org/eap/media/2916/file/maltreatment.pdf. Accessed 21 September 2023

WHO (2022) Child maltreatment, who.int. https://www.who.int/news-room/fact-sheets/detail/child-maltreatment. Accessed 19 May 2024

Involving Members of the Public in Health Service Evaluations

Katherine Knighting, Antoinette Bewley, and Lucy Bray

Abstract

This chapter explores the value, impact, and best practice of patient and public involvement and engagement (PPIE) in health service evaluations, with a focused look at the challenges in commissioned evaluations. Taking a solution-focused approach, the chapter provides examples of evidence-based responses to challenges around offering inclusive opportunities, working together in a meaningful way, and capturing the impact of engagement, along with top tips for being involvement-ready. The chapter does not assume prior knowledge and will be of interest to those who are new to public involvement and those who are interested in reflecting on their practice or trying new approaches. Quotes from patients and carers who collaborate with us in our research and teaching are woven throughout the chapter to share their voices.

Keywords

Patient and public involvement · Community engagement · Co-production · Inclusive opportunities · Measuring impact · Evaluation

The aim of the chapter is to introduce and critically discuss the involvement of members of the public in the planning, delivery, and dissemination of health service research and evaluations, identify the challenges this may have in commissioned work and discuss potential solutions based on the published evidence and the

K. Knighting (✉) · A. Bewley · L. Bray
Edge Hill University, Ormskirk, Lancashire, UK
e-mail: knightk@edgehill.ac.uk; bewleyt@edgehill.ac.uk; Brayl@edgehill.a.c.uk

A. Kaehne, J. Feather (eds.), *Handbook of Health Services Evaluation*,
https://doi.org/10.1007/978-3-031-87869-5_29

authors' experience. We hope this chapter adds to the established wealth of published work linked to the involvement of the public in health service evaluations while at the same time focusing on public involvement within commissioned health evaluation projects which are commonly time-sensitive, with boundaries already set, and linked to a specific service, program, or intervention. The discussion is presented under the headings of background to public involvement, inclusive opportunities, working together, measuring and reporting impact, and our top tips to be patient and public involvement-ready for commissioned evaluations. The chapter is written for an international audience and does not assume prior knowledge. It therefore aims to be of interest to those who are new to public involvement and those who are interested in reflecting on their practice or trying new approaches. While writing this chapter, we have spoken with patients and carers who collaborate with us in our research and teaching to gather their thoughts. With permission, quotes and their names are woven throughout the chapter to share their voices.

1 Background to Public Involvement

This background section will begin to set the scene by discussing what public involvement is, the range of terminology and definitions used internationally, and the evidence-based rationale for involving members of the public in health service evaluations.

1.1 What Do we Mean by Public Involvement?

The concept of the involvement of members of the public in research, often referred to as patient and public involvement (PPI) or patient and public involvement and engagement (PPIE), has evolved over time. The roots of PPI can be traced back to key historical developments since the rise of patient advocacy movements in the 1960s and strengthened during the 1980s when HIV/AIDS activism and community engagement demanded greater involvement in research and policy decisions (Epstein 1995; Herek et al. 2003). The philosophical underpinning of public involvement in research is linked to the principles of democratic governance and social justice which emphasize the need for inclusivity, transparency, autonomy, and respecting and valuing lived experience through collaboration and empowerment. Public involvement is aligned with a paradigm shift from a traditional hierarchical model of healthcare and research, where experts make decisions on behalf of patients and the public who are service users, to a more democratic and collaborative model where individuals actively participate in decisions and research affecting them (Abma et al. 2017; McLaughlin et al. 2020). This is reflected in the commonly shared definition of PPI coined by the National Institute of Health Research (NIHR) in the United Kingdom (UK) in that it is research being carried out "with" or "by" members of the public rather than "to", "about", or "for" them (National Institute for Health Research (NIHR) 2021).

The public involvement approach seeks to address power imbalances and promote social justice by ensuring that a diverse range of voices, including those from marginalized and underrepresented groups, contribute to and shape the research process (Boivin et al. 2018; Domecq et al. 2014). This includes those traditionally viewed as "vulnerable" and therefore less involved in decision-making such as children (United Nations 1989; Lundy and McEvoy 2012) and individuals with learning or intellectual disabilities (Beighton et al. 2019) to ensure that the development and delivery of research is relevant, appropriate, and respectful of their rights and perspectives. Underpinning PPI is the principle of respecting autonomy and the need to move away from a paternalistic model to one where the contributions of all individuals who possess valuable knowledge about their experiences and preferences are valued (Staniszewska et al. 2017; Tritter and McCallum 2006). Public involvement should aim to empower individuals to have a meaningful impact on research, while recognizing that empathy and understanding of the lived experience of participants is important (Brett et al. 2014). The emphasis on collaboration, inclusivity, and the recognition of the value of diverse perspectives has become integral to contemporary research practices. Duffy and Beresford (2020) remind us that "Involvement is not some kind of academic exercise. It is about real change for the better in real people's lives, in the real world… based on service user's experiential knowledge and their lived experience" (p. 15). Since the early 2000s, the term "patient and public involvement" emerged and aimed to reflect a broader and more inclusive approach to involving individuals in the research process, leading many research institutions, funding organizations, and journals to recognize its importance (Brett et al. 2014).

While the importance of PPI is acknowledged internationally, it is uneven in its implementation (Biddle et al. 2021) with variations influenced by attitudes, policies and societal expectations, and countries have different infrastructure, policies, and initiatives to foster collaboration with the public. The UK formalized and promoted public involvement in research through organizations like INVOLVE (est. 1996) and the NIHR Centre for Engagement and Dissemination (est. 2020 https://evidence.nihr.ac.uk/) and has been a leader in publishing work and discussion about PPI (Staley 2009; Biddle et al. 2021). Other countries have also made significant strides in the last few decades to integrate patient and public perspectives into research and policy, establishing initiatives, guidelines, and infrastructure to support involvement, with examples of innovative work taking place in the Netherlands and Scandinavian countries (Biddle et al. 2021), and the establishment of organizations such as The Guidelines International Network (GIN) (est. 2002 https://g-i-n.net/toolkit) and the Patient-Centered Outcomes Research Institute (PCORI) in the USA (est. 2010 https://www.pcori.org/). Additionally, European and International initiatives and networks, such as the International Association for Public Participation (https://www.iap2.org), the European Patients' Forum (est. 2003 https://www.eu-patient.eu/), The European Young Persons Advisory Group Network (eYPAGnet) (https://eypagnet.eu/), MESH community engagement network (est. 2017 https://mesh.tghn.org) and International Network for Public Involvement and Engagement in Health and Social Care Research (est. 2017), contribute to the exchange of best practices and the promotion of patient and public involvement in research across borders.

At this point, it is important to acknowledge how the terminology and language used to describe public involvement activity (Table 1) and the individuals involved within health research and evaluation (Table 2) have evolved and can differ across disciplines and countries. Terms such as "public involvement", "patient engagement", and "community engagement" are often used interchangeably or have nuanced differences to indicate the context and goals of the activity itself. For

Table 1 Definitions of common activity terms used within the landscape of public involvement and engagement

Activity terms	Definitions commonly used
Public engagement (PE)	Raising awareness of research with the public (Holmes et al. 2019)
Public involvement (PI)	Actively involving people in research (Holmes et al. 2019)
Patient engagement (PE)	Meaningful and active collaboration in governance, priority setting, conducting research, and knowledge translation (Canadian Institutes of Health Research (CIHR) 2016)
Patient and public involvement (PPI)	When the research is being carried out "with" or "by" members of the public rather than "to," "about," or "for" them (Patient-Centered Outcomes Research Institute (PCORI) 2019)
Patient and public involvement and engagement (PPIE)	The active and meaningful collaboration of patients, service users and members of the public in the research process from planning, conducting to dissemination to ensure research is relevant, responsive and respectful of the needs and priorities of those it seeks to benefit (Brett et al. 2014; National Institute for Health Research (NIHR) 2024a)
Spectrum of public participation	The IAP2's Spectrum of public participation is a continuum of five levels of public participation: Inform, consult, involve, collaborate, and empower https://www.iap2.org
Community engagement	Community engagement is a process of developing relationships that enable stakeholders to work together to address health-related issues and promote well-being. It involves the exchange of information and opinions, and actively seeks the input of community members (World Health Organization (WHO) 2019)
Patient-centered research	Patient-centered research is conducted with and for patients rather than to, for, or about them (Patient-Centered Outcomes Research Institute (PCORI) 2019)
Co-production	A collaborative approach which puts the public and patients at the heart of decision-making to combine the expertise and perspectives of all participants to create research that is grounded in real-world experiences and meets the needs of the intended beneficiaries. It involves all stakeholders working together *throughout* a project and sharing power in decision-making (National Institute for Health Research (NIHR) 2024b)
Co-design	A collaborative approach like co-production, but involvement is focused on the *design phase* to develop the aim, methods, interventions, and dissemination plans to create relevant and impactful outcomes with user-centered solutions (National Institute for Health Research (NIHR) 2024b; Sanders and Stappers 2008)

Table 2 Definitions of common terms for individuals used within the landscape of public involvement and engagement

Individual terms	
Public advisers/ contributors/ representatives	Members of the public who represent the broader public to provide advice, input, insights, and perspectives to the decision-making and research process (Domecq et al. 2014; National Institute for Health Research (NIHR) 2024a)
Public collaborators	Those working with the public in every aspect of a decision-making process, e.g., identifying the preferred solution and sharing some degree of control, management, or decision-making authority (IAPT2 2024)
Patient partners	Individuals with lived experience of a health condition or users of healthcare services who collaborate with researchers (Canadian Institutes of Health Research (CIHR) 2016)
Community representatives/ experts	Individuals from specific communities who draw on their expertise to represent the interests and perspectives of those communities in the research (Agency for Healthcare Research and Quality (AHRQ) 2019; Forsythe et al. 2016)
Consumer advocates	Individuals who advocate for the perspectives and interests of consumers (patients, the public) in the research process (Baum et al. 2006)
Lay representatives/ members	Individuals without professional or specialized training who participate in the research process (Brett et al. 2014)
Experts by experience	Individuals who possess a unique and valuable understanding of a particular condition, situation, or aspect of life based on their personal, lived experiences (Tritter and McCallum 2006)
Lived experience collaborators	Individuals who actively engage and collaborate as active partners in the research process based on their personal, direct experiences with a specific condition, situation or aspect of life providing valuable insights, expertise and perspectives that arise from their first hand encounters, enriching the research with a depth of understanding that may not be captured through traditional, expert-driven approaches (Greenhalgh et al. 2019)
Consumers	Individuals who use or consume healthcare services, including patients, service users or members of the public and provide their experience, perspectives, or needs to ensure it is patient-centered and responsive to the concerns and priorities of the people it serves (Carman et al. 2013)
Service users	Individuals who are the recipients or potential recipients of health, social care or public services
Stakeholder	An individual, group, or organization that has a vested interest or "stake" in the research process, outcomes, or its potential impact and is crucial for enhancing the relevance, quality, and applicability of research findings to the diverse perspectives, and needs of those it may impact (Carman et al. 2013)
Co-researchers	Individuals who collaborate as an equal partner with researchers throughout the research process to ensure research is inclusive and grounded in the real-world experiences of those impacted by the issues being studied, bridging the gap between researchers and communities (O'Brien et al. 2014)

example, within the UK, members of the public may be described as patient or public advisors, experts by experience, lay members or representatives, whereas within North America and Australia terms such as patient partner, patient/community experts, patient/consumer advocates or community representatives may be more commonly used (Weiler-Wichtl et al. 2023). The lack of consistency in definitions and language used in relation to public involvement has been suggested as problematic (Weiler-Wichtl et al. 2023) as it can lead to confusion around roles, contributions, and expectations within individual projects and within the literature. Particularly of note is the adoption and popularity of terms such as co-production and co-design, which can have differing and inconsistent interpretations, although they are an important step in establishing more equal roles between researchers and public members in research (The PARTNERS2 Writing Collective 2020).

Talking to people who have been involved in health service evaluations highlights that preferences for terminology may be individual, and some members of the public express concern about some terms. We give some examples from our conversations with them below. Jo shared:

> I like the term "lived experience" but feel that "experts by experience" is sometimes misunderstood as being experts of a topic rather than their personal experience. (Service User, 2024, Personal Communication).

However, Nath prefers a different term:

> Personally, I prefer being called a "Service User" as it is easy to understand, i.e., you are a user of a service whereas terms like "Expert by Experience" is rather vague as it doesn't imply what you are an expert of. (Service User, 2024, Personal Communication).

Whereas Lynsey does not like this term:

> I don't mind the name "Carer" however "Service User" I am not keen on. It sounds too business like. I prefer "patients". (Service User, 2024, Personal Communication).

Ultimately, while members of the public who were health service users that we work with made clear how it is important for the terminology to be agreed with the people involved, it is typically not a deal breaker as Ad says:

> As long as I'm treated with respect, the title does not matter. (Service User, 2024, Personal Communication).

As highlighted above, the clarity of terms can be important, an example of this being when "patient" and "public" advisors are discussed within health research as a homogenous whole, and how this can fail to recognize the different perspectives and roles "members of the public" and/or "patients" bring to the table the importance of representativeness (McCoy et al. 2019; Domecq et al. 2014). It has been argued that rather than using broad encompassing terms, there should be a clear distinction between "patient involvement" that involves individuals on the basis of their "experience with a particular condition" and "public involvement" which involves individuals based on them being "members of a relevant population" (McCoy et al. 2019).

There has also been considerable debate over the years about the differences and sometimes blurred boundaries between the activities of consultation, engagement, involvement, and participation, with frameworks and models often presenting different "levels" of public involvement according to hierarchies, continuums, or spectrums (Arnstein 1969; Hart 1987; IAPT2 2024). These models often depict different "levels" of public involvement according to working practices, power dynamics and the aims of public involvement (Greenhalgh et al. 2019; O'Brien et al. 2014; Green 2016). While these hierarchies, continuums, or spectrums can be useful to help researchers reflect, in practice, a project may involve and work with members of the public in different ways, for different purposes and at different "levels" simultaneously (Rouncefield-Swales et al. 2021). Transparent reflections on how we are working with members of the public within projects and how we report this are picked up again later in the chapter.

In this chapter, we have chosen to use the term public involvement to capture the different roles members of the public can have within health service evaluations as we believe this picks up the broad range of engagement, consultation, and involvement practices. The term "service users" is used throughout to indicate members of the public including patients and carers.

1.2 Why Involve Members of the Public in Health Service Evaluations?

The engagement, consultation, and involvement of members of the public in health research has gained increased recognition over the last 20 years, with a strong body of evidence demonstrating the benefits of such involvement to research (Crocker et al. 2018; Pizzo et al. 2015), policy (Pagatpatan and Ward 2017; Baumann et al. 2022), members of the public (Brett et al. 2014; Froggatt et al. 2015) and research team members (Aries et al. 2021; Staley et al. 2017). Involving members of the public in all aspects of research has been shown to reduce "research waste," by improving the design, conduct, and outcomes of research leading to meaningful benefits for patients (Slattery et al. 2020). When research and health evaluations are designed "with" or "by" members of the public they are likely to be more relevant, of higher quality, adopt more acceptable and accessible methods (Hoddinott et al. 2018) and be more transferable and impactful (Weiler-Wichtl et al. 2023). Working with service users from diverse backgrounds helps to ensure evaluations are designed to enable people to share their views, addresses common gaps with equity, diversity and inclusivity (EDI) and respects the rights of people to be involved in ensuring health services meet their needs.

Aside from the many benefits described above, another driver for increasing public involvement has come from funding organizations. Increasingly, health policy and research funding applications require evidence of the active involvement of service users in the research process (McMenamin et al. 2022). While practice as a whole is moving from consultation with members of the public to a more partnership approach, there is not a "one size fits all," and this chapter will discuss different ways of working to integrate public involvement in health research and commissioned evaluations and encourage researchers to critically reflect on their practice.

1.3 How Is PPI Different in Commissioned Evaluations of Health Services and Programmes to Research?

The integration of public involvement within health research is now widely accepted. However, health service evaluations are often commissioned within short timescales and within prescribed boundaries, which can create challenges between funding requirements and developing equitable involvement practices to work with patients or members of the public to shape the evaluations' design, conduct, and reporting (Smith et al. 2023).

A key challenge is that commissioned or tendered evaluation projects may have tighter timelines that do not provide adequate time for members of the public to fully engage and contribute to the process (Beresford 2019). This can lead to rushed or sub-optimal involvement, with key decisions being made without the involvement of service users, potentially compromising the quality of the evaluation. As noted by Audrey:

> I have been asked to give my input into both research bids and service and organizational evaluations. In the main I have been contacted at what seems to be the last minute. This does not seem as though my input is really valued or needed; it's about speed, get it done, tick the box, and it's not really acceptable. What is the point in asking me if you really don't give me time to respond having a good grasp of what it's all about. (Service User, 2024, Personal Communication).

In addition to short timelines, public involvement in commissioned work is often "boundaried," with the aims and approaches already being defined; this can lead to some key decisions which would usually be made with members of the public or patients already having been made, limiting the opportunities for service users to shape and direct some aspects of the work. Despite the challenges, there are published examples of commissioned health evaluations which have engaged with the public and patients, including evaluation of national programmes demonstrating various methods and benefits for both the research and the people involved (e.g., Hawkes et al. 2023; Ellins et al. 2023). Likewise, while there are differences in the nature of health research and commissioned evaluations such as the context, goals, and timings, there are also commonalities in involvement practice such as meaningful engagement, inclusivity, and transparency, and these are highlighted in Table 3.

The challenges highlighted above mean that it is important for commissioned evaluation teams to adapt public involvement approaches to fit the specific context and goals of each evaluation, and it is equally important to be transparent with service users about any limits associated with the commissioned work. Despite the challenges, we believe that incorporating the lived experiences of those who have

Table 3 An overview of similarities and differences in public involvement within commissioned evaluations of programmes and services, and researcher-led funded research

	Commissioned evaluation	Funded research
Context	Typically initiated by external organizations, such as government agencies, non-profits, or private entities, to assess the effectiveness or impact of specific programmes, interventions, or policies	Research projects are often initiated by researchers or institutions to generate new knowledge, test hypotheses or explore specific questions
Goals	To provide an independent and objective assessment of the commissioned programme or intervention PPI may focus on ensuring that the evaluation addresses relevant questions and considers the perspectives of those affected by the programme	The primary goal is to advance knowledge in a particular field PPI may be integrated into various stages of the research process, including identifying research questions, designing studies and interpreting findings
Timing	PPI may be initiated after the evaluation is commissioned, with a focus on informing the design and methodology to ensure relevance and inclusivity rather than purpose	PPI can be initiated at the outset of the research design, ensuring that the study is relevant and addresses the needs and concerns of the target population. It may continue throughout the research process and into dissemination
Inclusivity	Both can benefit from inclusivity in decision-making and design, ensuring that diverse perspectives are considered	
Transparency	Both can benefit from transparent communication about the goals, methodologies, and outcomes of the project, fostering trust and accountability	
Reciprocal relationships	Both can benefit from building reciprocal relationships with stakeholders, acknowledging the value of their contributions	

direct knowledge or experience of the issue, service, or programme being evaluated can significantly enhance the relevance, validity, and impact of a commissioned evaluation.

There is still important work to be done to continue to move public involvement beyond tokenism and consultation to models where participation is an integrated and valued part of commissioned health evaluations on the same scale as funded research. The following sections of this chapter are intended to provide information and guidance on how to provide inclusive opportunities, meaningful working together and suggestions for measuring and reporting impact, with consideration of the potential challenges specific to evaluations and how they may be reduced or overcome.

2 Inclusive Opportunities: Involving the Right People

Involving the right people in evaluations through inclusive opportunities is vital to ensure that the experiences and views of all members of the relevant population are considered. Historically, public engagement to inform health research and commissioned health evaluations has often relied on consultation with, and involvement of, service users or patients from established advisory groups and forums. Such groups have a wealth of expertise and are often formally trained, supported, and facilitated with sustained, trusted relationships which act as a facilitator for meaningful public involvement (Preston et al. 2023). Consulting with established advisory groups can be useful for time-limited evaluations where the opportunity to identify and recruit service users and develop relationships is limited. These established groups have, however, been noted to include less representation of service users from underserved or marginalised groups and those who may face the highest levels of inequity (Reynolds et al. 2021; Gilfoyle et al. 2023; Keane et al. 2023) such as people who are homeless, who do not speak the dominant language, refugees, and or from ethnic minorities who may live on the periphery of society and experience inequalities in many areas of life including health (O'Donnell et al. 2016). The absence of these service users' voice in guiding health evaluations creates further inequality as evaluation methods may exclude people from taking part due to adopting methods which are not culturally sensitive or accessible. There is increased recognition for a need to reach out to involve people within communities who have historically been less engaged in research rather than adopting a model where academic and health teams expect service users to come to events and workshops organized by them (Preston et al. 2024). Previously literature has discussed terms such as "less heard" or "hard to reach" in relation to certain populations and communities (Ellard-Gray et al. 2015), but recent debate has highlighted that such communities are not necessarily "hard to reach," just that there has often been less effort and time invested by researchers in reaching them (Keane et al. 2023).

In addition to marginalised groups, some people are excluded from public involvement due to being considered potentially "vulnerable" or the topic being perceived as being too sensitive or challenging such as end of life care, bereavement, and criminal behavior. The definition of vulnerability can vary but typically applies where there may be a risk to the person or where the person may not have autonomy or the ethical or legal capacity to consent. Groups often considered potentially vulnerable in research include people with serious mental health conditions, learning, or communication difficulties, the elderly, those who are critically ill, and children and young people; however, their lived experience may be central to an evaluation. As people who receive services, they have a right to be offered opportunities to help inform the focus and design of evaluation projects through public involvement. Working with potentially vulnerable groups to shape evaluations can be very rewarding and successful. An example of such practice is where people receiving palliative care collaborated through public involvement in all aspects of research planning, delivery, and dissemination (Chambers et al. 2019), with their involvement supported by the use of flexible methods, finding those with relevant experience, and the importance of developing relationships and providing a safe space. Due to the sensitive and sometimes upsetting topic, additional considerations for emotional support of service users, such as debrief meetings and embedding regular opportunities to check in with them, were found helpful to support involvement (Johnson et al. 2021). The meaningful involvement of children and young people in shaping projects can empower them to share valuable and unique insights (Preston et al. 2019, 2024), and teams need to ensure that they offer opportunities for genuine involvement taking into account children's other commitments such as education or treatment. Finding children to join public involvement activities often depends on parents or other adults to facilitate or signpost them to opportunities, and so reaching out to schools, youth clubs, home education groups and "where children and young people are" can reach those excluded when recruitment relies on social media targeting parents.

Finding the "right people" from the public, including those considered vulnerable or marginalised, to shape and inform commissioned health evaluations can involve additional time and investment in developing relationships with community members less used to being consulted. This is especially important when involvement is required from people with very specific lived experiences. As discussed above, this time is often not available or is constrained within commissioned health evaluations with tight timelines and deadlines, so teams may have to work harder to reach out to established groups within communities to ensure that relevant voices are heard. Continuing to exclude members from communities historically less involved means that health evaluation teams may miss opportunities to shape their work to engage with, and hear from, those facing the highest inequalities, perpetuating structural drivers of inequity.

The inclusion of members of the public from underserved communities or vulnerable groups in health evaluations introduces a range of diverse skills and perspectives, and there are specific reasonable adjustments which need to be considered to ensure equitable access to public involvement opportunities. Teams need to carefully and critically consider how decisions they make can inadvertently exclude some people from being able to join in consultation or involvement activities. For example, venues which are planned for activities may be difficult for people with disabilities or specific needs to reach and access. There may be poor signage, limited access to public transportation, entrances without ramps or lifts, a lack of accessible toilets or clearly marked accessible parking spaces. In emergency situations, a lack of planning and preparation for the inclusion of people with disabilities can be particularly dangerous. Audible and visible fire alarms, well-rehearsed evacuation plans and consideration for medical and cultural requirements are all essential for ensuring everyone's safety and inclusion (Batty et al. 2022). Jan's experience highlights the importance of clear and regular communication and consideration of appropriate venues to facilitate inclusive involvement:

> I identify as being disabled and run a small independent living charity that assists other disabled people to access services including financial state benefits and social care. As such I and the members of the charity have been involved in several service evaluations. My

> experience has not fully demonstrated that the people with lived experience involved in the evaluations have been fully involved in the planning, or implementation of the evaluations but rather become a tick box exercise to show that there has been some involvement. To make the work meaningful there must be clear and inclusive dialogue between researchers, stakeholders and service users. The selected venue needs to be accessible for all and timing of the meetings also considered, far too often the way that items are presented to service users, including language and acronyms used precludes the service user from being an active participant and the whole exercise fulfils the agenda of the organizers only. (Service User, 2024, Personal Communication).

There is also a need for evaluation teams who wish to be inclusive to take time to plan and budget to "reach out" and work with community members such as "community navigators" (Shommu et al. 2016), "health navigators" (Menendez et al. 2022) or "community champions" (Lofters et al. 2023) to establish important links between teams and communities. Engaging with members of the community can also facilitate a greater depth of exploration and better involvement for service users. As Jill highlighted:

> The [organization] facilitated these sessions, but I couldn't help but wonder if the interviewer or researcher should have had more specialised knowledge about poorly children. Perhaps having someone with expertise or experience in this area would have allowed for more in-depth and meaningful discussions with the parents, ultimately providing richer insights for the final report. (Service User, 2024, Personal Communication).

Health evaluation teams may also find frameworks such as the Race Equality Framework (National Institute for Health Research (NIHR) 2022a) and the Equality, Diversity and Inclusion toolkit (National Institute for Health Research (NIHR) 2022b) useful to reflect on whether the "right people" for the project are involved considering equality and diversity across all elements, also considering the diversity of the core evaluation team including collaborators and public advisers (National Institute for Health Research (NIHR) 2022b). Commissioners of health evaluations need to adopt a proactive approach to enable funds and "space" within commissioned calls to enable teams to involve and work with members of the public with experience of health inequalities and poor health outcomes during the initial phase of the project (Porroche-Escudero and Popay 2021). Table 4 summarizes some top tips to support inclusive public involvement.

Involving the right people can be rewarding for both the evaluation and the public advisors who support the project. Jill spoke of her experience and how her lived experience enriched a national evaluation:

> I was invited to sit on a panel as a parent representative for a long-term ventilation evaluative study… I was proud to be asked. There were doctors and consultants who were so interested in making the journey for families like mine better. I felt really valued in the meetings which took place over a couple of years. I felt like one of the team and an expert in being the parent of the child on ventilation. I had answers that consultants didn't know about lived experience, for example how certain discussions feel to parents when news is delivered or when your child's options are being discussed. I was really proud to be involved … and I could add opinions that professionals couldn't. It's good to feel valuable. (Service User, 2024, Personal Communication).

Table 4 Tips for improving inclusive involvement

• Consider the membership of the team working on the project where possible
• Identify what lived experience is required by service users for the evaluation research
• Understand and address any barriers to involvement identified in the scoping stage to inform public involvement plans
• Be flexible in the recruitment and engagement approaches so they are accessible and inclusive, including partnerships with others to reach into communities
• Work to establish equity in relationships, e.g., cultural competence and sensitivity, building trust, mutual respect, acknowledge, and address power imbalances
• Communicate clearly from the start, carefully considering language and terminology, e.g., commitment, timeline, payments
• Be clear about engagement options and commitments, e.g., in person, online, email, telephone
• Consider travel needs if meeting in person and reduce the need for service users to travel to the evaluation team
• Ensure all venues are accessible and appropriate for any needs of service users
• Incorporate feedback mechanisms throughout a project to keep people informed and to allow for changes to meet people's needs, and opportunities to capture any impact from public involvement

3 Working Together: Building, Sustaining, and Valuing all Contributions

If commissioned health evaluation teams can overcome challenges in connecting with service users from diverse backgrounds and lived experience, the next step is to establish ways of working with advisors in a way that values all contributions, and that builds and sustains mutually respectful and productive relationships. There is no one right way to involve people, and the approaches and methods need to be flexible and responsive to the needs of those involved.

Establishing working relationships between service users and evaluation teams usually starts with building trust and rapport and getting to know each other. Within health research, there is increased recognition of the importance of "taking time" to build relationships (Rouncefield-Swales et al. 2021) and learning ways of working together. Spending time to develop relationships helps provide a safe space for service users to share honest and open views with researchers. However, within commissioned evaluations, this time may be limited, and as mentioned above, this may mean that evaluation teams may have to rely on working with "connectors" or established groups who already have developed relationships with members of the public and already know "what works" to enable people to share their views and get involved. At this point, it is important to recognize that not all public involvement will occur in the form of formal and organized meetings, whether online or in person, depending on the preferences and needs of the members. Much can be learned from service users through individual interactions, informal attendance at existing group events and reaching out online to hear from community members. As identified above, attendance at formal organized meetings may not suit busy lives, communication preferences or appeal to service users.

Establishing working relationships enables the evaluation team to learn more about any adjustments which are needed to enable service users with disabilities or specific needs to engage and become involved. In relation to in-person involvement, the team will have to consider the physical environment when working with service users, and this would include the accessibility of the venue, buildings, and room. Careful consideration also needs to be given to sensory elements such as lights, sounds/echoes, and smells within the space, which can be particularly important for autistic people or those with visual and hearing impairments. There will also be cultural considerations linked to the timing and organization of planned meetings, and cultural competency is needed to inform discussions around health and illness, family and spirituality (Gopalkrishnan 2018). Facilitators should also check that any venue provides induction loops (assistive listening systems that transmit sound directly to hearing aids or cochlear implants) which can greatly improve the listening experience for individuals with hearing impairments, allowing them to better understand speech and participate fully in discussions. Similarly, a sign language interpreter may be required for participants who are deaf, and specialised computer programmes may need to be provided for those with visual impairments. Online engagement should be offered as an alternative to attendance at in-person events, as this can be more accessible for some service users. It is important to recognize that some participants may require the assistance of a companion in order to fully participate in the event. Planning accessible ways to work together can come with additional costs, and so it is important to include these within project budgets. As highlighted above, team members need to ensure that an individual's dietary needs (allergies, cultural aspects) are accounted for and, by doing this, demonstrate their commitment to inclusivity and ensure that all individuals feel valued and consulted. As noted by Audrey:

> I have recently been involved in an evaluation of sexual health services. I'm hearing impaired, I've got hearing aids but the place where I was asked to go to do the evaluation didn't have hearing loops, so many people were talking, and there was no consideration of those who couldn't hear, so it was a tick box exercise! (Service User, 2024, Personal Communication).

Information underpinning consultation with service users may need to be translated, provided in easy-read formats or shared as an audio file. The acronyms and complex language which dominate the research world can make it incredibly hard for members of the public to understand conversations and documents. The IAP2's Spectrum of Public Participation stresses key issues of information being given to the public in clear, accessible, and unbiased forms (IAPT2 2024), and teams need to make sure that information and communication uses clear and simple language and any information should be shared with service users before a meeting and not just "sprung on them" to enable equity for those people who may need a longer processing time.

Initial engagement will need to allow time for evaluation teams to get to know people and find out the reasons why service users have volunteered to join in and also what they would like to get out of becoming a public advisor. In many cases, people will engage for altruistic reasons (Ashcroft et al. 2016), linking back to notions of citizenship. However, some people may be looking to gain skills, link into teams or provide evidence for their curriculum vitae. People's expectations and goals are really important to establish to ensure a meaningful working relationship. These initial conversations will also help identify any training needs or knowledge gaps a person may have, which may impact on how they are able to engage. These "getting to know you"conversations are important as they enable evaluation teams to address any expectations, goals and training needs and ensure everyone is on the same page. These initial conversations and meetings will also help establish and set mutually agreed-upon boundaries and ways of working together. An example of the importance of evaluation teams having "getting to know you" conversations when working with children and young people can be that a quick conversation may identify that they have been "volunteered" by a parent but they are not actually keen to be involved, or that they do not really want to join a meeting but are happy to share their views via a WhatsApp group or that they have amazing creative skills and would particularly like to focus on helping to disseminate the evaluation findings.

When working together, team members need to acknowledge the emotional aspects of discussing what can be sensitive and personal issues in the process of developing and conducting commissioned evaluations. Service users may become upset or experience conflict with other team members. While researchers may have detailed action plans or distress protocols on how to support research participants who become upset, this is of equal importance when consulting and working with members of the public. Team members need to have contact details for relevant support networks available and consider whether specialised training or support is required for staff or service users involved in the project, and this should be factored into the evaluation and budgetary considerations right from the beginning. Furthermore, it is crucial to establish a clear framework for resolving disagreements and differing opinions, and this should be communicated to all involved from the outset of working together with service users. It is imperative to create an environment where personal opinions are heard and respected.

4 Remuneration, Reward, and Recompense

An important issue when involving service users in research or commissioned evaluation projects is remuneration and how individuals are rewarded, recompensed and thanked for their time and contributions to the project. Expenses, access, and support requirements are crucial for promoting equity, and it is essential to acknowledge and reward all service users for their contributions. This can be done through monetary compensation or vouchers. However, there is a noticeable disparity among organizations that offer financial incentives to individuals for their time spent on completing service evaluations, both in terms of amounts paid and processes. Project leads need to carefully plan the budget required to support engagement with the public from the very beginning of a project. Team members need to also be prepared and informed to assist members who may need help completing pay claims forms and be aware of any potential impact on state monetary benefits that members of the public may receive as a result of their payments. Therefore, it is recommended to provide comprehensive and easily accessible guidance to members of the public, including email addresses, direct internet links, relevant phone numbers and contacts within the organization's payroll department where appropriate. It is important to recognize that the processes associated with payments for public involvement can be bureaucratic, lengthy, and difficult to navigate for many people, and therefore, teams need to try and make sure that service users are supported throughout the process. Being clear on any delays for payment or the process involved aims to ensure that people have the necessary support and information to make an informed decision about whether they would like to be involved as service users on a project (Ball et al. 2019). There is useful guidance on the UK National Institute for Health and Care Research website which details hourly rates for specific activities, and while these relate to research, they are applicable and relevant for any activities involving members of the public (NIHR 2023). While the focus may be on monetary reward and thanks for participation, there may be additional or alternative methods of saying thank you to service users for their contributions including refreshments or equipment or provisions. Additional consideration will need to be given to how children and young people or people who do not manage their own budgets are thanked for their contributions.

It is paramount to ensure, right from the beginning of any project, that there are adequate resources, skills, and flexible timescales in place (Hawkes et al. 2023) to facilitate meaningful and supported involvement of members of the public in health evaluations. Table 5 presents some top tips to support strategies you may develop as a team and in your organization.

5 Measuring and Reporting PPI Impact

Historically, there has been less attention paid to considering and reporting the impact of public consultation and involvement as part of health evaluations. This had led to a lack of critical discussion on the challenges and opportunities faced in relation to the involvement of service users in commissioned projects. Over the last 10 years, there has been a noticeable shift and increase in publications linked to the evaluation of public involvement within health service research, and this is leading to improvements in the sharing of practices, improved understanding of the benefits and challenges of public involvement in health research (Gibson et al. 2017) and what makes good involvement practices (Crocker et al. 2017; Moult et al. 2024). However, evaluation and PPI reporting are not consistent, and a recent review of PPIE in the UK in relation to research with children and young people highlights that the current reporting of involvement in health research is very poor (Preston et al. 2024). Reporting and evaluation of PPI impact is often even less evident within commissioned projects. The evaluation and subsequent reporting of the process and impact of PPIE means that research teams and the public advisors they are working

Table 5 Tips for working together in the right way

• Promote equality, diversity and inclusivity in the team and public involvement to encourage and respect different lived experiences, beliefs, and opinions • Ensure evaluation team members are trained and have the necessary skills and understanding to engage and work with service users • Adopt inclusive and flexible approaches that consider the needs and preferences of service users to support their involvement • Clear and transparent communication will provide a solid foundation and clear direction for all involved. This includes telling people about the evidence base for decisions and being clear about resource limitations and other constraints • Check service users' understanding of the evaluation and expectations from the beginning • Support the empowerment of service users through training and support as needed to ensure a shared understanding of the evaluation and process • Value people's lived experience and use all the strengths and talents that people bring to the table, working towards shared goals and aiming for constructive and productive conversations, being mindful of power dynamics • Provide clear information (plain language) and seek to facilitate involvement by all, recognizing that everyone has different needs • When information has to be kept confidential, explain why • Invest in partnerships with ongoing dialogue and avoid tokenism; provide information, support, training, and the right kind of leadership so everyone can work, learn, and improve together • Consider safeguarding, governance, finances, and be clear on how these will be managed • Consider the development of accessible public involvement "rules of engagement" which will provide all information in one source to all service users at the beginning of the relationship • Incorporate support and feedback mechanisms throughout a project to allow for changes and opportunities to capture any impact from public involvement

with can openly acknowledge and learn from things which have worked well during a project and what could have been better.

There are several comprehensive frameworks and tools which have been developed to support the evaluation of public involvement (Popay and Collins 2014; Boivin et al. 2018) including the CUBE (Gibson et al. 2017). These frameworks have been designed specifically to evaluate PPIE impact, but reviews have highlighted that these tools and frameworks may ironically have not been developed with service users or using robust scientific approaches (Boivin et al. 2018). As well as the increasing number of formal tools to evaluate public involvement, there are broader frameworks which may also be of value in considering how public advisors are meaningfully involved in shaping the design of commissioned evaluations. An example of this would be the Lundy Model, which was derived from considering children's right to express their views, have their views heard, be paid attention to and influence outcomes (Lundy 2007). Another framework developed to support the evaluation of patient, family, and caregiver engagement in health systems is the Engage with Impact Toolkit (Abelson et al. 2023) which seeks to support organizations to self-assess the impact of their engagement work. Using models and frameworks like this can help teams plan, conduct, and evaluate their public involvement work (Faux-Nightingale et al. 2024). It is valuable to work with service users to plan

Table 6 Tips for measuring and reporting public involvement impact

• Work with service users to agree on ways to gather information about the impact of the public involvement work • Be open, honest, and transparent about the PPI contributions throughout the evaluation • Review experience (positive and negative) and learn from it to continuously improve how people are involved • Recognize, record, and celebrate people's contributions and give feedback on the results of involvement; show people how they are valued

any public involvement evaluation; while the research team may have ideas for creative evaluation methods, service users may prefer a short anonymous survey or to share their views in a particular way.

There are now increased expectations around the reporting of public involvement. The transparent reporting of who was involved, how, and the impact of that involvement in published papers and reports is important to drive forward understanding of public involvement and practices which support involvement, work well and could be improved upon. The GRIPP tools (Staniszewska et al. 2017), both short and long forms, are commonly used to provide important details about public involvement. Some top tips for planning and reporting impact are in Table 6.

Many community members will discuss how they have experienced researchers coming in and gathering information from them and they never hear from them again. While the above sections discuss formal evaluations of public involvement impact, public involvement members require feedback throughout a project to understand how what they have shared and discussed has impacted on the project and evaluation team. This may be in the form of "you said, we did" type feedback or more formal reporting of how public involvement has shaped each part of the commissioned evaluation.

6 Being PPI-Ready for Health Service Evaluations

As with all public involvement, the planning and execution of involvement activities as part of health service evaluations, particularly commissioned evaluations, takes careful thought and effort if it is to work well. While the tight timescales and budgets often associated with commissioned work can provide additional challenges, if teams are fully committed to working with service users in a meaningful and authentic way, then the opportunities for shared learning and benefits to the team, the project and the service users greatly outweigh additional work. We hope that the information presented in the previous sections and the contributions shared by the service users from their experiences have highlighted the range and flexibility of public involvement and the key things to consider if you are to be PPI-ready for future commissioned evaluations.

This chapter has shown that public involvement work can hinge on finding the right people to work with, identifying stakeholders as early as possible. This may involve connecting with existing networks and groups (sometimes referred to as "piggybacking"), reaching out to engage with new communities or establishing your own group for the team or individual project.

For teams who are new to public involvement but want to embed public involvement within their work, we recommend trying to access training or colleagues who have more experience to advise and guide them. Having a person assigned to lead the public involvement activities within the team to ensure good and consistent communication and so service users know who to contact when needed is vital and can support development of a more trusted relationship with them.

Flexibility is a key part of public involvement work and is important to make sure that service users can get involved according to their strengths and preferences. Flexibility can take many forms in public involvement work, from using different ways for people to share their views, going to different places, different members dipping in and out of different parts of a project and unanticipated directions raised by service users. If a team can embrace and adapt to this flexibility, then public involvement is likely to be more inclusive and result in greater impact.

Transparent working practices and reporting are equally important, and as highlighted above, commissioned work comes with some challenges for public involvement, but it is imperative that teams can work with service users to acknowledge these limitations and recognize how decisions along the way may have excluded some people from being involved. If you engage in public involvement work, capturing its impact for the team, service users, and the project using available tools can help to demonstrate its relevance within organizations and to funders, in addition to supporting the ongoing development of public involvement in evaluations.

To give our service users the last word(s), Jan was very clear that to make the work meaningful for them, there must be clear communication throughout between the researchers, stakeholders, and service users:

> Any impact of the evaluations or our role in it is rarely noted or reported back to those service users involved. To make the work meaningful there must be clear and inclusive dialogue between stakeholders and service users throughout. (Service User, 2024, Personal Communication).

Jill also spoke of the importance of understanding the impact of their involvement and the evaluation outcome:

> I'm not entirely sure how valuable the other parents felt their participation was in the evaluation... Despite it being an enjoyable day, one where my voice was heard and I was included in the plans of the day; the results were never fed back to me, it would have been interesting to know the outcome. (Service User, 2024, Personal Communication).

Ultimately, involvement should be enjoyable as Alex says:

It was my first time being involved like this, having a voice on what was important to me and how to do it. The people were really nice, helping me get involved in the groups, and it was fun! I recommend it to anyone who is interested. (Young Person Service User, 2024, Personal Communication).

7 Conclusion

This chapter has been written to support researchers to engage with the patients and the public in the planning and delivery of health service evaluations. It provides a review of the evidence, along with examples from our own practice and the voices of some of the people we have worked with. The guidance and suggestions made can be applied to all health service evaluations, but we have intentionally highlighted the challenges in commissioned evaluations, and the potential solutions, as there is less work published in this area of evaluation. We hope that this chapter will be helpful when considering how you—and your team or organization—can offer inclusive opportunities to patients and the public to engage with you, work together in a meaningful way for all involved and capture the impact of engagement on the evaluation ahead of embarking on this journey.

Acknowledgements With thanks to the service users from the Service User and Carer Group of the Faculty of Health, Social Care and Medicine at Edge Hill University (Jo Clough, Audrey Cushion, Jill Evans, Nath Fernandes, Ad Gridley, Alex, Lynsey Harmon), Jan Thomas from The FDF Centre for Independent Living, the Tracheostomy Support Group UK and individual projects. Names have been used with permission.

References

Abelson J, Tripp L, MacNeil M, Lang A, Fancott C, Ganann R, Granieri M, Hofstetter C, King B, Kristy BL, Maybee A, Smith M, You J (2023) Development of the engage with impact toolkit: a comprehensive resource to support the evaluation of patient, family and caregiver engagement in health systems. Health Expect 26(3):1255–1265. https://doi.org/10.1111/hex.13742

Abma TA, Cook T, Rämgård M, Kleba E, Harris J, Wallerstein N. (2017) Social impact of participatory health research: collaborative non-linear processes of knowledge mobilization Educational Action Research 25(4): 489–505 https://doi.org/10.1080/09650792.2017.1329092

Agency for Healthcare Research and Quality (AHRQ) (2019) Chapter 3. Strategies for effective stakeholder engagement. https://www.ahrq.gov/research/findings/evidence-based-reports/stakeholderengagement/chapter3.html. Accessed 3 November 2024

Aries AM, Bailey P, Hunter SM (2021) The mutual benefits of patient and public involvement in research: an example from a feasibility study (MoTaStim-foot). Res Involve Engage 7:87. https://doi.org/10.1186/s40900-021-00330-w

Arnstein SP (1969) A ladder of citizen participation. J Am Inst Plan 35(4):216–224

Ashcroft J, Wykes T, Taylor J, Crowther A, Szmukler G (2016) Impact on the individual: what do patients and carers gain, lose and expect from being involved in research? J Ment Health 25(1):28–35

Ball S, Harshfield A, Carpenter A, Bertscher A, Marjanovic S (2019) Patient and public involvement and engagement in research. In: enabling meaningful contributions. RAND Corporation, Santa Monica. https://www.rand.org/pubs/research_reports/RR2678.html. Accessed 24 November 2024

Batty G. Humphrey G, Meakin B. (for Shaping our Lives), (2022) Tickboxes and tokenism? Service user involvement report 2022. https://shapingourlives.org.uk/wp-content/uploads/2022/02/Tickboxes-and-Tokenism-Feb-2022-1.pdf Accessed 13 May 2025

Baum FE, MacDougall C, Smith D (2006) Participatory action research. J Epidemiol Community Health 60(10):854–857

Baumann LA, Reinhold AK, Brütt AL (2022) Public and patient involvement in health policy decision-making on the health system level—a scoping review. Health Policy 126(10):1023–1038. https://doi.org/10.1016/j.healthpol.2022.07.007

Beighton C, Victor C, Carey IM, Hosking F, DeWilde S, Cook DG, Manners P, Harris T (2019) 'I'm sure we made it a better study…': experiences of adults with intellectual disabilities and parent carers of patient and public involvement in a health research study. J Intellect Disabil 23(1):78–96. https://doi.org/10.1177/1744629517723485

Beresford P (2019) Public participation in health and social care: exploring the co-production of knowledge. Front Sociol 3(41):1–12. https://doi.org/10.3389/fsoc.2018.00041

Biddle MS, Gibson A, Evans D (2021) Attitudes and approaches to patient and public involvement across Europe: a systematic review. Health Soc Care Commun 29:18–27. https://doi.org/10.1111/Hsc.13111

Boivin A, L'Espérance A, Gauvin FP, Dumez V, Macaulay AC, Lehoux P, Abelson J (2018) Patient and public engagement in research and health system decision making: a systematic review of evaluation tools. Health Expect 21(6):1075–1084

Brett J, Staniszewska S, Mockford C, Herron-Marx S, Hughes J, Tysall C, Suleman R (2014) A systematic review of the impact of patient and public involvement on service users, researchers and communities. Patient-Center Outcomes Res 7(4):387–395

Canadian Institutes of Health Research (CIHR) (2016) Strategy for patient-oriented research (SPOR) patient engagement framework. http://www.cihr-irsc.gc.ca/e/documents/spor_framework-en.pdf. Accessed 24 November 2024

Carman KL, Dardess P, Maurer M, Sofaer S, Adams K, Bechtel C, Sweeney J (2013) Patient and family engagement: a framework for understanding the elements and developing interventions and policies. Health Aff 32(2):223–231. https://doi.org/10.1377/hlthaff.2012.1133

Chambers E, Gardiner C, Thompson J et al (2019) Patient and carer involvement in palliative care research: an integrative qualitative evidence synthesis review. Palliative Medicine 33(8):969–984. https://doi.org/10.1177/0269216319858247

Crocker JC, Boylan AM, Bostock J, Locock L (2017) Is it worth it? Patient and public views on the impact of their involvement in health research and its assessment: a UK-based qualitative interview study. Health Expect 20(3):519–528. https://doi.org/10.1111/hex.12479

Crocker JC, Ricci-Cabello I, Parker A, Hirst JA, Chant A, Petit-Zeman S, Evans D, Rees S (2018) Impact of patient and public involvement on enrolment and retention in clinical trials: systematic review and meta-analysis. Br Med J 28:363. https://doi.org/10.1136/bmj.k4738

Domecq JP, Prutsky G, Elraiyah T, Wang Z, Nabhan M, Shippee N, Brito JP, Boehmer K, Hasan R, Firwana B, Erwin P, Eton D, Sloan J, Montori V, Asi N, Dabrh AM, Murad MH (2014) Patient engagement in research: a systematic review. BMC Health Serv Res 14:89. https://doi.org/10.1186/1472-6963-14-89

Duffy J, Beresford P (2020) Critical issues in the development of service user involvement. In: McLaughlin H, Beresford P, Cameron C, Casey H, Duffy J (eds) The Routledge handbook of service user involvement in human services research and education. Routledge, Abingdon, pp 9–17

Ellard-Gray A, Jeffrey NK, Choubak M, Crann SE (2015) Finding the hidden participant: solutions for recruiting hidden, hard-to-reach, and vulnerable populations. Int J Qual Methods 14:5. https://doi.org/10.1177/1609406915621420

Ellins J, Hocking L, Al-Haboubi M, Newbould J, Fenton SJ, Daniel K, Stockwell S, Leach B, Sidhu M, Bousfield J, McKenna G, Saunders K, O'Neill S, Mays N (2023) Early evaluation of the children and young people's mental health trailblazer programme: a rapid mixed-methods study. Health Soc Care Deliv Res 11(8):1–137. https://doi.org/10.3310/XQWU4117

Epstein S (1995) The construction of lay expertise: AIDS activism and the forging of credibility in the reform of clinical trials. Sci Technol Hum Values 20(4):408–437

Faux-Nightingale A, Somayajula G, Bradbury C, Bray L, Burton C, Chew-Graham CA, Gardner A, Griffin A, Twohig H, Welsh V (2024) Coproducing health information materials with young people: reflections and lessons learned. Health Expect 27(3):e14115. https://doi.org/10.1111/hex.14115

Forsythe LP, Ellis LE, Edmundson L, Sabharwal R, Rein A, Konopka KE (2016) Patient and stakeholder engagement in the PCORI pilot projects: description and lessons learned. J Gen Intern Med 33(9):13–21. https://doi.org/10.1007/s11606-015-3450-z

Froggatt K, Preston N, Turner M, Kerr C (2015) Patient and public involvement in research and the cancer experiences collaborative: benefits and challenges. BMJ Support Palliat Care 5(5):518–521. https://doi.org/10.1136/bmjspcare-2013-000548

Gibson A, Welsman J, Britten N (2017) Evaluating patient and public involvement in health research: from theoretical model to practical workshop. Health Expect 20(5):826–835

Gilfoyle M, Melro C, Koskinas E, Salzburg J (2023) Recruitment of patients, carers and members of the public to advisory boards, groups and panels in public and patient involved health research: a scoping review. BMJ Open 13(10):e072918. https://doi.org/10.1136/bmjopen-2023-072918

Gopalkrishnan N (2018) Cultural diversity and mental health: considerations for policy and practice. Front Public Health 6:179. https://doi.org/10.3389/fpubh.2018.00179

Green G (2016) Power to the people: to what extent has public involvement in applied health research achieved this? Res Involve Engage 2(1):1–13

Greenhalgh T, Hinton L, Finlay T, Macfarlane A, Fahy N, Clyde B, Chant A (2019) Frameworks for supporting patient and public involvement in research: systematic review and co-design pilot. Health Expect 22(4):785–801. https://doi.org/10.1111/hex.12969

Hart RA (1987) Children's participation in planning and design. In: Space for children, the built environment and child development. Plenum Press, New York, pp 217–239

Hawkes RE, Sanders C, Soiland-Reyes C et al (2023) Reflections of patient and public involvement from a commissioned research project evaluating a nationally implemented NHS programme focused on diabetes prevention. Res Involve Engage 9:42. https://doi.org/10.1186/s40900-023-00447-0

Herek GM, Capitanio JP, Widaman KF (2003) HIV-related stigma and knowledge in the United States: prevalence and trends, 1991-1999. Am J Public Health 92(3):371–377. https://doi.org/10.2105/ajph.92.3.371

Hoddinott P, Pollock A, O'Cathain A, Boyer I, Taylor J, MacDonald C, Oliver S, Donovan JL (2018) How to incorporate patient and public perspectives into the design and conduct of research. F1000Research 7:752. https://doi.org/10.12688/f1000research.15162.1

Holmes L, Cresswell K, Williams S, Parsons S, Keane A, Wilson C, Islam S, Joseph O, Miah J, Robinson E, Starling B (2019) Innovating public engagement and patient involvement through strategic collaboration and practice. Res Involve Engage 5(30):1–12. https://doi.org/10.1186/s40900-019-0160-4

IAPT2 (2024). https://www.iap2.org/mpage/Home. Accessed 24 November 2024

Johnson H, Ogden M, Brighton LJ, Etkind SN, Oluyase AO, Chukwusa E, Yu P, de Wolf-Linder S, Smith P, Bailey S, Koffman J, Evans CJ (2021) Patient and public involvement in palliative care research: what works, and why? A qualitative evaluation. Palliative Med 35(1):151–160. https://doi.org/10.1177/0269216320956819

Keane A, Islam S, Parsons S, Verma A, Farragher T, Forde D, Holmes L, Cresswell K, Williams S, Arru P, Howlett E, Turner-Uaandja H, MacGregor I, Grey T, Arain Z, Scahill M, Starling B (2023) Understanding who is and isn't involved and engaged in health research: capturing and analysing demographic data to diversify patient and public involvement and engagement. Res Involve Engage 9(1):30. https://doi.org/10.1186/s40900-023-00434-5

Lofters A, Prakash V, Devotta K, Vahabi M (2023) The potential benefits of "community champions" in the healthcare system. Healthc Manage Forum 36(6):382–387. https://doi.org/10.1177/08404704231179911

Lundy L (2007) 'Voice' is not enough: conceptualising article 12 of the United Nations convention on the rights of the child. Br Educ Res J 33(6):927–942. https://doi.org/10.1080/01411920701657033

Lundy L, McEvoy L (2012) Children's rights and research processes: assisting children to (in) formed views. Childhood 19(1):129–144. https://doi.org/10.1177/0907568211409078

McCoy MS, Warsh J, Rand L, Parker M, Sheehan M (2019) Patient and public involvement: two sides of the same coin or different coins altogether? Bioethics 33(6):708–715. https://doi.org/10.1111/bioe.12584
McLaughlin H, Beresford P, Cameron C, Casey H, Duffy J. (Eds.) (2020) The Routledge handbook of service user involvement in human services research and education. Routledge
McMenamin R, Isaksen J, Manning M, Tierney E (2022) Distinctions and blurred boundaries between qualitative approaches and public and patient involvement (PPI) in research. Int J Speech Lang Pathol 24(5):515–526. https://doi.org/10.1080/17549507.2022.2075465
Menendez T, Barragan NC, Kuo T, Morrison JL (2022) Using health navigators to connect at-risk clients to community resources. J Public Health Manag Pract 28(2):E397–E403. https://doi.org/10.1097/PHH.0000000000001396
Moult A, Knight N, Medina N, Babatunde O, Kingstone T, Duffy H, Fryer K, Canvin K, Swaithes L, Brading L, Bray L (2024) An evaluation of a public partnership project between academic institutions and young people with black African, Asian and Caribbean heritage. Res Involve Engage 10:31. https://doi.org/10.1186/s40900-024-00564-4
National Institute for Health Research (NIHR) (2021) Briefing notes for researchers-public involvement in NHS, health and social care research. https://www.nihr.ac.uk/briefing-notes-researchers-public-involvement-nhs-health-and-social-care-research. Accessed 18 July 2024
National Institute for Health Research (NIHR) (2022a) The race equality framework: a practitioner's guide for public involvement in research. https://www.nihr.ac.uk/documents/NIHR-race-equality-framework/30388. Accessed 18 July 2024
National Institute for Health Research (NIHR) (2022b) The equality, diversity and inclusion toolkit. https://www.rssleicesterresources.org.uk/edi-toolkit. Accessed 18 July 2024
National Institute for Health Research (NIHR) (2024a) Going the extra mile: improving the nation's health and wellbeing through public involvement in research. https://www.nihr.ac.uk/going-the-extra-mile
National Institute for Health Research (NIHR) (2024b) Guidance on co-producing a research project. https://www.learningforinvolvement.org.uk/content/resource/nihr-guidance-on-co-producing-a-research-project/. Accessed 10 December 2024
O'Brien P, McConkey R, García-Iriarte E (2014) Co-researching with people who have intellectual disabilities: insights from a national survey. J Appl Res Intellect Disabil 27(1):65–75. https://doi.org/10.1111/jar.12074
O'Donnell P, Tierney E, O'Carroll A et al (2016) Exploring levers and barriers to accessing primary care for marginalised groups and identifying their priorities for primary care provision: a participatory learning and action research study. Int J Equity Health 15:197. https://doi.org/10.1186/s12939-016-0487-5
Pagatpatan CP, Ward PR (2017) Understanding the factors that make public participation effective in health policy and planning: a realist synthesis. Aust J Prim Health 23(6):516–530. https://doi.org/10.1071/PY16129
Patient-Centered Outcomes Research Institute (PCORI) (2019) What we mean by patient-centered research. https://www.pcori.org/about-us/our-programs/patient-engagement/what-we-mean-patient-centered-research. Accessed 24 November 2024
Pizzo E, Doyle C, Matthews R, Barlow J (2015) Patient and public involvement: how much do we spend and what are the benefits? Health Expect 18(6):1918–1926. https://doi.org/10.1111/hex.12204
Popay J, Collins M (2014) The public involvement impact assessment framework. http://piiaf.org.uk/documents/piiaf-guidance-jan14.pdf. Accessed 24 November 2024
Porroche-Escudero A, Popay J (2021) The health inequalities assessment toolkit: supporting integration of equity into applied health research. J Public Health 43(3):567–572. https://doi.org/10.1093/pubmed/fdaa047
Preston J, Stones SR, Davies H, Preston J, Phillips B (2019) How to involve children and young people in what is, after all, their research. Arch Dis Child 104(5):494–500. https://doi.org/10.1136/archdischild-2018-315118

Preston J, Biglino G, Harbottle V et al (2023) Reporting involvement activities with children and young people in paediatric research: a framework analysis. Res Involve Engage 9:61. https://doi.org/10.1186/s40900-023-00477-8

Preston J, Lappin E, Ainsworth J, Wood CL, Dimitri P (2024) Involving children and young people as active partners in paediatric health research. Paediatr Child Health 34(1):11–15. https://doi.org/10.1016/j.paed.2023.10.003

Reynolds J, Ogden M, Beresford R (2021) Conceptualising and constructing 'diversity' through experiences of public and patient involvement in health research. Res Involve Engage 7:53. https://doi.org/10.1186/s40900-021-00296-9

Rouncefield-Swales A, Harris J, Carter B, Bray L, Bewley T, Martin R (2021) Children and young people's contributions to public involvement and engagement activities in health-related research: a scoping review. PLoS One 16(6):e0252774. https://doi.org/10.1371/journal.pone.0252774

Sanders EBN, Stappers PJ (2008) Co-creation and the new landscapes of design. CoDesign 4(1):5–18. https://doi.org/10.1080/15710880701875068

Shommu NS, Ahmed S, Rumana N, Barron GR, McBrien KA, Turin TC (2016) What is the scope of improving immigrant and ethnic minority healthcare using community navigators: a systematic scoping review. Int J Equity Health 15(6):1–12. https://doi.org/10.1186/s12939-016-0298-8

Slattery P, Saeri AK, Bragge P (2020) Research co-design in health: a rapid overview of reviews. Health Res Policy Syst 18(17):1–13. https://doi.org/10.1186/s12961-020-0528-9

Smith J, Ellins J, Sherlaw-Johnson C, Vindrola-Padros C, Appleby J, Morris S et al (2023) Rapid evaluation of service innovations in health and social care: key considerations. Health Soc Care Deliv Res 11:11. https://www.ncbi.nlm.nih.gov/books/NBK595722/. Accessed 24 November 2024

Staley K (2009) Exploring impact: public involvement in NHS, public health and social care research. Involve, Eastleigh

Staley K, Abbey-Vital I, Nolan C (2017) The impact of involvement on researchers: a learning experience. Res Involve Engage 3:20. https://doi.org/10.1186/s40900-017-0071-1

Staniszewska S, Brett J, Simera I, Seers K, Mockford C, Goodlad S, Altman DG, Moher D, Barber R, Denegri S, Entwistle A, Littlejohns P, Morris C, Suleman R, Thomas V, Tysall C (2017) GRIPP2 reporting checklists: tools to improve reporting of patient and public involvement in research. Br Med J 358:3453. https://doi.org/10.1136/bmj.j3453

The PARTNERS2 Writing Collective (2020) Exploring patient and public involvement (PPI) and co-production approaches in mental health research: learning from the PARTNERS2 research programme. Res Involve Engage 6:56. https://doi.org/10.1186/s40900-020-00224-3

Tritter JQ, McCallum A (2006) The snakes and ladders of user involvement: moving beyond Arnstein. Health Policy 76(2):156–168. https://doi.org/10.1016/j.healthpol.2005.05.008

United Nations (1989) United Nations convention on the rights of the child. United Nations, Geneva

Weiler-Wichtl LJ, Leiss U, Gojo J, Kienesberger A, Hansl R, Hopfgartner M, Schneider C (2023) Good to know—this is PPIE! Development of a training tool for public and patient involvement and engagement in pediatric oncological research. Cancer Rep 6(6):e1835. https://doi.org/10.1002/cnr2.1835

World Health Organization (WHO) (2019) Community engagement. https://www.who.int/publications/i/item/9789240010529. Accessed 24 November 2024

New Frontiers in Health Service Evaluation: Navigating Health, Agency, and Artificial Intelligence

Axel Kaehne and Julie Feather

Abstract

This concluding chapter explores emerging frontiers in health service evaluation, reflecting on critical themes of patient agency, evaluator leadership, and the transformative potential of artificial intelligence (AI). It contextualizes the tension between the scientific and societal purposes of evaluation, highlighting how values and public policy imperatives may shape evaluation practices in the future. By examining the evolving landscape of health services, the chapter draws on emerging paradigms such as co-production and patient-centered approaches. It also outlines how AI is potentially reshaping the evaluator's role, challenging established methodologies and democratizing access to evaluation tools. These dual developments—redefining health as a value proposition and the rise of AI—are positioned as critical for the future of health service evaluation, offering both challenges and opportunities.

Keywords

Health service evaluation · Artificial intelligence · Patient agency · Co-production · Evaluation leadership · Personalized care

---

A. Kaehne (✉)
Evaluation and Policy Analysis (EPA) Unit, and Medical School, Edge Hill University, Ormskirk, UK
e-mail: Kaehnea@edgehill.ac.uk

J. Feather
Evaluation and Policy Analysis (EPA) Unit, Edge Hill University, Ormskirk, UK

A. Kaehne, J. Feather (eds.), *Handbook of Health Services Evaluation*,
https://doi.org/10.1007/978-3-031-87869-5_30

In *Evaluation Studies: Review Annual* from 1986, David S. Cordray and Mark W. Lipsey sketched the well-known difference between research and evaluation. They wrote that researchers investigate the mechanisms and causes of interventions (such as public health programs) whereas evaluators probe their merit (Cordray and Lipsey 1986, p. 22). Their characterization of research and evaluation encapsulated in a nutshell the challenges of evaluation of health services even to this day. The last decades have witnessed a significant increase in the use of theory-led methodologies and approaches in evaluation, yet its main purpose remains the same: to assess the impact and effect of programs on their beneficiaries and to provide recommendations for future policymaking (Nilsen 2015). Despite the fact that evaluations are now generally theory-informed and utilize often complex models of cause and effect or impact, their main motive remains tethered to their paymaster's will: to conclude whether or not a public policy intervention was worth the investment.

In a way, this tension between scientific ambition and economic purpose frames the wider context in which evaluators have operated for a long time. Yet the ideas that shape public policy programs have also left their mark on the way in which evaluations are defined, conducted, and perceived by those inside and outside the evaluation community of practice. Our handbook has brought together a wide array of contributions which are reflective of these ideas and forces in society which currently inform public policy programs and evaluation practice alike, be they notions of inequality of resource distribution, cultural sensitivity, or individual or collective trauma.

In this concluding chapter we will reflect on what some of these novel perspectives mean for the practice of health service evaluations, as well as try to embed them in the wider context of providing health services. We will frame this through the lens of new frontiers opening up which, at times, may transpire to be old frontiers indeed, fundamental to our understanding of how to provide health services in a free society. The attribute 'free' is an important one, as we will argue throughout this chapter. Gaining a better understanding of the role of patients and their needs is an often professed goal of health professionals. Perhaps too readily, evaluators align their practice with this ambition and assume it as a given.

Many of the contributions in this handbook and, most recently, to the wider debate on public policy impact reveal a skepticism as to the underlying claim that health care services are by definition responsive to, and compassionate of, their clients (Abbasgholizadeh Rahimi et al. 2019; Gautier et al. 2022). Repeatedly, policy drives are launched to 'localize' the commissioning, design, and delivery, which arguably reflect a shift to a more sophisticated understanding of the relationship between health services, professionals, and patients. Co-production or co-design approaches speak of this impetus as do the long-standing debates around patient choice and shared decision-making in medical care (Michie et al. 2002; Voorberg et al. 2015; Kaehne et al. 2018; Waddell et al. 2021; Saut et al. 2023).

In this chapter we will try to make sense of these intersecting ideas and sketch how they may influence health service evaluations. We will do this by, initially, zooming out of the picture and critically reflect some aspects of the wider discourse on health in society. We believe this will enable us to understand better the concrete practice of evaluating health services and its recent innovations. In the last section we will then zoom back in to the practice of health service evaluation and explore the role and impact of artificial intelligence, which arguably challenges our core professional identity, role, and competencies.

1 The Tyranny of Health

It is difficult to think of a value statement more easily accepted and supported than the one that human beings seek to live a healthy life. The statement appears to capture the primary importance of one of our most fundamental desires which is closely linked to the wish for human happiness. To understand its real import, consider for a moment how this notion of health as a primary objective of human life informs our understanding of health care. Where health services exist free of charge, it strains our imagination that somebody would not want to avail themselves of those. But we know that some people decide not to use health services. This mismatch between foundational value statement (health is of primary importance to life) and reality reveals a tension between preconceived value and the individually defined merit of health.

Universal payer health services such as the NHS in England are a case in hand. Health care professionals only recently developed a better understanding of why some individuals or communities decide not to use local services on offer (Akbar et al. 2010; Nicholson and Cooper 2011; Seeleman et al. 2015). Our difficulty to comprehend conscious disengagement with health services reflects a wider, much more deeply engrained perception of health services as a benevolent, compassionate, caring, and responsive public offer to patients. This perception extends to how we assume people relate to health care organizations as well. Through a health system policy perspective, services are seen as facilitators of health improvement, responsive to needs. It is only recently that we have begun to appraise the sometimes limiting and forbidding effects of organizations, be that in clinical practice, or in the design of hospitals, as services prove to be challenging to navigate for those with hearing or visual impairment or cultural differences (Hunt et al. 2004; Krahn and Drum 2007; Akbar et al. 2010).

It is here that the slightly bombastic earlier argument we introduced about freedom and liberty conflicts with our value statement of benevolent and compassionate health services. Two decades ago, John LeGrand put forward an interesting metaphor for this clash between aspiration and reality. He argued that health care professionals may see themselves as knights, where patients are the knaves to be taken care of (LeGrand 2003). It may be argued that we have long overcome this paternalistic view of health care services. But the many novel contributions in our handbook challenging the paternalistic service narrative demonstrate how much the illusion of benevolent health services is still with us.

At heart, however, the misperception of health services as a public offer benevolent by nature is more than an act of harmless mistaken self-belief. More fundamentally, it echoes a widespread conviction that health as first-order value ought to be, and hence is, the primary goal of human conduct. This collides, however, with the idea of personal freedom as any doctor or nurse working in an emergency department can tell you. Health services are in the center of this collision, navigating this as best they can.

The divergence between ambition and reality extends to how organizations respond to patient needs. Here we find the tension between standardization of care and the desire to create services sensitive and responsive to patient needs. As chronic conditions and multi-morbidities are rising, the need to resolve this tension becomes ever more urgent requiring more resources. It is encapsulated in the fight between the efficient cookie cutter design and the genuine person-centered care (Kaehne and Nies 2021; Cribb and Woodcock 2022).

Consider the most recent attempt to reduce smoking in the UK by progressively banning the sale of tobacco products to anybody born 2010 or later. The thrust of the argument put forward in defense of this public policy suggested by the Westminster government is that, firstly, it reduces the costs caused by smoking to the NHS and, secondly, that this improves the health of future generations. It reflects the paternalistic vision of public policy as regulatory mechanism to bring about improved health outcomes. But how to evaluate this public health policy?

The challenge for evaluators here is thrown into sharp relief. They may choose one of two approaches. Once the policy is implemented and bedded in, they may assess its impact as defined by the narrowly frame policy intent: reduced health expenditure and improved health outcomes for those age groups banned from purchasing tobacco products. Alternatively, evaluators may choose to cast their net more widely. They may ask about the impact of the policy and define impact through the lens of policy 'beneficiaries', co-producing as it were the model of impact to be investigated and tested. The latter option reframes the value of the policy by redefining its benchmark. What was originally perceived as an incontrovertible priority of a public good (improved health) is now aligned with individual preferences (health, happiness) for specific values often at conflict with each other.

The critical insight here is that the effect of public policies such as the smoking ban for specific generations requires awareness of this clash between health as ultimate value and individual preferences shaped by personal or collective experiences. Assessing the impact of the generational smoking ban, in turn, calls upon evaluators to select the wider investigative frame rather than asking about the policy's narrow effect. There is a range of evaluation approaches and methods on offer now which speak to this need to broaden the perspective beyond the narrow policy goal. Realism is one (Punton et al. 2016; Pawson 2020); principle-based investigations are another example.

Yet this example also highlights where the future frontiers are located for evaluation practice. Within the restraints of commissioning evaluations, evaluators need significant leadership skills to navigate the Scylla of predefined health policy goals and the Charybdis of unlimited exploratory investigations. It is this leadership competence that will increasingly define the status and position of evaluation practice in the wider societal field of conflicting policy narratives jostling for legitimacy through marshalling evidence.

While recognizing the freedom of patients vis-à-vis organizational constraints and laudable policy narratives is one side of the medal, the other is preserving agency for evaluators themselves. Conventionally, this is framed as protecting the independence of evaluators in the pursuit of robust and reliable evidence of the impact of a service or program. Yet it may be useful to lift our gaze briefly and recognize that there are wider forces at work now which may present challenges not yet acknowledged.

2 The Impact of AI

It has been only a couple of years that the latest and most powerful iteration of artificial intelligence (AI) tools have been released. In November 2022, OpenAI revealed its first model of Large Language Models (LLM), ChatGPT, and Alphabet followed suit with Gemini. Normally, the old adage should hold true that it takes generations to arrive at a reliable judgement of how new technology affects a human practice. As Mark Twain once warned, prediction is difficult, particularly when it involves the future. Yet, even a simple reflection about the speed of current developments reveals that the impact of LLM has been nothing but revolutionary and, arguably, that AI will challenge the foundations of scientific practice, whether we like it or not. In our handbook, discussion related to AI is still confined to the issue how AI can support evaluation, yet, arguably, the impact of AI may be much wider for health services.

Consequently, evaluators will need to get a grip on these rapid changes quickly. AI is not just changing the health service practices, requiring novel techniques of evaluation, yet also questioning the role of evaluators as agent and catalyst of considered judgement. In a nutshell, we believe AI will democratize evaluation practice, making it possible for many professionals to conduct most evaluation tasks such as data cleaning, data coding, data analysis, synthesis of findings and evidence, in an automated way, using AI tools (Wang and Hsu 2024). This will challenge our understanding of professional identity. Take the example of data analysis.

Most evaluators are data analysts priding themselves of having hands-on experience of how to collect data, how to analyze it and how to synthesize findings. These activities allow them to develop skills yet are also sources of professional identity and pride. In addition, they are intricately connected with evaluators' claim to produce rigorous and reliable evidence. It is the human judgement based on a protocol led and regulated scientific activity which stands at the heart of evaluation practice as a discipline.

Given the meteoric rise of AI tools in the last couple of years and their spread and adoption in key fields of evaluation activity such as theory of change or logic model development, thematic or framework data analysis, as well as their already ubiquitous use for predictive modelling and probabilistic analysis in quantitative science, it is easy to predict that AI will shake the foundations of evaluation practice to the core (Mrowinski et al. 2017; Fischer and Steiger 2020; Chen et al. 2021; Ge et al. 2024; Reddy 2024). Some may conceive this as jeopardizing practitioners' identity and livelihood. Yet others may see it as an opportunity to free themselves from repetitive and time-consuming tasks (Qureshi et al. 2023; Issaiy et al. 2024). Whichever interpretation you prefer, evaluation practice is likely to be a new, rapidly moving frontier with its pace determined not by humans but solely dictated by the capacity of AI solutions to learn and improve. This may be an unnerving scenario for some. It may be argued that AI tools hold significant promise for evaluation practice if evaluators are clear eyed about how they may change evaluation tasks and alter evaluation roles while establishing new methodological, theoretical and, indeed, empirical boundaries.

We believe it is these twin developments, the questioning of an agent-free value proposition of health and the emergence of AI undermining the agency of evaluation practitioners, which demarcate the outer frontiers of evaluation practice in the years to come. The chapters in this handbook carry a strong echo of these issues, and, through the lens of their own disciplinary field, contributors are trying to find answers to the vexed question of patient agency in delivering health services as well as increasing methodological sophistication in evaluation practice. It seems to us that these are exciting times to be an evaluator of health services.

References

Abbasgholizadeh Rahimi S, Zomahoun HTV, Légaré F (2019) Patient engagement and its evaluation tools – current challenges and future directions comment on "metrics and evaluation tools for patient engagement in healthcare organization- and system-level decision-making: a systematic review". Int J Health Policy Manag 8(6):378–380. https://doi.org/10.15171/ijhpm.2019.16

Akbar F et al (2010) A mixed-methods assessment of health care service access and delivery to youth with special health care needs attending exceptional student education schools in Duval County, Florida. Int J Child Health Hum Dev 3(4):423–436. Available https://liverpool.idm.oclc.org/login?url

Chen Y et al (2021) Professionals' responses to the introduction of AI innovations in radiology and their implications for future adoption: a qualitative study. BMC Health Serv Res 21(1):1–9. https://doi.org/10.1186/s12913-021-06861-y

Cordray DS, Lipsey MW (1986) Program evaluation and program research. Eval Stud Rev Ann 11:17–44

Cribb A, Woodcock T (2022) Measuring with quality: the example of person-centred care. J Health Serv Res Policy 27(2):151–156. https://doi.org/10.1177/13558196211054278

Fischer I, Steiger HJ (2020) Toward automatic evaluation of medical abstracts: the current value of sentiment analysis and machine learning for classification of the importance of PubMed abstracts of randomized trials for stroke. J Stroke Cerebrovasc Dis 29(9):105042. https://doi.org/10.1016/j.jstrokecerebrovasdis.2020.105042

Gautier L et al (2022) Patient- and community-centered approaches as the cornerstone of health service evaluation in the 21st century. Int J Health Plann Manag 37(Suppl 1):4–7. https://doi.org/10.1002/hpm.3568

Ge L et al (2024) Leveraging artificial intelligence to enhance systematic reviews in health research: advanced tools and challenges. Syst Rev 13(1):269. https://doi.org/10.1186/s13643-024-02682-2

Hunt C et al (2004) Access to secondary care for people with learning disabilities. Nurs Times 100(3):34

Issaiy M et al (2024) Methodological insights into ChatGPT's screening performance in systematic reviews. BMC Med Res Methodol 24(1):1–11. https://doi.org/10.1186/s12874-024-02203-8
Kaehne A, Nies H (eds) (2021) How to deliver integrated care. A guidebook for managers. Emerald Publishing, Bingley. Available https://books.emeraldinsight.com/page/detail/How-to-Deliver-Integrated-Care/?k=9781838675301
Kaehne A, Beacham A, Feather J (2018) Co-production in integrated health and social care programmes: a pragmatic model. J Integr Care 26(1):87–96. https://doi.org/10.1108/JICA-11-2017-0044
Krahn L, Drum E (2007) Translating policy principles into practice to improve health care access for adults with intellectual disabilities: a research review of the past decade. Ment Retard Dev Disabil Res Rev 13(2):160
LeGrand J (2003) Motivation, agency, and public policy of knights and knaves, pawns and queens. OUP, Oxford
Michie S, Dormandy E, Marteau TM (2002) The multi-dimensional measure of informed choice: a validation study. Patient Educ Couns 48(1):87–91
Mrowinski MJ et al (2017) Artificial intelligence in peer review: how can evolutionary computation support journal editors? PLoS One 12(9):e0184711. https://doi.org/10.1371/journal.pone.0184711
Nicholson L, Cooper S-A (2011) Access to healthcare services by people with intellectual disabilities: a rural-urban comparison. J Intellect Disabil 15(2):115–130
Nilsen P (2015) Making sense of implementation theories, models and frameworks. Implement Sci 10(1):1–13. https://doi.org/10.1186/s13012-015-0242-0
Pawson R (2020) The relevance of realism in the pandemic. The denial of complexity. Available https://www.ramesesproject.org/media/WP3_-_Denial_of_complexity.pdf
Punton M, Vogel I, Lloyd R (2016) Reflections from a realist evaluation in progress: scaling ladders and stitching theory. CDI Pract Paper 18:1–11. Available https://opendocs.ids.ac.uk/opendocs/bitstream/handle/123456789/11254/CDIPracticePaper_18.pdf;jsessionid=FD8312F306BA82467A283D51DB13BFB6?sequence=1
Qureshi R et al (2023) Are ChatGPT and large language models "the answer" to bringing us closer to systematic review automation? Syst Rev 12(1):10–13. https://doi.org/10.1186/s13643-023-02243-z
Reddy S (2024) Generative AI in healthcare: an implementation science informed translational path on application, integration and governance. Implement Sci 27:1–15. https://doi.org/10.1186/s13012-024-01357-9
Saut AM et al (2023) How did healthcare professionals define patient engagement in quality management? A survey study. BMC Health Serv Res 23(1):1–13. https://doi.org/10.1186/s12913-023-09098-z
Seeleman C et al (2015) How should health service organizations respond to diversity? A content analysis of six approaches health policy, reform, governance and law. BMC Health Serv Res 15(1):510. https://doi.org/10.1186/s12913-015-1159-7
Voorberg WH, Bekkers VJJM, Tummers LG (2015) A systematic review of co-creation and co-production: embarking on the social innovation journey. Public Manag Rev 17(9):1333–1357. https://doi.org/10.1080/14719037.2014.930505
Waddell A et al (2021) Barriers and facilitators to shared decision-making in hospitals from policy to practice: a systematic review. Implement Sci 16(1):74
Wang W, Hsu W (2024) Integrating data sources for AI-based long-term care service evaluation. Appl Syst Innov. https://doi.org/10.21203/rs.3.rs-3265279/v1

Index

A

B

A. Kaehne, J. Feather (eds.), *Handbook of Health Services Evaluation*, https://doi.org/10.1007/978-3-031-87869-5

D

E

Q

R

GPSR Compliance
The European Union's (EU) General Product Safety Regulation (GPSR) is a set of rules that requires consumer products to be safe and our obligations to ensure this.

If you have any concerns about our products, you can contact us on

ProductSafety@springernature.com

In case Publisher is established outside the EU, the EU authorized representative is:

Springer Nature Customer Service Center GmbH
Europaplatz 3
69115 Heidelberg, Germany

www.ingramcontent.com/pod-product-compliance
Lightning Source LLC
Chambersburg PA
CBHW062358280826
50469CB00035B/33
* 9 7 8 3 0 3 1 8 7 8 6 8 8 *